COGNITIVE PROCESSES IN EDUCATION:
A Psychological Preparation for Teaching and Curriculum Development

COGNITIVE PROCESSES IN EDUCATION:
A Psychological Preparation for Teaching and Curriculum Development

WITHDRAWN

Sylvia Farnham-Diggory

CARNEGIE-MELLON UNIVERSITY

HARPER & ROW, PUBLISHERS
New York, Evanston, San Francisco, London

COGNITIVE PROCESSES IN EDUCATION: A Psychological Preparation for Teaching and Curriculum Development
Copyright © 1972 by *Sylvia Farnham-Diggory*

STANDARD BOOK NUMBER: 06-041999-7
LIBRARY OF CONGRESS CATALOG CARD NUMBER: 70-178105

For
Lola, James, Matthew, *and* Jonathan
who educated me
in that order
and
to the memory of
Albert

CONTENTS

FOREWORD
by Jerome S. Bruner

This book represents a new departure in "educational psychology." It is a volume conceived and organized around the practical question — What is known about the nature of mental growth and functioning that might be of use to specialists in education, be they concerned with teaching or curriculum making or evaluation? It is a book at once bold and learned, and it is good that it is both. For Dr. Farnham-Diggory does not limit herself to the conventional topics of educational psychology but goes as far afield as need be to harvest research findings and theoretical formulations that may be of help to the student of the educational process. She is not only bold in the scope of her gathering but also in the coherence of the plan that guides her search. She is programmatically committed to a point of view that has come to be called "cognitive psychology," a view that treats man as a searcher after, processor of, and indeed, creator of, information. She is not trying to "sell" a particular theory of information processing — how human beings achieve, retain, and transform knowledge. Her approach, rather is "heuristic" in the sense that she poses models of how man's traffic with knowledge might work, what alternative ways he might use in getting on with his enterprise, and how one may evaluate various contemporary "theories" that assert the "basic" nature of the underlying psychological processes. It is a view that is firmly based in modern thinking about the hypothetical nature of theoretical models; and it is marked by a delightful combination of seriousness with respect to attempted explanation and scepticism about grand theories.

The reader will be struck by the comprehensiveness of this volume, its scholarly coverage — linguistics, theories of growth, the role of group interaction, theories of perceptual recognition and feature extraction, ideas about the role of the self, concern about the nature of memory — all explored with a firm concern on the part of the author for their relevance to the building of curriculum, the conduct of a class, the presentation of a subject matter. Dr. Farnham-Diggory's scholarliness is neither "high falutin'" nor drily abstract. It has a purpose, and the purpose is the educational enterprise in its myriad guises.

It was the character of educational psychology a generation ago that it exhibited a slavish reliance on what was rather over-generously called "learning theory." Most of learning theory during that period was based on the performance of organisms, human and animal, in tasks that presented recurrent regularities that were to be recognized and mastered — a maze to be run repeatedly until the blinds could finally be eliminated and the true path alone followed, a discrimination task involving learning how to tell the relevant cues from the irrelevant, a list of words or syllables to be retained or recognized no matter in what order they were encountered. It was most usually made to seem that, though such tasks were not quite like what one found in schools, the principles being derived would one day be extended to them, that the simple tasks of the laboratory were somehow the "paradigm" case, school being but a heaping together of many little instances of the same kind. Several things have come to change this view in a major way. One was surely the computer and the emergence of computer sciences; it was plain that the program of even rather dull computer routines would have to be more intelligent and less linked to the environment than most of the learning theories proposed for complex organisms. Moreover, close inspection indicated the importance of the order of encounter with material to be learned — the curriculum, a matter not often of concern to standard learning theories. A second source of change was modern linguistics, particularly the growth of transformational grammar and studies by psycholinguists of its acquisition. Again, there was serious question as to whether the body of rules informing language could be "learned" or whether, rather, they were inferred from a few instances of encountered speech embodying the rules. Once language could be conceived of as the mastering of a body of concepts and rules, the way was open to conceiving of many other activities in the same spirit. Thirdly, the field of developmental psychology underwent a revolution, sparked principally by the classic work of the Geneva school, but generally built around the proposition that the growth of the child was not simply a learning of new responses or new habits that were added to or differentiated out of old ones. Rather, development consisted of the emergence of new strategies — new ways of coping with and processing information; it was not a continuous accretion of small changes or of bits of knowledge. The greatest problem was to match what a child had to learn with his way of going about learning. Finally, and perhaps in response to these trends, there emerged a new emphasis in personality theory, a concern for the development of competence or effectance, for the conditions that allowed a child to feel his own power rather than feeling a victim.

All of these changes ring clear and true in these pages. It is a thoroughly "modern" book in this sense, a text in educational psychology that serves the student of education with knowledge of how man comes to know and to control his world — and what the troubles are that he meets on the way.

One final note. Sylvia Farnham-Diggory, in addition to being an able psychologist, is a human being of great zest, with an evident and long-term attachment to the working of the human mind, in whatever guise. She has worked with children, handicapped and gifted; she has been a professional actress and has some sense of the human resources not usually touched in the laboratory experiment. This volume is full of the life she brings to her work.

Cambridge, 1971

ACKNOWLEDGMENTS

Page

6   Figure 7 from *Higher cortical functions in man* by A. R. Luria, © 1966 Consultants Bureau Enterprises Inc. and Basic Books, Inc., Publishers, New York.

13   From Bruner, J. S., Olver, R. R. and Greenfield, P. *Studies in cognitive growth.* New York: Wiley, 1966. By permission of John Wiley & Sons, Inc.

17   Figure 1 from Farnham-Diggory, S. and Bermon, M. Verbal compensation, cognitive synthesis, and conservation. *Merrill-Palmer Quarterly of Behavior & Development,* 1968, 14, 215–228.

18   From Bruner, J. S., Olver, R. R. and Greenfield, P. *Studies in cognitive growth.* New York: Wiley, 1966. By permission of John Wiley & Sons, Inc.

19   Figure 14 from Wapner, S. and Werner, H. *Perceptual development.* Worcester, Mass.: Clark University Press, 1957.

22–23 From Mehler, J. and Bever, T. G. Cognitive capacity of very young children. *Science,* 1967, 158, 141–142. Copyright 1967 by the American Association for the Advancement of Science.

27   Figure 5 from Rohwer, W. D. Images and pictures in children's learning. In Reese, H. W. (ed.), Imagery in children's learning: a symposium. *Psychological Bulletin,* 1970, 73, 393–403.

29   From Montessori, M. *Dr. Montessori's own handbook,* p. 29. Cambridge, Mass.: Bentley, 1964.

32   From Weir, M. W. and Stevenson, H. W. The effect of verbalization in children's learning as a function of chronological age. *Child Development*, 1959, 30, 143–149.

37   From Hooper, F. H. Piagetian research and education. In Sigel, I. E. and Hooper, F. H. (eds.), *Logical thinking in children*, p. 427. New York: Holt, Rinehart & Winston, 1968.

39–40   From Bruner, J. S., Olver, R. R. and Greenfield, P. *Studies in cognitive growth*. New York: Wiley, 1966. By permission of John Wiley & Sons, Inc.

49   From *Higher cortical functions in man*, p. 9, by A. R. Luria, © 1966 Consultants Bureau Enterprises Inc. and Basic Books, Inc., Publishers, New York.

55   From *Higher cortical functions in man*, pp. 139 and 140, by A. R. Luria, © 1966 Consultants Bureau Enterprises Inc. and Basic Books, Inc., Publishers, New York.

55   From Paine, R. S. and Oppé, T. W. Neurological examination of children, pp. 62 and 77. *Clinics in Developmental Medicine*, Double Vol. 20/21. London: Heinemann, 1966.

60   Figure 1 from Sterritt, G. M., Camp, B. W. and Lipman, B. S. Effects of early auditory deprivation upon auditory and visual information processing. *Perceptual and Motor Skills*, 1966, 23, 123–130. Reprinted with permission of author and publisher.

65   Figure 5 from Tanner, J. M. Human growth and constitution. In Harrison, G. A., Weiner, J. S., Tanner, J. M. and Barnicot, N. A. *Human biology: an introduction to human evolution, variation and growth*. New York: Oxford University Press, 1964. By permission of author.

82   From *Plans and the structure of behavior*, pp. 171–172, by George A. Miller, Eugene Galanter and Karl H. Pribram. Copyright © 1960 by Holt, Rinehart & Winston, Inc. Reprinted by permission of Holt, Rinehart & Winston, Inc.

86   From *The conditions of learning*, p. 181, by Robert M. Gagné. Copyright © 1965 by Holt, Rinehart & Winston, Inc. Reproduced by permission of Holt, Rinehart & Winston, Inc.

89–90   From *Plans and the structure of behavior*, p. 26, by George A. Miller, Eugene Galanter and Karl H. Pribram. Copyright © 1960 by Holt, Rinehart & Winston, Inc. Reprinted by permission of Holt, Rinehart & Winston, Inc.

96   From Diggory, J. C. *Self-evaluation: concepts and studies*. New York: Wiley, 1966. By permission of John Wiley & Sons, Inc.

97   Table 8 from Pepper, S. C. *The sources of value*. Berkeley, Calif.: University of California Press, 1958.

104–106   From Fenton, E. (ed.). *The Americans: a history of the United States*. New York: Holt, Rinehart & Winston, 1970.

112   From Polya, G. *How to solve it: a new aspect of mathematical method*, pp. 6–8, 12. Princeton, N. J.: Princeton University Press, 1945. Reprinted by permission of Princeton University Press.

114   From *Macromolecules and behavior*. Edited by John Gaito. Copyright © 1966 by Meredith Publishing Company. Reprinted by permission

of Appleton-Century-Crofts, Educational Division, Meredith Corporation.

116 From *Plans and the structure of behavior,* pp. 126–127, by George A. Miller, Eugene Galanter and Karl H. Pribram. Copyright © 1960 by Holt, Rinehart & Winston, Inc. Reprinted by permission of Holt, Rinehart & Winston, Inc.

119 From Brown, R. and McNeill, C. The "tip of the tongue" phenomenon. *Journal of Verbal Learning & Verbal Behavior,* 1966, 5, 325–337.

120 From Mace, C. A. *The psychology of study.* London: Methuen, 1932.

128–132 From Bruner, J. S. and Olver, R. R. Development of equivalence transformations in children. In Wright, J. C. and Kagan, J. (eds.), Basic cognitive processes in children. *Monographs of the Society for Research in Child Development,* 1963, Ser. 86, 125–141.

143–145 From Suchman, J. R. Inquiry training: building skills for autonomous discovery. *Merrill-Palmer Quarterly of Behavior & Development,* 1961, 7, 147–169.

146–147 From Fenton, E. (ed.). *Developing a new curriculum: a rationale for the Holt social studies curriculum.* New York: Holt, Rinehart & Winston, Inc., 1967.

150–153 From *Taxonomy of educational objectives: handbook I, cognitive domain,* by B. S. Bloom and D. R. Krathwhol. New York: David McKay Company, Inc., 1956. Used by permission of the David McKay Company, Inc.

156 From Bruner, J. S. Some elements of discovery. In L. S. Shulman and E. R. Keislar (eds.), *Learning by discovery,* pp. 101–102. Chicago: Rand McNally & Company, 1966.

179–180 Figure 1 from Staats, A. W., Finley, J. R., Minke, K. A. and Wolf, M. Reinforcement variables in the control of unit reading responses. *Journal of the Experimental Analysis of Behavior,* 1964, 7, 139–149. Copyright 1964 by the Society for the Experimental Analysis of Behavior, Inc.

182–183 Reprinted from Social learning through imitation by A. Bandura. In Jones, M. R. (ed.), *Nebraska symposium on motivation,* pp. 211–269, 1962, by permission of the University of Nebraska Press.

184 From Bandura, A., Ross, D. and Ross, S. A. Imitation of film-mediated aggressive models. *Journal of Abnormal & Social Psychology,* 1963, 66, 3–11.

186 From Bandura, A. and Menlove, F. L. Factors determining vicarious extinction of avoidance behavior through symbolic modeling. *Journal of Personality & Social Psychology,* 1965, 2, 698–705.

194–195 From *The achievement motive* by D. C. McClelland, J. W. Atkinson, R. A. Clark and E. L. Lowell. Copyright © 1953 by Appleton-Century-Crofts, Inc. Reprinted by permission of Appleton-Century-Crofts, Educational Division, Meredith Corporation.

197 From Rosen, B. C. and D'Andrade, R. The psychosocial origins of achievement motivation. *Sociometry,* 1959, 22, 185–218.

200–201, 203 From Diggory, J. S. *Self-evaluation: concepts and studies.* New York: Wiley, 1966. By permission of John Wiley & Sons, Inc.

204–205   From Prentice, W. C. H. Some cognitive aspects of motivation. *American Psychologist,* 1961, 16, 503–511.

206–207   From Berlin, I. N. Learning as therapy. *Saturday Review,* October 15, 1966. Copyright 1966 Saturday Review, Inc.

207–208   From Ott, J. F. The story of Esther. *Saturday Review,* October 15, 1966. Copyright 1966 Saturday Review, Inc.

213   From Aronson, E., Turner, J. A. and Carlsmith, J. M. Communication credibility and communication discrepancy as determinants of opinion change. *Journal of Abnormal & Social Psychology,* 1963, 67, 31–36.

218   From Heron, W. The pathology of boredom. *Scientific American,* 1957. Offprint No. 430.

219–220   From Bexton, W. H., Heron, W. and Scott, T. H. Effects of decreased variation in the sensory environment. *Canadian Journal of Psychology,* 1954, 8, 70–76.

223–224   From White, R. W. Ego and reality in psychoanalytic theory. *Psychological Issues,* 1963, 3.

225   Figure 2 from Berlyne, D. E. Curiosity and exploration. *Science,* 1966, 153, 25–33. Copyright 1966 by the American Association for the Advancement of Science.

230   From Mussen, P. H., Conger, J. J. and Kagan, J. *Child development and personality.* New York: Harper & Row, 1969.

236, 238   From Berlyne, D. E. *Structure and direction in thinking.* New York: Wiley, 1965. By permission of John Wiley & Sons, Inc.

247–248,   Reprinted from Competence and the psychosexual stages of develop-
251   ment by R. W. White. In Jones, M. R. (ed.), *Nebraska symposium on motivation,* pp. 97–140, 1960, by permission of the University of Nebraska Press.

252   From Grimes, J. W. and Allinsmith, W. Compulsivity, anxiety, and school achievement. *Merrill-Palmer Quarterly of Behavior & Development,* 1961, 7, 247–269.

246–253   From Erikson, E. H. Identity and the life cycle. *Psychological Issues,*
passim   1959, Monograph No. 1.

257   From Kagan, J., Rosman, B. L., Day, D., Albert, J. and Phillips, W. Information processing in the child: significance of analytic and reflective attitudes. *Psychological Monographs,* 1964, Whole No. 578.

259   Figure 1 from Yando, R. and Kagan, J. The effect of teacher tempo on the child. *Child Development,* 1968, 39, 27–34.

260   Figure 1 from Palkes, H., Stewart, M. and Kahana, B. Porteus maze performance of hyperactive boys after training in self-directed verbal commands. *Child Development,* 1968, 39, 817–826.

262   From *How children fail* by John Holt. Copyright © 1964 by Pitman Publishing Corporation. Reprinted by permission of Pitman Publishing Corp.

266–267   From Kagan, J. and Moss, H. The stability of passive and dependent behavior from childhood through adulthood. *Child Development,* 1960, 31, 577–591.

271–273   From Patterson, G. R., Littman, R. A. and Bricker, W. Assertive behavior in children: a step toward a theory of aggression. *Monographs of the Society for Research in Child Development*, 1967, 32, Ser. 113.

280–282   From Kagan, J., Moss, H. A. and Sigel, I. E. Psychological significance of styles of conceptualization. In Wright, J. C. and Kagan, J. (eds.), Basic cognitive processes in children. *Monographs of the Society for Research in Child Development*, 1963, 73–111, Ser. 86.

283   From *Human information processing: individuals and groups functioning in complex social situations*, by Harold M. Schroder, Michael J. Driver and Siegfried Streufert. Copyright © 1967 by Holt, Rinehart & Winston, Inc. Reproduced by permission of Holt, Rinehart & Winston, Inc.

286   From Gordon, I. J. *Studying the child in school.* New York: Wiley, 1966. By permission of John Wiley & Sons, Inc.

287   Bieker, H. *Using anecdotal records to know the child.* Washington, D.C.: 1950 Yearbook of the Association for Supervision and Curriculum Development, pp. 184–202.

287–288   From Sachs, B. M. *The student, the interview, and the curriculum.* Boston: Houghton Mifflin, 1966.

299   Reprinted with the permission of the publisher from Millie Almy's *Ways of studying children* (New York: Teachers College Press), copyright 1959.

303   From Atwood, G. A developmental study of cognitive balancing in hypothetical three-person systems. *Child Development*, 1969, 40, 73–85.

306–307   Table 1 from Deutsch, M. Socially relevant science. *American Psychologist*, 1969.

308   From Bales, R. *Interaction process analysis.* Reading, Mass.: Addison-Wesley, 1950. By permission of the author.

309   From Massialas, B. G. and Zevin, J. *Creative encounters in the classroom: teaching and learning through discovery.* New York: Wiley, 1967. By permission of John Wiley & Sons, Inc.

310–312   From Waimon, M. D. The study of teaching behavior by prospective teachers. In Corrigan, D. (ed.), *The study of teaching,* pp. 55–63. Washington, D.C.: The Association for Student Teaching, 1967.

311   From Amidon, E. J. The use of interaction analysis at Temple University. In Corrigan, D. (ed.), *The study of teaching,* pp. 42–54. Washington, D.C.: The Association for Student Teaching, 1967.

312   From Flavell, J. H. *The development of role-taking and communication skills in children.* New York: Wiley, 1968. By permission of John Wiley & Sons, Inc.

318–319   From Maier, N. R. F. Assets and liabilities in group problem solving: the need for an integrative function. *Psychological Review*, 1967, 74, 239–249.

326   From Lesser, G. S., Fifer, G. and Clark, D. H. Mental abilities of children from different social-class and cultural groups. *Monographs of the Society for Research in Child Development*, 1965, 30, Ser. 102.

327–329   From Hertzig, M. E., Birch, H. G., Thomas, A. and Mendez, O. A. Class and ethnic differences in the responsiveness of preschool children to cognitive demands. *Monographs of the Society for Research in Child Development*, 1968, 33, Ser. 117.

343   From Rheingold, H., Gewirtz, J. and Ross, H. W. Social conditioning of vocalization in infancy. *Journal of Comparative and Physiological Psychology*, 1959, 52, 68–73.

350   Table 1 from McNeill, D. Developmental psycholinguistics. In Smith, F. and Miller, G. A. (eds.), *The genesis of language*. Cambridge, Mass.: M. I. T. Press, 1966.

353   From Berko, J. The child's learning of English morphology. *Word*, 1958, pp. 150–177. Reprinted by permission.

364–366   From Furth, H. *Thinking without language: psychological implications of deafness*. New York: Free Press, 1966.

373   Figure 5 from Kiss, G. R. Words, associations, and networks. *Journal of Verbal Learning & Verbal Behavior*, 1968, 7, 707–713.

387   Figure 1 from Kohlberg, L., Yaeger, J. and Hjertholm, E. Private speech: four studies and a review of theories. *Child Development*, 1968, 39, 691–736.

389–391   From Whorf, B. L. *Language, thought and reality*. Cambridge, Mass.: M.I.T. Press, 1956.

392–393   From Osborn, J. Teaching a teaching language to disadvantaged children. In Brottman, M. A. (ed.), Language remediation for the disadvantaged preschool child. *Monographs of the Society for Research in Child Development*, 1968, 33, Ser. 124.

399–400   From Blank, M. and Solomon, F. A tutorial language program to develop abstract thinking in socially disadvantaged preschool children. *Child Development*, 1968, 39, 379–389.

407–408   From McCabe, B. J. A program for teaching composition to pupils of limited academic ability. In Shugrue, M. F. and Hillocks, G. (eds.), *Classroom practices in teaching English*, pp. 39–46. Washington, D.C.: National Council of Teachers of English, 1965. Copyright © by the National Council of Teachers of English. Reprinted by permission of the publisher and Bernard J. McCabe.

419   From Gibson, J. J. *The perception of the visual world*. Boston: Houghton Mifflin, 1950.

424   From Miller, G. A. *Psychology: the science of mental life*. New York: Harper & Row, 1962.

425   From Pritchard, R. M. Stabilized images on the retina. Copyright © 1961 by *Scientific American, Inc*. All rights reserved.

426   Figure 3 from Guthrie, G. and Wiener, M. Subliminal perception or perception of partial cue with pictorial stimuli. *Journal of Personality & Social Psychology*, 1966, 3, 619–628.

430   From Dwyer, F. M. Adapting visual illustrations for effective learning. *Harvard Educational Review*, 1967, 37, copyright © by President and Fellows of Harvard College.

433   Page 26 from McKee, P. *The teaching of reading*. Boston: Houghton Mifflin, 1948.

437 From Gibson, E. Learning to read. *Science*, 1965, 148, 1066–1072. Copyright 1965 by the American Association for the Advancement of Science.

437–438 From Selfridge, O. and Neisser, U. Pattern recognition by machine. Copyright © August, 1960, by *Scientific American, Inc.* All rights reserved.

441 From Dunn-Rankin, P. The similarity of lower-case letters of the English alphabet. *Journal of Verbal Learning & Verbal Behavior*, 1968, 7, 990–995.

442–444 From Geschwind, N. The anatomy of acquired disorders of reading. In Money, J. (ed.), *Reading disability*, pp. 115–129. Baltimore, Md.: Johns Hopkins Press, 1962.

445 From Kahn, D. and Birch, H. G. Development of auditory-visual integration and reading achievement. *Perceptual and Motor Skills*, 1968, 27, 459–468. Reprinted with permission of author and publisher.

447 From Jeffrey, W. E. and Samuels, S. J. Effect of method of reading training on initial learning and transfer. *Journal of Verbal Learning & Verbal Behavior*, 1967, 6, 354–358.

449–450 From Gibson, E., Osser, H. and Pick, A. D. A Study of the development of grapheme-phoneme correspondences. *Journal of Verbal Learning & Verbal Behavior*, 1963, 2, 142–146.

451 From SRA Basic Reading Series *A hen in a fox's den* by Donald E. Rasmussen and Lenina Goldberg. © 1964, 1965, by Donald E. Rasmussen and Lenina Goldberg. Reprinted by permission of Science Research Associates, Inc.

454 From *Linguistics and reading* by Charles C. Fries. Copyright © 1962, 1963 by Charles Carpenter Fries. Reprinted by permission of Holt, Rinehart & Winston, Inc.

458 From Ashton-Warner, S. *Teacher*. Copyright © 1963 by Sylvia Ashton-Warner. Reprinted by permission of Simon and Schuster.

459–460 From Stauffer, R. G. *Directing reading maturity as a cognitive process*. New York: Harper & Row, 1969.

466 From Goodenough, F. L. *Measurement of intelligence by drawings*. New York: Harcourt Brace Jovanovich, 1926.

467 From *Development of the perceptual world*, p. 166, by Charles M. Solley and Gardner Murphy. © 1960 by Basic Books, Inc., Publishers, New York.

468 From Cameron, N. Functional immaturity in the symbolization of scientifically trained adults. *Journal of Psychology*, 1938, 6, 161–175.

469–470 From Dart, F. E. and Pradhan, P. L. Cross-cultural teaching of science. *Science*, 1967, 155, 649–656. Copyright 1967 by the American Association for the Advancement of Science.

470 From Chapanis, A., Garner, W. R. and Morgan, C. T. *Applied experimental psychology: human factors in engineering design*. New York: Wiley, 1949. By permission of John Wiley & Sons, Inc.

471–472 From Vernon, M. D. Learning from graphical material. *British Journal of Psychology*, 1945, 36, 145–158.

480 From *Graphs and their uses* by Oystein Ore. Copyright © 1963 by Yale University. Reprinted by permission of Random House, Inc.

481–482   From Berry, P. C. Pretending to have (or to be) a computer as a strategy in teaching. *Harvard Educational Review*, 1964, 34, copyright © by President and Fellows of Harvard College.

488   From Brune, I. H. Language in mathematics. In Fehr, H. F., *The learning of mathematics*, pp. 156–191. Washington, D.C.: The National Council of Teachers of Mathematics, 1953.

499   From Ghiselin, B. The creative process. Originally published by the University of California Press, Berkeley, Calif.; reprinted by permission of The Regents of the University of California.

503   From Harris, D. B. The development and validation of a test of creativity in engineering. *Journal of Applied Psychology*, 1960, 44, 254–257.

504   From Myers, R. E. and Torrance, E. P. *Invitations to speaking and writing*. Boston: Ginn, 1962.

508   From *Creative person and creative process* by Frank Barron. Copyright © 1969 by Holt, Rinehart & Winston, Inc. Reprinted by permission of Holt, Rinehart & Winston, Inc.

509   From *Apes, angels and victorians* by W. Irvine. Copyright 1955 McGraw-Hill Book Company. Used with permission of McGraw-Hill Book Company.

516–522   *The productive thinking program* by Martin V. Covington, Richard S. Crutchfield, Lillian Davies, and Robert M. Olton, copyright 1972 by Charles E. Marrill Publishing Co., a Bell & Howell Company. Selected pages from Basic Lesson 7 reproduced by permission of the publisher.

525, 527–528   From Bruner, J. S. *On knowing: essays for the left hand*, 1964. By permission of The Belknap Press of Harvard University Press.

526   From Turner, E. M. *Teaching aids for elementary mathematics*. New York: Holt, Rinehart & Winston, 1966.

529   From *The medium is the massage* by Marshall McLuhan and Quentin Fiore, copyright © 1967 by Marshall McLuhan, Quentin Fiore, and Jerome Agel, by permission of Bantam Books, Inc.

532, 534   From Kris, E. *Psychoanalytic explorations in art*, 1952. By permission of International Universities, Press, Inc.

535   From *Creative person and creative process* by Frank Barron. Copyright © 1969 by Holt, Rinehart & Winston, Inc. Reprinted by permission of Holt, Rinehart & Winston, Inc.

536–537   From Gardner, J. W. *Self-renewal*. New York: Harper & Row, 1963.

540   From Ray, W. S. *The experimental psychology of original thinking*. New York: Macmillan, 1967. By permission of the author.

541   From Houston, J. P. and Mednick, S. A. Creativity and the need for novelty. *Journal of Abnormal & Social Psychology*, 1963, 66, 137–141.

546–547   From Iscoe, Ira and Pierce-Jones, John. Divergent thinking, age, and intelligence in white and Negro children. *Child Development*, 1960, 31, 577–591.

548–549   From *Teaching the "unteachable."* Reprinted with permission from *The New York Review of Books*. Copyright © 1967 Herbert Kohl.

This is the task of natural science: to show that the wonderful is not incomprehensible, to show how it can be comprehended—not to destroy wonder. For when we have explained the wonderful, unmasked the hidden pattern, a new wonder arises at how complexity was woven out of simplicity.

Herbert A. Simon

INTRODUCTION

In September 1970, Charles Silberman published *Crisis in the Classroom,* a dramatic, scholarly account of the current American educational scene. Many thousands of readers reacted with a sigh of genuine gratitude: "He's saved me years of research. . . . He's documented a situation I knew existed." Most of these readers were speaking from professional experience or personal observation. A few of them—a very few—were also speaking from a knowledge of scientific psychology.

Where has psychology been during the development of our classroom crises? In academic laboratories, as it properly should have been. No one expects medical research to take place in a downtown cafeteria, a shirt factory, or a public schoolroom. Psychological research also requires special technical conditions for the isolation of important causes and effects. However, once our scientific knowledge has been adequately formulated and tested, it should—like medical knowledge—move quickly into the world. The president of the American Psychological Association has said:

> As a science directly concerned with behavioral and social processes, psychology might be expected to provide intellectual leadership in the search for new and better personal and social arrangements. In fact, however, we psychologists have contributed relatively little of real importance—even less than our rather modest understanding of behavior might justify. We should have contributed more; although our scientific base for valid contributions is far from comprehensive, certainly more is known than has been used intelligently.
>
> This is the social challenge that psychologists face. In the years im-

mediately ahead we must not only extend and deepen our understanding of mental and behavioral phenomena, but we must somehow incorporate our hard-won knowledge more effectively into the vast social changes that we all know are coming. (George Miller, 1969, p. 1063)

Devotees of newspaper Sunday supplements and women's pages, daytime serials, and numerous books and magazines written on psychological topics might find Miller's mandate surprising. Have they not been reading for years about psychological principles? Is there any doubt that bad behavior stems from a bad early home life? that practice makes perfect? that women are happier when they are fulfilling their natural biological role? that children should not learn to read until they are "ready"? that men need to feel they are the household masters? Indeed, our teenagers can rattle off psychological truisms with a fluency their parents often find astonishing.

But somehow the social muddle persists. Some wonderful children come from appalling homes; some terrible children come from splendid homes. Practice may have a limited relationship to perfection—at least it cannot substitute for talent. Women are not happy when they are required to pretend that a physical function is equivalent to a mental one. Many children teach themselves to read years before they are supposed to be "ready." Many men would not dream of basing their self-esteem on "cave man" prowess. And despite their verbal glibness, teenagers seem to be in a worse mess than ever.

What has gone wrong? Are the psychological principles invalid? Are they too simple for a complex world?

The Need for Double Specialists

Like the modern world, modern scientific psychology is extremely technical and complex. The application of any particular set of psychological principles to any particular real problem requires a double specialist: a specialist in the scientific area, and a specialist in the real area.

Not many such double specialists exist. The relationship of a child's current behavior to his early home life, for example, is not a simple problem—Sunday supplement psychology notwithstanding. Many variables must be understood and integrated: special ("critical") periods of brain sensitivity, nutrition, genetic factors, the development of attention and perception, language, time factors (for example, the amount of time that elapses between a baby's action and a mother's smile), and so on. Mastery of these principles is a full-time professional occupation. The professional application of these principles—in, say, a day care center—is also a full-time occupation, and one that is foreign to many laboratory psychologists. Indeed, a laboratory psychologist may not even recognize his pet principles when they are realized in a day care setting.

The ability to recognize psychological principles in changed settings is extremely important. Psychology's failure to respond adequately to social problems may be in part a recognition failure. The principles that we already know something about from a research standpoint are often not recognized in their real-world guises. The psychologist is so busy working with his theories and his carefully controlled laboratory definitions that he fails to recognize the real forms his concepts may take.

The real-world specialist may suffer from the opposite lack. He may know little or nothing about the scientific principles he is applying in an actual situation. He may not even want to know anything about them. Many real-world specialists have developed comfortable systems for living by their wits and intuition. They "know what works"; never mind why it works. Yet their powers and insights would be greatly increased by theoretical knowledge.

What is needed is a coming together of real-world and laboratory specialists that will require both better communication and more complete experience. The laboratory specialist must spend some time in a real setting; the real-world specialist must spend some time in a theoretical laboratory. Each specialist needs to practice thinking like his counterpart. Each needs to practice translating theory into reality, and reality into theory.

Double Specialists in Education

The problem is especially visible and acute in education. Classroom crises like those documented by Silberman (1970) are almost entirely predictable on the basis of our present psychological knowledge. We know from research what happens to individuals who are placed in sensory-deprived settings—and the bland, timeless, boring setting of many classrooms is equivalent to that of a sensory-deprived laboratory. We know what frustration and failure do to people, child and teacher alike. We know many things about authoritarianism and the factors controlling obedience. Most of our schools are bad for reasons that can be theoretically as well as sociologically documented.

It follows that good schools can be built on theoretically sound principles, *if* the psychological specialist and the classroom specialist are willing to do their respective parts. The psychologist must be willing to plunge into the real world of a busy school system, to let it wash over him and absorb him until he can find connections between human behavior in that world and the behavior studied in his laboratory.

The classroom specialist must temporarily put aside his comfortable intuitive systems, at least long enough to question and analyze them theoretically. This may be a risky undertaking. If you are swimming in turbulent waters, you may quite naturally panic at the suggestion that you stop swimming and analyze the current scientifically. And yet you know full well that knowledge of the currents could save your life. The solution, of course, is to climb into a boat during the analytical period. A college course in educational psychology is such a boat.

Role of This Text

This text has been written for temporarily boated educational swimmers. They may be experienced or prospective swimmers. They may be interested in teaching, curriculum development, program design, administration, or some educational specialty, such as remedial reading or teaching the deaf. The text principles are sufficiently general and basic to be applicable to many areas, wherever and whenever they are needed. However, only those psychological principles that are of actual use have been included.

How were the choices made? On the basis of experience in classrooms and with school personnel of all kinds. On the basis of immersion in educational materials of all kinds. On the basis of confrontations with experienced educational personnel. On the basis of experience developing curriculum and teaching it in public school settings. At the same time, the psychological literature was scanned for answers to recurring questions: This is the problem. What do psychological specialists know about it? . . . This is the behavior we see in classrooms. What do psychologists know about it? . . . This is the educational program. What do psychologists know about factors involved in it? . . . This is the classroom material. What do psychologists know about relevant principles?

The book that has resulted may not look very much like a traditional educational psychology text because of its real-world orientation and its emphasis on the newest principles of cognition, creativity, and development.

"New" Psychology

Psychological science, like all modern science, has changed rapidly in recent years. Technological advances, such as computers and other kinds of sensitive electronic equipment, have made possible more precise tests of human behavior and the factors affecting it. Theoretical breakthroughs, such as new concepts for studying child language, have opened up more comprehensive ways of thinking about human behavior. In general, psychology has rather suddenly evolved to the point where it can handle complex variability more adequately. That is, psychology is better

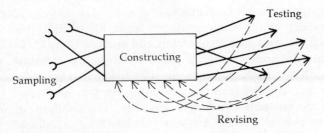

Figure I.1

equipped than it used to be to explain the complex behavior that occurs in educational settings.

The most important new theoretical concept is that of a human being as a sampler of the information around him (Bruner, Goodnow, and Austin, 1956; Miller, Galanter, and Pribram, 1960). We are born into a world of constantly fluctuating stimulation. We sample from this flux, we do not experience it totally. We formulate ideas about our sampled "bits." We relate them and organize them in various ways. We construct expectations and concepts. We test these concepts in various ways, and often revise them on the basis of our tests. Essentially, this sampling, constructing, testing, and revision is the basis of human mental growth. The process is diagrammed in Figure I.1

"Old" Education

Where does formal education fit in? Traditional education does not seem to fit in anywhere. During the school day, very little opportunity is provided for pupils to sample from a rich environment of information. The child sitting in a traditional classroom stares at a set of relatively unchanging walls, and listens to lecture materials entirely selected by his teacher. His own sampling mechanisms are only weakly involved. They are not strengthened, encouraged, or guided. This is particularly evident in terms of reading opportunities. Access to libraries is severely restricted in most traditional schools, despite the fact that libraries constitute our richest intellectual environments. The child who is taught through a basal reader is not permitted to sample from a rich range of written and spoken language; he must learn only the vocabulary selected for him by others (Chall, 1967).

Throughout his development, the child's own construction mechanisms are barely activated. Informally, we say, "Schools do not teach reasoning and problem solving or permit creativity." More formally, we may say, "The child is not allowed to formulate his own concepts and test them out." Of course, this does not mean we expect children to reinvent our entire culture; we are talking simply about a child's opportunity to strengthen and develop his own reasoning abilities. Most students—and this is the major problem on the college level as well—are shut out of the reasoning process. They are fed only the products of the teacher's reasoning. How, then, can we expect our schools to produce citizens capable of reasoning about the complex problems of their everyday lives? Should we be surprised by the flight of our adolescents from the realities of their world? What have we done to help them learn techniques for mastering confusion? for solving problems? for gaining a foothold? for developing systems of organizing their own experiences?

A human being in his everyday activities is an information-sampling, theory-building planner. He operates independently a great deal of the time, inside his own head. He may be interacting with others, but the decisions controlling his interactions are made inside his head. The housewife, the working man, the growing child all sample from the world around them, formulate ideas about it, act on the basis of those ideas, and make revisions on the basis of their experiences.

Our traditional American educational system does almost nothing to assist this natural mode of intellectual growth. Most such growth—if it happens at all—takes place in spite of the educational system, not because of it. Growth does not happen in many cases because it has been permanently stunted or warped by traditional schooling. In a sense, we may say that our citizens must learn to overcome the handicap of a schooling program that systematically impedes the process of natural mental growth.

Sound Educational Revolutions

National awareness of this problem has been developing rapidly in recent years. Many of the so-called romanticists (Schrag, 1967) of the educational literature such as John Holt (1964) and Jonathan Kozol (1967) have alerted us to the issues, but the psychologist often worries about the substitution of emotional hopes for realistic principles. It is therefore the job of the psychologist to communicate his unemotional, unromantic principles in a competitively readable style that does not sacrifice information for interesting prose. Much of the impact of Jerome Bruner's educational monographs (*The Process of Education, Toward a Theory of Instruction*) may be traced to their literary beauty, but this beauty is something of a dangerous lure. Many readers have rushed from the library to the classroom, only to find that Bruner's principles are like will-o'-the-wisps. They vanish in the noise and confusion of the typical school. The reason is simple. Bruner's principles are derived from a vast storehouse of knowledge that is not shared by the average reader. Nor is it presented in his monographs, except by brief allusions. Indeed, if one set oneself the task of explaining how Bruner derived his statements—where his ideas came from in psychology, how they have been documented and evolved, and how they are interrelated—the result would fill a number of technical volumes.

This text is an attempt to provide some of the background necessary for a sound educational revolution. It is not a blueprint for this revolution, partly because a blueprint is the wrong kind of guide. Whether old or young, human beings in educational systems are sampling, constructing, testing, and revising organisms. A blueprint would cripple the natural functions and skills of teachers and administrators as it does those of children. Readers will find psychological principles that should help them formulate solutions to their own problems. But the final solution—and it should always be a temporary, dynamic one—must be a product of their own tests and revisions. The educator is like a symphony conductor or an entrepreneur. He is always organizing and harmonizing the creative processes of others. There is no blueprint that can possibly predict his experiences, but there are principles that can help him organize and respond to them in ways that are consistent with psychological reality. If he can learn to utilize these principles in a dynamic, responsive way, he will find himself being carried along on a great wave of natural motivation. The natural capabilities of students, teachers, or program planners will be unleashed. He will be swimming with the current, instead of against it, and the current itself will carve meaningful and beautiful educational structures.

The Design of This Text

The relevant psychological principles sort themselves handily into six major categories that form the six parts of this text: development; basic systems of information processing; motivation, personality, and culture; language; reading and mathematical thinking; and creative thinking. They should be read in that order, since each part will build upon concepts previously explained and illustrated. Each part has its own introduction and summary. In a final concluding section (epilogue), I have outlined some of the applications of all the foregoing material to the design of an open school primary and preprimary program.

Although the text is based on experimental science, it is not simply a list of experiments and their results, it is an attempt to guide the reader through the analytical processes of the psychologist concerned with educational principles. When an experiment is mentioned, it will usually be explained in detail so that its results will be thoroughly understood. The model experiments selected are sometimes famous ones, sometimes not. They have been selected to illustrate critical points, not to flesh out a bibliography. The information explosion in the areas of educational, developmental, and cognitive psychology has been so great that it is not possible to cover everything in a single book. All the author can hope to do is to build a framework inside the reader's head. The reader should then be able to sort his additional, supplementary reading (which presumably will continue for the rest of his life) into the cubbyholes of this framework.

Some readers may be startled by the lack of frequent reference to the vast educational literature. This is partly the result of a decision, and partly the result of human weakness. I was simply unable to cope with the problem of sorting through that literature. Chall's (1967) introduction to her book on reading reflects my sentiments quite well; she describes the difficulties involved in making judgments about large numbers of methodologically poor studies. Many extremely gifted educators, whose intuitions I trust implicitly, have not paid much attention to experimental methodology. Citing their papers as illustrations of scientific principles therefore proved problematical. There are some exceptions, but in general I stayed with a psychological literature that is familiar to me and that meets the current standards of the scientific community to which I belong.

Acknowledgments

The major impetus for this text stemmed from a summer spent with the Education Development Center's *Man: A Course of Study,* a curriculum development project which was then under Jerome Bruner's direction. It was during that summer that I became fully aware of the need for a text of this sort. All my colleagues there contributed to the formation of this book, especially—through his inspiration and unrelenting encouragement ("You have to learn it all," he would say, "you have to learn it all!")—Jerome Bruner.

My colleagues at Carnegie-Mellon University and in the Pittsburgh schools have helped me grow, and helped this book to grow, to such an extent that I feel as if I have had many collaborators. I only hope they will forgive the errors that would not have been made had they been formal participants. In particular, June Delano has guided me wisely and patiently through the thickets of public schooling, and Herbert Simon, in his tireless quest for the "partially concealed pattern" of psychological lawfulness in real-world problems, is an enduring model.

Sylvia Farnham-Diggory
Carnegie-Mellon University

Part I COGNITIVE DEVELOPMENT

The human brain is a living, growing, changing
organ. It can even carry out its own repairs to
some extent. But it is bound by the inexorable
evolution of its functional aptitudes, and no one
can alter this, not even an educator or
psychiatrist. One can draw up a functional
timetable for the brain of a child. One might
well say there is a built-in biological clock that
tells the passing time of educational
opportunity.

WILDER PENFIELD

OVERVIEW

The student in the classroom is a growing organism, subject to laws of physical and mental development. As yet, we understand very little about those laws, but this much we do know: Our methods of teaching must take them into account, although there is no simple prescription for doing so. We cannot say, "Up until the age of such-and-such, use concrete materials; after that age, the child can understand lectures." In some areas, even adults can benefit from concrete materials; in others, even very young children can benefit from verbal directions. All the educator can do is learn as much as possible about critical features of mental growth and educational methods. Putting the two together then involves what J. McV. Hunt (1961) calls "the problem of the match"—the match between the child's inner state and the educator's program.

In Part I, we will survey a basic set of developmental principles, as well as some relevant educational materials, and consider the problem of putting the two together.

Stages of Development

The term *cognitive development* refers generally to changes in thinking abilities. These changes arise from the interaction of "outside" stimulation with ideas the child already has ("inside" structures of knowledge). The interaction itself is very much limited by the physical state of the brain, that is, by its anatomical structure and growth. Since the physiological reality of the brain is so crucial to thinking abilities, we will discuss that topic first. The physical structure of the brain, however, is only part of the story. Development proceeds in other ways as well. Thinking skills, like all skills, improve with practice and build upon each other. As his experiences multiply, it becomes necessary for the child to organize his ideas. If he did not do so, mental chaos would result—and indeed does result in cases of schizophrenia or brain damage, where the capacity for thought organization is fundamentally impaired.

Developmental theorists like Jean Piaget of Switzerland, Heinz Werner, late of Clark University, and Jerome Bruner of Harvard have been struck by the fact that children seem to progress through systematic stages of thought organization. They have described these stages in useful ways, and we will refer to their work frequently in the pages that follow.

A word of warning about the term *stage*, however. Kessen (1962) has pointed out that the term is used in many ways and that not all of them are valid. Stage, for example, may be a sort of metaphor: we may say a child is in a "chimpanzee stage," when we really mean that he is developing climbing skills and likes to exercise them. We may use the term as a synonym for age, saying "He's in the smiling stage," when we really mean that a child is about 3 months old and has not yet developed a fear of strangers. In its most meaningful sense, stage should refer to the principles or rules governing a large part of a child's behavior. For example, the 3-month-old baby smiles at strangers because a smile is his way of representing a complex relationship with adults. The fact that a baby has a physically organized method of representing complex ideas is the important principle, not the fact of the smile.

Symbolic Growth

During the early years, many of the child's concepts are physically organized. This fact has important implications for education, but it has an important theoretical implication as well. If a human's first modes of thinking take a certain form, then his later modes may take a similar form. This is like saying that the systems you used in learning to walk and to talk may be outlines or schemes for the systems you use in studying algebra. Of course, we cannot be sure this theory is true, but it is a useful working concept. Chapter 1 will spell it out in more detail.

As the brain "ripens" and the child's experiences increase, he learns to build upon them. His thought organizations become more sophisticated. He begins to symbolize his world in images and language. Chapters 2 and 3 detail this progress and its interaction with education.

Chapter 4 will sharpen our concepts of normal development by confronting us with problems of defective development—what may cause it and what kinds of educational remedies may help relieve it.

We must not forget, however, that the child perceives himself to be a unified, continuous creature. The striking changes in him that we may see (from age 4 to age 10, for example) are not obvious to him. What is his own central focus? What is his own unifying theme? Quite simply, understanding and predicting the world. The child is an information-sampling, theory-building planner. He constantly seeks clues to the nature of his universe. He constructs hypotheses about his universe and about his own relationship to it. He tries them out. Because he is inexperienced, many of his hypotheses are wrong. When he discovers this, he changes. Always, he is evolving toward greater competence in representing his world to himself and in coping with it.

Ideally, the educational process should help him in ways that are compatible with his own natural coping and developing systems; frequently, it does not (Silberman, 1970). Preschool and elementary education, as well as secondary education, all too often require the *cessation* of natural systems. The child is required to sit passively in a classroom and *turn off* his mind—except for a listening, receiving part—rather than engage in active hypothesis-testing and revision. By the time you have read Part I, you may understand enough about the process of mental development to make needed changes in that part of the educational system you can affect. Perhaps you will at least try.

Chapter 1 BASIC SENSORIMOTOR DEVELOPMENT

THE GROWTH OF THE BRAIN

The brain grows from the inside out. That is, the parts closest to the neck—the parts sometimes called the "old brain," because they are similar to the brains of lower animals—mature first. Many of these areas are mature at birth. This is necessary to the newborn's survival, since these brain areas control autonomic functions—heartbeat, breathing, sucking, and the like. There are also centers here for hunger and thirst and fear. Perhaps this "older" area is even the location of what Freud called the *id,* the biological self-gratifying impulses that civilized man must learn to control (see Chapter 14 for more about Freud).

Another important structure in this area is the general arousal system (the reticular activating system, or RAS), which is extensively involved in the processes of attention. The RAS mediates alertness and the focus of thought. It is the part of the brain that wakes the sleeping mother when her baby cries, but lets her sleep when the telephone rings; that wakes her doctor-husband when the telephone rings, but lets him sleep when the baby cries.

As our species evolved, "new brain"—the great folds of cortical tissue—developed. This is largely what Penfield (1964) calls "uncommitted" at birth. Human infancy and childhood are long so that complex learning, or cortical mapping, will have time to take place. Within the cortex, there are *primary* sensory and motor areas. These are the central receiving stations of internal (from the body) and external (from the world) information. How do they make connections with each other? How does the sensation "hot" make connections with the motor area governing "pull-back-finger"? By means of *secondary* cortical areas, a more widespread network of brain neurons (nerve cells). Each primary area has a secondary system, which means that some of these secondary systems are overlapping. For convenience, some neuropsychologists refer to these overlapping areas as *tertiary* systems.

After birth, the primary brain areas mature first—that is, they become functional first. Their respective secondary areas (otherwise known as *association areas*) lag behind. According to Tanner (1964), the primary motor area develops first, then the primary sensory area, then the visual area, then the auditory area. These are roughly sketched in Figure 1.1. The speech areas are apparently not "ready" until about 18 months, when language normally begins. However, as Lenneberg (1967) emphasizes, language is probably a complex result of several kinds of brain developments, not just the development of the speech area. Indeed, that is the critical clue to brain development as a whole; it involves complex coordinations of many types.

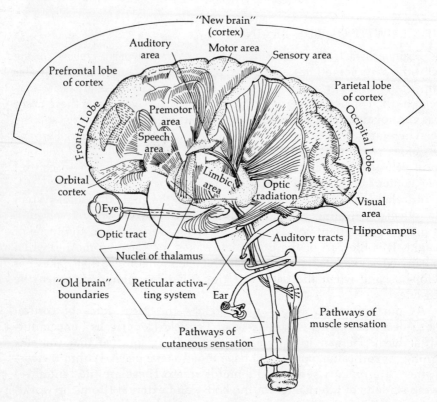

Figure 1.1   A diagram of brain areas and interconnections. (After Luria, 1966a)

Brain Coordinations

We have long since disproved the unsophisticated view of brain function as localized in special areas, even though such areas (like the speech area) can be located. The use of language involves concepts of many kinds. The word *run*, if it has any meaning at all, must refer to a motor and visual experience. Speech neuron patterns for *run* must be connected to the sensory and motor neuron patterns—located, probably, in other areas of the brain—for comprehension to occur. These patterns seem to be electrochemical in nature, and they can be detected in more than one part of the brain simultaneously (John, 1967) by instruments sensitive enough to pick up brain waves. Thus, the brain-wave pattern for *square* may be different from the pattern for *diamond.* When *square* is spoken, its pattern may appear in both the speech area and the visual area—at least that is the theory. Similarly, the sight of a familiar face ("Aunt Lulu! What are you doing back in Nebraska?") means that patterns in the occipital area (see Figure 1.1) must make connections with patterns in the speech area. Otherwise, the connection of face with name may not occur (as, alas, it often does not).

Neurological growth therefore refers more to the development of coordinations than to the maturation of specific cortical areas. Since these coordinations are dependent upon secondary and tertiary association areas, however, they cannot take place until the association networks are "ready." They are not fully "ready" until a child is about 13 years old—and, indeed, some associative tissue continues to mature throughout adulthood (Milner, 1967). *But readiness may never occur at all in the absence of appropriate "outside" stimulation,* a fact we will come back to repeatedly. As detailed in the pages that follow, work in many laboratories is showing that brain tissue is enriched, and its connectivity increased, by learning experiences and opportunities.

SENSORIMOTOR THINKING

Throughout the first year of life, the infant's concept of the world depends upon his sensory and motor functions. The term *sensorimotor stage* comes to us from Piaget (1967) who, like Werner (1961), has a strong biological orientation. Piaget has written eloquently of the ways in which sensorimotor experiences define the infant's subjective world:

> The infant is not content to suck only when he nurses; he also sucks at random. He sucks his fingers when he encounters them, then whatever object may be presented . . . and finally he coordinates the movement of his arms with the sucking until he is able to introduce his thumb into his mouth systematically. . . . In short . . . his initial behavior can be described by saying that for him the world is essentially a thing to be sucked. In short order, this same universe will also become a thing to be looked at, to listen to, and, as soon as his own movements allow, to shake. (Piaget, 1967, p. 9)

Piaget named these early representational systems *schemas.*

Sensorimotor Schemas

The infant who has developed a sucking schema can apply it to many new objects, as every frantic mother knows. What every mother does not realize, however, is that this is baby's way of defining each object. It is either a "suckable," or it does not exist, at least until the infant is old enough to have "bangables," "slappables," and "scratchables." Then, even if an object cannot be sucked, it can be known in other ways.

These schemas are critically important basic building blocks of conceptual development. Not only do they make it possible for baby to understand the world, they also lead to more general concepts, such as concepts of space, causality, time, and the permanence of objects. One of the most charming demonstrations of this latter general concept (the permanence of objects) can be seen at about 6 or 7 months, when the baby can sit up by himself. Put a favorite toy on his lap (such as it is). Just as he is reaching for it, drop a handkerchief over it (but not over his hand), so that the object disappears from his view. Baby will look around with a "Where did it go?" expression. *Out of sight, nonexistent* is the rule at this age. Objects have not yet developed as nonsensorimotor concepts.

Within a few months, however, baby will no longer fall for that trick. He will deftly toss the handkerchief aside. His concept of the object will not be destroyed by the object's disappearance. He will remember what it was and where it was, and search for it. His concept of the object will be something more permanent, like an image. But these are not ordinary visual images. They are what Piaget calls *action images,* or *motor memories.* They develop out of the experience of touching and reaching for objects. The general concept of the permanence of objects develops from many, many experiences of that sort. The general concepts of time, space, and causality develop in similar ways.

Of course, there is no way we can formally teach an infant about time, space, and object permanence. We can guide him to some extent by organizing his environment and by encouraging him to notice certain things, but basically we must rely on the infant's own capacities to make sense of his world. Let us now consider some features of these capacities. As mentioned in the introduction to Part I, these very early learning systems may be the prototypes of more advanced forms.

DIFFERENTIATION AND INTEGRATION

Stated simply, one important developmental principle says that we often learn first by recognizing or practicing parts of something and then by coordinating the parts. In learning to ride a bicycle, we may begin by plunging into a whole, undifferentiated experience (and by immediately plunging off one critical aspect of it). Gradually, we "distill" certain balancing and steering cues from the general muddle. These new awarenesses may be partly in our muscles and partly in our eyes. Then, sometimes rather suddenly, we become able to coordinate these signals, to put them together in a fairly well-organized way. We may wobble for a while, but the first stage of differentiation and integration has been passed. Your first teaching experience could probably be described in a similar way; the growth of your teaching skills proceeds by a process of differentiation and integration of critical cues and skills.

When you were an infant, you learned in essentially the same way. A good example may be found in the development of visually directed grasping abilities (*prehension*). At first, the infant can move only his entire arm in the direction of an object. We can see his great interest in reaching it, and we can infer that this interest, or goal, will polarize his efforts. Over the first one or two months of his life, the subpatterns necessary for visually directed grasping are differentiated out of the baby's global interest. The baby becomes able to follow an object (if it is moving) with his eyes, and even to anticipate the movement. Since he will direct his grasping with his eyes, this subpattern is very important. During this same period, the baby has learned to hold objects that are placed in his hand and to explore them manually. But the sight of the object does not trigger these manual activities. Then the first integrative activity occurs: The baby begins to watch his own hands (when he is about 3 months old). At about the same time, we begin to see "swiping" behavior—a close-fisted lunge that is often well aimed at the object of interest. But the baby has still not differentiated finger movements out of his global reaching urge. When this occurs (at about 4 months), we see a charming partial integration. The baby looks at the object, and his hands grasp each other! Finally, the baby succeeds in fully integrating the subpatterns of this system and attains adult-like reaching just prior to 5 months of age (White, Castle, and Held, 1964).

Evolutionary Steps
Clearly, these important developments are related to the growth of coordinating areas of the brain. They may also be related to the evolution of our species. Some anthropologists see the prehensile capacity, and its extension into tool using, as the most significant feature of human evolution. It may have been the ability to use tools—to bash smaller animals with stones—that helped develop the brains of our primate ancestors.* One eminent scientist has said:

> With man . . . one is started upon a new chapter in the history of the universe. It is as though nature had chosen to bypass all her previous experiments in the making of limbs, paddles, teeth, and fins save for one thing: to place a manipulative forelimb under the conscious control of the brain, to totally encephalize the hand. The brain and hand alone will now order the environment that once ordered them. Trees will be cut, fires will be started, flint will fly. (Eiseley, 1958, pp. 321–323)

*A readable review of this fascinating proposition may be found in the *Early Man* volume of the Life Nature Library, published by Time-Life Books.

The development of infant prehensile capacities may give us some hints about the complexities of those evolutionary steps. Each stage of differentiation and integration accomplished by our species may have taken thousands of years.

Emotional Differentiation

In considering the infancy of modern children, we need to remember that the differentiation and integration processes occur on an emotional and interpersonal level as well. Physiologically, the primary sensory and motor systems and the "old brain" emotional systems may function together in young infants. Perhaps this is why a 3-month-old may smile at almost any visual stimulus. He has not yet differentiated one kind of visual experience (mother's face) from another (the lampshade) in terms of its emotional significance. As Werner points out, the young human may also fail to differentiate parts of himself from parts of his surroundings:

> A relatively undifferentiated functioning . . . is characteristic of the earlier stages of childhood . . . many of the young child's activities can be understood only through the assumption that the motor-emotional and sensory factors are blended into one another. If it is admitted that the things of a child's world are created as much by his motor-affective activity as by objective stimuli, it becomes intelligible, for instance, why a child can seriously consider a few wisps of straw to be a doll or a bit of wood to be a horse. . . . His experience of a doll does not need to contain a head with two eyes, a nose, a mouth, and so on. . . . The affective and motor behavior of the child impresses itself on the world of things and fashions it. (Werner, 1961, pp. 59–65)

As the child grows, the elements of his experience become differentiated. Straw becomes straw, wood becomes wood, and his own interests become clear to him. He is then able to integrate all three. He can carve a horse from the wood and glue the straw to it (for a tail) because the construction of an animal interests him.

The General Model

This may be the model for general cognitive development. First, the differentiation and practice of fragments of a total response—fragments that in Piaget's system would be called schemas; then, under the pressure of a strong need or goal, the development of a system for integrating the fragments. We will meet this model again and again, especially in our study of language development (Part IV). Now let us see how these basic processes appear in Piaget's theory of sensorimotor development.

THE GROWTH OF SENSORIMOTOR INTELLIGENCE

According to Piaget, the very young infant moves through several stages of sensorimotor evolution (Piaget and Inhelder, 1969, pp. 6–12). These stages appear to involve the progressive differentiation of subpatterns and the integration of these subpatterns into increasingly complex behavior.

The first stage is one of simple reflex. The baby can activate his basic reflexes, such as sucking, grasping, and turning his head. As he practices these reflexes, they are refined and improved. Now the infant is able to begin to coordinate them into simple habits—turning his head to find a nipple, for example. This signals the onset of stage 2 in Piaget's system. At stage 3, about 4½ months of age, the baby appears to become aware of the fact that his actions have consequences. When he shakes his hand (which happens to have a rattle in it), a sound occurs. He then repeats the motion many times. Now he moves toward a higher stage of differentiation—he must differentiate the parts of the global hold-rattle-shake-sound experience. When he does so, we see, in stages 4 and 5, the earliest forms of instrumental behavior. The baby does something as a means to the goal of achieving something else. We call this *means-end awareness.* Of course, the earliest forms of this behavior are not necessarily logical; the baby may also use his rattle-shake schema in an attempt to make a light go on. But he gradually distinguishes one instrumental action from another and becomes able to integrate the right means with the right end. When he reaches stage 6, the end of the sensorimotor period, he is able to test mentally the suitability of various means. We can see this in the behavior of an infant facing a problem—a ball out of reach on a table, for example. Instead of activating a whole series of schemas (kicking, shaking the table, crying) in an effort to get the ball, the infant (who is about 18 months old) may sit still for a moment, obviously pondering. We can guess that he is trying out various ball-retrieving systems in his head. Suddenly, he reaches for the tablecloth and pulls it, pulling the ball to him at the same time. True intelligence—the ability to perform *mental* integrations of various behavior patterns—has begun. We will follow its progress in Chapter 2.

SENSORIMOTOR SYSTEMS IN SCHOOL

The principles of differentiation and integration have an extremely important implication for schooling, especially early schooling, for *children must be given adequate opportunity to differentiate and integrate their own learning experiences.* Otherwise, although they may be learning certain facts and skills by rote, their own minds will not be developing.

Learning Is Active

Becoming aware of critical cues in the general muddle of a learning situation is something each individual must do for himself. A good instructor can help, but he cannot do the job. This is easy to see in programs of physical instruction. For example, a swimming coach can provide important pointers and guidelines, but he cannot do the swimming for the individual. The principle is less apparent in programs of mental instruction because so much of the "swimming" is happening invisibly inside heads. We can often delude ourselves and our students into believing that cognitive development has occurred when a pupil has memorized a schema the teacher differentiated for him or performed a mechanical integration the teacher demanded, but we know that the child who practices kicking at poolside, blowing under water, and performing both actions to a rhythm clapped out by his instructor may nevertheless fail to develop the natural coordination of a good swimmer.

Actions Are Prototypes

Physical education analogies also illustrate the theory that an early, physical form of learning may be a prototype of a later, mental form of learning. Let us see if this theory works in terms of Piaget's sensorimotor stages.

Suppose you decided to take up the study of Roman history. First, you activate some well-learned habits, such as those of moving your eyes over a page (reading). This would be analogous to Piaget's stages 1 and 2. Gradually, you become aware of the fact that certain key figures and concepts are emerging from the general picture. To consolidate that awareness, you begin searching for other examples, and you take notes. Such behavior is analogous to Piaget's stage 3—the differentiation of certain schemas and their consequences. Now, as in sensorimotor stages 4 and 5, you begin to organize your material with the intention of achieving a certain summary statement ("All Gaul was divided . . . ."). At first, your subcategories are lumped together; later, your material is classified under various subheadings. Some of your notes, in other words, are discovered to be relevant to one topic; others are recognized as relevant to another topic. Most of the time you are working from notes, but finally you become able to put them aside. You have several concepts so clearly in mind that you can juggle them around mentally, trying them first in one relationship and then in another. At some point, you might have a sudden insight into the best relationship. That moment would be analogous to Piaget's stage 6.

There are many ways in which a good teacher can assist in such a process, and many ways in which the process can be carried out effectively. But if a child's natural learning systems are to grow, they must be exercised by each child for himself. We must remind ourselves of this constantly, because it is so easy to confuse the *product* of learning (the fact: Gaul was divided) with the *process* of learning (the stages of development described above).

ENACTIVE REPRESENTATION

Bruner has drawn our attention to the important fact that sensorimotor thinking is never totally abandoned; there are always concepts that we can represent best through action, rather than through words or images. He describes this phenomenon as *enactive representation*:

By enactive representation I mean a mode of representing past events through appropriate motor response. We cannot, for example, give an adequate description of familiar sidewalks or floors over which we habitually walk, nor do we have much of an image of what they are like. Yet we get about them without tripping or even looking much. Such segments of our environment—bicycle riding, tying knots, aspects of driving—get represented in our muscles, so to speak. (Bruner, 1964b, p. 2)

With respect to a particular knot, we learn the act of tying it and, when we "know" the knot, we know it by the habitual pattern of action we have mastered. The habit by which the knot is represented is serially organized, governed by some sort of schema that holds its successive segments together, and is in some sense related to other acts that either facilitate it or interfere with it. There is a fair amount of sensorimotor feedback involved in carrying out the act in question, yet what is crucial is that such a representation is executed in the medium of action. . . . It is possible for such habit patterns to become programmatic. . . . Such a programmatic pattern is best illustrated by skilled tool-using. What is at first a habitual pattern for using sensorimotor activity to achieve some end later becomes a program in the sense that various "substitutes" can be inserted without disrupting the over-all act. Even a chimpanzee who is unable to get a hand into an opening to extract a desired object can substitute a stick in place of reaching [See Chapter 7]. Or in skilled tool-using by humans, the carpenter who forgets his plane can substitute a chisel in the smoothing routine, a pocket knife, or the edge of a screwdriver, if need be.

We generally speak of such motor skills as "know-how," but they might better be called generative habits in the analogy of the generativeness in language, referring to the capacity to recombine and substitute elements to produce a rich area of language from a relatively small stock of language elements. (Bruner, Olver, and Greenfield, 1966, pp. 6–8)

Enactive Systems in Adulthood

We know many things enactively, even as adults. We may have developed and refined some forms of enactive knowledge to a high degree—as, for example, a ballet dancer has. But in a less extreme sense, much of our knowledge of the world has been constructed by our actions toward that world. In many ways, what we know is what we do, and what we do is what we know. Piaget's statement about the newborn infant, "The world is essentially a thing to be sucked," can be generalized to all of us, in one version or another. For some of us, under some conditions, the world is a thing to be pushed, pulled, beaten, climbed on, outmaneuvered, molded, patterned, arranged. We have little systems, or schemata, for knowing our world in these ways, and we learn to integrate them when necessary.

ENACTIVE THINKING IN SCHOOL

As far as classroom instruction is concerned, the two best-known systems of formal enactive pedagogy are *eurhythmics* and *mime.* Eurhythmics was developed by Jaques-Dalcroze as a system for bodily expression of ideas and feelings:

> The aim of all exercises in eurhythmics is to strengthen the power of concentration, to accustom the body to hold itself . . . in readiness to execute orders from the brain. . . .
>
> The aim of eurhythmics is to enable pupils at the end of their course to say, not "I know," but "I have experienced." (Jaques-Dalcroze, 1921, p. 118)

As might be predicted from our discussion of cognitive development thus far, eurhythmics has become important in modern teaching of young and retarded children. Enactive thinking, through eurhythmics, may be closer than verbal thinking to the capabilities of retardates. Further, in Jaques-Dalcroze's system, the gradually developing awareness of bodily expressions follows the principles of differentiation and integration. Children become aware of certain rhythms in themselves, then become able to control and integrate those rhythms. For retardates in particular, such practice may be an important foundation for mental development.

In mime, the direct expression of thought through action may take a more sophisticated form. The performer may first abstract key behaviors from a larger set of actions—behaviors that symbolize critical aspects of a situation or a relationship. Marcel Marceau, a famous modern French mime, has developed a scene called "David and Goliath." He portrays both characters, disappearing briefly behind a stage prop for the change from David to Goliath. He signals this change primarily by standing tall and by slowing his movements. Because (like all classic mimes) he wears a mask of white make-up, only his bodily movements can express the difference between the characters. Such miming is not merely the direct bodily expression of a concept; it is also symbolic. The young child may move toward the development of his own symbolic abilities in a similar way, as we will see in Chapter 2.

Summary
In this first chapter, we surveyed some of the principles governing early forms of thought. At birth, and for some months thereafter, thought is limited by the infant's lack of "ripe" associative brain tissue and also by his lack of experience. Gradually, through the important processes of differentiation and integration, he gains control over his skills and concepts. He begins to coordinate them, and his ability to behave intelligently increases accordingly.

These early forms of thinking may never be completely left behind, for we continue to use our sensorimotor systems in more advanced ways. But such advancement depends upon our opportunities to exercise the basic sensorimotor structure, at first directly, and later symbolically. Let us now consider the implications of this in more detail.

Chapter 2 THE EMERGENCE OF SYMBOLIC ABILITIES

EARLY SYMBOLIC SYSTEMS

One of the most difficult problems facing our three theorists is that of explaining how a child moves from his earlier concrete conceptual procedures to more abstract ones. The difficulty is of the following sort: Consider the individual (a child, for example) who is thinking primarily with his sensorimotor system—who is, according to Werner, responding in terms of an affect-laden action; or who is, according to Piaget, constructing concepts by means of sensorimotor schemata; or who is, according to Bruner, enactively representing his world. Regardless of our descriptive system, one thing is certain: The child is responding slowly. The time taken to perform an action, even a quick one, is much, much longer than the time taken to think about that action—assuming we have a brain capable of thinking about it. The problem facing all three theorists is to get from the slow action to the fast thought; to explain what happens inside a growing human's head that makes it possible for him to transform physical actions into mental actions which can be "run off" more quickly. Indeed, if such transformations did not take place, man would long since have been exterminated by physically superior animals. Man has somehow evolved an ability to represent his world mentally so that decisions, predictions, and estimations can be made instead of (or in advance of) action. The fact that other forms of animal life lack this ability is the only reason man is in control of his planet—at least for the most part.

But what is this ability? And how does it develop?

Forms of Early Symbolism

According to Piaget, we can see this skill emerging in the *symbolic play* of the young child:

> *Symbolic play* appears at about the same time as language but independently of it. . . . For example, the first symbolic play observed in one of my children consisted of his pretending to sleep. In order to go to sleep he always held a corner of his pillowcase in his hand and put the thumb of the same hand into his mouth. One morning, sitting wide awake on his mother's bed, Laurent noticed a corner of the sheet and it reminded him of the corner of his pillowcase. He grabbed the corner of the sheet firmly in his hand, put his thumb in his mouth, closed his eyes, and while still sitting, smiled broadly. (Piaget, 1967, p. 89)

Piaget has also described two other kinds of early symbolic thought: *deferred imitation* and *imagery*. One can observe deferred imitation constantly in the housekeeping play of young children. (Mothers, expect to see your bad habits acted out in detail!) Imagery will be discussed in more detail later in this chapter. When a young child (around the age of 2) has begun to represent his world in these primitive symbolic ways, Piaget says he has entered the *preoperational* stage of development; that is, the child is still limited in the number and types of mental operations he can perform with his crude symbols, but at least he is on his way.

PREOPERATIONAL THINKING

According to Piaget, the preoperational period lasts for about six years, from the age of 2 (or thereabouts) to 7 or 8. The quality of a preoperational child's thinking is suggested by the conservation experiments invented by Piaget to illustrate his theory.

Conservation Experiments

As shown in Figure 2.1, conservation of liquids (or conservation of continuous quantities) is illustrated by pouring liquid from a container of one shape into a container of a different shape. The child is told that one glass is his, and one is the experimenter's. Before the liquid is poured, the experimenter asks the child, "Do we have the same amount? Or do you have more, or do I have more?" No pouring takes place until the child agrees that the original glasses contain exactly the same amount.

The child's liquid is then poured into a container (or set of containers) of a different size. Again the child is asked, "Now, do we still have the same amount? Or do you have more? Or do I have more?" The preoperational child always decides that he has more *if* his glass of liquid has been poured into a taller, thinner beaker. He fails to *conserve* quantity when the shape of its container changes. When asked why, he explains readily that he has more because it goes up higher. He fails to take another perceptual cue into consideration: the fact that his higher glass is also thinner.

Implications for Thought

This inability to coordinate more than one perceptual feature at a time is an important characteristic of preoperational thinking. A good deal of differentiation has taken place, but it cannot be properly coordinated. For example, as Piaget and Inhelder (1969) point out, a child of 4 or 5 knows his right hand from his left hand perfectly well, but it will be about three years before he understands that a tree on his right when he is going one way will be on his left when he returns. This is essentially the same problem faced during the sensorimotor stage: the problem of differentiation and integration. Now that the child has fragments of symbolic thought at his disposal, he must learn how to organize them into systematic programs. Piaget calls such organizations *operations,* and we will hear more about exactly what he means in Chapter 3.

One can get the impression in reading Piaget that the preoperational stage is characterized more by negative than by positive aspects, but this is misleading. The preoperational child is learning how to use perceptual cues as symbols for more general concepts. He is taking a very important step toward mature symbolic thought.

To understand how this happens, we need to consider two aspects of

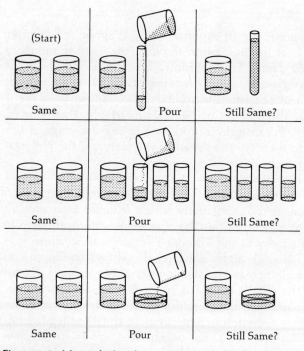

Figure 2.1 Materials for the conservation of liquids experiments. (Farnham-Diggory and Bermon, 1968)

preoperational behavior in detail: the young child's perceptual sensitivities, including visual and tactual sensitivities, and his perceptual strategies.

PERCEPTUAL SENSITIVITIES

Along with his growing use of various forms of imagery, the young child develops a new relationship to the spatial or visual cues in his environment. Although we have no clear neurological evidence on this point, the developments may signify new and rapid maturation of some parts of the visual association areas of the brain. Certainly the young child seems strangely dominated by the visual aspects of the world around him, as is evident in this description of a typical 3- or 4-year-old:

> The child's perceptual attention is highly *unstable*. He is notoriously distractible. Perhaps this trait accounts for the short supply of research on early perception! For young children can be astonishing in their distractibility. They are victims of the shifting sensory vividness and of the novelty of their environments. . . . It is as if the young child, having achieved a perceptual world that is no longer directly linked to action, now deals with the surface of things that catch attention. (Bruner, Olver, and Greenfield, 1966, p. 25)

One important aspect of this period is the child's changing sensitivity to illusions.

Sensitivity to Illusions

Figure 2.2 shows the materials for an experiment by Wapner and Werner (1957). Children saw each of the figures on the left (the "sitting mouse") moving at a certain speed past a little window. The figures on the right (like the "running mouse") were actually moving at the same speed, but the children were given the opportunity to adjust their speed to make it subjectively match that of the first set of figures. Invariably, they slowed down the running figures. Because the action cues in the drawings of the running figures seemed to increase the speed of the pictures, the children adjusted them by slowing them down.

Early in his career, Piaget himself made an extensive investigation of children's susceptibility to illusions and discovered an important fact: During the preoperational period, sensitivity to the Mueller-Lyer illusion (shown in Figure 2.3) is at a peak. But as the child makes the transition to operational thinking, sensitivity to the Mueller-Lyer decreases, while sensitivity to the so-called Titchener circles illusion (also shown in Figure 2.3) increases. This paradoxical increase in illusion sensitivity comes about, Piaget believes, because the child's maturing perception is *decentrating*, or becoming more differentiated. At the age of 4 or 5, children *centrate* on figures—they perceive them as wholes. Sensitivity to the Meuller-Lyer illusion is at its peak. But as the child decentrates, and—in effect— perceptually separates the ends of the Mueller-Lyer figure from its middle line, the illusion loses its effectiveness. The same tendency toward decentration, however, increases the susceptibility to the Titchener circles illusion because that illusion depends on attention to the outer circles. When the outer circles are larger, the inner one looks smaller. If the child is centrating on the figure as a whole, rather than noticing its separate parts, he will not perceive the illusion as strongly. A similar shift appears in tactual perception from attention to "wholistic" textures to the finer details of shape.

Sensitivity to Tactual Cues

Gerald Fisher (1965) has shown how very young children make judgments on the basis of textural information when feeling objects they are not allowed to see. Experiments on tactual perception are carried out by having subjects put their arms through a screen that rises above their eye level. The armholes are fitted with sweater-like cuffs so that nothing can be seen through them.

Figure 2.2   Materials used for testing children's susceptibility to action cues in visual materials. (Wapner and Werner, 1957, p. 32)

Fisher developed his experiment in an attempt to explain a mystery he had observed:

> When making the first tactile contact with shapes, the very young child, up to the age of about 2.5 years, depends for recognition upon such chance discoveries, or cues, as poking his finger through a hole or accidentally feeling an edge, indentation or point. Children of this age do not handle shapes or objects in the sense of exploring them with the finger tips and moving them around within the grasp, but grip them tightly making little or no attempt to conduct a detailed tactile examination of objects. ... It seems difficult to understand, however, how these very young children were able to recognize, or identify, the complex configurations of which the shapes of even ... simple, common objects are composed, with such a high frequency of accuracy, if cues to their profiles are afforded only by stimuli of the apparently chance nature suggested. (Fisher, 1965, p. 70)

He called this curious fact the *nonmanipulation paradox,* and he hypothesized that the explanation for it must lie in the children's use of textural cues. To test that hypothesis, he developed wooden models of thirty household objects that pilot studies had shown to be known even to his very young subjects, such as a book, a rubber ball, a saucer, a hammer.

Using the testing procedure described above, each one of these familiar objects was presented to children ranging in age from 1½ to 5 years.

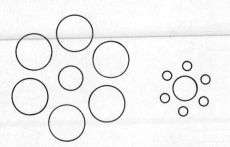

(a)

(b)

Mueller-Lyer Illusion

Titchener Circles Illusion

Figure 2.3   Illusions used to study the changing perceptual sensitivities of children.

Wooden models of the same items, identical in shape, size, and weight, were also presented to the children. Table 2.1 shows which items—the objects themselves or their wooden models—were recognized. Out of 120 trials, the six children under 2 years of age recognized the objects about 32 times, but the models only about 12 times. With age, frequency of recognition of both objects and models increased, but not until about the age of 5 were children as efficient in recognizing common items from their shape alone as they were in recognizing them when both shape and textural cues were present.

Table 2.1
Number of Normally Textured Objects and Wooden
Models Recognized Tactually by Very Young Children

AGE RANGE (YEARS)	NUMBER OF CHILDREN	OBJECTS	MODELS
1.5-1.9	6	31.6	12.1
2.0-2.9	10	64.0	35.4
3.0-3.9	10	102.0	75.4
4.0-5.0	16	112.8	109.2

SOURCE: Based on data in Fisher, 1965.
Note: The difference between object and model recognition was statistically significant, by Fisher's tests.

PERCEPTUAL STRATEGIES

Growth toward mature symbolism may depend greatly upon the young child's special perceptual sensitivities. The preoperational child may be learning to use a "shorthand" mental system for symbolizing information. For example, the child who fails a conservation-of-liquids test (Figure 2.1) may fail it because he is "outsmarting himself." He has learned that something higher is usually more than something lower. His reasoning is incomplete, but his intuitive perceptual guess is a good start toward the efficient use of symbols. He has selected one piece of a total perception and is basing his concept on it. Using that particular perceptual piece (the height of the liquid) is a mistake in this case, but it is a good mistake.

Iconic Thinking

To Bruner, such a child is beginning to use a second major mental system, one that will, like the enactive representational system, be available to him throughout life. Bruner calls this the *iconic representational system* because of its imagerial or iconlike characteristics.

If iconic strategies are, in fact, a step toward even more advanced symbolic abilities (the ability to handle the notion of conservation of quantity in this form, for example: $x + 3 = 3 + x$, or $x + 3 = 1 + 1 + 1 + x$), it should be possible to show that *younger* (less than 3 or 4 years old) children do not use them. Experimentally, this could have astounding results by showing that younger children, not being misled by the perceptual display, will show the same conservation ability as 8-year-olds, whereas the 3- to 4-year-old, busily developing his strategy and an easy victim of perceptual illusions, may not show it at all. Exactly this experiment was performed by Mehler and Bever (1967).

The Mehler-Bever Controversy

Consider Figure 2.4. In the top box (*a*), we see a display of clay pellets laid out in one-to-one correspondence. Children of any age will readily agree that there are the same number of pellets in the top row as in the bottom one. But then, as shown in (*b*), the experimenter may add some pellets to the bottom row and at the same time push them closer together. The top row remains spread out. When Mehler and Bever then asked, "Which row has more?" the child with conservation would say, of course, "The bottom one"; the child without conservation would say, "The top one."

Figure 2.5 is a bar graph showing the percentage of children in each age group who showed conservation. It can be seen that the bars march steadily downward and then back up again as the age of the children increases. All of the youngest group (about 2½ years old) showed conservation, but the bar for the second group (about 2¾ years old, on the average) is lower. Fewer of these children showed conservation. The downward trend continues until about the age of 4 years, when the conservation ability begins to reappear.

You might well wonder if there is a tendency in these very young children (2- and 3-year-olds) to favor small rows of things. Perhaps they tend to select something they feel is their own size. To test this possibility, a third condition was introduced (illustrated in (*c*), Figure 2.4). Here, the greater number of pellets has been placed in the longer row. The results show that 2-year-olds still select the greater number of pellets when asked

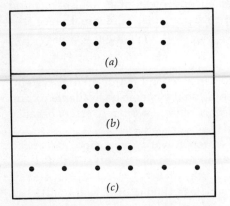

Figure 2.4 Materials for conservation of quantity experiment. (Mehler and Bever, 1967, p. 141)

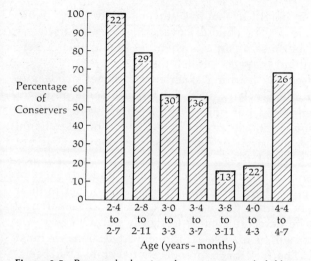

Figure 2.5 Bar graph showing the percentage of children who conserve quantity in seven age groups. Numbers within bars show the number of children in each group tested. (Mehler and Bever, 1967, p. 142)

which row has more. Mehler and Bever summarized the implications of their discovery as follows:

> Our results indicate that the inability to conserve quantity is a temporary phase in the developing child. The child does not gradually acquire quantity conservation during his 4th year [as Piaget has maintained]; rather, he reacquires it. The fact that the very young child successfully solves the conservation problem shows that he does have the capacities which depend on the logical structure of the cognitive operations. . . . We think that the temporary inability to solve the conservation problem reflects a period of overdependence on perceptual strategies. (Mehler and Bever, 1967, p. 142)

Piaget disagrees quite strongly with Bever's position. Interested readers can pursue the controversy—surely one of the most fascinating of this decade—in the following sources (in this order): Mehler and Bever, 1967; Beilin, 1968; Bever, Mehler and Epstein, 1968; Piaget, 1968; Mehler and Bever, 1968.

TEACHING OPERATIONAL LOGIC

Many attempts have been made to free young children from their illogical responses to conservation experiments. For example, in Piaget's own laboratory, efforts have been made to teach preoperational children to conserve liquids by using apparatus like that shown in Figure 2.6. The child starts with the top two glasses, which are filled with an equal quantity of liquid. If he opens the taps and lets the liquids into the middle glasses (which are unequal in size), the liquids will reach different levels. If the liquid in b' is made equal in height to that in b, then some of the b' liquid will have to be left behind in a'. The child discovers this. He also discovers that the amount he will be missing in c', when the liquid finally gets there, will be the same amount that was left behind.

By means of such discovery learning experiences, Piaget's colleague Bärbel Inhelder (Inhelder and Sinclair, 1969) did produce some improvement in preoperational thinking, but only if the children were about to outgrow the preoperational stage anyway. A solid preoperational child—one who is showing no signs of operational development—is not persuaded by such learning experiences.

Does this mean we should not try to teach children under the age of about 7 any abstract notions? Does it mean that they are so "set in their ways" intuitively that they cannot possibly break free of an apparently stupid overresponsiveness to perceptual cues? Certainly not. Of course we should teach them—but, as will be made clear in the next section, we must be careful how we do so. The fact that a preoperational child has special difficulties with the sorts of materials that Inhelder was using does not mean he will show the same reasoning deficiencies if the teaching strategies are changed.

We will see some examples of wise pedagogy shortly. But first, it is important to understand clearly the special neurological problems that the preoperational child is facing, problems requiring him to learn how to integrate visual, motor, and verbal information. Because of differing rates of brain maturation, some of these integrations are easier than others and

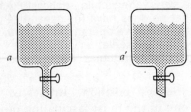

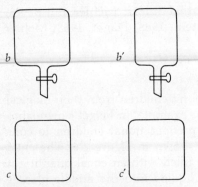

Figure 2.6   Apparatus used in Inhelder's experiments on training children to conserve quantity.

can pave the way for the others. The relationship is the great clue to good preschool teaching.

ACTION, PERCEPT, AND WORD

A significant feature of the preoperational stage is the emergence of language. This, too, is a representational system. The 4-year-old child, then, can represent his experiences in his actions (enactively), in his images (iconically), and in his words (verbally). A number of experiments, some of which are described below, have shown us how best to help the preoperational child utilize these systems in learning and thinking.

In general, the problem is this: During the preoperational phase, the child's special sensitivity to perceptual cues may trap and confuse him. The best strategy, then, would be to shield him from perceptual distractions whenever possible. Encourage him to rely upon his actions and his language, rather than upon his visual systems. If this is impossible, then show him how to use action and/or language as supportive systems.

The "Shielded" Conservation Experiment

Imagine that the beakers in Figure 2.1 were placed behind a screen so that only their tops were visible to the child. Under these conditions, after watching the experimenter pour the liquid but being unable to see the newly filled beakers, 4-year-olds will say, "Of course it's still the same. You only poured it!" or words to that effect. They seem perfectly capable of making the operational judgment that the amount of liquid will be conserved despite changes from container to container. But if the screen is then removed so that the children now see the differences in the shapes of the beakers and how much higher the water is in the tall, thin beaker, they may change their minds and say, "Oh, I was wrong. There really is more water in that high one now."

Bruner (1964b) believes such experiments show that the ability to think logically is actually present in young children as long as they can handle the information in a way that is free of misleading iconic cues. In this case, they handled it correctly on the basis of language and remembered action ("you only poured it").

Does this mean that iconic cues themselves cannot help guide learning? Of course they can, so long as they do not function as distracters. The research evidence would seem to indicate that preoperational children need special help in organizing their perceptual skills. Unless they have such help, younger children may not benefit from highly iconic instructional materials as much as older children do.

Visual Model Experiments

Corsini, Pick, and Flavell (1968) gave young children the opportunity to use paper visual models as an aid in remembering a block pattern. Although kindergarten children never spontaneously did so, many of them learned how through training. Flavell believes experiments of this type show that young children may not always lack the ability to use iconic cues in thinking or remembering tasks, but may lack awareness of the fact that they *should* be using them.

In a similar experiment using still younger children and less abstract materials than blocks (models of zoo animals), Ryan, Hegion, and Flavell (1969) taught preschoolers how to use pictures as cues for remembering the spatial locations of toys. The children simply learned to prop a picture beside a cage as a cue for placing the zoo animals properly.

Of special interest is the fact that among the very young children (3-year-olds), verbal explanation was more helpful than nonverbal modeling by the experimenter. If the experimenter did nothing but prop up the pictures of the animals, the 3-year-olds were not likely to understand his system. But if he also explained what he was doing, they were helped. This is an example of verbal guidance in the use of perceptual information.

Word-Picture Experiments

The most detailed and extensive experimentation on verbal vs. iconic learning has been carried out by a group of experimenters who gave a symposium in 1969 entitled *Imagery in Children's Learning* (Reese, 1969); we will consider here only the series of experiments presented by Rohwer (1969).

To help children learn paired lists of words, like *shoe-chair,* Rohwer put the words together in sentences like "The shoe *and* the chair" (a conjunctive relationship), or "The shoe is *under* the chair" (a prepositional relationship), or "The shoe *taps* the chair" (a verb or action relationship). In a number of careful experiments he and his colleagues established that the action relationship produces the best learning in children of preschool and kindergarten age, as well as in older children and adults.

Why should this be? Intuitively, it would seem that the image of the shoe tapping the chair is somehow more powerful or interesting than the imagery evoked by the other two conditions (conjunction and preposition). If that were the case, Rohwer reasoned, then pictures of the relationships should help learning in the same way—pictures of a shoe *and* a chair, a shoe *under* a chair, and a shoe *tapping* a chair. He found that the same relationship appeared: Pictures of a shoe tapping a chair helped learning best. He then decided to compare the verbal training condition with the pictorial condition, to test which was the more effective. The results are shown in Figure 2.7 for children in kindergarten through sixth grade. Each child saw a picture and heard a sentence in different combinations. The children who heard an action sentence ("The shoe taps the chair") learned better, regardless of the type of picture they saw. Although the best learners saw the action picture and heard the action sentence, their learning was not a great deal better than that of children who heard the action sentence and saw a nonaction picture.* Note the inter-esting crossover, however, among children composing the two middle curves. These children either heard an action sentence (dotted line) or saw an action picture (solid line). The younger children (kindergarten and first grade) were helped more by hearing the action sentence; the older chil-dren were helped more by seeing the action picture. Rohwer believes this happened because the older children had developed skill in using their ac-tion imagery efficiently:

> . . . it seems to me that the available data converge in suggesting that mental imagery is one of the processes whereby children represent and store information. It also seems to me, however, that a preference for and a capacity to make effective use of visual representation and storage de-velops later than is the case for verbal modes of representing and storing information. . . . The child's competence for understanding and producing relatively complex linguistic structures — sentences — emerges earlier than his competence even to copy, much less produce, relatively simple geo-metric forms, such as a diamond [Abercrombie, 1965]. . . . (Rohwer, 1969, p. 401)

*Note how much easier it was for you to understand that paragraph than to interpret Figure 2.7. Now practice coordinating the statements in the paragraph with the curves in the graph. These are the same problems facing the preoperational child. There will be more about the ability to read graphs in Part V.

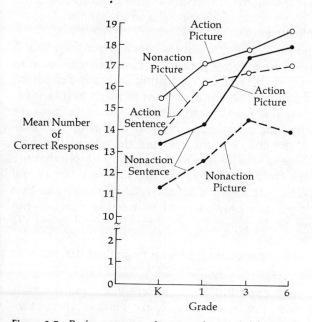

Figure 2.7   Performance as a function of type of elaboration and grade level. (Rohwer, 1970)

Word-Picture Conflicts

Perhaps the main problem is that young children do not easily connect pictures and words. The verbal representational system is located in the front-left-middle portion of the brain, and the visual or iconic system is located in the back. Connections between these two areas may depend on the development of associative brain tissue, development that is still not complete in the preoperational child. The child may therefore rely upon one system at a time.

Some very interesting work with children who have strong imagery has been reported by Haber (1969), who has studied those rare children who have what is called *eidetic* imagery. Such children can continue to see pictures as vividly as if they were still looking at them for several minutes after the pictures have been removed. What is of interest in our context is that Haber says eidetic children lose their images if they label them verbally. As soon as they give their images names, the images disappear. When the verbal representational system takes over, the iconic system "lets go." In some cases this would be unfortunate, but in the case of the preoperational child, involvement of the verbal systems may help free him from the dominance of misleading iconic cues.

THE "THINKING CHILD" IN PRESCHOOL

We have reviewed a great deal of the psychological literature. What does this literature tell us about the mental capacities of the child in preschool and about the best ways of teaching him? (Social and personality characteristics will be discussed in Part III.)

First of all, it is important to distinguish between what the child is capable of learning and what we may want to teach him. We may want to teach him some social skills, such as how to get along with other children, how to wait his turn, and so forth. Or we may want to teach him to read, to perform simple mathematical calculations, and similar feats. Because the choice of objectives depends upon many factors, including the availability of trained teachers, the child's home life, and the parents' wishes, no attempt will be made here to specify them. The point is simply that the teacher's objectives and the child's capacities are two different things and should not be confused. The teacher should not argue, for example, that preschool children should practice only social skills because they are not "ready" to read. If reading is the objective, ways can be found to get the child "ready" (more on this subject in Part V).

We can, however, make the following general recommendations with reference to cognitive objectives:

1. Provide the child with opportunities to differentiate and integrate his own experiences. Do this in all areas—music, art, blocks, letters. Provide him with materials that interest him and guide him in recognizing

important cues, but do not drill him in rote use of the materials. Let him make his own discoveries.

2. Expect him to become more sophisticated in his use of such materials. His block structures will become more intricate, his paintings will show more detail. Expect him to become better able to use materials in carrying out a plan (achieving a goal by exercising a means). Guide him to do so, but do not dictate a procedure.

3. Remember that the preoperational child is easily distracted and misled by visual materials. Select materials with care. Montessori materials, for example (Figure 2.8), provide strong perceptual cues that are not

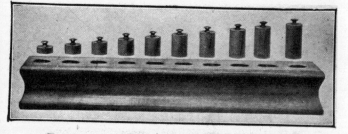

FIG. 5.—CYLINDERS DECREASING IN DIAMETER ONLY.

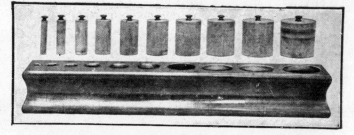

FIG. 6.—CYLINDERS DECREASING IN DIAMETER AND HEIGHT.

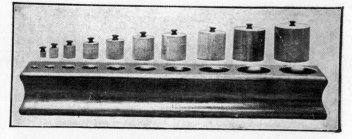

FIG. 7.—CYLINDERS DECREASING IN HEIGHT ONLY.

Figure 2.8 Montessori apparatus for teaching dimensional characteristics. (*a*) Cylinders decreasing in diameter only; (*b*) cylinders decreasing in diameter and height; (*c*) cylinders decreasing in height only. (Montessori, 1964a, p. 29)

misleading. Montessori's general emphasis on a prepared environment is designed to minimize perceptual distractions (Montessori, 1964a, 1964b). A large number of new preschool materials have been assembled on the same principles. Remember that even though the child must perform differentiations and integrations for himself, we can help him by eliminating environmental confusion. A table with a single task on it, a small rug with two books on it, a block corner that does not "spill over" into the housekeeping area—these preparations decrease visual confusion and distraction.

4. Remember also that conceptual development builds on actions. The young child must be physically involved if his mind is to grow. Counting by stamping and clapping, eurhythmics, and manipulation of all sorts will build brain as well as body.

5. Encourage the early forms of symbolization—symbolic play and deferred imitation. The housekeeping corner, puppets, and various kinds of dress-up activities are important in this respect.

6. Encourage verbal development. Remember, the preoperational child has sophisticated verbal systems that need to be exercised and extended.

7. Encourage the coordination of action, picture, and word. Ask the child to talk to you about pictures and about his actions. Encourage him to act out his words and to find pictures of words. Many preschool materials (such as the kits developed by the Peabody School of Education) encourage such coordinate growth.

Many good preschool programs can be designed within the framework of these general recommendations. One has been described in the concluding section of this book. We move now into first grade.

Chapter 3 TRUE CONCEPTUAL THINKING

EARLY CONCEPTUAL STRATEGIES

As in the case of the child growing from basic sensorimotor thinking to the use of basic perceptual strategies, the child who is advancing toward further conceptual sophistication may sometimes appear stupider than one who is not.

Are 5-year-olds Smarter than 9-year-olds?

Consider the following experiment carried out by Weir and Stevenson (1959). The subjects consisted of 128 preschool and elementary school children ranging in age from 3 to 10 years. All these children performed a simple task involving pictures of animals. The subjects were seated before a set of panels that could illuminate five pairs of slides—for example, a monkey and a cat, or a goose and an elephant. Unknown to the subject, one member of each pair had been designated by the experimenter as "right." If the child pushed the panel of the "right" slide, the light behind the panel went off. If the child pushed the panel of the "wrong" slide, the light remained on. The subject's task, therefore, was to learn which animals "turned off the light." Since in any given series of slides the same animal always "turned off the light," the task was basically quite a simple one, especially for the older children.

Simple tasks of this sort sometimes reveal a curious fact: Older children may perform less well on them than younger children do (Figure 3.1). Although the number of correct responses increased markedly from age 3 to age 5, they declined from age 5 to age 9. This held true whether or not the children had been instructed to verbalize the animal names, although the 5-to-9 decline seemed somewhat less for the verbalizers. What happened? Why should such a trivial task not be performed perfectly by 9-year-old children when 5-year-olds are correct 90 percent of the time? The researchers proposed this explanation:

> The possibility that seems most tenable is that older Ss developed complex hypotheses concerning the solution of the problem and that these hypotheses hindered their development of the more simple, correct solution. These Ss made such statements as, "I thought that it was going to be a pattern," and "I thought you were going to change them all around." The older Ss responded more slowly . . . than younger Ss, indicating that they may have been expecting a harder task and found it difficult to learn that the same response was always correct. (Weir and Stevenson, 1959, p. 148)

The remarkable fact is that the increasingly complex mind may project its own complexities onto a simpler-minded world. What is remarkable, of course, is that the complexities exist and that they grow.

Sheldon White (1965) has summarized an extensive amount of experimental evidence which supports the view that there is a major, qualitative transition in thinking behavior between the ages of 5 and 7. It is illustrated by the following experiment, carried out by Michael Zeiler (1964).

Are 3-year-olds Smarter than 7-year-olds?

Zeiler's subjects were children at three age levels: 3, 5, and 7 years old. These children also learned a very simple task—that under a particular block, a red plastic chip was hiding. Their task was to figure out which block. For some of the children, only one block *shape* was correct, either a round block or a triangular one. This group learned to pay attention to a perceptual cue. For the rest of the children, a particular *place* was correct,

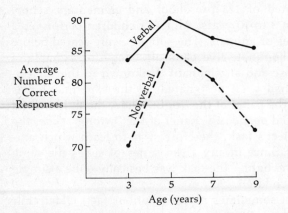

Figure 3.1   Average number of correct responses to animal concept study by children from 3 to 9 years of age. (Weir and Stevenson, 1959)

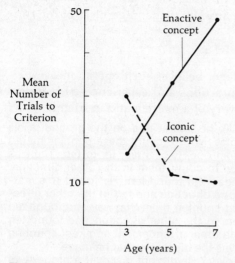

Figure 3.2   Subjects at three age levels learning a simple enactive or iconic concept. (Based on data from Zeiler, 1964)

either the block on the right or the block on the left, regardless of which block it was. These children learned a position cue.

Already we can see that in Bruner's terms, the children learning the position cue were developing an enactive concept; those learning the perceptual cue, an iconic concept. Did the age of the children matter? Would we predict that there would be a difference in the capacities of the children to learn in a particular modality?

Figure 3.2 shows that the younger children took longer to learn the perceptual concept and the older children took much longer to learn the position or enactive concept—presumably, again, because they refused to believe the learning problem was "that easy." The 7-year-olds learning the position concept required an average of 46 trials; the 3-year-olds learning the same concept required only about 18 trials. (Imagine the consternation of a 7-year-old who so thoroughly failed to beat little brother.)

But like the preoperational child whose conceptual abilities are in fact greater than those of the sensorimotor child, Zeiler's 7-year-olds are way ahead of their little brothers. The older children are entering what Piaget calls *the stage of concrete operations.*

CONCRETE OPERATIONAL THINKING

The stage of concrete operations begins about the age of 7 or 8 (Piaget and Inhelder, 1969). *Operations* are essentially groupings of schemas. They are called operations when the groupings have special interrelationships —for example, a reversible relationship (illustrated below). As a principle, reversibility will affect reasoning in many situations, regardless of the content of the situation.

The Origin of Concrete Logic

It is important to understand that Piaget believes such operational principles grow out of the individual's own actions and experiences. For example, he describes the childhood discovery of a mathematician friend:

> When he was . . . a small child, he was seated on the ground in his garden and he was counting pebbles. Now to count these pebbles he put them in a row and he counted them one, two, three, up to ten. Then he finished counting them and started to count them in the other direction. He began by the end and once again he found ten. He found this marvelous fact that there were ten in one direction and ten in the other direction. So he put them in a circle and counted them that way and found ten once again. Then he counted them in the other direction and found ten once more. So he put them in some other arrangement and kept counting them and kept finding ten. There was the discovery that he made.
>
> Now what indeed did he discover? He did not discover a property of pebbles; he discovered a property of the action of ordering. The pebbles had no order. It was his action which introduced a linear order or a cyclical order, or any kind of an order. . . .
>
> For the sum the same principle applied. The pebbles had no sum; they were simply in a pile. To make a sum, action was necessary—the operation of putting together and counting. He found that the sum was independent of the order. In other words, that the action of putting together is independent of the action of ordering. He discovered a property of actions and not a property of pebbles. . . . (Piaget, 1964, p. 11)

In the course of many experiences, a child develops certain basic rules for thinking logically. One such rule is that an idea can be the same in different forms. This is the principle of conservation discussed in Chapter 2—a principle the *preoperational* child has not yet developed. One hallmark of concrete operations—a signal that a child has entered the concrete operational stage of development—is his use of the conservation principle in solving various kinds of problems. Other principles were mentioned in Chapter 1—the principle of the permanence of objects, for example. Again, the sensorimotor child must learn that principle for himself; there is no way we can teach it to him.

Principles of Concrete Logic

There are four principles Piaget believes characterize operational thought. Lovell (1966), in his book about scientific and mathematical teaching, has provided an especially clear summary:

> Before systems of actions carried out in the mind (i.e., systems of operations) can be stable, they must, according to Piaget, have certain properties; unless these are present, thought will show inconsistencies. These properties are . . .
>
> 1. Closure—Any two operations can be combined to form a third operation. E.g., all boys and all girls equals all children; $3 + 4 = 7$.

2. Reversibility—For any operation there is an opposite operation which cancels it. E.g., all boys plus all girls equals all children, but all children except all boys equals all girls; $3 + 4 = 7$ and $7 - 4 = 3$.

3. Associativity—When three operations are combined it does not matter which two are combined first; or the same goal can be reached by different routes. E.g., all adults plus all boys and girls equals all boys plus all girls and adults; $(1 + 4) + 2 = 1 + (4 + 2)$.

4. Identity—This is a "null operation," and is performed when any operation is combined with its opposite. E.g., all human beings except all those who are human beings equals nobody; $5 - 5 = 0$. (Lovell, 1966, p. 147)

It is because these principles are missing from the thinking of preoperational children that their thought (Piaget believes) is illogical.

Concrete Logic in Conservation

The child whose thought is characterized by an awareness of reversibility will recognize that the amount of liquid in a high, narrow beaker can be the same as that in a low, wide beaker. He knows that the level of liquid can be reversed by the act of pouring, and he comes to that knowledge as a result of having done a great deal of pouring himself. He has also had other reversible experiences, so that by the age of 8 or 9 the concept is quite a general one.

Concrete Logic in Seriation

Suppose a child is given ten sticks of different sizes and asked to place them in order, from smallest to largest. The preoperational child separates the sticks into little groups and seriates each of them, but cannot put all the groups together in a single seriation. The child on the verge of operational thought may manage the whole pile by trial and error. The operational child will behave quite sytematically. He will look for the smallest element, and place it; then look for the next smallest and place it beside the first stick; then look for the smallest of those still remaining in the pile, and so on. His thought is characterized by reversibility, for his behavior indicates that he recognizes stick 2 to be *simultaneously* greater than stick 1 and smaller than stick 3.

Concrete Logic in Classification

Changes in classification behavior are also important clues to the development of operational thought. If you give a young child a large set of things to classify and ask him to put together the things that belong together (or words to that effect), he will make what Piaget calls a "figural collection." He will pay attention to similarities and differences, but overlook many of them by arranging the things spatially in rows, squares, and so forth. He makes them "belong together" more in a figural rather than a conceptual sense. The slightly older child may be able to group things conceptually, but he will still fail to grasp an essential point. Suppose he is classifying many different kinds of flowers, including a group of daisies (say, ten), three primroses, four tulips, and two violets. If you ask him, "Are there more daisies or more flowers?" he will reply, "More daisies." Not until he is 8 or 9 will he recognize the principle of the size of one class in relation to a class that includes it.

The concrete operational child is therefore capable of reasoning about many different kinds of things. It is because of these new powers that the child may overcomplicate simple situations. His mind is getting ready for bigger ideas.

FORMAL OPERATIONAL THOUGHT

The *concrete* operational child, who is between the ages of about 8 and 12, will "still need his pebbles." He can reason much more logically than the preoperational child, but it is still a reasoning about things. It is as if the concrete materials help him differentiate and integrate concepts. The *formal* operational child, who is 13 or 14, is free of concrete dependencies, and the possessor of other abilities as well.

Thought Takes Wings

Formal thought is characterized by an "all possibles" awareness. The 14-year-old youngster seems suddenly freed from dependency on reality. He can work with the imaginary as logically as he can work with reality. But in the beginning, this new logical freedom can also produce errors. The cognitive transitions are, as we have seen, often most clearly revealed by errors in thinking.

One summer, my teenager (a political liberal) met an ardent advocate of Ayn Rand's "objectivism," a political and moral philosophy of extremely conservative tone. My son was captivated by the paradoxical qualities of the objectivist argument, which makes many traditional nonvirtues (like selfishness and pride) into virtues. But he was equally captivated by liberal arguments—for social security, for example—that objectivists find abhorrent. For most of the following winter, an objectivist and a liberal lived side-by-side in my son's head—quite harmoniously, because they were not even nodding acquaintances. The arguments themselves were all that mattered. The fact that one argument (as delivered by my son) might wholly contradict another argument (as delivered by the same son) was never noticed (by said son—his father became thoroughly addled). When the young adolescent mind discovers its new logical wings (to use Piaget's terms), it may fly off in all directions at once until the urge to consolidate takes over. Again, we recognize a high-level differentiation and integration problem.

Complex Interrelations Are Understood

The "all possibles" awareness affects the child's perception of relations, classifications, combinations, and propositions. He becomes able to turn the world on all four corners and look at it from any direction. Notions of

balance, proportion, and probability become at once complex and stabilized. In the following excerpt from a paper by Hooper, Piaget's concepts
are related to the teaching of social studies:

Cognitive Prerequisite	Social Science Concepts
(1) Probabilistic reasoning	The fundamental uncertainty of his-torical predictions of outcomes.
(2) Multiple classification	Governmental tables of organization, authority relations, and related classi-fications of a hierarchical type.
(3) Multiple causation	Causal structure of historical or political outcomes. Concepts of causes continuously operating across extended time periods.
(4) Conservation	Generalization about historical or political processes — for example, common causal patterns involved in any revolution.

Multiple classification and relational understanding probably underlie
most abstract thinking or cognition as we normally conceive them. The
child of ten to eleven years has mastered the rational manipulation of
classes, relations, unit measurements, and numbers insofar as concrete
media are concerned. As he makes the transition to analogous operations
on the Piagetian formal level, he is capable of meaningful use and comprehension of certain abstract terms and concepts. As an example, the
child cannot grasp the essence of an organization table (chain of command, spheres of jurisdiction, interlocking authority) unless he has some
mastery of relational structures and superordinate, part-whole classifications as described in systems of logic. Competence in multiple, simultaneous classification and hierarchical relations is the cognitive prerequisite
for the acquisition of the concept of multiple causality. In other words, if a
student writing about Cardinal Richelieu wishes to be as objective as possible about his life, he must consider the implications of being both a
Frenchman and a member of the Catholic church. A "balance" must be
made by the student, just as it had to be made by the historical figure in
question. (Hooper, 1968, p. 427)

Analysis of the thinking processes that may be involved in formal operational activity is the province of Part II. There we will return to problems
of classification, hierarchical relationships, causality, and so forth.

A Note about "Readiness"
Later in Part I, and at other points throughout the book, we will take up
the question of readiness implied by writings such as Hooper's. Is it really
the case (as it seems) that we must wait until adolescence before introducing children to important historical and social concepts?

One researcher was recently heard to explain the importance of a
double classification principle to a group of social scientists. He presented
a curriculum to teach the principle to disadvantaged children, on the assumption that such a curriculum would increase their operational thinking.

Listening to this presentation was a skeptical anthropologist, who insisted that the disadvantaged children in question already knew how to perform double classifications. "No," answered the psychologist; "My test results—using colors and shapes—prove that they don't. The average disadvantaged child in my sample couldn't correctly classify red diamonds, blue diamonds, red squares, blue squares, and materials of that sort." The anthropologist shrugged. "I don't know about your squares and diamonds," he said, "but any ghetto child knows that black is good, and policemen are bad, and that when he meets a black policeman he has a problem. *That's* a double classification."

There are, indeed, many kinds of operational thought. We must not be too quick to assume that only the Piagetian materials exemplify them.

SYMBOLIC FUNCTIONS

In contrast to Piaget's emphasis upon logic in development, Werner has emphasized its biological nature. Biological development, Werner felt, illustrates the general form of cognitive development. The differentiation and eventual control of fine finger movements, for example, may be a model for the differentiation and control of thinking. One important implication of this is the continuing connection of the control system to the organic roots from which it emerges. The symbol (Werner says) already exists in the "primordial diffusion" of early thinking. The symbol must be *distilled from* the original impression, not *attached to* it. The word *chair*, for example, is distilled from the "sitting tone" and postural-affective state associated with the object.

An "Organic" Experiment

A surprising experimental demonstration of Werner's concepts was carried out by Langer and Rosenberg (1966). They used nonsense syllables that a pool of subjects considered to have color connotations. Over a hundred subjects decided:

> RED was the color implied by the syllables ZAH, KLAK, SKAF
> BLUE was the color implied by MUMLE, OOM, SOOL, MU
> GREEN was the color implied by TUR, ISH, NERD

In the experiment, the nonsense syllables were printed in colors that differed from their "organic" or true colors. ZAH, for example, was printed in green; MUMLE was printed in red. The subjects called out the name of the color the syllable was printed in, not the name of the syllable. Langer and Rosenberg believed that the organic color connotations of the syllable (its true color) would set up interference and make it difficult to call out the "false" color. They compared the subjects' abilities to call out false colors to their abilities to call out true ones. Oddly enough, they were right. Subjects had special difficulties calling out the name of the color a nonsense syllable was written in unless it was the "true" organic color.

As improbable as that experiment may sound, it does serve to illustrate Werner's main point, that symbolic forms may not be as arbitrary as we think. Symbols may be connected in our minds to the "stuff" they symbolize. Sylvia Ashton-Warner's so-called organic reading method illustrates a Wernerian type of pedagogy (see Chapter 21). She chooses as beginning words those a child finds intensely meaningful. The child's skills in using symbols is thereby linked to his emotional world.

Universal Symbolic Functions

Bruner also sees a link, but not of the same kind. He feels instead that the symbolic functions of language are also found in other kinds of cognitive behavior and that they may be practiced in these other ways before language becomes dominant. Bruner (in Bruner, Olver, and Greenfield, 1966) mentions the following aspects of a universal symbolic function which he believes to be expressed in speech, but not limited to it:

> *symbol reference:* the idea that there is a name that goes with things.
> *classification principles:* the idea that a name can refer to a class or category of things, not just to a single thing.
> *grammatical relations:* that things (nouns) can have actions (verbs), or be affected by modifications (adjectives and adverbs), or be the objects of actions.
> *experimental alteration of the environment:* "What if there were never any apples?" a four-year-old asked upon finishing one with gusto! (Bruner, Olver, and Greenfield, 1966, p. 37)

> "I would argue that language itself is not what is 'imposed' on experience. . . . Rather, language comes from the same basic root out of which symbolically organized experience grows." (Bruner, Olver, and Greenfield, 1966, p. 43)

Bruner goes on to point out that the experiences of organizing our world—by naming, classifying, relating (in a lawful way), and experimentally altering—may be disconnected from language organization for a while. This would arise, as we have seen, from the partial disconnection of verbal, visual, and motor representational systems in the brain. The coordination of these representational systems becomes more probable in adolescence, because the brain is more fully developed (Milner, 1967).

The Role of Schooling

Even in older children and adolescents, schooling is of critical importance. Without help, biologically mature humans will not necessarily develop adequate symbolic representational systems. Again, Bruner makes the point:

> One is thus led to believe that, in order for the child to use language as an instrument of thought, he must first bring the world of experience under the control of principles of organization that are in some degree isomorphic [in one-to-one correspondence] with . . . [language] princi-

ples. . . . Without special training in the symbolic *representation of experience*, the child grows to adulthood still depending in large measure on the enactive and iconic modes of representing and organizing the world, no matter what language he speaks. (Bruner, Olver, and Greenfield, 1966, pp. 43–48)

What does this imply for schooling?

THE "THINKING CHILD" IN SCHOOL

By way of summary, here are some general school applications of the information in this chapter.

1. The birth of concrete operational capacities in children signals the beginning of their interest in systems and rules. The child now has principles of thought organization in a more clearly formed state. He likes to use these systems, just as a sportsman likes to use his muscles and skills. The first general recommendation would therefore be to provide the child with numerous opportunities to exercise his interest in systems.

2. Remember, however, that during the early school years these systems should be (a) action-oriented and (b) exercised through the use of concrete materials. Put simply, the systems should give the child a great deal to do and a great deal to manipulate.

3. Of special importance is the principle of *isomorphism,* a matching of "outside" materials and activities to "inside" mental development. There is no way of exactly predicting these matches. The best way to find out about them is to provide schoolchildren with many kinds of tasks and then watch to see what absorbs their attention. If attention is absorbed, then the task is a good match for the inner mental systems. (In Part III, we will learn more about principles of self-motivation in learning tasks.)

4. Of course, even among normal children, the matching process cannot be left entirely to the child. Sometimes a child must be encouraged to pay attention to a task long enough to discover that he likes it. Sometimes he must be encouraged to exercise a skill long enough to discover that he actually has it. But there is a very great difference between that kind of guidance and being forced to carry out an entire day's worth of adult-selected school procedures.

5. The onset of concrete operations also signals the child's new interest in symbolization processes. He becomes fascinated by letters, numbers, drawing, and so forth. If this interest is properly managed, the child will voraciously practice symbolic skills—writing, reading, arithmetic, and drawing.

6. The most important aspect of proper management is matching these symbolic interests to the child's activities and emotional states. The child should be able to write about, or copy, ideas that interest him; to use numbers with reference to activities (such as measuring himself) that are meaningful to him; to read (or pretend to read) books about concepts that are important to him. Because commercial materials are not sufficiently

individualized, the good teacher must frequently generate appropriate materials. This is perhaps the most important skill a teacher can possess: the ability to build on a child's own interests, to develop materials that relate his interests to our cultural symbol systems.

7. The principles of differentiation and integration continue to operate, but at a higher level. The "thinking child" in elementary school can coordinate his skills and abilities much more successfully than the "thinking child" in preschool. That is because they are more clearly differentiated within his own head. The elementary school child can, with perhaps a little help, recognize when he has a rule that can be applied to new situations. The preschool child is less able to abstract a rule; for him, rules remain "stuck" to particular materials (*that* stove is hot).

8. By high school, these abstracting capacities have reached a high level. The adolescent has "free-floating" rules of reasoning that can be attached to almost anything, real or not. This is (or should be) the heyday of seminars, debates, discussion clubs, and forensics of all sorts. Unfortunately, the authoritarian pressures against free-floating rules seem crushing in many high schools (Silberman, 1970). Youngsters are discouraged from exercising their reasoning capacities with reference to matters of greatest interest to them—their own schooling, for example. Further, because their elementary years in traditional schools have blocked them from building their own minds on the basis of their own interests and activities, many high school students are incapable of reasoning wisely. Their reasoning capacities have been, in effect, crippled.

In Part II, we will learn more about the formal nature of the reasoning systems naturally used by human beings. In Parts III, IV, and V, we will learn more about motivation, language, and perceptual symbolization (reading, mathematics, and pictures). In Part VI, we will take up the problem of creativity. With that general background, we will be better able to understand the nature of the total process of normal conceptual development. More, then, can be said about appropriate forms of schooling at the primary, secondary, and college level.

In the next chapter, we will take up the problem of abnormal conceptual development and its implications for schooling.

Chapter 4 READINESS AND REMEDY

The constant interaction of experience and neurological potential jointly shapes a child's potential. In this chapter, we will look at the problem from several vantage points. What are some effects of genetic influences? of brain damage? of sensory deficits such as deafness or blindness? of early experience deprivations? Can such effects be counteracted in schools?

NEW RESEARCH IN PSYCHOGENETICS

In the early 1920s, John B. Watson, the father of behaviorism in American psychology (see Chapter 5), made a famous declaration:

> Give me a dozen healthy infants, well-formed, and my own specified world to bring them up in and I'll guarantee to take any one at random and train him to become any type of specialist I might select—doctor, lawyer, artist, merchant-chief, and yes, even beggar-man and thief, regardless of his talents, penchants, tendencies, abilities, vocations, and race of his ancestors. (Watson, 1930, p. 82)

Although few psychologists (then or now) would agree that such a sweeping statement is justified, many would share the sentiment that learning or environmental causes are the primary shaping forces of human behavior. Watson's declaration represented a rejection of genetics, instincts, or inborn tendencies of any sort as acceptable scientific explanations of human behavior. It is easy to see why such a step was necessary in the evolution of psychological science. If we explain behavior as inherited in some vague sense, we are not likely to advance our knowledge of it or our ability to affect it educationally. But now, our biochemical knowledge of genetic mechanisms has been greatly deepened, and a genetic explanation of behavior is not a mere "cop out." We are beginning to understand what genes really are and how they operate.

Transmitting the Genetic Code

Strictly speaking, behavior cannot be inherited. A child does not really inherit Uncle Arn's sluffy walk, but he may inherit the bodily characteristics that would inevitably result in such a walk. These characteristics exist within a gene in the form of a biochemical code, or program, for development. Figure 4.1 shows (in a vastly oversimplified way) the steps by means of which this code is transmitted.

We begin with a cell—any cell. Within that cell is a biochemical code for the full amount of genetic information received from the male sperm and the female egg of the parents. The information is stored in the form of a spirally bonded set of chemicals. (Some chemicals go together like salt and pepper, or magnets and iron filings, because of certain atomic "needs.") The name for this chemical spiral (see J. D. Watson, 1968, for a full explanation) is deoxyribonucleic acid, or DNA for short. The chemicals that make up DNA can be arranged in many ways. DNA itself acts as a sort of master planner or architect; it *shows* the cell-manufacturing process what to do, by means of itself. It acts as a living blueprint.

The "contractor" for the manufacturing process is a cousin, *ribonucleic acid,* or RNA. We will meet RNA again in our discussion of memory (Chapter 7), for it is now believed to be an important substance in learning. RNA is widely distributed throughout each cell, and in some of its forms it can act as a message carrier for the DNA processes.

When a cell multiplies itself—which is, of course, the basic step in growth of all sorts—it does so in response to RNA's instructions, and RNA is, in turn, following DNA's blueprint. The cell takes in nutrients, breaks them down by metabolic processes, and reassembles the broken-down products into the same kinds of biochemical chains modeled by DNA. This entire process is triggered by hormones of various types, which are, in turn, affected by growth and by triggers of their own located in the brain.

Coded Interactions

All the characteristics that can genetically govern the behavior of human beings are carried in the form of a chemical code, but of course, complex behavior does not occur within a single cell. Also coded are instructions for how various cell-multiplication processes are to be interrelated to produce complex body parts and governing mechanisms. If the entire genetic lot is stored in each cell, how does the cell know which part of it to activate? and how long to continue multiplying?

The mechanism is by no means fully understood, but it has to do with the same processes of differentiation and integration that we have been using as a model of psychological development. As some cells develop, they operate as *leader cells* that tell other cells what to do. We know this because under some conditions, and to a very limited extent, these cells can be transplanted to new tissue and will cause the new cells to begin to

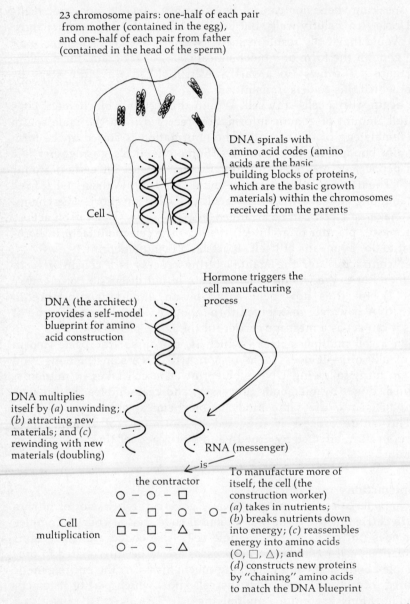

23 chromosome pairs: one-half of each pair from mother (contained in the egg), and one-half of each pair from father (contained in the head of the sperm)

DNA spirals with amino acid codes (amino acids are the basic building blocks of proteins, which are the basic growth materials) within the chromosomes received from the parents

Cell

Hormone triggers the cell manufacturing process

DNA (the architect) provides a self-model blueprint for amino acid construction

DNA multiplies itself by (a) unwinding; (b) attracting new materials; and (c) rewinding with new materials (doubling)

RNA (messenger)

is

Cell multiplication

the contractor

O – O – □
△ – □ – O – O –
□ – □ – △ –
O – O – △

To manufacture more of itself, the cell (the construction worker) (a) takes in nutrients; (b) breaks nutrients down into energy; (c) reassembles energy into amino acids (O, □, △); and (d) constructs new proteins by "chaining" amino acids to match the DNA blueprint

Figure 4.1   Diagram of the way a cell multiplies in response to instructions from the genetic program.

operate on a master plan they would not ordinarily follow. But timing is critically important. If the new cells have grown beyond a certain period (called a *critical* period), they may be "set in their ways" and refuse to take further orders from transplanted cells. If the new cells have not yet achieved a critical stage, they will not take orders either. The question of "readiness" actually goes back to such biological concepts, although the term is used in a much looser way educationally.

From Code to Behavior

There are a very large number of biological processes that may be governed by a genetic biochemical code received from the male and female parents. When we say "intelligence is inherited," for example (a statement that may or may not be true), what we mean is that certain genetically controlled programs for the development of the brain may underlie the potential for certain kinds of thinking.

> It is possible that intelligence may be a function of efficient neural chemistry, the rapid formation perhaps of synaptic [connecting] conductors, and the prompt removal of the waste products of neurochemical reactions. Efficient oxygen transport and utilization might be another aspect of this neurophysiology. Gene-derived enzymes could presumably be important in these reactions. . . . (Nash, 1970, p. 26)

Nash provides excellent, readable coverage of psychobiological principles of all sorts. His chapter on genetics (pp. 17–45) is especially recommended.

We know for a fact that processes of this sort can be involved in certain kinds of retardation (*phenylketonuria*)—happy news because of the additional fact that then biochemical remedies can be used. A simple test for the presence of a biochemical abnormality, followed by diet control, can prevent retardation of this particular type, provided it begins immediately after birth. If the condition is not diagnosed early, retardation (from cellular brain damage) will inevitably and irreversibly result. Similar progress is being made in understanding the genetic biochemical mechanisms in the thought disorders known as *schizophrenia,* which is actually a catchall term for many kinds of mental abnormalities. The research into the genetics of schizophrenia has also served as a model for another important principle: the concept of *heritability.*

What Is Heritability?

Heritability is determined by twin studies, not by family trees. While it may be true that everyone in Uncle Arn's family has the same sluffy walk, we cannot be sure that the walk or the bodily factors associated with it were inherited. It may be that the sluffiness resulted from particular child-training procedures that were passed on in the same family not genetically, but through direct instruction. Uncle Arn's great-great-grandmother may have started a family tradition that babies should push themselves around in strollers for six months before they are allowed to practice walking, even if they are already able to walk. Maybe both the tradition and the stroller were handed down.

To find out about such possibilities, we will have to imagine that Uncle Arn had a monozygotic (one-egg) twin who was adopted and reared by a family with a different set of traditions. If the same sluffy walk appeared in both Uncle Arn and Uncle Zeke, we would be a step closer to determining its genetic elements. But there are other factors—nutrition, for example. To control for that, we should imagine that other twins besides Uncle Arn and Uncle Zeke are involved in our study. One quarter of them, while being brought up in one kind of family tradition, are also receiving one kind of nutrition; one quarter of them, in the same kind of family, are receiving another kind of nutrition. A similar division operates in the other family tradition. In summary form, the experiment looks like the chart.

Twins (AA, BB, CC, etc.)

	Nutrition Y	Nutrition Z
Family Tradition W	A, B, C, D, E, F, G, H	A, C, F, I, J, K, L, M, N, O
Family Tradition X	B, D, G, I, J, K	E, H, L, M, N, O

At the age of 10, everybody gets tested for sluffy walks. By means of special statistical techniques, it is possible to estimate the extent to which nutrition, family tradition, and genetic inheritance (shared by each twin pair) each contributed to sluffiness. The latter portion of the sluffiness would be called sluffiness heritability. It is a statistical estimate for a population, remember, not a prediction for an individual twin. It takes all the twins in the study to compose the statistical estimate.

You can see that some of the main requirements of such a study are lots of twins and rather careful control of their environmental experiences. Such studies are difficult to carry out, but they have been done.

Heritability of IQ

On the basis of twin studies, it has been determined that performance on IQ tests (which may or may not be a fair measure of intelligence; see Chapter 9) has a *heritability coefficient* of about .80. That is to say, about 80 percent of the variation in IQ in a given population is determined by genetic factors. Although this has been known for some time, it has emerged again in connection with racial issues. Arthur Jenson (1969) and others have argued, on the basis of heritability evidence, that Negro populations may be afflicted with genetic mental deficiencies. This is why, they say, Head Start and other remedial programs are not working.

It is important to separate the racial, genetic, and educational problems entangled in this controversy. In the first place, if a remedial educational program for whites, blacks, browns, yellows, or reds is not working, then something is wrong with the program. It is clearly ridiculous to blame the failure of such a program on whatever problem may have made it necessary. This would be as absurd as saying a transfusion failed because the patient was bleeding. Of course he was bleeding; why else would he need a transfusion? We do not abandon transfusions under such conditions; we find another way of coping with the problem. In the second place, all the heritability studies that I have been able to locate have been carried out on white populations. It is entirely possible that the heritability coefficients that have been calculated for white populations are not generalizable to blacks, browns, yellows, or reds. Certainly the burden of proof is on the geneticist, and in the meantime we can only guess. In the third place, any educational program for human beings of any racial or ethnic stock must cope with genetic predispositions of many, many kinds. Some of these may be far more critical than IQ.

Heritability of Personality Traits

Not only mental abilities, but temperamental characteristics too are genetically preprogrammed to varying degrees. Schizophrenic behavioral tendencies are strongly controlled by genetic codes, the nature of which, like the nature of intelligence codes, is poorly understood. We know the genetic influence is there because of the heritability studies (Heston, 1970). Personality traits like interest in sociability (sometimes called extroversion) have heritabilities of about 40 percent. Other personality characteristics, as measured by a test called the Minnesota Multiphasic Personality Inventory (MMPI), also show substantial heritabilities. Some traits sampled by this test may have heritabilities as high as 68 percent (Gottesman, 1963).

Democratic Concerns

At the present time, heritability statements may be regarded with great consternation by many psychologists who have been professionally educated in behavioristic or humanistic traditions. We find it emotionally and professionally disturbing to be told that our children may be growing up in accord with genetic programs which our environments—including our schools—cannot control. Like Watson, we want to believe that *we* are producing the architects and the thieves; we do not like to hear that architects may be produced by a genetically controlled spatial ability and that thieves may be produced by an inherited lack of sensitivity to hormones that produce feelings of anxiety. Humanistically, we feel somehow that it is not fair to condemn a child to a limited potential because of his genetic programming. Consequently, both humanists and behaviorists may be angered by the psychogeneticist's quiet and relentless collection of heritability evidence.

Environmental Influences

It should be emphasized, however, that the psychogeneticists have never said that genetic influences are the only influences on human behavior. In fact, the genetic factors may themselves produce special susceptibilities to environmental influences. A very good example of this has emerged from the Berkeley Growth Studies—longitudinal studies of children who have been followed into adulthood. In 54 cases, they have been followed for almost forty years. Repeated measures of the intelligence of these children, along with other information, have produced a curious finding: Factors that are associated with the IQ of girls may differ from those associated with the IQ of boys. In girls, vocalization measures (When did she begin to babble? How many words did she know by 19 months?) have a consistent, positive association with IQ. In boys, this association does not appear. Early verbal abilities are not clearly associated with IQ scores in males. For them, the critical associations seem to be between IQ and quality of the mother-child interaction before the age of about 4. Ratings of maternal warmth, hostility, rejection of child, and so on were available, and these seemed to be quite directly associated with IQ development:

> These sex differences in patterns of correlations led us to the suggestion that there are genetically determined sex differences in the extent to which the effects of early experiences (such as maternal love and hostility) persist. The girls appeared to be more resilient in returning to their own characteristic inherent response tendencies. Boys, on the other hand, were more permanently affected by the emotional climate in infancy whether it was one of warmth and understanding or of punitive rejection. (Bayley, 1968, pp. 14–15)

In the next sections of this chapter, we will review some of these nongenetic influences on cognitive development—early experience, sensory opportunities, and the like. In the final analysis, we are very far from fully comprehending the nature of the complex interaction between genes and environmental factors, and we must consider any contribution to our understanding of these matters to be a helpful step toward the preparation of effective educational procedures. We will never construct remedies if we refuse to face frankly and courageously the full extent of the problem. Would we rather have a vaccine for polio, or a nursing staff which sentimentally refuses to admit that paralysis cannot be cured by massage and hot blankets, or a militant group of polio victims who argue that in a democratic society, crippled people should have the right to enter track meets? Polio, of course, is not inherited. That is why absurdities regarding its treatment are easier to detect. Disorders produced by genetic mechanisms rather than by a virus may also be curable. Stubbornness, sentimentality, and misguided militancy are just as absurd in their case as well—and just as unfair to the afflicted population.

BRAIN INJURY

The Brain Function Controversy

A hundred years ago it was believed that the brain was divided into parts and that each part was responsible for a piece of human behavior. (Figure 4.2 illustrates the kind of "brain map" such a theory generated.) But as time went on, these concepts were recognized as too fanciful. In 1929, for example, a researcher published the diagram shown in Figure 4.3; it illustrates the centers of functional localization generally recognized at that time.

Although such behaviors as perfectionism were no longer considered

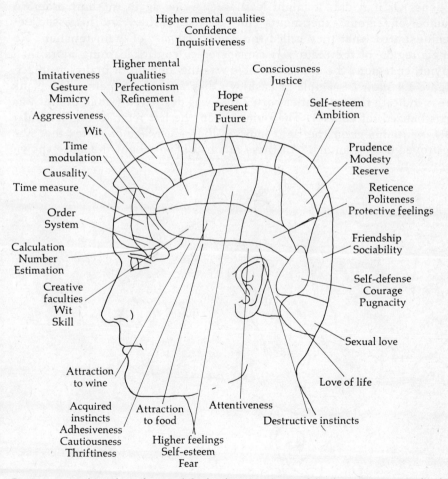

Figure 4.2   A phrenological map of the localization of mental faculties, as conceptualized in the middle of the nineteenth century. (Luria, 1966a, p. 9)

to have brain centers of their own, other forms of complex mental behavior like word reading were still thought to be localized. What led to
such beliefs? Suppose an individual with a brain tumor lost his ability to
read. When he was operated on and the tumor removed, his ability to read
returned. The surgeon might then decide that the tumor was located in an
area of word reading ability. If the evidence were experimental rather than
clinical, it might consist of the following: A cat might be operated on, and
part of its brain in the section labeled "visual guidance" removed. The cat
might then lose its ability to walk along a narrow ledge or to avoid
bumping into walls.

But even this convenient picture of the brain proved much too simple.
The operated-on cat just might *not* lose its ability to visually guide its own
actions. Or. if it did, it might learn such skills again in short order. A
number of famous experiments done by Karl Lashley and his associates
demonstrated what they called the *equipotentiality* of brain function: No
single region of the brain was considered to control learning more than
any other region; the critical variable was the amount of brain left intact.
Figure 4.4 shows a sample of Lashley's diagrams of rat brains. The blank
areas indicate the amount of cortex that was destroyed (while the rat was
anesthetized, of course). The numbers on the left refer to the particular
rat; the numbers on the right indicate the percentage of cortex that was
destroyed in that animal. All these rats had been taught the maze shown

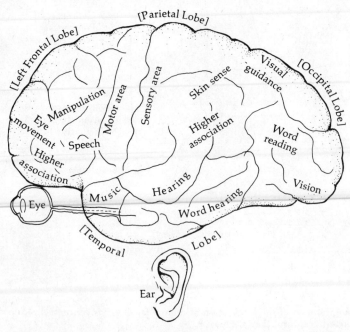

Figure 4.3 Diagram of the cerebral cortex showing function localization as it was conceptualized in the 1920s.

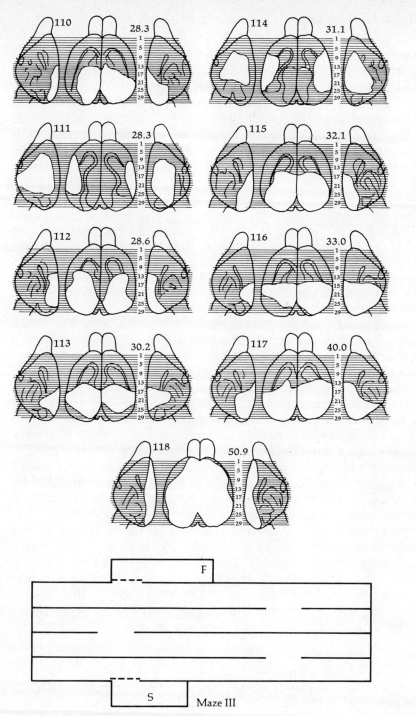

Figure 4.4 A sample of Lashley's diagrams of the location and extent of brain injuries produced in rats who had learned Maze III. Each rat's ability to relearn the maze after its operation was affected more by the amount of the damaged area than by the location of the damage. (Lashley, 1963, p. 31 and Plate X)

at the bottom of the figure. All had difficulty relearning the maze after their operations, but the degree of difficulty was directly proportional to the *amount* of brain injury, not to its location (Lashley, 1963).

From about 1930, when Lashley's book was first published, until about 1950, psychologists generally believed that learning was not localized in any one part of the brain, but could take place almost anywhere. If one part of the brain was injured, another would take over eventually; the brain's potential for learning was believed to be solely a matter of its available mass.

New Theories of Brain Function

With the close of World War II, new technological equipment began to change old conceptions of brain function. For one thing, it became possible to record the electrical activity taking place in a single brain cell; for another, computers could "collect" very faint electrical activities recorded from the skull and thereby locate a special mental activity inside the head of a person, without performing any sort of surgical operation. The electrical activity would "pile up" in a certain place, and a recording device placed on the head of a subject could detect it. The development of these more precise methods of measurement and detection was accompanied by more precise methods of experimentally damaging the brains of animals. Now a lesion could be produced in an exact spot; in Lashley's day, the injuries were less well controlled. In addition, microscopic electrodes could actually be placed within the brains of both animals and people without causing pain or damage. Weak electrical stimulation from these electrodes might then produce certain kinds of effects—a person might, for example, report hearing a familiar strain of music, or a cat might jump as if something had frightened it. The particularized responses could be produced by stimulating only certain areas of the brain. Findings of this sort suggested that Lashley's theories of equipotentiality could not be wholly true.

In recent years, a major attempt to synthesize the localizationist and nonlocalizationist theories of brain function has been undertaken by a Russian neuropsychologist named Luria. He has mastered not only the extensive animal studies of brain physiology, but also the fields of neurological diagnosis and psychological testing of brain injury in humans. Although not everyone agrees with Luria's theorizing, no one has surpassed his prodigious knowledge of cortical function in man (Luria, 1966a and 1966b).

Luria's Theory of Brain Function

Luria's view is that complex thinking is the result of *working constellations* of brain cells that might be located in widely separated areas. He calls these constellations "functional centers," but by this he means not a geographic location, but rather sets of cells that "fire" together, even though they are in separate parts of the brain.

Complex behavior, then, would result not from the amount of brain that was involved, but from particular portions of the brain that were involved together. Consider, for example, what happens when you write down an assignment: First, you have to acoustically analyze the sounds. This probably involves articulating some of those sounds to yourself—repeating to yourself some of the instructions. Next, you must recode the sounds into their visual representations (letters) and arrange them spatially. This is done before you begin the act of writing. Writing involves recoding your images of letters into what Luria (1966a) calls a "kinesthetic melody" of motor actions. As you write, you constantly check sound and letter patterns through feedback systems.

This complex process may involve widely separated working constellations of brain cells, in an "orchestration" of many brain areas. Clearly, the primary areas concerned with hearing, articulating, touching, and seeing are involved. The coordination of these areas is accomplished by means of the secondary and tertiary association areas, but the matter does not end there. How is the task (writing down an assignment dictated by the teacher) planned? Is there any physiological basis for the idea of a beginning, an ending, and a series of intermediate steps as applied to a particular task? Luria and others believe that such planning requires the participation of the frontal lobes—also by means of tertiary association areas—especially when serial processes are necessary. In addition, there is a simultaneous act of recognition at many points of task performance: recognizing the written word, for example, or even recognizing the individual letters. This kind of simultaneity, Luria believes, is mediated by the parietal and occipital lobes at the top and back of the brain. Again, such participation is carried out by means of the "overlapping" tertiary association areas.

How does Luria support his contention that such different and widely separated brain areas must be involved in a higher mental coordination? He has made an extensive study of the writing behavior of patients who have suffered wounds or tumors in various parts of the brain, and he reports that although writing behavior is affected by lesions in many areas, it is affected differently. If the wound is in the auditory area, for example, the patient may be able to write only highly automated words—words his writing muscles "know" as well as his ears. But such a patient will find writing words from dictation impossible, because he will be unable to identify (analyze) the sounds that he hears.

A Clinical Example

Figure 4.5 shows a letter my husband and I received from my father-in-law shortly after he had suffered a stroke. You can see that the language functions—spelling, sentence construction, and the like—are impaired. He notes that it took him an hour to "right this." You can also see that there is nothing wrong with his arithmetic skills. Being worried about his hospital bill, he was asking us to repay a small loan ($200) that he had made to us ten years before. He had correctly computed the compound interest (at 6 percent) on this loan over a ten-year period.

This would indicate that the area of stroke damage was probably limited to the left temporal region (language area). The interesting fact that calculation skills may not be affected by the same injuries that affect language functions supports the view that mathematical thinking is more spatial in nature. If that were so, then injuries to the back part of the brain (the occipital areas) should be more likely to impair arithmetical abilities, and that is often the case.

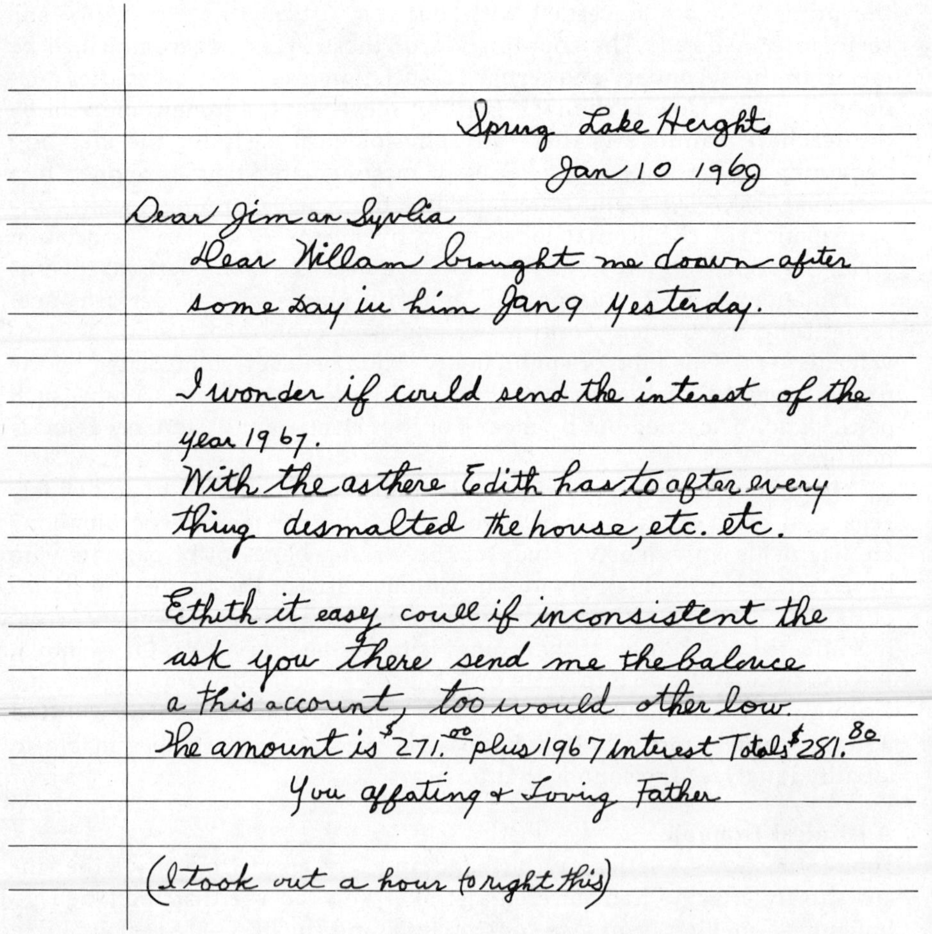

Spring Lake Heights
Jan 10 1969

Dear Jim an Sylvia
Hear Willam brought me doown after
some day in him Jan 9 Yesterday.

I wonder if could send the interest of the
year 1967.
With the asthere Edith has to after every
thing desmalted the house, etc. etc.

Ethith it easy coull if inconsistent the
ask you there send me the balance
a this account, too would other low.
The amount is $271.00 plus 1967 interest Totals $281.80
You affating & Loving Father

(I took out a hour to right this)

Figure 4.5 Letter written by a patient who had recently suffered a cerebral hemmorhage, illustrating disruption in his ability to write down his thoughts, but no disruption of his ability to calculate interest on a loan.

Other Symbolic Disorders

Injuries to the occipital areas can impair other functions (Figure 4.6). One of the frequent problems an educator faces may involve reading difficulties, or *dyslexia*. It is not clear if this results from brain injury, from inher-

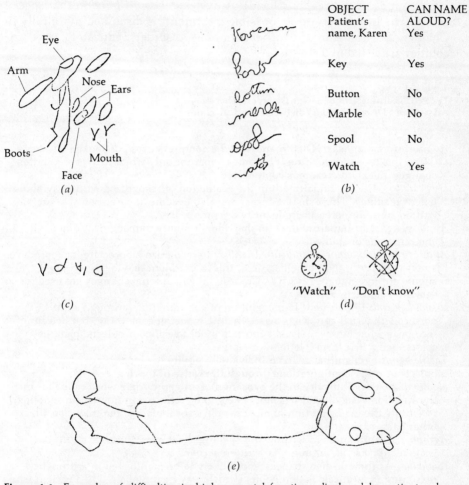

OBJECT Patient's name, Karen	CAN NAME ALOUD? Yes
Key	Yes
Button	No
Marble	No
Spool	No
Watch	Yes

(a)   (b)

(c)

"Watch"   "Don't know"

(d)

(e)

Figure 4.6 Examples of difficulties in higher mental functions displayed by patients who have been injured in various cortical zones.
(a) Patient was damaged in the visual area. His drawing of a man shows how he could not integrate the idea of a man—he drew the man in separated pieces. (Luria, 1966a, p. 140)
(b) Distorted handwriting of a 7-year-old girl with developmental aphasia. Note that she is able to write the names of some objects shown her when she was unable to name them aloud. (Paine and Oppé, 1966, p. 62)
(c) Seven-year-old boy with chronic brain syndrome writes his name, David, with letters out of order, upside down and backwards. (Paine and Oppé, 1966, p. 77)
(d) Disturbance of perception of crossed-out figure in patient with optic agnosia. (Luria, 1966a, p. 139)
(e) 90° rotation of human figure lying on its side, but described by the patient as a drawing of a man walking upright along the street.

itance (reading difficulties frequently run in families, but the relevant heritability studies have not been done), from some sort of developmental
failure, or from poor teaching. The difficulty itself seems to result from a
lack or loss of associative connections of spatial representations (the way
the word looks on the page) with verbal representations (the way the
word sounds in the reader's head). A dyslexic is *word blind* in that special
sense. The problem, and its possible treatment, is discussed more fully in
Chapter 21. Some of the other symbolic disorders educators may encounter are listed in Table 4.1.

Table 4.1
Types of Learning and Behavior Disorders That May
Arise from "Disconnections" Between Cortical Zones

Auditory verbal aphasia: Disturbances in the comprehension of spoken language.
Often this type of impairment becomes apparent only when the speech content
changes quickly or becomes complicated.

Dyslexia (or *Alexia*): Impairment in the evaluation of recognized written symbols
(silent reading). These disturbances may also become apparent only as the
written content increases in quantity or complexity.

Auditory agnosia: Impairment in an individual's ability to recognize sounds or
combinations of sounds.

Auditory musical agnosia (*amusia*): Inability to recognize, appreciate, or reproduce
a musical pattern. Not tone deafness, this impairment may be especially
significant in languages, such as Chinese, in which tonal changes are used for
semantic distinctions.

Visual agnosia: Impairment in recognition of configurations through sight. A
person with visual agnosia is aware that he is seeing something, but he cannot
recognize what he sees; visual agnosia may be specific for objects, pictures,
colors, geometric forms, letters, or words.

Tactile agnosia: Disturbance in an individual's ability to recognize or identify
objects or other configurations through the sense of touch.

Nominal aphasia: Difficulty in the evocation of an appropriate word called for by
the situation. The difficulty is most likely to be reflected in nouns, since nouns
constitute the major portion of most people's vocabularies, but may also affect
other parts of speech.

Agraphia: Disturbances in writing and spelling. Examples: *suppose* might be
written *suppoise, occur* might be written *accour.*

Acalculia: Arithmetic disturbances, more likely to be manifested in arithmetic
reasoning than in calculation habits (which may be unimpaired in a patient who
cannot reason about numbers).

Paraphasia: Errors of commission or omission relative to grammar, word
substitutions, sound substitutions, or sound or letter reversals—similar to "slips
of tongue."

Dysarthrias: Defects of articulation, which tend to be aggravated as word or
sentence length increases.

Apraxia: Disturbances characterized by disability in the voluntary and intended use
of tools, such as brushes, hammers, and knives.

SOURCE: Based on Berry and Eisenson, 1956.

Remedial Strategies

Unless they are extremely severe, all these disorders can be at least partially overcome by the application of a simple principle: The injured person must develop *alternate brain pathways* for handling the same information. In the *Restoration of Function after Brain Injury,* Luria (1963) discusses a number of ways to help brain-injured patients. For example, following a certain type of injury to the frontal lobes (see Figure 1.1), patients often sound like eighth-grade students facing their first English composition assignment: "I can't think of a thing to say . . . I've got no ideas . . . I don't know what to say first." To help such patients restore the flow of thought, Luria first engages the patient in a dialogue ("What next? And then what happened? What else?"), and then teaches the patient to carry out this sort of dialogue with himself. Another technique was to write transitional phrases ("However . . ." "Whereas . . ." "Although . . ." "After . . ." "Since . . .") on a large card. When the patient was stuck, he was shown the card and asked to select a phrase that "moved him along." Eventually, the patient could use such a card for himself, and then dispense with the card entirely. When ideas were fragmented, a patient would be encouraged to write the fragments on separate file cards and then arrange them (classify them) spatially—spread out on a table in front of him.

Many of these strategies sound like those that have been used by good English teachers for many years. But English teachers may not realize that they activate alternate mental pathways inside the heads of their students. Here is one simple example: Reach as high as you can, straight up. Now do it again, but this time try to touch a spot on the ceiling. To an observer, your actions would not look very different, but inside your head, different brain patterns were activated. The principle underlying the development of alternate instructional systems of any sort is to set up alternate mental coordinations. If the student's brain has been injured, the alternate systems may be his only hope. If he can be helped to develop them, his behavior may become completely normal.

It is important to understand that brain injuries do not necessarily result from major accidents like falling from a playground swing. One of the most common sources of damage is simply the act of being born. A few seconds of oxygen deprivation at the moment of birth may kill some strategic brain cells—those crucial to certain kinds of language connections, for example—that are not able to replace themselves. Or perhaps a fever during infancy damages some brain cells. The parents may have no knowledge of these cerebral accidents. It may be that many of the children in public school "special classes" are suffering from various kinds of undiagnosed brain damage.

We will return shortly to the question of what the nonspecialist educator can do about occasional problems that appear in his classroom. The solution is not always to summon the school psychologist and pass the educational problem on to someone else.

SENSORY DEFICIENCIES

In the following two studies, we will consider the effects of early sensory loss (blindness or deafness) on later problem-solving abilities.

Some Effects of Blindness on Cognitive Development

The first study was carried out by Drever (1955) in England. His subjects were teenage boys and girls. One group was normally sighted, and there were two groups of blind subjects. The *early blind* group had been born blind or had lost their vision within the first five years of life. The *late blind* group had lost their sight with the second five years of life. Using appropriate materials, Drever tested the IQ of all his subjects, and there were no differences between the blind and sighted groups in this respect. All three groups were above average (IQ of approximately 118).

The sighted children were all blindfolded for the following tests. First, Drever handed his subjects (one at a time) two wooden half-circles, one in each hand. These stimulus objects could be put together to make a complete wooden circle, but the subjects were not allowed to do that. After they had handled the original objects, the experimenter took them back and handed the subject a complete wooden circle, and a square or a rectangle, also one at a time. The subject was then asked to state which of the latter objects could have been constructed out of the first two objects. (Of course, Drever did not limit this problem just to circles; the subjects were also tested on squares, rectangles, and so forth.) The test required the subjects to integrate mentally their perceptions of parts of an object. By the age of Drever's sample, this test was quite easy, but a difference between the groups nevertheless appeared.

Table 4.2 shows the scores of the three groups on this first test, called *object integration* (we will discuss the pegboard problem shortly). You can see that the sighted children made the fewest errors (0.9, on the average), the late blind children made the next fewest, and the early blind children made the most. Apparently, visual abilities acquired during the first five years of life helped develop the mental skills necessary for this problem.

Table 4.2
Mean Number of Errors in the Sighted, Early
Blind, and Late Blind Groups on Two Tasks

TASK	SIGHTED	LATE BLIND	EARLY BLIND
Object-integration	0.9	1.4	2.9
Pegboard patterns	41.2	26.2	39.6

SOURCE: Based on data in Drever, 1955.

In Drever's second study, this same blind group (late blind) proved superior to the sighted as well as to the early blind. The subject was presented with a pegboard on which the experimenter had constructed some simple peg patterns. (They included two pegs placed vertically, horizontally, and diagonally; three pegs making right angles; four pegs making a square; and so forth.) After the subject had felt the pattern, the pegs were removed, the board was turned half-way around, and the subject was told to replace the pegs in the holes they had occupied when he touched them the first time. This task therefore required the youngsters to hold the image of a simple pattern in their minds and to re-create that image in an altered position. Table 4.2 shows the number of errors made by the three groups. You can see that the most errors were made by the sighted and the early blind groups. We might conclude that early opportunity to see is important, but that later loss of vision forced the super-development of the pegboard-type skill (we might think of this as a skill in maintaining map-like images from tactual information). Drever was quite impressed with the skill of the late blind group. He pointed out that no sighted person had ever been able to solve the problem with fewer than 20 errors, and some of the late blind youngsters reduced their errors to 8.

Since the tasks clearly require a mental operation on tactual "inputs," we might wonder whether the difference between the sighted and blind subjects arose from differences in the perceptual system itself or from differences in the ability to perform the necessary mental operations. In the following study, the effect of early deafness on the ability to process visual information was investigated. It suggests one answer to the question.

Some Effects of Deafness on Cognitive Development

This experiment was carried out by a group of researchers (Sterritt, Camp, and Lipman, 1966) at the University of Colorado Medical Center. Their subjects were nine children with profound hearing losses, five girls and four boys ranging in age from 3 to 8 years; and nine hearing children matched in sex and age to the deaf group. The deaf children had lost their hearing (as nearly as was known) within the first few months of life or had been born deaf.

All the subjects learned to reproduce, by pressing a telegraph key, a light-generated pattern of dots and dashes. Forty test stimuli ranged from simple to complex. Six of the forty consisted of single dots and dashes (stimulus complexity level 1); six were double dots or double dashes (level 2); eleven were triple dots, triple dashes, dot-dash, or dash-dot (level 3); and seventeen were triple dot-dash combinations (level 4). Figure 4.7 shows how well the deaf and hearing subjects could perform the task. As it became more complex, all the subjects performed less well, but on all levels the deaf children were inferior to the hearing ones.

Blindness vs. Deafness

These two studies illustrate a complex and important fact: that auditory deprivation seems to produce more widespread conceptual difficulties than visual deprivation. Deaf children may appear to be more retarded than blind children. Usually this is assumed to arise from the deaf child's language deficiency, but as the Sterritt study shows, language does not always seem to be involved. The retardation problem may also arise from the failure to develop connections between visual and speech areas.

The fact that early blindness produces more mental slowness than late blindness may arise from the same cause. If a child has the first five years of his life with at least some sight, many important connections can develop. Loss of sight after that time may not prevent images (or image-like patterns) in the visual brain areas from associating with language patterns. The connections have been built; the associations are possible. The fact that the visual patterns no longer come from the outside through the eyes may not matter as far as conceptual thinking is concerned. Concepts can still be formed on the basis of tactual information that may activate images which can then be associated with language.

In deaf children, especially profoundly deaf children, the language area itself may fail to develop. Mental slowness may be an inevitable result unless some alternate associative systems are developed. If deaf children learned a manual language, their slowness might be greatly overcome. Manual or motor brain areas are located near language areas (Figure 1.1). Visual-motor connections might be almost as helpful to later concept development as visual-language connections; at least the visual-motor (manual-language) practice would build up symbolic associations of one sort.

Deafness and Retardation

Unfortunately, manual languages are seldom taught to deaf children at an appropriately early age. Their mental slowness may result as much from

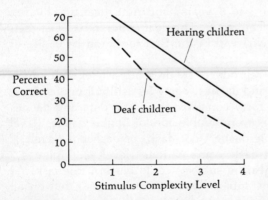

Figure 4.7 Mean visual pattern reproduction scores, expressed as percent correct, in deaf and hearing children. (Sterritt, Camp, and Lipman, 1966, p. 127)

that serious teaching lack as from their own physiological handicap (this is discussed further in Chapter 17). The fact that special educators (teachers of the deaf) have themselves been poorly educated in brain function is the basic problem. They simply do not understand that the use of sensory and motor brain areas in coordinated ways is the basis of later thinking ability. The child who spends the first five years of his life in silence or in darkness is not just bored. He is failing to develop—through use or "exercise"—the actual brain "stuff" that is necessary for good thinking.

EXPERIENCE DEFICIENCIES

Rat Studies

A few years ago, David Krech and his colleagues at the University of California at Berkeley began a series of experiments on the effects of various kinds of early stimulation on brain development. In a typical experiment, rats from the same litters would be randomly assigned to enriched Head Start environments or to unstimulating environments. The Head Start rats live in cages equipped with running wheels, ladders, and creative playthings. As they grow older, they are given various learning tasks to master and are rewarded with bits of sugar. The deprived rats live in barren cages and are rarely handled or given any stimulation at all. Both groups of rats, however, have unlimited access to the same standard food, so they are equally well-nourished physically.

At the end of about three months, the rats are sacrificed, and their brains are analyzed microscopically and chemically. The analyses show that the typical Head Start rat has a heavier and more expansive cortex than his deprived brother. Part of this is accounted for by an increase in nutritional brain cells, part by an increase in the size of the brain cells, and part by an increase in the blood supply. The Head Start rats with the bigger brains are also smarter, by rat standards.

> What does all of this mean? It means that the effects of the psychological and educational environment are not restricted to something called the "mental" realm. Permitting the young rat to grow up in an educationally and experientially inadequate and unstimulating environment creates an animal with a relatively deteriorated brain—a brain with a thin and light cortex, lowered blood supply, diminished enzymatic activities, smaller neuronal cell bodies, and fewer [nutritional] cells. A lack of adequate educational fare for the young animal—no matter how large the food supply or how good the family—and a lack of adequate psychological enrichment results in palpable, measurable, deteriorative changes in the brain's chemistry and anatomy. (Krech, 1968, p. 50)

Implications for Children

Those of us who have observed how children from culturally deprived backgrounds struggle with standard school requirements are quite willing to assert the plausibility of a comparable situation in the human species.

Many of these children appear to be brain-damaged or organically re-tarded. Might not some of this retardation arise from socially induced cor-tical deterioration? Might we not suppose that early childhood deprivation results in brain damage, not merely in motivational damage?

Of course, we cannot answer the question for certain without autop-sies on children of the same age from advantaged and disadvantaged envi-ronments. But we can make some sophisticated guesses. The actual com-ponents of brain tissue in all animals—including man—is the same. If early experience can be shown to increase the actual brain substance of rats, then it probably also increases the actual brain substance of humans. Further, if mental abilities in rats are correlated with the amount of brain substance, then mental abilities in people probably are too. At least we know this much: Children who are deprived of early experiences do not grow up to be as intelligent as children who lead a richer, fuller early life.

The Skeels Orphanage Study

A dramatic demonstration of institutionally produced retardation was car-ried out by a psychologist named Skeels in the 1930s. Because of permis-sive state laws, Skeels was able to carry out an extraordinary experiment. As a staff psychologist, he was in charge of testing infants at an or-phanage. Like most institutions of the 1930s, its conditions were unstimu-lating for the children. Babies were given only minimal attention. They had nothing much to look at or to play with, and were almost never rocked. Toddlers were kept in larger cribs and had few play materials and opportunities.

At one point, two baby girls were committed to the orphanage. They were emaciated and inactive, and had developmental quotients (baby IQs) of about 6 months, although they were over a year old. Since they were considered feebleminded and unadoptable, they were transferred to a state school for the mentally retarded. As it happened, this environment turned out to be much more stimulating for the infants. The babies were placed on a ward of older women who had mental ages of about 10 years—just the right age for playing with babies. The infants were showered with affection and attention. Six months later, when Skeels tested them again, they were approaching developmental normalcy.

Skeels and his colleagues then arranged to have eleven more such children placed in institutions for the mentally retarded as "house guests." Because of the stigma that would have been attached to formal commit-ment to such an institution, the experimental children were still main-tained on the rolls of the orphanage. But they went to live on a ward with retarded women, as the first two little girls had done. All eleven of the experimental children were, in fact, testing retarded at the time of their placement. In addition, for various reasons some of the nonretarded chil-dren at the orphanage were never placed in adoptive homes. From this group, Skeels later selected twelve children who could serve as a statistical control or contrast group for the children who had been placed in the homes for the retarded. Most of the control children were not retarded at the time of their first test.

The length of the experimental period differed for each of the children who had been placed in a home for the retarded. For some children, it was approximately six months; for others, it was over four years. On the average, the enrichment period was between a year and a half and two years. As soon as a child showed normal mental development as measured by tests and observations, his experimental period was considered completed. He was either returned to the orphanage or placed in an adoptive home.

The effects of the warm and stimulating environment at the hands of the retarded women were startling. The IQ changes are plotted in Figure 4.8. From the first IQ test (administered when the children were approximately 18 months old) to the final one for the experimental period (administered when the children were approximately 3 years old after an experimental period of a year and a half), the experimental group showed gains of about 30 IQ points. The contrast group, which had remained in the orphanage, showed losses of about 26 IQ points.

About two and a half years later, IQ tests were administered again, in

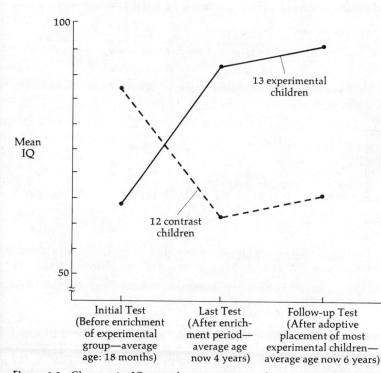

Figure 4.8 Changes in IQ over three testing periods in an experimentally enriched group and a contrasting deprived group of children. (Based on data from Skeels, 1966)

the adoptive homes of children who were no longer institution residents, or in the institutions themselves if the children were still living there. As Figure 4.8 shows, gains of only about 4 IQ points were shown for the experimental group, while gains of about 6 IQ points were registered for the contrast group (some of whom had been transferred, at this late stage of their development, to better institutions). Even with this slight gain, the contrast group still showed a total loss (from initial test to follow-up) of over 20 IQ points, while the experimental group showed a total gain of about 32 IQ points—most of which was clearly attributable not to the adoptive homes, but to the preadoptive placement in a warm and stimulating environment between the ages of 1 and 4 years. This is not by any means to minimize the importance of adoption. The adopted families must have been responsible for teaching the children middle-class ways, because most of the experimental children married and had normal families of their own.

The Follow-up Study

Table 4.3 lists the results of the follow-up study that was done about twenty years after the original experiment. In occupational status and education, the experimental group was quite representative of the United States population as a whole. The contrast group (the seven who were

Table 4.3
Follow-up Data on Children from the Experimental and Contrast Groups, 20 Years Later

FOLLOW-UP DATA	EXPERIMENTAL GROUP	CONTRAST GROUP
Number remaining in orphanage	1	3
Number transferred to schools for retarded	1	9
Number adopted	11	0
Education: average grade completed	12.0	2.8
Number who married	11	1
Number who had children	9	1
Number who were self-supporting or married	13	7
Median income (for 1959)	$4224	$1200

SOURCE: Based on data in Skeels, 1966.

finally out of an institution) were totally unskilled "hewers of wood and drawers of water" (Skeels, 1966, p. 55). On the average, they did not get beyond third grade, and only one married and had a family of his own. None had ever been adopted; they grew up in an orphanage. As Skeels points out:

> The right of every child to be well born, well nurtured, well brought up, and well educated was enunciated in the Children's Charter of the 1930 White House Conference on Child Health and Protection [and many times since then]. . . . Though society strives to insure this right, for many years to come there will be children to whom it has been denied and for

whom society must provide both intervention and restitution. There is need for further research to determine the optimum modes of such intervention and the most appropriate ages and techniques for initiating them. . . .

The unanswered questions of this study could form the basis for many lifelong research projects. If the tragic fate of the 12 contrast-group children provokes even a single crucial study that will help prevent such a fate for others, their lives will not have been in vain. (Skeels, 1966, pp. 56–57)

IMPLICATIONS FOR NORMAL DEVELOPMENT

Growth Rates of Body vs. Brain

Consider Figure 4.9, which shows the growth curves for different body parts, including the brain. Notice how the reproductive organs grow very little for the first ten to twelve years, then grow rapidly in the years from ages 14 to 20, when their final adult weight is reached. Now notice the lymph tissue. It grows extremely rapidly up until about the age of 10, when both the rate of growth and the relative amount of lymph tissue (relative to the amount in the fully adult body) decreases. (Remember those enlarged tonsils you used to have?) General growth (the second

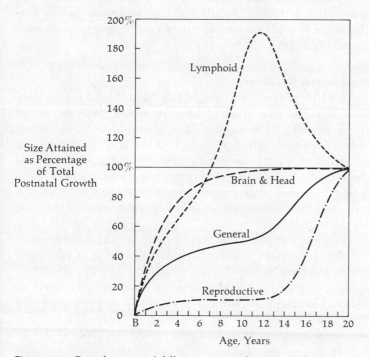

Figure 4.9 Growth curves of different parts and tissues of the body, showing the four chief types. (Tanner, 1964)

curve from the bottom) refers to muscles, digestive organs, bones, and so forth. That curve moves rather slowly upward until the adolescent "growth spurt" that parallels reproductive development. Now look at the curve for brain and head. These grow extremely rapidly for the first four years of life, and then the growth rate begins to level off. By the age of 6, when formal schooling normally begins, the human brain has completed 90 percent of its growth.

Interaction of Growth Rate and Environmental Help

We know from the work of Krech, Skeels, and others that early experience deprivations may be associated with retardation. Quite possibly this is because the deprivations are occurring at a time when the brain is undergoing its growth spurt. Stimulation of both the sensory and educational variety may have its greatest effect when the brain is developing physically. At a later time, when the physical growth has slowed down, such stimulation may have less of an effect.

Nutritional deficiencies have a similar effect. When a baby is half-starved during the first six months of his life, he may be permanently stunted physically. If the starvation occurs after he is 2 years old, there is likely to be no permanent physical damage (Eichenwald and Fry, 1969). For this reason, psychologists and educators are now deeply concerned about early educational (as well as nutritional) opportunities for all citizens. Many of them are less concerned about forcing children educationally than about depriving them.

Modern Attitudes Toward Readiness

Years ago, the concept of educational "readiness" dominated elementary education. We were afraid to encourage children to read before the age of 6, for example, and parents were warned that attempts to push formal school learning could seriously damage children. There is, of course, no question but that pressure to do something you are not able to do has damaging psychological consequences. Frustration, unhappiness, and physically damaging tensions can result. But withholding educational opportunities from children who are eagerly seeking them can have equally disastrous consequences.

Nowadays, our concept of education has changed sufficiently to make readiness concerns less important. We are no longer thinking of education in terms of the rote learning of words and numbers. Ideally, education means opportunities to explore and manipulate, to discover and invent, to practice and develop. This happens with toys among young children and with ideas among the older ones. As long as education means the exercise of normal interests and abilities, the child will always be "ready" for it. The trick, then, is to design an educational program consistent with the interests and abilities of children at various stages of development.

Bruner's Famous Hypothesis

In 1960, Bruner made a statement that has probably been more frequently quoted (and misquoted) than any modern educational maxim:

> We begin with the hypothesis that any subject can be taught in some intellectually honest form to any child at any stage of development. (Bruner, 1960, p. 33)

This is, of course, a *proposition,* not a fact. It is to be balanced against another proposition, one that has been dominant in our American school system for a number of years:

> Much American education begins with the hypothesis that educational information and experiences should be withheld from a child until he reaches a state that the school system defines as *readiness* for that particular kind of learning.

This unproved proposition has been treated as fact in many schools, to the disastrous miseducation of many children. Bruner's hypothesis is, from a psychologist's point of view, the only logical alternative. Since we do not know exactly what a child can learn and in what form he can best learn it, we should try everything. The child will let us know what his readiness actually is. He is a much more reliable guide than a state law or an educator's curriculum book, if only we can learn to read his signals.

TEACHING THE CHILD WITH THINKING DISABILITIES

But what of brains that do not grow normally? What of the day when you, as a teacher, recognize the signs of brain damage in one of your children? What of the child whose own experience background or genetic or sensory deficiency has trapped him in a slower rate of development? What of the child who is said to be emotionally disturbed, or even prepsychotic, but who still attends a normal school, possibly because there is no place else for him to go or because a physician believes a normal atmosphere is best for him? What, then, is the classroom teacher to do?

The child with a mildly or moderately defective brain is still a child with a brain that will follow the same laws of development that influence every brain. First, review the recommendations for "The 'Thinking Child' in Preschool" and "The 'Thinking Child' in School." Then make the following adjustments for children whose development is slow or disabled:

1. Even though the child may be chronologically past the preoperational stage, he may be highly susceptible to perceptual distractions. This can include social distractions. The sight of another child picking up a red crayon, for example, may trigger an outburst from a mentally disabled child ("I want the red crayon!"). For such children, the environment should be kept as simple and nondistracting as possible. This can mean removing a child from a normally sociable environment, which may be overstimulating to a child whose perceptual sensitivities are still keen. The environment may be providing him with more informational "inputs" than he can comfortably integrate.

2. Base the child's curriculum on as much motor involvement as possible. Eurhythmics is ideal. Sports training of various kinds is good for older children. Bringing the body under coordinated control is a good foundation for learning—perhaps the only foundation in cases of severe retardation.

3. Continue to provide opportunities for symbolic play—blocks, housekeeping, and dramatic opportunities of various sorts. These opportunities also provide foundations for symbolic thinking, since they are its early forms.

4. Give the child special help in abstracting rules and systems; do not count on his ability to perform these abstractions for himself. He will need help in the concrete forms of these rules (using concrete materials to practice counting, for example) as well as in the abstract forms (learning the digits from 1 to 10). And he will need special help integrating ideas and materials. He will not easily make the leap from the concrete, intuitive idea to its abstract form.

Here, teachers of special education can be extremely helpful to the regular classroom teacher. Over the years, an experienced, successful special teacher will have evolved materials and systems for helping children develop concepts of various sorts. A two-hour conversation with a good special teacher can save you years of personal trial and error.

5. Give your mentally disabled child special help in integrating word, action, and percept. He may have special difficulties with writing, drawing, or reading. In all cases, he is suffering from integrative defects. If possible, help him develop alternate systems for handling these forms of symbolization. For example, the child who cannot draw a house can be encouraged to first list verbally the things that a house has (windows, doors, steps) and then to list the locations of these elements. In that way, he will be coordinating his pencil with a verbal list, which may be much easier for him, rather than with a visual memory image he cannot handle.

6. Enlist help from everyone you can. There are several million high school students who would love to help a dyslexic child practice reading. Most of them are probably smart enough to do so with minimal supervisory instruction from a teacher. Parents can also help. With learning disabilities, practice, practice, and more practice may be the only way of developing alternate cortical systems to handle symbolic information. (Language defects are discussed more fully in Chapter 17.)

7. Trust your own ideas. If you have read Part I carefully and understood it, you have enough basic information to develop some reasonable educational programs for afflicted children. You know that the basic physiological principle is the development of associative "brain stuff" through practice and experience of various kinds. You know that the basic psychological principle is movement from concrete to abstract thinking. Given

those two basic principles, almost any experimental curriculum will be worth a try.

8. Let the child's responses be your guide. Can he do it? Does he respond fairly well? Does he enjoy what he's doing enough to keep at it? Does he ask for more? Pay attention to the child, not to any special theory. The theory may be improved someday by the observations you are making.

In the next sections, you will find additional guidelines that may help you cope with problems of special education. But there is no substitute for your own sympathetic, experimental spirit.

SUMMARY

What does development have to do with education? Some answers may
seem obvious ("Children have to be old enough to learn certain things"),
but they are based on complex principles. Generally, these principles involve "the problem of the match" (Hunt, 1961), the problem of providing
a human being with an educational milieu appropriate for his stage of development.

Such stages imply a number of things. First of all, they imply something about physiological development. The brain grows, and thought
changes as it grows. Opportunities to think (to exercise the brain) may
even affect that growth (Krech, 1968). Brain growth after birth mostly involves associative rather than primary tissue. This associative tissue makes
possible connections and coordinations between different brain areas.

Prior to the time when these associations are fluent, the child is limited in his thinking abilities. Piaget (Piaget and Inhelder, 1969) refers to
this very early period as the *sensorimotor stage* of mental development.
The individual knows the world in terms of what he can do to the world
and in terms of the sensations he has about the world.

Partly as a result of practice exercising these forms of thinking and
partly as a result of brain growth, thought becomes better organized. Even
during the sensorimotor period, growth toward organization can be observed. The basic process involves the extremely important growth principles of *differentiation* and *integration,* principles that continue to characterize mental development throughout our lives. The stages of thought
organization Piaget has described for the sensorimotor period may be a

prototype or model for more advanced thinking. The way in which an infant learns to organize his mind may be a general system he will continue to use. One aspect of this organization is the system for representing our concepts through physical action. Bruner (1964b) calls this the *enactive representational system.* It is formally taught through eurhythmics and mime.

As growth continues, the child becomes able to represent his world to himself symbolically. The earliest forms of this new ability may be seen in the child's imitative play. At this point (about the age of 2), Piaget says the child has entered the *preoperational stage* of development. Preoperational thinking is characterized by a child's failure to use certain kinds of information logically, by adult standards. For example, he believes that quantities are changed when their spatial organization changes.

This illogic is associated with perceptual sensitivity of various kinds, particularly to visual cues. It is also associated with a strategy of making guesses about the world on the basis of a perceptual cue (such as height). This strategy may be an important step toward the development of the ability to use symbols. Bruner (1964b) refers to these sensitivities and strategies as the *iconic representational system.*

Although it has generally proved impossible to teach preoperational children to respond logically to certain Piagetian tests, this does not mean that no teaching at all should occur. Teaching the preoperational child correctly involves helping him use language and action as aids to logic, rather than letting him rely upon his temporarily oversensitive (and therefore misleading) iconic system. A number of experiments that show how language and action can aid iconic learning have pointed the way toward effective teaching.

During the preoperational period, the systems of language, action, and percept are somewhat disconnected, probably for neurological reasons. As the child becomes older and better able to coordinate his ideas, he enters what Piaget calls the *concrete operational stage.* Many new logical skills appear rather suddenly at that time (about the age of 8). The child becomes much more skillful in using principles and rules and enjoys exercising these powers, even when the power may be inappropriate. By the age of 12, the child is moving into the *formal operational stage,* where he is able to separate his logical powers from any concrete dependency. In Piaget's words, "thought takes wings" (Inhelder and Piaget, 1958).

Another aspect of this growth process is the child's developing skill in using what Bruner calls the *symbolic representational system.* Werner also emphasizes this skill, and he has been particularly impressed by its organic roots. To Werner, symbols grow out of the "primordial diffusion" of early experience. To Bruner, symbolic representational skills involve the ability to match language to actions and percepts. He does not believe this matching process will develop extensively without schooling.

In general, schooling must involve opportunities to actively experience the classroom world. The organization of that experience must be guided by a wise teacher, but it cannot be done *for* the child. The child must be able to sample from his world, put together trial organizations, and get feedback from his teacher (and from the world) on the validity of his "trial balloons." Under these conditions, operational thought (in Piaget's terms) and symbolic thought (in Werner's and Bruner's terms) will grow organically. Under conditions of passive rote learning, mental growth will happen only in sporadic and limited ways; in effect, the mind will be crippled by lack of exercise, nourishment, and meaningful guidance.

Of course, the mind may be crippled by other things before schooling even begins. There may be faulty genetic programming, sensory deficiencies, brain damage, or experience deficiencies. Separately or in combination, these influences can damage thinking abilities. The classroom teacher will need to apply principles of early mental development to the education of such damaged children. For example, the teacher may need to give the child special help in overcoming perceptual distractibility.

This first section of the text should provide a general background in the principles of cognitive development, principles that may continue to operate in different forms throughout the educational period. Part II will be concerned with the basic systems of formal thought that people use. In Piaget's terms, these would be operational systems, but our analysis will extend beyond his concepts to a larger body of modern American theory and research relevant to education.

Part II BASIC SYSTEMS OF INFORMATION PROCESSING

Most of our skill in dealing with the environment is embodied in elaborate *heuristics,* or rules of thumb, that allow us to factor — approximately — the complex perceived world into highly simple components, and to find — approximately and reasonably reliably — the correspondences that allow us to act on that world predictably. This is the skill that the adult businessman uses when he makes a decision, the skill of a scientist in his laboratory, the skill of a child learning to speak.

HERBERT A. SIMON
ALLEN NEWELL

OVERVIEW

The normal human being samples from the environmental information around him and then operates upon his data in some way. His operational system will depend upon many things: his goal, his past experience, his energy level, and the resources available to him. So many variables are involved that it may seem impossible to understand how his mind is working. Yet, miraculously, we can often predict the mental activities of others. "I know how his mind works . . ." "He's a slow learner . . ." "He's very quick . . ." "He has to figure everything out first, before he'll do anything . . ." "He has a mind like a steel trap . . ." One can make any number of statements like these to describe the thinking styles of the people one knows. Within two weeks, an experienced teacher can fairly accurately describe the mental characteristics of every student in a new class. How is this done? What is being described? What is the evidence upon which judgments about mental abilities are based?

Part II opens with these questions: How can we tell if thinking exists? How can we organize our descriptions of it?

In Chapter 5 we will examine the problem of deciding if thinking can exist apart from the behavior of thinking. We will also examine the complex problems of differences between the products of thinking and the process of thinking. These days, so-called process curricula are often in the news. Finally, we will look at two basic systems for describing educational programs: a static system, composed of products, and a dynamic system, composed of processes. These are the skeletons of most modern curricula.

In Chapters 6, 7, and 8, we will turn to systems of human thinking. There do not appear to be a very large number of such basic systems—perhaps only five: scanning and holding, problem solving, remembering, generating and classifying, and ordering and relating. Most forms of human information processing involve one or more of these basic programs. If we can understand them and how schooling relates to them, we will have gained a powerful set of analytical tools.

We will also have a better framework for understanding the logic and implications of IQ tests. Not much space will be devoted to the mechanics and statistics of mental testing, since such excellent reviews are available elsewhere (Anastasi, 1968, for example). But the logic of these testing procedures is of great importance to educators. Do we, as members of a democratic society, have the right to make predictions about the future achievements of children? Can we make useful predictions? Will children be helped by them?

It is the thesis of this entire book that schooling should be suitable for the youngster engaged in it. Many children—not merely those whose intelligence test scores are abnormally high or low—are trapped in educational systems that do not fit their interests or needs. Part II will help outline a way of analyzing those needs so that they can be met on any level, and by all educational personnel. If we were to do this well, who knows what our intellectual upper limits may actually be?

Chapter 5   THE STUDY OF THINKING

BEHAVIOR AND THOUGHT

Mental Elements

When psychology was beginning to take shape as a formal science during the latter half of the nineteenth century, it was philosophically fashionable to talk about "mental elements." These were, for the most part, sensations or bits of sensations that could be combined (theoretically) into more complicated structures by the "glue" of associations. How were they discovered and verified? through introspection. Try it for yourself: If you close your eyes and concentrate, you may be able to detect the very basic elements of consciousness. You may also be able to detect the sensations that bind these elements together. Of course, it may take a good deal of practice, but eventually you should be able to report on your introspections quite scientifically—scientifically, that is, by the standards of Wilhelm Wundt, the originator of psychological science:

> Wundt's introspections held a great fascination for his students. Who would have guessed that anything as familiar as one's own mind could harbor all these shadowy and unexpected elements? Who could guess what other pumpkins might turn into coaches when examined with the marvelous inner eye? Wundt's talent for making the perfectly familiar seem completely novel and mysterious—by stripping off its meaning and cutting it up in pieces—was the source of both his strength and his weakness as a psychologist.
>
> Note how hard it is to disprove his claims. If your own introspections give you a different result, how can you decide who is right? Perhaps you

misunderstood his description of his experience; perhaps you paid attention to the wrong things; perhaps you do not know how to introspect properly; perhaps you and Wundt are not made the same way; and so on. His experiments, unlike experiments elsewhere in science, do not insure agreement among all those who witness them. Introspective observation is essentially private, and disagreements cannot be settled by repeated observations.

But scientific psychology had to start somewhere. (Miller, 1962a, p. 22)

So it began with mental elements; these were the first building blocks out of which mental structures were (theoretically) created. As scientific sophistication increased, discontent with such structures also increased. A more objective research methodology was needed. By the early 1900s the *reflex arc* was beginning to supplant the mental element as the basic building block of a scientific psychology.

Stimulus and Response Units
A reflex arc is an automatic connection of a sensory stimulus and a motor response, abbreviated S-R. You blow in my eye (stimulus) and I will blink (response). You tap my patellar tendon, and I will kick. These simple S-R systems could be demonstrated in behavior that was visible to everyone. Such demonstrations provided a much more satisfactory basis for a scientific psychology. In a sort of "declaration of independence from mentalism," John B. Watson, the father of behaviorism in America, wrote in 1913:

Psychology, as the behaviorist views it, is a purely objective experimental branch of natural science which needs introspection as little as do the sciences of chemistry and physics. It is granted that the behavior of animals can be investigated without appeals to consciousness. The position is taken here that the behavior of man . . . must be considered on the same plane. . . . It can dispense with consciousness in a psychological sense. The separate observation of "states of consciousness" [in the absence of behavior observable to others] is . . . no more a part of the task of the psychologist than of the physicist. (Watson, 1913, p. 177)

Behaviorism as a Method
From then on, mental activities of all sorts were translated into behaviors—or they did not exist for scientific purposes. In school settings, knowledge was redefined as the behavior of writing test answers that are 90 percent correct, for example. Nowadays, when a psychologist sits down with an educator to work out an evaluation program, the psychologist will typically say: "Now, what are your objectives? How will you know when they are achieved—that is, what kind of student behavior will you accept as a signal that your objectives have been reached?" The educator who answers, "Well, I just know intuitively about things like that. I *feel* it when a student understands something. . . ." is going to face a difficult adjustment problem. Feelings are not objective evidence. If, however, the

psychologist can devise a way for the educator to express his feelings on a rating scale, the educator's *rating behavior* becomes scientifically promising—provided that it agrees well enough with the rating behavior of other experts. (In scientific terms, we say, "If the ratings are technically *reliable*," as determined by a controlled scientific evaluation of them.) The educator who feels insulted by the need for controlled scientific evaluations and who reacts as if he were being attacked by those who do not understand the "art of education" does not himself understand the nature of the scientific method in psychology. It is not intended to insult him by doubting his judgment, it is intended merely to bring out educational concepts and intentions so they can be publicly studied. If they remain subjective, like Wundt's mental elements, we can never really understand them.

Behaviorism as a Theory

Note that we have been discussing behaviorism as a *method* of objective study. We have not been saying anything about behaviorism as a *theory* in itself. Behaviorism as a theory has two general forms: (1) S-R theory, which refers to the building of simple behavioral units into more complex learning structures, and (2) Skinnerian theory, which refers to the shaping or control of behavior as an end in itself.

S-R Behavior Theory

Traditional learning theory, or S-R theory, has been psychology's major emphasis for many years. No attempt will be made to summarize it here, since summaries are readily available in any basic textbook. (Especially recommended, however, is George Miller's *Psychology: The Science of Mental Life.* This is an absorbing account of psychology written by one of its most famous innovators.) Many of the experiments discussed in this book have arisen from the S-R theoretical system, and in the next section of this chapter we will look at the special theories designed to show how simple S-R units (like a reflex arc) can grow into the behavior of complex thinking. This is not, as you might imagine, an easy fact to explain.

Skinnerian Behavior Theory

Skinner's theory of behavior is something else again. It is less an actual theory than a program or set of recipes for affecting behavior. Skinner does not feel the need for any special theory to account for "invisibles" such as thinking or learning. He simply changes the behavior itself by means of rewards, punishments, or other reinforcement principles (see Chapter 10). Little behaviors (like holding a pencil) can be connected to other behaviors (like reading an arithmetic problem) to produce still other behaviors (writing the answer to the arithmetic problem). These behaviors can be taught, or "shaped up," by means of a series of reinforcements. In Skinner's view, we do not need to say that a child has "learned to solve an arithmetic problem." We say merely that the child has "learned appropriate arithmetic behaviors."

We can define terms like "information," "knowledge," and "verbal ability" by reference to the behavior from which we infer their presence. We may then *teach the behavior directly*. Instead of "transmitting the information to the student" we may simply set up the behavior which is taken as a sign that he possesses information. Instead of teaching "a knowledge of French" we may teach the behavior from which we infer such knowledge. Instead of teaching "an ability to read," we may set up the behavioral repertoire which distinguishes the child who knows how to read from one who does not.

To take the last example, a child reads or "shows that he knows how to read" by exhibiting a behavioral repertoire of great complexity. He finds a letter or word in a list on demand; he reads aloud; he finds or identifies objects described in a text; he rephrases sentences; he obeys written instructions; he behaves appropriately to described situations; he reacts emotionally to described events; and so on, in a long list. He does none of this before learning to read and all of it afterwards. To bring about such a change is an extensive assignment, and it is tempting to try to circumvent it by teaching something called "an ability to read," from which all these specific behaviors will flow. But this has never actually been done. (Skinner, 1964, pp. 49–50)

His position may seem extreme, but it really depends on how irascible Skinner is feeling at the particular time. Actually, he is a brilliant, original, and wise man. (Some of his disciples, like those of any great man, may seem less brilliant, and far less wise.) Skinnerian principles have the extremely discomforting habit of working. Behavior that is positively reinforced will often increase if other factors are not interfering. When positive reinforcement is withheld, the behavior often decreases. All kinds of behavior, from the babbling of an infant (see Chapter 16) to aggression in children (see Chapter 14) to therapeutic self-insight (Chapter 17), may be "shaped up" by reinforcement procedures. Knowing how to use such procedures can be invaluable to a teacher and to a parent, especially when the true cause of a behavior is not understood.

What Causes Behavior?

It is precisely here that many of us depart from the Skinnerian tradition. We may agree that Skinnerian techniques are of great practical value, but we may be unwilling to give up hope that there is an underlying cause from which the behaviors do in fact flow. We cling stubbornly to the belief that there *is* something called "an ability to read" and that it *can* be taught. Why? Because that ability might be a basic law, or set of principles, that can be expressed in a wide variety of behaviors. The principles of photosynthesis, for example, express the behavior of many thousands of different plants. Knowing these basic principles gives us great power; we can predict many different reactions of these plants to changes in sunlight, water, soil conditions, and so forth. It would be highly inefficient, scientifically, to chart the behavior of each plant separately, even though each little chart would give an accurate picture. It would be far more efficient to discover and apply the general laws that lie behind the information on each chart.

Similarly, we may hope that the discovery of underlying principles of mental skill will give us the power to predict many kinds of learning behavior:

> Given that a man can multiply, why should one want to ask after processes that enable him to do so? . . . Let me suggest that the reason why one searches for the mechanisms behind a regularity is that they are usually there, waiting to be found. And when found, they usually provide a theory with vastly increased scope. . . . One can find a mechanism for producing the light that shines from the stars. One can find a mechanism for photosynthesis. . . . And one can expect to find a mechanism that enables an organism to follow learned complex rules. . . . The psychological mechanisms are there, confronting us. If we were ingenious enough, they would yield up their secrets. . . . To believe that we should proceed only with descriptions of [behavioral] regularities, and avoid any attempt to see in them the processing that is involved, seems to me almost a failure of nerve. (Newell, 1967, pp. 250–252)

Our irascible Skinner, however, would remain unconvinced.

> I think the main objection to behaviorism [of the Skinnerian variety] is that people are in love with the mental apparatus. If you say that doesn't really exist, that it's a fiction and let's get back to the facts, then they have to give up their first love. . . . You are asking them to throw away their lifework. Or their only confidence. . . . They're interested in the mental apparatus. To ask them to give that up would be like asking an engineer to go into sculpture. You may convince him that sculpturing is more important than building bridges, but he's a bridge builder. He wouldn't know how to start something over. (Skinner, 1967, p. 69)

The theoretical war between cognition and behaviorism has a long psychological history and will probably never be wholly resolved. It is essentially a recapitulation of the mind-body problem, a venerable philosophical issue. Is there a mind that is separate from the physiological reality of the brain? Does thought still unexpressed in behavior actually exist?

Behaviorism Reviewed

While we cannot answer that question, we can be careful to distinguish the kinds of behavior it implies. To review briefly, three kinds of behaviorism may be implied by the term: (1) behaviorism as a method of objectivity common to all modern psychological theories, including cognitive theories; (2) behaviorism as a label for traditional learning, or S-R theory; and (3) behaviorism as a label for Skinnerian theory. Educators in particular must take care to distinguish the ways in which the term may be used. When a psychologist announces that he is a "behaviorist," ask him: "Do you mean in the general experimental sense? the S-R sense? or the Skinnerian sense?" If he does not know enough psychology to be able to answer that question, get yourself another expert.

Now, assuming you are willing to look for behavioral evidence of thinking in your students, what kind of behavior will it be?

PRODUCT VS. PROCESS

A *product* of a thinking activity would be the result or outcome of that activity—a set of answers on an arithmetic test, for example. Much behavioral evidence of thinking is in the form of products. Frequently, however, an arithmetic teacher will request students to show their work as well as their answers. If the course has been well taught, the steps in mathematical reasoning shown by the student will be useful diagnostic aids. The instructor will be able to spot errors. He may even be able to predict the most likely errors and to teach students routines for checking special trouble spots for themselves. The course emphasis in general in good mathematics courses is on the quality and the direction of the mathematical thinking process, not on the correctness of the answer.

Several kinds of processes may be emphasized in the instruction. In the "old math" days, we learned "recipes" for multiplying fractions, solving algebra problems, developing geometric proofs, and so forth. Such recipes might be guaranteed systems for getting right answers on examinations, but they often bore little relationship to the logic of mathematics itself. If you were to ask us, "*Why* do you invert and multiply as the rule for dividing fractions?" we would look quite blank. We never knew why. We never understood that there was a logical relationship between multiplication and division. We simply memorized and followed a recipe.

Suppose we are now faced with a problem for which there seems to be no recipe—the four-color map problem, for example. It is a fact that we need no more than four colors in coloring a map to guarantee that no two adjoining countries will be the same color. Any map, even imaginary ones. Get yourself a box of crayons and try it, but note your thinking processes at the same time. What do you think of first? second? What do you *do* first? Even though you have not been taught a recipe for handling this problem, you will not behave randomly. You may try one thing and then another, but you will keep track of what you are doing, compare your achievements with your goal, and try to think of fresh alternatives, in more systematic ways than you may imagine.

Three Kinds of Thinking Processes
We have indicated, then, three different types of thinking processes:

Type 1. A behavioral recipe (like "invert and multiply") for achieving the goal of getting a right answer
Type 2. A logical process (like the relationship between multiplication and division) that exists in the subject matter
Type 3. A process of reasoning (which may be seen in the coloring problem) that is psychological in nature

The first two kinds of processes apply formal rules, or *algorithms.* The third process applies a rule of thumb, or *heuristic.*

Algorithms vs. Heuristics

There are algorithms for many activities—playing chess, for example—although experts may differ on which are the best. Heuristics, or rules of thumb, are nothing so elegant. The discomfort of trying to work out heuristics has been well described by Miller, Galanter, and Pribram in their book, *Plans and the Structure of Behavior:*

> In ordinary affairs, we usually muddle ahead, doing what is habitual and customary, being slightly puzzled when it sometimes fails to give the intended outcome, but not stopping to worry much about the failures because there are too many other things still to do. Then circumstances conspire against us and we find ourselves caught failing where we must succeed—where we cannot withdraw from the field, or lower our self-imposed standards, or ask for help, or throw a tantrum. Then we may begin to suspect that we face a problem. But at first it is not clear what the problem is, or what test would have to be satisfied by any solution. There is an important kind of thinking that goes on at this stage—the stage in which the problem becomes defined. . . . We search about, exploring a hunch, gambling that we might get a good idea if we spent some time on this or that, fiddling with a few examples . . . but never being certain precisely what we are searching for. . . . It is a little like trying to develop a good filing system without knowing exactly what the file will be used for (Miller, Galanter, and Pribram, 1960, pp. 171–175)

The personal rules that we develop (or invent) for handling muddles of that sort are called heuristics. We are actually storehouses of heuristic systems for handling information. The study of these personal systems makes up a large part of modern research into human thinking. Ideally, the reasoning processes emphasized in school situations should take natural heuristic systems into consideration. That is, the ideal method of teaching the division of fractions, for example, should involve both type 2 and type 3 of the processes defined above. The instructor might begin by letting children exercise their natural reasoning skills about the division of fractions; he might supply them with Cuisenaire rods or other concrete materials as vehicles. As the children's natural logic developed, our ideal instructor could then relate their reasoning to the logic of arithmetic (Methods C and D in Figure 5.1).

Structure vs. Content

Controversies in education about the structure vs. the content of a discipline are generally arguments about process vs. product. These controversies can be difficult to settle, however, because the three types of processes are not clearly distinguished. Structure usually refers to type 2, above—the logical processes involved in a body of knowledge. Content can refer to knowledge of these processes (rules of the number system, for example) or to other facts and concepts. Educators who "teach process" may be confused because they are confusing type 2 and type 3. The process of thinking about the number system is not identical to the number processes themselves. (Piaget has been trying to connect the two, but we need not go into that here; see Chapter 23). People's heuristic processes will not necessarily be related to the logical processes of a scholarly discipline, but they will be related to the heuristic processes of other people—and therein lies the clue.

We can teach students how to use the heuristic processes of experts, and we can teach them this by letting them begin with their own inexpert heuristic systems and then educating the systems. This is very different from teaching the processes as if they were products or facts to be memorized (Rule 1: Poe wrote his poems by . . .), teaching the products directly (Poe's first six poems were . . .), or teaching algorithmic processes (the first step in writing your poem is . . .). Figure 5.1 may clarify the connections between content, product, the three types of processes, and structure.

Laboratory methods that use only method A have been the mainstay of traditional schooling. Laboratory methods that use combinations of methods C and D make up most of the "new" curricula—new biology, new physics, and the like. This is why two lab courses that both claim to

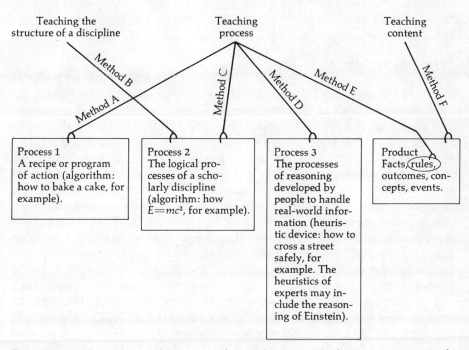

Figure 5.1 Some meanings of *process, product,* and *structure,* as these terms are currently used in educational theory.

"teach process" may be doing very different things and may be very differently viewed by students. For the most part, sharing in the thinking processes of experts is rewarding and exciting, especially when we have the opportunity to test them against our own reasoning. The history course in which the professor says, "How would you feel about Aaron Burr if you were in Hamilton's shoes?" may be remembered as "The best course I ever took in my life," while that in which the professor says, "Aaron Burr and Alexander Hamilton were enemies." may be remembered as the dullest. When teachers shut us out of the reasoning processes by giving us only the resulting products, we often feel resentful and vaguely insulted.

Of course, no good teacher wants to insult his students. The problem arises from the decision by schools and parents to accept product behavior, instead of process behavior, as evidence of thinking. Most curricula are defined in terms of sets of products, usually test answers. Building a curriculum on process behavior is the goal of many new courses, but it is a difficult one to achieve. Let us look at this difficulty in more detail.

BRICKS, TOTES, AND HIERARCHIES

We have been making some careful distinctions: between three kinds of thinking processes, between three kinds of behaviorism, and so forth. Now we need to make another one: a distinction between *static* and *dynamic* cognitive structures.

Snapshots vs. Moving Pictures

To put it briefly: A static cognitive structure is like a building composed of bricks and scaffolding. The whole edifice may be complete and beautiful, but it does not move. A dynamic cognitive structure is like a roller coaster. The target process moves, sometimes quite rapidly, but through a well-charted region. We know where the target is going and how it will return.

Both S-R and Skinnerian theories rely on static models. They construct complex mental behaviors out of the bricks of little mental behaviors. The more modern cognitive theories rely on dynamic models. They construct complex dynamic systems out of small dynamic systems. Both the cognitive theories and the modern S-R theories build their big behaviors out of little ones in a hierarchical manner. That is, an egg goes into an egg box; the egg boxes go into crates; the crates go into truckloads; the truckloads go into trainloads; and the trainloads converge in a single railway market. Note that although the number of eggs increases, each step in the hierarchy decreases the size of the symbolic unit. There are 12 eggs in 1 egg box; the ratio of symbol (egg box) to unit (egg) is therefore 1 to 12, or .08. If there are 10 egg boxes in one crate, the ratio of symbol (crate) to unit (egg) is going to be 1 to 10 × 12 (1 to 120), or .008. Each time the egg is "recoded" symbolically, the symbol stands for larger and larger numbers of eggs. This represents an extremely important basic cognitive process—the ability to recode many little things (like all the automobiles in the world) into a single concept (the word *automobile*).

It is not clear that Skinner's constructions are hierarchical. Skinner will shape up whatever behavior seems necessary to shape up the next most complex behavior, and he is not concerned with whether or not this process is hierarchical in nature. This will become clear as we look at examples of S-R, Skinnerian, and cognitive structures.

S-R Structures, Illustrated by Gagné's Theory

Robert Gagné, now at Florida State University, has theorized that there are eight types of learning, beginning with the very simple S-R units, which can be built up hierarchically (Gagné, 1966). They are as follows:

Type 1. Signal Learning. A particular stimulus (a peeled onion) always elicits a particular response (tears); eventually, the very sight of the onion (or even the word *onion*) may evoke the response.

Type 2. Stimulus-Response Learning. A slightly more complex type of learning built out of simple signals, it is what we normally call instrumental or operant conditioning. A child says "goo-goo," Mommy smiles, and the "goo-goo" is repeated, since it brought a rewarding outcome.

Type 3. Chaining. S-R units, formed as in Type 2 learning, are connected. A child learns to make a verbal response (*doll*, for example) and also learns to discriminate between the doll and the dog. The word is then connected to the right object, and a chain has been formed.

Type 4. Verbal Association. This is actually a subvariety of chaining. The meaning of one word, say, is discovered by recognizing its connection to another word. Thus, *alumette* is chained to *lum* which in turn is chained to *illu-mi*nation. Learning of the French word may take place for that reason.

Type 5. Multiple Discrimination. There are stimulus-response chains that work in combination. A child may discriminate among cars by recognizing that car A has a special type of headlight in combination with a special type of grille; Car B has a different headlight, different grille, and white-wall tires.

Type 6. Concept Learning. Sets of multiple discriminations come together under a verbal label. A concept may also represent multiple verbal discriminations. Many different uses of the word *middle* are finally learned as a concept, for example.

Type 7. Principle Learning. This is a chain of concepts. The principle of gravitation, for example, involves many concepts.

Type 8. Problem Solving. This is combining principles into novel, higher-order principles.

An example of a Gagné hierarchy is shown in Figure 5.2. The development of an instructional program for ordering numbers would proceed from top to bottom: The curriculum writer sets his top objective, and then says to himself, in effect, what do you need to know to order numbers? Well, how to form sets and how to join sets. What do you need to know to perform those operations? Among other things, concepts of adding, subtracting, same, different, and so forth. Finally, at the very bottom level, the most basic necessary knowledge is marking with pencils. The instructional program is then set up to match these theoretical steps. It may be, of course, that some of the steps are wrong; that will become evident as

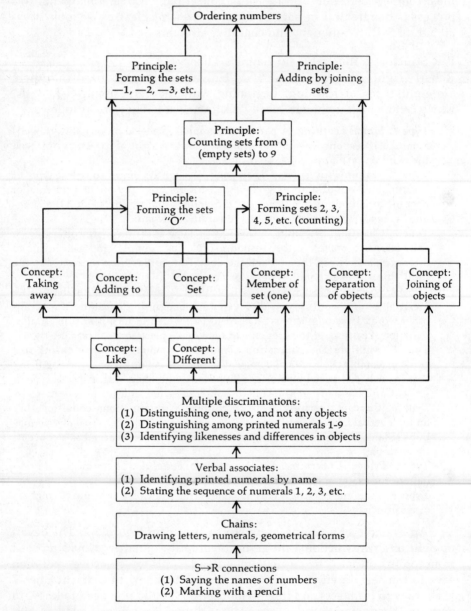

Figure 5.2   A learning hierarchy for number operations. (Redrawn from Gagné, 1965, p. 181)

the instructional program is tested. For example, it may be that saying the numerals when they are presented (item 1 of the third box up) is actually easier than saying the names of numbers by heart (item 1 of the bottom box). In that case, the diagram and the instructional program will be changed to conform to reality.

The student starts from the bottom and works up. He first learns the names of the numbers, and then he learns to write them. When he has passed tests showing that he can do these things, he moves up the ladder to harder tasks. Finally, when he reaches the top box, he can be almost perfectly sure of success since he has demonstrated knowledge of all the foregoing concepts, multiple discriminations, chains, and S-R connections.

The hierarchy is static because it does not contain a system for "swinging back through" earlier structures if the learner needs to recapture lost information. If you think of the structure as representing the structure of knowledge in a student's head, you can see that it is fixed. Knowledge is accumulated on one "floor" at a time and contributes brick by brick to a sum total. It is a collection of products.

Skinnerian Structures, Illustrated by a Teaching Program

The development of teaching machines has been one of the most dramatic outgrowths of Skinnerian theory. Skinner did not invent teaching machines; a hundred years ago, Prince Louis-Napoleon of France used one to learn to read. However, the precise control offered by a machine met Skinner's theoretical needs very well, as he explained in *The Technology of Teaching:*

> The machine itself, of course, does not teach. It simply brings the student into contact with the person who composed the material it presents. It is a laborsaving device because it can bring one programmer into contact with an indefinite number of students. This may suggest mass production, but the effect upon each student is surprisingly like that of a private tutor. The comparison holds in several respects. (1) There is a constant interchange between program and student. Unlike lectures, textbooks, and the usual audiovisual aids, the machine induces sustained activity. The student is always alert and busy. (2) Like a good tutor, the machine insists that a given point be thoroughly understood, either frame by frame or set by set, before the student moves on. Lectures, textbooks, and their mechanized equivalents, on the other hand, proceed without making sure that the student understands and easily leave him behind. (3) Like a good tutor, the machine presents just that material for which the student is ready. It asks him to take only that step which he is at the moment best equipped and most likely to take. (4) Like a skillful tutor, the machine helps the student come up with the right answer. It does this in part through the orderly construction of the program and in part with such techniques as hinting, prompting, and suggesting. . . . (5) Lastly, of course, the machine, like the private tutor, reinforces the student for every correct response, using this immediate feedback not only to shape his behavior most efficiently, but to maintain it in strength in a manner which

the layman would describe as "holding the student's interest." (Skinner, 1968, p. 39)

Without going into the technicalities of program construction (see DeGrazia and Sohn, 1964; DeCecco, 1964; and Markle, 1969, for references to theory, research, and techniques of programming), we might consider Figure 5.3 as an example of a Skinnerian program for teaching the same ordering abilities shown in Figure 5.2. The program would, of course, go on for a much longer time, the child filling in progressively more complicated blanks of number sets. Conceivably, the program could

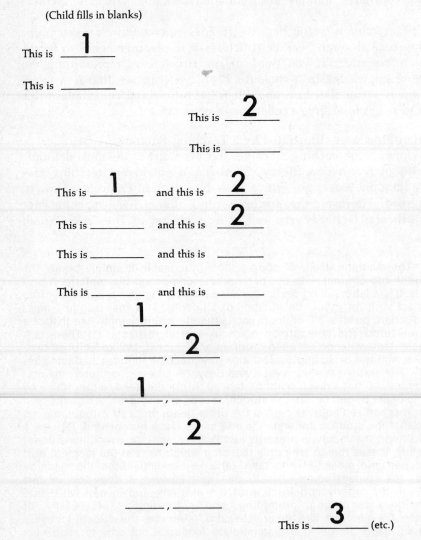

Figure 5.3 An example of a Skinner-type teaching program for learning to order numbers.

match Gagné's if the programmer, who works empirically, discovered that the steps described by Gagné were the most efficient way of approaching the goal of learning to order numbers. However, it is likely that Skinnerian programmers would not feel a need to match anyone's theory of what the correct sequence should be. Skinner looks upon programming as something of an a-theoretical art; his only interest is in shaping up the behavior itself.

Skinnerian programs are also collections of products. As each new bit of behavior is mastered, it is added into the total. When a sufficient number of behavioral products have been collected, complex learning is said to have occurred.

A Dynamic Structure, Illustrated by a Flow Diagram

We come now to a new topic, one that will be pursued in detail in the following pages. We have been discussing two kinds of behaviorists, the S-R type and the Skinnerian type. Cognitive psychologists are not usually called behaviorists, but they are, in the general experimental sense. They also believe that thought must appear in behavior for careful study to be made. A cognitive behaviorist, however, differs from an S-R behaviorist and from a Skinnerian behaviorist in one essential way: He does not believe that learning structures are static collections of products. He sees each learning episode as a dynamic system composed of simpler or related dynamic systems.

Basic to the dynamic theories of cognitive psychologists is the notion that the building blocks of human behavior are *feedback loops* (Wiener, 1948). These are self-regulating systems rather like thermostats; when something does not match a particular criteria (a set temperature), an operation is instituted (the furnace goes on or off) to correct the situation.

Miller and his colleagues (1960) have conceptualized the basic building block of a dynamic mental structure as a feedback loop they call a TOTE (which is an acronym for test-operate-test-exit). Figure 5.4 shows their basic TOTE diagram. Suppose you are hungry. You go to the refrigerator and test it for sandwich materials. If the test fails—if, in the language of the diagram, an incongruity is found between the state of the refrigerator (empty) and your objective (food)—you institute an operation.

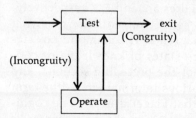

Figure 5.4   The test-operate-test-exit (TOTE) unit. (Miller, Galanter, and Pribram, 1960, p. 26)

You go to the store and buy sandwich materials. Returning home, you place the materials in the refrigerator, thereby testing it a second time. This time, the test is successful; the makings of a lunch are found. This congruity between your objective and the state of the refrigerator then leads you to exit from this particular unit. Your next unit, presumably, would be the production of lunch. First test: Is lunch prepared? Incongruity: No. Operation: Fix lunch. Re-test: Is lunch now prepared? Congruity: Yes. Next unit: Eat. As you can see, complicated tests-within-tests can easily be set up. The final goal, or top objective, might be survival. Leading to it would be many meals and many ways of getting them, including the feedback units involved in getting to the store, working to get the money to buy food, growing vegetables in the back yard, and so forth. Linking all these steps is something Miller and his colleagues called the *flow of control:*

> What flows over the arrows [Figure 5.4] . . . is an intangible something called *control.* Or perhaps we should say that the arrow indicates only succession. This concept appears most frequently in the discussion of computing machines, where the control of the machine's operations passes from one instruction to another, successively, as the machine proceeds to execute the list of instructions that comprise the program it has been given. But the idea is certainly not limited to computers. As a simple example drawn from more familiar activities, imagine that you wanted to look up a particular topic in a certain book in order to see what the author had to say about it. You would open the book to the index and find the topic. Following the entry is a string of numbers. As you look up each page reference in turn, your behavior can be described as under the control of that list of numbers, and control is transferred from one number to the next as you proceed through the list. The transfer of control could be symbolized by drawing arrows from one page number to the next, but the arrows would [indicate] . . . the order in which the "instructions" are executed. (Miller, Galanter, and Pribram, 1960, pp. 28–29)

In addition to the flow of control, another important aspect of human information processing is implied in the TOTE unit: continuous evaluation or *monitoring.* We constantly monitor our own behavior, even our own thinking behavior. Further, we monitor it with special reference to the goals we are trying to achieve.

If these processes are in fact basic to human thinking, then a number-ordering program would look quite different from the hierarchies developed by Gagné or Skinner and shown in Figures 5.2 and 5.3, respectively. To show this kind of program, we need a set of conventions somewhat like those used in drawing computer flow diagrams. The diamond box signifies the test; the closed rectangle signifies states of knowledge or concepts (content or product, in the language of the preceding section), and the open rectangle signifies operations of various informal kinds (the term is not being used here in the special sense that Piaget uses it). The cognitive psychologist, for reasons that will become clear in the next chapter, is not likely to teach number ordering in the same way as Gagné and Skinner. Instead, he would suggest that the child draw into his immediate ordering problem an analogous skill of some kind. ("If you don't know how to order numbers, do you know how to order anything?" "Yes," the child replies, "I can make blocks go from big to little." "Fine," says the cognitive psychologist, "do that.") Unless a child is demented, if he is old enough to learn how to order numbers, he already knows how to order a lot of other things. In order to simplify the diagram, we will also assume he already knows how to count. What he does not know how to do is attach increasing orders of numbers to increasing orders of blocks. Once he has his blocks in order, the psychologist (or the Montessori teacher) then shows him how to say the littlest number while touching the littlest block, the next number while touching the next block, and so forth. Figure 5.5 shows such a process in the diagram form.

As you can see, Figure 5.5 illustrates a dynamic structure because it allows for movement back through earlier structures if necessary. Further, it has taught the child a basic rule of thumb: If you do not know how to do something, think of something like it that you *do* know how to do, and ask the teacher to help you connect it to your goal. The procedure should teach the child how to organize his own flow of control—how to program himself to solve a number-ordering problem. He does this by activating smaller, familiar dynamic systems (ordering blocks), and tying them together in a larger dynamic whole.

The Three Systems Compared

Three types of instructional hierarchies have been illustrated: Gagné-type theories, Skinner-type theories, and cognitive theories. Each has some advantages and some disadvantages.

The Gagné-type learning hierarchy may contain some irrelevant steps. It is not always clear that early steps in the hierarchy are actually necessary to later steps. The same may be true of Skinnerian programs, which often suffer from the additional drawback of being stupifyingly oversimplified. Skinner (rather like a Christian Scientist) does not believe that people should rehearse error, so each step is designed to have an obviously correct answer. Because the next step differs from it in very small ways, the next answer is also easy to recognize. After a few minutes of this, boredom can set in.

However, both the Gagné- and Skinner-type learning programs have the advantage of precise specification. They are, in effect, algorithms for the development of instructional systems. You follow Gagné's or Skinner's rules, and you come up with a clearly structured curriculum. You know where you are and where you are going; if things are wrong with the program, you will find that out and can make corrections. Better education will often happen as a result.

Cognitive instructional programs are messier. Because an effort is made to involve a student's natural heuristic systems and because these systems are not very well understood, the learning program is likely to be unpredictable and spotty. We simply do not know enough yet to turn our own heuristic methods for developing curricula into algorithms. But knowledge is accumulating. In Chapter 6, we will attempt to compile what information we have about natural heuristic systems—systems for solving problems, scanning and classifying information, reasoning inductively, and so forth—in an effort to make it more immediately applicable to educational endeavors.

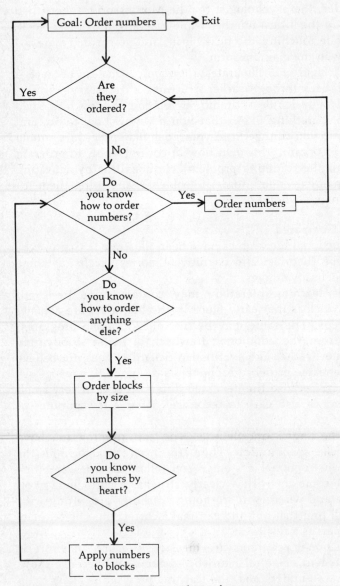

Figure 5.5   Flow diagram of a number-ordering process.

Chapter 6 BASIC HUMAN PROGRAMS

COMPUTERS THAT (WHO) THINK

Given three requirements—heuristic processes, behavioral specifications, and dynamic hierarchies—how can we construct a theory of human thinking? How can we test it?

Computer Simulations

The most ingenious answer to this difficult question has been developed by the cognitive researcher who specializes in *computer simulations.* The details of a dynamic heuristic process are enormously complicated, but one machine that is able to handle at least some of them is the computer. If a researcher works out a theory of human problem solving and translates that theory into a computer program (a set of instructions for the computer to follow), the computer can test the theory for him. If, for instance, the theory says that in looking for solutions, people vacillate, trying first this approach, then that one, the instructions to the computer might be: Here is a problem, here are several possible solutions, try first this one and then that one, but make the decision randomly. The computer, in obeying the instructions, writes out a "trace" of its actual behavior. That trace can then be compared to the behavior of a person solving the same problem. If the theory has been carefully worked out, the two traces will agree reasonably well. The random choice of the computer in this example may agree fairly well with the subject's choice, which would suggest that the subject may also be operating randomly. It is important to understand that the theorist does not write out every step for the computer; in effect, he tells the computer to apply a certain set of principles. The behavior of the computer and the behavior of a human subject are tests of those principles as applied to different kinds of information.

Educators may gain a useful glimpse into the method by asking themselves a series of questions such as these: Suppose I want to teach a robot to solve a problem. What information and ideas and abilities would I have to put into the robot? What concepts would it need? What kinds of "thinking" operations would it have to perform: Comparing? testing? searching? How would it know when its goal had been achieved? Just thinking about academic information in this way can be very revealing. For example, how would you teach a robot to memorize the names of the American presidents? to answer questions like "What is the mood of a poem?" to perform tasks such as classifying the good and bad aspects of urban living? It is a sobering experience to realize how much we expect of unknown processes in the heads of our students. We assume something will happen inside their heads, but we often do not have the foggiest notion of what it should be.

In the pages that follow we will consider some of the basic principles of human information processing that have come out of the field of computer simulation, as well as other relevant research. Our goal will be to learn how to analyze dynamic heuristic systems—*human programs,* for short—in an educational setting.

Basic Human Programs

The student who walks into a college brings with him an enormous variety of natural human programs. He knows how to drive a car (a program which is in itself a complex integration of iconic, verbal, and enactive elements), how to introduce people, how to type, how to use complex communication equipment, how to write papers, how to read books, how to cut his eight o'clock class, how to make love, how to spread the rumor that the Dean is in failing mental health, and so forth. We are all positively extraordinary storehouses of programs, bits of programs, obsolete programs, untested programs, and programs for inventing new programs.

We have been developing these programs since birth. Piaget calls simple programs *schemas,* and more complicated ones *operations.* Luria calls programs *functional systems.* Miller, Galanter, and Pribram (1960) call them *plans.* Others have called them *cognitive maps* (Tolman, 1932), *schemes* (Bartlett, 1964), *life-spaces* (Lewin, see Chapter 15), *games* (Berne, 1964; Mead, 1934). We will think of human programs as involving the components described below:

Goals—which are more or less valued

Elements—the "things" involved in the program, like numbers in an algebra problem, or musical ideas in composing

Operations—the activities, mental or otherwise, necessary to the program

States of knowledge—concepts, ideas, notions

Rules—constraints or limitations, such as the law of gravity

Tests—Do I know how to do something? Have I done it yet? Is there anything more to do?

Our conventions for sketching or diagramming a program have already been mentioned: closed rectangles house states of knowledge, including rules and goals; open rectangles house operations (when we see an open rectangle, we know it contains an instruction to do something); diamonds enclose tests; and arrows indicate the flow of control.

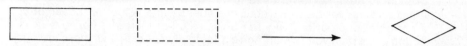

This procedure for diagramming human programs has been taken from the field of computer programming. The procedure does not duplicate the operations of a computer; it is simply a convenient analogy that makes it possible for us to compare different human programs more easily, very much as we might parse a sentence in order to show how one kind of sentence (active) differs from another (passive or interrogative).

We begin with the important matter of goals and values.

GOALS AND VALUES

Fundamental to all basic processing systems is an intent of some sort. It may not be conscious; it may not be admirable; it may have nothing to do with the intent of the teacher or the curriculum developer. But if organized mental activities are occurring—that is, if mental activities are not psychotic or dreamlike—a goal is somehow involved.

Instrumental Values

The various ways in which a goal polarizes human behavior are discussed in Part III, but here we confront the problem of value as one critically intertwined with human programs. The length and complexity of a program, the number of subgoals it contains, and the persistence with which it is activated result from the value of the ultimate goal. Does this imply that human programs may be faulty and weak if their objectives are not valued? Indeed it does. But it also means that the way to increase value is to make a goal relevant to another important goal. The source of value is *instrumental relevance* to other values. We value this because it helps us to get that. We value it even more if it helps us to get that and that and that. Diggory's explanation of this point is helpful:

> The objective study of value must start with the facts of purposive behavior. Value must always be defined in terms of some goal or objective of an individual organism, however that goal is instituted or chosen. Values are assigned to objects in terms of their usefulness in achieving these ends or goals. This is a utilitarian theory of value. Whether it is also

a materialistic one is decided by the nature of the goals, and these can range from building a house to controlling one's temper or cultivating religious experiences.

This theory of valuation can be validated by experiment and observation on behavior. This is the best test to make of it, because the reason we need the word *value* in the first place is to refer to certain aspects of behavior. . . . The notion of value implied here is consistent with the following propositions:

The value of anything is a function of the purposes of the user. Most simple hand tools illustrate this point well. A hammer can be used as a nail driver, nail puller, ice crusher, metal shaper, nutcracker, paperweight, or plumb bob. If we never need to do any of the things a hammer can do, it has no value for us. Now, let us consider people. A football coach brings a premium price at any Big Ten university, but there are colleges in this country to which you couldn't *give* a football coach, just as there are businesses which have no use for machinists or physicists.

The value of an object is to some extent independent of its immediate usefulness. We may value a thing simply because we *expect* to use it sometime in the future, not because we need to use it now. This is most obvious in the case of food, which is generally supplied in advance of immediate demand, but it also holds for tools and equipment of various kinds and for people with special skills as well. The value of an object goes from positive to zero or negative only when we permanently abandon the expectation that it will be used again.

Other things being equal, *the greater the number of goals to which an object is relevant, the greater its value and the longer its value will be maintained.* This is precisely the source of the value of money in our society—it can be traded for so many things. It is also the basis for the indisputably supreme value of individual human beings, particularly young human beings. They are multi-purpose machines, self-starting, and insatiable in their curiosity, always coming up with something new to amaze and dismay their jaded, know-it-all elders. There is no telling what they might do or what they might become if they are given adequate opportunity to transform their talents into skills and to use them effectively. The greater the number of skills and amount of information a man has the more likely he is to be useful, and hence, valuable, to himself and to others. (Diggory, 1966, pp. 88–90)

Utilitarian theories of value may strike you as rather cold and unsentimental, which indeed they are. But sentiment in this area rapidly draws us into what C. S. Pierce (1878) called "a rich mud of conceptions." To be useful to educators, value concepts must be clearly linked to reality and to plans of action—their own, and their students'. Describing human values in any other way yields poetic beauty or literary charm, rather than concepts we may apply in an educational setting.

Pepper's Theory of Value

The most recent proponents of the utilitarian theory, which has long been a controversial philosophical issue, are John Dewey (1939) and Stephen Pepper (1958). Pepper's contributions are especially valuable because they were worked out with the help of his close friend Edward Tolman (1932), one of the best and earliest cognitive psychologists. It was Tolman who developed the idea of "cognitive maps" and who carried out experiments challenging psychologists who maintained that only mindless habit structures existed. (This is, of course, another version of the cognitive-behaviorist controversy described in Chapter 5.)

Following a rigorous philosophical argument, Pepper (1958) concluded that there were seven major sources of value operating in the world today. Each value system has both a positive and a negative pole; we move toward the positive pole and away from the negative one. Thus, we move toward success and away from failure, or toward pleasant feelings and away from unpleasant ones. The seven types of values are shown in Table 6.1. Each value has certain built-in *selective systems* through which it operates. Social congeniality, for example, is a value that groups will automatically strive toward, using the avenues provided by the group situation. Some value systems may take precedence over others. We can see, for example, that a ghetto survival system may dominate a system powered mainly by the affective value of middle-class manners and cleanliness. Middle-class schools may therefore be totally unsuited to a ghetto culture. The force of Pepper's argument lies in his seeing this type of conflict as inevitable. It is not a matter of individual choice; pursuit of certain values is automatically a product of certain social systems.

Table 6.1
Pepper's Sources of Value and Their Selective Systems

TYPE OF VALUE	SELECTIVE SYSTEM ACTIVATED
Affective: pleasant vs. unpleasant feelings	Consummatory (pleasant) and riddance (unpleasant) behavior patterns
Achievement: success vs. lack of success	Purposeful structures
Prudential: prudent vs. imprudent	Personal situation (Lewinian life-space)
Character: integrative vs. unintegrative	Personality structure
Social: congenial vs. uncongenial	Social situation
Cultural: conforming vs. nonconforming	Cultural pattern
Survival: adaptive vs. unadaptive	Natural selection

SOURCE: After Pepper, 1958, Table 8, p. 673.

Manipulation of value structures is the topic of Part III, which is concerned with motivation, personality, and culture. The general rule is to begin with the values students already hold and work from there. For now, we will focus on only the cognitive aspects of human programs; the continuing importance of goals and values will be assumed.

HUMAN ACADEMIC PROGRAMS

The student in a school setting will be using his natural heuristic skills to cope with educational problems. If he is lucky, he will become good at adapting these natural skills to academic requirements. If he is unlucky, he may never even realize this adaptation is possible. Skilled counselors are sometimes available to help with study problems, but in most cases, school learning difficulties are not recognized as problems of personal program construction. Remembering content will result only if a good program for remembering has been constructed; relating information will result only if a good program for relating has been constructed. Academic requirements—as defined by examinations, themes, note taking, library research, and problem solving—are basically requirements for efficient, intellectual self-programming.

Basic Systems

When a student learns something, what does he do? What does the act of learning actually mean? Probably one or several of the following:

1. Constructing a program for scanning information and holding it in mind (underlining the key words in a text, or taking lecture notes)

2. Constructing a program for solving problems (algebra)

3. Constructing a program for recalling information (examinations)

4. Constructing a program for generating and classifying information (library research)

5. Constructing a program for ordering and relating information (composition of a theme)

The student may not do any of these things expertly, and he may not be at all aware of the fact that he does them. But it is difficult to decide what else learning may be, if it is not these processes.

The list represents what we will call *basic systems of information processing.* It is probably not exhaustive, but there is every reason to believe that the human mind is not capable of constructing an infinite number of programs, just as the human body is not infinitely bendable. The mind probably uses a few basic prototype (model) programs as master patterns for the others. Most of these prototypes are represented by our basic systems. If we study thoroughly *scanning and holding, problem solving, recalling, generating and classifying,* and *ordering and relating,* we will at least have made a good start. We will have a conceptual tool kit for critically examining, comparing, and evaluating educational materials and experiences of many kinds.

Chapter 7 PROGRAMS FOR REMEMBERING AND SOLVING

We will begin our survey of the basic human programs necessary to academic success with memorizing, problem solving, and scanning information. Two more, to be considered in the next chapter, involve the organization of information into concepts and rules.

SCANNING AND HOLDING

A program basic to almost all academic and real-world situations involves our need to sample information. When we listen to people talking, we are, in effect, selectively scanning sound waves. A critical sound ("Fire!") causes us to react appropriately. We scan the visual environment in a similar way. When we spot the cue (that greenish snubby shape) that the bus is on the way, we move toward the curb. The other vehicles temporarily disappear from awareness.

The Phenomenon of Set

The selectiveness of our scanning systems is well illustrated by the phenomenon known as *set*. For example, unscramble these words in the order given: LECAM, NELIN, NEDOZ, SDLEN, PACHE. Do this before looking at the footnote below. Now read the footnote.*

---

*Did you develop a system for unscrambling the words? Did that system lead you to unscramble the last word as CHEAP? Why not PEACH? Probably you did not even see peach, because your *set* was for unscrambling the word by starting with the middle consonant. In your head, there was a little program controlling your scanning behavior.

Instructions that set or "tune" the scanning process before the information is presented generally have a stronger effect than instructions received after the information has been scanned. That seems obvious, but the reason for it is important: In the latter situation, all the information must be held in mind until the instructions are received. This is generally impossible, for human minds are extremely limited in what is called *short-term memory*.

The Span of Apprehension

In a famous psychological paper called "The Magical Number Seven: Plus or Minus Two," George Miller (1965) demonstrated that we have only about seven "slots" in our immediate or short-term memories. This limitation applies to many kinds of scanning and judging operations. For example, we can discriminate differences between only five to seven shades of red; beyond that number, we lose track. We cannot hold in mind more than about six different slots for redness. Similarly, if you drop a handful of coins on the table, you may be able to count about four of them at a glance. One clump will just "look like four" without any counting procedure on your part. Perhaps you can see five in the same way. But beyond about seven, you will have to do something else, like counting, in order to know how many coins are there. When you count, you have actually *recoded* a spatter of coins into a single word (ten) that stands for the whole. Now you are using only one of your short-term memory slots, whereas before you were unsuccessfully trying to cram ten things into seven slots. The great secret is recoding.

Recoding Operations

Consider the problem of learning Morse code. At first, you try valiantly to remember streams of dots and dashes, then they begin to recode themselves into patterns. Where before you were trying to remember ten separate signals, now you remember only three basic patterns. Then the patterns "chunk" themselves into words, and now the three patterns are heard as a single word. Six short-term memory slots are again open for new information. A selective listening skill has been established.

It should be clear from the example why *familiarity* and *high probability* improve scanning-and-holding efficiency (see, for example, Maccoby and Konrad, 1967, for experimental evidence). If we know what to expect and are familiar with the information, our recoding skills are probably greater. More slots for short-term storage will be available. But other factors are important, too.

Visual, Auditory, and Motor Spans

A great deal of highly technical research is now being done on the nature of the short-term (holding) memory system. It is felt that there are important differences between a short-term *visual* holding operation and a short-term *auditory* one. The fact that these channels are separate will become evident as you perform the following experiments, which also involve *motor* channels.

Consider the sentence, "A bird in the hand is not in the bush." Suppose you were instructed to hold that sentence in your mind and then say "Yes" if the words (in sequence) were nouns, and "No" if they were non-nouns. The sequence would be: "No, yes, no, no, yes, no, no, no, no, yes." (Try it; the experience provides a good test of the difference between a holding and a recoding operation.) Now suppose that instead of saying the words *yes* and *no,* you were instructed to signal noun by tapping with your left hand, and non-noun by tapping with your right hand. In this case, a motor system is involved in the recall of verbal material. In the former case, a verbal system was involved in the recall of verbal material. Which would you expect to be easier?

Suppose you were shown a visual figure that looked like this:

Now, from memory, say whether each dot (going from top right to bottom) is at the extreme top, the extreme bottom, or in between. Say "Yes" for extreme top and bottom, and "No" for in between. The sequence would be: "Yes, yes, yes, no, no, no, no, no, yes." As an alternative response system, you could tap with the right hand for extreme outside and with the left hand for in between. In another alternative system for both the sentence and the dot pattern, you might point to a sequence of Ys and Ns (for Yes and No) written down on a piece of paper. Such a response would involve some motor elements, but would be primarily a visual one.

All told, the procedures involve two kinds of short-term memory (auditory and visual) and three kinds of recoding systems (verbal, visual, and motor). The results of an actual experiment carried out by Lee Brooks of McMaster University in Ontario are given in Table 7.1. The results tell us that using a verbal response system for short-term auditory memories slows down the recoding process. It is faster if the subjects are permitted to use either visual (pointing to Ys and Ns) or motor (tapping) recoding systems. But the same is not true for the visual materials. In this case, using the visual recoding system slowed down the recoding operation. The fact that the tapping responses also utilized some spatial ideas—"Yes"

Table 7.1
Speed of Recoding (Seconds)

TYPE OF MATERIAL	TYPE OF RECODING		
	VERBAL	VISUAL	MOTOR
Auditory (sentence)	13.8	9.8	7.8
Visual (dot pattern)	11.3	28.2	14.1

SOURCE: Based on data from Brooks, 1958.

was tapped by the right hand and "No" by the left—probably accounted for the recoding rate being slower for the visual material when tapping was the response system. The fastest rate of recoding for visual material appeared to be in the verbal mode.

This means that the program works more efficiently if scanning takes place in one mode and recoding in another. You can see from the diagram in Figure 7.2 that both scanning and recoding operate out of short-term memory simultaneously. If it is possible to use "separate" perceptual channels, program efficiency may be increased. Another factor affecting efficiency, however, is the sheer capacity of short-term memory. Psychologists have long known that people differ greatly in this particular capacity, which is measured by *digit span*.

The Significance of Digit Span
Sets of numbers are displayed at a fixed speed, one at a time, visually or aurally. The subject says them back immediately.

As Miller (1956) pointed out, most normal adults can remember about seven digits at a time—6, 8, 2, 4, 7, 5, 1, for example—but digit span is much lower for young children. In an experiment by Whimbey and Ryan (1969), it was found that digit span was related to subjects' ability to recode logical statements into visual diagrams (Figure 7.1). The subjects were trained to use Venn diagrams to recode such statements as "All men are human; Jack is a man; therefore Jack is human." The diagrams were then used to determine whether the statements were true or false.

Because the syllogism has to be held in mind while the diagram is being constructed, we would expect short-term memory deficiencies (lower digit-span abilities) to interfere with the construction of the diagrams, and this was what Whimbey and Ryan found. But the important point was that the deficiency affected the ability of students to learn how to carry out a recoding process (constructing Venn diagrams).

A Scanning-and-Holding Flow Diagram
Figure 7.2 summarizes the principles we have discussed and shows their implications for education. We can see that a scanning-and-holding program involves sampling information, holding some of it in mind, and recoding it at the same time so that a portion will be available for later refer-

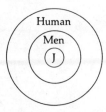

Figure 7.1

ence or later cognitive use of some kind. Because more information must be sampled even while the recoding process is going on, the short-term holding operation is in a sense divided.

This is essentially the program that students use when they take notes during a lecture or from reading material. It is the program they use when they summarize the main points of a debate or restate something a teacher has said. It is the program that is used in "paying attention," which is surely more than just orienting in the direction of a teacher, a book, or a TV screen.

Pedagogical Strategies

How can we help students develop more efficient scanning-and-holding programs? Research suggests the following:

1. Begin training with highly familiar material so that students will already have some recoding skills available.

2. Provide some organizing principles in advance to help students establish a preparatory set for attending selectively.

3. Locate these principles in a different cognitive mode, if possible. In learning to take notes from a lecture, for example, young children (or slow students) will be helped by having spatially cued outlines in front of them

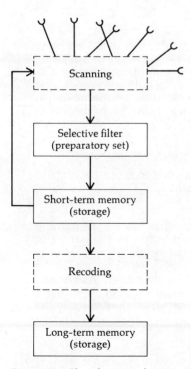

Figure 7.2 Flow diagram of a scanning-and-holding process.

(which the teacher might prepare on Ditto sheets). In learning to attend selectively to a slide presentation, however, the principles should be in the form of auditory memories. (Remember to look at the slide carefully, from left to right, and whisper the name of each different kind of fruit to yourself.)

4. Remember that program deficiencies may result from short-term memory deficiencies, not necessarily from "poor motivation" or the like. Short-term memory problems are probably physiological in nature. It is not known to what extent they can be fixed—through drill procedures, for example—and in any case the critical factor is the way short-term memory fits into a total program. The best kind of practice will involve a total program, not merely separate memory drill.

Various other aspects of scanning-and-holding programs are discussed elsewhere in the text. In Part V, particular attention is paid to problems of recoding verbal material into spatial forms (constructing visual representations) and recoding spatial material into verbal forms

---

PART **8**

THE UNKNOWN IN 1492—A POPULAR TALE

You have seen which parts of the world were unknown in 1492. The following reading shows how some people felt about those unknown parts of the world.

The reading is from a tale which was very popular before the time of Columbus. Although the tale was not true, many people believed it. The tale is from a book a man wrote about what he thought the unknown world was like. The author, of course, had never been to the unknown parts of the world.

As you read, think about these questions:

1. How did the unknown appear to the author of this tale?

2. Why do you think many people believed what they did about parts of the world which were unknown to them?

*

In one of these islands are very tall people. They are giants, horrible and ugly to look at. They have but one eye, and that is in the middle of their face. In another island are ugly men without heads. They have eyes in their shoulders. Their mouths look like horseshoes, and are in the middle of their chests. In another island are other ugly men without heads. Their eyes and their mouths are behind their shoulders. In another island are ugly men who have a bottom lip so large that when they sleep in the sun, they cover their whole face with that lip.

NOW, TURN TO PAGE 11 IN YOUR WORKBOOK.

Figure 7.3 A text scanning-and-holding program with verbal instructions. (Fenton, 1970, p. 12)

(comprehending a graph). The general problems of the development of verbal, visual, and motor systems covered in Part I affect scanning-and-holding programs quite directly. The further use of materials that have been put in long-term storage is a later topic in this chapter.

Illustrations from Social Studies

Two illustrations of scanning-and-holding programs are shown in Figures 7.3, 7.4, and 7.5. They are taken from a curriculum for slow learners at the high school level developed by Edwin Fenton and his colleagues and called *The Americans: A History of the United States.*

The first illustration (Figure 7.3) uses verbal instructions as a preparatory set for scanning and holding with reference to verbal materials (a text paragraph). Note how difficult it is to keep the set instructions in mind while you are reading. On the workbook page (Figure 7.4) is the recoding assistance the students will need. Note how the workbook page is organized spatially, and how it guides the students to scan the paragraph for a specific point: Each question tunes or sets the student to select a special type of information. The information is then recoded in the student's own words so that he can refer to it later.

PART **8** TEXT PAGE 12

THE UNKNOWN IN 1492—A POPULAR TALE

QUESTIONS

1. Describe what the unknown was like according to the author of the tale.__

_____

_____

_____

2. Why do you think people believed stories like this about the unknown?__

_____

_____

_____

3. What kind of man would sail into unknown oceans near unknown continents if he had heard stories like this?_____

_____

_____

Figure 7.4   Workbook page corresponding to Figure 7.3 (Fenton, 1970)

PART **10**

THE UNKNOWN IN 1492—PICTURES

Below are two drawings about the unknown. They were made almost 500 years ago. Like the stories you have read or listened to, they show how men felt about the unknown world before Columbus made his voyage. As you look at them, think about:

1. How you would describe each picture.

2. Why the artist drew the unknown that way.

Picture 1

Figure 7.5 A scanning-and-holding program with pictures. (Fenton, 1970)

Picture 2

NOW, TURN TO PAGE 13 IN YOUR WORKBOOK.

In another example from the same curriculum (Figure 7.5), the student is directed to scan pictures with particular verbal instructions in mind. Note how much easier it is to keep the instructions in mind while a picture rather than verbal text is being scanned. (The corresponding workbook exercise provides for recoding and long-term storage, as in the previous illustration.) The students are being charted through a slow-motion program similar to the advanced programs used by history scholars.

Of course, scanning-and-holding programs are important subprograms in many kinds of cognitive processing. To solve a problem, for example, one must first scan the problem and hold its key aspects in mind in order to formulate the nature of the problem itself. Scanning and holding can also be greatly affected by motivational factors, as we shall see in Part III.

PROBLEM SOLVING

When you decided what suit to wear this morning, you solved a little problem. When you steer your car through traffic, you solve many problems. Waiting in line at the supermarket or at the barber shop, you think of something or read something to pass the time. You are solving another problem, that of boredom. Do these human problem-solving programs have anything in common?

The General Problem Solver

The foremost researchers in the field of computer simulation, Herbert Simon and Allen Newell, believe they do. (See their 1962 paper for a good summary relevant to child development.) To demonstrate this, they designed a computer program that simulates human problem solving. It is called the General Problem Solver, or GPS for short. The program enables a computer to solve new, unfamiliar problems in ways that match (reasonably well) the problem-solving behavior of human beings. What does the model reveal?

First, that a *goal* of some sort must be represented (in the head, or in the computer). Second, that the *present state* of the individual must also be represented. How do we know we are not at the goal? Because we know where we are now and that it is not at the goal. This awareness of a gap, or *discrepancy,* between where we are now and the goal makes up the third major component of the GPS program. To close a gap, we institute an *operation* of some sort. We move a chess piece or look up something in a dictionary. These operations must be represented as problem-solving resources. The *rules* or conditions of the problem must also be represented in the mind of the problem solver. And then, of course, there are the *elements* of the problem—mathematical symbols, scientific apparatus, the ingredients of a recipe, or whatever. Finally, methods of *evaluation* (are we at the goal yet?) are necessary; these too must be represented in the mind of the problem solver.

When these components are assembled, the program can begin to run. What happens first? According to GPS, the subject first tests himself. He compares where he is (on the ground) to where he wants to be (on the roof, where the football is). If he has not achieved his goal (that's a 40-foot gap), he then formulates a subgoal: finding some means of getting closer to where he wants to be. If he needs something—a ladder, for example—he then formulates still another subgoal: constructing the thing he needs. He may set numerous additional subgoals and generate many different kinds of operations and tests that are gradually ticked off, one by one. If the suboperations are complicated and extensive, keeping track of progress and next steps may in itself become a problem for which new problem-solving procedures will be necessary. At all times, the subject is constrained by rules of one sort or another (the laws of gravity, for example).

As he completes each subgoal, the subject rechecks his position. Has he achieved the subgoal of constructing the ladder? If not, continue with the building; if so, apply the ladder to the next subgoal, climbing to the roof. Is he there yet? No? Then keep climbing. Yes? Good! Has the goal been achieved? Not quite—the football is over there behind the chimney. Achieved yet? Yes! (Now whatever became of that ladder. . . .)

A Problem-Solving Flow Diagram

The flow diagram for this procedure is shown in Figure 7.6. Discussions of academic problem solving usually seem much more muddled than our simple football on the roof because many different basic programs may be summoned to help with a problem. Scanning and holding, generating and classifying, and remembering all may function as subprograms in an overall problem-solving program.

Yet the basic problem-solving format is as simple as a football on a roof: You have a goal; you are not achieving it; you set up a series of subgoals to help you achieve it; you institute whatever operations are necessary to achieve your subgoals; you keep track of where you are in the overall operation by a series of continuing tests until your goal is finally achieved. What makes a problem a problem is that this program is not clearly perceived. Once it is, the person is on his way toward a solution.

Means-End Awareness in Köhler's Chimpanzees

One major difficulty may be that the problem solver fails to recognize that the components of a solution are in fact available to him. One famous historical example described in the 1920s concerned a colony of primates. The animals—chimpanzees and apes—were used in a series of experiments carried out by a Gestalt psychologist (see Chapter 20) named Köhler (1927). In one experiment the chimps had to learn to pile boxes to get a piece of fruit; in another, they had to use both boxes and a stick, sometimes retrieving the stick from another place. That in itself was an interesting problem; at least in the beginning, sticks were not perceived as tools unless they were visually close to the fruit. After a while, sticks would be fetched from any place; they had developed a "tool function" in the minds of the animals.

Köhler's best-known chimp was Sultan. Sultan was the first to discover that one stick could be put into another to make a stick sufficiently long to retrieve a banana outside the cage.

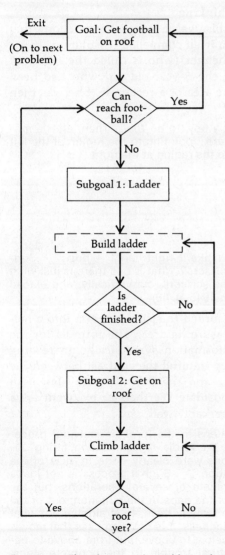

Figure 7.6 Flow diagram of a problem-solving process.

> After his first success Sultan repeated the act a number of times, without stopping to eat until he had drawn into his cage, not only all of the fruit, but also a number of other things. He appeared to enjoy the act, and he retained the method of solution so well that on the following day he was able to construct a still longer stick from three bamboo stalks. (Koffka, 1946, p. 218)

This sounds very similar to Piaget's *secondary circular reaction,* discussed in Chapter 13. In all these cases, the components of the problem-solving program were there; all the animals had to do was recognize them.

Wertheimer's Theory of Productive Thinking

The Gestalt psychologists believed this was a *wholistic* function, that something in the nature of the problem itself compelled its solution. In his book *Productive Thinking,* Max Wertheimer (who is called the father of Gestalt psychology) cited the case of the 5-year-old girl who had been shown a simple formula for finding the area of a rectangle. She was then shown a parallelogram:

> She said, "I certainly don't know how to do *that.*" Then, after a moment of silence: "This is *no good here,*" pointing to the region at the left end; "and *no good here,*" pointing to the region at the right.

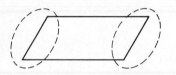

> Hesitatingly she said: "I could make it right here . . . but . . ." Suddenly she cried out, "May I have a scissors? What is bad there is just what is needed here. It fits." She took the scissors, cut vertically, and placed the left end at the right. (Wertheimer, 1945, p. 48)

This was an intuitive solution. Having turned the parallelogram into a rectangle, the child was then able to measure its area. The formula for the problem accomplishes the same transformation symbolically. In reading Wertheimer's explanation (below), keep in mind the contrast between the Gagné hierarchy shown in Figure 5.2 and the flow diagram shown in Figure 7.6. Although the flow charts postdate Wertheimer by twenty-five years, they illustrate his reasoning remarkably well.

> What are the operations, the steps in the [problem-solving] procedure? . . . Regrouping with regard to the whole, reorganization, fitting. . . . The steps were taken, the operations were clearly done in view of the whole figure and of the whole situation. . . . Such a process is not just a sum of several steps, not an aggregate of several operations, but the growth of one line of thinking out of the gaps in the situation, out of the structural troubles and the desire to remedy them, to straighten out what is bad, to get at the good inner-relatedness. It is not a process that moves from pieces to an aggregate, from below to above, but from above to below, from the nature of the structural trouble to the concrete steps. (Wertheimer, 1945, p. 50)

The components of the solution were there; all the child had to do was recognize their relationship to each other.

A number of experiments have explored the factors that affect this basic ability. One of them is suggested by the finding that Köhler's chimps had to develop a new concept of stick-as-tool.

Duncker's Concept of Functional Fixedness

Karl Duncker, one of Wertheimer's colleagues, took as his major research emphasis the fact that familiar materials may have a *functional fixedness* about them. We simply fail to recognize how they can be arranged or used in a new way that facilitates the discovery of a solution. He used the case of the chimpanzees:

> A chimpanzee who stands in need of a stick (something long, firm . . .) sometimes has difficulties in recognizing the stick in a branch still growing on the tree, in seeing it as a percept apart. . . . On the tree it is a "branch," a part of the visual figural unit "tree," and this part-character — more generally, this *fixedness* — is clearly responsible for the fact that to a search for something like a stick, the branch on the tree is less "within reach" than the branch on the ground. (Duncker, 1945, p. 85)

In one experimental attempt to study this question, Duncker presented his subjects (who seemed to be adult college students) with little problems that could be solved with the materials displayed on a table. For example, one problem was that of fastening candles on a door at eye level, ostensibly for use in some kind of visual experiments:

> With each problem there lay on the table . . . all kinds of material, partly . . . unsuitable for the solution, such as paperclips, pieces of paper, string, pencils, tinfoil, old parts of apparatus, ashtrays, joints, pieces of wood, etc. . . . The objects lay in apparent confusion, but in definite places. The crucial objects never occupied a prominent place. (Duncker, 1945, p. 87)

For the candle problem, the crucial objects were some little cardboard boxes and some thumbtacks. The boxes could be tacked to the door and the candles placed in them.

This solution was readily discovered by most of the subjects when the little boxes were lying about on the table empty. In one experimental condition, however, Duncker put some of the miscellaneous apparatus (paper clips, string) in the little boxes so that they functioned as containers. In this case, subjects less frequently thought of them as potential candle-

Table 7.2
Number of Solutions in Duncker's Test of Functional Fixedness

	NUMBER OF SOLUTIONS	NUMBER OF FAILURES
Boxes empty	7	0
Boxes filled	3	4

SOURCE: Based on data from Duncker, 1945.

holders. The experiment results appear in Table 7.2. The functional fixedness of the boxes was determined simply by presenting them first as containers. If they were not "fixed" in this way, they could be more readily perceived as candleholders. Once subjects have participated in an experiment like this, or even read about one, however, they are forever on the alert for functional un-fixedness. This awareness is an important clue for education.

Learning Problem-Solving Systems

Problem solving can be learned by solving problems, even problems for which no algorithms exist. It helps if the first problems are simple ones and if some of the rules learned are general ones. Scandura and Durnin (1968) have shown in several experiments that although subjects can

---

HOW TO SOLVE IT

UNDERSTANDING THE PROBLEM

First.
You have to
understand the
problem.

What is the unknown? What are the data? What is the condition? Is it possible to satisfy the condition? Is the condition sufficient to determine the unknown? Or is it insufficient? Or redundant? Or contradictory?

Draw a figure. Introduce suitable notation.

Separate the various parts of the condition. Can you write them down?

DEVISING A PLAN

Second.
Find the connection
between the data and
the unknown.
You may be obliged
to consider auxiliary
problems if an
immediate connection
cannot be found.
You should obtain
eventually a plan of
the solution.

Have you seen it before? Or have you seen the same problem in a slightly different form?

Do you know a related problem? Do you know a theorem that could be useful?

Look at the unknown! And try to think of a familiar problem having the same or a similar unknown.

Here is a problem related to yours and solved before.

Could you use it? Could you use its result? Could you use its method? Should you introduce some auxiliary element in order to make its use possible?

Could you restate the problem? Could you restate it still differently?

Go back to definitions.

Figure 7.7   (Polya, 1945, pp. 6–8, 12)

transfer a rule originally relevant to specific problems, it is more efficient for them to learn a general rule to begin with. In Sultan's terms, discovering that two sticks could be put together was a general operation that could be applied to many situations. But in the beginning the rule had a very specific form for him: Two sticks were a thing-to-get-that-particular-banana-with. Transfer was slower as a result.

Polya's System

What are the best general rules for learning how to solve problems? One of the clearest statements is Polya's, whose little book *How to Solve It* (1957) has applications far beyond mathematics. His basic outline is reproduced in Figure 7.7. The book should be carefully studied by educators interested in the heuristics of good problem solving and how to teach them.

If you cannot solve the proposed problem try to solve first some related problem. Could you imagine a more accessible related problem? A more general problem? A more special problem? An analogous problem? Could you solve a part of the problem? Keep only a part of the condition, drop the other part; how far is the unknown then determined, how can it vary? Could you derive something useful from the data? Could you think of other data appropriate to determine the unknown? Could you change the unknown or the data, or both if necessary, so that the new unknown and the new data are nearer to each other?

Did you use all the data? Did you use the whole condition? Have you taken into account all essential notions involved in the problem?

CARRYING OUT THE PLAN

Third.
Carry out your plan.

Carrying out your plan of the solution, *check each step.*

Can you see clearly that the step is correct? Can you prove that it is correct?

LOOKING BACK

Fourth.
Examine the solution obtained.

Can you *check the result?* Can you check the argument?

Can you derive the result differently? Can you see it at a glance?

Can you use the result, or the method, for some other problem?

Figure 7.7 *(Continued)*

Now look back at Figure 5.5. You should understand why the flow diagram represented a pedagogical situation in which the teacher was saying to the child, "Do you know how to order something *else?*"

REMEMBERING

The ability of man to remember, despite rival claims from the ranks of the computers, remains one of the most remarkable of his powers.

The greatest of the giant machines, cramming and crowding its tapes and wheels, and dials, and relays, into cubic meters of space, cannot remember, select, and forget, in the integrated creative way the brain does with its kilo-and-a-half of matter. This extraordinary power which we call memory has engaged, over all recorded history, the attention of those given to inquiry and contemplation—the Greek philosophers, the great poets of the post-Renaissance period, and the scientists emerging in the 19th century—neurologists, neurosurgeons, and psychiatrists, and more lately, the psychologists, biochemists, and the new men, bred of the merging of many fields.

Of all those multitudinous events which start when coded information enters the central nervous system, and terminate with later readout into conscious experience, none has captured the imagination as has that central and fundamental phenomenon, the memory trace—how is it formed, how is it preserved, where is it located? . . . While it is impossible to say when man first began to speculate on the physical basis of memory, speculation can nonetheless be found as far back as the writings of Paramenides, about 540 B.C. . . . Plato's wax tablet hypothesis . . . appeared some 200 years later, and . . . [has been followed by] a great array of subsequent theories, each becoming progressively modified as knowledge of neurophysiology and psychological functioning has increased. Despite this progression of knowledge, there has been no agreement on a general theory of memory. Indeed, one must be struck alike by the multiplicity of theories of memory and by the unevenness of progress of our knowledge of this function.

. . . One finds an extraordinary number of competing hypotheses, one being that memory may be stored in reverberatory circuits . . . or in assemblies of cells, in changes occurring at the synaptic junction or in some substance in the brain in which a lasting trace might be formed. Much of the support for these ideas, however, has been quite limited and contradictory. But in the 1950's the long-held belief that the memory trace is held in structural [chemical] form began to receive important support, and that support has grown with impressive rapidity. (Cameron et al., 1966, pp. 129–130)

RNA Experiments

The support has been primarily the discovery that ribonucleic acid, or RNA, is involved in memory storage. RNA is intimately involved in protein synthesis and therefore has something to do with almost all possible structural modifications of all cells. It has thus been difficult to learn exactly what it does to which cells located in what part of the brain, and exactly how this affects memory storage. We do know, however, that if an animal is deprived of sensory stimulation in one of its modalities (such as vision), the nerve cells in the sensory (visual) area of the animal's brain will not develop biochemically. The anatomy may appear normal, but the nerve cells may be deficient both in RNA and in protein. It was because of such evidence that RNA first began to be considered an important biochemical in learning. There have also been some other interesting experiments; for example, a rat that learns to climb up a string to a food platform will be found (upon postmortem analysis) to have increased RNA production in those brain cells involved in making the string-climbing response.

Another group of experimenters (Babich et al., 1965) at the University of California, Los Angeles, trained a group of rats to approach a food cup when they heard a click, but only when they heard a click. They trained them quite vigorously, and by the end of training each rat approached the food cup promptly and swiftly from wherever it happened to be when the click was sounded. But the trained rats never or rarely approached the cup in the absence of the click. After this training was completed, the rats were sacrificed, their brains were removed, and RNA was extracted from a certain portion of the brain tissue. Approximately eight hours later, the RNA extract from the trained rats was injected into a group of untrained rats. In addition, a control group was formed to test the effects on untrained rats of just having plain old RNA injected into their brains. Rats who had had no training in the food-click response were also sacrificed, and the RNA extracted from their brains was injected into a second (control) group of untrained rats.

Now we have two new groups of rats, both of which have had no previous training in responding to clicks and both of which have had RNA injections. One group has been injected with "smart" RNA from previously trained rats; the other group has been injected with "dumb" RNA from previously untrained rats. The question is: What will these two new groups do when they are placed (one by one) in a cage with a food cup and hear a click? Let us consider the control group first.

There were nine rats in the control ("dumb" RNA) group. When these rats heard the click (presumably for the first time in their lives), they approached the food cup on the average of once. Compare that to the performance of the "smart" RNA group: When they heard the click, they approached the food cup on an average of 6 times. In fact, only one rat approached the food cup less than 3 times; one rat approached the cup just 3 times; another approached 7 times; another, 8 times; another, 9 times; and two rats approached the food cup 10 times. This happened without any training of their own; the only way they differed from the control rats was that they had been injected with "smart" RNA.

Other studies of this sort have been carried out, not always with similar results. There are many controversies about methodology and training procedures, but enough evidence is in to indicate that in the relatively near future, we will have some solid information about the biochemistry of remembering.

What then? Suppose memory pills can be developed and dispensed at schools like free lunches. Is the job of teaching finished? Obviously not, but the important question is why not? What is there about the process of remembering that is important pedagogically?

Learning to Remember (Without Pills)

One clue can be found in the following description by Miller, Galanter, and Pribram:

> If you ask a man who has just memorized his first list of nonsense syllables to tell you what he did in order to master the list, he will have quite a lot to say. And he will usually be eager to say it. In fact, the only part of the task that has any interest or appeal to most subjects concerns the discovery and use of a technique for solving the problem. He will say that he was trying to connect things up and make sense of them. Of course, you knew that he had to connect them up, but how did he make sense out of the carefully chosen nonsense he was given? Well, it wasn't easy, but he did it. Now, that first nonsense syllable, BOF, was just plain remembered the way it came, but the second one reminded him of "XAJerate," the third one turned into "MIBery," and the fourth turned from ZYQ to "not sick." So he had a kind of sentence, "BOF exaggerates his misery because he is not sick," instead of the cryptic BOF, XAJ, MIB, ZYQ, and he could imagine a hypochondriac named BOF who continually complained about his health. That MIBery-misery association wasn't too good, however, because for two or three trials through the list he remembered MIS instead of MIB. But he finally worked it out by thinking of "mibery" as a new word meaning "false misery." The fleeting thought that ZYQ was a strange way to spell "sick" was just amusing enough to fix the fourth syllable. Now the fifth and sixth syllables went together, too. . . . And so the subject chatters on, spinning out long descriptions of the various ideas, images, associations, and connections that occurred to him during the learning. Is it nothing but chatter? Or is this the sort of data that psychologists ought to study most carefully? (Miller, Galanter, and Pribram, 1960, pp. 126–127)

In old-fashioned theories of learning, programs for remembering were of little interest because it was believed that the fundamental memory process was some kind of physiological "trace." As we have seen, modern biochemical research (in RNA) suggests that these older theories may be right. But more modern theories of thinking are also concerned with the way in which a subject constructs a program for remembering materials that will be useful to him. This is the problem of *long-term* memory.

Moving information from a short-term holding operation into long-term storage is essentially a recoding problem—and the word *problem* is important here. As Miller and his colleagues suggest, remembering something may mean *solving the problem of retrieving it.* Presumably an item of information is stored in some chemical form, or perhaps as an electrical pattern. The problem is not storing it; the problem is getting it back. In the example, the subject stored each item of information (each nonsense syllable) with *retrieval cues.* He stored MIB with the cue "misery," ZYQ with the cue "not sick," and so forth. When he needed to pull the nonsense syllables from his long-term storage system, he activated the cues and out came the syllables. Note also that the cues themselves went together in a little story. A context, or *framework,* was established. These two factors—retrieval cues and a unified framework—are the major organizing principles of long-term memory.

Personal Organizing Principles

The principles are illustrated in most mnemonic systems, including the ones you have invented for remembering your Social Security number, license plates, mother-in-law's maiden name, and other material of that sort. A simple system is to put some strange object on the floor as a reminder of whatever it is you are supposed to remember, like "Call the grocer about that ridiculous bill." Even though the object on the floor is an ashtray, it will jog the memory quite efficiently. You look at the ashtray, think to yourself, "Now what in the world is *that* doing on the floor?" and back into consciousness pops the ridiculous grocery bill.

Other systems are described in Norman's *Memory and Attention* (1969), a highly readable book that will give you more details about modern memory research. Elaborate mnemonic systems always have a framework of some sort that assists in the retrieval of an indefinite amount of material. Rhyming systems (thirty days hath September . . .) pull a lot of information back; so do spatial systems (think of the memory items as attached to the spokes of a wheel . . .).

In a famous book called *Remembering,* F. C. Bartlett (1932) explored the nature of complex verbal memory by having subjects read a story and then asking them to recall it repeatedly, over many years in some cases. He found that personal organizing principles strongly controlled the retrieval process. For example, one student of anthropology recalled the story as containing ideas about "ancient Egyptian beliefs," which in fact it did not. Students attempted in various ways to straighten out confusions in the story and to structure their recollection around outstanding details, including humorous aspects. It was clear from Bartlett's reports that students actively organized the information and stored it with special retrieval cues.

A Computer Program Called EPAM

The most detailed theorizing about the nature of remembering programs has been carried out by Herbert Simon and his former student E. A. Feigenbaum. They developed a program that caused computers to remember in ways that simulated human remembering. The program is called EPAM, for Elementary Perceiver and Memorizer (see Feigenbaum, 1963, for a summary of the details).

Simon and Feigenbaum conceived of human remembering as a process of sorting through a *discrimination net,* clue by clue, until a unique "storage bin" is reached. This sorting process is actually a series of tests, very much like a network of TOTE units. Suppose, for example, you were trying to remember the name of someone you recently met. "Did it begin with an R," you might ask yourself, "or an L?" The first test, then, would be between those two letters. Even if you were not sure exactly which one was correct, you might select one and "try out" vowel sounds (Ra, Ri, Ro) until you discovered one that "sounded right" (passed your second test). Then you might try out another letter, or even a whole syllable (Ro*ber* or Ro*ger*).

This explains the process for retrieving. What about the process for *storing?* According to Simon and Feigenbaum, learning or remembering is accomplished by *growing the discrimination net.* That is, the individual begins with the capability for remembering only what he already knows; when something new is to be added, he constructs a new "storage bin" (*node*) for it. In order to determine if this is necessary, the new information must first be checked against what is already stored. If it matches, it goes into an old bin. If it does not match, the new bin must be constructed, and it must capitalize on the special features that distinguish the new information from the old. These are the new cues stored with the information. In effect, they are the way the bins are decorated, or flagged.

The storage system illustrates another aspect of memory programming—why people with a lot on their minds tend to forget new information, or why, for example, children may have better memories than adults for some material. There is a bin problem. Suppose you have a lot of similar bins. According to the theory behind EPAM, an item of new information will automatically locate itself in a bin that has other similar information in it. (You may have one bin for onions and one for potatoes. Now a sweet potato may be automatically sorted into the potato bin, unless you consciously construct a new bin and tag it "for sweet potatoes only.")

As is customary in simulation research, Simon and Feigenbaum have compared the performance of the computer (the "trace," or machine record) with the performance of people learning the same material. The comparison is favorable. The computer even shows some of the same oscillation behavior characteristic of people—remembering something one time, forgetting it the next, and then remembering it again.

Tip of the Tongue (TOT) Phenomena
One study of special interest was carried out by two other experimenters who were not specifically testing EPAM, but who discovered the process EPAM describes in the behavior of students suffering from what they call the "tip of the tongue phenomenon" (TOT).

William James wrote, in 1893: "Suppose we try to recall a forgotten name. The state of our consciousness is peculiar. There is a gap therein; but no mere gap. It is a gap that is intensely active. A sort of wraith of the name is in it, beckoning us in a given direction, making us at moments tingle with the sense of our closeness and then letting us sink back without the longed-for term. If wrong names are proposed to us, this singularly definite gap acts immediately so as to negate them. They do not fit into its mould. And the gap of one word does not feel like the gap of another, all empty of content as both might seem necessarily to be when described as gaps."

For several months we watched TOT states in ourselves. Unable to recall the name of the street on which a relative lives, one of us thought of *Congress* and *Corinth* and *Concord* and then looked up the address and learned that it was *Cornish*. The words that had come to mind have certain properties in common with the word that had been sought (the "target word"): all four begin with *Co;* all are two-syllable words; all put the primary stress on the first syllable. . . .

We thought it might pay to "prospect" for TOT states by reading to *S* definitions of uncommon English words and asking him to supply the words. The procedure was given a preliminary test with nine *S*s. . . . In 57 instances an *S* was, in fact, "seized" by a TOT state. The signs of it were unmistakable; he would appear to be in mild torment, something like the brink of a sneeze, and if he found the word his relief was considerable. While searching for the target *S* told us all the words that came to his mind. He volunteered the information that some of them resembled the target in sound but not in meaning; others he was sure were similar in meaning but not in sound. The *E* intruded on *S*'s agony with two questions: (a) How many syllables has the target word? (b) What is its first letter? . . . Outcomes encouraged us . . . to devise a group procedure that would . . . speed up the rate of data collection. (Brown and McNeill, 1966, pp. 325–326)

Fifty-seven Harvard and Radcliffe undergraduates from a general education course volunteered for two-hour evening test sessions in which they were given definitions for infrequent words and asked to fill out a questionnaire the instant they felt themselves to be in a TOT state. The questionnaire not only asked for the initial letter of the target word and the number of syllables, but also for any words that seemed to them to be closest in sound or meaning to the target word. The former were called SS (similar in sound) words, and the latter were called SM (similar in meaning) words.

To convey a sense of the SS and SM words, we offer the following examples. When the target was *sampan,* the SS words (not all of them real words) included: *Saipan, Siam, Cheyenne, sarong, sanching,* and *sympoon.* The SM words were *barge, houseboat,* and *junk.* (Brown and Mc-Neill, 1966, p. 328)

The results of this study supported the kind of word filing system postulated by EPAM. First of all, subjects in the TOT state produced fewer SM (95) than SS words (224), which suggests that the sound similarity is critical during the period immediately preceding the emergence of the word. (In some cases the subjects did not always find the word for themselves, but were later able to recognize it from a list read by the experimenter.) Second, the subjects in the TOT state were able to recall with significant success the number of syllables in the target word, its initial letter, the location of syllabic stress, letters in the last positions, and chunks like suffixes. In particular, the ability of TOT-state subjects to recall accurately the first and last letters of the target word suggests the gap that James was describing and also supports the *noticing order* that Simon and Feigenbaum built into EPAM and that has been demonstrated in other psychological experiments. The first and last bits of a long item of information tend to be remembered best. Altogether, the TOT experiment could be said to have shown that something like the series of tests—of letters, sounds, and syllable patterns—does in fact go on when we are trying to recall isolated words.

Classroom Implications

If a system of this sort is used by students, what does it imply for the classroom? First of all, it tells us that successful memorizing (of such things as dates, names, places) has a creative, constructive aspect. The individual must build a network of distinctive cues at the time he is memorizing, or he will not be able to retrieve the information. Second, the memory program should have a unified framework. The same principles hold for complex material.

Verbal rehearsal of one's own summaries seems to provide the best method of capitalizing on both principles. Complex information—whether in text or lecture or film or conversation—should be summarized in the briefest possible form. (Remember the "magic number 7" problem, and condense accordingly.) Then it should be rehearsed, aloud and actively:

> There is much that would tempt us to say that the seat of the memory is not in the mind but in the muscular system. It resides, at least, not so much in the receptive as in the responsive side of our nature. We learn by doing, and we learn by *expressing.* We retain information by making use of it, just as we maintain the strength of our muscles by giving them work to do, and as we retain dexterity by continued dexterous action.
>
> Some form of action or of expression would seem to be essential to unimpaired retention. It seems that good conversationalists and great talkers generally have good memories. It is over-simple to suppose that this is due to the fact that, having good memories, they are well supplied with topics of conversation. The reverse connexion would seem to be involved. What is talked about is more firmly impressed upon the mind. Such men when they read a book immediately discuss it with a friend, thus unconsciously employing the potent principles of active repetition.
>
> One of the best ways of mastering a book, as every teacher knows, is to give a lecture on it. In this fact a special principle is involved. Each of us possesses an active and a passive vocabulary. A man's active vocabulary is constituted by those words he habitually uses in speech and writing. His passive vocabulary is constituted by the words he under-

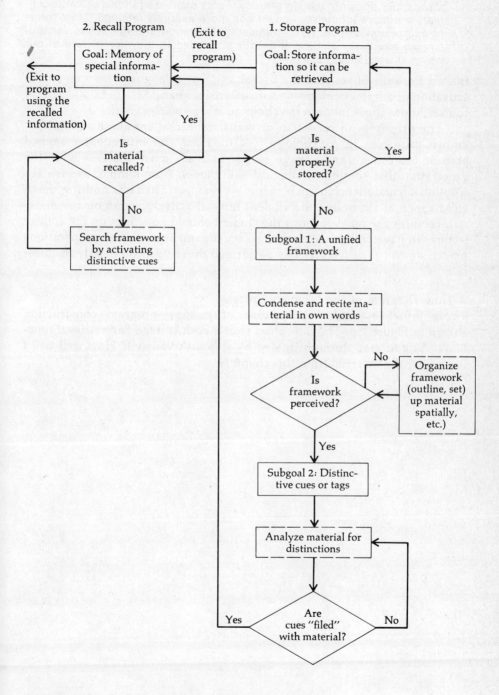

Figure 7.8   Flow diagrams of storage and retrieval processes.

stands, but does not usually employ. Facts expressed in the active vocabulary are more intimately known and more securely retained. Most forms of expression compel us to translate information into the active vocabulary we habitually employ. It is thus embodied in the very texture of our being. (Mace, 1932, pp. 41–42)

In Part IV, we will see that the use of one's own language may mean the activation of a framework even more extensive than Mace (who did not, of course, know about modern psycholinguistic principles) realized.

The principles of recitation or verbal rehearsal are among the oldest known principles in psychology, yet they are still infrequently applied both at pre-college and college levels. Instead, most students have the expectation that something magical will happen from simple, passive absorption of material. No such magic will happen; in fact, nothing much will happen at all, unless the student himself actively works on the material. Lectures are no exception; the student should not count on the college lecturer to have performed the necessary organizing and cueing operations *for the student.* The lecturer has performed those operations only for himself.

A Flow Diagram of the Memory Process
These principles underlie the type of memory-program construction shown in Figure 7.8. The flow chart shows both storage and retrieval functions. As you read through it, step by step, ask yourself: How well will I remember the material from this chapter?

Chapter 8 PROGRAMS FOR ORGANIZING INFORMATION

Technically, all the programs in the preceding chapter organize information. Remembering, scanning and holding, solving problems—all are programs for orderly thinking. But they are fairly specific programs. Two other programs are more general systems for coping with large amounts of information.

GENERATING AND CLASSIFYING

Have you ever seen two faces exactly alike? Have any two people ever experienced two events in exactly the same way? Did you know there are more than seven million discriminably different colors? One of the most remarkable aspects of the human mind is its capacity for making fine discriminations. Yet, as you know from our discussions of short- and long-term memory, the human mind is also sharply limited in its capacity to retain conscious awareness of different events. As far as short-term memory is concerned, we can hold only about seven things in mind simultaneously. Although no one knows how much may be stored in long-term memory, retrieving it usually requires careful advance programming. How do we explain the paradox of a machine that can make fine discriminations, but then cannot hold all of them in mind?

Recoding into Concepts

The solution, as you might guess, lies in the human mind's equally remarkable capacity for *recoding* information. We do not need to hold two million different shades of blue in mind when we have the word *blue* to represent them. We do not need to experience new events when we have experienced similar ones; instead, we can share a common code for them—a *concept*. My concept of an event will, to be sure, differ in certain ways from yours, but we have our code in common. We have *classified* our experiences in a similar way:

> This hodgepodge of objects is comprised in the category "chairs," that assortment of diverse numbers is all grouped together as "powers of 2," these structures are "houses" but those others are "garages." What is unique about categories of this kind is that once they are mastered they can be used without further learning. . . . If we have learned the class "house" as a concept, new exemplars can readily be recognized. The category becomes a tool for further use. The learning and utilization of categories represents one of the most elementary and general forms of cognition by which man adjusts to his environment. (Bruner, Goodnow, and Austin, 1956, pp. 1–2)

Criterial Attributes

How do we decide if something belongs in a particular category or not? How do we tell a house from a garage? A 2 that is used to signify "the powers of 2" from a 2 in "one potato, two potato"? We make judgments on the basis of what psychologists call *criterial attributes*—or critical cues, for short.

What are the critical cues for houses? To answer that question, we might start with a list like this:

> Place to live
> Some form of protection against weather
> Usually has furniture
> Usually has people, or some other form of living creature

A garage?

> A car's house
> Place where a car lives when it is not in use
> Some form of protection against weather
> No furniture (except things that are stored there)
> No people (maybe spiders, but they are not relevant)

A house, then, is defined by any abode that fits its list of critical cues; a garage is defined by any abode that fits another list of critical cues. Of course, we are not conscious of these cues at the time we perform a classification, but they are nevertheless operating. We can retrieve lists of critical cues relevant to any concept with very little effort in most cases, but unless we put our mind to the task of retrieval, many of the cues will operate quite unconsciously. Sometimes these lists are called *sets,* or *frames of reference.* We often become acutely conscious of list differences when we try to translate a concept from one language into another. Different languages have different words for what appears to be the same concept because the list of critical cues is different. (See Chapter 18 for further discussion of the effects this may have on thinking.)

Individual Differences in Criterial Lists
Cultural differences may be enormous, even within a single linguistic group. For example, a middle-class child's list of cues for the concept *postman* may be the following:

> A nice man
> Wears a blue suit
> Brings me letters from Granny
> Comes from a little brick house that has stamps to lick and a little window
> Likes our dog
> Smiles a lot at Christmas

A ghetto child may have quite a different concept of *postman:*

> A mean man
> Wears a blue suit
> Brings the welfare check, which makes Mom and Dad fight
> Comes from a giant house where everybody yells at you and you can't find anything
> Kicks our dog
> Doesn't come around on Christmas

Because the lists are different, the concepts are different, even though the same code word may be used.

Finding Our Way Through Lists of Lists
Note that in discussing the definition of concept, we generated a list of other concepts. Presumably, the concept came into existence in the first place because it was needed to recode a list of experiences. In that case, life generated the experiences, but in other situations—library research, for example—the list is generated by carrying out special procedures.
We go to the *card catalog*

and look for the alphabet letter *S*

under *S*, we look for *Shakespeare*

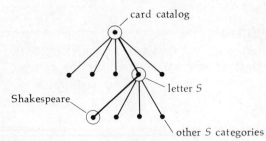

and under *Shakespeare*, we look for *women*

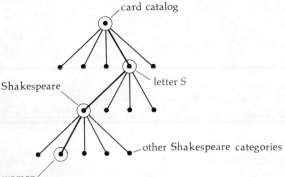

This is a *decision* or *a search tree,* a common human program for sorting one's way through a long list of possible alternatives. In this case, the list was generated by the library, and the problem was to find a path through it to a smaller list located at the last node.

From the list of *women* cards we compile a bibliography, which is, of course, a list. We may then subdivide the list by forming categories: laws affecting Shakespeare's women, customs affecting them, clothing and styles, furnishings used in women's quarters, and so on. Having generated the bibliographic list, we perform various kinds of classification operations on it. Finally, using our new categories, we might make up a theme ("Shakespeare's Women") that represents a new category and is defined by listing the various topics of which it is composed (laws, clothing, customs).

Through all these steps, we have been using the basic program of generating and classifying. The two operations are necessary to the whole program, because if we do not have a list of some sort, the act of classification is not necessary. The important psychological principles involve the elements on the list (the critical cues) and the ways in which such lists come into existence.

Generating a Criterial List

According to Bruner, Goodnow, and Austin (1956), there are four major ways in which a criterial list may be developed:

1. By Laws of Nature. If you eat a mushroom that looks like *that,* you will die; the list of critical cues is matter of fact, not opinion.

2. By Custom or Consensus. *This* is honest, *that* is dishonest; the list of critical cues is generated by group agreement.

3. By Consistency. *This* goes with this, but *that* doesn't; the list of critical cues for classifying subjects of sentences, for example, are the other words in the sentences—the verbs, adjectives, and so forth.

4. By Emotional Consistency. *This* is art, because I *like* it; the list of critical cues is personal and emotional, and may give rise to arguments with people who have other cues on their affective lists.

How would we analyze the following illustration?

Below are listed some foods. Group them in a way you believe to be proper.

Applesauce, baked apple, biscuits, chocolate-cream pudding, cinnamon toast, cranberry-jelly sauce, creamed dried chip-beef, cream of tomato soup, custard, egg nog, fruit-jello mold, hot chocolate, leafy salad, macaroni-supreme salad, melon, muffins, omelet, oven-fried chicken, popcorn balls, steak, vegetable-oil pastry, waffles.

(Student responses)
1. Fruits, breads, meats, dairy, and vegetables.
2. Fruits, desserts, breads, meats, eggs, soups, salads.
3. Foods I like and foods I dislike.
4. Desserts, beverages, breads, proteins, and vegetables.
5. Fattening foods and nonfattening foods.
6. Breakfast, lunch, dinner, and snack foods.
7. Solids and liquids.
8. Foods that require cooking and foods that may be eaten uncooked.
9. Foods cooked on top of the stove and foods cooked in the oven.
10. Foods served cold and foods served hot.
11. The basic four: breads and cereals, meat, dairy, fruits and vegetables.

Analyze each of the above groupings. Can you determine on what basis or principle the groups were selected? Look at the eleven groups themselves carefully. Do you see a way of grouping them? (Raths et al., 1967, p. 154)

The students in this case were all capable of abstracting critical cues from the food list and subdividing the cues into new small lists or categories (foods I like, desserts). But this ability is not necessarily found among younger children. Bruner and Olver (1963) performed an experiment that shows how this capacity develops. Because it should be helpful for teachers to have a picture of the way basic classification skills grow, we will give the Bruner and Olver experiment in some detail.

The Bruner-Olver Experiment

The experiment used two lists of words.

banana		bell
peach		horn
potato		radio
meat	or	newspaper
milk		book
water		painting
air		education

Each subject was asked about the words one at a time. First, "In what way are banana and peach alike?" After answering, the subject was presented with the third word and asked, "How is potato like banana and peach?" Then the subject proceeded through the list, explaining, with each new addition, how the whole set was equivalent. The types of relationships the subjects generated depended very much on their age. We quote first from the description given by Bruner and Olver (1963) of their earliest experiment:

> I would like to describe some of the different forms of grouping that have nothing to do with the content used in the grouping.

I. SUPERORDINATE CONCEPT FORMATION

The first form of grouping is called *superordination.* Items are grouped on the basis of one or more attributes common to them all. The basis is one of genuine conceptual grouping. The attributes can be functional properties, perceptible qualities, some common affective reaction, etc.

GENERAL SUPERORDINATE

Grade I.   "Both something that makes noise."
Grade IV. "You can get information from all of them."
Grade VI. "They all communicate ideas."

[The table above] shows the *general superordinate* grouping. . . . That is one type of superordinate concept formed for grouping the set.

[The table below] shows the *itemized superordinate* grouping, where the elements have a generalized property that ties them all together, but where there is explicitly stated the basis on which each term qualifies. . . .

ITEMIZED SUPERORDINATE

Grade I.   "Bell makes noise; horn makes noise too—bell says ding ding; horn says doo doo."

Grade IV. "They're all alike because you learning something from each one of them – telephone you learn by talking, bell you learn, horn you learn how to use them, book you learn news from, newspaper you learn from."

Grade VI. "You hear things from them – bell, horn, telephone, radio hear things by doing something to them, newspaper you have to read."

II. COMPLEX FORMATION

The examples of superordination given are to be contrasted with a range of responses that I refer to as *complex formations.* The characteristic of complex formation as a general strategy is that the subject uses selected attributes of the array without subordinating the entire array to any one attribute or set of attributes. We have been able to distinguish five clearly discernible complex-forming maneuvers, and these five can be used with a wide range of filler content.

The first one . . . is the *association complex.* . . . The subject uses a bond between two elements as the nucleus to form a group. . . .

ASSOCIATION COMPLEX

Grade I.   "Bell and horn are music things, when you dial telephone it's music a little."

Grade IV. "Bell, horn, telephone, radio make sound you can hear, when a person talks from a newspaper it is actually a sound too."

Grade VI. "Bell, horn, telephone, radio all make noises, if you fold back a newspaper then it will crackle and make a noise."

The *key ring* complex [below] consists of taking an element and ringing all of the others on it by choosing attributes that form relations between one item in the list and each of the others. . . .

KEY RING COMPLEX

Grade I.   "Painting, one thing is book's got some painting in it, newspaper's got some black paintings – printings, radio's got painting on it, telephone's got painting on it, horn well there's a little painting on it, bell is also the color of paints."

Grade IV. "In an education you learn how to do painting, you read books and gradually you learn how to read newspaper, how to use radio, how to use telephone, and horn and bell the same way."

Grade VI. "Germs are in banana, peach, potato, meat, milk, water and air."

. . . The *edge matching* complex . . . is also an interesting one. . . . It consists of forming associative links between neighboring items. . . . The associations pile up in linked pairs.

EDGE MATCHING COMPLEX

Grade I.   "Banana and peach look alike—yellow, potato and peach are round."

Grade IV. "Telephone is like a bell because telephone has bell inside it, it's like a horn because you put your mouth up to a telephone and you put your mouth up to a horn."

Grade VI. (None.)

The *collection* . . . consists essentially in finding complementary, contrasting, or otherwise related properties that all the things have, but not quite tying them together in terms of the attributes that are shared. . . .

COLLECTION COMPLEX

Grade I.   "Bell is black, horn is brown, telephone is sometimes blue, radio is red."

Grade IV. "Newspaper you can read, book you can read, telephone you get messages over, radio you get messages over, you can blow a horn and ring a bell."

Grade VI. (None.)

Last is the *multiple grouping* complex . . . where several subgroupings are formed. . . . Multiple groups are thus formed within the list. The child will draw the line at some point, forming two or more separate groups, but refusing to bridge the gap between them.

MULTIPLE GROUPING COMPLEX

Grade I.   "Telephone is like a radio, I know that, bell is like a horn because they both make sounds, but I don't know about a newspaper."

Grade II. "Newspaper, book, painting tell stories; bell, horn, telephone, radio make sounds."

Grade VI. "You eat banana, peach, meat; you drink milk."

III. THEMATIC GROUPING

The last form of grouping . . . yields very beautiful structures . . . that are about as uneconomical as anything the subject could do with the stimuli. The sequence coat, sweater, umbrella, house, infection yielded the following example of thematic grouping: "If you get an infection, you wouldn't go out of the house, but if you did, you'd take an umbrella if it were drizzling and wear a coat and sweater." The story, of course, can continue to incorporate almost any additional items that are provided on the list.

THEMATIC

(Bruner and Olver, 1963, pp. 128–133)

Bruner then goes on to point out that the complexity of the classification systems increases as one goes from the superordinate to the thematic. A superordinate rule is very simple; a thematic rule is very complex. How would you explain the reasoning that led to the "coat . . . infection" classification? How would you explain the reasoning that would lead you to connect one thematic classification with another? more complex themes? Bruner explains that in the child, the growth of intellect moves in the direction of less burdensome classification skills. The child intuitively seeks classification rules that reduce cognitive strain, rather than rules that increase it.

In support of their hypothesis, Bruner and Olver pointed to the frequency of grouping by either a superordinate or a complexive strategy. It can be seen in Table 8.1 that the more economical, cognitively simpler superordinate classifications increase as one goes from first to sixth grade, while the complexive, hard-to-remember classifications decrease. This would be in line with Kagan's finding (Chapter 14) that, in boys, analytic attitudes increase while relational attitudes decrease over approximately the same age range. As a matter of fact, if the Bruner and Olver data are separated by sex, their experimental effect also appears more strongly in boys, as Table 8.2 shows. For the boys, the increase in superordinate categorization from Grades I to VI is 43; for the girls, the comparable increase is 13. For the boys, the decrease in complexive categorizing over the same grade range is 31; for the girls, the decrease is only 8. These two studies, taken together, suggest that the ability to find more economical and efficient categorizations increases systematically with age, especially among males.

Table 8.1
Types of Classifications Made by Children in the Bruner and Olver (1963) Study

| | NUMBER OF GROUPINGS (CLASSIFICATIONS) | | |
	GRADE I	GRADE IV	GRADE VI
Superordinate	65	103	121
Complexive	57	30	18

SOURCE: After Bruner and Olver, 1963, p. 134.

Table 8.2
Increase in Superordinate Classifications from Grades I to VI in Boys and Girls

| | Boys | | | Girls | | |
	Grade I	Grade IV	Grade VI	Grade I	Grade IV	Grade VI
Superordinate	19	50	62	46	53	59
Complexive	38	16	7	19	14	11

SOURCE: After Bruner and Olver, 1963, p. 135.

Of course, this sort of development can be affected by cultural factors. Some of Bruner's students found, for example, that children from rural Mexico failed to develop superordinate classification systems the way American children (Boston suburbs variety) do (Maccoby and Modiano, 1966). We will take up these social influences on cognition in Part III, where we can explore in more detail the complicated issue of *how* social influences translate themselves into cognitive styles and systems. For the moment, the point is simply that development in classification abilities can take place and may be affected by a variety of factors, such as age, sex, and culture.

Piaget considers classification skills to be closely related to general mental development. For him, the stage of concrete operations is partly defined by a child's incomplete classification abilities. By the stage of formal operations, a normal child is able to classify much more extensively and fully. Theoretically, he is able to take all possible critical cues into consideration and make decisions about his classifications on a broad basis. The young child, as we have seen from Bruner's illustrations, selects cues on a more immediate and perceptual basis.

A Flow Diagram of the Concept-Formation Process

The chart in Figure 8.1 shows how we might conceptualize the adult classification process (note that the use of flow diagrams is also a way of classifying information). As you read through the flow diagram, you will note that the *classification* process, as diagrammed, is actually the same thing as a *concept-formation* process. When we discover a new concept, we have performed a classification—either by inventing a new class ("This, this, and this are all widgets") or by recognizing that a new item belongs in an old class ("You mean *that's* a widget too?"). A concept is, in Carroll's (1966) terms, "an internal representation of a certain class of experiences." A concept is, in fact, a category into which we can put ideas, rather like we might put food in one basket and flowers in another.

What Influences Concept Discovery?

The discovery of new concepts—the invention of new classes—is an important part of education. Bruner (in Bruner, Goodnow, and Austin, 1956), has suggested that the following factors influence the concept-formation process in significant ways:

1. The definition of the discovery task. What does the student think he is supposed to do? What is the objective?

2. The nature of the examples (concept) the student encounters. Do they occur randomly? In systematic order? Are there other irrelevant or distracting materials thrown in with them? Does each example contain a lot of information, or just a little?

3. The nature of informative feedback. Does the student receive any feedback as he goes along? Can his hypotheses (about the concept) be readily checked?

4. The consequences of trial hypotheses. If he makes a guess, will the student be penalized? Will he lead himself down a blind alley? Or will he benefit?

5. The nature of restrictions. Is there a time limit? Is the student allowed to keep a record of his progress, or must he try to remember it?

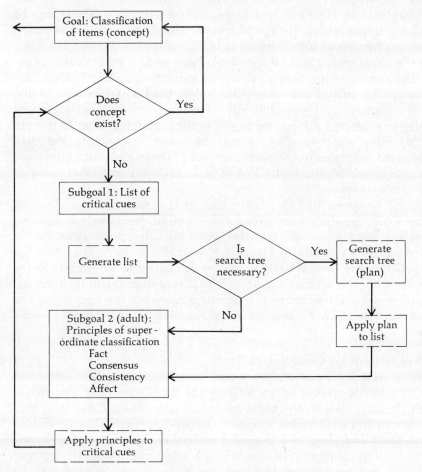

Figure 8.1   Flow diagram of a classification and concept-formation process.

In Chapter 15, there is a transcript of a class discussion recorded by Massialas and Zevin (1967). It is in that chapter because it is also an instance of classroom interaction and is studied there with reference to those social processes. Turn to it now and see how the class's progress toward concept attainment may be analyzed in terms of Bruner's conditions. Does the class understand the objective? What are the examples? What kind of feedback are they receiving?

Selection vs. Reception in Concept Attainment

The Massialas transcript illustrates what Bruner calls the *selection* method of concept attainment. All the examples (of the concept) are presented at once, and the student decides which ones to think about first, second, and so forth. An alternative to this is the *reception* method. The illustrations are presented one at a time by someone else (the teacher). There have been two experiments—one carried out by Huttenlocher (1962) and one carried out by Hunt (1965)—which suggest that reception methods may be easier for children under the age of formal operations and that selection methods may be easier for adults.

In the selection method, the students have to do a great deal of organizing and remembering that may impose an extra cognitive burden children are not capable of assuming. Otherwise, they might be able to discover the concept without difficulty. For children, teacher-presented examples of a concept ("What do moon, orange, and egg seem to have in common? How are they alike?") may be easier to conceptualize than child-selected examples of the same concept ("There are a lot of different things over there on the table. See if you can figure out what some of them have in common.").

Adults, however, find this latter kind of task easier. If an adult can organize a concept-attainment situation for himself, he is likely to discover the concept more efficiently than he would in a reception situation. In terms of our flow diagram in Figure 8.1, we can see why: The adult has developed his own concept-attainment style (personal program), and it may differ from the teacher's program. In a reception-learning situation, the adult may have two problems: figuring out what the concept is and figuring out the teacher's reasons for illustrating the concept in exactly that way.

Inductive Dialogues: Class Search Trees

Modern educators are turning more and more to the use of *inductive dialogues,* in which a class is led by a teacher to the discovery of a particular concept. In such classes, the usual procedure is for the teacher to open a discussion with a challenging question, record (on a chalkboard) various answers to it, and then lead the class in further discussion of what the answers have in common. For example, a teacher might begin: "Suppose I were to go into your houses and exchange things you have for things the other children in your block have. You would still end up with the same number of things, but they would come from different houses, not your own. Would you like that? How would you feel about it?" The teacher would record the class's answers and then say, "Well, you all seem to be pretty definite in your feelings. Johnny says he would fight me if I came into his room and took anything; Mary says no doll could ever take the place of her favorite doll." "What," the teacher would finally ask, "do you suppose this is telling us about all people? Would you say that all people feel a certain way about their possessions?" The teacher would lead the class to induce the concept of property rights and the importance of laws protecting them. (Is the classification principle here one of *fact, consensus, consistency,* or *affect?*)

Such a procedure is essentially a generate-and-classify program, using a search tree. In guiding a discussion of that sort, the teacher will begin with a question that generates a *limited* set of responses—too large a set, and the discussion will get out of hand. Figure 8.2 shows the sequence in search-tree form. After the teacher has selected one of the responses (or a set of several responses), she uses it as a "trigger" for the next question. "Several of you have said that you would fight me if I tried to take your things. Suppose I arranged to take them when you were out of the house. How would you feel when you came back and found them gone?"

By means of such advance planning, the teacher can control the inductive learning situation. But, you may say, is this not merely a way of getting the class to generate answers the teacher already has in mind? The fact that a teacher knows his students (or similar students) well enough to

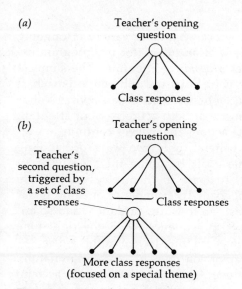

Figure 8.2 A search-tree sequence.

anticipate some of their responses and plan accordingly does not mean that the responses exist only in the mind of the teacher. It means, rather, that the teacher is helping the class select, from the list of responses it is generating, those that "go together" into concepts. This particular kind of selection may be just what a class—especially if it is responding enthusiastically—may have difficulty doing for itself. The teacher is, in effect, demonstrating to the class how to carry out a generate-and-classify program. Quite possibly, such training may eventually be internalized and become an inner skill for each student, rather than just a social (classroom) skill. (Evidence for that possibility is discussed in Chapter 19.)

ORDERING AND RELATING

Man operates serially. He can handle only a few items at a time and in a serial manner; he cannot process information in many different ways simultaneously. He cannot read and play the piano at the same time. He cannot play an entire piece of music simultaneously. If he tries to get on a bus and girl-watch at the same time, he may land in a manhole. He must learn to program his attention.

Such ordering-and-relating programs are severely limited by the actual capacity of the brain. Any type of academic ordering program—whether ordering the lines of a sonnet, comparing one list of items with another, following a recipe, writing a theme, setting up a biology experiment, or grading test papers—is critically affected by the fact that the mind must handle a few items of information at a time. The basic ability to order information is common to most enterprises.

Simon's Theory of Serial Behavior

According to Herbert Simon (1967), we can handle a variety of ongoing activities only through the development of an integrator or "program executive" that supervises and organizes *alternating* attention. The simplest way to sense this executive is to pat your head and rub your stomach at the same time. Something (the executive) coordinates the activity. Notice how you cannot be simultaneously aware of both actions—your attention switches back and forth—although the actions themselves continue.

Our mental executives have, in general, only two ways of handling complex information: one is to queue goals by lining them up in serial fashion; the other is to select goals that are in themselves all-purpose enough to achieve more than one subgoal. An example of queuing is our daily activities: we get up, eat breakfast, go to work, eat lunch, and so on. Each of these little programs runs off in sequence when the right time comes around. Many queuing operations are time-locked in this sense.

The second major system of program control is hierarchical in nature. The overall goal of making a chess move, for example, takes into account a number of subgoals: protecting some men, preparing for certain future moves, developing control of the center. The subgoals themselves must be monitored in serial fashion, but each one must be checked before the overall goal of making the move is achieved. Many of our daily and academic activities are also of that form.

A consideration of serializing activities leads to another interesting problem: How do we know when to move from one subgoal to another? Simon suggests the following four criteria:

1. A subroutine may terminate when its *subgoal has been achieved* in some clearcut manner.

2. A subroutine may terminate when its *subgoal has been achieved "well enough"*—in a manner that reaches some minimum requirement.

3. A subroutine may terminate when *a certain amount of time has been used up* in trying to achieve it.

4. A subroutine may terminate after *a certain set of processes has been used,* whether successful or not.

These criteria may be directly applied to educational situations. Do our students "give up too soon" or "hang on too long" with reference to subroutines in their problem-solving or memory programs? Perhaps this is because their executives have not clearly conceptualized appropriate termination rules.

Simon goes on to point out that provision must be made for an *interrupt system.* The executive must be able to switch to an emergency program in case of difficulty. To make sure this will be possible, our scanners must continue to operate while a special program is being carried out. These scanners are alert to environmental cues, and to internal cues as well—a sudden thought that we forgot to feed the dog, for example. As soon as an interrupt cue is noticed, a new program is activated and the old one is temporarily set aside.

An important aspect of human development involves the ability to learn how to cope with interrupting goals—how to fit them into ongoing programs without disruption:

> For example, an unskilled bicyclist who tries to carry on a conversation frequently interrupts his conversation to attend to the road. With greater skills, he time-shares between the conversation and the cycling without often interrupting the former. In effect, the earlier single-purpose program [carrying on a conversation] with frequent interruptions [falling off the bicycle] has been replaced with a program having the goal: "Carry on the conversation while keeping your balance." As learning proceeds, not only does the amount of interruption decrease but evidences of emotional behavior become less and less frequent and intense, as well. (Simon, 1967, p. 36)

School Applications

Interrupting goals forces us to develop recoding plans of this sort. If school days were under our control, we would probably do one thing at a time (grade all the test papers, and *then* interview the independent study students). But since interruptions are inevitable, we have been forced to develop executive routines (grade test papers and interview students at the same time) that integrate multiple subroutines (or become hysterical).

One might also ask: Is it better to have "study periods" that signal the onset and end of particular study routines or to let students develop their own executive systems for organizing study, library research, class attendance, and recreation? Does a school supervisor prefer to have the subroutines of teachers and students organized by simple serial programs? Is he unwilling to develop for himself a broader executive routine that could incorporate interrupt systems? Little research has been done on such questions.

Relationship Rules
Some research has, however, been done on the perception of relations—that is, on the recognition of the fact that one thing is related to something else on a particular basis. Although this is a form of classification, the relation between concepts is more often thought of as a rule or law. For example, we can have the following sorts of relations, each of which results from the application of some kind of rule:

Causal: Things that belong together because one makes the other happen.
Probabilistic: Things that may belong together under certain conditions.
Temporal: Things that belong together because one has a connection with the other in time.
Spatial: Things that belong together because one has a connection with the other in space.
Inclusive: Things that belong together because one includes the other.
Exclusive: Things that belong together because they specifically exclude other things.
Ordinal: Things that go together in a particular order.
Identity: Things that belong together because they are really the same thing.

Then there are *transitive* relations (I like Billy; Billy likes Johnny; therefore I like Johnny—see Chapter 15); *symmetrical* relations (I like my mother; my mother likes me); *asymmetrical* relations (my mother-in-law likes me); *inverse* relations (hot weather is lovely; cold weather is unlovely), and so forth.

Experiments on Rule Learning
In one experiment on relationship rules, Haygood and Bourne (1965) compared the effects of learning a concept with the effects of learning a rule for relating concepts. For example, subjects might be shown two colors (red and blue) and asked to discover the rule for relating them. The rule might be conditional: If blue appears, choose red. Or, subjects might be told that a conditional rule is operating (If something appears, choose something), but then have to learn what the concepts (red, blue) are.

Haygood and Bourne found generally that rule learning in this sense was easier than concept learning. They also found that some rules were harder to learn than others. A study by Neisser and Weene (1962) helps explain why. They devised an experimental situation that illustrated several types of relations (rules) which subjects had to discover. In informal terms, some of their rules were as follows:

LEVEL I

1. Presence	*A* must be present.	Vertebrate: Must have a backbone.
2. Absence	*A* must not be present.	Invertebrate: Must not have a backbone.

LEVEL II

3. Conjunction	Both *A* and *B* must be present.	Good quality: Both material and workmanship must be first-class.
4. Disjunction	Either *A* or *B* or both must be present.	Allergenic: a food that contains either tomatoes or strawberries.
5. Exclusion	*A* must be present; *B* must not be present.	Eligibility for driver's license: Must have passed test and not have committed felony.
6. Disjunctive absence	Either *A* or *B* or both must be absent.	Poor quality: Either material or workmanship or both is not first-class.
7. Conjunctive absence	*A* and *B* must both be absent.	Nonallergenic: A food that contains neither tomatoes nor strawberries.
8. Implication (negative form)	*A* may be absent, but if *A* is present, then *B* must also be present.	If he is ineligible for a driver's license, then he must have failed his test or committed a felony.

As you can see, many of the Level II rules include Level I rules; the list is hierarchical in nature. This is why (according to Neisser) some rules are harder to discover than others.

Harlow's Learning Sets

From an educator's standpoint, learning to induce (discover) a simple set of relations would prepare students for learning more complex ones. For example, on one level, students might discover a rule; on the next level, students might discover a second rule—that rules change. Some experiments by Harry Harlow (1949 a,b) illustrate this hierarchy.

Harlow analyzed the nature of the concept-learning process in primates (usually monkeys). In one series of experiments, he taught monkeys the rule: The raisin is always under the red block, no matter where the block is located on the tray. Then he taught a higher-level rule: The raisin is always under a block of a particular color. The monkeys learned this by discovering that the raisin stopped appearing under the red block and started appearing under the blue block. Then it would appear under a yellow block for a while, and so forth, until the monkey had learned the general rule: The raisin is always under a block of a particular color, but the colors may change; if you don't find it under the usual color, check another one. Harlow said that sort of higher-level rule should be called a *learning set.*

A human adult would develop such a set quickly. One glance under the red block that found the raisin missing would immediately lead him to check the blue block, where the raisin would be found. From then on, the adult would choose the blue block without error. The result would show that the human probably already knew the higher-level rule and simply applied it. But many experiments have shown that children, like monkeys, learn higher-level rules with difficulty. A great deal of research on this point has been carried out by the Kendlers (1967).

The Kendler Reversal Learning Studies

Using a variety of research techniques, the Kendlers have shown that young children (preoperational children, in Piaget's terms) may have special difficulty learning higher-level rules that use the same perceptual cues as lower-level rules. For example, they would have difficulty learning to switch colors in the block-and-raisin experiment. But suppose one of the blocks (the red one) was little, and the other block (the blue one) was big. And suppose the rule switch was: The raisin is always under the little block. To illustrate that rule, the experimenter would present only big and little red blocks. Young children find that kind of switch very easy.

The interesting problem is this: Older children find the first kind of switch easier than the second. The Kendlers believe this is because older children are already using a higher-level rule. They are not saying to themselves, "Red has the raisin," but rather, "Color of one sort has the raisin." Thus, it is easy for them to make the switch to blue because they are still saying, "Color of one sort has the raisin."

When the rule changes to size differences, however, older children have difficulty because they must change their higher-level rule to "Size of

one sort has the raisin." The preoperational children have no difficulty
with this, because to them the second situation (blocks of different sizes)
is not related to the first situation (blocks of different colors) anyway.
They were never using a higher-level rule. The Kendler experimental plan
is shown in Figure 8.3.

Practice or Variability?

These higher-level discoveries seem to be forced into existence by situa-
tional changes. But whenever the situation changes, it also leads to more
practice. So one might well wonder if the *variability* is producing the
learning of a new, higher-level rule or if the *amount of practice* is producing it.

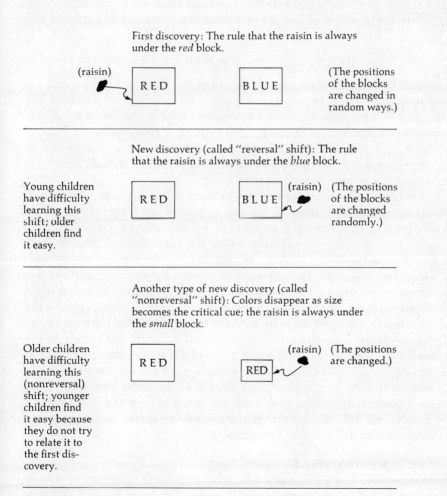

Figure 8.3 content:

First discovery: The rule that the raisin is always
under the *red* block.

(raisin) RED   BLUE   (The positions of the blocks are changed in random ways.)

New discovery (called "reversal" shift): The rule
that the raisin is always under the *blue* block.

Young children have difficulty learning this shift; older children find it easy.

RED   BLUE (raisin)   (The positions of the blocks are changed randomly.)

Another type of new discovery (called "nonreversal" shift): Colors disappear as size becomes the critical cue; the raisin is always under the *small* block.

Older children have difficulty learning this (nonreversal) shift; younger children find it easy because they do not try to relate it to the first discovery.

RED   RED (raisin)   (The positions are changed.)

Figure 8.3 The type of experimental plan developed by the Kendlers (1967) for studying rule learning in children.

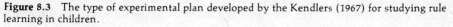

Exactly this question was asked by Duncan (1958). He gave different groups of college students either a little training on a lot of rule-discovery tasks or a lot of training on a few tasks. All subjects were then tested on new (transfer) tasks. *The subjects who had been trained on a variety of tasks showed the best transfer.* They had developed the most efficient ordering-and-relating programs. They expected to discover something new and went about doing this more skillfully than the group that had had the same amount of practice on a single task.

Discovering Pattern Rules

In the final experiment to be discussed here, Simon and Kotovsky (1963) pinpointed some additional factors that may affect the development of good ordering-and-relating programs. Consider the type of problem found in many tests of so-called inductive reasoning. The subject fills in the blanks:

$$c\,d\,c\,d\,c\,d\,\_\_\quad\text{or}\quad m\,n\,l\,n\,k\,n\,j\,n\,\_\_$$

The second pattern is, of course, harder than the first, but Simon and his colleague found that both sequences have certain things in common. In the first place, they both require a knowledge of the alphabet—a list of letters in a particular order. Second, they require a recognition of "sameness" and of "nextness." Third, both sequences require the ability to cycle—to recognize a small subpattern that is repeated. Finally, both require some kind of monitoring system.

If you practiced on a large number of such exercises, you would eventually develop a program for handling inductive problems. You would probably begin by searching the sequence for repeating cycles, then look for systematic "jumps" on your alphabetic list (does it jump four letters? two?), and so forth.

Simon and Kotovsky formalized their theory by putting it in the form of a computer program. The computer was not only able to solve some pattern problems, it also failed to solve some problems for essentially the same reasons that people do. The authors found that—for both computer and person—there were three major sources of difficulty with some of the problems: (1) They required keeping one's place on several lists simultaneously (abc, cdd, efe requires keeping one's place on the list ab__, cd__, ef__, and on the list __ __ c, __ __ d, __ __ e at the same time). (2) They contained false relationships that were not really part of the main pattern to be discovered. (3) The length of the period, or cycle, was too long to keep in immediate (short-term) memory.

Summary of Rule-learning Research

To summarize the foregoing materials: Man processes information serially and cannot handle very many ideas at once. Yet, in order to survive in today's demanding world, he must organize and monitor multiple ongoing activities. He cannot finish one before beginning another, much as he might like to. He copes with this problem by tying smaller programs together into larger ones. This is his basic ordering-and-relating system.

He has a number of tactics for achieving larger organizations. For one thing, he can organize his goals; he can go from one to another in time or let some goals include others. He has a set of rules for deciding when to move from one goal to another. He broadens his organizing skills by admitting interrupts and redesigning his organization to take them into account. Man also has sets of basic relations that tie one program to others (or tie one subprogram into a larger one). He recognizes causes, probabilities, time relations, spatial relations, and so forth. These are the rules for connecting one concept to another.

Research has indicated that some of these rules are harder to learn than others. (1) Some rules are more complex than others—they are actually composed of simpler rules. (2) Some rules are more abstract than others—they are "higher-order" or more general rules. (3) Because of their developmental limitations, children find some rules (more complex and abstract ones) harder to learn than others. (4) The higher-order rules can be learned best from practice in a variety of situations so they will not be thought of as limited to specific ones. (5) Higher-order rules must not overload capacities (short-term memory), deal with too many irrelevant cues, or require too long a wait before a cue appears in a sequence of events.

School Applications

Basic ordering-and-relating systems appear in many school activities. In writing a theme, for example, why does one paragraph follow another? The first paragraph may set up a list of ideas that the following paragraphs will illustrate. Or the first paragraph may describe a situation that causes something described in the second paragraph. Or the first paragraph may refer to something that occurs earlier in time than the events in the second paragraph. These kinds of relationships may tie together aspects of the overall program.

Ordering-and-relating programs frequently occur in scientific material. Here, as in English, the major pedagogical problem may be to help students develop their own ordering-and-relating schemes, rather than simply providing them with recipes to be memorized (see the discussion of different kinds of process teaching in Chapter 5).

Inquiry Training: Inducing Complex Relationships

Some examples of an *inquiry-training program* developed by Suchman (1961) follow:

> I shall first describe one of our films so that we can consider the answers to these fundamental questions with a specific example at hand. Typical of our demonstrations is one we call "The Bimetallic Strip." (The

children are never given the film titles.) The apparatus is made of two thin strips of metal, one steel, one brass, fused together into one strip that looks rather like a long narrow spatula. It is held, steel side down, in a Bunsen burner flame by means of a wooden handle. Almost immediately the strip begins to bend downward in an increasing arc which approaches 90°. Next, the strip is dipped into a large tank of cool water whereupon it straightens out quite abruptly. The strip is flipped over and once again held in the flame. This time it bends upward, forming the identical arc, as before, but inverted. Once again it straightens out when placed in the water. The problem question: "Why does the strip bend and then straighten out again?" . . .

THE NEED FOR INQUIRY TRAINING

In a series of preliminary studies of about 50 fifth-grade children whose intelligence was considerably higher than average we were able to determine some of the major difficulties that interfere with discovery through inquiry. To begin with, there was a marked lack of autonomy and productivity, stemming—we believe—from children's dependence upon authorities, teachers, parents and books to shape their concepts. When given new data, or a situation in which such data were available, the children rarely organized what they had, rarely gathered more data, rarely raised and tested hypotheses or drew inferences. Instead they blocked completely, began to offer unsupported conclusions, or produced a string of stereotyped probes that led nowhere. Accustomed to having concepts explained to them in discussions, pictures, films, and textbooks, the children were unwilling or unable to plan and initiate action with the purpose of discovering new concepts for themselves—even when all the data necessary for such discovery were available on demand. . . . To help children attain the objectives we had set, we designed the following schema. . . . This schema is not a recipe for discovery, nor is it even a rigidly prescribed sequence of operations. Each new problem calls for the collection of different kinds of information in different sequences. What the child must adopt, however, is a sequence of *goals* such that the attainment of the first provides the basic material for the pursuit of the second, and so forth. This is precisely what our subjects are taught. Each of the three stages of the schema has as its goal discovery at a higher order of abstraction and generality.

Stage I is called *episode analysis*. The goal . . . is the verification of the facts of the filmed demonstrations. . . . Temperature, volume, length, pressure and position are examples. . . . When episode analysis has been carried through, the result is a tabular organization or matrix of objects and their conditions at critical points during the demonstration. . . . As this matrix takes shape, it is recorded on the blackboard to serve as a reference . . . and reduce cognitive strain. (Suchman, 1961, pp. 155–159)

The matrix is shown in Table 8.3; you can see that it makes possible the induction of relationships of various kinds—although of course the students would be guided in their use of the matrix.

Inquiry Training in Social Science
Social scientists have also evolved systems for analyzing and evaluating data, and again the pedagogical problem is how to guide students to the

Table 8.3
Episode Analysis Matrix for "The Bimetallic Strip" Inquiry Training Film

| | CONDITIONS/EVENTS | | | | | | | | |
| | AT START OF DEMONSTRATION | | | AFTER BLADE IS HELD IN FLAME | | | AFTER BLADE IS PLACED IN WATER | | |
OBJECTS/ SYSTEMS	TEMPER- ATURE	SIZE	SHAPE	TEMPER- ATURE	SIZE	SHAPE	TEMPER- ATURE	SIZE	SHAPE
Bimetallic strip	Room temp.	Normal	Straight	>Room temp.	Normal	Curved	Room temp.	Normal	Straight
Metal A	Room temp.	Normal	Straight	>Room temp.	Normal	Curved	Room temp.	Normal	Straight
Metal B	Room temp. (A=B)	Normal	Straight	>Room temp. (A>B)	Normal	Curved	Room temp. (A=B)	Normal	Straight
Tank of water	Water temp. = Room temp.			Water temp. = Room temp.			Water temp. = Room temp.		
Bunsen burner	Produces heat			Produces heat			Produces heat		

SOURCE: Suchman, 1961, p. 160.

development of their own ordering-and-relating programs, rather than to the application of a rote recipe. The social studies curriculum developed by Edwin Fenton and his colleagues (now called the *Holt Social Studies Curriculum,* and published by Holt, Rinehart & Winston) has adopted the inquiry-training guide illustrated in Figure 8.4.

Throughout their high school courses, social studies students practice the skills outlined in Figure 8.4 on a variety of materials ranging from political science to economics to history. Their practice is guided by special questions that they use to guide their own hypothesis formation (Figure 8.5).

A Flow Diagram of Ordering and Relating

In general, both these programs have flow-chart characteristics similar to the ones shown in Figure 8.6, which, in turn, is related to the concept-attainment program shown in Figure 8.1. These may be thought of as "guided discovery" systems that combine the generating of ideas with systems for holding them in mind and putting them together. In Figure 8.1, a search tree helps with the latter two processes. In Figure 8.6, a diagram of relationships may help in a similar way. Suchman's matrix (Table 8.3) is one such diagram. The list of Primary Analytical Questions (Figure 8.5) is also a kind of diagram—cultures that answer those questions in one way can be related to cultures that answer them in another. Thus it may be seen that regardless of the type of ordering-and-relating involved and regardless of the type of material used, the basic cognitive program may be similar.

INQUIRY SKILLS

Our third major set of objectives stresses the ability to use a mode of inquiry for the social studies. In a world where the total knowledge of mankind doubles each decade, a student who has not mastered inquiry skills may well find himself on the human scrap heap ten years after he leaves school. Cramming facts and generalizations from a textbook into his head cannot meet the challenge of the knowledge explosion. Unless a student can inquire independently of the questions which teachers use to cue him, he is not equipped to be an independent thinker and a responsible citizen of a democracy.

We have identified six major steps in a process of inquiry for the social studies. They are as follows:

A Mode of Inquiry for the Social Studies

1. Recognizing a problem from data

2. Formulating hypotheses
   Asking analytical questions
   Stating hypotheses
   Remaining aware of the tentative nature of hypotheses

3. Recognizing the logical implications of hypotheses

4. Gathering data
   Deciding what data will be needed
   Selecting or rejecting sources on the basis of their relevance to hypotheses

5. Analyzing, evaluating, and interpreting data
   Selecting relevant data from the sources
   Evaluating the sources
      Determining the frame of reference of the author of a source
      Determining the accuracy of statements of fact
   Interpreting the data

6. Evaluating the hypothesis in light of the data
   Modifying the hypothesis, if necessary
      Rejecting a logical implication unsupported by data
      Restating the hypothesis
   Stating a generalization

Figure 8.4 Inquiry training in social studies. (Fenton, 1967, p. 6)

Primary Analytical Questions

A. Stressed first in *Comparative Political Systems*

1. *Leadership*—That position in society having the authority to determine how the power of government will be used.

   a. Who are the leaders? What are their personal characteristics? Their social backgrounds?

   b. How does society recruit its leaders? How does it persuade people to accept leadership positions? What formal and informal rules does the society establish for granting leadership?

   c. What must a person do to obtain and keep a leadership position? To whom does he appeal? How does he appeal to these people? How does he maintain support?

2. *Decision-Making*—The process by which a political system determines for what purposes governmental power will be used and how power will be exercised.

   a. What are the formal rules for making decisions? The informal rules?

   b. In what leaders and institutions does decision-making power reside?

   c. What factors influence decision-making? How does ideology influence it? The personal attributes of leaders? Institutions? The desires of citizens?

   d. How does information flow to the decision-makers? What influence does it have?

   e. How are decisions carried into effect? What sanctions are used to enforce decisions?

3. *Institutions*—Organizations and well-established practices which distribute authority to make decisions about how power shall be used.

   a. What are the institutions of a society? What functions does each institution have?

   b. What official authority has been given to an institution? What authority has an institution accumulated informally?

   c. How do institutions influence decisions?

4. *Citizenship*—The rights of individuals to influence how societal power will be used, their obligations to submit to governmental power, and the processes by which they accomplish these two functions.

   a. How does a citizen influence how public power is used? Does he have a role in the decision-making process? How does he obtain access to decision-makers? What influence does he have over them?

   b. How does a citizen get information about government?

   c. How does government affect the life of the citizen? How does it restrict his freedom? How does it enlarge his freedom?

Figure 8.5 Special questions for inquiry training. (Fenton, 1967, p. 10)

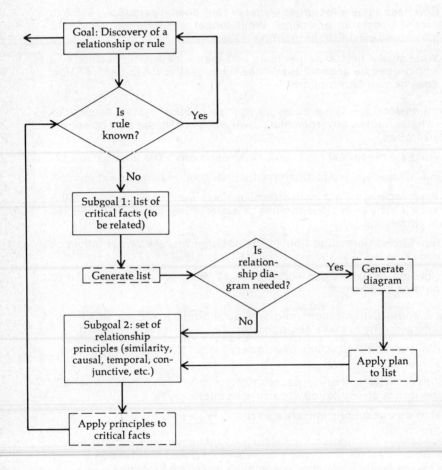

Figure 8.6   Flow diagram of a relationship or rule-discovery process.

Chapter 9 EDUCATIONAL IMPLICATIONS

BLOOM'S COGNITIVE TAXONOMY

Once you develop a learning set (to use Harlow's term) for types of basic human programs, it is possible to learn to recognize them, frequently "hidden" behind misleading labels and distracting details, in school materials. Educators refer to lessons as "classification" or "problem solving," for example, as if these were different processes. When the basic cognitive programs are analyzed, they may turn out to be exactly the same. Educators frequently fail to recognize scanning-and-holding programs in their own materials.

Bloom's Taxonomy

The following examples, taken from the *Taxonomy of Educational Objectives, Cognitive Domain* (Bloom, 1956), are presented (like the case material in Chapter 14) to give you some practice in discovering the programs hidden in school materials. You must learn how to diagnose thinking requirements and prepare training lessons without regard for the labels that educators and curriculum developers use in describing their objectives.

Bloom's objectives are to develop ways of testing for the existence of certain types of cognitive skills, and he is ingenious in accomplishing them. His emphasis is on behavior in one of the senses described in Chapter 5: He is a cognitive behaviorist, not an S-R or Skinnerian behaviorist. His emphasis is also on hierarchical development along the lines of Gagné's work (Figure 5.2). Here is Bloom's taxonomy:

1.00 Knowledge
    1.10 Knowledge of specifics
        1.11 Knowledge of terminology
        1.12 Knowledge of specific facts
    1.20 Knowledge of ways and means of dealing with specifics
        1.21 Knowledge of conventions
        1.22 Knowledge of trends and sequences
        1.23 Knowledge of classifications and categories
        1.24 Knowledge of criteria
        1.25 Knowledge of methodology
    1.30 Knowledge of the universals and abstractions in a field
        1.31 Knowledge of principles and generalizations
        1.32 Knowledge of theories and structures
2.00 Comprehension
    2.10 Translation
    2.20 Interpretation
    2.30 Extrapolation
3.00 Application
4.00 Analysis
    4.10 Analysis of elements
    4.20 Analysis of relationships
    4.30 Analysis of organization principles
5.00 Synthesis
    5.10 Production of a unique communication
    5.20 Production of a plan or proposed set of operations
    5.30 Derivation of a set of abstract relations
6.00 Evaluation
    6.10 Judgments in terms of internal evidence
    6.20 Judgments in terms of external criteria

Before you decide you will never understand these distinctions, refer back to the discussion of process vs. content in Chapter 5. For the most part, Bloom is making inferences about mental skills on the basis of a *product*—a single test answer. He is not necessarily testing for steps in the reasoning *process.* Nevertheless, many of the steps involved in the reasoning that leads to the product are similar to those of the basic human programs we have discussed. For example, the following test item illustrates what Bloom calls "analysis of relationships":

    The college committee in charge of social regulations was holding an open meeting on a proposal that the rule on chaperoning coeducational outings (wiener roasts, overnight hikes, campfires, etc.) should be more strictly applied. A student in the audience got the floor and made this speech:
    (A) This whole discussion is ridiculous,
    (B) for we shouldn't have chaperones at all!
    (C) You see, any chaperone you get will either arrange not to see what

happens or he will be so badly outnumbered he can't keep track of what is going on.

(D) But chaperones are supposed to guarantee that what goes on is respectable.

(E) So the chaperonage system is utterly ineffective and full of hypocrisy.

(F) Besides, collegians will never develop maturity unless they are given responsibilities to exercise and are really trusted with these responsibilities.

[Test questions]

The student offered (A) as a reason for

1. B
2. C
3. D
4. E
5. None of these

The student offered (B) as a reason for

1. A
2. C
3. D
4. E
5. None of these

(Bloom, ed., 1956, p. 155)

Try to answer the questions and analyze your reasoning process at the same time. Note what you are doing, and see how it compares to the flow diagram in Figure 8.6.

Your goal is the discovery of a relationship between two statements.

Do you know what it is? No, not immediately.

Your first subgoal, then, is the list of critical facts—B, C, D, E, and, of course, A.

Do you need a diagram to help you recognize the relationship of A to B, C, D, and E? No, not as long as you can continue to stare at the test question. (If you had to remember it without reading it again, some kind of diagram or notational system would be needed.)

Your second subgoal is to hold in mind the type of relationship that will exist between those facts. It is a type of logical relationship; in common sense terms, we can call it a "because" relationship. It takes this form: B is true because A is true, or C is true because A is true, and so forth. There is also the possibility that neither B, C, D, or E will follow from A after all, since the last multiple-choice item is "None of these."

You then apply the "because" relationship test to each of the facts: "We shouldn't have any chaperones at all, *because* this whole discussion is ridiculous. . . . So the chaperonage system is utterly ineffective and full of hypocrisy, *because* this whole discussion is ridiculous."

As it turns out, none of the "because" relationships make sense. How about the second test question? Analyze it by means of the same flow diagram.

Most of Bloom's "knowledge" questions would seem to be recall questions, but actually they do not test a student's storage programs. For example:

> Jean Valjean was first sentenced to the galleys for stealing
> 1. The bishop's candlesticks
> 2. A loaf of bread
> 3. A few sticks of wood
> 4. A widow's cow
> 5. The cloth from off the altar

> The Monroe Doctrine was announced about ten years after the
> 1. Revolutionary War
> 2. War of 1812
> 3. Civil War
> 4. Spanish-American War

(Bloom, ed., 1956, p. 79)

As you try to recall answers, you will notice that you are searching for the distinctive cues or tags stored with the information. You may think to yourself, "Now I remember seeing a picture of Monroe signing that document. Was he wearing a ruffled shirt? or a three-cornered hat?" A good teacher should have taught Monroe Doctrine facts in such a rich informational framework that better cues than mine will be available.

Some of Bloom's "comprehension" questions fit into our generate-and-classify programs. For example:

> When a beggar justifies his begging by the claim that the world owes him a living, he is
> A. Behaving like a psychotic person
> B. Showing a paranoid symptom
> C. Having an hallucination
> D. Making a typical infantile reaction
> E. Rationalizing

(Bloom, ed., 1956, p. 100)

Assuming you know a little abnormal psychology, you will probably tackle that question by generating a list of critical cues (symptoms) for each of the classes: psychosis, paranoia, hallucination, infantile reaction, and rationalization. You will not need a search tree because the lists are short, but you may make a few notes on the margin of your test paper. You will recognize that (at least as far as psychiatrists are concerned) a consensus principle is involved. A particular set of symptoms is said to define a particular type of illness (or, in technical language, *nosological category*) by common agreement among medical experts. Then you ask your first test question again (first in the diagram in Figure 8.1): Does a concept (nosological category) relevant to the beggar's behavior exist? The answer is yes, the category of rationalization. The beggar is, in fact, rationalizing his behavior.

Problem-solving programs are easy to recognize, and Bloom has several in his "Application" category. What is the cognitive program involved in the following example, as compared to the flow chart in Figure 7.6?

> Suppose an elevator is descending with a constant acceleration of gravity "g." If a passenger attempts to throw a rubber ball upward, what will be the motion of the ball with respect to the elevator? The ball will
> 1. Remain fixed at the point the passenger releases it
> 2. Rise to the top of the elevator and remain there
> 3. Not rise at all, but will fall to the floor
> 4. Rise, bounce off the ceiling, then move toward the floor at a constant speed
> 5. Rise, bounce off the ceiling, then move toward the floor at an increasing speed
>
> (Bloom, ed., 1956, p. 136)

Note how your subgoals involve little programs such as: Recall such-and-such principle of physics. . . . Generate and classify such-and-such. . . . Relate such-and-such. It is in this sense that problem-solving programs involve many subprograms. Note also how useful Polya's heuristic "recipes" are (Chapter 7) and how important scanning-and-holding programs are in all the Bloom examples. In an experiment with Broder (Bloom and Broder, 1950), Bloom himself found that a major difficulty among students who do not perform well on examination questions of the sort above is that they rush too quickly from the question to the answer. They fail to analyze the question well enough for a proper program to be set up.

"DISCOVERY LEARNING"

These examples of typical questions help us recognize why process instruction (in the sense of method D, Figure 5.1) may be superior to content instruction (methods E and F) in helping students prepare for examinations—that is, in helping them master information. The cognitive processes involved in answering an examination question should be practiced during the course, not just on the examination. This is not difficult to arrange if we first analyze the examination questions, as we have been doing in these pages.

Although *discovery learning* as a concept has many meanings, it is usually thought to be related to process teaching. Process and discovery are often erroneously assumed to be the same. We certainly cannot be sure that students will discover good reasoning processes (good heuristics) if they are left to their own devices. On the other hand, they certainly will not discover them if they never practice any reasoning at all—if they simply learn by rote whatever material (content or algorithms) the instructor presents to them. These three types of pedagogy—*rote learning* (rule-and-example learning), *laissez-faire discovery,* and *guided discovery*—have been compared in many educational experiments. One of the best was done by Gagné and Brown (1961).

Gagné's Experiments on Discovery Learning

The subjects were boys in grades 9 and 10. They all worked individually, and the materials were presented by means of an informal teaching machine—sets of file cards, in a prearranged sequence, clipped to a board.

The task was to learn formulas for finding the sum of such series as 1, 2, 4, 8, 16, __ and 1, 3, 7, 15, 31, __. A formula or rule for finding the sum of the first series, for example was to predict the next number, 32, and subtract 1 from it. Different series had different formulas.

In the rule-and-example (R&E) program, the correct formula was stated, and the subject then proceeded through a series of examples. In the discovery (D) program, the subject was asked, "What is the rule? . . . Try to do this by yourself." Hints were available if he needed them. In the guided discovery (GD) program, the subjects first rehearsed the subconcepts necessary to the discovery of the rule. For example, the subject might be asked (on the file card): "In this series, the sum is 31. What is the next term that would go into the blank? (32) If you have 32, you can get 31 by _____." A strategy for analyzing the patterns was actually taught.

Gagné and Brown asked two main questions: How fast did the subjects learn formulas by these three methods? And how well were they then able to discover the formulas for new number series they had never seen before? This last question refers, of course, to transfer skills—can the subjects transfer their method for learning formulas (whatever that method might be) to new problems?

Table 9.1
Data from Experiment on Discovery Learning

	TIME TO LEARN FORMULAS[*]	
LEARNING CONDITION	ORIGINAL LEARNING	TRANSFER TIME
Rule-and-example	28.8	27.4
Guided discovery	33.2	16.7
Discovery	18.5	19.8

SOURCE: Based on data in Gagné and Brown, 1961.
[*]In minutes. Long time = slow learning.

The experiment results for the first question are shown in Table 9.1. According to the table, the discovery method resulted in the fastest learning. Did it also produce the fastest transfer? Look at the Transfer column of Table 9.1. It is clear that for transfer, the guided discovery method resulted in the fastest new learning. But note that the total learning time (original learning plus transfer learning) was shortest for the discovery (with hints) condition.

The authors believed that the major factor in the success of the guided discovery program was that the subjects rehearsed "pieces" of the solution process. Gagné and Smith (1962) demonstrated a similar phenomenon, using a different kind of problem.

Subjects in this second experiment were also boys in grades 9 and 10, but this time they were working on a three-circle problem very similar to the "Tower of Hanoi" game. Subjects must transfer circles or disks from one area to another, always keeping a little disk on a large one.

The rule for solving the problem (which the subjects were to discover) was this: If the number of disks is odd, move first to the circle you want to end on. If the number is even, move first away from this circle. Always move disks with odd numbers in a clockwise direction, and disks with even numbers in a counterclockwise direction. If the rule was not discovered, the problem could not be solved.

The two questions the researchers asked of this experiment were slightly different from those in the Gagné and Brown study. If the subjects verbalize what they are trying to do, will that help them solve the problem (discover the principle) more efficiently? And if we tell the subjects that there *is* a principle and that they are to look for it, will that help them find it? There were actually four groups of subjects: Group 1 verbalized their moves—tried to explain the reasons behind them. In addition, this group was instructed to look for the rule. Group 2 only verbalized; nothing was said to them about looking for a rule. Group 3 only looked for the rule; they did not verbalize. And Group 4 did nothing at all except try to solve the problem. After a training period, all groups were tested on their ability to solve the problem and on their ability to say what the rule was. The outcomes are shown in Table 9.2.

Table 9.2
Data from Experiment on Verbalization and Problem Solving

GROUP	TIME TO SOLUTION, FINAL TEST	COMPREHENSION OF RULE		
		INADEQUATE	PARTIAL	COMPLETE
Verbalized and looked for rule	4.2*	0	3	4
Verbalized only	3.8	0	5	2
Looked for rule only	10.1	1	6	0
Nothing—solved problem only	10.0	6	1	0

SOURCE: Based on data in Gagné and Smith, 1962.
*Data in minutes.

This experiment tells us that the verbal rehearsal of the solution process may help speed it along and that the instruction to look for a rule may help the subjects discover it. Looking for the rule may also mean that subjects are rehearsing parts of the rule as they discover them. In fact, the subjects were practicing a scanning-and-holding program (Figure 7.2).

We recognize in both these experiments examples of ways to teach students to develop good heuristic techniques similar to the basic academic programs shown in Figures 7.2 through 8.6. Such techniques ensure that students in so-called discovery learning situations will benefit from them.

Bruner's Position on Discovery Learning

Much controversy over the benefit question has resulted from a misunderstanding of Bruner's (1960) position. Bruner's point has always been that heuristic techniques must be taught, and one of his more recent statements clarifies this:

> You cannot consider education without taking into account how a culture gets passed on. It seems to me highly unlikely that given the centrality of a culture in man's adaptation to his environment . . . that, biologically speaking, one would expect each organism to rediscover the totality of its culture—this would seem most unlikely. Moreover, it seems equally unlikely, given the nature of man's dependency as a creature, that this long period of dependency characteristic of our species was designed entirely for the most inefficient technique possible for regaining what has been gathered over a long period of time, i.e., discovery.
>
> Assume, for example, that man continues to adjust when he learns a language and certain ways of using tools. At that particular point, evolution becomes Lamarckian in the sense of involving the passing on of acquired characteristics, not through the genes, but through the medium of culture. On the other hand, it becomes reversible in that one can lose parts of culture in the way that Easter Islanders or the Incas of Peru seem to have lost some of their techniques. Culture, thus, is not discovered; it is passed on or forgotten. All this suggests to me that we had better be cautious in talking about the method of discovery, or discovery as the principal vehicle of education. Simply from a biological point of view, it does not seem to be the case at all. We ought to be extremely careful, therefore, to think about the range of possible techniques used for guaranteeing that we produce competent adults within a society that the educational process supports. Thus, in order to train these adults, education must program their development of skills, and provide them with models. . . . All of these things must be taken into account, rather than just taking it for granted that discovery is a principal way in which the individual finds out about his environment. (Bruner, 1966, pp. 101–102)

WHAT EXACTLY IS IQ?

Controversies surrounding the discovery learning issue have been equaled, in recent years, by controversies surrounding the IQ issue. Particularly because of the current emphasis upon education for the disadvantaged, equal job opportunities, equal college opportunities, and so forth, this question repeatedly arises: Are there some people who cannot benefit from these increased opportunities, regardless of public interest and public funds? In a word, are some people just too dumb to cope with twentieth-century civilization?

The Difficult Moral Issue

The answer to that question is neither simple nor easy. There are, among other things, large amounts of tax money at stake—money that might be funneled into other endeavors likely to produce cures for equally important areas of human suffering. Should we deny the gifted child who is dying of leukemia the tax dollars that would support research in his disease in order to provide an expensive education for a disadvantaged youngster who may not have the basic intellectual capacity to get very much out of it?

Such questions—like those of population control, censorship, abortion, mercy killings, and capital punishment—require us to confront questions of human values, questions that citizens of a democracy find most uncomfortable. It is all very well to say that everyone should have an equal right to life-supporting materials (such as food and education). But suppose there is not enough to go around? Who gets it? How shall we, the people who elect our government, decide?

The Nature of Binet's IQ Test

Historically, IQ tests were invented in an effort to help answer that question. In the early 1900s, Alfred Binet invented a type of intelligence test (still in use today) in order to weed out retarded children who could not benefit from traditional French education. Since there was also a traditional French system for the education of retarded children, such a weeding process would be to their benefit as well. Once discovered, these children could be placed in special educational environments better geared to their needs and skill requirements.

Binet's method for developing an intelligence test was a simple one, and it is still used in developing mental and personality tests of all sorts. He put together a lot of questions that seemed to be reasonable samples of a child's ability. He said the questions that 50 percent of a 6-year-old group, for example, could answer revealed "average 6-year-old abilities." Questions that 50 percent of a 7-year-old group could answer revealed "average 7-year-old abilities," and so forth. This is what we call an *empirically based* test. There was no particular theory behind it; Binet did not decide in advance that these are the sorts of questions a 6-year-old should be able to answer because of specific theoretical reasons. That was one reason why Piaget, who began his study of children under Binet's direction, parted company with him. Piaget believed that such levels could be theoretically predicted and set himself the task of discovering the theory; Binet was content to pay attention to what children could actually do, and never mind why. Piaget was fascinated by the theoretical clues in the mistakes children made when they tried to answer Binet's questions; Binet was interested only in whether or not the answers were correct.

A test was constructed by Binet's method with average ability levels from approximately 2 years to adulthood. The psychologist who administers such a test to a child scores the child as "passing the third, fourth, or fifth year levels," for example. The test continues until the child fails a series of questions, thereby revealing that his upper limit has been reached.

Computing the Intelligence Quotient

The child's upper limit defines his *mental age.* At the chronological age of 7, for example, a child may have a mental age of 7, or 3, or 12. This mental age is then divided by his chronological age to give a measure of the relationship of mental age to chronological age. That is why it is called an *intelligence quotient,* or IQ for short. The resulting number is then multiplied by 100 as a matter of convenience (it gets rid of the decimal).

You can see that the 7-year-old with a mental age of 7 will have an IQ of 100, which is normal for his age: mental age = 7, chronological age = 7. Therefore:

$$7 \div 7 = 1.00 \times 100 = 100$$

The 7-year-old with a mental age of 3 will have an IQ of

$$3 \div 7 = .43 \times 100 = 43 \text{ (retarded)}$$

The 7-year-old with a mental age of 12 will have an IQ of

$$12 \div 7 = 1.71 \times 100 = 171 \text{ (gifted)}$$

A Population of IQ Scores

Since the questions for average 7-year-olds were selected by asking 7-year-olds (not the same ones, of course) those same questions in the first place, it is easy to understand why most 7-year-olds can answer them. Most people have average IQs of around 100, because they can answer the same questions that most of the other people their age can answer. In Figure 9.1, if we let *P* stand for Person, we find that they pile up around the average IQ level.

This is the so-called normal statistical distribution. The line drawn around it shows why a normal distribution is referred to as "bell-shaped." You can see that it is symmetrical; there are roughly as many people above the average as below it. We can refer to the distance from the average (middle point) as a *deviation.* There is a statistical method for determining what the average deviation is, known as the *standard deviation.*

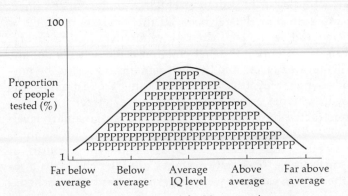

Figure 9.1   A normal distribution of the IQ scores of persons.

Most people will be found within two average or standard deviations (on each side) from the mean. People who are far from the mean on either side are extremely rare.

Culture and Intelligence

Now what about intelligence? Are you willing to say that people who can answer most of the questions that other people their age can answer are *normally intelligent?* That seems to be a reasonable way of measuring something, but is it measuring intelligence? Or is it measuring average amounts of information, known by average people, who have had an average amount of practice figuring out answers to the kinds of questions that people their own age can usually answer?

Psychologists who are concerned about disadvantaged populations worry about the latter possibility. What chance does a slum-reared, half-starved 7-year-old have of knowing the average amount of information known by average 7-year-olds who have had average amounts of practice figuring out answers to the kinds of questions that 7-year-olds can usually answer? A slum child may have spent most of his seven years just learning how to stay alive in very un-average ways. In some cases, the fact that such a child survives at all is striking testimony to his intelligence.

Nevertheless, *that* kind of intelligence is unfortunately not the kind he will need in a traditional school. The plain fact of the matter is that high scores on Binet-type intelligence tests predict high grades in school. The tests do exactly what Binet intended them to do—they tell us who is going to benefit from a traditional type of schooling and who is not. Why, then, do we not call them "traditional-school-prediction tests" instead of intelligence tests? And why do we not eliminate traditional schooling for individuals who are not expected to succeed in such a setting?

Perhaps we should. But there are other factors to consider. Both Binet-type IQ and schooling are correlated with occupation, with income, with achievement of various kinds, with success as a parent, and so forth. People who can do the kinds of reasoning that average people can do—only better—and who also (for that reason, perhaps) have a successful school career are likely to live richer, fuller, more interesting lives than below-average people.

Should we change our society? In the first place, it is not clear that we can. As we will see in Part III, people may come biologically equipped with motivations to develop competence, to achieve, to discover interesting things to do, to satisfy curiosity, and so forth. Even if we were able to impose on ourselves a world in which everyone was automatically equipped with all good things so that personal achievement or problem-solving ability no longer counted for anything, it is not clear that we would be happy. People need to strive, to exercise their abilities, to develop them, to feel a sense of satisfaction in their growth. We probably

beat out the dinosaurs because that achievement urge accidentally occurred in our forebears' genes.

Along with those achievement-urge genes, there are also genes for
intelligence (see Chapter 4). These genes do not exclusively control intelligence, but they interact with environmental factors (such as nutrition,
early experiences, and parental attention) to set limits. For all these reasons and many more, individual differences in intellectual ability are going
to continue to exist. Given any kind of educational system, any kind of
occupational system, any kind of human endeavor, some people are going
to be better at it than others.

General vs. Special Mental Abilities

According to Binet and others who have developed Binet-type IQ tests,
there is a *general* ability level (*g* for short) that will appear in an individual
no matter what he is doing. That general ability is what they believe IQ
tests of the Binet type actually measure. According to others who have
been pioneers in the mental testing movement—J. P. Guilford, for
example—people have clusters of special abilities rather than one general
ability. Guilford (1959) looks for spatial abilities, verbal abilities, symbolic
abilities, and so forth. He believes there are many kinds of intelligence,
and that each kind needs to be measured by special tests.

He may be right, but the *g* theorists simply reply: "Look, if you give
an individual twenty different tests and he obtains a score on each of
them, the *co-variation* in his test scores describes the amount of *g* that individual has." The amount of *g* for some individuals will be more than for
others, the *g* theorists explain, because those individuals have higher
(than average) scores on most or all of the tests. The common "upness"
(variation) is *g*. "Nevertheless," the special ability theorists argue, "it can
be useful to look at a *profile* of special abilities rather than at a single
Binet-type test score." These theorists invented IQ tests like the Wechsler
Intelligence Scale for Children (WISC) and the Illinois Test of Psycholinguistic Abilities (ITPA) in order to provide such profiles.

The ITPA is especially appealing to cognitive psychologists because it
measures short-term memory of verbal and auditory kinds, fluencies
(which Guilford believes to indicate creativity—see Chapter 24), grammatical development (see Chapter 16), concept attainment of various kinds,
and so forth. Although it uses questions similar to those on the Binet test,
it groups them in ways that show a student's cognitive strengths and
weaknesses. Two individuals who have an equal total ITPA score may
obtain that total score in different ways. Three ITPA profiles are shown in
Figure 9.2.

Can We Improve IQ Through Teaching?

At this point, the educator may be wondering: since an IQ test (whether
general or specific) is merely a set of questions, can we not improve IQ by

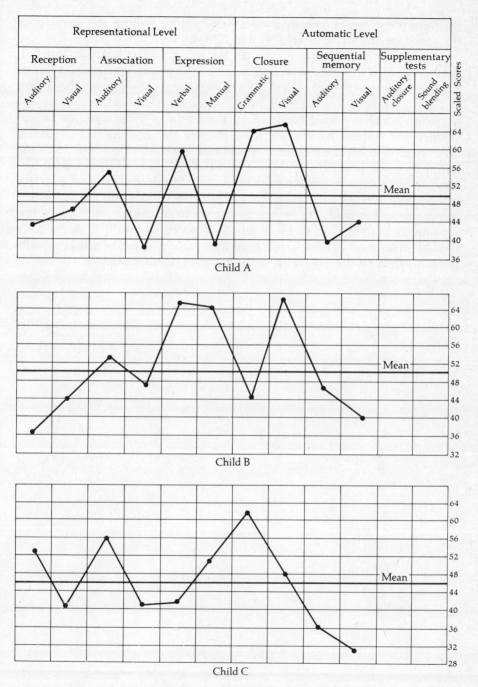

Figure 9.2 Illinois Test of Psycholinguistic Abilities (ITPA) profiles of three kindergarten children, showing how the same approximate mean level (horizontal line) can be obtained from different patterns of abilities.

teaching the answers to similar questions? Or by drilling and developing the special abilities (like memory) that IQ tests use?

The only honest answer is that we still do not know for sure, although research in that direction is proceeding (my own, for example, Farnham-Diggory, 1970). Certainly the first step is to analyze the nature of IQ questions. After that, methods of improving the particular type of thinking, which we have been calling basic human programs, can be developed and tested. But it is not necessary for this practice to be separate from general academic training. We do not teach someone how to think, and then teach him how to think about biology, how to think about history, and so forth. In teaching the subject matter itself, the good educator will become aware of the basic human programs hidden in the reasoning of experts in his field. As he teaches these to his pupils, he will be improving their abilities to think about other matters as well. It seems quite possible that good academic teaching in a variety of fields will eventually have an effect on the general ability, or g, that IQ tests sample.

SUMMARY

In this section of the text, we have pursued further the question of basic information-processing systems—that is, basic ways in which we think as we move through our world of experiences.

Human beings do not have an infinite number of thinking styles and possibilities. We are really quite limited in how much we can remember, how many different ways we can relate information, and the number of ideas we can generate. We cope with the world because we have developed systems for handling our own deficiencies. Because we can hold only a few ideas in mind simultaneously, we have learned how to think in concepts. One basic idea (like the idea of an automobile) can generate many special instances (like my car, your car, the policeman's car). And we have learned other mental efficiency strategies.

The psychological study of such strategies implies an interest in the process of thinking, as well as in its products, or answers. In everyday life, these processes are heuristic in nature—that is, they are naturalistic rule systems. In academic life, they may be algorithmic in nature—that is, they may be recipes of various kinds taught by teachers. Knowledge itself is composed of products as well as of heuristic and algorithmic processes and it is important for educators to distinguish one aspect of knowledge from another.

To do this, we must obtain some kind of behavior. We cannot tell if any thinking is going on when it remains entirely within the head of the thinker. This kind of general, experimental behaviorism is common to all modern psychologists. There are also special theories of behaviorism in modern education—S-R theory and Skinnerian theory. Cognitive psychologists, though behaviorists in the general experimental sense, are not behaviorists in the sense of S-R and Skinnerian theories because their interest is in the dynamic processes of thought, as opposed to the static products of thought.

S-R theory views knowledge as composed hierarchically of little bits of knowledge. Skinnerian theory views thought itself as nonexistent; Skinnerians are interested only in the behavior of thinking. Cognitive psychologists view thinking processes as large systems composed hierarchically of smaller systems. They see the act of thinking as a goal-directed sequence of related mental activities, or programs—to use computer terminology.

Cognitive theorists frequently express their theories as computer programs, on the assumption that teaching a machine to think the way people do helps us specify the nature of thinking. We have borrowed some of these same assumptions in attempting to specify the nature of basic academic thinking.

Once a goal has been selected and valued (and its value depends to a large extent on its instrumentality), basic human mental programs go into operation. In a school, they are generally of five types: scanning and holding, problem solving, remembering, generating and classifying, and ordering and relating. Most classroom activities involve one or more of these basic information-processing systems.

Scanning-and-holding systems refer to our ability to sample the information around us and then to do something with it in order to hold it available for mental use. Such programs are greatly affected by intention, or preparatory set; by modalities (vision, auditory, or tactual); by the familiarity of the material being processed; and by basic physiological limitations, indicated by "the magic number 7."

Problem-solving systems are simple in outline. Once a goal has been selected, a series of actions, subgoals, tests, and retests should be instituted in order to achieve it. The "problem" with a problem is that these steps are not clearly perceived. The necessary steps and materials may be right at hand (mentally or physically) and yet not recognized, perhaps because they have functions we fail to associate with the immediate problem. The general problem-solving system developed by Polya strives to help students bring into awareness the connections between problems so that old skills and solutions can be reused.

Remembering has two related aspects, storing and retrieving. Programs for storing information involve the use of informationally rich cues and a unified, organized framework. Programs for retrieving activate the cues and move through the framework. What we do in this case is not ectoplasmic; it involves the construction of a biochemical trace or pattern. Verbal rehearsal of one's own summaries seems to be the best way of producing these patterns with complex academic material.

Generating and classifying information is the heart of conceptual thinking. When we classify two things together, we generate a list of things they have in common. They may have these things in common because of some fact of nature, because we "feel" as if they do, because a group of us got together and decided they do, or because they are consistent with something else. If the lists are complicated—as they will be with most verbal material—we may need a plan or search tree for moving through them systematically. As children grow, their ability to recognize a single common factor, even in a complex list, improves.

In a classroom, the student's ability to discover underlying concepts will be affected by many factors, including the teacher's skill in presenting the critical information. Young children may discover a concept more efficiently if the teacher selects information points for them; adults may perform more efficiently if they choose their own. When this is being handled through inductive discussions, the teacher should be prepared to guide, with skill and interest, the information points (or list of critical factors) the students themselves are generating.

Ordering and relating is the heart of human programming itself. It requires, first of all, an "executive planner" that can make decisions about how to relate one aspect of a program to another and how to handle interruptions of various kinds. More complex relationships and routines may be produced by interruptions if they are accepted rather than ignored. That is how the executive improves.

Second, ordering-and-relating programs make use of types of relations that human beings seem to be naturally capable of recognizing—similarities, causes, time relations, and so forth. More complex relations may be built out of simpler ones. So-called higher-level relations (or rules) may be built from experience with elementary ones. Skills develop as students practice the discovery of relationships on a wide variety of materials, so that the discovery process itself becomes independent of the material. Rules are then known in a highly useful abstract form.

Training in these programs, like training in all programs, must take into account natural human limitations and make available aids of various kinds. A relationship diagram like a search tree may be necessary to efficient ordering and relating.

To illustrate the existence of basic human programs in academic material, a few test questions from Bloom's *Taxonomy* were analyzed. As a concluding note, the relationship of basic information-processing skills to IQ was discussed. This relationship is an empirical one. IQ tests simply include examples of basic information-processing skills. If a person can demonstrate an average amount of skill of his own, he will have an average IQ. The question of changing that basic ability is the fundamental proposition of education itself.

Part III MOTIVATION, PERSONALITY, AND CULTURE

Schoolrooms are not and should not be the place where man learns only scientific techniques. They are the place where selfhood . . . is created. Only such deep inner knowledge truly expands horizons and makes use of technology, and not for power, but for human happiness. . . . As the capacity for self-awareness is intensified, so will return that sense of personal responsibility which has been well nigh lost in the eager yearning for aggrandizement of the asphalt man. . . . Let it be admitted that the world's problems are many and wearing, and that the whirlpool runs fast. If we are to build a stable, cultural structure above that which threatens to engulf us by changing our lives more rapidly than we can adjust our habits, it will only be by flinging over the torrent a structure as taut and flexible as a spider's web, a human society deeply self-conscious and undeceived by the waters that race beneath it, a society more literate, more appreciative of human worth than any society that has previously existed. That is the sole prescription not for survival, which is meaningless, but for a society worthy to survive.

LOREN EISELEY

The new teacher, nervously awaiting the first day of school, is probably most worried about one thing: the control of the classroom. Will there be chaos? Will the principal walk in and find screaming disorder? How does one force young human beings to sit quietly in chairs and listen for six hours at a stretch?

One important aspect of Silberman's book, *Crisis in the Classroom,* is the author's emphasis upon "education for docility" (pp. 113–157). He points out that schools of all types share a preoccupation with order and control. Learning and development must be made secondary to timetables, rules, regulations, and administrative convenience. Because pupils and teachers are cogs in a presumably efficient machine (or at least an orderly machine), they are dehumanized.

It is difficult to force young human beings to accept dehumanization passively. That is why it is difficult to control them in classrooms of the traditional type. The nontraditional classrooms described by Silberman—and visible in many cities across the nation—do not have serious obedience problems, because they do not require obedience to a dehumanizing system.

The nontraditional classroom may, of course, have problems of classroom management and public relations; no human enterprise is free of those. Some pupils lack social skills of various kinds; some have motivational difficulties; some have personality problems and/or cultural backgrounds that make schooling problematical. But these are not traditional hickory-stick obedience problems. They are problems that require more subtle forms of insight and understanding on the part of school personnel.

The purpose of Part III is to provide some guidelines for the understanding and management of *human* beings in classrooms.

We begin with questions of obedience. Do we want it? What might it lead to? How can we get it? Psychologists know quite a bit about controlling human behavior through conditioning and modeling programs. Should these techniques be used to instill obedience? Can they be used in other ways? Chapter 10 will cover these topics.

Chapter 11 introduces motivational topics of a deeper nature: achievement drives, aspirations, expectations, and competence. Are they awakened in your students? Can you arrange a program to awaken and/or guide them? Can you, in effect, "unleash" a student's natural drive to develop mental competence? An important aspect of this will be the student's own curiosity and need for mental stimulation. Chapter 12 presents what is currently known about these factors.

Chapter 13 takes up the complex problem of the interaction of curiosity and competence motives in what we are describing generally as *self-motivating learning cycles*. There are two important theories of such cycles—one by Piaget and one by Berlyne. We will analyze them, and then look at school applications.

Chapters 14 and 15 provide more detailed clues to matters of personality and social background as they may influence schooling. Some personality problems seem to appear in almost every classroom: the student who is excessively dependent, for example, or the student who is physically aggressive (in both these cases, conditioning procedures may be helpful). Socially, we have both home and school factors to understand and to include in educational planning.

Throughout Part III, we will be asking one basic question: If we were to design a school that capitalized on the natural motivational systems of human beings, what kind of a school would it be? How can we base schools upon the natural desires of human beings to learn, to master their own confusion and uncertainty, to become mentally skillful? How can we design human educational programs instead of dehumanizing ones? The teacher who can find answers to these questions may find that the problem of obedience no longer exists.

Chapter 10   THE QUESTION OF OBEDIENCE

THE MILGRAM OBEDIENCE STUDIES

In 1963 and for several years thereafter, some startling experiments on obedience were carried out at Yale University by a psychologist named Stanley Milgram.

The subjects of the first experiment were forty men between the ages of 20 and 50. They were obtained through a newspaper advertisement offering $4.50 for participation in a psychological experiment, and they came from New Haven and the surrounding community. Those who responded believed they were to participate in a study of learning and memory at Yale University. A wide range of occupations were represented: postal clerks, high school teachers, salesmen, engineers, and laborers. Some had not finished elementary school; some had professional degrees. Although the subjects were paid, they all understood that the money was theirs regardless of how long they participated in the experiment. They were never under the illusion that they had to complete the experiment, or even any portion of it, in order to get their money. This is an important fact to remember.

The experiment was conducted in an elegant laboratory on the Yale campus. The role of the Experimenter was played by a high school biology teacher, one whose manner was impassive and a bit stern. The role of one subject was played by a 47-year-old accountant, a mild-mannered and likable man. This subject was interviewed with each of the real subjects, who did not know he was a confederate. During their joint interview, the confederate subject and the real subject were told that the experiment concerned the effects of punishment on learning. "Actually," the bogus experimenter told them, "we know very little about the effect of punishment on learning because almost no truly scientific studies have been made of it in human beings. For instance, we do not know how much . . . difference it makes as to who is giving the punishment. Or whether an adult learns best from a younger or older person, and many things of this sort. So in this study we are bringing together a number of adults from different occupations and ages, and we are asking some of them to be teachers and some of them to be learners. We want to find out just what effect different people have on each other as teachers and learners, and also what effect punishment will have on learning in this situation. Therefore, I am going to ask one of you to be the teacher here, and one of you to be the learner." The subjects then drew slips of paper from a hat to determine who would be the teacher. The drawing was rigged so that the real subject was always the teacher, and the fake subject was always the learner.

Immediately after the drawing, teacher and learner were taken to an adjacent room, and the learner was strapped into a chair. The experimenter explained that the straps were to prevent excessive movement while the learner was being shocked. An electrode was attached to the learner's wrist, and electrode tape was applied. The subject was told this was done to avoid blisters and burns and to prevent permanent tissue damage.

The real subject was then taken to an adjoining room and shown an imposing "generator," which was said to deliver shocks to the learner. The instrument panel of the "generator" consisted of thirty lever switches set in a horizontal line. Each switch was clearly labeled with a voltage designation that went from 15 to 450 volts. In addition, the switches were marked in the following way: the first four switches were labeled Slight Shock; the next four were labeled Moderate Shock; the next four, Strong Shock; then, Very Strong Shock; then, Intense Shock; then, Extreme Intensity Shock; then Danger. There were two more switches after this, marked simply XXX. When a switch was depressed, a red pilot light was illuminated, an electric buzzing was heard, a blue light labeled Voltage Energizer flashed, the dial on the voltage meter moved, and various relay clicks were sounded. All details of the instrument were carefully designed to look authentic, even to precision engraving and brand names. No subject in the experiment ever suspected that the instrument was a fake—which, of course, it was.

After he learned how to work the switches, the subject was told that his job was to teach a list of words to the learner (the fake subject) sitting strapped to his "electric chair" in the next room. The subject was also told that he was to administer a shock to the learner every time he made a mistake. Further, he was told to increase the voltage with each error. The subject was also told to announce the voltage level aloud prior to administering the shock to make sure the subject was fully aware of the fact that the voltage was increasing.

The experiment began. The confederate turned out to be a poor learner. He made only one correct response out of four on the average. He was therefore supposed to get shocked about 75 percent of the time. The real experimental question was: Would the true subject pull those levers? Would he administer an increasingly strong shock to an older man who was strapped to a chair? Would he continue to administer shocks even after the man began to cry out in pain?

In Milgram's first experiment, there was no cry of pain until the 300-volt shock level was reached. When that happened, the learner pounded on the wall of the room, and the sound could be heard by the subject. The learner then ceased giving any answers at all. At this turn of events, the subject usually asked the experimenter what to do; he was told to treat the absence of a response as a wrong answer and to continue to shock the learner, increasing the voltage as usual.

If the subject said anything more, the bogus experimenter replied in fixed ways and in a fixed order. He said first, "Please continue" or "Please go on." If the subject appeared reluctant, he added, "The experiment requires that you continue." If that was not enough, he then said, "It is absolutely essential that you continue." And if *that* was not enough, he finally said, "You have no other choice, you must go on." If the real subject then refused to obey the experimenter, the experiment was terminated. It is important to remember that no force, no coercion, no threat was exerted on the subject. The experimenter was not even angry. His voice was firm, but not impolite.

How would you have reacted? Would you have kept on shocking the hapless learner? Would you have decided that you did, in fact, have another choice—the choice of stopping the experiment and walking out of the building?

In an average classroom poll, the majority of the students usually believe only about 2 percent of the subjects would continue to shock the learner up to the 450-volt XXX level. In actual fact, more than 50 percent of the real subjects did exactly that.

Of course the subjects suffered; they perspired, they moaned and groaned, they displayed many signs of tension and anxiety—but they kept on going. Certainly they had all learned from childhood that it was wrong to hurt another person against his will. And certainly they all knew that the man pounding on the wall was being hurt against his will. Yet, the majority of the subjects abandoned this teaching to follow the instructions of an authority *who had no special power to enforce his requests.*

Before each subject left, the true nature of the experiment was fully explained to him. Subjects who had administered the full range of shock usually protested that they had done so because of the scientific respectability associated with Yale. Milgram did not believe this mattered as much as the subjects said it did, and to prove his point he performed the experiment all over again far from Yale—in a not-so-respectable office in a commercial section of Bridgeport, Connecticut. The same thing happened. There was no significant difference between Yale and Bridgeport in the number of subjects who administered the full range of shocks.

Milgram tested a number of other factors he believed to be important. In one experiment, for example, the experimenter was not physically present, but gave his instructions by telephone. Many subjects cheated under these conditions—they said they were shocking the learner, when they were not. Why, Milgram wondered, did they not just walk out? (They had already been paid.) Why *pretend* to do something you believe is wrong, when no one has the power to force you?

In another experiment, Milgram varied the distance of the subject from the learner. In the first condition (as described above), the learner was in another room and could not be seen by the subject, although he was heard pounding on the wall. In the second condition, the subject was in the same room with the learner, about 2 feet away from him. And in still another condition, the learner received a shock only when the subject forced his (the learner's) hand down on a shock plate.

As Milgram expected, obedience was significantly reduced as the victim was moved closer. When the subjects were close to the victim, about 60 percent of them refused to obey the experimenter. When the subjects were required to force the victim's hand onto the shock plate, 70 percent refused to obey. However, the fact remains that even in that final condition, 30 percent—that is to say, 30 men out of every 100—did voluntarily force the hand of another man onto a shock plate which they believed to be giving an extremely painful electric shock.

The results of these experiments were deeply disturbing. (They have since been discontinued.) As Milgram points out:

> They raise the possibility that human nature, or more specifically the kind of character produced in American democratic society, cannot be counted on to insulate its citizens from brutality and inhuman treatment at the direction of malevolent authority. A substantial proportion of people do what they are told to do, irrespective of the content of the act, and without limitation of conscience, so long as they perceive the command comes from legitimate authority. If, in this study, an anonymous experimenter could successfully command adults to subdue a 50-year-old man and force on him painful electric shocks against his protests, one can only wonder what government with its vastly greater authority and prestige can command of its citizenry. (Milgram, 1965, p. 262)

How much of this obedience has been instilled by schools? Where else might it come from? Can we control behavior in schools without producing a citizenry that takes orders, without question, from anyone perceived to be an authority? To answer these questions, we will need to understand the dynamics of *conditioning*.

THE CONTROL OF BEHAVIOR

How does obedience begin? Infants are certainly not born obedient. They must learn how to become that way, and the learning is often stormy. Almost from birth, therefore, some kind of obedience training is being given the child. A nursing schedule may be recommended by a doctor or a nurse, and the mother then trains her baby to accommodate to it by the simple expedient of not feeding him until a certain period of time has passed. Even very young babies can adjust their biological rhythms (up to a point) to the clock. A baby on a "demand schedule," however, may train his mother to be obedient. He does this in a very efficient and systematic way: He rewards her (with a burp of satisfaction) for doing what he wants, and punishes her (with cries of anguish) for not doing what he wants. Such a baby is practicing a system of *instrumental conditioning*—sometimes called *operant conditioning* or *contingency management.* If rewards and punishments are contingent upon certain behavior, the behavior tends to come under the control of the reinforcement system.

Principles of behavior control have grown out of psychological theories of conditioning. Beginning with the work of Pavlov in Russia, an immense body of literature now describes many facets of *classical* conditioning. Skinner's research has centered upon instrumental conditioning (he calls it operant conditioning). Rather than describing here the basic laboratory procedures (they can be found in any introductory psychology textbook), we will consider instead some modern applications.

Classical Conditioning

The mother who trains her baby to be hungry on schedule is practicing a form of classical conditioning. If you feel hunger pangs when the noon bell tolls, you have also been classically conditioned. The principle is simply this: A naturally occurring response (like hunger or an eyeblink) has been attached to an arbitrary signal (like a bell). The conditioning process (the attaching procedure) involves the pairing of the natural stimulus (say, a puff of air) with the arbitrary signal. This pairing happens many times, until the arbitrary signal can elicit the natural response by itself. (Every time you hear the bell, you blink.)

In recent years, psychiatrists and psychologists have been using conditioning techniques as tools for the reeducation of neurotic response systems. One early case (reported in Hilgard and Marquis, 1940) involved a 32-year-old unmarried schoolteacher who had been in an auto accident. As a result of both the shock of the accident and some personal emotional problems, the teacher had developed a hysterical paralysis of her left arm. For six years, her left arm had been entirely useless to her, despite the fact that there was nothing organically wrong with it. The arm was also totally anesthetic.

Why she waited so long before seeking psychiatric help is not clear, but at any rate, the standard type of psychiatric help was not effective. Finally, her doctor decided to employ a conditioning procedure. Two electrodes were used, one for each hand. With her good hand, the teacher held down a key, and on signal that key was electrified. If the teacher received the signal, she could withdraw her finger in time to avoid a shock.

What was the signal? A slight shock to the paralyzed, anesthetic hand. Would feeling be restored? Would the anesthetic hand "learn" to feel again in order to save the good hand a shock? The answer was yes; sensitivity gradually returned to the insensitive hand and arm. The conditioning procedure was then reversed: The normal hand was given a light shock and the paralyzed hand was given a more severe shock, unless it learned to move in time. It did. Through this classical conditioning procedure, natural reflexive behavior was restored.

School Phobias

It may be that many emotions are "attached" to objects and events through inadvertent classical conditioning procedures. One of the earliest demonstrations of the process was carried out by J. B. Watson (see Chapter 5). Watson and Rayner (1920) showed that a baby could be conditioned to fear any white, fuzzy object by pairing one of those objects with a loud clanging noise (hitting an iron bar). Since the noise frightened the baby, he connected his fear to all white, fuzzy objects and developed a (temporary) phobia of them.

What are now called *school phobias* may develop in a similar way. Parents or teachers or peers may inadvertently condition strong anxiety to school events, particularly if the child has a large amount of general anxiety (see Chapter 14 for a discussion of anxiety). Of course, we all know of extreme cases: One teacher, for example, locked second-graders in dark closets for misbehavior; this naturally produced school phobias in some of the children. Although such extreme forms of teacher conditioning can be dealt with administratively (and firmly!), even genuinely humane teachers (and parents) may accidentally frighten children in a way that "hooks" their fright to a school event. The otherwise harmless event may then continue to evoke irrational fright and lead to school-phobic behavior.

In very young children, school phobias may be related to separation (from mother) fears and can perhaps be better understood within the framework of Freudian developmental theory (see Chapter 14). A summary of this particular viewpoint may be found in Paulson (1957), and in Sarason et al. (1960, pp. 50–60). We will not emphasize it here because modern treatment of school phobias seems to be moving away from psychoanalytical concepts toward behavioral conditioning concepts, even with young children. (In the case of very young children, of course, there is no need to face the problem at all; they should not be forced to attend school if they are frightened by it.)

Among adolescents, who may be experiencing severe anxieties related to problems of identity (see Chapter 14), the attachment of this general fear to school events may produce such severe phobias as to cause runaway or other truancy behaviors. The true fears are often masked by role behaviors fashionable for a particular peer group, and the truancy may be attributed to causes other than the basic fear, even by the youngsters themselves.

Desensitization Therapy

Nowadays, phobias of all sorts are often treated by *desensitization* procedures, which are actually forms of deconditioning. The treatment involves teaching a patient how to become deeply relaxed and how to safely imagine himself in states similar to those that evoked his phobic anxiety. In one case (Kushner, 1966) a high school boy had been involved in an accident and was afraid to get back in his car. During his first therapeutic session, he was instructed to relax, then to imagine himself looking at his car, then sitting in the car with the ignition off. In subsequent sessions, he imagined himself driving in the car, driving it himself, and finally, driving it under conditions that led to the original accident. As soon as he could imagine that fully without anxiety, he was cured. This treatment is something like a reversal of the conditioning process: The patient learns to dissociate (separate) a natural response (anxiety) from the events originally paired with it (like driving a car).

Deconditioning (desensitization) procedures attempt to lead a school-phobic child gradually to "unhook" his anxiety from school events. A young phobic child, for example, might first play school with dolls and toy furniture, then with other children until he could tolerate the situations without fright, before being returned to the real school situation (Patterson, 1966). Similarly, desensitization procedures rather than legal enforcement may be more appropriate ways of handling some adolescent truants. Two principles, however, must be kept in mind: (1) Desensitization programs should always be carried out under the supervision of a psychiatrist or clinical psychologist who specializes in therapy of this sort. (2) The behavior problems of childhood and adolescence may have complex causes and complex cures; school personnel should beware of oversimplified explanations and treatment recommendations.

With proper supervision, schools may be able to develop extremely useful psychological procedures for handling emotional problems in their students. We will have more to say about such programs in later discussions of personality. Now, let us continue with our study of conditioning procedures.

Instrumental Conditioning (Contingency Management)

Whereas the fathers of classical conditioning are Pavlov (in Russia) and Watson (in America), the father of instrumental conditioning is B. F.

Skinner (1968). Skinner's basic conditioning rule is a simple one: What you do is governed by its consequences. Behavior that is instrumental in achieving a goal tends to be repeated. It is an *operant*.

If you are rewarded for a particular kind of behavior, it increases; if you are punished for it, the behavior decreases. More important, if a reward is withheld (that is, if you are not rewarded), the behavior also decreases. Rewards can take many forms—the giving of attention, for example. If it is attention that is rewarding, even the attention associated with punishment may be sought. For this reason (in Skinner theory), misbehavior may increase, despite the fact that it is being punished.

Teachers often produce the very behavior they are trying to eliminate by inadvertently rewarding it. Suppose, for example, you want your third-graders to sit quietly in their seats reading, while you work with a few children at the blackboard. If someone jumps out of his seat, you will probably reward that behavior by saying, "Johnny, sit down!" But you may forget to reward the good behavior of the other children by saying, "Bobby (or Mary, or Susie, or Jack) I certainly like the way you are sitting quietly and reading!" You should not then be surprised if not only Johnny, but also Mary, Susie, and Jack jump out of their seats more and more frequently. (Imitating the rewarded behavior of other children may produce a sense of vicarious reward, as we will see in the next section of this chapter.)

At first glance, Skinnerian principles may seem to contradict the principles of desensitization discussed above. Truancy, you may be thinking, will increase if it is not punished. This is the basis of most forms of legal retribution. But punishment can take many forms, and one kind of punishment may be an escape from another. If Johnny is bored by his book, his teacher's statement, "Johnny, sit down!" may provide a welcome escape from the punishment of having to sit still and read. Similarly, a visit from a truant officer, a scolding from a parent, or expulsion from school may provide a welcome escape from the punishment of facing a cruel fear or sense of failure. In this sense, then, a lesser punishment may function as a reward and increase the very behavior it was intended to erase. Desensitization would be designed to change the controlling fear.

Homme's Illustrations of Contingency Management
The fact that "one man's punishment may be another man's reward" (and no reference to masochism is intended) has been emphasized by Homme (1966) in a report on contingency management. Homme pointed out that any behavior an individual likes may serve as reinforcement for behavior he does not like. How do we know what he likes? By his frequency of choice: High-probability behaviors are the ones he is most likely to engage in; low-probability behaviors are the ones he is least likely to engage in. It is therefore assumed that the high-probability behaviors are the rewarding ones. As Homme points out, the high-probability behaviors can

be used to reinforce the low-probability ones. Here are some of his examples:

THREE NORMAL MIDDLE-CLASS THREE-YEAR-OLDS

. . . The high probability behaviors used as reinforcers were of the sort generally suppressed by the environment, e.g., running and screaming. The contracts specified by the contingency manager [say, a teacher] were of the sort, "Sit quietly and watch what I do at the blackboard; then you may run and scream until the timer goes *ding.*"

TWO CHILDREN OF POVERTY

There is no dearth of authorities to explain how and why children of the poor are different. To find out if they obeyed a different set of behavioral laws, staff members of this department sought out two Negro boys, five and six, of poor families. . . .

What was most striking to us in this pilot project was the speed with which these children from a different culture learned middle-class behaviors. They learned instantly, for example, to knock on a door and inquire, "May I come in?" when entering the reinforcing event area was contingent on this behavior. They cheerfully fulfilled small contracts of the usual sort: "Execute some low probability behavior (find another letter that looks like this one), and then you can execute some high probability behavior." We were prepared to find that different high probability behaviors would have to be used to reinforce these children, but this was not the case. The usual program of water colors, crayons . . . pushing a castor-equipped chair, and so forth, served to reinforce behaviors very nicely.

TWENTY-THREE ADOLESCENTS

Guidance counselors were used to recruit subjects for a study of adolescents who were high school dropouts or judged to be potential dropouts. These adolescent had the behaviors usually associated with "street kids." They spoke a hip jargon, some of them were discovered to be carrying knives, some of them wore their sun glasses at all times, and so on. The low probability behavior for these subjects was getting themselves through programed instructional material in subjects like arithmetic and reading. Most of the high probability behavior used to reinforce these were of the conventional sort: time for a break, coffee, smoke, coke, and so on. However, there were some surprises. For some of the subjects, going through a program in Russian proved to be a reliable high probability behavior. When this was discovered, their contracts would take a form like the following: "Do 20 frames of arithmetic; then you can work on Russian for 10 minutes." This does serve to illustrate that one need not know why a high probability behavior exists in order to use it as a reinforcer. My own speculation about why street kids' high probability behavior is learning Russian is that perhaps fuzz cannot read messages written in Russian. (Homme, 1966)

These reinforcement strategies do not, of course, say anything about the choice and sequencing of the material to be learned. Such sequences have been discussed in Chapter 5. You will recall that Skinnerian learning sequences are carefully developed to move the learner through a step-by-step series of behaviors. The learner's response repertoire is slowly increased until he is capable of emitting complex responses (like "3.14159") on cue ("How much is pi?"). In this section we are concentrating on the motivational rather than the structural aspects of Skinnerian systems.

Teaching Technologies

Programming low-probability behavior is not a simple matter in many cases, because the ratio of reinforced to unreinforced behaviors may be wrong. Students may have to wait too long before reinforcement is dispensed, or they may not have to wait long enough. If reinforcement is too frequent, habits of sustained work or work apart from the reinforcing situation may be difficult to establish. Skinner's book *The Technology of Teaching* (1968) contains many examples of operant conditioning problems in classrooms.

Figure 10.1 shows an application of reinforcement theory by Staats et al. (1964) to the study of reading. The teaching machine in this case involved the presentation of stimulus materials (words) in the windows at the back of the booth. The children pressed various buttons to signal their

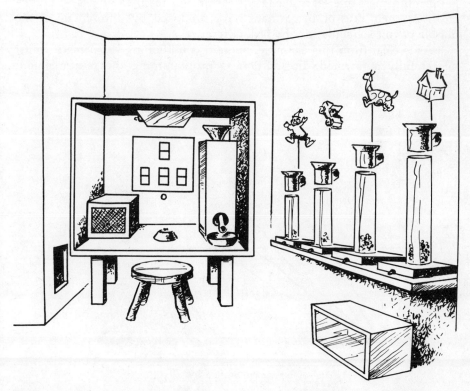

Figure 10.1   Laboratory apparatus for the experimental study of operant reading. (Staats et al., 1964)

responses. (Equipment of this sort can be programmed to teach reading in a variety of ways.) If the responses were correct, they received a marble in the dispenser at the right. They could receive a trinket delivered immediately in the bin at the extreme left by depositing the marble in the top funnel of the marble dispenser, or they could "buy" a toy on the right by depositing their marbles in the plastic tubes beneath them; when a tube was filled, the toy was theirs.

The children's responses were recorded by a cumulative recording device, which adds up the responses as it records them. On the first trial a graph of the responses would be low; on the twenty-fifth trial, the graph would be high. The important point about such a graph is the rate of increase. If the graph line is steep, the subject is responding rapidly; if it is shallow, the subject is responding slowly.

Figure 10.2 shows differences in response rate produced by four schedules of reinforcement: continuous reinforcement for every correct response, variable interval reinforcement (reinforcement is delivered every few minutes), variable ratio reinforcement (reinforcement delivered for a varying proportion of responses: sometimes 1 out of 6, sometimes 1 out of 3), and extinction (no reinforcement). Remember that the children are performing the same learning task (learning to read) in all cases. Differences in their rate of performance are produced by differences in the marble payoff schedule, not by task differences.

As is clear from this example, operant conditioning experiments must be carefully performed. In addition to programming the reinforcement

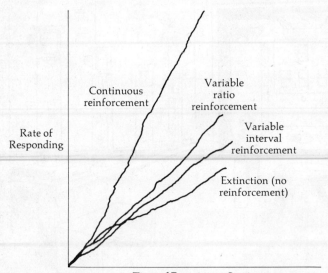

Figure 10.2 Examples of differences in response rate produced by different schedules of reinforcement. (Staats, 1968, with modifications)

rates, exact measures must be made of baseline response rates—the amount of responding that occurs before reinforcement is introduced or before a reinforcement is withheld. For example, suppose you want to try to eliminate crying in a preschooler. You may discover that the crying is being sustained by the reinforcement of loving attention from a teacher. Every time the child cries, the teacher may respond with a reassuring hug. Before asking the teacher to change her reinforcement strategy and hug only when the child is *not* crying, you must get baseline measurements of the amount of crying that is actually going on. Then when the reinforcement strategy is changed, you can tell if it works.

After having determined that crying rate is responsive to a change in reinforcement contingencies, you should go back to the old reinforcement system temporarily, to see if the crying rate reverts to its former high response level. If it does, you can feel sure you have control of the behavior (by manipulating reinforcements). The final step would be to reinforce again (with hugs) only the behavior of *not* crying, until that behavior predominates.

Effective Reinforcement

There are difficult technical problems involving both the appropriate type of reinforcement and its appropriate schedule. Children introduced to such apparatus as illustrated in Figure 10.1, for example, may respond eagerly for a short while and then become bored, no matter how the reinforcement schedule is manipulated. They may decide they do not want any of the toys and refuse to work for them. How do we convince such a child that there are other rewards in learning to read? How do we transfer a child who has been working for toys to working for praise, for gold stars, or for grades? These are some of the technological puzzles reinforcement theorists are trying to solve.

You will note that we have been talking generally about three kinds of reinforcements: *extrinsic rewards* (like candy, money, or other payment, and being praised publicly); *intrinsic rewards* (like being right, studying Russian, and satisfying one's curiosity); and *aversive consequences* (loss of reward and punishment). Most Skinnerian teaching programs use some combination of extrinsic and intrinsic rewards and simply withhold them when the desired behavior is not forthcoming.

Young children (preschoolers) are generally responsive (their behavior increases) to praise and attention; older children may be more responsive to the intrinsic reward of being right. In chapters to come, we will learn more about the important motivational properties of competence development and discovery opportunities. In the Skinnerian scheme, any motivator can be used to control and program behavior.

Other Reinforcement Studies

In Part IV, you will read about an operant conditioning experiment that increased babbling in 3-month-old infants. Many others are reported in two books by Ullman and Krasner (1966, and Krasner and Ullman, 1967): experiments to control isolate behavior, aggression, excessive crying, refusal to eat, stuttering, thumbsucking, and so forth. Recent studies of all kinds may be found in *The Journal of Applied Behavioral Analysis.*

What about self-reinforcement of one's own behavior? When you tell yourself to read ten more pages of this book and then have lunch, you are applying operant conditioning principles to your own behavior. Are they successful? Can you program your own study habits by managing your own reinforcement schedules? This important clue to school management will be discussed further at the end of this chapter.

IMITATION AND SELF-CONTROL

Another important way of controlling behavior is through a process of sharing vicariously in the rewards of another. Some basic work in this area was carried out by Bandura and Walters (1963) and is reported in their book, *Social Learning and Personality Development.* Although they do not disagree with Skinner's basic principles, they point out that instrumental conditioning procedures would not be sufficient to teach many responses in the absence of imitation. Bandura presents his case in this way:

> As a way of illustrating the gross inefficiency of operant [instrumental] conditioning procedures in human learning let us imagine an automobile driver training program based on [Skinnerian principles]. . . .
>
> As a first step our trainer, who has been carefully programed to produce head nods, resonant hm-hms, and other verbal reinforcers, loads up with an ample supply of candy, chewing gum, and filter-tip cigarettes. A semi-willing subject who has never observed a person drive an automobile, and a parked car complete the picture. Our trainer might have to wait a long time before the subject emits an orienting response toward the vehicle. At the moment the subject does look . . . this response is immediately reinforced and gradually he begins to gaze longingly at the stationary automobile. Similarly, approach responses in the desired direction are promptly reinforced in order to bring the subject in proximity to the car. Eventually, through the skillful use of differential reinforcement, the trainer will teach the subject to open and to close the car door. With perseverance he will move the subject from the back seat or any other inappropriate location chosen in this trial-and-error ramble until at length the subject is shaped up behind the steering wheel. It is unnecessary to depict the remainder of the training procedure beyond noting that it will likely prove an exceedingly tedious, not to mention an expensive and hazardous enterprise.
> . . .
> Let us now contrast the process of social learning described above with a program of driver training based upon modeling procedures. First, the model performs the necessary orienting and approach responses toward the automobile, opens the car door, and sits behind the steering wheel. A single demonstration along with a verbal description of the sequence of responses necessary to start, to accelerate, to stop, and to control the movement of the automobile will greatly curtail unnecessary and

dangerous experimentation. This substantially increases the probability that both the subject and the trainer will survive the learning process. The subject, in turn, will have acquired a substantial portion of the repertoire of responses essential for successful motoring simply by observing the behavior of the model without performing any overt responses or experiencing any response-consequences. By contrast, the process of shaping motoring behavior by means of differential reinforcement is very likely to unshape the driver, the trainer, the automobile, and the surrounding environment. (Bandura, 1962, pp. 213–214)

In an extensive series of experiments, some of which are discussed below, Bandura and others have shown that many factors will influence imitation learning.

Children Imitate People Who Have Been Rewarding to Them

In this basic experiment, a model (the person who was to be imitated) brought the child to the experimental room and then did one of two things: She either gave the child some toys and then busied herself with her own work, or she played with the child for a while. After this experience, the child was tested for imitation in the following way: The experimenter told the child that they were going to play a game, the object of which was to guess which of two boxes contained a picture. The model always had the first turn, which the child watched. In executing each trial, the model always did irrelevant things, like saying "march, march, march" as she walked to the box, or knocking off a doll sitting on the lid. The child then took his turn.

The experimental question was, how many of the model's irrelevant behaviors would the child imitate? The major question was whether the child would imitate the model who had played with him (the rewarding or nurturant model) more than he would imitate the model who had given him toys, but remained otherwise indifferent. The subject children imitated the nurturant model more, and even continued to imitate her (for example, saying "march, march, march" on their way back to their classroom) after the experiment was over.

Children Imitate Aggressive Behavior They See
in Real Life, Films, and Cartoons

The basic condition concerned a Bobo doll (a life-sized inflated doll that bounces back up when you knock it down). The various models all behaved toward the Bobo doll in specific ways that children were otherwise unlikely to think of: For example, the model sat on Bobo, pounded his nose, and hit him repeatedly with a wooden mallet.

This experiment was repeated in three forms: In the *real-life* condition, the children "happened" to be playing in a room when the model came in and knocked Bobo around in the prescribed manner. In the *film* condition, the model was shown on film doing the same thing. In the *cartoon* condition, the model was costumed as a black cat and the setting and music were characteristic of cartoons, but the aggressive behaviors were the standard ones.

After exposure to the modeled aggression, each child spent 20 minutes alone in the test room with Bobo, while observers secretly rated his aggressive behavior. The amount of aggression was extremely high, as illustrated in Figure 10.3, regardless of the type of exposure. Whether watching a real-life demonstration, a film, or a "funny" cartoon, children can learn to behave in aggressive ways they would not have invented by themselves. Studies of control groups who were not exposed to modeled aggression showed that the amount of aggression when a child was left alone in a playroom for 20 minutes was ordinarily quite low, even when Bobo was present.

Children Imitate Aggressive Behavior of Other Children

In a study by Hicks (1965), children observed the same Bobo attacks as those described above, but this time, they watched either an adult or a child (peer) model. Imitation was measured twice: immediately after the modeling film and six months later. It was measured in the usual way; the subject was left in the playroom with Bobo, and his attacks on Bobo were secretly recorded by the experimenter.

Immediately after the film, the children who had observed another child displayed the most aggression, especially children who had observed the aggression of a boy their own age. Six months later, back in the same

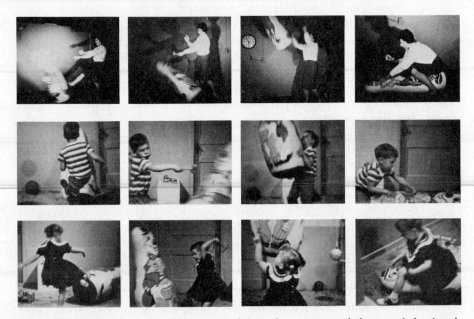

Figure 10.3 Photographs of children reproducing the aggressive behavior of the female model (top row) they had observed on film. (Bandura, Ross, and Ross, 1963)

playroom with the same materials (Bobo, a wooden mallet, and so on), all the children's imitative behavior had lessened. However, children who had observed the adult male still displayed more aggression than their controls. Hicks concluded that peers may be more influential than adults in producing immediate imitation in other children, but that adult example may have the more lasting effect.

Children Are Less Likely to Imitate Aggressive Behavior They See Punished

In still another version of the filmed Bobo experiment, rewarding and punishing scenes were added. Bandura (1965) describes these in the following way:

> [After the aggression against Bobo was completed, the film went on to show the model being rewarded or punished for his actions.] For children in the model-rewarded condition a second adult appeared with an abundant supply of candies and soft drinks. He informed the model that he [the model] was a "strong champion" and that his superb aggressive performance clearly deserved a generous treat. He then poured him a large glass of 7-Up, and readily supplied additional energy-building nourishment including chocolate bars, Cracker Jack popcorn, and an assortment of candies. While the model was rapidly consuming the delectable treats, his admirer symbolically reinstated the modeled aggressive responses [talked about the attacks on Bobo] and engaged in considerable positive social reinforcement.
>
> For children in the model-punished condition, the reinforcing agent appeared on the scene shaking his finger menacingly and commenting reprovingly, "Hey, there, you big bully. You quit picking on that clown. I won't tolerate it." As the model drew back he tripped and fell, the other adult sat on the model and spanked him with a rolled-up magazine while reminding him of his aggressive behavior. As the model ran off cowering, the agent forewarned him, "If I catch you doing that again, you big bully, I'll give you a hard spanking. You quit acting that way." (Bandura, 1965, p. 591)

As predicted, the children who viewed the punishment sequence displayed much less aggression toward Bobo themselves when they were left alone with him in the playroom.

Thus far, we have considered only behaviors of play or aggression. Is there any evidence that children can learn to develop more mature and positive behaviors through imitation?

Children Imitate Courageous Behavior

In the first part of this experiment carried out by Bandura and Menlove (1968), children who were afraid of dogs were identified. The decision about the degree of fearfulness was made in two ways: from mothers' evaluations and from a real-life test situation involving a cocker spaniel (the children were asked to pat the dog, climb into the pen with her, and so on). Following this assessment, the children watched a film displaying fearless behavior toward the dog, as modeled by another child. The experimental children were then tested again in the real-life dog situation.

A significant number of fearful children showed improved courage as a result of their film observations (Figure 10.4). Bandura and Menlove point out that an important aspect of the modeling treatment was the gradualness of the filmed child's approach to the dog and the gradualness of the test. Real-life modeling situations (carried out by parents, for example) may be erratic and overwhelm the child as a result:

> A not uncommon domestic modeling scene is one in which a parent is busily petting a dog that is jumping about while simultaneously pressuring the child, who is clinging fearfully, to touch the bounding animal. . . . Had the [experimental film] modeling sequence been presented [in such a fashion] . . . the vicarious [fear] extinction outcomes might have been relatively weak and unpredictable. (Bandura and Menlove, 1968, p. 106)

Children Imitate Self-control Toward Rewards

Mischel (1958) has carried out a number of studies exploring the capacity of individuals to wait for a delayed but large reward, rather than settling for a smaller, immediate reward. Bandura and Mischel (1965) showed that children will imitate delay behavior.

As in the cocker spaniel study, children were first selected on the basis of their natural preferences for either a small, immediate reward (as described in a test booklet) or a larger, delayed reward. The children who preferred immediate rewards were then paired with a model who preferred

Figure 10.4 Photographs of children who were apprehensive about dogs engaging in fearless interactions with dogs after exposure to the series of therapeutic films. (Bandura and Menlove, 1968, p. 104)

delayed rewards; the children who preferred delayed rewards were paired with a model who preferred immediate ones. The experimental treatment went like this:

> With the high-delay children, the model consistently selected the immediately available rewards, and in several instances commented briefly, according to a prearranged script, on the benefits of immediate self-reward (e.g., "Chess figures are chess figures. I can get much use out of the plastic ones right away"). In addition, after the fourth item, the model casually summarized his immediate-gratification philosophy of life as follows: "You probably have noticed that I am a person who likes things now. One can spend so much time in life waiting that one never gets around to really living. I find that it is better to make the most of each moment or life will pass you by."
>
> . . .
>
> With low-delay children the procedure was identical to that described above except the model consistently selected the more valued delayed rewards. The model likewise commented periodically on the virtues of self-imposed delay (e.g., "The wooden chess figures are of much better quality, more attractive and will last longer. I'll wait two weeks for the better ones"), and expounded his postponement-of-gratification philosophy of life in the following manner: "You have probably noticed that I am a person who is willing to forego having fewer or less valuable things now, for the sake of more and bigger benefits later. I usually find that life is more gratifying when I take that carefully into account." (Bandura and Mischel, 1965, p. 701)

The models then left the experimental setting so that the subjects would not feel their own performances were being observed. Each child's preference for immediate or delayed reward was then reassessed, using a booklet method of testing. Between 50 and 60 percent of the children altered their responses in the direction of the model's, despite the fact that the model's preferences were originally opposite to their own. Over half the children who originally expressed preferences for immediate rewards changed to preferences for delayed rewards, and vice versa.

Children Imitate Self-critical Responses

This experiment was carried out by Herbert, Gelfand, and Hartmann (1969) at the University of Utah. The apparatus used was a miniature bowling game, which was actually preset to give everyone the same series of good and bad scores. Adults also played this game and modeled the self-critical responses by saying such things as "Boy, that was a stupid thing for me to do." Models also *voluntarily* (not as part of the game instructions) gave up tokens they were issued at the beginning of the game. Since the tokens were to be exchanged for candies and pennies, giving up a token for a bad shot meant giving up a promised reward.

Compared to children who did not observe self-critical models, children who did observe them imitated the self-critical behavior to a significant degree. They also gave up tokens just as their models did, thereby depriving themselves of a reward, when their scores were poor.

Children Imitate When They Need Help

In 1958, Turnure and Zigler carried out an important experiment demonstrating that retarded children and children who have a history of failure are more *outer-directed* than normal children and children who have a history of success. An adult model worked a puzzle alongside a child who was also working a puzzle. The retarded and failing children attended much more frequently to the behavior of the model. Sometimes this outer-directedness improved performance, sometimes not—when the model was working on a different puzzle, for example.

The experiment results tell us that children may be especially responsive to modeling opportunities when they need help. Ordinarily, this behavior is treated as a problem in schools. Children who do not know the answers to tests are likely to copy from another's paper if they are not watched or moved out of copying distance. The effectiveness of modeling as a teaching procedure is not usually exploited. By modeling, a teacher or an expert child could demonstrate the behaviors of good task performance to a child who is having difficulties. Unlike the more direct teaching methods, the modeling procedure has two advantages: (1) It does not call attention to the target child's difficulties and (2) it permits the target child to decide for himself which of the behaviors he wishes to imitate and which he will carry out on his own. One would hope that in the future, educators will take more advantage of the powerful imitative influences that can be brought into the classroom, instead of leaving them entirely to the extracurricular world of parents, neighborhood gangs, and television.

Adults Imitate Too

Lest you leave this chapter with the conviction that only children imitate, consider the following experiment carried out by Wagner and Wheeler (1969) on Navy enlisted men.

The subjects were told that the purpose of the study was to test a new target detection system. Through a one-way intercom, they received signals from someone in another room (someone who was actually an experimental confederate, like the "victim" in the Milgram experiments) and transcribed them. This went on for 15 minutes. During the next 5 minutes, the subjects remained in the experimental room, filling out a questionnaire. The intercom was left on, and the subjects "accidentally" overheard someone come into the next room and carry on a conversation with their experimental partner. The partner then became the experimental model.

The stranger asked the model to contribute some money to a fund. In one case, the model agreed to give $20 and was told by the stranger that his donation was indeed very generous. In the other case, the model said he did not ordinarily give money to charities and would not give to this one either. The solicitor said, "You mean you won't give anything at all?"

and the model reasserted his refusal. Then the solicitor, ostensibly going down the hall, came into the real subject's room and made the same pitch. The major question was whether or not the real subject would imitate the behavior of the model. Generally, he did. The subjects who had overheard the generous model were more generous; the subjects who had overheard the selfish model behaved more selfishly.

Imitation Learning in the School

Imitative conditioning is, of course, a school mainstay. Several important principles have been illustrated experimentally in the Bandura and Walters (1959, 1963) studies:

1. The affectionate, warm teacher is more likely to be imitated by students than the indifferent teacher.
2. Students will imitate both positive and negative behavior.
   A. They will imitate courageous actions, self-control, and self-criticism.
   B. They will imitate aggressive behavior of both adults and children, whether seen in real life or in fantasies.
   C. They are less likely to imitate aggressive behavior they see punished.
3. Students imitate when they need help; the provision of helpful models may be a useful pedagogical aid.

The deliberate application of such principles may result in a better-managed classroom. The principles will be operating anyway; the teacher's choice is between letting them operate randomly and using them to advantage. Children of all ages imitate other children; much classroom behavior is "contagious" in that sense. The wise teacher will try to arrange for the spread of productive, academically useful behavior, rather than spitball throwing, illegal whispering, cheating, and drug abuse.

CONDITIONING IN THE SCHOOL

In this chapter we have surveyed some of the ways in which behavior can be controlled without the full awareness of the subject. The basic classical, operant, and imitative conditioning procedures have been described and illustrated in detail.

Despite their fancy terminology and laboratory applications, most conditioning procedures may seem intuitively familiar. Do the right thing, and you get rewarded (one way or the other); do the wrong thing, and you get punished. Do what other people do, and whatever happens to them will also happen to you. What is so special and technical about that? What has scientific psychology really added to our folk knowledge?

The Importance of Scientific Studies

In the first place, scientific studies have shown that basic conditioning principles are in fact principles: they are independent of specific personalities and conditions. Almost any kind of behavior will increase when rewarded and decrease when unrewarded, regardless of the nature of the behavior or the reward.

Second, science has isolated certain critical factors—timing, for example. If the consequence of a behavior is delayed, the behavior is less likely to be affected. Feedback (in the form of reward or punishment) needs to be swift if it is to be maximally effective. Other more subtle timing factors have also been discovered. One good example is that partial reinforcement may make a behavior more lasting than continuous reinforcement. Once the individual learns that reinforcement will not occur after each action, he is more willing to continue the behavior for no reinforcement at all. "Someday . . ." he may be saying to himself. If that expectation exists, nonreinforced behavior may be extremely persistent.

A third important scientific contribution is perhaps a somewhat negative one: Controlling complex human behavior has proved to be extremely difficult, if not impossible. There are too many influences, and too many of them counteract each other. No one can really gain complete control of anyone else on the basis of conditioning alone. If such control exists, other factors (affection, for example) have contributed to it. In the laboratory, only small bits of relatively simple behavior can be fully conditioned. In the classroom, even when operant conditioning procedures are carefully installed, conditioning is frequently disrupted by other social influences. Children or prisoners who earn tangible rewards (such as trading stamps or money) for schoolwork are not really being controlled by such procedures. They engage in them because they want to, and frequently they do not want to for prolonged periods. Perhaps the aversive activity of studying negatively conditions the joy of collecting trading stamps! A conditioning principle is, after all, a conditioning principle.

In sum, laboratory studies have helped us recognize that although conditioning procedures are useful general tools, they are relatively superficial ones. In the Milgram obedience studies, the experimental conditioning principles alone could not have produced that kind of obedience on the part of human adults.

Guidelines to Classroom Conditioning

The tools of conditioning and the objectives of conditioning are two different things. If we want our schools to be places where children learn to be obedient to an authority just because he is an authority, conditioning tools can help produce that kind of obedience. If we want our schools to be places where children learn to direct their own activities and development, conditioning tools can help them learn how to do so. The basic principles of conditioning can be integrated with motivational and cognitive factors of all kinds.

If conditioning is to be effective, however, such integration should be thoughtfully planned by the relevant school personnel. All too often, conditioning procedures are used in careless ways that may defeat their actual purpose. The following guidelines may be helpful:

1. If school is a place where unpleasant things happen, students will be conditioned to dislike and/or fear school. If school is a place where pleasant things happen, students will be conditioned to like school. Such conditioning is not especially rational. Once a student has been conditioned to hate school, his hate may color almost everything about the school situation. Where there has been pervasive, negative conditioning of large numbers of students, education becomes almost impossible. Drastic renovations will be required if the school is to be salvaged.

2. Engineering a good conditioning (or reconditioning) program should be done in concert with the students themselves. In the first place, it is important to teach students how to carry out such engineering for themselves; in the second place, self-engineering will be much more effective than school engineering. One effective system involves "contracts": A student may agree to learn a set of mathematical or grammatical principles, either by himself or by carrying out certain procedures. When the contract is fulfilled, the student is rewarded appropriately (rewards himself), usually by engaging in learning behaviors he likes better.

There are many good ways of developing contract programs, depending upon the age and capabilities of the students, the materials, and the number of teachers available. Once a teaching staff begins to think in terms of contracts, ideas come rapidly. Try out as many as you can, and keep the ones that work best. (There are some commercial contract programs available, but these are tailored neither to particular students, nor to special teaching interests.)

Contract programs usually require more flexible school periods. The regimented march of 50-minute hours should be replaced by more flexible modular programming schedules. (Flexible schedules are, of course, desirable for many other reasons.) If notions of "contracts" and "modular scheduling" are new to you, contact your local school board for the locations of schools that have such programs in operation. If your school board has no such information and does not know how to refer you, then (1) worry about the knowledgeability of your school board and (2) read Silberman (1970) and contact the schools he praises for further information and visiting schedules.

3. Model the behaviors you want your students to imitate. This often means that you will engage in *mutual learning* situations with your students, rather than in *I teach—they learn* situations. If you want your students to learn how to learn effectively, then give them the opportunity to watch you learning—really learning, not just going through a set of rote procedures. Similarly, if teaching helps you learn (it should), then give your students the opportunity to teach and to model their own teaching behaviors on yours.

There are other ways in which conditioning principles can be used to achieve nonauthoritarian school objectives, but these suggestions should give you a start. Before going further in your planning, you will need to learn more about the important motivational influences of competence, curiosity, and their interaction (Chapters 11, 12, and 13).

Chapter 11   COMPETENCE AND ACHIEVEMENT

White's Theory of Competence Motivation

In 1959, Robert W. White published an article called "Motivation Reconsidered: The Concept of Competence." In it, he considered many theories of motivation, many experiments, and many anecdotal accounts of motivated behavior. On the basis of this evidence, he concluded that there existed in human beings a biological drive toward mastery of the environment—a basic *competence motivation:*

> According to Webster, competence means fitness or ability, and the suggested synonyms include capability, capacity, efficiency, proficiency, and skill. It is therefore a suitable word to describe such things as grasping and exploring, crawling and walking, attention and perception, language and thinking, manipulating and changing the surroundings, all of which promote an effective—a competent—interaction with the environment. It is true, of course, that maturation plays a part in all these developments, but this part is heavily overshadowed by learning in all the more complex accomplishments like speech or skilled manipulation. I shall argue that it is necessary to make competence a motivational concept; there is a *competence motivation* as well as competence in its more familiar sense of achieved capacity. The behavior that leads to the building up of effective grasping, handling, and letting go of objects, to take one example, is not random behavior produced by a general overflow of energy. It is directed, selective, and persistent, and it is continued not because it serves primary drives, which indeed it cannot serve until it is almost perfected, but because it satisfies an intrinsic need to deal with the environment. (White, 1959, pp. 317–318)

193

We read in Part I of the stages of cognitive development described by Piaget, Bruner, and Werner. In Chapter 14 we will read of the stages of personality development described by Freud, Erikson, and White, for White believes that the growth of competence has characteristic effects on the human personality. Whereas Freud accounted for these effects in terms of sexual motivation and Erikson accounts for them in terms of drives for security and identity, White sees them as an accompaniment to changes in an individual's ability to have an effect on his environment. Probably all three theorists are right to some extent, which is why we will consider them together.

In this present section, our emphasis will be on factors that affect the sense of competence, as well as on the significance of competence for other kinds of behavior.

McClelland's Theory of Achievement Motivation

Closely related to competence theory is another theory that also originated at Harvard (White was a Harvard professor)—the theory of *achievement motivation* defined originally by Henry Murray (1938) and extended by David McClelland. According to McClelland (1955), achievement motives differ from competence motives in two ways: (1) They include a standard of evaluation (not merely doing a job, but doing a *good* job) and (2) they produce an emotion (sense of joy or satisfaction or anxiety) which is a result of personal acceptance of that standard.

McClelland and his associates have devised a number of ways of assessing the need for achievement (sometimes abbreviated *nAch*). Originally, it was done through an analysis of stories told to a special group of pictures. For example, the following two stories were told to a picture of a boy with some school books, staring off into space.

[HIGH ACHIEVEMENT IMAGERY]

The boy is thinking about a career as a doctor. He sees himself as a great surgeon performing an operation. He has been doing minor first aid work on his injured dog, and discovers he enjoys working with medicine. He thinks he is suited for this profession and sets it as an ultimate goal in life at this moment. He has not weighed the pros and cons of his own ability and has let his goal blind him to his own inability. An adjustment which will injure him will have to be made.

[LOW ACHIEVEMENT IMAGERY]

A young fellow is sitting in a plaid shirt and resting his head on one hand. He appears to be thinking of something. His eyes appear a little sad. He may have been involved in something that he is very sorry for. The boy is thinking over what he has done. By the look in his eyes we can tell that he is very sad about it. I believe that the boy will break down any minute if he continues in the manner in which he is now going. (McClelland, Atkinson, Clark, and Lowell, 1953, pp. 118–121)

Of course, not all stories are as clear-cut as these, but the scoring system is nevertheless a reliable one. Its development has made possible many studies of the way in which the drive to master one's environment may be associated with other behavior.

BEHAVIOR ASSOCIATED WITH ACHIEVEMENT DRIVE

Although achievement motivation is probably biological in origin, its direction and intensity may be greatly affected by learning and circumstances. Even basic measurement procedures must take this fact into account.

Ego-Involvement and Achievement Drive

In order to obtain a reasonably accurate estimate of a subject's achievement motivation, McClelland found it was necessary to present the picture task in a particular way that involved the *arousal* of the achievement motive by *ego-involvement instructions* relevant to a preliminary task of some sort. For example, in one experiment the following instructions were given:

> The tests which you are going to take indicate, in general, a person's level of intelligence. They were taken from a group of tests which were used to select Washington administrators and officer candidates for the OSS during the past war. Thus, in addition to general intelligence, they bring out an individual's capacity to organize material, his ability to evaluate situations quickly and accurately—in short, these tests demonstrate whether or not a person is suited to be a leader. (McClelland, Atkinson, Clark, and Lowell, 1953, pp. 102–103)

The task that followed was simply anagrams (word-building), but the subjects apparently took it quite seriously. After the anagrams, the subjects were administered the achievement test pictures and wrote their stories. Note that the ego-involving instructions did not refer directly to the pictures. If they had, then subjects (particularly college freshmen) might have been frightened into a "freeze"—an inability to write any stories at all.

Family Influences

The fact that achievement motivation may not appear clearly unless circumstances have aroused it suggests that family and social arousal conditions are important. Even though the drive may be a natural one, it may be elicited more by some conditions than by others.

The earliest study of family influences was carried out by Marian Winterbottom in 1953. She obtained stories from children (boys) between the ages of 8 and 10 and correlated intensity of achievement motive with the questionnaire responses of the mothers. Brown has given an excellent summary of this study in his *Social Psychology:*

Each mother was asked to tell by what age she expected her child to: (1) know his way around the city; (2) try new things for himself; (3) do well in competition; (4) make his own friends; and attain other such goals.

On the four items listed above mothers of high-scoring sons expected the accomplishment at a markedly earlier age than did mothers of low-scoring sons. However, there were not differences of this kind on all of the demands about which Winterbottom inquired. The demands yielding such differences all seem to be concerned with doing *new* things independently. Demands that a child take over certain necessary care-taking tasks from the parents were not made at an earlier age by mothers of high-scoring sons. Such tasks as getting dressed and getting ready for bed are duties a parent must perform if a child does not. Mothers of high-scoring sons are not concerned with unloading these duties at an early age. Their concern is rather that a boy should begin early to move out on his own, to acquire skill and explore possibilities. Winterbottom conceptualizes their attitude as a concern with early independence training. (Brown, 1965, p. 447)

A Family Experiment by Rosen and D'Andrade

In a subsequent study, Rosen and D'Andrade (1959) pointed out that in addition to independence training, parents may also provide direct achievement training, both in the goals and standards of excellence they set for their children and in the methods of control they use to make sure these standards are maintained. Rosen also emphasized the importance of the father in these matters.

To explore these related issues, Rosen and his associates visited forty boys between the ages of 9 and 11 in their homes. Half these boys had (on previous testing) been found to be high in achievement motivation, and half were low. Rosen then administered a special block-building task in the home under the parents' supervision. Each child was blindfolded and asked to build a tower out of irregularly shaped blocks. The parents were told that this was a test of their son's ability to build things and that they could say anything to help their son, but must not physically help him by touching the blocks. A standard was introduced by telling parents that the average boy could build a tower of eight blocks under these conditions. Thus, we have the ego-involvement (on the part of both parents and children) necessary to the arousal of the achievement motive, and we have several possible ways in which parental influence could be expressed: as achievement training, independence training, or direct behavior control.

In general, Rosen found that there was less evidence of independence training (for example, withholding verbal directions) on the part of the parents than of direct achievement training. Parents of boys who had shown high need for achievement on the picture tests typically set higher standards for their boys on the block-building task, expected more improvement, and controlled behavior more directly—by expressions of warmth or rejection—than did parents of boys with low achievement needs. Further, there were interesting differences between the fathers and mothers, as shown in Figure 11.1.

The profiles in Figure 11.1 must be carefully related to the labels; note, for example, that some of the characteristics are labeled "more," and some are labeled "less." The general picture of differences between mothers and fathers in responding to boys of high and low achievement motivation is clear, however. Parents seem to respond in complementary ways to their children. Whereas the fathers of high *nAch* boys tend to offer fewer directions, less push, more autonomy, and more warmth, the mothers of high *nAch* boys tend to be opposite in all these behaviors except warmth.

The reverse pattern appears for the parents of low *nAch* boys. The fathers give more specific directions, push more, interfere more (less autonomy), and are more rejecting; whereas the mothers tend to be opposite in these behaviors, except for rejection. Like the fathers, the mothers withhold warmth from children with low need for achievement.

Changes in Family Influences

Complex patterns of this sort generally appear in any carefully analyzed study of home influences. Educators must beware of oversimplifying the joint role of parents in affecting a child's achievement motivation; the role of even one parent may change when a longer span of development is considered.

Six years later, Feld (1967) went back to visit some of Winterbottom's 1953 subjects, who were now about 15 years old. Feld retested both the boys and their mothers and found that, whereas the degree of achievement motivation remained fairly consistent (the boys who were below or above average on the childhood measure also tended to be below or above

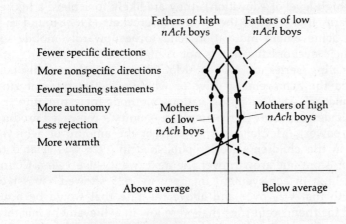

Figure 11.1 Profiles of mothers and fathers of boys with different degrees of achievement motivation. (Rosen and D'Andrade, 1959, pp. 205–206)

average on the adolescent measure), the mothers' attitudes were no longer the same. There was no longer a clear correlation between independence training (or the mothers' attitudes toward independence) and adolescent achievement motivation. The inconsistency may have arisen from chance errors of measurement, or it may represent a real change. Mothers who encourage independence in childhood may worry more about it during adolescence; mothers who encourage dependence in childhood may push toward independence in adolescence. More longitudinal studies of this type will be needed before we can be sure.

Culture and Achievement Drive
In addition to family influences, social class may affect achievement motives and behavior. Rosen (1956) studied high school boys who differed in both level of achievement need and socioeconomic background. He found that 64 percent of the middle-class boys were high need-achievers, but only 26 percent of the lower-class boys fit into that category. However, when it came to school grades, only 66 percent of the high need-achievers in the middle-class group obtained a B average or better; 75 percent of the high need-achievers in the lower class group did so. The implication, then, is that although fewer lower-class boys will be highly motivated toward achievement, the high need-achievers can succeed academically as well as middle-class children. (Some of the factors that may produce low nAch in lower-class students are discussed in Chapter 15.)

As one might expect, level of achievement motivation is associated with the amount of education one obtains. Veroff and his colleagues (1960) found that subjects who were above average in achievement motive were more likely to go on to college. Similarly (and perhaps because of their relatively high level of education), they are likely to achieve a higher occupational status than that of their fathers. Crockett (1962) found that people high in achievement motivation tend to be upwardly mobile socially, even if their level of education is not as high as it could be.

In a fascinating series of studies, McClelland (1961) and his colleagues assessed the achievement drive of whole societies by analyzing folklore and children's stories. Using various methods for estimating the rate of economic development (for example, a country's increased production of electric power), McClelland showed that the amount of achievement imagery in the children's stories published in 1925 was related to predicted rate of economic growth over the next twenty-five years. Countries that were high in achievement imagery in 1925 showed a burst of economic growth that was over and above the rate that would be ordinarily predicted for them; countries that were low in achievement imagery showed less than the predicted economic growth. Some of the countries are listed in Table 11.1.

Interestingly, the achievement imagery found in children's stories published during 1950 did not show a backward relationship to the coun-

Table 11.1
Rate of Economic Growth and Level of Achievement Imagery in Children's Stories, 1925

COUNTRY	ACHIEVEMENT IMAGERY LEVEL IN CHILDREN'S STORIES	GAIN OR LOSS OVER PREDICTED ECONOMIC GROWTH
Sweden	2.19	+ 3.17
United States	1.90	+ 1.86
Great Britain	2.10	+ 1.65
Hungary	1.29	− .26
Greece	0.38	− .52
Spain	0.81	− .63
Russia	0.95	− 1.26

SOURCE: Based on data in McClelland, 1961.

try's economic achievement; only the 1925 measure of achievement imagery was correlated with the economic spurt (or lack of it). McClelland concludes:

> It is difficult to argue from these data that material advance came first and created a higher need for achievement. Rather the reverse appears to be true—high [achievement imagery] levels are associated with subsequently more rapid economic development. Marx appears to have been somewhat premature in dismissing psychology as a major determinant in history. (McClelland, 1961, p. 93)

You can probably think of several interpretations of this phenomenon. You might guess, for example, that the achievement imagery in the books influenced the children who read them to become highly motivated toward achievement. Although McClelland believes such influences exist, it is not likely that he would have agreed with this interpretation of the children's literature, simply because there was not enough time for the influence to have taken effect. The countries began to show economic spurts before the children who were reading the books had grown up. McClelland believes, rather, that the books revealed the achievement motivation level of the adults who were writing them. The same adults who wrote the books pushed the society to higher economic levels.

McClelland also wondered if there were differences in the *type* of achievement imagery between high- and low-achieving countries. The scoring categories include such imagery as anticipations of success or failure, positive or negative emotions, and help by another person, as well as instrumental imagery—imagery about means to obtaining goals and obstacles. The countries that showed an unusually high economic spurt also showed an unusually high preoccupation (in the children's stories) with *instrumental* imagery:

> Psychologically speaking, what such findings seem to mean is that [the achievement imagery] . . . from more rapidly developing countries . . . is more apt to be "means" oriented . . . than goal oriented. The achievement sequence [in the story] more often dwells on obstacles to success and specific means of overcoming them, rather than on the goal itself, the

desire for it, and the emotions surrounding attaining or failing to attain it. The adaptive quality of such a concern with means is obvious: a people who *think* in terms of ways of overcoming obstacles would seem more likely to find ways of overcoming them in fact. At any rate that is precisely what happens: the "means" oriented stories come from countries which have managed to overcome the obstacles to economic achievement more successfully than the other countries. (McClelland, 1961, pp. 104–105)

The general principle of *means awareness* has important implications for a variety of motivational situations.

ASPIRATION AND FAILURE

To understand achievement behavior, we need to be familiar with two other theoretical constructs: *level of aspiration* and *fear of failure*. The former is associated with Kurt Lewin and his students (Lewin, Dembo, Festinger, and Sears, 1944); the latter, with John W. Atkinson and his students and colleagues (Atkinson, 1965) and also with S. B. Sarason and his colleagues (Sarason et al., 1960), who have developed a measure of anxiety that Atkinson adopted as a way of estimating fear of failure.

What Is a Level of Aspiration?

Informally, a level of aspiration may be revealed by a person's goal or by his behaviors in pursuit of it. If you ask a student, "What grade are you trying for on the next history quiz?" and he says "An A," then you know what his level of aspiration is for that particular event. You might also infer his level of aspiration from the fact that he is spending three hours a day in the library studying history.

Laboratory investigations of levels of aspiration have shown that they generally tend to go up with success, as one might predict. If the student got his A, he might try for the Dean's List by attempting to pull up his grades in all his courses. But success may lead to other kinds of aspiration changes as well. The subject is primarily characterized by a high degree of personal absorption, if he is permitted to set and adjust his own goals.

If a person freely chooses his own goals, his behavior is based on certain contingencies which he confronts in the course of his action. If he chooses an activity which he never attempted before, his first attempts will be purely exploratory. He will test his skills, the materials, the time requirements, and the tools and equipment. He will discover minor problems and solve them if he can. He is likely to make only a minimal commitment to the task. The question of success or failure does not arise because his goal, if he has one, is merely to see whether or not the thing is possible at all. Once this exploration ends and he begins a more or less systematic attempt to produce something, he very likely will set implicit or explicit *levels of aspiration* for his successive attempts; then he can define success or failure. He seldom needs anyone to tell him when he succeeds or fails because he sets his own standards of performance. At first these standards are likely to be modest, relatively easy to achieve, but he moves always toward standards more difficult to achieve. The standards he uses are quite varied and may change from one attempt to the next. Now he tries to produce a result as good as the last one, but quicker. Next, he may disregard time altogether and try to improve the product. Later he may concentrate on the smoothness of the process and attempt to swing elegantly through a well-ordered and efficient routine. He may discover and invent new processes, or adapt new materials or new methods of work. To the casual uninterested observer this may all seem repetitive and dull, but the operator, the worker, may be intensely interested because he never has exactly the same goal on two successive trials. He is in charge of the goals and their general trend is upward, always ahead of his actual performance, always aimed at doing something better. By this process of gently spurring himself to successively higher achievements, he approaches mastery of himself and his environment. He is making himself a better man. (Diggory, 1966, pp. 125–126)

Expectation of Eventual Success

The behavior described above may be one subroutine in a larger routine of overall achievement. It may, for example, refer to a sawing operation that is part of the larger operation of building a boat. Diggory (1966) has emphasized that success or failure on such suboperations will have a strong effect on the immediate aspiration level (the very next goal), but may not change the overall expectation of success. Even if one is not good at sawing, one may still expect to succeed in boat-building. One may even experience a succession of failures in various suboperations (sawing, nailing, and planing) without giving up hope for the boat. Other suboperators may be employed (a carpenter, for example), or the suboperations may be declared unnecessary (as in a prefabricated boat).

Several of Diggory's students have studied the effects on overall success expectancy of using up one's alternatives. As one would predict, success expectancy remains relatively high as long as alternatives exist; but when they are all used up, hope of success may plunge *unless another overall goal can be substituted*. Two basic strategies, then, may keep morale high, even when achievement is proving difficult: (1) Look for alternative methods, or suboperations, for achieving the goal and (2) if alternative methods are all used up, try to substitute a new, equally attractive goal for the original one.

Fear of Failure

While it seems clear that these aspiration strategies are powered by the positive hope of success, it may be less clear that another motive is also at work: fear of failure. These two motives may have quite different effects. If the desire to achieve is strong, work may be undertaken with zest and persistence. If the fear of failure is strong, work may be abandoned; the best way to avoid failure may be not to undertake a task at all.

But a sense of failure can also be avoided by a form of magical thinking. One may hope that some exceptional thing (a fairy godmother?) will occur and make success happen. For that reason, individuals with a very strong fear of failure may react in a way that is opposite to task avoidance: They may unrealistically plunge into tasks that are far too difficult for them.

Failure and Unrealism

This phenomenon was illustrated in a study by Mahone (1960) of the vocational aspirations of college students. First, the achievement motivation of students was measured by the picture method described above. In addition, fear of failure was measured by a test anxiety scale similar to one that will be discussed in Chapter 14. The scale measures anxiety about testing situations as well as the subject's awareness of the extent to which anxiety interferes with his test performance. An illustrative item is: "In a course where I have been doing poorly, my fear of a bad grade cuts down my efficiency."

Test anxiety is generally not correlated with achievement motivation. Subjects may be high in one but not the other, high in both, or low in both. Mahone separated his subjects into groups of that sort and looked to see how their vocational aspirations varied. Each subject had also filled out a vocational questionnaire that indicated his objectives, his concept of the skills required, and an estimate of his own relative skill. These answers were then compared to the estimates made by two experienced clinical psychologists of the subjects' *actual* abilities (based on grade point average and other factors).

The results are shown in Table 11.2. Subjects who were high in failure anxiety were much more likely to be unrealistic about their vocational futures: 10 out of 55 of the unrealistic subjects were underaspiring (that is, their levels of aspiration were lower than they should have been, according to the psychologists); and 45 out of 55 were unrealistic in the opposite direction—they were overaspiring. Subjects who were low in failure anxiety were more often realistic about their vocational aspirations—especially if they were also high in achievement motivation.

This experiment illustrates a general pattern that may follow failure: The aspiration level may not go down; instead, it may show a paradoxical increase. Of course, this is not true of all individuals, but the existence of confusion about what to do next and of magical thinking of various kinds makes the teacher's management of failing students especially difficult.

Table 11.2
Achievement Motivation, Failure Anxiety, and Realism of Vocational Aspiration

| TESTED LEVEL | | | VOCATIONAL ASPIRATIONS, | |
| ACHIEVEMENT MOTIVATION | FAILURE ANXIETY | NUMBER OF SUBJECTS | PERCENTAGE OF GROUP | |
			REALISTIC	UNREALISTIC
High	High	31	48%	52%
High	Low	36	75	25
Low	High	28	39	61
Low	Low	40	68	32

SOURCE: Based on data in Mahone, 1960.

Failure and Frustration

Another aspect of failure, one that has received special attention from psychologists, is frustration. Largely because of Freud's emphasis on it (see Chapter 14), frustration has become something of a hobgoblin in child-rearing and education. It has been considered the root of many negative behaviors—aggression, hopelessness, immature play behavior, and confusion. (The classic studies are reviewed in Mussen, Conger, and Kagan, 1969, pp. 331–335.) While it is certainly true that these negative behaviors can occur, it does not follow that frustration is entirely responsible for them. Some failure, and some resulting frustration, is bound to happen in classrooms and elsewhere. Teachers will want to remove unnecessary frustration as much as possible, but another part of the job will be to help students learn how to respond to frustration. This will generally involve rethinking the situation, trying to find alternative paths to the goal, or trying to find a substitute goal that is just as satisfactory. A student who lacks the grades to become a laboratory biologist may find an equally rewarding life in the forestry service, for example.

In many cases it will be possible to help a student handle his own frustration by teaching him how to work out a realistic program of achievement. His frustration may be arising primarily from his confusion about how to get what he wants. Many young people, for example, have rather magical expectations—if their wishes do not instantly come to pass, frustration and discouragement result. The problem may not be lack of ability, but simply lack of realistic planning. We will pursue the point in the next two sections of this chapter.

Failure and Depression

One final point about failure must be made first, however: the problem of serious emotional depression. A teacher may discover that a particular failing student is totally unresponsive to various suggestions for planning a new or alternative enterprise, whereas another student, with perhaps an even worse record, is responding eagerly:

> If we put together our general impressions of objective failure situations which we have witnessed or experienced, it appears that there are two general classes of reactions. In one case, a single failure seems to crush the individual so that he behaves and talks as though he were not good for anything, in spite of all evidence to the contrary. Other people seem to shrug off failures and quickly take up some other task in which they become equally absorbed. . . . [Similarly], after success some people are in a state of very high elation; judging from their words and actions, there is nothing they could not do or would not dare. Others who have succeeded, though they may act quite pleased, have a more sober or moderate reaction, and they quickly take up the pursuit of some other goal. In short, it appears that for some people, or in some conditions, either success or failure will generalize . . . to many other aspects of a person's goal-striving attitudes, but in other cases this generalization is much more limited, if it occurs at all. (Diggory, 1966, pp. 229–230)

To account for this "spread of effect," Diggory has hypothesized that we each have personal capacities (he calls them *alpha capacities*) that are especially important to us because they are especially relevant to the achievement of our major goals. For example, playing the piano may be critical to a potential (she hopes) Miss America, but not at all critical to a football player. The sportsman does, however, have several alpha capacities of his own. *Failure of an alpha capacity may have catastrophic effects on the human personality.* In effect, the individual may say to himself: "Well, if I'm no good at *that*, then I'm no good at *anything*." This would be the condition, then, for a sense of failure to spread throughout the personal universe.

One mark of our ignorance of human motivation lies in our inability to detect individuals' alpha areas in advance. In schools, industrial organizations, neighborhoods, and supermarkets there are people whose casual behavior may be far more critical to their general morale than we realize. Of course, they do not wear signs saying, "Watch out! I'm expressing my alpha capacities!" but we should know more than we do about how to detect their special vulnerabilities. In the absence of such knowledge, all a teacher can do is think long and hard about the problem of a student's personal reaction to failure. In many cases, the psychological sting of a failing enterprise may produce that extra effort necessary for success; the prospect of an embarrassing defeat may mobilize a student's resources in a powerful way. But in another case, it may lead to suicide. This may happen to only one student in a hundred thousand. The trouble is, we do not know which one.

COGNITIVE AVAILABILITY OF PATHS TO A GOAL

When we have selected a personal goal, how clear are we about the steps involved in achieving it? Frequently we are not clear at all, even when we have had some experience tackling goals of the same type. The situation is more muddled when we have had no experience at all. The intensity of our motivation to achieve that goal may be very much influenced by the clarity of our instrumental concepts. If we know how to get there, we set off with greater zest. W. C. H. Prentice takes up the point in illuminating detail:

> The setting of personal goals seems to be enhanced by the opportunity to see a graded series of achievements. . . . Let me illustrate. If I asked a 15-year-old boy to attempt to high jump 7 feet, he would almost certainly give up very soon. But if I let him start with a height that can be achieved and show him how practice and training can help him to inch his way upward over a period of years, I may be able to make a high jumper out of him. Or suppose I invite you to run for President. A realistic view of what that would mean were you to set out on your own would probably make the program unappealing. It would fall in the "too difficult" category. But the apparent degree of difficulty might change if I presented you

with a series of stratagems leading to successive subgoals of precinct leader, city chairman, governor, etc.

Our knowledge in this area is slight, indeed, but we do have a few facts. Studies of level of aspiration show that success typically leads to the setting of higher sights but that success also leads to more realistic goals than failure does. Apparently it is important to permit the aspirant to very distant goals an opportunity to avoid the cognitive confusion that can be produced by failure. It is necessary not only for a properly graded series of steps to exist, but also for them to be apprehended. And that fact emphasizes the importance of recognizing the motivational differences that may exist [not only] between clearly presented situations and less clearly presented ones, but also between people capable of understanding what lies ahead and those unable to do so. The attractive progression from subgoal to subgoal can occur only when it is *cognitively available* to the actor.

It may be valuable in this connection to note that in games we typically arrange things so that the direction of paths to the goal is much clearer than it is likely to be in life's ordinary tasks. Even in a game like chess or bridge, where uncountable combinations of steps are available, the game provides strict constraints, and the shrewd player may know within reasonably narrow limits the probabilities of success on any one play. The dull player will probably find the same game confusing and, therefore, unattractive. It seems likely that the clarity of paths toward the goal is part of the attractiveness of the entire enterprise. At least we may note that people who are skillful in handling human beings make regular use of this motivational principle. . . . The salesman or politician will typically attempt to diminish uncertainties for you with respect to the next step and where it will lead, while at the same time showing you the magnificent possibilities of the steps to come. Any theory of motivation will have to find room for an assessment of the clarity with which the path to the goal is delineated. (Prentice, 1961, p. 508)

As Prentice himself immediately goes on to explain, this clarity can reach the point of aversive dullness. Many of us, for example, would not feel especially motivated by the prospect of three years of high-jump training, no matter how clearly the steps were explained. The point to be emphasized here is the extent to which we often overlook cognitive clarity, or cognitive confusion, as an important factor in achievement motivation.

Culture, Clarification, and Hope

The problem may be most vividly illustrated in contemporary life by the failure of many work-training opportunities to remotivate people who have lived all their lives in disadvantaged situations. In many underprivileged areas—from the depressed agricultural lands of the South to Appalachian mining towns and Northern ghettos—motivation is not produced by the introduction of shiny new government programs to upgrade skills and increase salary potential. Nor is education "for the better life" welcomed and utilized. On the contrary, the programs typically perish for lack of attendance, at spectacular cost to taxpayers.

What is going wrong? Why is it that undereducated, underemployed, even starving people will not grab at a free opportunity to move upward?

To a large extent, these motivational deficiencies may be produced by cognitive confusions of the sort described above. If we do not know where we are going or how to get there, it may be better not to move at all.

Successful programs have usually become part of the life of the particular area and attempted to achieve only one small step upward at a time. They have not taught a whole new method of building a house, but rather how to repair the already-existing houses. What is being taught is the *idea* that a person can be instrumental in the achievement of his own goals and the *idea* that goals can be achieved by taking one small, satisfying step at a time. This amounts to cognitive reprogramming of emotional and motivational systems: First you change your thinking about a problem, and then you discover that you feel like tackling it. Cognitive reprogramming is opposite to the usual procedure, in which first your feelings are changed (by the promise of special rewards), and then you work on the problem. The point about cognitive reprogramming is that it may unleash natural competence and achievement drives far more powerful than the promise of an extrinsic reward.

Classroom Clarification Strategies

Good teachers have always known how to "get a student started" on a long series of tasks by showing him where he is going and how he can get there. To some students, learning how to read, for example, is an undifferentiated muddle. So is the arithmetic workbook. The teacher who helps such a student by showing him a system for moving ahead may be startled by a sudden display of eagerness and concentration.

In many cases, however, the problem is not merely the student's lack of system, but his desperation. He will not let himself use a system he already knows about. In the next section, we will consider a case of that type and see how it was handled by a wise teacher.

THE CASE OF ESTHER

In a recent series of articles, the problem of the urban school failure was analyzed by both a psychiatrist and a teacher. The psychiatrist first pointed out that the student's background produced special problems involving expectation and achievement:

> My convictions came from experiences with families of such students. It had become clear that often these parents had serious personal problems. Their own unhappiness and dissatisfactions made them unable to provide any model for successful, productive living for their child. The bitter socio-economic realities under which many of them lived served to increase their own feeling of failure, of being unloved, both in their own childhood and now. Each parent felt angry at the bitter reality and the inability of the other parent to make him happy, and therefore had little sustained love to give an infant. They were unable to enjoy, praise, and encourage their child's discoveries and early adventures in learning. Such a simple and vital experience as being aided to persist in their learning

efforts until they could master a task was not theirs. The parents either hastily did it for the child so as to be done with it, or left the child alone to experience continual frustration until he gave up. In either case the child felt dissatisfied, disgruntled, and finally wanted someone else to do it for him. Such a child had a valid belief *that someone owed him something*. Thus, working on his own and for himself was very difficult.

Their early disgruntled, angry feelings often have prevented the mastery of the fundamentals of schooling. They usually cannot read well. Mathematics seems an insurmountable obstacle. All learning requires some application and since they have not experienced satisfactions that come from perseverance and the completion of tasks, they become restless and easily distracted. They also feel continually unhappy and angry at the persons who require that they undergo such frustrations. Underlying all of this, too, is the desire to be able to do the tasks, to experience the pleasure others seem to get, and to be able to feel adequate and worthwhile in the school setting. Such students are therefore in constant conflict with themselves and with their environment.

The monumental task of helping them to begin to learn and to want to go on learning requires an endless patience. Thus, the teacher by his persistence provides the necessary living model for the student: a parental model who believes the student can learn and who is willing to take the time to stand by and help him learn. The youngster hopefully experiences for the first time an adult who will not react to the angry, bitter, and hostile expression of his internal conflicts and frustrations with retaliatory anger and hurt self-esteem. Such a teacher's firm insistence on what he knows must be done by the student, so that he begins to learn, results in the gradual achievement of those satisfactions that come from mastering tasks. . . .

One of the obstacles to [this] learning process is the student's recurrent hope that magically he will acquire the skills in which he is deficient. This wishful fantasy, that by magic rather than by hard work he will get something, was acquired from repeated experiences with his parents, who themselves could only express wishes for solutions to their troubles. When such a student meets a teacher who has a similar hope—that is, that a teacher's transient interest and concern will magically cause the student to learn—then both student and teacher are inevitably disappointed. The teacher feels hurt, let down, and angry that his concern carried no magical cure for the student's learning problems, and the student has again encountered an adult who could not help him learn. He feels angry, hopeless, and distrustful of all adults who promise much but never come through. (Berlin, 1966, p. 78)

The impressive thing about magical expectations is that they are easier for the teacher, too. The sentimental hope that one's love will cause a youngster to start learning is much more enjoyable than the hard work (and at least temporary unpopularity) involved in making sure that he does. Let us look at one example of the daily record of an unsentimental teacher in Dr. Berlin's project:

I had to build and strengthen Esther's academic skills. She was a poor reader. Her attention span was short. She had no success in class. My biggest job with Esther, as indeed with all these youngsters, was making her stick to a job until it was finished.

I remember the morning Esther graduated from short division to long division. The word *long* in long division had defeated Esther in elementary school. She had never really tried to master these problems. She was terribly afraid of failing. I had told her the day before that we were going to move on to long division. She had told me that she could not do it. Never could and never would. She came into the room quietly, put her head down on her folded arms and closed her eyes. It took about fifteen minutes to get the rest of the class settled with questions answered and work well under way. Then I told Esther to get her work out.

"I got a headache, Mr. Ott. I wanna see the nurse."

"Oh, come on, Esther. I just saw you playing softball last period. You're just afraid of this division."

"I can't do that old stuff."

"Come on. Get your paper and pencil and I'm going to show you that all you have to remember are three simple steps and there isn't any number you can't divide."

When she had gone through a problem once without my help I left her and went back to the other students. In two or three minutes Esther was at my desk.

"I have to get a drink of water."

"Let's see your problem. Did you finish it?"

"No. I can't do that old stuff."

"You just did one. You sit down and finish this problem. If you still have to have water then I'll let you go."

"That's chicken, Mr. Ott."

"Go on now. Sit down and do the best you can."

Two or three minutes and she was back. "I gotta go to the toilet."

"You haven't finished that problem?"

"No. But honest-to-god, I've gotta go bad, Mr. Ott."

"Then it's going to be too bad for all of us because I expect you to knuckle down to this work."

We went back and forth like this for a few minutes. I was chicken and a dirty rat, but she finally understood that she was going to stick to that work until she whipped it. I knew there was no way I could make her work but I would not go on with anything more until we had made it up this step. This took the better part of a week, but we made it. There were many other steps, but somehow with this experience behind us the others never really seemed too tough.

Esther graduated last semester. She came back to visit some weeks ago with the news that her grades in junior college were good enough that she was accepted into a nursing college. . . . She is a bright girl who has more and more turned her intelligence to academic progress, but two years ago I would not have given two cents for her chances of lasting out the semester. As a matter of fact, the odds on me were not much better. (Ott, 1966, pp. 78–92)

Many of the theoretical principles we have discussed so far in Part III are illustrated in Ott's record: contingency management (getting a drink of water after you finish a problem), modeling, cognitive clarification (the three steps in a long division problem), and so forth. You can probably think of other techniques that might have helped—a teaching machine, for example, that set up Esther's drill problems for her. But then there is the question of whether the machine would have been able to provide the steady human expectation that Esther could, in fact, achieve what others could achieve and become a worthwhile person.

Human expectation can have a profound effect—when it is not magical. Nonmagical expectation must always be accompanied by a *plan of action* and a *method of evaluating results.* Where neither of these conditions have been met, you can be sure that only magical expectations are being displayed.

Let us consider that assertion in more detail.

MAGICAL EXPECTATIONS

It is September, and school is beginning. In a typical first grade, two-thirds of the children will fall within a range the teacher considers normal. Of the remaining third, half will be gifted, and half will be extremely slow.

In an atypical first grade, say, a ghetto or Appalachian school, from one-half to two-thirds of the children may fall into the extremely slow range, by the teacher's standards. That is, the teaching techniques that have been developed for average children will not work. The children will not learn.

Unless she is a saint of some kind, the teacher will rapidly become extremely discouraged and decide that the situation is almost hopeless. Many of the other teachers (perhaps all of them) in the school will agree. The administration will agree. By the end of October, the entire system will have decided that 50 to 60 percent of the first-grade children are too slow to achieve very much. The system may then treat the children, in subtle and not-so-subtle ways, as failures. For the rest of their schooling period, the system and most of the people in it will be set for these children to fail.

This is an extremely damaging situation, but it is important to understand that it is a real situation, not a magical one. The simple mental act of expecting a student to succeed is no remedy at all. A student cannot succeed if the system has no resources for guiding him—specifically, if it can provide no alternative ways of teaching him.

The Rosenthal and Jacobson Report

One recently published report on some effects of simple changes in teacher expectation is completely misleading on this point. Like many apparent panaceas, it has been widely quoted. Because it is important to understand what is methodologically wrong with this report, we will consider it in some detail. The book in question is *Pygmalion in the Classroom,* by Rosenthal and Jacobson (1968).

The authors begin by summarizing evidence that shows how experimenter bias can affect experimental results. Psychological experiments, unlike those in chemistry or physics, often depend upon direct human interactions between experimenter and subject. If the experimenter is tired and tries to hurry a subject through the experiment, or if he signals by his voice or attitude that a particular sort of experimental result is good, he may bias the outcome of the study. Good experimenters build in checks and balances of various kinds to keep such biasing effects to a minimum, but the fact remains that many subtle behavioral cues may be detected by a responsive subject and acted upon. Is the same cueing effect taking place in classrooms? Rosenthal believes it might be.

In an attempt to test that possibility, Rosenthal and Jacobson (1968) administered a test to children from grades 1 through 6. In reality, it was a multi-aptitude test (TOGA, or Tests of General Achievement, developed by Flanagan). Rosenthal told teachers, however, that it was the Harvard Test of Inflected Acquisition, designed to discover children who were likely to show an IQ spurt in the following year. He then casually showed teachers a list of children the test had supposedly "discovered." These were the children, Rosenthal said, who could be expected to show the spurt; perhaps their teachers would be interested in knowing who they were. Nothing else was said or recommended. The experimenters withdrew. They returned the following spring, and the spring after that, to remeasure the children's IQ on the TOGA tests. In reality, the "spurters" had been selected randomly. There was no scientific reason whatsoever to assume that an IQ spurt was in fact expected of any of them. All that was really being manipulated was teacher expectation. Would the IQs of the children show an actual increase because of that expectation?

As one reads through this little book, a number of disturbing questions arise. For one thing, the teachers later said they actually did not remember who the experimenter said was supposed to show an IQ spurt and who was not. They only looked briefly at a list the experimenter showed them, and (like many teachers who participate in psychological experiments) dismissed it as irrelevant and got on with their jobs. Rosenthal believed the dismissal showed how teacher expectation will continue to function on an unconscious level. But it could also be argued that teacher expectation was never really affected to begin with, if the teachers could not even remember who their expectations were supposed to be about.

At any rate, the results of the study were said to show that first- and second-grade children did increase in IQ as a result of their teachers' expectations. That is, a child who had been expected to increase did increase, even though the expectation was not justified. (Rosenthal had designated "expectees" randomly, remember.) The experimenters believed this demonstrated the power of expectation. Perhaps it did, but this particular experiment could not really prove it.

To begin with, children in third, fourth, fifth, and sixth grades did not show any response to teacher expectancy. Although this might indicate that only young children are responsive, there are other possibilities. In a close examination of the actual IQ data, Snow (1969), another psychologist who reviewed the *Pygmalion* book, discovered a serious problem. The particular IQ test used (TOGA) does not have adequate published IQ norms for young children, especially for those from lower socioeconomic backgrounds. Rosenthal and his assistants therefore had to estimate IQs from the test scores, rather than by referring to published IQ tables. Some of these estimates were very strange. One child, for example, was alleged to have an original (before teacher expectancy was manipulated) IQ of 17. Such a child should have been little more than a vegetable. After the experimental period, the same child showed an IQ of 148. Was there really that enormous an increase? Or was the true IQ incorrectly estimated to begin with?

The average IQ for all first-grade children was originally estimated to be 58. Some children must therefore have been way below the IQ required for institutionalization. Did these children truly respond to teacher expectancy? Or was their true IQ correctly measured only the second time around? Did the third-, fourth-, fifth-, and sixth-grade children fail to show a response to teacher expectancy simply because their IQs had been correctly estimated from published tables the first time around?

In a way, Rosenthal proved his own thesis better than he intended. Wishes, hopes, expectations do alter the outcomes of experiments; but they do not alter them magically. They alter them through a chain of behaviors. In Rosenthal's case, belief in his thesis may have led to IQ estimates that would make the thesis work. Expectation, in other words, may have produced an alteration in the mathematical behavior of the researchers themselves.

Expectations and Plans

If teacher expectations matter, they matter because they affect behavior. The teacher who expects a child to fail probably behaves differently toward that child than toward a child who is expected to succeed. If you have given up on a child, you may not take that extra three or four minutes to explain something; you may not remember to praise him, even when he does something right. ("After all," you may think, "it won't last anyway.") You may not schedule him for the field trip. ("He has enough trouble keeping his mind on his work as it is.") You may not let him have the special art period. You may become angry at his behavior, not recognizing that it stems from failure and frustration, and punish him excessively. Research that can show us how teacher expectation produces teacher behavior which in turn affects pupil behavior is certainly needed. But until we understand the mechanisms of the effect of expectation, we will do better to concentrate on remedial strategies.

The teacher who wants a child to succeed will need to do more than change an expectation. The teacher who expects a child to succeed should have a plan for achieving that success and a way of knowing (evaluating) progress. The positive-thinking teacher also needs a variety of strategies for keeping that progress going. Without a solid pedagogical system, expectation may have no effect. With a solid pedagogical system, expectation is translated into a realistic program of action.

COMPETENCE TO ARGUE AND DOUBT

Subtle problems of teacher expectancy may be less serious, in the long run, than overt problems of teacher intention. Some teachers, alas, simply do not want their students to learn everything they could learn. The reason is simple: Students may develop the competence to disagree with the teacher.

As the Milgram studies (Chapter 10) seem to indicate, people generally do what they are told to do when they perceive the instruction to come from a reasonably legitimate authority. But information may interfere with the obedient response. Certainly, information as to the true nature of the Milgram experiments would have stopped subjects cold. Similarly, information may help us build up resistance to propaganda of various kinds, even teacher propaganda.

Competence to Resist Indoctrination

An experiment by Lewan and Stotland shows that even moderate amounts of information may increase resistance to an emotional appeal. The subjects were senior high school students in a social studies class. The main part of the experiment required them to listen to a speech about a small country called Andorra. Their attitudes toward Andorra were measured both before and after the speech. Half the students, however, received a fact sheet about Andorra before they heard the lecture; it contained such relatively neutral and dull information as the following:

> The country . . . uses both French and Spanish currencies since there is no such thing as Andorran coinage or money. Postal service is free within the country, being financed by the sale of Andorran stamps to stamp collectors. (Lewan and Stotland, 1961, p. 451)

The lecture, on the other hand, was anything but neutral.

> . . . The Arkansas hillbilly would be a sophisticated "man of the world" compared to the average Andorrese. It is revealing that the national economy is based upon immorality, is based upon smuggling, blackmarket, and theft to a large extent. In fact, if you were to ask a well-informed person what is the one thing for which Andorra is noted, the answer would probably be "the absence of morality." (Lewan and Stotland, 1961, p. 451)

Needless to say, after such an unfavorable description, all subjects changed their attitudes about Andorra in a negative direction. But the students who had received the neutral fact sheet were less negative than the students who had not. Even a little information may help students resist the influence of a prejudiced appeal.

Facts, however, may not be sufficient in themselves. In another study, Aronson, Turner, and Carlsmith (1963) showed that information itself may be used to produce mental acquiescence to so-called authorities.

Indoctrination and Authority

The subjects of the experiment were college students who volunteered to participate in an "experiment on esthetics." They met in small groups and were told that the experimenter was interested in how people evaluate poetry. First, the subjects were asked to rank nine stanzas from best to worst, according to how they felt about the poet's use of *alliteration* (for example, "in a summer season when soft was the sun").

Then the subjects read an essay entitled, "The Use of Alliteration in Poetry." The essay consisted of general statements about the good and bad uses of alliteration and used, as an example, a particular stanza that the experimental subjects had already ranked. The essays were cleverly prepared in advance so that the illustrative stanza "happened" to be the stanza each subject had ranked eighth—next to worst, in the subject's judgment.

For some of the subjects, the essay indicated that this particular verse was average (which would have been fifth instead of eighth in the ranking); for other subjects, the essay indicated that the particular verse was above average; and for still other subjects, the essay called the illustrative verse the best example of the use of alliteration in the whole sample. The essays were thus set up with varying degrees of contradiction of the subject's own judgment.

In addition to the contradiction, the credibility of the authority was varied. For half the subjects, the essay was said to have been written by T. S. Eliot. The rest were told the essay had been written by Miss Agnes Stearns, a student at Mississippi State Teachers College and a cousin of the experimenter. Miss Stearns planned to become an English teacher,

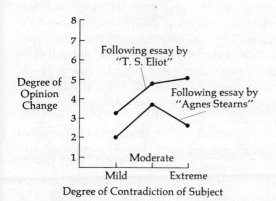

Figure 11.2 Degree of opinion change reported by students after reading an essay on poetry by one of two "authors." (Aronson, Turner and Carlsmith, 1963)

and she had asked her cousin to show the essay to some students to find out if it helped them evaluate poetry.

After the students had finished reading the essay, they were asked to rank the stanzas again. The main experimental question was whether or not they would change their opinion of the stanza they had ranked next to worst and whether or not the amount of change would be affected by the credibility of the authority. (The subjects, of course, knew nothing of this.)

As Figure 11.2 shows, the subjects changed their rankings more when they believed the essay had been written by Eliot than when they believed it to have been written by Miss Stearns, especially when the degree of contradiction was extremely high. Under the extreme condition, subjects who had read Miss Stearns' essay decided that *she* was wrong and were not affected by her judgment. In the less extreme condition, the subjects trusted Miss Stearns' judgment somewhat more than they trusted their own.

Defending a Judgment

What kind of teaching might have led students to defend their judgments against both Miss Stearns and Mr. Eliot? More or different information about alliteration? That might have helped, as we saw before. But another important factor might have been practice in defending a judgment. The competence to argue and doubt T. S. Eliot, or any other authoritative figure, partly arises from practice in arguing and doubting in the classroom. The teacher who is willing to provide both information and practice in doubting it will be going a long way toward the development of truly competent thinking in students.

The seminar program at St. John's College in Annapolis, Maryland, provides a good model for the development of such competence in college students. The model could easily be extended to high schools. At the first freshman seminar, students are told by the leader that they are responsible for everything they say throughout the year and that they must defend their statements. As a result, they develop skill in evaluating their own words before they speak them. This skill transfers to the evaluation of statements by others. For example, a student might state, "Anarchy is a bad political system." What, his fellow students will ask, do you mean by *anarchy*? by *bad*? and by *political system*? *Bad* when and under what conditions? Once a system of meanings has been established, the student must argue logically within that system.

The seminar leader is as liable to attack as the students. He too must argue logically within a fixed system of definitions. He may question students and force them to question their own statements. He models critical skills for his students, as well as thoughtful self-analysis. Leaders are not permitted to be subject-matter specialists. Good thinking is expected to be good thinking, no matter what the field. Logical thought (so the argument goes) can be exercised with reference to all types of content. As a teacher, you must develop the general competence to argue and doubt and to teach your students to argue and doubt. You are not permitted to cloak yourself in an aura of superior knowledge that your students may not question. After even a few weeks of such training, students would be better prepared to resist "authoritative" indoctrination. So would teachers.

COMPETENCE AND ACHIEVEMENT IN SCHOOLS

All students possess a drive to achieve something, somewhere, sometime. A major school problem, however, may be to awaken that drive with reference to education. Let us see how the principles we have discussed can be applied to school learning:

1. If, as White suggests, there is a basic need to deal with the environment competently, students should come equipped with a basic need to deal competently with school environments. We do not have to instill such a need through promises of rewards—but we do have to be careful to recognize the true nature of the school environment. It includes, for example, peer goals and influences that may be quite separate from those set by the school. A student's need to deal competently with one set of factors (say, drug pressures) may jeopardize his ability to deal competently with another (academic pressures).

2. The achievement needs of individual students can be assessed—by a trained psychologist if necessary, but also, informally, by teachers. Where academic achievement needs seem to be low, it may be helpful to contact fathers, since fathers seem to be more willing than mothers to give low *nAch* children a push.

3. Achievement needs appear to be affected by social class and by more general facets of modern culture. The current counterculture of many of our teenagers may signify a true shift in our society's orientation toward traditional achievements. Consequently, schools should be on the alert for newer relevancies: How are academic skills and concepts instrumental to new goals? Where teachers can help adolescents make such connections, new achievement drives may be unleashed.

4. Another way of stimulating achievement drives may be to let students set a series of goals for themselves. Teachers can judge aspiration levels in such cases. Are they realistic? Do students respond realistically to success and failure? If not, the student in question may be characterized more by fear of failure than hope of success.

5. When failure, frustration, and/or depression occur, try to help the student find equally satisfying alternate or substitute goals. Be on the watch for the spread of depression that may follow failure of an alpha capacity.

6. When failure has occurred, renewed hope and energy may follow clarification of the program. Once a series of goals become cognitively available to a student, his interest in achieving them may sharply increase.

7. The teacher's expectations for success in a student, when these expectations are realistically implemented, can be effective and important. But magical expectations will just lead to disillusionment on the part of both student and teacher.

8. Have the courage to let true competence develop in your students—the competence to argue skillfully with their teacher.

Chapter 12   THE NEED FOR STIMULATION

Competence may have drawbacks other than unpopularity with teachers. The highly competent student may have motivational problems precisely because of his competence. He may be bored silly.

Like achievement drives, the urge to terminate boredom is now considered to have organic roots. It is in the nature of the human brain to be stimulated; if stimulation is lacking, we seek it out. A condition of stimulus deprivation is felt to be highly aversive—as people who spend a long time in hospitals, mental institutions, jails, and poor classrooms will be quick to point out.

EXPERIMENTS ON SENSORY DEPRIVATION

In 1951, a series of experiments on the effects of sensory deprivation began at McGill University.

> Male college students were paid to lie 24 hours a day on a comfortable bed in a lighted, semisoundproof cubicle which had an observation window. Throughout the experiment, the students wore translucent goggles which admitted diffuse light but prevented pattern vision. Except when eating or at the toilet, they wore cotton gloves and cardboard cuffs which extended from below the elbows to beyond the fingertips, in order to limit tactual perception. A U-shaped foam rubber pillow, the walls of the cubicle, and the masking noise of the thermostatically regulated air-conditioner and other equipment severely limited auditory perception. . . . [The experimental conditions are shown in the figure.]

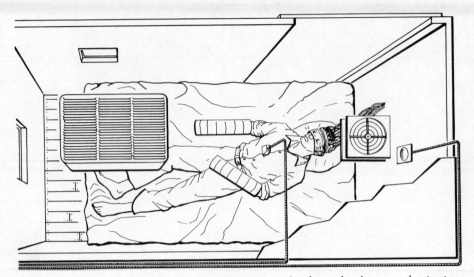

Experimental cubicle constructed at McGill University for the study of sensory deprivation. (Heron, 1957)

The subjects were asked to stay as long as they could (usually 2–3 days) and during this period they were prevented as far as possible from finding out the time. An experimenter was always in attendance and the subjects were told that if they needed anything, they had only to call for it. They were fed and went to the toilet on request. Meals were eaten from a tray beside the bed and the toilet was in an adjacent room. These breaks occupied, on the average, 2–3 hours a day. (Heron, 1961, pp. 8–9)

Subjects were paid as much as $20 a day to lead this life of ease and comfort, but oddly enough, they were not anxious to continue it. Obtaining data on their reactions to sensory deprivation proved to be more difficult than expected, because many subjects would not stay around long enough to provide it.

The experimenters were interested in three kinds of reactions: (1) Thinking ability, as measured by simple tasks like anagrams, mental arithmetic, and drawing maps; (2) hallucinations or other illusory sensory responses; and (3) susceptibility to propaganda. One of the main reasons for embarking on the experimental program was the information about brainwashing then coming from Korea. The reports indicated that prolonged periods of isolation were making prisoners more susceptible to Communist propaganda. The Canadian experiments did not go to such extremes, nor did they use Communist propaganda material. Instead, they offered subjects an opportunity to listen to arguments (recorded) favoring psychic beliefs—ghosts, poltergeists, telepathy, and the like. Before and after the recorded "brainwashing," subjects' attitudes toward psychic phenomena were tested.

Thinking Difficulties

Figure 12.1 illustrates the types of difficulties sensory deprivation produced in thinking ability. The subjects were simply making up words from a list of letters. During the isolation period, sensory-deprived subjects seemed to lose their ability to handle a simple problem of this sort compared to controls (matching students who were not sensory-deprived) and to their own pretest level. There were similar difficulties in the subjects' abilities to perform simple calculations, match block patterns, recognize peculiarities in pictures, and so forth. The experimenters concluded:

> The maintenance of normal, intelligent, adaptive behavior probably requires a continually varied sensory input. The brain is not like a calculating machine operated by an electric motor which is able to respond at once to specific cues after lying idle indefinitely. Instead, it is like one that must be kept warmed up and working. . . . The subjects reported that they were unable to concentrate on any topic for a long while in the cubicle. Those who tried to review their studies or solve self-initiated intellectual problems found it difficult to do so. As a result they lapsed into day-dreaming, abandoned attempts at organized thinking, and let their thoughts wander. There were also reports of "blank periods" during which they seemed unable to think of anything at all. (Bexton, Heron, and Scott, 1954, p. 70)

Does that make you think of your own mental reactions to a boring lecture? Perhaps the report quoted on the following page will too.

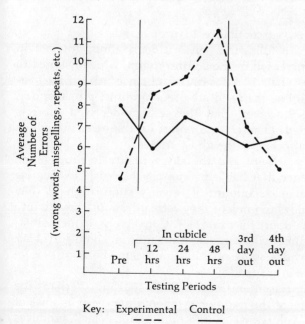

Key: Experimental - - -   Control ———

Figure 12.1 Mean word-making error scores for experimental and control subjects before, during, and after the sensory deprivation period in the cubicle. (Bexton, Heron and Scott, 1954, p. 73)

Hallucinations

Among our early subjects there were several references, rather puzzling at first, to what one of them called "having a dream while awake." . . . The last 14 subjects were [therefore] asked to report any "visual imagery" they observed. . . . Levels of complexity could be differentiated as follows: in the simplest form the visual field, with the eyes closed, changed from dark to light colour; next in complexity were dots of light, lines, or simple geometrical patterns. All 14 subjects reported such imagery, and said it was a new experience to them. Still more complex forms consisted in "wallpaper patterns," reported by 11 subjects, and isolated figures or objects, without background (e.g., a row of little men with black caps on and their mouths open . . .) reported by 7 subjects. Finally, there were integrated scenes (e.g., a procession of squirrels with sacks over their shoulders marching "purposefully" across a snow field and out of the field of "vision" . . .). Three of the 14 subjects reported such scenes. . . .

There were also reports of hallucinations involving other senses. One subject could hear the people speaking in his visual hallucinations, and another repeatedly heard the playing of a music box. Four subjects described kinesthetic and somesthetic phenomena. One reported seeing a miniature rocket ship discharging pellets that kept striking his arm, and one reported reaching out to touch a doorknob he saw before him and feeling an electric shock. (Bexton, Heron, and Scott, 1954, pp. 73–76)

Apparently, the sensory systems attempt to provide their missing stimulation for themselves. In a less extreme form, we may do the same thing when we daydream during a dull class.

Susceptibility to Propaganda

In the McGill experiments, susceptibility to propaganda about psychic matters appeared to increase following sensory deprivation. Interest in psychic phenomena also increased in the control group, which listened to the same recorded lectures. This is not surprising, since it is an intrinsically interesting subject (unlike many forms of Communist propaganda). The experiments showed, however, that the sensory-deprived subjects were more intensely affected. (There is no report on the extent to which hallucinatory activity was affected by the ghost stories!)

Both the hallucinatory activity and the susceptibility to propaganda illustrate the kind of evidence that has led some psychologists to theorize that individuals need a balanced amount of sensory stimulation. If they are in a situation that provides too much, they retreat from it (they go into a quiet room and close the door, for example). Conversely, if their situation is too unstimulating, they will seek out stimulation of some sort. Hallucinating presumably provides some of this stimulation. So might a lecture, even though it is pure propaganda.

The analogy to boring classrooms seems quite startling: Perhaps the sensory-deprived conditions of the traditional schoolroom, with its rows of desks, plain windows, tan-colored walls, and monotonous clock, produces a susceptibility to educational indoctrination. The stupified child may believe what he hears and sees because his brain has been partly "turned off" through lack of stimulation, not because it has been "turned on" by the teacher's presentation. A truly turned-on brain requires stimulation—interesting wall decorations, curtains and carpets (to deaden random noise), pictures, engaging sounds, and the opportunity to become intellectually involved, through questions and arguments, with the information made available.

INDIVIDUAL DIFFERENCES IN NEED FOR STIMULATION

Of course it is the case that some people need more stimulation than others. We all know individuals, for example, who seem to need constant social stimulation; who cannot eat meals without reading or watching television; who cannot read without listening to music; who cannot listen to lectures without doodling. In various ways, these people are telling us that their sensory needs are relatively high.

There may be actual physiological differences between individuals who have a high need for stimulation, and individuals whose need for stimulation (abbreviated *nStim*) is low. This can be seen from the way they are identified.

Assessing Need for Stimulation Experimentally

In one method, subjects are first blindfolded; then they are handed a rectangular wooden block (say 1½ inches wide) and asked to estimate the size of the block in the following manner: The hand that is not holding the block is placed at the base of a wooden wedge which increases in width from about ½ inch to 4 inches. The subject is asked to run his hand up the block and say when he reaches a width that corresponds to the test block he is holding. After doing this several times, the subject is given a second test block, which is larger. He indicates its width in the same way. Then the subject is given the small block again. The major question is this: Will his estimate of the small block now show the influence of the larger block he has just measured? If there is an influence, it may be of two kinds. The subject may reduce or increase his estimate of the size of the small block. If he reduces it, we say his need for stimulation is high—it would require a bigger block to cause him to give the same measurement he gave the first time. If he increases it, we say his need for stimulation is low—the size of the larger block easily caused him to overestimate the size of the smaller block; stimulation from one source was directly generalized to another.

There has been a good deal of interesting research on this phenomenon. Ryan and Foster (1967) showed that high school contact athletes (like football players) tend to be reducers on the block task. Their need for stimulation is high—presumably because they manage to diminish the intensity of stimulation when it occurs. Possibly that is why they enjoy the intense stimulation of contact sports.

Petrie, McCulloch, and Kazdin (1962) reported that juvenile delinquents tended to be reducers—that is, to have a high need for stimulation. Perhaps this is why they seek thrills, even at the expense of their own eventual well-being. They must suffer particularly in the monotonous environment of a jail cell.

Sales (1971) has summarized a series of experiments on the correlation of *nStim* level with other behaviors. He reports that individuals with high *nStim* like complex patterns, psychedelic experiences, music, lots of friends, coffee, and as little sleep as possible. Individuals with low *nStim* like simpler patterns, calm experiences, little music, less coffee, and more sleep. Of special relevance to education was the finding that study habits appeared to differ between the two groups: high *nStim* students liked to study with other people and with the TV or music turned on. Low *nStim* students preferred isolation and quiet. Further, individuals high in *nStim* tended to learn more from complex auditory materials than low *nStim* students did. (But the converse did not hold: low *nStim* students did not learn more from simpler materials.)

It is important to understand that the experimenters who studied this phenomenon do not believe that the level of *nStim* is significantly affected by immediate experience. Of course we may welcome peace and quiet after battling the rush hour traffic or a crowded department store. We might similarly assume that children who come from intensely overstimulating slums would welcome the peace and quiet of a classroom. But this is not always the case. Whether produced genetically or learned from experience, *nStim* may be more of an enduring personality trait than a momentary result of immediate experience.

nStim vs. Arousal

Rush hour traffic and the tension of the slums may produce an effect better termed *arousal* than *nStim*. As you recall from Chapter 1, arousal, attention, and what Russian scientists call *orienting responses* involve the reticular activating system (RAS), shown in Figure 1.1. Factors that affect arousal—noise, for example—may affect high *nStim* people differently from low *nStim* people. The slum child with a high need for stimulation may not register or "take in" a loud noise that drives his teacher (who may have a lower need for stimulation) to distraction. If high *nStim* runs in families, as it may, then noise in a home may be generated more or less deliberately by the family itself—otherwise, they may feel sensory-deprived.

Stimulus devices designed to arouse the interest and attention of average *nStim* groups may leave high *nStim* students in a state of boredom and may overwhelm the low *nStim* students with a rush of ideas they scarcely know how to organize. Individual differences in the need for stimulation may interact with arousal conditions to produce marked differences in student behavior.

CURIOSITY AND EXPLORATORY MOTIVES

Studies of the effects of sensory deprivation (which people with a high need for stimulation will feel most keenly) have shown that the motivation to escape boredom is a strong one. Put more positively, living organisms (at least those high up the phylogenetic scale) are motivated to seek stimulus variation. In its simplest form, animals will work (learn mazes, for example) just for the reward of being able to change the level of illumination. In a more complex form, many animals—especially primates—are "turned on" by the opportunity to explore and manipulate their environment. New psychological theory and experimentation in this area has been concisely summarized by White:

> It requires no special study to appreciate the fact that many animals are given to exploration, manipulation, and playful activity. If there is a puppy in the house its playfulness will detract noticeably from one's scholarly work, and even if one allows a quiet, well-fed cat to sit purring on one's writing table it will not be long before pencils and erasers are delicately moved into a position where they may serve to demonstrate the properties of freely falling bodies.

Photograph courtesy Roc Walley*

*This is an entirely candid snapshot taken while I was an undergraduate at Berkeley. I was typing a term paper and left the room to get a cup of coffee. When I returned, I found our cat, Tiger, investigating the typewriter. Tiger, now aged 15, is alive and well and living in Canada. Unfortunately, his typing behavior has extinguished.

About twenty years ago . . . there was a marked renewal of interest in animal curiosity. . . . Older ideas concerning an instinct of curiosity and an exploratory drive were brought back to life, and a whole series of investigations was directed at this aspect of animal behavior. . . .

Exploratory behavior on the part of rats was studied by Berlyne (1960) by putting the animals in unfamiliar places and later introducing a variety of unfamiliar objects. Each novelty evoked characteristic behavior of approaching, sniffing, and examining from all sides. Interest in any one object lasted only for a short while, but the introduction of a fresh novelty brought an immediate renewal of exploratory action. Montgomery (1954) placed rats in a simple maze offering the choice between a blind alley with a quick return to the living quarters and another alley that led into further unfamiliar maze territory suitable for exploration. The animals learned to favor this second alley in preference to the first. With a similar design Miles (1958) has shown that kittens reared in small cages, which more or less prevented play, would learn to prefer the route that led them to balls of paper, pieces of string, and other choice feline toys. . . .

In such experiments the attempt is made to rule out the participation of primary drives [hunger, thirst, sex, and fear] by satisfying them beforehand. When the animal subjects are tested they are well fed, sexually inactive or satisfied, apparently comfortable, and not noticeably anxious after the first few moments in a new situation. Yet their behavior cannot be properly described as merely random, idle, or restless, nor can it be interpreted simply as responses to proffered stimulation. It exhibits qualities of direction, selection, and persistence that are generally taken as signs that behavior is motivated. Given a choice, the animals elect to go where they will encounter objects and novel surroundings, where there will be an increase in stimulation rather than the quickest possible return to inactivity. (R. W. White, 1963, pp. 25–27)

Similar effects in people seem too obvious to require documentation. Vast entertainment, hobby, and travel industries have grown up in response to human exploratory and curiosity needs. And yet, the exact characteristics of these needs are not as obvious as one might think. Why, exactly, do we prefer one game or television program to another? What are the characteristics of furnishings or pictures that interest us, as compared to those that do not?

Qualities of Interesting Events

Berlyne (1960) believes that interesting stimuli—materials that lead us to explore or to play—have one or more of four qualities: novelty, uncertainty, conflict, and/or complexity. They may have these qualities to a greater or lesser degree, and not all degrees are equally interesting to all people. But in any case, Berlyne believes the behavior of exploration or curiosity results because the novelty, uncertainty, conflict, or complexity leads to a type of conceptual conflict people are motivated to resolve. We put a puzzle together because we are disturbed by the conceptual conflict aroused by the loose puzzle pieces. We gamble because we are trying to resolve the uncertainty of the slot machines (in our favor, of course). We look longer at pictures that display incongruity, complexity, or asymmetry—as illustrated in Figure 12.2, for example—because we are

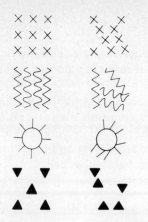

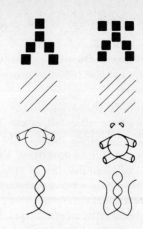

A· IRREGULARITY OF ARRANGEMENT

B· AMOUNT OF MATERIAL

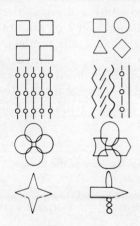

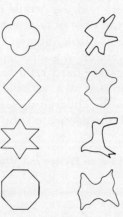

C· HETEROGENEITY OF ELEMENTS

D· IRREGULARITY OF SHAPE

F· INCONGRUOUS JUXTAPOSITION

E· INCONGRUITY

Figure 12.2 Visual patterns representing various collative variables used in experiments on exploratory and curiosity behavior. (Berlyne, 1966)

trying to resolve the conceptual conflict they induce. Simple, symmetrical patterns cause us to lose interest more quickly because they do not arouse conflict of any sort.

Berlyne refers to these conflict producers as *collative variables* or *collative displays,* because they all seem to have in common an integration requirement. The variables need to be put together in a new way; the display needs to be resolved somehow. Where there is interest and attention, Berlyne says, a collative display of some sort is probably involved.

The Hayes Experiment

One charming example of this has been provided by John R. Hayes' (1958) experiment using preschool children.

The task was simply pressing a button to turn on a picture of a cat. The children were told they could play this picture game as long as they liked. Some of the time only one button was available; some of the time six buttons were available. Some of the time the cat picture was turned on every time the button was pressed; some of the time it was turned on every fourth press (a fixed ratio schedule); and some of the time it was turned on according to a variable interval schedule (Figure 10.2). The number of times the children pressed the buttons and the amount of time they stayed with the game are shown in Table 12.1.

Table 12.1
Average Number of Button Presses and Minutes Spent, Various Versions of the Picture Game

	SCHEDULE OF PICTURE PRESENTATION		
NUMBER OF BUTTONS	EVERY TIME	EVERY FOURTH TIME	VARIABLE RATIO
1	8.0 presses	55.0 presses	77.5 presses
	0.51 min	6.19 min	4.95 min
6	47.0 presses	224.0 presses	441.0 presses
	1.60 min	8.19 min	13.29 min

SOURCE: Based on data in Hayes, 1958.

As you can see, turning the game from a sure thing (picture on every time) into a mystery (picture on with every fourth press, regardless of which button) greatly increased the children's interest in the task. When the picture was controlled by an essentially random program (the variable ratio schedule), the children were even more fascinated. Changing the number of buttons and the rates of reinforcement changed the game from picture-looking to puzzle-solving: Which button turns on the picture?

The experiment shows that interest can be controlled by a graded series of events; it is not an on-or-off phenomenon, as it sometimes appears to be. Gradations are also shown in Figure 12.2. Some pictures have more elements than others, some are more heterogeneous than others, and so forth. But finding the point (the degree of complexity) of maximal interest for any individual is still a trial-and-error undertaking.

These same collative variables of uncertainty and complexity are probably also critical to our appreciation of humor and art.

Qualities of Humor and Art

Humor always involves some degree of uncertainty or surprise, but the difficulties of predicting exactly what will be funny further illustrates the trial-and-error factor. We do not yet have a science of humor, any more than we have a true science of curiosity and interest.

The collative properties of humor can be recognized in jokes that bring together concepts not usually associated, as in Samuel Johnson's observation: "A woman's preaching is like a dog standing on its hind legs. It is not done well, but you are surprised to find it done at all."

The delicacy involved in finding exactly the right degree of surprise is well illustrated by the Chaplin films. The little tramp frequently repeats his choice scenes. He repeats them once, so you can savor the surprise anew; he then begins to repeat them a second time, but is deflected into a new behavior pattern. Many of the silent film comics had an exquisite sense of optimal repetition—they repeated just enough to keep you simultaneously surprised and satisfied.

The collative properties of art are well expressed in theories of esthetics that have emphasized such concepts as "unity in diversity." Descartes is quoted as saying: "That sensation or arrangement, interval or rhythm pleases which neither bores nor fatigues. The extremes to be avoided are those of the confusing, intricate figure, laborious and tiring, on the one hand, and of monotony and unfulfilled desire, on the other." And Graves (1951), in a book called *The Art and Color of Design,* says: "Conflict is the aesthetic conflict or visual tension between opposing or contrasting lines, directions, shapes, space intervals, textures, values, hues. . . . Visual conflict or tension, also called opposition, contrast or variety, is used to produce stimulus or interest." (Both examples are taken from Berlyne, 1960, pp. 232–233. His entire chapter on art and humor should be read by anyone with a scholarly interest in the psychology of art and humor.)

Tests of creative ability may capitalize on an artistic person's preference for an optimal degree of complexity or surprise. Materials similar to those shown in Figure 12.2 may be used in such a test. Artistic people prefer collative displays that offer the "right" degree of conceptual conflict.

Summary

Curiosity and exploratory motivational systems appear to arise from a biological need for a balanced amount of sensory stimulation. We are motivated to act on our environment (or on ourselves) when that stimulation rises above, or falls below, the amount optimal for us. This optimum may differ among individuals because of (possibly physiological) differences in their need-stimulation thresholds. But generally, curiosity and interest will be aroused by collative displays—conditions that produce the "right" amount of conceptual conflict by displaying something surprising, uncertain, complex, or novel.

If the arousal is too great, we will dislike the stimulation and retreat from the object; if the arousal is too little, we will be bored and seek elsewhere for adequate stimulation. But the optimal amount of conceptual conflict will hold our interest.

Chapter 13   SELF-MOTIVATING LEARNING CYCLES

The most difficult and interesting human problem is not to show that exploratory and curiosity motives exist, or that competence motives exist, but to show how they interact to produce prolonged attempts at learning and understanding. Under some conditions, young children will display an almost obsessive preoccupation with tasks or activities that appears to be the same kind of motivation displayed by scientists who win the Nobel prize. The shocking tragedy of much formal education is that it may systematically destroy the natural motivational systems human beings bring with them into the world.

How can teachers capitalize on these natural systems? First of all, by trying to understand them, both theoretically and within themselves. From the theoretical standpoint, the most general principle is a simple one: *The growing human's interest in the complexities of his environment increases with his ability to coordinate his responses to them.* This basic principle can be seen very early in life, in an infant's response to pictures, for example. Look at Figure 13.1. Two-month-old infants may look longer at the normal faces, while 4-month-olds may prefer to stare at the scrambled ones. As the baby's own schema for faces matures, he is intrigued by having that schema challenged. The puzzle of recoordinating the elements of a face is intriguing only after the coordination ability is developed; before then, the puzzle arouses no interest.

The Enriched Crib Experiment
The principle has been further illustrated in an experiment carried out by Burton White and his colleagues (B. L. White, 1963). White carried out his

experiment in an orphanage, where it was possible for him to enrich the environment of some of the babies in controlled ways. Due to circumstances in many infant institutions, the children live very unstimulating lives. For hygienic reasons, the rooms are often painted white and pictures or other visual objects are at a minimum. Cloths are draped over the sides of cribs in order to cut drafts, decreasing visual stimulation even further. The baby exists in something like a white cocoon except for 15-minute feeding periods, when a bottle is propped and a diaper is changed.

White was interested in the visual curiosity of institutionalized babies. What did they look at? How often did their gaze shift? He attempted to stimulate curiosity in two ways. Some of the babies were rocked regularly, at least 10 minutes in every 2-hour period. Other babies were placed in enriched cribs of the sort shown in Figure 13.2. Babies who were rocked

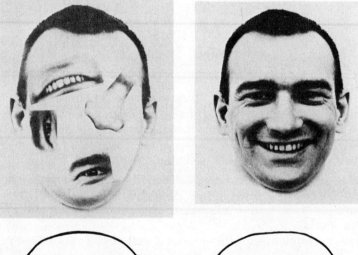

Figure 13.1   Scrambled faces used for studying the visual interest of infants. (Mussen et al., 1969, p. 164)

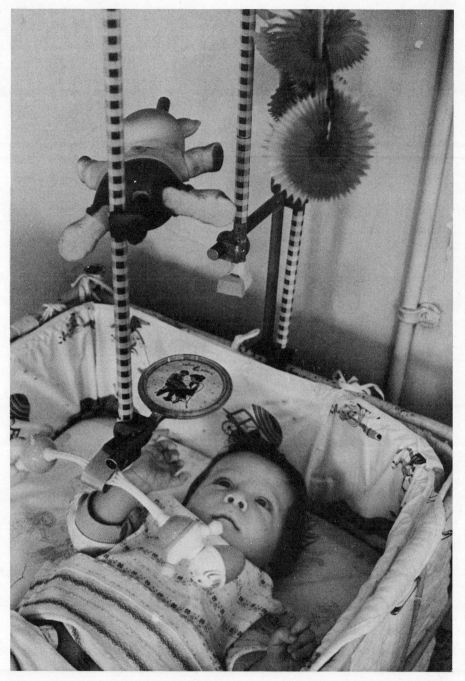

Figure 13.2 Enriched visual ecology of infant in study by White and Castle, 1964. (Leonard McCombe, *Life* magazine, © Time Inc.)

were lightly blindfolded so that only tactual stimulation was increased by the rocking.

Visual curiosity was tested over a three-month period. It changed in very interesting ways, as shown in Figure 13.3. The rocked (or handled) infants, when placed back in their cribs, showed the most visual curiosity from the age of about 1½ months until the age of about 2½ months. They showed more visual curiosity than the babies in the enriched cribs and than control babies (who were being neither rocked nor visually enriched). The enriched crib babies were, in fact, the least curious of the three groups up until the age of about 2½ months. At this point, shown clearly on the graph where the lines cross, the enriched crib babies shot ahead in visual curiosity. Over the last month of measurement, the enriched babies were far superior in visual exploration to both rocked babies and control babies. The other groups were actually showing a decline, or loss of interest (a visual discouragement, perhaps).

What happened at 2½ months? At this age, babies become able to direct their own motoric systems toward things that interest them. In White's terms, they become able to *swipe*. A swipe is a closed-fisted reach—the baby is not yet able to grab things—that can be aimed quite well. The onset (physical maturation) of swiping abilities made the enriched babies far more visually responsive to their environment. Once

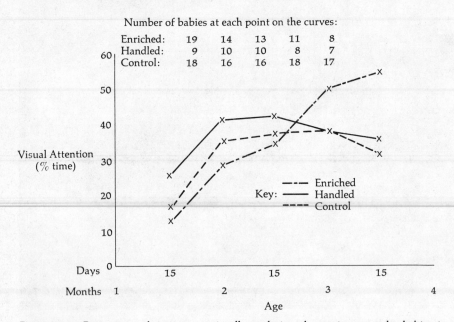

Figure 13.3 Percentage of time spent visually exploring the environment by babies in an enriched environment, babies who had been given extra handling, and control babies. (B. L. White, 1963)

they became able to reach out toward the stimulation, they became extremely curious about it.

The experiment beautifully illustrates our general principle: The growing human's interest in the complexities of his environment increases with his ability to coordinate his responses to them. That principle is the keynote of self-motivating learning cycles. Two scientists who have done detailed work on such cycles are Jean Piaget and Daniel Berlyne. We will consider their theoretical positions first, and then conclude with a note on the joy that accompanies successful completion of a cycle.

PIAGET'S EQUILIBRIUM THEORY

In his studies of infant development, Piaget (1952) described the development of *circular reactions*—repetitive and self-reinforcing actions we often see in infants. A *primary* circular reaction is the simplest type: It consists of mere repetition of an action that was enjoyed, such as banging a rattle to make an interesting noise happen. *Secondary* circular reactions (which, according to Piaget, begin to appear between 3 and 6 months) are more sophisticated: They appear to use one response as a means to another—banging a rattle as a way of making mother smile. Piaget describes an instance when his baby daughter kept pulling a string on her crib in order to make daddy dangle his watch again. Presumably, these secondary circular reactions are the infant's first experience of instrumental power. White (1959) sees them as the earliest display of competence motivation.

The *tertiary* circular reactions appear around 10 or 11 months. They differ from secondary reactions in that they are less repetitive. The secondary reactions attempted to make something new happen by repeating a response that worked on something else. The tertiary reactions contain the element of variability: The infant may deliberately change his manipulation or action in order to make something new happen. One familiar example of this is banging with a spoon. Everything gets banged—the plate, the high chair, the bottle, the dog, and Mommy's head when she bends down to console the dog. We might call this the onset of the scientific attitude.

In the course of his experiments, the child discovers that some ideas have unfortunate or confusing outcomes (banging Mommy's head, for example). As a result, the child changes his idea; he seeks a concept of his experiences that produces equilibrium rather than confusion. In this example, he would presumably arrive at a concept of the form: "Some things are all right to bang with the spoon, and some things are not." But even that concept would eventually have to be revised in the light of experience; some things can be banged lightly, and some things can be banged hard.

Piaget sees this *practice-expand-practice* behavior cycle as the basic "engine" of conceptual development. He explains it more generally as the need to find an appropriate balance between the processes of *assimilation* and *accommodation*.

The Search for Equilibrium

The infant who is banging everything is assimilating the world to his newly developed schema of banging. The infant who is learning not to bang Mommy's head is accommodating his schema to the reality of the world.

Assimilation often seems like play. It seems easier, more satisfying. Accommodation seems more like work and may be stressful. In our own self-governing behavior of learning (picking out books in a library, for example), as well as in our teaching of others, we strive to find a balance between the two processes. Too much activation of a well-practiced schema (reading books we have read before) produces boredom; too much accommodation stress (reading books that are too technical) produces abandonment of learning. There is, however, one aspect of accommodation that seems more like play than like work, and that is *imitation*.

Imitation in Piaget's system is seen as the rehearsal or reactivation of a newly accommodated idea. Thus, the role playing of young children is their way of practicing adaptation to the real world. As we know from Part I, Piaget (1962) sees this kind of imitation as an important step toward the full development of symbolic abilities.

Most formal instruction is based on the idea of balance between the taking in of new information and the practice of information already learned. In Piaget's terms, we can see that each of these processes has two aspects:

1. The "taking in" process:
   A. Is the new information easily assimilated to existing mental structures?
   B. Does it require the mental structure to "bend," "shift," or accommodate?

2. The practice or expressive process:
   A. Is it a playful exercise of the new idea without regard to reality?
   B. Is it an imitative exercise of an accommodation requirement?

Most instructional programs incorporate some of each, rather like a random shopper. More thoughtful programs strive to relate these four aspects of learning in a way that generates self-motivating learning cycles. In Piaget's terms, such a cycle might be diagrammed as follows:

A PIAGETIAN SELF-MOTIVATING LEARNING CYCLE

PLAY (activation of a schema) → ACCOMMODATION (adjusting to a newly discovered bit of reality) → IMITATION (practicing the adjustment) → ASSIMILATION (applying the revised schema to a new situation) → PLAY (activation of the more advanced schema) → ACCOMMODATION (adjusting to another newly discovered bit of reality) → IMITATION (practicing the new adjustment) → ASSIMILATION (incorporating still more information into the new schema) → and so on.

By means of these processes, Piaget believes, knowledge grows. It is clear that the system is seeking an equilibrium; it keeps moving because the equilibrium continues to be disturbed. Even if nothing happens in the outside world to upset a complacent set of ideas, other ideas might intrude. Further, because of our need for stimulation, new experiences may be sought. Constant assimilation and play may become as uninspiring as chewing one's cud.

Operational Balance

The balanced grouping of ideas that Piaget calls *operational structures* has been described in Part I. You will recall that the balance is characterized by possible or potential movements, not necessarily actual ones. If a particular movement (pouring water into three small beakers) could be reversed in thought (mentally pouring the water back into the single large beaker), the resulting judgment would be in a state of logical balance (quantities stay the same no matter what their containers look like).

The development of a system that will maintain this sort of dynamic equilibrium comes about through the exercise of the self-motivating learning cycle presented above. The child discovers through his own activities (play) that certain aspects of reality will no longer fit his preconceptions (schemas). He then adjusts his ideas and practices the adjustment (sometimes by imitating others or himself, sometimes by applying his adjusted notions to new situations). Eventually, he discovers *principles* of adjustment. That is how reversibility, compensation, and other principles of operational logic are discovered, according to Piaget. Most important, Piaget believes this may be the *only* way they can be discovered. If just one part of the process (say, accommodation in the form of rote drill of arithmetic rules) is practiced, true operational logic will never develop.

Another view of this same problem is provided by a second self-motivating learning cycle, one that has a good deal in common with Piaget's, but offers some alternative concepts.

BERLYNE'S THEORY OF EPISTEMIC MOTIVATION

We have already been introduced to Berlyne's general theory of exploratory motivation—that a conceptual conflict, induced by collative variables, will move a person to resolve it in order to restore himself to a comfortable state of arousal. Berlyne (1965) extended his theory to explain *epistemic* (knowledge-seeking) *motivation* as the motivation to reduce a conceptual conflict by learning something.

Of course, not all types of conceptual conflict are resolved in this way (the conflict between ice cream flavors, for example). Berlyne has listed the following types of conceptual conflict as the major sources of epistemic behavior:

Doubt. There is . . . the conflict between tendencies to believe and to disbelieve the same statement. Doubt will presumably create maximum conflict when the tendencies to believe and to disbelieve are equal in strength. . . . The agonies of Othello illustrate the point admirably. . . .

Perplexity. When there are factors inclining the subject toward each of a number of mutually exclusive beliefs, e.g., when there is some evidence favoring each of them but no way of knowing for certain which is true. . . . (Berlyne, 1960, pp. 286–287)

Contradiction. This is a particularly intense kind of conflict. . . . The subject is under the influence of factors that . . . imperatively force on him two incompatible beliefs. . . .

Conceptual incongruity. This occurs when a subject believes that two properties, A and B, . . . are unlikely to occur together, and yet factors are present that lead him to believe that a certain object possesses both. . . . An example would be the condition of a person who hears about a fish (the mudskipper) that walks on dry land when he has been trained to believe that no fish can survive or move about after leaving the water.*

Confusion. This condition is produced by information whose implications are not clear. . . . Ambiguous verbal material [for example]. Confusion will overlap with perplexity whenever the subject recognizes a number of alternative possibilities and the information . . . is insufficient to specify the correct one. At other times, however, he may be left wondering what the truth could possibly be, without being able to name any alternatives.

Irrelevance. This kind of perceptual conflict is extremely hard to define or analyze. It can apparently be distressing and motivate searches for . . . escape from it in the course of directed thinking. . . .

. . . Whenever a subject is faced with a question to which he can supply no possible answer whatever . . . we assume he will not be entirely bereft of thoughts. . . . Some symbolic material will inevitably be conjured up by associative processes . . . most or all of which will be irrelevant. We can thus infer that there will be a high degree of conflict due to irrelevance. (Berlyne, 1965, pp. 257–258)

Berlyne believes there are four major ways of resolving conceptual conflicts of this sort. These are the processes that underlie epistemic or knowledge-seeking behavior.

Resolving Conceptual Conflicts

First of all, something may happen that affects the strength of the competing responses so that one of them "wins." This process is called *disequalization.* A state of doubt may be disequalized when we receive new information; the doubt is resolved in favor of one of the alternatives. But sometimes an entirely new alternative appears, wiping out doubt or perplexity by a process Berlyne calls *swamping.* Conflicts arising from confusion or irrelevance are often resolved this way. In our confusion, we cast about for a way out, and the confusion itself is swamped out of existence

---

*In *The Immense Journey,* Loren Eiseley describes how his wife reacted to the report of a similar species with the worried murmur, "They ought to be watched. . . . They ought to be watched."

by the solution that is discovered. A third type of conflict resolution comes from *conciliation,* in which the competing responses are reconciled with each other. Everyone wins, so to speak. This is frequently a higher type of solution and may be involved in creative thinking to an important degree (see Chapter 25). The final type of resolution process is simply to drive one arm of the mental conflict underground. *Suppression,* Berlyne says, is normally a desperate measure. Nevertheless, it may be characteristic of certain types of personalities.

These conflict-reducing processes may not operate in a simple, straightforward manner. Sometimes the effort to gather new information increases the conflict by introducing new alternatives, strengthening weak ones, or challenging cherished beliefs. In any case, the quest for knowledge that reduces the conflict continues. Epistemic motivation thus generates epistemic or knowledge-seeking behavior. When the conflict is finally resolved, the individual will have advanced in knowledge. He will know, at least, the solution to one kind of puzzle. But now his more advanced concept is open to challenge or conflict, and the whole cycle may begin again on a higher level. The self-motivating learning cycle suggested by Berlyne's theory might be presented as follows:

BERLYNE'S SELF-MOTIVATING LEARNING CYCLE

COLLATIVE DISPLAY (puzzle, uncertainty, complexity) → CONCEPTUAL CONFLICT (doubt, contradiction, perplexity) → EPISTEMIC BEHAVIOR (asking questions, gathering information) → CONFLICT REDUCTION (swamping, conciliation) → KNOWLEDGE (mudskippers *are* a type of fish) → NEW COLLATIVE DISPLAY (new mystery about mudskippers) → NEW CONCEPTUAL CONFLICT → MORE EPISTEMIC BEHAVIOR → CONFLICT REDUCTION → NEW KNOWLEDGE → and so on.

Experimental Studies of Epistemic Motivation

There are several American and Russian experimental studies of the factors affecting epistemic motivation. In one study, Berlyne (1954) asked high school students to indicate which of forty-eight questions about animals they would most like to have answered. Much more curiosity (Berlyne would call it epistemic curiosity) was evoked by familiar animals than by unfamiliar ones, especially when the questions indicated that the animals possessed unlikely characteristics. This experiment showed that greater conceptual conflict may be aroused about something familiar, presumably because the subject has some concepts to conflict. One can hardly feel aroused by a statement like, "It is surprising to realize that a French cartouche was more often made of paper than of wood, as was popularly believed." But a firearms scholar who already possesses a number of ideas about such matters might feel quite aroused.

In a related study, Maas (as described by Peel, 1961) presented students with museum objects of an exotic and mysterious nature. Students indicated the strength of their interest by marking a five-point scale. Maas then presented the objects again, this time giving more information about them. Students indicated the strength of their interest again, and it had increased. The more they knew, the more their ideas could be challenged. Epistemic motivation was thus increased.

In a Russian study by Marozova (cited by Berlyne, 1965), children ranging in age from 11 to 15 were shown different kinds of textbook materials about latitude and longitude. Marozova measured mastery of the material and interest, and found that both were greatest when the text described a child hero who was faced with the problem of finding out his own location and experienced difficulties of various sorts. In general, Marozova concluded that the best teaching materials met the following conditions:

1. What is read must raise a question that the reader finds hard to answer.
2. There is a hero who is faced with the question.
3. The hero is engaged in an active search for an answer.
4. There is a central element of "struggle" against difficulties and perplexities.

There must . . . be the makings of conceptual conflict, and the possibility of identifying with a hero enables the reader to experience the conflict vicariously. The hero's successful efforts to overcome the difficulties and resolve the conflict appear not only to satisfy the reader's desire to know the answers to the specific questions involved but also to stimulate an eagerness for further knowledge about the same topic.

Marozova also inquired which books were and were not in heavy demand in the school library. The books for which there was not a great call consisted largely of declarative statements, simply purveying information; they raised few questions, offered few chances to guess answers, and required no thought on the part of the child. The books for which there was a great demand, and which the children presumably found interesting, were ones that raised questions and stimulated efforts to think out answers to the questions before the information to be assimilated was supplied.

As Marozova's work has continued (personal communication), there has been still more emphasis on the key role of conflict or "struggle." She stresses the pedagogical and interest-inducing value of first giving children some information and then acquainting them with facts that apparently discord with the information. They may, for example, hear about Spartacus and what a stalwart leader of the Roman slave population he was. But then they are told that he hesitated to lead a revolt against the patricians. They may be told how plants require sunlight for the photochemical processes on which their growth and survival depend. It is then pointed out to them that there are plants, namely fungi, that can live in the dark. Once they have been confronted with these apparently inconsistent facts and have made some attempts to resolve the conflict, they are given the appropriate explanations and, it is reported, both interest and retention are thereby brought to a peak. (Berlyne, 1965, pp. 263–264)

PEDAGOGICAL MODELS

In America, some excellent self-motivating learning kits have been developed by the Education Development Center, Cambridge, Massachusetts, and are now marketed by McGraw-Hill. These are the Elementary Science Study kits. They can be "plugged into" a traditional science program or used as the foundation for a science course.

A more comprehensive program has been developed by the Science Curriculum Improvement Study group under the direction of Dr. R. Karplus, a physicist at the University of California, Berkeley. The SCIS materials are now marketed by Rand McNally. They are quite remarkable in their spiral qualities—that is, in the way in which they build on children's previous knowledge. For example, the earliest natural science unit, called *Organisms,* is the foundation for a second unit, *Life Cycles,* which in turn provides the foundation for a later unit called *Populations.* An example from *Populations* should give you an idea of the quality and impact of this program.

The students have built a terrarium and stocked it with crickets (available from Rand McNally, but don't drop the box!). After a few lessons on crickets and other population problems, chameleons are introduced into the terrarium. The crickets, of course, disappear. Then the chameleons are removed. The students are somewhat dismayed and saddened, but they have learned several important lessons about nature's way of controlling population. Because the terrarium is pretty, the teacher suggests that the class continue to water it, even though it is empty. The class does. Then one day, an apparent miracle occurs. The crickets reappear! Baby crickets, from eggs that had been laid before the population was wiped out. Thus the class learns the critically important lesson that a species may live even though every member of a population has been destroyed. You can imagine the interest in scientific details that would be generated by such an experience. The children are insatiable.

The SCIS program constantly builds in that way upon the students' experiences, moving them to extend their own knowledge in response to conceptual conflicts and surprises. Read Karplus and Thier (1967) for details of theory and program development.

In the social studies area, the best-known self-motivating learning program is *Man: A Course of Study,* developed by the Education Development Center, Cambridge. This is essentially an anthropology course comparing several cultures along dimensions of interest to children. Bruner (1966, pp. 73–101) has described some theoretical aspects of the course, and some excerpts from trial versions may be found in Jones (1968). The engineering details of the course follow the self-motivating learning principles that have been discussed. The children's view of normal life is challenged (frequently through the use of special films). The course then builds on their surprise and curiosity. The children master enormous amounts of anthropological information in order to achieve a new, more well-balanced and comprehensive view of "normal life."

Spontaneous Academic Persistence

Of course, it is not possible to pinpoint each stage of the cycle as it occurs in the head of each student. But with a little practice, a teacher can learn to recognize the course of interest development and willingness to work in an individual student. A suggestion here, a word of encouragement there, a bit of help will be all that is necessary to keep the student going, provided that his natural cycle has been activated.

The most surprising aspect of such cycles to many teachers is the amount of spontaneous self-drilling that may appear. The reason for this is beautifully illustrated in the following excerpt from Montessori's writings. She is describing the "explosion into writing" that is said to occur sometime after the children have mastered separate parts of the writing process—they have learned how to make letters, how to use writing tools, and which letters go with which sounds. In the Italian language, these phonetic rules are regular, and the Montessori children eventually discover that they know how to write everything (or almost everything) they can say. The moment of this discovery is up to the children. The teachers plan for it, but they do not teach it directly.

> One beautiful December day when the sun shone and the air was like spring, I went up on the roof with the children. They were playing freely about, and a number of them were gathered about me. I was sitting near a chimney, and said to a little five-year-old boy who sat beside me, "Draw me a picture of this chimney," giving him as I spoke a piece of chalk. He got down obediently and made a rough sketch of the chimney on the tiles which formed the floor of this roof terrace. As is my custom with little children, I encouraged him, praising his work. The child looked at me, smiled, remained for a moment as if on the point of bursting into some joyous act, and then cried out, "I can write! I can write!" and kneeling down again he wrote on the pavement the word "hand." Then, full of enthusiasm, he wrote also "chimney," "roof." As he wrote, he continued to cry out, "I can write! I know how to write!" His cries of joy brought the other children, who formed a circle about him, looking down at his work in stupefied amazement. Two or three of them said to me, trembling with excitement, "Give me the chalk. I can write too." And indeed they began to write various words: *mama, hand, John, chimney, Ada.*
>
> Not one of them had ever taken chalk or any other instrument in hand for the purpose of writing. It was the *first time* that they had ever written, and they traced an entire word, as a child, when speaking for the first time, speaks the entire word.
>
> . . . Such was our first experience in the development of the written language in our children. Those first days we were a prey to deep emotions. It seemed as if we were walking in a dream, and as if we assisted at some miraculous achievement.
>
> The child who wrote a word for the first time was full of excited joy. He might be compared to the hen who has just laid an egg. Indeed, no one could escape from the noisy manifestations of the little one. He would

call everyone to see, and if there were some who did not go, he ran to take hold of their clothes forcing them to come and see. We all had to go and stand about the written word to admire the marvel, and to unite our exclamations of surprise with the joyous cries of the fortunate author. Usually, this first word was written on the floor, and then the child knelt down before it in order to be nearer to his work and to contemplate it more closely.

After the first word, the children, with a species of frenzied joy, continued to write everywhere. I saw children crowding about one another at the blackboard, and behind the little ones who were standing on the floor another line would form consisting of children mounted upon chairs, so that they might write above the heads of the little ones. In a fury at being thwarted, other children, in order to find a little place where they might write, overturned the chairs upon which their companions were mounted. Others ran toward the window shutters or the door, covering them with writing. In these first days we walked upon a carpet of written signs. Daily accounts showed us that the same thing was going on at home, and some of the mothers, in order to save their pavements, and even the crust of their loaves upon which they found words written, made their children presents of *paper* and *pencil.* One of these children brought to me one day a little note-book entirely filled with writing, and the mother told me that the child had written all day long and all evening, and had gone to sleep in his bed with the paper and pencil in his hand. (Montessori, 1964b, pp. 286–289)

It is worth remembering that these were slum children.

Self-drilling following the discovery of one's own coordinating powers can be extreme. As noted, interest in environmental complexities increases with our ability to coordinate our responses to them. Montessori's "explosion" is really an explosive new interest in one's own language, with all of its complexities. This explosion is contingent upon the discovery of coordination skills.

In Piaget's system, this would be the *assimilation* phase: the children are assimilating their own language to their new writing schemas. In Berlyne's system, it could be described as the *knowledge* phase following conflict reduction. Although the Montessori children were probably not put into a situation of deliberate doubt or perplexity, the struggle to read and to write—to master cultural symbol systems—is highly perplexing and worrisome to most young children. They are puzzled by the "secret rules" of our symbol systems and eager to "break" them.

Eagerness to practice writing, reading, number facts, scientific facts and tables, and so on frequently follows a breakthrough of this sort—a breakthrough that the teacher will recognize as a new coordination plateau, a new equilibrium developed by the child as a way of resolving conceptual challenges.

Preparing the Environment

More and more self-motivating pedagogical materials are becoming commercially available, and the teacher will find many helpful resources in designing programs that capitalize on natural practice-expand-practice cycles. As should be clear from all the foregoing examples, however, a great deal of thoughtful preparation is involved. Self-motivated classrooms are not sentimental accidents. Breakthroughs happen because the teacher arranges for them to happen.

Just as I wrote this, I noticed a child—about 5 years old—across the street from my office window, writing his name in giant letters with a stick in the unseeded lawn before his home. His mother has now emerged angrily from the house and is scolding him for damaging the lawn. Unfortunately, environments prepared for the lawns of civilization are frequently unprepared for the discoveries of childhood.

We have a long way to go before we understand how to guarantee educational joys for all children, how to prepare exactly the right learning environment for everyone. But one thing is clear: Any educator who has watched a youngster experience such joy will never again doubt the fact that a properly designed education can be a profoundly self-motivating one.

Chapter 14   THE PROBLEM OF THE PERSON

According to Freud, the cognitive processes described in Parts I and II of this book are *secondary processes* that flow out of the confrontation of primary biological instincts with cultural reality. The *primary processes* may be loosely identified with "old brain" systems—activation, hunger, sex, reflexes. The secondary processes may be loosely identified with the higher "new brain" systems—language, intellect. Freud believed the secondary processes were in fact secondary to the "real" life of the mind—the energies and urges of instinctual systems.

Although modern neuropsychologists would modify that point of view, it is certainly the case that deeper personality factors of various kinds affect the ability to profit from instruction. It is also true that the instruction, in turn, affects further personality growth. In point of fact, it is not really possible to separate personality from thinking and learning. The personality is going to be involved in anything we teach, whether we like it or not. The only question is whether it is actively involved or just "tags along" like an unwanted second cousin. In this chapter, we will consider some of the basic principles that can help you deal skillfully with the fact that you will be teaching not only subject matter and minds, but people.

Personal Reaction Systems

Personalities and personality problems do not happen in a vacuum; a personality is revealed by patterns of behavior toward an event. Each student who comes into a classroom brings with him a unique set of personal reaction systems. The teacher creates the instructional events, and it is in the student's reactions to these events that his special personality patterns are revealed. Some students, for example, respond to an assignment slowly and methodically; some are impulsive. Some students study only what interests them; others show an unusual capacity to take different points of view. Some students have special problems with anxiety; others never seem to be anxious enough.

Despite the many differences in personal reactions, they are not infinitely varied. An experienced teacher will recognize some of the patterns as they appear again and again. A wise teacher will make adjustments in both instructional programs and his own expectations that take these patterns into account. A prepared teacher will consider a range of possible reaction patterns even before classes begin. We cannot cover all possibilities, but the personality dimensions given special emphasis here are those selected as critical because they have a direct bearing on instructional decisions and because they seem to be represented in most classrooms.

1. Activity level, including persistence and impulsivity
2. Anxiety and defensiveness
3. Passive-dependent behavior
4. Assertiveness, aggression, and hostility
5. Egocentrism and self-esteem
6. Cognitive styles of analyzing and organizing information

We have already considered some additional critical dimensions—achievement drive, need for stimulation, competence and curiosity drives, and so forth—and in the next chapter on social and sociological factors, we will consider still others. In combination, these chapters should give the prepared teacher a rich framework for analyzing the problem of the person. One important aspect of such a framework is the chronological age of the student. Personalities change with growth in ways that are at least as predictable as changes in cognitive abilities. The foremost architect of personality development was Sigmund Freud, but his views have since been constructively modified by Robert White (1960) and Erik Erikson (1959) in a direction relevant to education. So we will consider Freud, White, and Erikson together.

GROWTH OF THE PERSONALITY

Birth to Two Years
The trauma of birth (if it is a trauma) may have more far-reaching consequences for the personality than we fully understand. In particular, there may be problems resulting from an overwhelming bombardment of the sensory systems. The infant must somehow learn to cope with this extraordinary stimulation, and his early methods may extend into later life. Sleep, for example, is one way of coping. The adult individual who "turns off" anxiety by getting sleepy (and thus, perhaps, is unable to study for

exams) may have mastered that coping technique in infancy. What may have been a good technique originally becomes maladaptive in an adult. More generally, *nStim* thresholds, if they are not wholly biological, may have been set shortly after birth as a way of coping with the sensory bombardment of the real world.

As the infant grows older, he enters into what Freud called the *oral stage.* The infant's focus on eating is the key to this period, but there is another important aspect to it, and that is the infant's inability to tell the difference between himself and the source of his greatest pleasure—his food. This inability leads to two primitive concepts: the concept (on the infant's part) that he is the primary source of his own pleasures, a concept Freud called *primary narcissism;* and the infant's sense of his own *omnipotence.* (When we meet a certain type of egocentricity in adults, we may well wonder if these early concepts are not still operating.)

The most important characteristic of the oral stage is the child's *dependence.* The infant is totally unable to care for himself. If something goes wrong, he must accept it. (Even worse, he may come to expect it, a point that is the cornerstone of Erikson's theory, as we will see shortly.) But he may not like it. Freud believed that infants may become *orally aggressive* (bite mother's nipple, for example) during the weaning period. Both dependency and aggression may therefore characterize an individual's later so-called oral behavior, as Baldwin explains:

> Any feature of an individual's behavior, especially his pleasure-seeking behavior, that resembles some feature of the oral stage is viewed in psychoanalytic theory as possibly stemming from the oral period. . . . Some are literally oral, kissing, smoking a pipe, nail biting. Some are metaphorically oral like "biting" sarcasm. Some, like "eating jags" replicate the fact that the oral stage is concerned largely with food. Some, like compulsive overfeeding of one's children, may be oral because they seem to equate food with love. Still others re-create the basic oral attitude toward love objects, the imperious demand for the love object [the bottle] when desire is high together with ignoring it the rest of the time. In still another version of orality the emphasis may be on the passivity of the oral stage. For example, a passive, unrealistic optimism that someone will appear to solve one's problems may be an oral trait.* (Baldwin, 1967, p. 367)

Erikson, like Freud, views personality development as an outgrowth of a series of personal crises. If the personality weathers and resolves these crises, development is normal. If a crisis is not resolved, the personality may remain "stuck" in a futile attempt to continue to resolve it.

Basic Trust and Schooling The reports of teachers who have been working in Head Start programs suggest that some deprived children may be struggling to resolve oral problems, especially of the sort Erikson describes. Erikson believes that "the *firm establishment of enduring patterns*

---

*See Chapter 11 for a description of such magical expectations in relationship to schooling.

for the balance of basic trust over basic mistrust is the first task of the budding personality" (Erikson, 1959, p. 63). Naturally, it is the mother who is primarily responsible for the successful accomplishment of this task:

> Mothers create a sense of trust in their children by that kind of administration which in its quality combines sensitive care of the baby's individual needs and a firm sense of personal trustworthiness within the trusted framework of their community life style. . . . Parents must . . . be able to represent to the child a deep, an almost somatic conviction that there is meaning to what they are doing. (Erikson, 1959, p. 63)

The confusion and turmoil of our urban slums may not transmit trustworthiness to mothers or to their children. Such children may arrive at day care centers with a profound disbelief in the fact that they are places of security. Sometimes their distrust may be manifested as an excessive degree of affection toward any stranger, rather than as fearful withdrawal. Severely disadvantaged children may be so preoccupied with their need to make sure a teacher will in fact care for them, no matter what, that they constantly demand attention and affection and seem unable to settle down to any task that does not involve cuddling, clinging, or other forms of physical dependency (Mattick, 1965).

Competence and Trust While it is clearly important to provide a trust-starved child with reassurance, we should not lose sight of the fact that competence development may also be at stake. It is not a foregone conclusion that all disadvantaged children are trust-starved. Many families, though poor in the material sense, are rich in playfulness and affection, especially for infants. Some children who appear to have great dependency needs may have nothing of the kind; they may simply be applying to their new school situation habits of affection and personal interaction that have characterized their home life. Their problem may be the development of trust in their own competence.

As we will see in Chapter 15, sociocultural backgrounds may differ in the degree to which they prepare children to perform tasks of various kinds, including tasks of the sort that are required in preschool settings. Montessori developed her "practical life" curriculum to mirror the self-care and home-care tasks (such as shoe tying and folding towels) that middle-class parents were careful to teach their children. She did this for two reasons. One was the need to teach basic hygiene to slum children sent to her school on a day-care basis; the other was her realization that the skills involved in these practical tasks were easily generalized to more advanced activities and provided a foundation for them (Montessori, 1964a, 1964b).

White would agree that the basic competence developed in practical areas is an important feature of childhood. In fact, he believes the growth of competence to be a critically important feature of the oral stage, as Freud defines it:

> Something else, some other need . . . [may] encroach upon pure oral gratification. For one thing, there are clear signs [by the time a baby is a year old] that additional entertainment is desired during a meal. The utensils are investigated, the behavior of spilled food is explored, toys are played with throughout the feeding. . . . At one year of age a toy in each hand is the only guarantee that a meal will be completed without housekeeping disaster. . . . More important, however, is the infant's growing enthusiasm for the doctrine of "do it yourself." He assists in his own nourishment by holding the bottle and by active finger feeding. Around one year there is likely to occur . . . "the battle of the spoon," the moment "when the baby grabs the spoon from the mother's hand and tries to feed itself." From . . . the spoon's "hazardous journey" from dish to mouth we can be sure that the child is not motivated at this point by increased oral gratification. He gets more food by letting mother do it, but by doing it himself he gets more of another kind of satisfaction — a feeling of efficacy, and perhaps already a growth of the sense of competence. (White, 1960, p. 110)

If the mother, because of her lack of awareness or because of other pressures, prevents this early sense of competence from flowering, the child may come to mistrust his own abilities to carry out such tasks. When he finally arrives at a day care center, his primary needs may be those that Montessori defined—needs involving mastery of small, practical tasks.

The day care center that offers only complicated, sophisticated playthings suitable primarily for middle-class, advantaged children may find its young charges behaving as if the goals of the task are not cognitively available to them. And indeed they are not. On the other hand, centers that provide only water to splash dolls in, sand to throw, blocks to kick, and chairs to climb on may be going to the opposite extreme—providing only tasks that have no goals at all. Failure cannot be experienced if success cannot be defined, but the disadvantaged child needs above all to experience a sense of genuine success on tasks that are simple enough and clear enough for him to understand. In this way, he will make up for lost time and provide himself with a sound foundation in both competence and trust.

Two to Four Years

During this period, if not before, toilet training becomes a major focus of the child's development. Freud called this the *anal period,* because he believed the child's emotional energies centered on the toileting process. Whether this concentration results from biological urges and pleasure or from parental concern, the process itself is believed to have important consequences for personality development.

First, there is the question of the child's own will. Getting to the toilet in time or performing when requested means gaining control of a previously autonomic function. It also means pleasing or displeasing the parent; it becomes a way of controlling the parent. Then there is the matter of messiness. Feces can be interesting to play with; they smear well. Mother's reaction to that particular discovery may explain why, a year or so later, the young child is still reluctant to smear finger paints. (It is also possible that young children resist finger painting because they do not understand that the paint will wash off.) Finally, the withholding of a bowel movement may (up to a point) be a source of pleasure that may generalize to other enterprises. Baldwin (1967) describes the adult personality that may have remained "stuck" in the anal phase of development:

> Miserliness is a pleasure in the accumulating and hoarding of possessions, which could have its historical origin in the pleasure of withholding feces. Stinginess is so common in certain kinds of people that it is one of a triad of traits constituting the *anal personality*. . . .
> A different feature of the anal period is the emphasis on cleanliness and neatness. . . . Cleanliness can thus become a major issue for the individual, either in the form of obsessive cleanliness or defiant messiness, or in an alternation between the two. . . .
> Often this cleanliness seems to be part of a more general fussiness and neatness, not only of physical possessions but also of thoughts. The anal personality is often pedantic. He tends to cling to tiny distinctions, to split hairs, and generally to be unable to tolerate any confusion or ambiguity. . . . [This may lead] to various sorts of maladjustment and to distortion of the individual's conception of the real world as he tries to make everything neat and tidy. Another related form of neatness is punctiliousness or clinging to the letter of the law. It is a form of literal obedience that may also stem from the experiences of toilet-training. (Baldwin, 1965, pp. 360–361)

Autonomy vs. Shame and Doubt Erikson sees this period as a three-way battle of wills—the will of the parent to train the child, the will of the body to evacuate when ready, and the will of the child to gain control of the situation. If he loses control to the parent, he will have lost his self-esteem; if he loses control to his body, he will be overcome by a sense of shame. It is the resolution of this crisis—autonomy vs. shame and doubt—that Erikson believes to characterize successful completion of the anal period. But White sees it as much more than that:

> Clearly we are dealing with important problems of development, but is it correct to place the decisive struggle in the bathroom? . . .
> Let us ask what the child accomplishes during the second and third years in the way of competent interactions with his environment. As regards locomotion he starts as an awkward toddler, but by the middle of the second year he becomes a restless runabout. . . . By the third birthday he may display his astonishing gains in coordination by starting to ride a tricycle. . . . One observes a constant activity of carrying objects about, filling and emptying containers, tearing things apart and fitting them together, lining up blocks and eventually building with them, digging and constructing in the sandbox. . . . In parallel fashion he begins new tests of his competence in the social sphere. (White, 1960, pp. 115–117)

These "tests of competence" may get him into trouble, at least with some of his friends and with his parents. Does he have the right to do what he wants to, when he wants to? What happens when he says no? What demands can he make? As the child experiments with primitive organizations of his own sense of competent selfhood, his battle for autonomy may grow intense.

White sees maladjustments stemming from this period as unresolved social conflicts. The adult who did not pass through this stage successfully may continue to place himself in opposition to social pressures, as if he were a stubborn child. It is as if his autonomy "froze" before it became mature. His personality may seem to be held together by a set of rules that take the place of more mature types of personality organization. And every time those rules are questioned ("George, why do we *have* to leave for the concert at exactly 7:29?"), they must be nailed down more firmly ("Because it takes us exactly fourteen and one-half minutes to reach the auditorium, and three minutes to park.") or the personality will dissolve into a shameful mess.

A popular theme in movies and plays is that of the stuffy businessman who lives by the clock and the stock market suddenly being transformed into a playboy by an uninhibited female. There may be more psychological truth than fiction to this plot; the way to "unfreeze" a prematurely rigidified personality may be to reawaken the early sense of playful exploration that White describes. As the reawakened energies are tested and personal competence begins to grow again, the personality may be able to reintegrate on a more mature, less rule-bound level. (Although few schools specialize in uninhibited females, they may be able to offer some engaging adventures in creative art.)

Four to Six Years
As the child becomes more aware of himself as a separate person with ideas and purposes of his own, he falls in love (in effect) with one of his parents. Thus, the stage is set for the reenactment of the Oedipus or the Electra conflict—the child sees the same-sex parent as a rival for the affections of the other parent. To understand this drama, we need to be aware of three aspects of the emerging personality—the *id* (or instinctual urges), the *superego* (or conscience), and the *ego* (or self). Freud saw the ego as a sort of compromise system that comes into existence as a way of gratifying id impulses without violating the superego's rules. (The same might be said about civilization in general.)

The id, of course, is around from the beginning; it is the nest of biological instincts the infant brings with him. The superego becomes crystallized during the Oedipal period—the so-called *phallic stage* of personality development (phallic because the child's focus has shifted from the mouth and the anal region to the genitals). The crystallization comes about in this way: The child's special love for the opposite-sex parent is viewed with alarm (the child believes) by his parental rival. The alarm is coupled with threats of punishment. In boys, this punishment is thought to be aimed at the genitals, and castration anxiety is the result. In girls, the castration is thought to have taken place already. Since these fantasied threats are severe and the child is tiny, a solution must be found. The child cannot tolerate the continuation of such a "war" with his dangerous parent.

Identification with the Parental Rival The solution is a straightforward one: The child develops a sense of psychological unity, or identification, with his rival—the father, in the case of a boy; the mother, in the case of a girl. The identification leads to the development of proper sex role characteristics. The boy becomes masculine, and the girl becomes feminine. Each takes his otherwise dangerous parental rival into himself (Freud's term for this was *introjection*) and paradoxically becomes protected against the same parent (the term for this is *identification with the aggressor*). Something that threatens us can no longer hurt us if it has become part of us.

The Birth of Primitive Conscience In a sense, the child is thought to have "swallowed whole" the parent's wishes, values, and standards, along with certain personality characteristics. Here is the source of the superego. But during this primitive phase of development, the child's superego may be more concrete and literal than his parents' actual rules. He still lacks abstract concepts of such things as justice and tolerance, as we know from his preoperational behavior. He may have difficulty digesting his own conscience:

> All of this may seem strange to readers who have only seen the sunnier side of childhood and have not recognized the potential powerhouse of destructive drives which can be aroused and temporarily buried at this stage, only to contribute later to the arsenal of a destructiveness so ready to be used when opportunity provokes it. . . . For the conscience of the child *can* be primitive, cruel, and uncompromising. . . . (Erikson, 1959, p. 79)

Erikson sees the Oedipal personality crisis as one of initiative vs. guilt. The child must begin to construct a harmonious relationship between his own impulses and the rules of his culture. If he weathers this crisis, his own personal initiative (discovered during the anal period) will flower. If he loses his battle to an overwhelming sense of guilt, his ego may be permanently crippled. It will not have healthfully survived the "war" between his id and his superego.

The Competence Problem White sees the crisis much more in terms of a competence rivalry. The 4- to 5-year-old child is developing many new motor, language, and role-playing skills. He is much better able to evaluate his skills in relation to those of others in his family and to realize that his are, in fact, frequently inferior:

> From the point of view of competence, of pride in being big, genital inferiority is by no means greater than many other inferiorities such as

stature, strength, speed of running, distance one can throw a ball. Father can start the power lawn mower and control it; he can drive the car; for the modern child these must be obvious and hopeless tokens of [father's] superiority. . . . [Although] there is clearly a sexual flavor to some of the child's activities and interests . . . [this should not be taken] as a matter so profound that the whole of emotional development hangs upon it. . . . (White, 1960, p. 124)

The role of schooling during this period may be critical. For most children, nursery school, Head Start, kindergarten, or first grade begins while their personal initiative-guilt struggle is still unresolved. The school that helps them to understand that growth in competence is possible may produce lifelong benefits to the personality. The school that adds to a child's already crushing sense of inferiority (as many cruel first grades do) may permanently warp his development. In a sense, the school has become a silent partner to the crisis:

> Parents often do not realize why some children suddenly seem to think less of them and seem to attach themselves to teachers, to the parents of other children, or to people representing occupations which the child can grasp: firemen and policemen, gardeners and plumbers. The point is that children do not wish to be reminded of the principal inequality with the parent of the same sex. They . . . look for opportunities where superficial identification seems to promise a field of initiative without too much conflict or guilt. (Erikson, 1959, pp. 81–82)

In his school, the child may (if he is fortunate) experience a type of collaboration with his teacher—a collaboration that convinces him he is equal in *worth*, if not in size or skill, to his adult models. The onset of formal schooling, then, because of its coincidence with a special type of personality crisis, may be a gateway to mental health.

Seven to Twelve Years
Because this period precedes the flowering of adult genital sexuality and follows the period of childish sexuality (the Oedipal period), Freud described it as the *latency period*. What is latent is the libido; what it is doing while it is latent is constructing an organized ego.

The struggle between the id and the superego continues and may intensify or counteract earlier struggles. The child is primarily turned outward, rather than inward toward his family. His interests are in peers, clubs, games with rules, Scouts, and so forth. It is as if the child were practicing and solidifying his earlier personality achievements by testing them in the world. Here, he learns again how trust operates (with peers and teachers, for example), what the limits of his own willfulness may be, what the sex role characteristics are outside of his family, and how much of his own initiative may be safely exercised without guilt or shame.

Both Erikson and White see this period as an exceptionally important one. Erikson describes it as the flowering of the sense of industry, and the accompanying personality crisis as one between industry and inferiority. The child wants to be industrious—to do real, not play work. If he is not successful during this critical birth of true enterprise, he may give up forever—or at least he may carry with him a lasting sense of inadequacy.

Since this period covers almost all the elementary school years, a great deal is said about it elsewhere in this book. It is Piaget's period of concrete operations, for example, and it is important for moral development. But we have no overall Freudian theory of the major lines of personality development over the latency years. Freud was primarily interested in origins (infancy) and outcomes (adulthood); he was not as convinced as later theorists (such as Erikson and White) that middle childhood mattered. As White says, "Freud seems to have found the [latency] period something of a bore" (1960, p. 127).

Curriculum Style and Mental Health The importance of personality theory for instructional strategies is indicated by a study in which Grimes and Allinsmith (1961) investigated the relationship of reading methods to personality characteristics. By means of personality tests, they identified third-grade children who were high and low in what they called *compulsivity*—orderliness, neatness, attention to detail, conformity—and children who were high and low in *anxiety*. We might guess that the highly compulsive children had not weathered the anal period very well and that the highly anxious children were still struggling with the competence problems of the Oedipal period.

The children were from two different schools—one a structured, traditional school with a relatively traditional curriculum; the other, a less structured school with a warmer, more permissive environment. In addition to environmental differences, the schools offered different types of reading programs. The structured school taught by a code method (see Chapter 21); the unstructured school, by a "look and say" or meaning method. As Figure 14.1 shows, *the influence of school and reading structure*

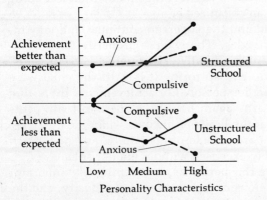

Figure 14.1 Reading achievement of anxious and compulsive third-grade children in two school environments. (Grimes and Allinsmith, 1961)

was beneficial as personality difficulties increased. The experimenters believed this was because the structured school offered a pattern of behavior to children who were still having difficulty working out their own individual patterns. We might say (with Prentice) that the steps involved in learning to read were made cognitively available to them.

The experiment illustrates the way in which an appropriate instructional strategy may interact with personality dynamics during the latency period. Quite possibly, an appropriate strategy would lead to personality improvement, although Grimes and Allinsmith did not pursue this point. At least we can speculate that an anxious or compulsive child who is taught to read by an inappropriate method may fail to develop exactly the sort of competence that would help him resolve his personality difficulties.

In the next section, we will take up other personality dimensions that may interact with instructional systems during the latency period and other periods. First, however, we need to look at the final phase of personality development.

Adolescence

The years from 12 to 18 or 20 are marked by a flowering of adult sexual potential. This is, of course, a period of great personal turbulence. Freud viewed it as a reactivation of all the earlier problems, except that the love object shifted from parent to someone outside the family. This is not a simple, easy transition, especially in our American society. Little transitional practice is permitted; the adolescent is expected to change from an immature family follower into a mature family leader, complete with job, purpose in life, and sexual competence, while spending most of his time boxed up in the artificial environment of a high school. The youngster who fails to make this transition comfortably becomes caught up again in problems of trust and dependence, guilt and shame, initiative, industry, and confusion. Erikson refers to this as *identity diffusion:*

> The danger of this stage is . . . as Biff puts it in Arthur Miller's *Death of a Salesman*, "I just can't take hold, Mom, I can't take hold of some kind of a life." Where such a dilemma is based on a strong previous doubt of one's ethnic and sexual identity, delinquent and outright psychotic incidents are not uncommon. . . . [But] if diagnosed and treated correctly, seemingly psychotic and criminal incidents do not in adolescence have the same fatal significance which they have at other ages. . . . (Erikson, 1959, p. 91)

There are several important aspects of the problem Erikson describes. First of all, identity diffusion leaves an adolescent prey to all his earlier conflicts and confusions. We may see symptoms of oral and anal conflicts—a youngster may become compulsive about certain food habits, for example. (Vegetarianism is common among youths in the counterculture.) Some of the old Oedipal fears may also arise, leaving the youngster fearful of too strong an attachment to the opposite-sex parent. Such a fear may produce excessive demands for independence.

Second, adolescents may help each other through their identity crises by banding together in cliques. Their behavior may become stereotyped. In effect, they create for each other an artificial, prosthetic identity. This is discussed further in the section on dependency behavior later in this chapter.

The Problem of Drug Abuse Nowadays, the natural developmental crisis of identity diffusion has been malevolently compounded by the use of drugs. Youngsters who might otherwise be banding together on the basis of harmless fads are becoming victims of chemicals that have effects far beyond their control. (A good general discussion of these effects may be found in Peter Laurie's *Drugs: Medical, Psychological and Social Facts,* published by Penguin Books.)

At this writing, the drug epidemic has become a national crisis that is still not fully recognized. Schools cannot, of course, solve the problem without substantial help from their communities. All a textbook of this sort can do is sound a call for understanding: Drug abusers in our high schools and colleges are undergoing developmental crises of various kinds; they are not criminals. They have discovered an escape from personal conflicts—an escape that works far too well and that may rapidly take them beyond a point of no return. Just having adolescents sit in a traditional classroom will do nothing. The job of the community and the school is to seek out and provide alternative routes for solving the identity development problem. According to some reports, one out of every five high school seniors uses hard drugs to a serious degree. Surely such statistics should galvanize our social institutions into purposeful, responsive activity.

Identity and Formal Operations The interaction of the identity crisis with formal operational skills sometimes produces articulate youngsters who can argue forcefully for points of view that are only temporary. They are described by Inhelder and Piaget as concerned with the theoretical and the abstract:

> Most [adolescents] have political or social theories and want to reform the world; they have their own ways of explaining all of the present-day turmoil. . . . Others have literary or aesthetic theories. . . . Some go through religious crises and reflect on the problem of faith. . . . Philosophical speculation carries away a minority. . . . A still smaller minority turns from the start toward scientific or pseudoscientific theories. . . . Of course, the girls are more interested in marriage, but the husband they dream of is most often "theoretical," and their thoughts about married life as well often take on the characteristics of "theories." . . .
>
> If we now step outside the student range and the intellectual classes . . . we can recognize the same phenomenon in other forms. . . . We would find . . . a lower degree of abstraction. But under different and varied exteriors the same core process can easily be discerned. . . . (Inhelder and Piaget, 1958, pp. 339–342)

These new operational skills may be an important clue for community-school adolescent programs. If youngsters can "try on" various theories and identities, why not provide them with constructive ways of doing so? Movie-making projects, for example, could provide ways of testing theories and identities of various kinds safely and meaningfully. Opportunities to travel, to participate in historical, scientific, and artistic projects, to work on real community problems—these should form a substantial part of adolescent education. The more formal, academic programs could be minimized, carried out on a contract basis, and integrated as much as possible with the projects, which would provide real-life models for adolescents struggling with identity problems. They would acquire models for living, not merely for classroom regimentation.

Personality and Schooling

This survey of the phases of personality growth is intended to provide a framework for "decoding" some general response patterns. When you teach youngsters of a certain age, it is reasonable to expect certain personality characteristics, just as you expect certain cognitive characteristics. Their exact form, of course, will vary from student to student. The concrete operational child will have a "sense of industry" along with an interest in rules and symbols, but depending upon his history, these characteristics may manifest themselves as an interest in school subjects or in street-corner hustling.

Ideally, a school should permit youngsters to use their own personalities in their own education. But this would require, just to begin with, more opportunity for the expression of personality in the school. Suppose teachers were expected, as part of their job, to relate to students in accordance with characteristic personality-growth needs. What would this mean?

First, during the early preschool period, the relationship of trust and security would be dominant. In disadvantaged communities, this emphasis might lead to the establishment of round-the-clock community schools so that a neglected child would never be abandoned. For older children who still have unresolved problems of trust and dependency, surrogate parents or tutors might be provided.

Second, as the child grows, his sphere of guided personal expression should be extended as far as he wishes it to go. Involvement in real-life enterprises on an apprenticeship basis should occur as a natural outgrowth of developing competence and confidence. By adolescence, the child of such a schooling program might be spending only a few hours a week in a formal classroom. The rest of his education would be occurring in surroundings compatible with his own maturing personality. His teachers, in that case, might need to be "certified" primarily as human beings.

How strange it might seem to construct a curriculum on such principles. Yet is it not equally strange that our school programs relegate almost all personality development to the home, or to somewhere, *anywhere* but the school? Can we really expect to educate minds that are not the minds of *persons*?

CRITICAL PERSONALITY DIMENSIONS IN THE CLASSROOM

Certain personality characteristics stand out in students of all ages. Hyperactivity, for example, may arise in young children as a result of unusual dependency (oral) needs; in adolescents, a similar condition may have a different cause or may arise from a reactivation of the old dependency needs. In any event, the condition must be dealt with in the classroom. In this section, we will pull special personality characteristics out of their overall growth framework and examine them separately.

Persistence, Impulsivity, and Hyperactivity

Perhaps the most visible critical personality dimension is the ability (or inability) of a student to persist at a school task. In primary school, we may see this in the restless, careless child; on the secondary level, the trait may be expressed in truancy and unfinished assignments. In many cases, of course, such behavior can be attributed to poor classroom conditions or to inappropriate assignments. But for a small number of children, the restlessness may be a personality characteristic that the school must cope with under all conditions.

Research since the 1930s has shown that infants differ from birth in activity level and that these differences persist for at least fifteen years (Schaefer and Bayley, 1963; Irwin, 1930). Clinicians label the most severe cases *hyperactives*. These children may have suffered actual brain damage to inhibitory neural areas. The condition may not be serious enough for institutionalization, but it may drive a teacher to distraction. In the midst of one's distraction, it is important to remember that the hyperactive child is not being "bad." He is a child with a handicap, not a character deficiency.

Kagan's Test of Impulsivity On a less serious level, restlessness may lead to habits of carelessness in school tasks. Kagan et al. (1964) have developed a test of impulsivity called the Matching Familiar Figures (MFF) test. Some items from it are shown in Figure 14.2. Subjects must find the figure that exactly matches the test (top) figure. Some subjects respond quickly and carelessly; others carefully check one figure at a time. Kagan believes that impulsivity or reflectivity is a consistent and relatively stable personality trait that may be evident by the time a child is 2 years old.

Scores on the MFF test are correlated with a variety of academic skills, as one might expect. Reading errors, for example, are more numerous among children who are impulsive on the MFF materials (Kagan, 1965). Impulsive children also make more errors on a variety of inductive reasoning tasks, where inferences must be evaluated (Kagan, Pearson,

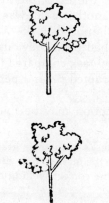

Figure 14.2   Sample items from the Matching Familiar Figures (MFF) test. (Kagan et al., 1964)

and Welch, 1966). The implication of such research is that the personality trait of impulsiveness, rather than intellectual deficiency, may be partly responsible for poor reading and reasoning ability.

Tolerance for Delay of Gratification Earlier, we discussed Mischel's (1958) concept of individual differences in tolerance for delays in reinforcement. This may also be a personality characteristic that operates in a variety of situations. Its cause is not clear. In one study (Farnham-Diggory, 1966), it was found that time perception was somewhat distorted in normal children who preferred the immediate reinforcement of a small candy bar to the delayed reinforcement of a large candy bar received a week later. The children indicated (through drawings) that intervals like three hours, two weeks, or one month seemed unusually long to them, compared to children who chose the delayed reward. Perhaps the extended time perspective made waiting for a reward more difficult.

Habits of Interruption Lack of persistence on a task may not be associated with rewards or impulsivity, however. It may arise from other causes. In another study (Farnham-Diggory and Ramsey, 1971), 5-year-old Head Start girls played for 10 minutes with ordinary toys—playdough, paints, bubbles, and the like. Just as they became interested in a toy—just as they were about to blow a bubble or to put a puzzle piece in place—the experimenter interrupted and said something like, "Why don't you try this?" or "Hey, you haven't done this yet." The interruption was not punitive, it was just annoying; the child could never carry out a plan of her own without being interrupted or nudged to press on to something else. (Some mothers are of this "smothering" variety; so are some teachers, as we will see in a coming example.)

Following the 10-minute play period, the experimenter went away, and the child was left (not entirely alone; another adult was sitting quietly in a corner of the room) to play with still another task—a new one that had not been seen before. Children who had been previously interrupted displayed very short persistence on the new task compared to control children. It was as if the interruption had disrupted natural persistence tendencies and set up habits of restlessness.

A chilling example of teacher interruption may be found in the following transcript:

> The children were sitting at their desks with their grammar books in front of them. The teacher was explaining the method by which the child was to associate the picture in the book with the correct spelling of the word represented.
>
> She directed a question to Robert. "Robert, can you spell *fork*?" Robert did not reply, his head bent down. She then directed her question to Terry, first asking him for the correct name of the object in the book. "Terry, what is this picture?" Terry answered, "Fork." The teacher then said, "Spell it." Terry raised his head from the book and started spelling the word. "F . . ."

and then hesitated. The teacher broke in, "Why don't you look in the book?" Immediately upon asking this question, she turned around and directed the question to Linda. "Linda, spell fork."

Throughout the school day, children in this classroom were almost never permitted to complete a response. Needless to say, they were extremely restless and disruptive.

To a less extreme degree, primary and secondary school environments systematically interrupt students. The bell rings or the period ends without regard for student preoccupation. Do such interruptions encourage habits of nonpersistence? Should we be surprised if students fail to persist at homework and lack concentration abilities?

Teaching Persistence On a more positive note, if nonpersistence can be taught, then so can persistence. As you know from Chapter 10, Bandura and Mischel (1965) showed that tolerance for reinforcement delay was responsive to modeling. A child who observed an adult express a preference for delayed rewards learned to express similar interests. Impulsivity is also responsive to modeling. Yando and Kagan (1968) investigated the

Figure 14.3 Sample item from the adult version of the MFF test. (Yando and Kagan, 1968, p. 29)

amount of change in first-graders' impulsivity from fall to spring as a function of the impulsivity of their *teachers.*

A sample from the MFF test for adults is shown in Figure 14.3. Twenty first-grade teachers were classified as impulsive or reflective on the basis of their responses to the test. The mean response time of the reflective teachers was about 60 seconds; that of the impulsive teachers, about 16 seconds. The results were clear: Over the school year, *children in the classrooms of reflective teachers changed significantly toward reflectivity themselves,* particularly if the teachers were experienced. Children in the classrooms of impulsive teachers either showed no change or changed in the direction of impulsivity.

Reflectivity can also be taught directly (Kagan, Pearson, and Welch, 1966), even in the case of hyperactives. Palkes, Stewart, and Kahana (1968) taught hyperactive children to use visual reminder cards like those shown in Figure 14.4 as self-instructional materials. The children re-

Figure 14.4 Visual reminder cards used with hyperactive students. (Palkes, Stewart, and Kahana, 1968)

hearsed the various self-commands aloud as aids on the MFF test and on another similar test. After practicing on these materials, the hyperactives were switched to another task (maze tracing). Although they did not use the visual reminder cards on the maze task, they showed improved control. Practice in self-instructed reflectivity had generalized to the next task.

Whether a so-called restless nature in a student comes from organic or social causes, it should be treated with understanding rather than punishment. In the case of both young children and adolescents, the student may be unable to "program" his own activities in an organized, self-controlled way. The wise teacher will have techniques for helping him learn how to do so.

Anxiety and Defensiveness
Anxiety is a general all-purpose signal that something is wrong. The signal system is generally an advantage, for some degree of anxiety is

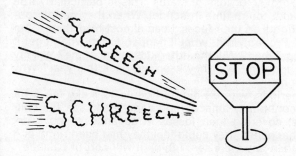

Figure 14.4   *(Continued)*

necessary to survival. Two other aspects of anxiety, however, are not so beneficial: (1) False or loose anxiety that seems to float around and block all forms of constructive behavior (the Freudians call this *free-floating* anxiety) and (2) response systems that prevent the individual from feeling anxiety and thus from solving the problems that produced it (Freudians call these *defense mechanisms*).

Free-floating anxiety probably arises from unresolved crises of personality growth. An identity crisis, for example, may generate anxiety that seems to attach itself to (or power) many kinds of behavior. In general, school situations that help to resolve the crisis will help to eliminate free-floating anxiety; those that intensify the crisis will increase the anxiety, sometimes to psychotic proportions.

John Holt in *How Children Fail* has written persuasively of school behaviors that may be adopted by highly anxious children:

> The strategies of most of these kids have been consistently self-centered, self-protective, aimed above all else at avoiding trouble, embarrassment, punishment, disapproval, or loss of status. This is particularly true of the ones who have had a tough time in school. When they get a problem, I can read their thoughts on their faces, I can almost hear them, "Am I going to get this right? Probably not; what'll happen to me when I get it wrong? Will the teacher get mad? Will the other kids laugh at me? Will my mother and father hear about it? Will they keep me back this year? Why am I so dumb?" And so on.
>
> Even in the room periods, where I did all I could to make the work non-threatening, I was continually amazed and appalled to see the children hedging their bets, covering their losses in advance, trying to fix things so that whatever happened they could feel they had been right, or if wrong, no more wrong than anyone else. "I think it will sort of balance." They are fence-straddlers, afraid ever to commit themselves — and at the age of ten. . . .
>
> These self-limiting and self-defeating strategies are dictated above all else, by fear. For many years I have been asking myself why intelligent children act unintelligently at school. The simple answer is, "Because they're scared." . . .
>
> . . . Perhaps most people do not recognize fear in children when they see it. They can read the grossest signs of fear; they know what the trouble is when a child clings howling to his mother, but the subtler signs of fear escape them. It is these signs, in children's faces, noises, and gestures, in their movements and ways of working, that tell me plainly that most children in school are scared most of the time, many of them very scared. Like good soldiers, they control their fears, live with them, and adjust themselves to them. But the trouble is, and here is a vital difference between school and war, that the adjustments children make to their fears are almost wholly bad, destructive of their intelligence and capacity. The scared fighter may be the best fighter, but the scared learner is always a poor learner. (Holt, 1964, pp. 48–49)

Systematic research on the behavior described by Holt is still scarce. We have very little evidence, for example, on the extent to which such behavior (pupil anxiety) may occur more frequently in some schools or classrooms than others. A teacher's personal impression that children are highly anxious may be a reflection of the teacher's own anxiety—possibly even of a teacher's *wish* to believe that his students are anxious. (Perhaps some insecure teachers are comforted by what they believe to be fear and uncertainty in their pupils.) Further, some private schools, or special classes in public schools, have an above-average number of emotionally or mentally handicapped children. Such children generally display a high degree of anxiety. We must be careful to bring objectivity into our assessment of anxiety in children.

The Test Anxiety Scale for Children One objective research program has been carried out by Seymour Sarason and his colleagues (Sarason et al., 1960). They have not studied all forms of school anxiety, but have concentrated on a critical type: anxiety about tests. To investigate this problem, they developed a measure called the Test Anxiety Scale for Children, or TASC.

The TASC is a self-report inventory. It contains such items as "Do you worry a lot before taking a test?" "When the teacher says she is going to find out how much you have learned, does your heart begin to beat faster?" "While you are taking a test, do you usually think you are not doing well?"

Sarason has also developed what he calls a Defensiveness Scale for Children (DSC), which contains items like these: "When you hurt somebody's feelings, does it make you feel badly?" "Do you wish your teacher paid more attention to you?" "Do you sometimes have arguments with your mother and father?" Children who usually answer "No" to questions of this sort are probably defending themselves against the experience of anxiety and/or guilt. Generally, there is a strong negative correlation between scores on the defensiveness scale and scores on the test anxiety scale. The more defensive a student is on the DSC, the less anxiety he admits to on the TASC.

Sarason and his colleagues found that TASC scores are negatively correlated with IQ, especially when the TASC scores are statistically corrected for the effects of defensiveness. There is a similar negative correlation between test anxiety and academic achievement. In other words, the less bright the child and the less successful he is in school, the more anxious he becomes about testing situations. This effect increases with age; the negative correlation between TASC scores and achievement is stronger in older children than it is in first- and second-grade children.

Stevenson and Odom (1965) examined the relationship between TASC scores and problem-solving abilities. They used five standard learning and problem-solving tasks, such as learning nonsense syllable pairs, concept attainment, and anagrams. They concluded that test anxiety had an especially disruptive effect on verbal tasks compared to tasks involving visual symbols (tasks that were more iconic in nature). Sarason et al. (1960) and Lynn (1957) also found a stronger relationship between test anxiety and reading skills than between test anxiety and arithmetic skills (which may also be visual in nature; see Chapter 23).

Of course, a correlation is not a causal relationship—that is, the fact that two scores are associated with each other does not prove that one caused the other. Test anxiety may be caused by failure in school subjects or by difficulties stemming from relatively low intelligence. On the other hand, the school failures, and even the IQ difficulties, may be increased by test anxiety.

One study by Waite, Sarason, Lighthall, and Davidson (1958) showed that highly test-anxious children *began* a task with as much skill as children with low anxiety, but deteriorated as the task progressed. By the end of the task, the highly anxious children were much worse than the others, who had demonstrated better ability to improve with practice. Both groups were equated for IQ, so the learning deficit seemed to result more from anxiety than from basic intelligence.

Coping with Anxiety in School In addition to test anxiety, there are many other forms of anxiety in the classroom. School phobias have already been mentioned (Chapter 10). The special crises attending the stages of personality development may all produce anxiety. In addition, anxiety may appear in the form of a defense mechanism. In this case, the student may not be conscious of his anxiety, but the teacher will recognize that it exists.

Freud defined several mechanisms of defense, including *repression* (blocking an anxiety-producing idea from consciousness); *denial* (admitting the idea, but denying that it is true); *projection* (placing the source of the idea elsewhere, rather than in oneself); and *rationalization* (accepting responsibility for the idea, but making socially acceptable excuses for it). Probably the last two mechanisms appear most frequently in classrooms. Psychosomatic symptoms such as those shown by Esther (Chapter 11) may also result from anxiety.

What is the teacher to do about anxiety? First of all, not let it increase his own. Some amount of anxiety is inevitable in today's world. It is possible that moderate amounts of anxiety, experienced in the comparative safety of a school situation, will help prepare individuals to cope with reality in the adult world. Test-taking experience in the early grades, for example, may help reduce anxiety in the later grades. Further, some degree of anxiety will definitely spur achievement. A realistic appraisal of college competition may make individuals anxious about mastery of high school subjects—and produce greater achievement as a result. The increased competence will, in turn, lower future anxiety. Anxiety that leads to increased competence is probably not damaging to the personality.

But what about anxiety that is severe enough to disrupt competence development? It goes without saying that severe anxiety should not be deliberately generated by teachers or school policies. Evidence of high anxiety on the part of a whole class (assuming the children are normal) should certainly be grounds for examining the school, not the pupils. Assuming a generally benign school atmosphere, however, what should a teacher do about especially anxious children who seem to have brought their anxiety with them into the classroom? The two basic therapeutic principles seem to be cognitive clarification and desensitization. We have discussed both earlier, and their application in a school setting is straightforward. Sarason et al. (1960) have urged teachers to assure test-anxious children that questions about test items will be answered and that ample time will be allowed. It is also suggested that a playlike atmosphere, rather than a testlike atmosphere, be created if possible. Curricula that emphasize retesting and mastery may also help reduce the sense of panic produced by the feeling that a test is irrevocable and final.

Desensitization may be partly accomplished by giving many small tests, rather than a few big ones. Some of these might be practice or trial tests. In severe cases (even among adults), simulating real test conditions may be helpful—even to setting time limits and gaining familiarity with special test rooms (auditoriums, for example). Simulations also have the advantage of increasing clarification because the student is learning more and more about the characteristics and requirements of real tests.

The anxiety hidden in defense mechanisms is more problematical. If the bluff is called ("Jenny, you know perfectly well that your D was your own fault and that the noise in the radiator had nothing to do with it"), the student may be forced to greater lengths to ward off the anxiety the defense mechanism is containing ("I'm going to tell the principal that you made me sit next to that radiator, just to make me fail!"). We can sometimes avoid confrontations of that sort by thinking of a defensive strategy as a *shield against fear.* If the shield is attacked, the student will hang on more tightly than ever. A better approach would be to give the student support and encouragement so that he will be willing to put aside his shield voluntarily. The most realistically satisfying shield is genuine competence.

A hopeful future sign is revealed in an experiment carried out by Sutter and Reid (1969), who measured the achievement of students participating in a computer-assisted instruction (CAI) program. Some of these students were high in test anxiety, and some were not. Some studied at the machine with a partner, and some studied alone. Sutter and Reid found that students high in test anxiety achieved more when they studied alone; students low in test anxiety achieved more when they had a partner. The study is hopeful because it shows us how personality characteristics may be taken into consideration in designing instructional programs. Even negative characteristics like anxiety may be "put to work" in the student's own interest, if they are recognized and respected.

Passive and Dependent Behaviors

A dependency trait may take a variety of forms. In the nursery school, we see it in the clinging child who seems to need constant support and attention from adults. In the upper grades, the characteristic may take more ominous forms, including drug addiction.

As you know, dependency needs are thought to originate in infancy, when dependency is a biologically necessary state. The transition to independence occurs gradually during early childhood; it may take an especially trying form during the toilet training period. Family efforts to produce independent behavior may vary between families, and from child to child within a single family. Dependency behavior is generally considered appropriate for girls and is encouraged. For that reason, it may persist as a visible character trait among women, but not among men.

Dependency and Growth Kagan and Moss (1960) examined longitudinal data from the Fels Research Institute for consistency of dependency behaviors. They obtained measures of dependency on the same individuals from 3 to about 25 years of age. The childhood measures were not, however, exactly the same as the adult measures. During childhood, the children were rated by observers; as adults, they were interviewed personally. Thus we have a comparison between observer reports of early childhood behavior and self-reports of adult behavior. The categories used by Kagan and Moss for measuring dependency behavior are quoted below because they are useful guides to the detection of dependency needs in the classroom.

[DURING CHILDHOOD]

Tendency to behave in a passive manner when faced with environmental obstacles or stress. . . . This variable assessed the degree to which the child was behaviorally passive in the face of external frustrations and failed to make any active mastery attempts to obtain desired goal objects following frustration. The rating of a passive behavioral reaction emphasized withdrawal from the frustration but included whining, crying, and soliciting help.

Tendency to seek support, nurturance, and assistance from female adults when under stress: general dependence. . . . This [referred to] . . . the subject's behavioral tendency to obtain assistance, nurturance, or affection from mother and other female adults when confronted with a threat to his well-being, a problem, or loss of a desired goal object. Dependent behavior included seeking out adults when faced with a problem or personal injury, reluctance to start a task without help or encouragement, seeking assistance of others, seeking affection from and close contact with female adults.

Tendency to seek affection and emotional support from female adults. . . . This variable assessed the degree to which the child sought affection or emotional encouragement from mother or mother substitute figures. Evidence included kissing, holding hands, clinging, seeking encouragement or proximity to female adults.

Tendency to seek instrumental assistance from female adults. . . .
This variable assessed the degree to which the child sought instrumental help with specific problems from mother, teachers, or other female authority figures. Instrumental dependent acts included seeking help with tasks, and seeking help when physically threatened. (Kagan and Moss, 1960, pp. 578–579)

During adulthood, the situation becomes more complicated. The interviewers in the Kagan and Moss study developed six categories of behavior (as self-reported), which they believed revealed the degree of dependency of the respondent.

[DURING ADULTHOOD]

Degree to which dependent gratifications were sought in choice of vocation. This variable assessed the degree to which security was an important aspect of job choice, the degree to which the subject looked to his employer for gratification of his dependent needs, reluctance to shift jobs because of temporary loss of security. For nonworking women, emphasis was placed on her attitudes about the importance of security in her husband's job.
Degree of dependent behavior toward a love object. This variable assessed the degree to which the subject sought advice and emotional support from a love object (sweetheart, husband, wife), degree to which the subject looked for stability and wisdom in a love object, degree to which responsibility for decision making was given to love object.
Degree of dependent behavior with parents. This variable assessed the degree to which the subject looked for advice, support, emotional encouragement, and nurturance from one or both parents.
Degree of dependent behavior toward nonparental figures. This variable assessed the degree to which the subject sought advice, emotional support, and nurturance from nonparental figures who were not love objects, e.g., friends, relatives, and teachers.
Tendency to display behavioral withdrawal in the face of anticipated failure. This variable assessed the frequency and consistency with which the subject tended to withdraw from tasks and situations which he thought were difficult to master and in which failure was anticipated.
Degree of conflict over dependent behavior. This variable assessed the degree to which the subject avoided placing himself in dependent positions, his derogation of dependent behavior in self and others and his emphasis on the value and importance of independent behavior. (Kagan and Moss, 1960, p. 580)

There are a number of ways in which the correlation of childhood and adult dependency behaviors can be tested. Of all those ways, 60 percent were significantly correlated for women; only 9 percent were significantly correlated for men. Kagan and Moss believed this difference to be due to the fact that American society encourages dependent behavior in women, who are thus freer to maintain dependency needs.

Dependency Behavior in School During the preschool and elementary years, dependency behavior can be handled in relatively straightforward ways. The teacher does not want to frighten a dependent child by "throwing him into the water," so to speak, and expecting him to learn how to swim by himself. A good teacher will therefore try to provide emotional support and assistance—but always with a view toward extricating himself from this parental role. Operant conditioning techniques may be useful here. Young dependent children may be lavishly praised for independent behaviors and less rewarded for dependent behaviors. This may seem contrary to the popular notion that the child will spontaneously become independent once his need for security is fulfilled. Because of factors beyond the teacher's control, with some dependent children that need will never be fulfilled. The child's goal will be to maintain a dependent relationship with the teacher; the more the teacher encourages this, the more dependent the child will become. Therefore, the technique of rewarding independent behavior and withholding reward for dependent behavior may be the only way of guiding such a child to independence, at least as far as the classroom is concerned.

During the high school period, dependency needs may be hidden in a variety of roles. Among girls, the behavior may still be visible, but it is usually directed toward other girls (cliques) or toward boys. There is less overt dependence on a teacher. Among boys, however, the behavior may become almost invisible; by this time, the culture is expressing pronounced disapproval of overt dependency behavior in males. If dependency needs are still strong, they may have to masquerade. They may even masquerade as exaggerated needs for independence.

It seems possible that this type of masquerade is basic to the formation of so-called hippie cults among high school and college students. If one analyzes hippie behavior in terms of the categories above, it becomes clear that a good deal of dependency behavior is actually being expressed, primarily in the area of withdrawal from possible failure. The youngster who drops out of high school prior to the college admissions competition, who says he does not want to go to college or to develop himself in any skilled or professional capacity is actually maintaining himself as a dependent. He may not be overtly dependent upon his parents, but he is dependent upon *someone,* since he has no means of supporting himself. Usually, the dependency is directed toward a peer group or a commune-type of home. Because everyone in the group may be lacking in maintenance skills, the whole group may be dependent upon society or upon some charitable organization. If society does not respond to the group's demands, group members may become ill and/or vengeful. Much hippie behavior seems to take the form of a nonverbal cry: "Take care of me, or I will die!" Or, in another version, "Because you are expecting me to be independent and take care of myself, I will punish you!" Punishment may take the form of embarrassing the family by dress and behavior, or worrying the family by running away, keeping late hours, associating with undesirable people, and so forth. The extreme form of withdrawal, dependency, and punishment may be drug addiction.

Parents are not often able to handle these extreme dependency problems; they may even have helped produce them. Schools may also have helped produce them by the repeated insistence upon passive acceptance of assignments, curricula, and other forms of regulation. Community agencies such as the Y or other social and athletic clubs are neither prepared nor staffed to carry out intensive reeducation. Unless the school is willing to develop a special educational arm to help the extremely dependent youngster, it may force him into a descending spiral of incompetence. The less he learns, the more dependent he becomes; the more dependent he becomes, the less willing he will be to accept the step-by-step challenge of true competence development.

A clue to appropriate reeducation strategies may be found in some of the more mature commune hippie societies. Some communes (Michaelson, 1969) have leaders or founders who display organizational and maintenance skills. They buy land, build houses, grow crops. Of course, data on the stability of these groups are not available. It is not known how long they last, what the rate of turnover is, and how much of the apparent stability is really just "nose-thumbing" sustained by tourists and publicity. Perhaps when the tourists become bored and the magazine writers stop coming around, the mature commune (like the immature one) will dissolve. In that case, we would have to classify it as just another angry reaction to a society that would not fulfill masquerading dependency needs.

But if a mature commune is a stable phenomenon, it may help us understand how to deal with youngsters who *are* masquerading. An adolescent's extreme need to depend on a model or leader could possibly be met by "hip" teachers who point the way toward genuine competence development. A commune type of school may be the logical outcome. The right to remain in the commune could be contingent upon mastery of steps toward competence. Group goals (building a house of one's own, developing special art forms) could be used to generate subgoals (learning engineering, mastering silkscreen methods) that are worthwhile skills. Skill development could then be seen as an instrument of self-fulfillment, not as an "independence trap." ("If I learn how to make a living as a commercial artist, then I won't be able to depend upon anybody any more. What's worse, *other* people may expect to depend on *me*.") Unless commune leadership is assumed by responsible adults, we may continue to lose many valuable young people to irresponsible, criminal individuals whose own psychopathic needs are complemented and nourished by the extreme dependency of others.

Assertiveness, Aggression, and Hostility

Almost opposite to the trait of dependency is the trait we wish some hippies would develop—normal aggression or self-assertiveness. This is, perhaps, the trait that student activists have too much of; our student society sometimes seems to have divided a single normal personality into separate strands of extremism.

Scientists now believe that aggression has biological foundations. In fact, evidence is mounting that individual differences in aggressive behavior may be directly related to something like hostility centers in the brain. Many lines of evidence point to the possibility that brains differ in sensitivity to aggressive stimulation and in the degree of inhibition. The sensitivity may, in turn, be controlled by hormones:

> Irritability is a frequent component of the premenstrual tension syndrome in the human female and is successfully treated by the administration of [the hormone] progesterone. It has also been shown that crimes of violence committed by women are related to the menstrual cycle. In a study of 249 women prison inmates, it was shown that 62 per cent of the crimes of violence were committed during the premenstrual week and only 2 per cent at the end of the period. [Another hormone] diandrone . . . increases confidence in adolescents with feelings of inferiority and promotes aggressive responses. . . .
>
> It is generally recognized that frustration and stress, particularly if prolonged, are likely to result in increased irritability and aggressive behavior. It may well be that . . . irritability results from the sensitization of certain brain areas by the particular hormone balance which characterizes the stress syndrome. Both the adrenal cortex [which secretes adrenalin] and the thyroid are intimately involved in the stress syndrome, and dysfunctions of either gland result in increased irritability. (Moyer, 1968, pp. 12–13)

But the biological evidence does not obviate the effects of learning or previous experience. The same authors who studied dependency (Kagan and Moss, 1962) also studied the stability of aggressive behavior. They discovered that whereas dependency was consistent for women over the age range of 3 to about 30, aggression was consistent for men. Presumably society expects and encourages aggressive behavior in men, so they are able to maintain natural tendencies. We also know from the Bandura experiments (Chapter 10) that aggressive behavior is responsive to modeling. Certainly men have more opportunities than women to observe aggressive behavior in other men.

Learning to Be Aggressive Patterson, Littman, and Bricker (1967) studied aggressive behavior in nursery school children. Their theoretical orientation was a Skinnerian one: They were looking for reinforcement factors that increased or decreased aggression in the school setting. They believed that aggression may be (1) taught in the home and then maintained or increased by a permissive school setting and/or (2) taught in the school by the children themselves. Home conditioning may begin very early:

> An example . . . observed by one of the writers was as follows: The mother sat holding her 7-month-old infant at the dinner table. In talking to another member of the family, she had been looking away from the infant

and did not observe his attempts to reach a glass of milk sitting on the table. He began pummeling her arm, upon which the mother reached over and gave him the glass of milk. A few minutes later, the infant did not reach for the milk that was again sitting in the middle of the table, but proceeded directly to pummel his mother's arm. In no case, of course, is a monster created by such a one-trial learning process. However, repeated events of this kind, in a variety of settings [might produce a highly assertive child]. . . . (Patterson, Littman, and Bricker, 1967, p. 6)

We recognize here an example of Piaget's *secondary circular reaction,* in which an infant uses one schema as an instrument for obtaining something else. If aggressive schemas are practiced in this way, it might be said that according to Piaget's theory, aggression is being built into a child's cognitive structure.

The learning process however, may be even more direct. Bandura and Walters (1959) reported the following excerpt from an interview with the father of an antisocially aggressive adolescent boy:

INTERVIEWER: How much of this sort of thing (verbal aggression) have you allowed?

FATHER: I don't allow him to get moody with me because he knows he wouldn't get away with it. They're too smart. They know what they can do and what they can't do.

I: Have you ever encouraged Earl to use his fists to defend himself?

F: Yes, if necessary. I told him many times that if someone wanted to fight with him and started the old idea of the chip on the shoulder, "Don't hit the chip, hit his jaw, and get it over with."

I: Has he ever come to you and complained that another fellow was giving him a rough time?

F: Yes.

I: What did you advise him to do about it?

F: I told him to hit him.

I: If Earl got into a fight with one of the neighbor's boys, how would you handle it?

F: That would depend who was at fault. If my boy was at fault, he'd be wrong and I'd do my best to show him that. But if he was in the right I wouldn't want to chastise him.

I: How far would you let it go?

F: I'd let it go until one won. See who was the best man. (Bandura and Walters, 1959, p. 122)

There is clear evidence here of reward and love (from the father) being contingent upon the expression of aggressive behavior by the son. Patterson and his colleagues found evidence that children may similarly reinforce each other, even when they are as young as 3. They found that approximately 75 percent of aggressive behaviors are responded to by the other children in ways that reward the aggressor. The attacked child might give up a toy or a territory, as well as cry, cower, or even respond aggressively in a way that was mutually stimulating. If such behavior was, in fact, reinforcing to the aggressor, then one would expect the aggressive child to "do it again" quickly. Patterson found extremely high frequencies of exactly that sort of repetition:

> . . . For example . . . [one aggressive child] struck [a victim] with an object, was reinforced by the victim, then repeated this response 18 times and was reinforced each time. On the nineteenth response [the victim] counterattacked, and the teacher intervened; [the aggressor] then terminated his aggression against [the first victim]. However, he immediately shifted to [a second victim] who had previously reinforced him. . . . [He] attacked his new victim twenty times in rapid succession and quit only when the teacher intervened. (Patterson, Littman, and Bricker, 1967, p. 31)

Even more disturbing were data showing that originally nonaggressive or even passive children learned to be aggressive around aggressive children. It depended on how much counterattacking they did; when passive children counterattacked and were reinforced (by cowering, for example, on the part of the original aggressor), they, too, began to experience rewards for aggression. Their own aggressive behavior thereupon increased. The passive child who was not successful in his counterattacks was less likely to develop aggressive behavior. Examples of individual children are shown in Figure 14.5.

Management of Aggression in the Classroom Patterson makes several suggestions about the management of aggressive behavior in children. In the first place, punishment will not be successful. It may stop aggression toward one child, but the aggressor is more likely to shift to another child than to stop completely. A better, twofold strategy is recommended: (1) Remove an aggressive child to a quiet, solitary place for a while, where his aggression cannot be reinforced by other children; this is called "time out" (from positive reinforcement). The removal should be swift so that it interrupts the reinforcing situation. (2) Positively reinforce behaviors that are incompatible with aggression, such as helping behaviors, expressions of sympathy and affection. As these incompatible behaviors build up, aggression is bound to go down. Control of the total situation is also important, as every good teacher knows:

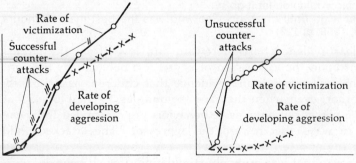

Figure 14.5 Cumulative frequency curves of passive children being attacked by aggressive children. (Patterson, Littman, and Bricker, 1967, pp. 24, 28)

> It was our impression that the *group output* of assertive-aggressive behaviors was mainly a function of . . . the program of activities. . . . For example, one of the teachers . . . was particularly effective in structuring the *kind* of interaction which took place. She frequently introduced play activities and games that provided . . . stimuli for a wide variety of nonaggressive behaviors. She also seemed able to anticipate social settings in which aggressive behaviors were likely to occur, and by removing one or more of the children or introducing a new activity she decreased the probability of aggressive behaviors. (Patterson, Littman, and Bricker, 1967, p. 19)

The occurrence of both aggression and restlessness also depends very much on the size of the room in which the children are confined. Playgrounds do much to decrease aggressive behavior in the school setting. The sad fact is, however, that in many schools the playground facilities are not utilized because overworked teachers find them "too much trouble." One wonders if the increasing aggression of normally passive children will not turn out to be equally troublesome.

Frustration and Aggression Theories of aggression as a conditioned behavior stand in contrast to theories of aggression as a consequence of frustration (Dollard, Doob, Miller, and Sears, 1939). The frustration theory is favored by psychoanalysts, who believe that the blockage of *id* (biological) impulses creates a frustrated, angry person whose hostility is directed toward the "blocker." If this is not safe (if the blocker is, say, a giant father), the hostility may be *displaced* onto someone else (weak little brother). The individual is then said to take it out on a *scapegoat* (long-suffering little brother). This is the explanation often advanced for chronically hostile people, from the bitter, angry child to the lynch mob. It is assumed that frustration and resentment are being "taken out on" scapegoats of one sort or another. The two theories lead to different prescriptions. If frustration is the basic problem, then meeting the frustrated needs (loving the child, guaranteeing jobs for the lynch mob) should eliminate the anger. If conditioning is the basic problem, then fulfilling needs would be exactly the wrong thing to do, since the fulfillment would reinforce the angry behavior.

As is the case with most psychological theorizing, there is probably some measure of truth in both propositions. The unfulfilled individual may be a more troublesome person in many respects than the fulfilled individual (leaving aside, for the moment, the question of what fulfillment means). If it is possible for a school to provide fulfillment, that may indeed remove some of the trouble. But it is probably advisable to make that fulfillment contingent upon the individual's *good* behavior, not upon his tantrums or other acts of anger. The school administrator who invites students to serve on the community school board *before* a student riot and who clearly specifies that the public honor is being conferred as a reward for honorable and responsible behavior may have forestalled school aggression in two ways: (1) He will have removed a source of frustration and (2) he will have reinforced peaceable behavior rather than hostility.

Egocentrism and Self-esteem

According to Piaget, *egocentrism* is a critical feature of cognitive development that accompanies each phase in progressively more sophisticated forms. During the sensorimotor stage, the infant is not able, Piaget and others believe, to tell the difference between himself and the rest of the world—"The world is a thing to be sucked." The world is, in fact, the experience of sucking and of other sensorimotor activities. During the second year, the child undergoes what Piaget calls "a miniature Copernican revolution" in which he becomes aware of the fact that the universe does not revolve around himself, but has a reality and a stability of its own. This awareness signifies the onset of the preoperational period. But even though the child has evolved beyond the egocentricity of infancy, his new cognitive life is characterized by an egocentricity of another sort.

An example of this can be found in language development. The 3-year-old talks to himself quite frequently. The course of egocentric speech is described in Chapter 19. Eventually, it "goes inside" to become silent inner speech (at least according to some theorists). Another example can be observed in the child's inability to take another's point of view. Imagine yourself sitting across a table from a 4-year-old with a toy elephant between you, facing the child. If you were to ask the child to describe what part of the elephant is closer to you, the head or the tail, he will say, "the head." He cannot "see" the elephant through your eyes and recognize that the tail is closer to you. The young child who believes his mother has shared his dream is showing a similar type of egocentricity. So is the child who believes the moon accompanies him on his walks.

As the child moves into the concrete operational stage, his preoperational egocentricity declines. His new concrete operational mental abilities lead him to recognize new causes and stabilities independent of his own viewpoint. Yet we would hardly describe the 10-year-old as coolly objective; his outlook may be decidedly egocentric.

By the age of 12 or 13, the child's earlier forms of egocentrism seem to have disappeared, but in their place appears the massive egocentrism of the adolescent. The systems built by the adolescent *are* the world, not just his interpretation of the world. For example, one young hippie was recently quoted as saying:

> We don't have this rational, logical way of looking at the world—we're more mystically oriented. The earth and sky and rain are holy to us, and when we work, we do it so we can live, so we can enjoy these things—not like the crazy, logical middle-class Americans who live only to work, and have fallen out of Nature's grace. (Michaelson, 1969, p. 17)

Apparently it never occurred to this young man that anybody's Nature but *his* Nature might also be natural.

The spiraling (toward more sophistication) process of increasing and decreasing egocentrism is an important aspect of Piaget's system, for the egocentrism signifies a centering or consolidation of new viewpoints. Just as an adult may become temporarily absorbed in a new creative enterprise, excluding many old interests and friends until the "obsession" has passed, so the growing child becomes absorbed in the newly discovered powers of his own brain. This kind of egocentrism is, then, a necessary stage in the development of cognitive skills that should not be disparaged as egotism. It does not signify bad character development, but merely a consolidation phase of mental growth.

In Our Stars or in Ourselves? The inability to distinguish clearly between one's own system of thought and the external world has been further explored in the so-called *locus of control* studies. Developed by Julian Rotter and his colleagues (Rotter, 1966), this personality scale tests the extent to which a respondent believes he is in control of his own fate. It is a *forced-choice* scale—the respondent must choose either (*a*) or (*b*) of items like the following:

(*a*) Without the right breaks, one cannot be an effective leader.
(*b*) Capable people who fail to become leaders have not taken advantage of their opportunities.

(*a*) I have often found that what is going to happen will happen.
(*b*) Trusting to fate has never turned out as well for me as making a decision to take a definite course of action.

(*a*) As far as world affairs are concerned, most of us are the victims of forces we can neither understand nor control.
(*b*) By taking an active part in political and social affairs, the people can control world events.

(*a*) Sometimes I can't understand how teachers arrive at the grades they give.
(*b*) There is a direct connection between how hard I study and the grades I get.

Scores on this personality test have been found to be correlated with many kinds of behavior. Hospital patients and prisoners who believed they were largely in control of their own fate obtained much more information (than "externals" did) about their institutions and their own conditions; "internals" were also more likely (than "externals") to take part in civil rights demonstrations and to stop smoking (Rotter, 1966).

The Crandalls (Crandall, Katkovsky, and Crandall, 1965) have developed a similar scale that focuses on academic achievement situations. They call their questionnaire the Intellectual Achievement Responsibility (IAR) scale. Here are some sample items:

If a teacher passes you to the next grade, would it probably be
    (*a*) because she liked you, or
    (*b*) because of the work you did?

Suppose you are showing a friend how to play a game and he has trouble with it. Would that happen
   (a) because he wasn't able to understand how to play, or
   (b) because you couldn't explain it well?

Suppose you're not sure about the answer to a question your teacher asks you and the answer you give turns out to be wrong. It is likely to happen
   (a) because she was more particular than usual, or
   (b) because you answered too quickly?

The test was originally administered to a large sample of children ranging in age from 8 to 18. The scores did not change a great deal with age, and they indicated a generally high sense of personal responsibility. The one exception to this rule was the large *decrease* in acceptance of personal responsibility for the positive items (like item 1, above) among boys from the tenth to the twelfth grades. The decrease looked like either modesty or uncertainty in the face of college competition. Girls are generally more "internal" than boys, especially as they grow older, but they do not decrease in acceptance of responsibility for their own positive achievements.

In a later study, McGhee and Crandall (1968) examined the relationship of IAR scores to academic performance. As far as grades (report cards) were concerned, there was a straightforward relationship between the acceptance of responsibility and good grades. But on more general standardized achievement tests, the relationship held just for the girls. For the boys, only acceptance of responsibility for the negative IAR items (like item 27, above) predicted a high achievement test score. The boys who assumed responsibility for their own failures performed more competently on the achievement tests than "externals" did.

Feelings vs. Behavior Findings of this sort lead us to wonder about the self-awareness of students: Perhaps some students fail because they honestly do not recognize the causes of failure within themselves. But what does that recognition involve? Attention to an internal feeling? or to one's own behavior? Similarly, what causes us to think well of ourselves? The external cues of other people's behavior? ("I must be a good guy; she smiled at me."); the internal cues of one's own behavior? ("I must be a good guy; I keep doing such nice things for people."); the internal cues of emotion and conviction? ("I must be a good guy; I feel like a good guy.")

These distinctions have a long psychological history. Festinger (1954) has summarized evidence in favor of his belief that *social comparisons* (external cues involving other people) are the major source of self-evaluation, especially when other cues are faint. He says, in effect, that we decide how good we are by comparing ourselves to others. Diggory (1966) has argued that the internal cues of one's own behavior are the critical sources of self-esteem ("I must be a good guy; I keep doing such nice things for people"). If we depend on the smiles or praise of other people or on our own feelings, self-esteem may evaporate. But if we base it on our own behavioral achievements, regardless of the achievements of others, it will be as solid as our achievements are.

However, Diggory believes, it may be that there are differences between people in the degree to which they depend on social comparisons rather than on their own achievements. To paraphrase Riesman, (1954), some people may be more "other-directed" than "self-directed" as far as evaluation is concerned.

In any event, the educator must be careful to distinguish between these various sources of information about one's own value: cues from the behavior of other people, cues from one's own behavior, and cues from one's own feelings. Teacher may hope that indiscriminate praise ("I tell him his picture is beautiful no matter what it looks like") will build self-esteem. Actually, it may build *feelings* of self-esteem that are not supported by any behavioral evidence and that lead eventually to confusion and loss of self-esteem. When praise is truly indiscriminate, it will make both social and personal behavioral cues more difficult for the child to sort out. What is it about other people that makes them praise a painting? Suppose other people do not praise a painting; are there any personal cues to tell a child the painting is nevertheless good? Indiscriminate praise may prevent a student from developing a realistic set of self-evaluative cues that will stand him in better stead than his feelings.

Pauline Sears (1964) has provided detailed case studies of factors related to the self-esteem of elementary school children, although she did not draw any final conclusions from her data. She quotes one of her teachers as saying:

> The pupils have to feel that they themselves are accomplishing something and that they're satisfied with it. If they do their best and their best doesn't satisfy me, then I think I have to do some adjusting. . . . If the child is really sure that this is the best work that he can do (now I realize this sort of evaluation is difficult for the child), I'll say, "Well, I don't think that this is your best. Now how do you feel about it?" And if the child can honestly say, "Well, I can't do any better, Mr. Ladd," then I accept it. . . . Children have to have standards that are reasonable and that they can see are worthwhile, not necessarily adult standards. (Sears, 1964, p. 26)

Pedagogy of this sort should help students become aware of the cues in their own behavior that are relevant to self-esteem. Students of all ages need to feel they are genuinely competent in something. Diggory (1966) would say that they need to feel they have the power to achieve goals of importance to them. Regardless of what is said by others, and regardless of his own feelings, the student's evaluation of his power may eventually depend on what he has actually accomplished:

> Many previous writers have emphasized that human beings value themselves on the skill, adroitness, or efficiency with which they accomplish their purposes. Man then might be viewed as a purposive instrument, and might evaluate himself in quite the same terms as he evaluates

any other instrument. Many people might object and say that this reduces man to the status of an implement and so degrades him. . . . However, if it is mystery and miracles we crave, then here is the mystery and the miracle right under our very noses. What a marvelous engine this is which is inherently no specific instrument but whose usefulness can range from counting bits of atoms to weighing the stars! (Diggory, 1966, p. 418)

Cognitive Styles of Analyzing and Organizing Information

An infant's ability to separate himself from his environment and an adult's ability to separate the internal causes of his own behavior from external "fate" are two aspects of a more general personality dimension. Some people seem to be naturally analytical; they perceive aspects of a situation to be separable from each other. Other people show what Witkin and his colleagues (1962) call *field dependence.* The field-dependent individual has difficulty, for example, finding a geometrical figure in a distracting pattern. He may also have difficulty detecting a statement that is buried in noise. If he is given the problem of adjusting a luminous rod in a luminous frame so that the rod is exactly vertical, he may have difficulty doing so if the frame is tilted, or if he (in his chair) is tilted.

The field-independent person, on the other hand, is less influenced by the frame or by other field influences. This kind of individual may be more analytic in his approach to various kinds of situations.

Kagan and his colleagues (Kagan, Moss, and Sigel, 1963) have developed a test of analytic attitude, some examples of which are shown in Figure 14.6. Note how the figures in each test box could be classified as pairs in several ways. In the top left box, we could classify the wooden chair and the table together "because they are both missing legs" or "because you sit on the chair to eat off the table," or we could classify the wooden chair and the easy chair together "because they are both chairs." Similarly, in the next test box we could classify the boy and the rabbit together "because they are both missing eyes" or we could classify the boy and the eyeglasses together "because boys wear eyeglasses."

There are differences between people in whether they prefer analytical or relational classification schemes. As Figure 14.7 shows, boys are generally more analytic than girls, but analytic responses increase with age in both boys and girls. Relational responses decrease with age in boys, but not in girls.

The same sort of effect appears in Witkin's theoretical framework. Boys are likely to be field-independent; girls are more field-dependent. In some ways, field dependence has educational disadvantages, but in other ways it has advantages: in reading, for instance, the context or background of an idea is important to its meaning. Girls are generally better readers than boys (Overview, Part V); perhaps this is because they are better able to respond to context (field cues) during the reading process.

There is also some evidence that a relational or field-dependent cognitive style is associated with personality characteristics different from those associated with independent styles. Field-dependent people may be somewhat less mature and self-aware:

> For example, in interviews with them, their lack of developed views of their own, and their consequent reliance on others for a definition of their attitudes and sentiments expressed itself. . . . When asked for their opinion on a given issue, they were likely to cite the judgment of a source which to them is authoritative. One child, asked "What are you like?" answered: "I don't know, my friends do." Another, asked how he liked his teacher, answered: "Everybody says she's nice."
>
> . . .
>
> [They] presented a picture of a strikingly low level of differentiation in over-all development. They showed poverty of resources, lack of enterprise and initiative, poorly developed interests, lack of well-structured [self] controls . . . and marked dependence on external sources of support and guidance. (Witkin et al., 1962, pp. 262–265)

The "Verbally Bright" Child One striking characteristic of a small number of field-dependent children is *verbal fluency*. The trait may also be found in field-independent people, but when it occurs in field-dependent people, its influence may be quite misleading. Psychologists once used the term "verbally bright" to characterize highly verbal individuals who lack what Piaget calls good operational development. The words may be there, but the reasoning ability is not. Such a student may be quite spectacular in terms of classroom discussions. The teacher may form the impression that the highly verbal but field-dependent youngster is quite bright. When quiz time comes around, the teacher is shocked to find that the student does not have a genuine grasp of the information; he may be unable to write down much of anything at all, or he may ramble incoherently in the hope that some of his verbiage will "hit" the correct answer.

Such a student is apparently good at picking up the field cues of a classroom discussion. When a topic is being bandied about, the field-dependent, verbally fluent youngster can pull right answers "out of the air," so to speak, and make the sort of comments the teacher likes to hear. But the ability to retain and digest and interrelate information is actually lacking, since all these skills arise from a basic ability to analyze. To think well, we must be able to organize and relate information, and that requires at least a moderate degree of analytical ability.

Schroder's Test of Cognitive Differentiation Another system for analyzing cognitive style has been developed by Schroder, Driver, and Streufert (1967). They see cognitive styles as involving two main features: the number of dimensions (or principles) an individual may think about with reference to a topic and the skill a person has in relating these dimensions to each other. For example, in thinking about internationalism, an individual may think about only one dimension—that of communism vs. democracy. Another individual may think about economics, military fac-

Figure 14.6 Sample stimuli used in conceptual style test for children, designed by Kagan, Moss, and Sigel (1963, pp. 80–81)

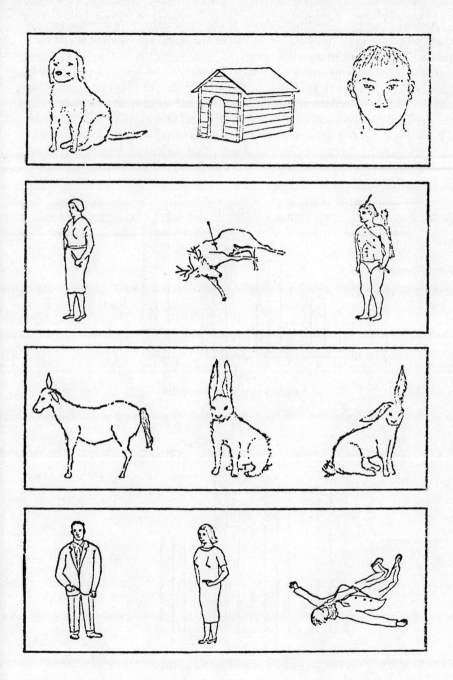

Figure 14.6 (*Continued*)

tors, history, but he may think about these factors in little compartments of their own; he may not be able to relate the various dimensions to each other in a flexible but integrated way.

Schroder diagrams such cognitive differences in the form shown in Figure 14.8. You can see that this scheme is similar to Piaget's conception of the factors involved in formal operational development, as well as to more general conceptions of differentiation and integration, but Schroder has been looking at a variety of additional personality and environmental factors. He has hypothesized, for example, that an environment that is too

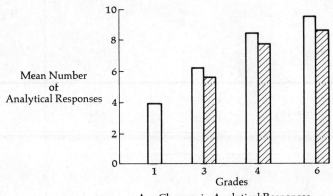

Age Changes in Analytical Responses

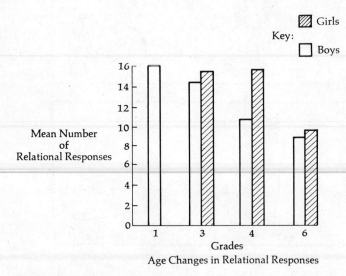

Age Changes in Relational Responses

Figure 14.7 Differences between boys and girls in age changes in analytical and relational classifications. No girls were available for the first-grade tests. (Kagan, Moss, and Sigel, 1963, pp. 90–91)

complex or too simple will inhibit the degree of cognitive development. Conditions that produce too many dimensions (too many different things to think about at once) may retard the development of integration systems; conditions that are too simple may have the same effect for the opposite reason—there are not enough ideas to integrate. Similarly, threats, costs, and rewards may at first increase but then as they grow overwhelming will decrease the development of a relatively high integration index.

Differences in personalities and attitudes may be seen in Schroder's measure of integrative development. He uses what are called *paragraph*

Dimensions

Only one way of relating them

Low Integration Index

Emergence of another way of relating dimensions

Moderately Low Integration Index

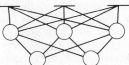

Many perspectives

More complex rules for comparing and relating

Moderately High Integration Index

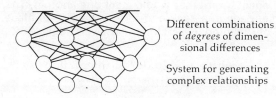

Different combinations of *degrees* of dimensional differences

System for generating complex relationships

High Integration Index

Figure 14.8 Diagrams of the degree of cognitive development. (Schroder, Driver, and Streufert, 1967)

completion tests. Individuals are given single words like "Rules . . ." or "Parents . . ." and told to write a paragraph to complete the thought. The individual with a low integration index may write something like the following:

> (a) [Rules] are made to be followed. They give direction to a project or life or anything. They should not be broken except in extreme circumstances.
>
> (b) [Rules] are absolutely ridiculous. Rules are restraining the human being who should be free and thinking for himself. Persons who make rules want to be masters and make others followers. I like to break every rule I can as long as there is no danger of getting caught. (Schroder, Driver, and Streufert, 1967, pp. 190–191)

It is clear that both paragraphs represent one-track minds: the first presents the positive pole, and the second, the negative pole. This sort of black-and-white, stereotyped viewpoint is characteristic of individuals with a low integration index. Such individuals are also quite convinced that "fate" causes most of their difficulties. Presumably they lack a sense of internal causation because they lack internal alternatives. Similarly, they lack a sense of conflict. How can one be conflicted if only one point of view is represented? The individual with a low integration index also attends primarily to information that already "fits his system." He cannot stretch his viewpoint (accommodate, in Piaget's terms) because he lacks the capacity to contain "stretching" information.

This cognitive style reminds us of political extremists. To quote the Overstreets (1964), who have made a study of extremist personalities:

> Those who make up [right-wing extremist groups] pretend to be serving a religion of love and a political heritage based on a Bill of Rights and an affirmation that "all men are created equal." . . . But their arguments add up to a ritual rather than to an ordered system of thought: the proof of this being the fact that their expressed dedication to our American heritage does not inhibit them at any point where expediency recommends a resort to un-American methods. The more we have studied the published output of the Right extremists, indeed, the more convinced we have become that their thinking is too compartmentalized, and too full of inner contradictions, to support any coherent theory, new or inherited. . . . The Right extremist cannot afford to let one lobe of his brain, so to speak, know what the other is doing. He cannot afford to have his self-contradictions pulled out into the open, where they would meet one another. Therefore he cannot afford to engage in a back-and-forth exchange of ideas in the open market places of the mind. (Overstreet and Overstreet, 1964, pp. 268–273)

Now consider the individual with a high index of integration, as illustrated by the same paragraph completion test:

> (a) [Rules] are necessary for a society to function well. However, rules should not be so strictly adhered to that they cannot be modified when circumstances alter. The purpose or effects of rules are more important than the rules themselves.

(b) [Rules] are made for everyone but are interpreted in many ways. It depends on the point of view of the interpreter. It is in this very process of interpretation that a society stays dynamic and changes and grows. (Schroder, Driver, and Streufert, 1967, pp. 191–192)

These individuals obviously have the capacity to contain many points of view and many ways of relating them. They would be more likely to accept responsibility for their own behavior and to feel conflicted at times. No doubt they disturb and annoy low integration people—very much as the liberal, tolerant individual worries extremists of any variety. We will come back to that point when we discuss authoritarian personalities.

Cognitive Style and IQ It is clear that in this section on cognitive styles of differentiating and integrating information, we have been talking about aspects of intelligence. But note how much more meaningfully we can now interpret IQ scores. Instead of saying, "Johnny has an IQ of 81," we can say, "Johnny has a field-dependent style and a low integration index. That means he is going to have difficulty detecting the main concepts in his reading—he will tend to muddle the information together. And he will also have difficulty thinking of alternative concepts. So I had better prepare a Ditto sheet or outline that will help him perform these abstractions and stimulate his thinking."

Current research in cognitive styles is moving more and more toward these richer descriptions of the way in which intelligence functions and the way in which it affects personal and social behavior.

CASE STUDIES

Now that we have established some principles for analyzing personality, it may be useful to practice applying them to samples of actual behavior. In the following case studies, consider these questions:

1. How would you interpret the behavior within the framework of the principles of motivation and personality discussed in Part III?

2. What instructional strategies would you employ to take into account the personality differences revealed by the behavior?

There is no officially right way of interpreting these materials. The important aspect of any interpretation is its consequence: What does the interpretation cause you to *do*? How does the interpretation lead you to improve educational procedures?

CASE NO. 1

[Five-year-old Michael]
     A group of six children were playing with dough. Michael had two cookie cutters and a rolling pin. Howard wanted one of the cookie cutters. He asked Michael for one of them. Michael said, "No, this is mine, I had them first." Howard said that he would give it back to him when he fin-

ished playing with it. Michael clutched the two cookie cutters close to him and then quickly grabbed the rolling pin and held it nearer to him. Howard grabbed at one of the cookie cutters and Michael held them still closer to him. His expression became more sullen. He clenched his mouth more tightly. Another child put a cookie cutter down on the table and Michael grabbed it and held on to it. Michael kept his face down. He moved his chair slowly from the table. Howard tried again to take it from him and Michael threw the cookie cutters and rolling pin on the floor. He hit Howard and kicked the chair. He looked penetratingly at the teacher and said to her that he was never coming to this school again and he didn't care if he didn't play with the dough. When the teacher did not reply to this statement, he walked away from the table sulking. He kept his hands in his pockets and held his head erect. (Almy and Cunningham, 1959, p. 48)

CASE NO. 2

[Eight-year-old Robin]

Mrs. M. [teacher] said, "Let's practice our parts for the skit tomorrow." The children were to portray a character from the reading they had done recently. Robin raised his hand as soon as Mrs. M. announced the event. He was the first to recite. He stood by his desk, leaning on his right arm, "I live in Sherwood Forest. I am always hiding out. I have a lot of trouble with the sheriff." He shrugged and continued "I'm Robin Hood." He sat down and smiled.

The next boy chose to be Bill Cody which was his real name. . . . He said, after he had recited, that the reason he had picked that particular character was because they were related.

Robin immediately held up his hand and waved it. Mrs. M. said, "We must go on." Robin still had his hand up and finally said, "Mrs. M. I want to say something." When she didn't stop him, he went on. "Ah well, ah the reason, ah, I chose *Robin Hood* for my book is that Little John is related to my mother." He turned to the boy across the table from him who asked him "How come?" "See, his real name was John Little an' my mother . . . "Ma'am?" he said to Mrs. M. who had spoken his name twice. "How did that come about?" said Mrs. M. "Well," said Robin, "I don't know 'cept somebody was talking. Johnny was saying he was related to some person, Thomas Jefferson, I think, so I asked mother someone famous we were related to and she said Little John."

Robert said from across the room, "Yeah, his mother's name is Little John," and snickered.

Robin held up his hand again. "Mrs. M.," he said, "I have two in mind. I don't know what to use, the one I already told or another one I have in mind." Mrs. M. answered, "You'll have to decide for yourself, Robin."

There were four other characters acted out and after each one, Robin held up his hand. He was never called upon. He chewed on his left forefinger during the portrayal of each character. (Gordon, 1966, pp. 81–82)

CASE NO. 3

[Eleven-year-old Jackie]

Jackie has a fresh shirt this morning. While the others are doing dictionary work he is trying to talk to Harvey in sign language—makes "catching" motion, sees me watching him, looks at his book. Makes motion as if rolling something on his desk.

"Jackie, have you finished your dictionary work?"

"No'm, I'm just fixin' to git it."

He got up and whispered to Bob, who sits in front of him. Bob handed Jackie a long red pencil.

At recess Jackie wrote his misspelled words quickly and was out ready to play softball, yelling "Play ball!" as he rushed out of the building.

. . .

We went on a field trip this afternoon. Jackie climbed up a tall pine to get needles and cones for the class. He climbed down and took some notes on a piece of paper which he laid flat on the ground and in which his pencil punched a few holes. I admired a small green pine cone Bruce had. Jackie climbed back up the tree and threw me several cones. He found "granddaddies" in the grass. He chased Maxine, who screamed, with one. Then he climbed another tree.

. . .

Our caterpillars have spun cocoons. . . . The first-grade teacher asked us to explain them to her group, and Jackie volunteered to present her with one. She asked him to explain it, and here is what he said, as near as she could take it down:

"This here worm-looking thing, it's a pupa. It used to be a green caterpillar we found on a hicker-nut tree. It et until it couldn't eat no more and then it turn brown and swivelled up. That there spider-web lookin' stuff, that's its cocoon it's a-spiting' out. It will wind itself up in them webs and next spring it'll bust out." (Bieker, 1950, pp. 188–190)

CASE NO. 4

[Sixteen-year-old Cathy]

Cathy, the subject of this interview, was introduced to me by an administrator as one of the "happiest girls in school." He later explained that . . . [she] was happy for several reasons. For one thing, she was . . . nearly certain to be valedictorian of the following year's graduating class. . . .

INTERVIEWER: How important are grades?

CATHY: To me, they're very important. They're my whole life.

I: Your whole life?

CATHY: Yes. It's all I have to do.

I: What do you mean? . . .

C: Day after day all I do is go to school and do my homework. So it has become my whole life, going to school.

. . .

I: Are you happy?

. . .

C: Happiness is a difficult term, but I don't believe I've ever been happy — ever been able to say I'm happy except a few times. Grades make me happy. After report cards I'm happy.

I: For how long?

C: For a few days.

I: And then what?

C: And then back to school again for the next report card. . . . I wouldn't say that I'm really happy. I'm content though. . . . I like to be on a schedule, sort of. And school does that. Regular homework in class makes you feel content, secure.

. . .

I: Why do you believe getting all "A's" is the thing to do?

C: Because it's the thing to accomplish. The "A's" are there, so if you don't achieve them, you're missing something.

I: What?

C: The honor of being the top.

I: Do you always intend to be the top?

C: As long as I'm able, yes.

I: Supposing you're not able?

C: Then I'll find some way to beat it.

I: And if you were not in the top, you wouldn't be very happy?

C: No.

I: But you're not happy being on top.

C: You're never on top. . . . There's always something to feel you're not on top in, so you always have to keep working.

I: And so you're always going to work?

C: Yes.

I: Are you going to get married?

C: I don't think so.

I: Why not?

C: Then I would have to stop working.

I: You'll never have any children?

C: Probably not. . . . I wouldn't want to have any children myself except to train [them]. (Sachs, 1966, pp. 106–116)

CASE NO. 5

[Sixteen-year-old Fred]

I'm all tense when I come home from school. How did I do in that test? What did I learn today? Look, I have a notebook. I started this when I came back from Christmas. . . . I got all my stuff down. I write it all down. I have a test on Thursday: Chapters 8, 9, and 10. I haven't taken that test yet. That was two weeks ago. . . . The thing is what I want. Maybe I'm completely abnormal. Maybe this isn't what any other kid wants. But what I want. Come home from school. If I'm tense, get something to eat, go off in the hills, talk to the trees, talk to the bushes. Relax. Say about five o'clock. Sit down. I'm all calm and relaxed. I calmly clear off my desk. I separate which is homework, which is extra work, which I should work on. . . . So I'll calmly sit back and relax, and I'll read . . . I calmly do things the way I want to without having people say, "You gotta do this right now. You gotta do this right now. Hurry, hurry, hurry." . . . Maybe I'm insane. Not insane, but maybe I'm not just normal in wanting to do these things slow, but it's the only way I can operate. Sure, in a place like my father's business, things have to be done. He has conferences at ten o'clock, a letter to be dictated to his secretary at 11:00, so on, and so on, like that. I can't do it. I just like to calmly sit down. . . . This is what I think it should be. (Sachs, 1966, pp. 234–236)

Chapter 15 CULTURE OF THE SCHOOL

Traditionally, motivation and personality are treated as if they influence classroom behavior, instead of the other way around. The teacher's presentation is the input, the child's response (on a test, say) is the output, and the personal and motivational mediating system is in between. (In previous chapters, we have been considering aspects of that system.) Although categorizing these interactions in the traditional order may be a convenient method of analysis, it is somewhat misleading. The school itself may mediate the person. That is, we might also think of the personal network as the input, the classroom as the mediating system, and the teacher's reaction as the output. Or we might think of the classroom situation as the input, the teacher as the mediator, and the personal reaction system as the output. In reality, a group of students with a teacher in a classroom is a dynamic social whole.

In this final chapter of Part III we will pay special attention to the social aspects of that whole, as these aspects are created by the classroom and as they are brought into the classroom in the form of preshaped attitudes. Questions of competition, affiliation, sex roles, prejudice, discipline, territoriality are social concepts of particular importance to the educator. What are those aspects of group and community life that facilitate education? What aspects have the opposite effect? Should the teacher be a "boss" or a "pal"? Many educational texts offer recommendations; we will focus here on psychological research that may help us sort opinion from fact.

THE FIELD THEORY OF KURT LEWIN

Leading the way in urging us to think of the person and his environ-ment as a psychological whole was Kurt Lewin, a fellow traveler of the Gestalt movement in the 1930s (see Baldwin, 1967, for a good review of Lewin's position). Lewin originated a way of looking at behavior that is called *psychological ecology*—the study of the person in his psychological environment. For example, suppose you are torn between two attractive goal regions—two good movies, let us say. Lewin would diagram your psychological state as in Figure 15.1 (*a*). The state includes your aware-ness of the films and the forces pushing you. These forces can be thought of as originating in the films, although of course they really originate in your wishes and interests. According to Lewin, the films, forces, and person constitute your momentary *life space.* He considered the major job of psychology to be that of describing (verbally and graphically) the life space of individuals.

It is important to understand that Lewinian life space does not signify only conscious awareness; a person might be affected by forces of which he is not entirely conscious. If the forces are affecting him, as evidenced by his behavior, then they exist in his life space. If they are not affecting him, even though someone else might know about them, they are not in the life space of the person.

In Figure 15.1 (*a*), the plus signs indicate the *valence* of a goal region (the two films). In this case, both goals have a *positive* valence. If one were positive and one negative, the person's life space might be dia-grammed as in Figure 15.1 (*b*). Here you can see that the forces affecting the person will drive him in the direction of the positive goal.

In Figure 15.1 (*a*), the person hangs suspended between two equally attractive goals. In Figure 15.1 (*c*), the person also hangs suspended be-tween two equally *negative* goals. In this kind of situation—say, the plight

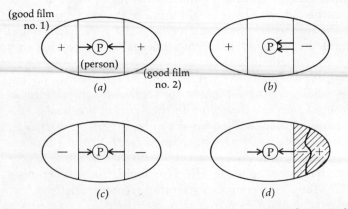

Figure 15.1 Lewinian life space diagrams. (*a*) An approach-approach conflict; (*b*) no con-flict; (*c*) an avoidance-avoidance conflict; (*d*) an approach-avoidance conflict.

of a bank robber who must face an armed policeman at both the back and the front doors of the bank—the person will tend to leave the field (head for the fire escape), unless he is prevented from doing so by barriers of various kinds. Children who face two equally distasteful tasks—learning the multiplication table or taking an F home on the report card—may also tend to leave the field (daydream, play hooky, develop a headache), unless special controls are applied by the teacher.

In a final type of conflict, shown in Figure 15.1 (d), we see the plight of the child who will be spanked for stealing cookies from the cookie jar. The goal has both positive and negative "charges." The force from the positive aspect propels him toward the cookie jar; the force from the negative aspect propels him away from it. Again, he will hang suspended for a while. (Experiments have shown that strongest valence will "win" eventually.)

The student in conflict may oscillate in complex ways. In the approach-avoidance conflict, both the positive and the negative valences increase as the person moves toward the goal region. If the negative valence is strong, the individual may move back from the goal just at the moment he seems about to achieve it. Some people may fear the consequences of success (increased responsibility, for example), while still being powerfully attracted by it. Oscillation (working hard, but not showing up at the prize-winning ceremonies) may appear in such cases.

Characteristics of the Life Space

Of course, a person's life space includes more than conflicts and goal regions. A region may be a physical area, an event happening to the individual, an activity, a group membership. If the person must move through several regions to accomplish a goal, then we can say he has traversed a path—a series of regions—to his goal. Sometimes barriers must be hurdled or avoided. Sometimes regions are numerous and highly differentiated; sometimes they are diffuse and large. In Lewin's day, his students argued long and happily over the ways in which psychological environments should properly be diagrammed. In our own day, it is still the case that analyzing the life space of an individual sensitizes us to his world:

> One of the basic characteristics of field theory in psychology, as I see it, is the demand that the field which influences an individual should be described . . . in the way in which it exists for that person at that time. . . . A teacher will never succeed in giving proper guidance to a child if he does not learn to understand the psychological world in which that individual child lives. To describe a situation "objectively" in psychology actually means to describe the situation as a totality of those facts and only those facts which make up the field of that individual. To substitute for that world of the individual the world of the teacher, of the physicist, or of anybody else is to be, not objective, but wrong. (Lewin, 1951, p. 62)

A child going unwillingly to a bad ghetto school might have a life space that looks like the diagram in Figure 15.2 (a); John Holt's frightened child might be trapped in the psychological environment of Figure 15.2 (*b*); the 16-year-old valedictorian lives in a school world that might look like that shown in Figure 15.2 (*c*). Once a teacher has an idea of the subjective school world of a particular child, concepts of instructional strategies may be easier to formulate. Look again at Figure 15.2. In the case of the ghetto child, for example, the life space needs to become more differentiated and less negative. The child needs to be helped to see that there are some good regions in his school day. (The community may need to enforce a few laws to change those valences, however.)

Similarly, the frightened child may need help in learning to perceive his surroundings as more positive and less imprisoning. Again, the school (or the teacher's) policy may need to be changed; the problem may not be entirely one of subjective perception on the child's part.

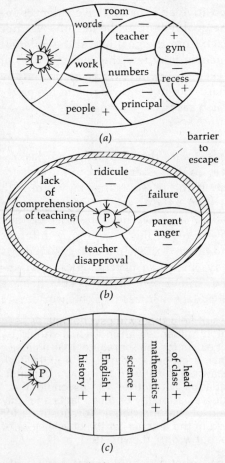

Figure 15.2   Analyzing life spaces. (*a*) The slum child; (*b*) the frightened child; (*c*) the "happy" valedictorian.

The world of the valedictorian poses more subtle problems. The neatness, order, and positive valences of that particular life space look too good to be true. The problem may be one of helping the student to recognize that the life space is partly unreal. Perhaps it should be diagrammed to include the fact that the student may be using grades and homework as a secure refuge from negative people in her life—people who let her down when she was younger (Figure 15.3).

Life Space and the School

Traditionally, regions of spelling, arithmetic, drawing, reading, social studies, and so forth are imposed upon students regardless of their natural locations in individual subjective worlds. It is little wonder that so many individual problems appear to arise as children find themselves trapped in systems of conflicts, barriers, and force-fields they can barely understand, much less cope with. In many places, more flexible schooling procedures are being developed in response to these difficulties.

One such system is that of the *open school,* now becoming popular in this country. It has been tried in many British primary (infant) schools over the past decade. (A good summary from a psychologist's standpoint is Gardner's *Experiment and Tradition in Primary Schools,* published in 1966.) In an open school, interest centers (mathematics, language arts) are set up in a large room. The students are free to work in any one center or to develop projects that combine several areas of learning. They are free to work with whomever they please. The teacher functions as an assistant or guide, rather than as a dictator, but he does keep watch over students and encourage them to develop a full range of academic skills.

If we were to picture the life spaces of a traditional and an open classroom, they might look like the diagrams in Figure 15.4. In the case of the open school, all regions are likely to have positive valences because they are structured by the child's own interests and activities. In the traditional school, more negative regions may appear. In the open school, there may be less differentiation of field areas; in the traditional school, there is a scheduled sequence of learning activities, and these activities may be perceived as separated from each other. Learning to add numbers has an

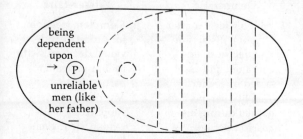

Figure 15.3 Rediagramming the valedictorian's life space.

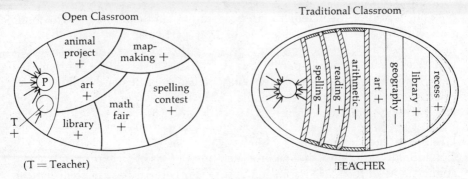

Figure 15.4   Life space diagrams of two school environments.

important relationship to basic economic concepts (learning to add the money a farmer gets for selling eggs and comparing that sum to the sum he might earn as a coal miner, for example); in the traditional school, the regions are so clearly separated that intersubject connections may be harder for a child to make.

Of course, open schools differ from traditional ones in other ways as well. The social forces that operate are different from traditional ones. Class or ethnic factors may be clearer than they are in a traditional setting. Competition, helpfulness, communication systems—all these may function quite differently in an open system. In the next sections of this chapter, we will consider some basic principles of social psychology that affect both traditional and open schooling. Wise decisions about classroom ecology—whether traditional or not—must be based on a firm understanding of these principles.

DEMOCRATIC VS. AUTHORITARIAN SOCIAL CLIMATES

In the late 1930s, two of Lewin's students carried out a set of experiments on the effects of authoritarian, democratic, and laissez-faire social climates. Several after-school clubs of 10-year-old boys were the subjects. The experimenters (Lippitt and White, 1943) and their graduate students were the leaders. The social climates were described as follows:

Authoritarian	Democratic	Laissez-faire
1. All determination of policy by leader.	1. All policies a matter of group discussion and decision, encouraged and assisted by leader.	1. Complete freedom for group or individual decision, with minimum leader participation.
2. Techniques and activity steps dictated by the authority, one at a time; future	2. Activity perspective gained during discussion period. General steps to	2. Various materials supplied by leader, who made it clear he would supply

Authoritarian	Democratic	Laissez-faire
steps always uncertain to a large degree.	group goal sketched; when technical advice needed, leader suggested two or more alternative procedures from which choice could be made.	information when asked, but took no other part in work discussion.
3. Leader usually dictated particular work task and work companion of each member.	3. Members free to work with whomever they chose; division of tasks left to group.	3. Complete nonparticipation of leader.
4. Dominator tended to be "personal" in his praise and criticism of work of each member; remained aloof from active group participation except when demonstrating.	4. Leader "objective" or "fact-minded" in praise and criticism; tried to be regular group member in spirit without doing too much of the work.	4. Infrequent spontaneous comments on member activities unless questions, and no attempt to appraise or regulate the course of events.

The group meetings were monitored by trained observers who recorded what happened. The authoritarian leader gave many more direct orders and many more commands that disrupted the wishes or ongoing activities of group members. He also criticized more and praised more—perhaps providing the positive and negative reinforcement that a Skinnerian would recommend for controlling behavior. The observers noted a further more subtle distinction between the praise or criticism given by the democratic leader and that given by the authoritarian leader: The democratic leader helped group members learn the criteria for evaluating their own work.

> LEADER: I think that's going to be a pretty wobbly [piece of furniture]. Can you guess why I think so?
> BOY: Maybe because there are so many bent nails and none that go through. (White and Lippitt, 1968, p. 325)

Counterparts of the direct ordering of the authoritarian leader were the guiding suggestions of the democratic leader and the information giving of the laissez-faire leader. Guiding suggestions were characterized by their attention to the activities of the boys themselves; the activity always came first, and the suggestion second. The large amount of information given out by the laissez-faire leader was in response to direct requests of members of his group. He offered no suggestions at all unless requested to do so.

Both the democratic and the laissez-faire leaders stimulated self-guidance to a much greater extent than the authoritarian leader did, but the democratic leader was more of a pal—he was jovial, confiding, and equalitarian.

Summary of the White and Lippitt Study
The following summary (adapted from White and Lippitt, 1968, p. 334) describes the results of the study.

1. Laissez-faire was not the same as democracy.
   a. There was less work done and poorer work.
   b. It was characterized more by play.
   c. In interviews, the boys expressed a preference for their democratic leader.
2. Democracy can be efficient.
   a. The quantity of work done in autocracy was somewhat greater.
   b. But work motivation was stronger in democracy.
   c. Originality was greater in democracy.
3. Autocracy can create much hostility and aggression, including aggression against scapegoats.
   a. The autocratic groups generally showed more "bossiness," more demands for attention, more destruction of their own property, and more scapegoating.
4. Autocracy can create discontent that does not appear on the surface.
   a. Four boys dropped out, and all of them did so during autocratic club periods in which overt rebellion did not occur.
   b. Nineteen of twenty boys preferred their democratic leader.
   c. "Release" behavior on the day of transition to a freer atmosphere suggested the presence of previous frustration.
5. There was more dependence and less individuality in autocracy.
   a. There was more submissive behavior.
   b. Conversation was less varied.
   c. Individual differences were less varied.
   d. There seemed to be a general loss of individuality.
6. There was more group-mindedness and more friendliness in democracy.
   a. The pronoun I was used less frequently in the democratic group.
   b. Spontaneous subgroups were larger.
   c. Group-minded remarks were more frequent.
   d. Friendly remarks were more frequent.
   e. Mutual praise was more frequent.
   f. The democratic group showed more readiness to share group property.

Additional Experiments
The White and Lippitt study still stands, thirty years later, as a classic demonstration of the value of a democratic classroom atmosphere. Since that time, however, we have learned even more about the nature of these advantages. Numerous studies have provided evidence that democratic teacher attitudes and procedures will have good effects on student development. Glidewell and his colleagues (1966) have reviewed research

showing that democratic atmospheres (a) stimulate more pupil-to-pupil interaction; (b) reduce interpersonal conflict and anxieties; (c) increase mutual esteem, rapport, and self-esteem; (d) induce a wider spread and flexibility of peer social power; (e) produce a greater tolerance for divergent opinions; (f) lead to more group cohesiveness; and (g) increase moral responsibility, self-initiated work, independence of opinion, and responsibility in carrying out assignments. These are essentially the same processes first noted by Lippitt and White.

Cooperation and Rules

The evidence further suggests that a democratic social climate matches naturally developing social and democratic tendencies. When do children become able to function cooperatively in groups? to see themselves as members of groups? Another aspect of the democratic attitude has to do with the formation of rules and with reactions to individuals who break the rules. What kinds of rules do children naturally develop? When do they develop them? What kinds of moral feelings accompany them?

Piaget (1967) has described how moral feelings develop in the same way that general operational thinking develops. Concepts of morality gradually become separated from concrete instances, and then come together into logical systems. Thus, a series of specific punishments for specific misdeeds would gradually develop into a code of laws independent of particular applications. Logical thinking about rules and morals would (in Piaget's theory) parallel logical thinking about the physical world (see Part I).

A group of inner-city kindergarten children recently generated the following set of rules, which their teacher wrote down and posted on the wall.

OUR RULES

1. Don't mess around.
2. Don't talk a lot.
3. Stop hitting people.
4. Don't make too much noise.
5. Don't throw blocks around.
6. Clean up and put the blocks away right.
7. Don't stomp around.
8. Don't be bad.
9. Don't take anyone else's blocks.
10. Don't tear up anyone's paper.

We can see the concrete, specific nature of their rules, but we can also see how certain general principles of acceptable classroom behavior can emerge from them.

We can therefore see why democratic groups give children an extremely important opportunity to practice their developing sense of genuine democracy. If during this special formative period they are required to submit to authoritarian principles, they may lose forever their zest for accepting citizenship responsibilities.

Of course, one cannot expect mature democratic principles from a group of elementary school age; some adult guidance will be necessary. Nor can one expect an altogether peaceful time of it. As anyone who has watched sandlot baseball knows, as much time may be spent arguing about the rules as playing the game. The acceptance of rules as a contract between group members may be as difficult at the level of the U.S. Senate, however. Can we expect a mature sense of citizenship to grow when schooling has taken place almost entirely within an authoritarian system? Should we not include as part of citizenship training democratic participation in the very institution (the school) that is responsible for that training? Can we be sure that mature citizenship will ever result if it is not practiced during the critical period of its development? or if natural concepts of justice, fair play, and mutual respect are exercised and developed only within the framework of the street-corner gang?

GROUP DYNAMICS IN THE CLASSROOM

The democratic process is not a random one, although it may seem wholly unpredictable at times. In addition to the developmental forces discussed previously, there are principles underlying the formation of coalitions, communication patterns, and group problem-solving processes. These principles are often referred to as the *dynamics* of group behavior. Unfortunately, group dynamics is still a young and fluid science. A teacher cannot be told to "take a pinch of this and add a pinch of that" in order to stir up a successful classroom group. But we do know a few basic principles that may help.

Cohesiveness and Friendship

A well-known tool for measuring interpersonal interests within a group is the *sociogram.* The construction of a sociogram begins by asking students such questions as, "Whom do you like?" or "Who would you like to sit next to you on the bus?" Students' choices can then be diagrammed, as in Figure 15.5. The arrows signify who was chosen by whom. In this case, each child had three choices; the question was, "Who are your three best friends in this school?"

Note that during the elementary years, girls are chosen by girls and boys by boys, to a great extent. Same-sex influences are strong in friendship patterns. Other types of similarities are also influential: social class, age, religion, and ethnic background, for example. Interest similarities have predictable effects on friendship patterns, as one might imagine, especially among older children. In general, popular children and adolescents share a cluster of positive characteristics. They are perceived by their peers as being "friendly," "helpful," "interested in you," "intelligent,"

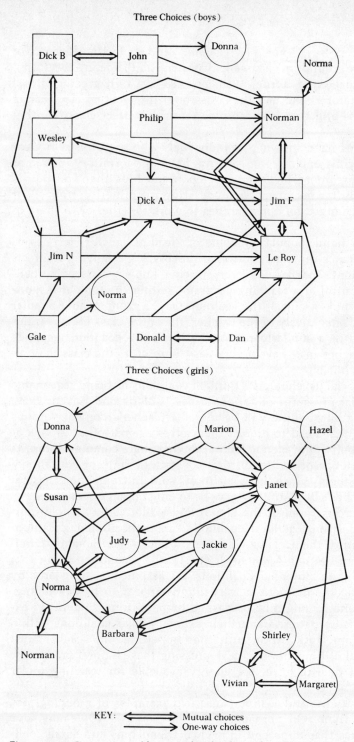

Figure 15.5 Sociograms of boys' and girls' three "best friends." (Almy and Cunningham, 1966, p. 18)

"attractive," "not bossy," "not quarrelsome," and so forth. (Reviews of this literature are found in Mussen, Conger, and Kagan, 1969, pp. 578–585; and Lindzey and Byrne, 1968, pp. 483–509.) Of greater importance to the educator is the fact that classroom interactions can change friendship patterns and that friendship patterns can affect classroom behavior.

Several studies have shown that individuals who are physically near to each other in terms of classroom seating, housing, dormitory rooms, or apartment units are more likely to develop friendships than individuals who are physically farther apart. Attitudes (toward minority groups, for example) can be changed by opportunities to work together or to share in activities.

On the other hand, popular students or "leading crowds" may exert considerable influence on the educational process, especially as it affects the more dependent students. As every teacher knows, classroom coalitions may take control of a teaching program, setting the tone of responsiveness for the whole group. If the coalition (say, a group of four popular students) responds negatively to the teacher, the entire class may be influenced to respond in a similarly negative way. If the coalition responds positively, the teacher may have a very easy time of it; the class may almost seem to teach itself.

In general, social psychologists think of coalitions as being reasonable responses to social pressures of various types (Collins and Raven, 1969, pp. 127–137). Not all of these will be under a teacher's control. Groups that wish power, that need to protect themselves against other groups or against the possibility of academic failure, or that share common interests (of a creative variety, for example) may coalesce in spite of educational pressures against them. Since these coalitions contain tremendous natural energies, the teacher's best strategy may be to enlist them directly.

A democratic classroom of the Lippitt and White variety would capitalize upon these strong, natural coalitions; an authoritarian classroom must seek to destroy them. Thus we have, in books like Schain's *Discipline: How to Establish and Maintain It* (1961), the recommendation that the teacher break up potential coalitions by assigned seating and by changes in seating the moment new coalitions appear to be developing. Far more useful energy might be unleashed by permitting students to express their friendship patterns and their extracurricular coalitions within an educational framework. In an authoritarian setting, the teacher must spend a great deal of time and energy repressing these natural groupings. Chances are that he will have less energy available for teaching under those conditions.

Friendship patterns and coalitions are two examples of grouping processes in the classroom. On a broader scale, the class as a whole may have cohesive properties that transcend individual friendships and small coalitions. How can a teacher increase class cohesiveness?

In general, attraction to a group is affected by the individual's perception of the rewards of membership. There are, of course, many kinds of rewards. Some students have more intense social needs than others; just being a member of a group—any group—may be rewarding to them. Other students see group membership as a way of achieving an important goal—producing a play, for example—that cannot be achieved in isolation. Still other students enjoy the thrill of competition; as long as their group is the winning group, cohesiveness is strong. (What happens when their group becomes the losing group is another story.) Finally, groups may be able to provide special rewards: money, privileges, and the like—as a union does, for example. (These factors are reviewed in more detail in Cartwright, 1968.) To the extent that a teacher becomes able to manipulate these factors, he can manipulate the cohesiveness of his classroom groups.

A Classroom Example One application of some of these principles was carried out in a required mathematics class for college freshmen (Hayes, personal communication). The subject was calculus, and the requirement was felt necessary in order to provide students with freedom to participate in advanced science courses. The administration reasoned that such freedom would be denied students who lacked the basic mathematical tools for science projects. Consequently, although the underlying philosophy was democratic in principle, the immediate application was somewhat authoritarian: The course was required, a level of proficiency was required, and the subject matter was dictated. The usual response to classes of that nature is resentment, resistance, and negative coalition formation—especially in this day of emphasis upon student freedom.

To overcome these negative group pressures, the classes were divided into four- to six-person groups. Everyone who passed the proficiency tests was to get a B, and the tests could be taken as often as necessary. But in order for anyone to get an A, everyone in the group had to get an A. In other words, the entire group had to develop a high level of proficiency if anyone in the group was to be rewarded for it.

This procedure was both popular and successful. Students with low mathematical aptitude became the targets of intensive helping processes, unlike their usual rejection as class "dunces." They felt a tremendous pressure to master the material for the sake of the group. Group competition was keen and fun, since everyone could be a winner. Talented group members had a chance to use their special abilities in constructive, unselfish ways and to sharpen their teaching or coaching skills at the same time. Groups were free to establish their own study periods and coaching procedures, so that some degree of democratic involvement was in fact possible. The entire procedure suggests a model that might be usefully applied (with some modifications) with different age groups and subject matters.

Theories of Social Balance

Social psychologists, like all scientists, have been searching for general principles of social behavior—principles that will be sufficiently universal to explain both individual and group behavior. Theories involving ideas of *balance* or *congruity* may have this generality:

> Common to the concepts of balance, congruity, and dissonance [or unbalance] is the notion that thoughts, beliefs, attitudes, and behavior tend to organize themselves in meaningful and sensible ways. Members of the White Citizens Council do not ordinarily contribute to [the] NAACP. Adherents of the New Deal seldom support Republican candidates. Christian Scientists do not enroll in medical schools. And people who live in glass houses apparently do not throw stones. In this respect the concept of consistency underscores and presumes human *rationality*. It holds that behavior and attitudes are not only consistent to the objective observer, but that individuals try to appear consistent to themselves. It assumes that inconsistency is a noxious state setting up pressures to eliminate it or reduce it. But in the *ways* that consistency in human behavior and attitudes is achieved we see rather often a striking lack of rationality. A heavy smoker cannot readily accept evidence relating cancer to smoking; a socialist, told that Hoover's endorsement of certain political slogans agreed perfectly with his own, calls him "a typical hypocrite and a liar." (Zajonc, 1960, p. 280)

Nevertheless, Zajonc and others believe, the behavior is not really irrational. It is simply obeying a less obvious set of principles.

Festinger, in his book *A Theory of Cognitive Dissonance* (1957), has said that people will behave in predictable ways in order to escape disequilibrium of various kinds. By *dissonance,* Festinger means any kind of dissonance—between a person and his own actions, between two persons, between two ideas, and so forth. When a dissonant state exists, an individual will strive to overcome it by changing his ideas, changing the situation, changing his evaluations, or perhaps trying to persuade others to change their evaluations.

Thus, a person who buys a house but is not sure he did the right thing studies the real estate ads more intensively *after* he makes a down payment. Presumably, he is looking for information that will reduce his dissonance. In a fascinating book, *When Prophecy Fails,* Festinger and his colleagues describe how a religious group avoided publicity during the period when it was predicting the end of the world, but *sought* publicity after its prophecy had failed. The group was attempting to resolve its own dissonance by persuading others to take up its cause. Prior to the dissonant state, it was not interested in proselytizing.

The Development of Balanced Social Concepts

The father of these theories in social psychology was Fritz Heider (1946), who introduced the notion of *balance* in perception and thought. We will illustrate Heider's work and consider its development at the same time by referring to a delightful study by Atwood (1969).

Heider's theory concerned the person (*P*), an other person (*O*), and an event (or "thing" or third person) known as *X*. *P*, *O*, and *X* can have either positive or negative relations with each other. In a balanced relation, *P* likes *O*, *O* likes *X*, and therefore *P* likes *X*. Similarly, if *P* likes *O* and *O* dislikes *X*, then *P* will dislike *X*—that is also balanced. But if *P* likes *O*, *O* likes *X*, and *P* dislikes *X*, the relation is unbalanced.

Heider believed that individuals tend to balance their view of their world, when possible. But until the Atwood paper was published, nothing was known about the development of this balancing tendency. Atwood, following the traditional manner of testing Heider's theory, told children these three stories:

1. Allen, who wanted to be on the baseball team very badly, walked up to Butch, the captain, and asked if he could play. "Shut up and get out of here, kid," said Butch. "You couldn't hit a baseball in a million years." Allen asked another child who was watching if he was on the baseball team. "No," said the other child. "Butch said I'm no good and he wouldn't let me play."
[QUESTION: Will Allen and the other child like each other? If the cognition balances, the answer would be Yes.]

2. On his birthday Jack received a brand-new basketball. He played often with his good friend Eric. They had fun playing ball. One day Eric's cousin Joe came over to visit Eric. Eric and Joe liked each other very much. Since they had nothing to do they decided to go over to Jack's house to play basketball. Jack sees Eric and Joe coming.
[QUESTION: Will Jack be glad to see Joe? Will he like him?]

3. One day Mike was playing peacefully on the sidewalk with his new marbles when Bob and Ray, who are very close friends, came down the street to where Mike was playing. Bob sees Mike and runs over and kicks the marbles as hard as he can. "Mike, you told on me at school and I hate you," yells Bob. "Take off," says Mike, "and don't ever let me see you again, Bob. Beat it."
[QUESTION: Will Mike want Ray to go away too?] (Atwood, 1968, p. 76)

Atwood skillfully questioned children, whom he had also tested on some of Piaget's tasks. He was sure the children understood the stories and got the names straight. He found—as Piaget would surely predict—that children who were still preoperational did not balance their cognition of the stories. Children who had reached the concrete operational stage balanced quite firmly. They were very sure about the likes and dislikes of the respective children.

[Example of a preoperational child; responses in italics]
Do Bob and Ray like each other? *Yes.* Do Bob and Mike like each other? *Bob and Mike don't like each other.* How about Mike and Ray, do they like each other? *Yes.* Why? *Because Ray didn't kick the marbles.*

[Example of a concrete operational child; responses in italics]
How would Ray and Mike feel about each other? *They probably wouldn't like each other.* Why? *Ray is Bob's friend.* Is it possible that they would like each other, Mike and Ray? *Ray might not like Bob kicking the*

marbles. He could be on Mike's side against Bob. (Atwood, 1968, pp. 79–80)

Note how this last child rebalanced the triad by finding a reason why Ray must share Mike's negative feeling toward Bob.

What does this signify to the teacher? That in their social relationships, as well as in their academic behavior, children grow in mental logic. The young child may be inconsistent, from an adult's point of view, in his choice of friends and in his evaluation of social forces. But as he develops, principles of logic will begin to function in his social behavior, as well as in every other area of his life. This logic may not reach the highest degree of which it is potentially capable; because of various teachings and pressures, a child may remain "stuck" in oversimplified social views and prejudices. Or he may develop a tight logical system (of hatred, say) that is harmful to society. But during the early years, growth in social reasoning is possible, and it follows developmental principles that make it easier to understand and predict.

Competition and Conflict

Competition and conflict may follow equally predictable principles. Morton Deutsch and his colleagues at Columbia University have developed a number of experimental models for studying the differences between competitive and cooperative situations. Their analysis, shown in Table 15.1, details the differences in the negative and positive dynamics activated by the two situations. Careful study of the table leads one to wonder how competitiveness (for grades, class standing, and so forth) ever became so entrenched in our school systems. Surely we have passed beyond such primitive "dog-eat-dog, survival-of-the-fittest" notions of social motivation.

Communication Networks

Consider the communication patterns shown in Figure 15.6. Each circle represents a person. Figure 15.6(*a*) is a typical classroom pattern, in which the teacher communicates to each student, and each student communicates directly to the teacher. There is little student interchange. Now consider the pattern in Figure 15.6(*b*), which is also fairly typical. The teacher has designated a class monitor who communicates with the other students, and then with the teacher. Students who are left "in charge of a class" during a teacher's absence have this communicative function; so do chairmen of class committees.

Now consider a typical discussion group, as shown in Figure 15.6(*c*). The discussion group is obviously messier and noisier. The teacher, being only another discussant, has no special path of control.

Different communication patterns are necessary for different group goals. Clearly, wars would never be won (or battles even launched) if armies were discussion groups. On the other hand, wars are not always being fought in classrooms. As far as problem solving is concerned, the discussion network—though noisier and messier—is more efficient; more and better solutions are achieved by groups that use such a network. They are also more popular and lead to greater cohesiveness. (Collins and Raven, 1969, pp. 137–155, provide the most up-to-date review of the extensive research on communication networks in group problem solving.)

Keeping Track of Interactions

The study of what actually happens during interpersonal communication is a difficult matter, simply because so much is taking place. Tape recordings or filmed sequences of communication behavior can be coded and scored in many ways, but it may not be possible to keep all the interactions in mind simultaneously (remember "the magic number 7").

There are several systems of interaction analysis suitable for class-

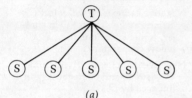

(a)

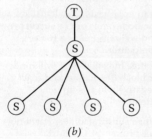

(b)

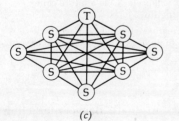

(c)

Figure 15.6 Typical communication patterns. (a) Teacher and students; (b) teacher, monitor, and students; (c) discussion group.

Table 15.1
Basic Concepts in the Analysis of the Effects of Cooperation and Competition

TYPE OF PERCEIVED INTERDEPENDENCE BETWEEN P AND O	TYPE OF ACTION BY O	EFFECTS OF O'S ACTIONS ON P
Cooperative: P's and O's goals are linked in such a way that their probabilities of goal attainment are positively correlated; as one's chances increase or decrease so does the other's chances.	Effective: (O's action increases O's chances of goal attainment and, thus, also P's.)	Positive substitutability: P will not need to act to accomplish what O has accomplished. Positive cathexis: P will value O's actions and will be attracted to O in similar, future situations (i.e., as a fellow cooperator). Positive inducibility: P will facilitate O's actions and be open to positive influence from O.
	Ineffective: (O's action decreases O's chances of goal attainment and, thus, also P's.)	Negative substitutability: P will need to act to accomplish what O has failed to accomplish. Negative cathexis: P will reject O's actions and will reject O in similar, future situations (i.e., as a fellow cooperator). Negative inducibility: P will hinder O's actions and be negatively influenced by O.
Competitive: P's and O's goals are linked in such a way that their probabilities of goal attainment are negatively correlated; as one's chances increase, the other's decrease.	Effective: (O's action increases O's chances of goal attainment and, thus, decreases P's chances.)	Negative substitutability: P will need to act to accomplish what O has accomplished. Negative cathexis: P will dislike the occurrence of O's successes and will reject O as a future competitor. Negative inducibility: P will hinder or block O's actions and react negatively to O's influence attempts.
	Ineffective: (O's action decreases O's chances of goal attainment and, thus, increases P's chances.)	Positive substitutability: P will not need to repeat O's mistakes. Positive cathexis: P will value the occurrence of O's failures and will prefer O as a future competitor. Positive inducibility: P will facilitate O's blunders and be ready to help O make mistakes.

SOURCE: Deutsch, 1969, p. 1078.

room groups. A simplified form of the "old, original" Bales interaction process analytical system is shown in Figure 15.7. It can be used to score group behavior without regard for who said what, or it can be used to score the behavior of a single member of a group. Time segments, names,

Table 15.1
(*Continued*)

SOME THEORETICALLY EXPECTED CONSEQUENCES OF AN
EXCHANGE OF *EFFECTIVE* ACTIONS BETWEEN P AND O
IN COOPERATIVE AND COMPETITIVE RELATIONSHIPS

Task orientation: Highlighting of mutual interests; coordinated effort with division of
labor and specialization of function; sub-
stitutability of effort rather than duplica-
tion; the enhancement of mutual power becomes an objective.

Attitudes: Trusting, friendly attitudes with a
positive interest in the other's welfare and
a readiness to respond helpfully to the
other's needs and requests.

Perception: Increased sensitivity to common
interests while minimizing the salience of
opposed interests; a sense of convergence of
beliefs and values.

Communication: Open, honest communication
of relevant information; each is interested
in accurately informing as well as being in-
formed; communication is persuasive rather
than coercive in intent.

Task orientation: Emphasis on antagonistic
interests; the minimization of the other's
power becomes an objective.

Attitudes: Suspicious, hostile attitudes with a
readiness to exploit the other's needs and
weakness and a negative responsiveness to
the other's requests.

Perception: Increased sensitivity to opposed
interests, to threats, and to power differences while minimizing the awareness of
similarities.

Communication: Little communication or misleading communication; espionage or other
techniques to obtain information the other
is unwilling to give; each seeks to obtain
accurate information about the other but to
mislead, discourage, or intimidate the other;
coercive tactics are employed.

or role labels can be written across the top. (For more details on how to
use this system, see Gordon, 1966, pp. 125–128, 137–139.)

Classroom Dialogues How would you use the Bales system (as shown
in Figure 15.7) to analyze the following classroom interchange? The

CATEGORIES																																	TOTALS
1 Shows solidarity, raises other's status, gives help, reward																																	
2 Shows tension release, jokes, laughs, shows satisfaction																																	
3 Agrees, shows passive acceptance, understands, concurs, complies																																	
4 Gives suggestion, direction, implying autonomy for other																																	
5 Gives opinion, evaluation, analysis, expresses feeling, wish																																	
6 Gives orientation, information, repeats, clarifies, confirms																																	
7 Asks for orientation, information, repetition, confirmation																																	
8 Asks for opinion, evaluation, analysis, expression of feeling																																	
9 Asks for suggestion, direction, possible ways of action																																	
10 Disagrees, shows passive rejection, formality, withholds help																																	
11 Shows tensions, asks for help, withdraws out of field																																	
12 Shows antagonism, deflates other's status, defends or asserts self																																	
Totals																																	

No. in group_____   Time of day_____
Topic_____   Date_____
_____   Other_____

Figure 15.7   Categories of interactions in Bales' system. (Bales, 1950, p. 18)

teacher has given the class a set of little verses which are actually *haiku* (Japanese poetry), although the class does not know that. Their problem, in fact, is to figure out what the poems are and where they come from.

CAROLYN: Well, they're all poems, so they must have been written by a poet.

BILL S.: That's some help! How do you know they're not written by one and the same poet? They all look the same to me, same three lines, same style, all short and vague.

CAROLYN: But they're on different subjects and they give different feelings. Each one gives me a different feeling.

BILL S.: Does that mean they can't be by one poet expressing himself on different subjects?

SYLVIA: I have a different idea. Maybe these poems are all by different poets, but may seem to be the same because of the style. What I mean is that maybe they are the usual kind of poem for this country.

GWEN: Or, it could just be the style of a particular poet.

JOHN: I think this is getting us nowhere. Let's forget about the poet and try to find out where it's from.

BOB: But these poems are too vague.

DIANE: We're back to that again.

TEACHER: Well, does everyone agree with this, or can someone offer advice or evidence to help us out? Where are these from?

SHARON: They are from Europe because an Emperor is mentioned, and lords are also mentioned a couple of times. This means there must have been an autocracy in this country. Many countries of Europe had monarchs and lords.

BERNARD: At one time almost every European country had this kind of government. Maybe these poems are from Russia. Russia had an Emperor and nobles running it for a long, long time.

DIANE: I think that this is from France or Germany, or Austria during the Middle Ages, because the lords seem to be very powerful; they are able to command cavalry men and to own large halls. Maybe the emperor referred to is Charlemagne.

GWEN: I think you're getting on the wrong track. This is no European set of poems, certainly not American!

TEACHER: Why?

GWEN: Well, you're missing a lot of important parts of the poems that seem not to be European at all. What about the mention of a temple? Since when are Medieval churches called temples? And what about the reference to rice in one of the poems? Rice wasn't one of the European's main dishes, at least as far as I know.

EDDIE: Rice is from the Orient, from China. The Chinese eat lots of rice. The poems must be translated from Chinese.

STEVE: They could also be from Japan or India. I've read somewhere that these two countries produce and eat rice as their main dish.

MARY: I read recently that Southeast Asia produces a lot of rice. Vietnam exports rice, and eats some of it.

HELEN: I have a suggestion, but not of another country. I think we should try to get the meaning and message of each poem and then find out where they're from. Let's start with poem 1 and work our way down. (Massialas and Zevin, 1967, pp. 76–78)

The group did eventually discover the type and origin of the poems. But more important from Massialas' standpoint, they practiced their communication and discovery skills. The value of a system such as Bales' is that it makes possible a comparison of different types of materials. Regardless of what a group is communicating about, it may show greater or lesser amounts of agreement (category 3), asking for opinion or suggestions (8 and 9), antagonism (12), and so forth (Figure 15.7). Although Massialas has not tested this, it should be possible to show that practice in what he calls "creative encounters" with problems will, in fact, improve communication skills, at least as compared to groups who have had no such practice.

A simplified version of the Bales system has been developed by Flanders (see the summary by Amidon, 1967). It is an interaction analysis system more suitable for the first or second communication pattern shown above—the more authoritarian patterns. The categories are shown in Table 15.2.

Try the Flanders system in coding the following transcript:

TEACHER: When you are ready, we will start! (Noise of desks, talk, etc., subsides gradually.)

SUSAN: Do we need our books out?

TEACHER: Just wait and I will tell you what you need.

TEACHER: You know, the longer we have to wait, the more time we waste. Do you think it is fair that some of us have to wait for others?

BILLY: Sh! Sh!

TEACHER: All right—Now today we are ready to discuss the Russian Revolution. Jack, what is a revolution?

JACK: It is when the people are very unhappy and they decide to get rid of the king or something?

TEACHER: Then what? Bill?

BILL: They usually kill the king or czar.

TEACHER: Yes. But what causes a revolution?

SUZY: (Raises hand, teacher nods.) Well, like Jack said, people are unhappy and they revolt against the government.

TEACHER: Oh, then what happens?

MARY: There is usually a lot of bloodshed and then probably the new people get to be the people in power.

TEACHER: And??

MARY: They set up their own government.

TEACHER: What revolutions do we know about?

TIM: We had one!

BUD: Yeah, we kicked the British out of the colonies!

TEACHER: All right, there was an American Revolution. Do you know of any others?

FRED: The French cut off a lot of heads.

TEACHER: When was that?

FRED: When they got rid of their king.

TEACHER: Okay, the American, the French and the Russian revolutions are three examples. Are there any going on now?

MARY: Cuba had a revolution a little while ago.

TEACHER: What about that?

MARY: Well, this man Tateeta (teacher corrects—Batista), ah, Batista kept all the money and land and finally there was a revolution.

TEACHER: Who can tell us more about this?

JACK: Castro is the dictator now.

BILL: He came out of the hills.

CHARLEY: He looks more like he came out of the trees.

TEACHER: That's enough of that (glares at Charley). Now, what happened in Cuba? Mary?

MARY: The people were poor and a few men had all the money—so,

Table 15.2
Categories of Interaction Analysis in Flanders' System*

TEACHER TALK	**INDIRECT INFLUENCE**	1. *Accepts feeling:* Accepts and clarifies the feeling tone of the students in a nonthreatening manner. Feelings may be positive or negative. Predicting or recalling feelings are included. 2. *Praises or encourages:* Praises or encourages student action or behavior. Jokes that release tension not at the expense of another individual; nodding head or saying "um hm?" or "go on" are included. 3. *Accepts or uses ideas of student:* Clarifying, building, or developing ideas suggested by a student. As teacher brings more of his own ideas into play, shift to category five.
	DIRECT INFLUENCE	4. *Asks questions:* Asking a question about content or procedure with the intent that a student answer. 5. *Lecturing:* Giving facts or opinions about content or procedure; expressing his own ideas; asking rhetorical questions. 6. *Giving directions:* Directions, commands, or orders with which a student is expected to comply. 7. *Criticizing or justifying authority:* Statements intended to change student behavior from non-acceptable to acceptable pattern; bawling someone out; stating why the teacher is doing what he is doing; extreme self-reference. 8. *Student talk—response:* Talk by students is response to teacher. Teacher initiates the contact or solicits student statement.
STUDENT TALK		9. *Student talk—initiation:* Talk by students which they initiate. If "called on" student is only to indicate who may talk next; observer must decide whether student wanted to talk. If he did, use this category.
		10. *Silence or confusion:* Pauses, short periods of silence, and periods of confusion in which communication cannot be understood by the observer.

SOURCE: Amidon, 1967, p. 47.
*There is *no* scale implied by the numbers. Each number is classificatory; it designates a particular kind of communication event. To write these numbers down during observation is to enumerate, not to judge, a position on a scale.

they started a revolution and threw out Batista, and now Castro runs the country and everything is just as bad as it was.

TEACHER: You mean nothing good came of the revolution?

MARY: Things are worse now, down there.

TEACHER: Well, maybe. But the important thing for us at this point is to realize that there was a revolution. So I think I have been hearing you say that revolutions arise when conditions are bad in a country—that the people or some group arms itself and deliberately sets out to gain control of the government of the country. When this happens we say that there is a revolution. Now, what about the Russian Revolution. Who knows some facts? (Waimon, 1967, pp. 58–59)

Research cited by Amidon (1967) suggests that training in interaction analysis helps student teachers to become less directive and more accepting of student responses—and that this sort of indirect teaching is associated with higher pupil achievement.

Laboratory Studies of Human Interaction

The study of interpersonal communication in a classroom setting overlooks a good deal, however. For example, it may not be possible to tell how the communicator is taking individual differences into account. How does the teacher change his communication to fit particular students? How do students change their modes of communication to fit particular teachers? How do communicators take feedback into account? For answers to questions of that sort, we must return to the laboratory.

In a series of studies of role taking and communicative skills in children, Flavell (1968) and his colleagues gave children such tasks as telling a fable ("The Fox and the Grapes") to a younger child and describing the displays shown in Figure 15.8 to someone (imaginary, shown in a photograph) who could not see them.

In the first task, there was a striking shift between the third and sev-

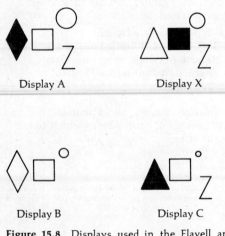

Display A   Display X

Display B   Display C

Figure 15.8 Displays used in the Flavell and Fry experiments on child communication. (Flavell, 1968, p. 130)

enth grade in the way the fable was phrased for younger children. It was recoded in simpler forms. These recodings could take three forms: They might be substitutions, additions, or deletions. Substitutions were most frequent ("walking" for "strolling"; "satisfy my thirst" for "quench my thirst"). The design task was scored for communications about position, size, color, and shape, and also showed progressive improvement from third to eleventh grade. That is, the older students were better able to take listener needs into account. They were more attuned to those needs.

The concept of *cognitive tuning* is a useful one in thinking about communication problems. Many factors might enter into such tuning: degree of egocentricity, information about the other person's knowledge or attitudes, information about his motivation, sympathy for him, motivation of the communicator, and so forth. The need to tune a communication may even affect the concepts of the communicator.

One experiment that demonstrated such an effect was carried out by Cohen (1961). The concept in question was that of another person's personality. Subjects were given lists of traits and asked to write out a personality description. Half the subjects were told they would eventually tell someone else about their concept (of the personality); half were told they would be receivers only—that someone would tell them about the personality, but that all they had to do was listen. The traits involved in the personality concept were these: very friendly, extremely generous, ruthless, extremely dependable, overly conceited, very kind, scheming, very cold, highly loyal, insincere. Since they are contradictory, forming a concept of this particular personality posed something of a problem.

How did the set to "send" a communication or to "receive" one affect the personality concept? The subjects who had been told they would "send" polarized around one aspect of the personality—either the good one or the bad one. The subjects who had been told they would "receive" remained more tolerant and open. The personality description they wrote was more accepting of the contradictions. Further, the "receivers" were more interested than the "senders" in obtaining additional information about the personality, when given an opportunity to do so.

> It is curious that people who have to transmit information concerning a complex impression to others do, in fact, want less additional information than those who are to receive others' complex impressions. Furthermore, the information they do want tends to be one-sided and narrowly defined, whereas those exposed to reception tuning desire material more on both sides of the issue. However, these results, as well as the results on the written impression [of the personality], become plausible once it is understood that transmission requires a tight and well-bound cognitive "package" which can be communicated to others. Additional and contradictory information about the person makes it more difficult to order a clear and unambiguous cognitive structure which can be passed on. When set to receive others' impressions, the person can entertain a more flexible and ambiguous picture, and may forestall the quick polarization demanded by the [sending] requirements. (Cohen, 1961, p. 244)

These findings suggest that it might be possible to *sharpen* communication skills more by speaking or "transmitting" than by listening or "receiving." Fry (1966) tested this hypothesis on 12-year-old students, using the Flavell picture materials shown in Figure 15.8. Some of his subjects were trained to improve their communications about these pictures by preparing and delivering communications about them and then receiving feedback about the adequacy of their presentation. Other subjects simply listened and delivered feedback, but prepared no communications of their own. Feedback involved both the visual feedback of seeing whether or not the listener could identify the correct picture and verbal feedback concerning these questions: Was enough information included to permit correct identification? Was additional unnecessary information included? Could the listener think of alternative ways of making the message a more effective one? Improvement in communication skills was tested both on that same task and on other tasks, to see if generalization to other tasks occurred.

Fry found that improvement occurred on the picture task regardless of whether speaking or listening had been practiced. But generalization (to new tasks) occurred only for speaking; children who had practiced the actual communicating were better able to apply their new skill to other tasks.

Stimulating Classroom Discussion

One other problem should be discussed here: the special problem of stimulating discussion in classrooms. In many cases, the first need is to get students talking. Improvement in their communication skills cannot be attempted until communication itself is begun.

Social psychologists have tested a number of principles believed to motivate communication (the work is summarized in Festinger, 1950). The principles are based on the general notion that people are uncomfortable when they perceive discrepancies or gaps between their own ideas and the ideas of groups which are important to them. Pressure to communicate then arises; the student wants to close the gap. (We recognize here something similar to Berlyne's *collative display,* in which the individual may be motivated to try to harmonize conflicting ideas.) According to Festinger, the following principles govern the pressure to communicate:

1. The pressure to communicate increases as the size of the gap (between self and group) increases.

2. The pressure to communicate about something in particular (item *x*) increases with the relevance of item *x*.

3. The pressure increases with the cohesiveness of the group; the tighter-knit the group, the greater the communication needs.

4. The force to communicate about item *x* to a particular member of the group increases as the gap between the communicator and that group

member increases. (Many more communications may be directed toward a group deviant, at least up until the time he is considered to be excluded from the group—as a deviant will be, eventually.)

5. The force to communicate will increase the more it is perceived that the communication will change the group member's opinion. (In other words, we argue harder when we think we may have an influence.)

With these as guidelines, we might make a number of classroom predictions and suggestions. For example, a class that contains a coalition (a subgroup or clique) will probably generate more discussion. If teachers can create coalitions (debate teams, committees), discussion will probably increase. If a teacher takes a deviant position but seems open to persuasion, more communication should be directed by the class toward the teacher. The need to communicate arises from one's concept of a situation; if a teacher can manipulate the concepts, he can manipulate communication needs.

Group Helping Processes

Strangely enough, despite all the work done on groups, we still do not know for sure if problem solving is better in groups or in isolation. There is evidence in support of both positions. For the most part, the studies indicate that "it depends"—on the kind of problem, the kind of group, the incentive conditions, and so forth. As an example of the type of research that is done, consider the brainstorming controversy. In 1953 a book called *Applied Imagination* by A. F. Osborn appeared on the market. Its subtitle was *Principles and Procedures of Creative Thinking,* and brainstorming was one of the procedures:

> "Brainstorm" means using the *brain* to *storm* a creative problem — and to do so in *commando* fashion, with each stormer audaciously attacking the same objective.
> Hundreds of such brainstorm sessions have been held from coast to coast, and nearly all have been worthwhile in terms of ideas produced. Fiascoes are usually due to failure of leadership. For example, if a group-chairman acts omniscient, he makes his more timid members afraid to open their mouths. Then, too, when a leader allows criticism to creep into the proceedings, he likewise fails to get the best out of his panel. He must always insist that the ideas produced be judged — not *during* the brainstorming session — but *afterward.* (Osborn, 1953, pp. 80–81)

Generally, the procedure is to get together in a group and generate all the ideas one can possibly think of that are relevant to the group's problem. No evaluation of the ideas is permitted at the time, but everything is recorded (on tape, or in shorthand). The group atmosphere should be gamelike, rather than critical; wild ideas are welcomed, and ideas that combine other ideas (or take them as a starting point) are also encouraged. The method can be applied in any kind of group, from U.S. Steel executives to Divorcees Anonymous.

Experimental Studies of Brainstorming One experimental study of the effects of brainstorming was carried out by Parnes and Meadow. They compared the problem solving of groups that had been given brainstorming and nonbrainstorming instructions:

> **Brainstorming Instructions.** You are to list all the ideas [about the use of various objects] that come to your mind without judging them in any way. Forget about the quality of the ideas entirely. We will count only quantity on this task. Express any idea which comes to your mind. As you go along, you may combine or modify any of the ideas which you have already listed, in order to produce additional ideas. Remember that quantity and freedom of expression without evaluation are the key points.
>
> **Nonbrainstorming Instructions.** You are to list all the *good* ideas you can think up. Your score will be the total number of good ideas. Don't put down any idea unless you feel it is a *good* one. (Parnes and Meadow, 1959, p. 172)

The experimenters found that significantly more good ideas were produced by the groups that had been given brainstorming instructions—especially by groups whose members had taken a course in creative problem solving. Since Osborn himself never performed systematic experiments of this type, the basic demonstration that brainstorming instructions can improve group problem solving is important. A more important question, however, may be whether or not *group* problem solving under brainstorming instructions would produce as many good ideas as *individual* problem solving under the same instructions.

The basic experiment testing this question was performed by Taylor, Berry, and Block (1958–1959). As in the Parnes and Meadow experiment, the subjects were college students. You might suppose that the comparison of groups and individuals could be made in a straightforward way by simply counting the number of responses given by the group and comparing them to the number of responses given by an individual. If you do that, you will find that the sheer number of responses is greater for the group. But does this prove that group participation facilitates problem solving? No; it proves only that there were more individuals in the group, so that the number of ideas produced is bound to be greater. Six individuals can produce more of almost anything than one individual can.

In order to carry out a fair test of group facilitation, Taylor and his associates combined individual subjects into artificial groups on paper *after* they had done their individual problem solving. The artificial groups had the same number of subjects in them as the real groups, but each member of the artificial group had actually done his problem solving in private. Table 15.3 shows the number of responses given by the individuals, the real groups, and the artificial groups. Clearly, the artificial groups produced the highest number of responses. In fact (according to Taylor), real group problem solving may *inhibit* the production of ideas. Nevertheless, it seems intuitively obvious that "two heads are better than one" under some conditions. The secret is to discover which conditions.

Table 15.3
Mean Number of Problem Solutions,
Individuals, Groups, Artificial Groups

	SOLUTIONS
Individuals	19.6
Groups (individuals working together)	37.5
Artificial groups (individuals working privately)	68.1

SOURCE: Based on data in Taylor, Berry, and Block, 1958.

Social Facilitation

Zajonc (1965), in reviewing the social facilitation literature, made one helpful discovery. Performance on the tasks in the following lists is *improved* when they are carried out under social conditions—either in front of an audience or in company with colleagues.

Type I Tasks

1. Pursuit-rotor: The subject must follow a small revolving target by means of a stylus he holds in his hand.
2. Radar scanning: A vigilance task.
3. Simple multiplication.
4. Word association.
5. Nest-building (ants).

Now compare these to the following tasks, which are performed less well under social conditions than in isolation.

Type II Tasks

1. Problem solving.
2. Learning a food source (birds).
3. Judging odors and weights.
4. Learning nonsense syllables.
5. Learning mazes (cockroaches).
6. Learning finger mazes (humans).

What characteristics do the Type I tasks have in common? They involve well-established, rather mechanical habits. Apparently, these habits are more strongly aroused by social stimulation. Type II tasks require the formation of new responses and habits; these are the tasks that are injured by the presence of an audience or of co-workers. Zajonc came to this conclusion:

> If one were to draw one practical suggestion from the review of the social-facilitation effects which are summarized in this article he would advise the student to study all alone, preferably in an isolated cubicle, and to arrange to take his examinations in the company of many other students, on stage, and in the presence of a large audience. The results of his

examination would be beyond his wildest expectations, provided, of course, he had learned his material quite thoroughly. (Zajonc, 1965, p. 274)

Productive Group Leadership

Of course, the group facilitation situation is not quite as simple as that. Maier (1967) has provided us with a useful set of analytical principles for deciding about the relative helpfulness of groups that can be quite directly applied to educational situations.

First of all, let us consider group assets: (1) There is a greater sum total of knowledge and information in a group. (2) There is a greater number of different approaches to a problem; group members can keep each other from getting stuck in one track. (3) If everyone has contributed to a solution, everyone is more likely to accept it. (4) Everyone is also more likely to understand it.

Now consider group liabilities: (1) Social pressures of various kinds (to conform, for example) may interfere with good problem solving. (2) A solution may build in attractiveness and be accepted, even though it is not objectively a good one. It is possible to compute what Maier calls a *valence index,* composed of the number of positive and negative comments about a solution. When this index reaches a certain positive intensity, the solution tends to be adopted by the group, whether it is objectively good or not. (3) Another disadvantage of leaderless groups is that one person may be too dominant—by participating more than the others do, by persuasion, or by fatiguing the opposition. The dominant individual may not, alas, be the best problem solver. (4) A final problem may arise when the goal of winning the argument is substituted for the original group goal of solving the problem.

Maier points out that a good leader (the teacher, for example) can help groups capitalize on their assets and sidestep their liabilities. He likens a good leader to the nerve ring of a starfish. Ordinarily, the nerve ring coordinates the movements of the separate rays. Even when the nerve ring has been surgically removed, however, the starfish can still manage to locomote. It does this through a sort of fake coordination—one leg moves, dragging the other legs, which then respond to the sensation of dragging. In a sense, the rays are still acting as a group, but they lack the higher type of coordination the nerve ring could provide. Maier's view of the leader's function is elaborated below:

> If we now examine what goes on in a discussion group we find that members can problem-solve as individuals, they can influence others by external pushes and pulls, or they can function as a group with varying degrees of unity. In order for the latter function to be maximized, however, something must be introduced to serve the function of a nerve ring. . . . We see this as the function of the leader. . . . His function is to *receive information, facilitate communications between the individuals, relay messages*, and *integrate the incoming responses* so that a single unified response occurs.

He must be receptive to information contributed, accept contributions without evaluating them (posting contributions on a chalk board to keep them alive), summarize information to facilitate integration, stimulate exploratory behavior, create awareness of problems of one member by others, and detect when the group is ready to resolve differences and agree to a unified solution.

. . .

If the leader can contribute the integrative requirement, group problem solving may emerge as a unique type of group function. This type of approach to group processes places the leader in a particular role in which he must cease to contribute, avoid evaluation, and refrain from thinking about solutions or group *products.* Instead he must concentrate on the group *process*, listen in order to understand rather than to appraise or refute, assume responsibility for accurate communication between members, be sensitive to unexpressed feelings, protect minority points of view, keep the discussion moving, and develop skills in summarizing. (Maier, 1967, pp. 245–247)

The leader who can function like a starfish nerve ring may utilize the following dynamics to move groups toward an effective solution: (1) He may be able to create a climate for disagreement that will encourage a search for solutions, rather than hard feelings. (2) He may be able to help group members with strong personal interests recognize and incorporate the mutual interests of the group. (3) He may be able to guide—in a constructive direction—the group's willingness to take risks (groups are generally more willing to take risks than individuals are). (4) He may be able to control discussion time effectively, allowing enough, but not too much. (5) He can make sure that social pressures do not repress minority views or good suggestions from shy group members.

With these basic principles in mind, re-read the discussion transcripts you used for interaction analysis. Ask yourself how you, as a good discussion group leader, would have handled those particular group problem-solving sessions. (You might also want to study an excellent review of leadership research by Gibb, 1968.)

In this section on group dynamics in the classroom, we have considered some of the major forces that affect the "care and feeding" of classroom groups. These are dynamics—forces of attraction, coalition, communication, and facilitation—that occur in the classroom itself. But there are many additional group or cultural influences that students (and teachers) bring into the classroom with them. Just as individuals have unique reaction systems that we call personality, so they also have unique outlooks and attitudes that have been shaped by sociological influences. It is to these that we now turn.

CLASS AND ETHNIC INFLUENCES

It has often been pointed out that public schooling in America is a middle-class operation. That is, public schools have been designed by middle-class people for middle-class children. Some schools, of course, do not meet this ideal—possibly because they are too poor, or too rich, or not enough of something. *Summerhill,* for example, is not a middle-class operation; neither are slum schools like those described in Kozol's *Death at an Early Age.*

One important aspect of the middle-classness of American education is the middle-class outlook of the average teacher. Most teachers are, however, a bit new to the middle class (Miller and Woock, 1970). Their parents were most frequently lower down the social scale—upper lower class, or even straight lower class. The parents of many teachers were not themselves very well educated. Of course this is not true of all, but it is frequent enough to set a tone: middle-class schools are largely run by middle-class teachers to whom middle-class status is an important personal achievement. Naturally, we are motivated to protect and maintain our important personal achievements. We also tend to assume they are (or should be) equally important to all.

Is the Middle-class Ideal Ideal?

The surprising fact is that two-thirds of the children attending our public schools are not from middle-class or upper-class backgrounds; they are from lower-class backgrounds (McCandless, 1967, p. 584). That means, quite simply, that they may not share the teacher's values. McCandless has provided us with a useful summary of the differences that may be involved:

Middle-class Values	Lower-class Values
1. Belief in God and regular church attendance. Most often Protestant, although this may vary regionally (the majority of teachers in New York City, for example, are Jewish).	1. Less likely to emphasize church, unless it is a fundamentalist one or the Roman Catholic Church.
2. Emphasis upon personal cleanliness—clean clothing, clean bodies, clean teeth, clean hair, clean fingernails (and clean minds, as we will see).	2. Less emphasis upon cleanliness in many large families, where there is little privacy, no bathroom, and nothing to get cleaned up for.
3. Belief in thrift, savings, and property. Luxuries and vacations are planned for, debts unpaid are shameful, and retirement security is a must.	3. Nothing to be thrifty with, and nothing to save for. "For the typical lower-class child, faith in the future has received little support. He has learned instead that he had better grab while the grabbing is good, because if he doesn't, one of his brothers and sisters, or his parents, or his

Middle-class Values

4. Intellect, rather than emotion, should control one's life. Reason and common sense are the best guidelines to action, which should be delayed and organized and planned, as reason dictates.

5. One should avoid expressing strong emotion, especially of a sexual or aggressive variety. "People should live peacefully and chastely together" (McCandless, 1967, p. 587). Sexual restraint is a matter of class pride. If aggression must be expressed, then it should be expressed in socially acceptable forms (perhaps in spectator sports, or games). Alcohol should be used very moderately.

6. Clean and correct language must be used—especially in the presence of children, or between the sexes. "Locker room talk" should never be used in the presence of women.

7. Language should also be scrupulously honest. Lying is a dreadful sin. So is stealing or cheating.

Lower-class Values

peers, will grab instead; and the supply is limited" (McCandless, 1967, p. 587).

4. "Reason has never won a street fight, nor enabled him to get the biggest share of the can of beans, nor served to keep his father from beating his mother when he got drunk. . . . Without immediate action and intense drive, the child may not survive in the tooth-and-claw existence that for him is almost routine" (McCandless, 1967, p. 587).

5. Strong emotion is constantly expressed and modeled. The lower-class child's world is full of fights, drunks, and sexual expression. "What is sacred and taboo for the middle-class teacher in the area of sex may be a matter of indulgence and free expression for the lower-class child. Hence, the child may pose a distinct threat to the controlled and perhaps inhibited teacher" (McCandless, 1967, p. 590).

6. "The lower-class child shares little, if any, of the middle-class teacher's horror of filthy talk, 'impure' accents, and messy grammar. He talks bluntly, in the argot he has learned in his particular portion of the wrong side of the tracks, and is interested only in communication, not in form" (McCandless, 1967, p. 590).

7. In both language and action, survival and desperation may lead to violations of the middle-class honor code. "If you are well-fed and have an amply stocked toy chest, it is easy not to snitch from the bakery stall or the notions counter; but if your stomach is growling, or you have never in

Middle-class Values	Lower-class Values
	your life owned a doll, the drive to do a little shoplifting is substantial" (McCandless, 1967, p. 591).
8. Hard work and self-discipline will bring success and happiness. "That is to say, if one is not impulsive, if one does not gratify his immediate needs for pleasure but postpones them for the sake of later satisfactions, he will in the long run be happier, have more money in the bank, and be more esteemed by the community and by himself. This middle-class ethic is as old as the fable of the grasshopper and the ant" (McCandless, 1967, p. 582).	8. "The lower-class child has little reason to believe that hard work and self-discipline result in success. Middle-class fathers do not put in eight hours of brutal labor swinging a pick. Such labor . . . is done in the heat and the cold; it is dirty; and it obtains relatively few of the world's goods. Nor is the unskilled and uneducated father likely to win conspicuous advancement by his diligence. He remains a day laborer . . . at the mercy of his boss, the times, and the weather. He does not get ahead. All he has to look forward to is more of the same. . . . In other words, our society is not organized to demonstrate to the lower-class child the virtues of hard work and self-discipline" (McCandless, 1967, p. 592).
9. Learning is a virtue in itself, and also as a mark of status and potential. Not finishing high school is a social disgrace. Nowadays, a college education—most frequently at a state college or university—is also pushed, even for girls. "Paradoxically, *too much* learning is viewed with suspicion. The United States seems most to esteem the well-educated but practical man. It is uneasy about the scholar . . ." (McCandless, 1967, p. 583).	9. "What is there in his life to teach a lower-class child that learning for the sake of learning is good? He grows up in a home where there are few, if any, books, magazines, or newspapers. His parents have probably done poorly in school and avoid . . . culture because their memories of their own school days are bitter. . . . Higher education, which might prepare the child for an 'easy' job, is out of the question for practical reasons (no money; no family backing, either practical or psychological; and, all too often, not enough ability). The pleasures of the lower-class child are therefore [not] likely to be those . . . that delight the mind or result in advancement through education" (McCandless, 1967, p. 592).

The Role of the School

There are large gaps, then, between the values of most teachers and the values of many children in public schools. This is reflected in every aspect of school, from the building to its textbooks; the middle-class institution that is the school bears little or no relationship to many of the other institutions that make up a lower-class child's community and family background.

Of course, the middle-class school atmosphere is much more natural to middle-class children. That means, in effect, that lower-class children will have a difficult social time of it. They can expect to be rejected and looked down upon by both middle-class children and their own lower-class peers who admire middle-class children greatly, and to have to endure this treatment in a middle-class setting. Further, if they manage to learn and adopt middle-class ways, they may be scorned by their families and communities for "putting on airs" or trying to "make it" up the social ladder. Such efforts always imply a rejection of the old ways, and rejection always hurts. The lower-class child is damned if he does and damned if he doesn't with respect to middle-class aspirations.

And yet the solution is obviously not to adopt lower-class values, as lower-class parents are the first to point out. For both middle-class and lower-class parents, the middle-class school is *expected* to teach and to model middle-class standards and aspirations. The problem is that in many communities—including many middle-class communities—it is simply not succeeding. What is taking place is something like a charade. The school administrators, teachers, curriculum developers, and parents are striving to keep alive the *picture* of the proper middle-class school serving proper middle-class children. But in reality, the children are living separate and often secret lives, in accord with psychological principles (of needs, dependencies, prejudices, and curiosities) that the schools are pretending do not exist. The real problem is not one of deciding for or against middle-class values, but one of facing honestly the values and behaviors that actually exist.

In a not-so-trivial way, the problem can be illustrated by the difference between pledge of allegiance controversies and what the pledge of allegiance actually means to the children who repeat it. Or the difference between school prayer controversies and what those prayers actually mean to the children who repeat them or listen to them. The true problem of education is the meaning of the pledge and the prayer, not lip service to court orders. This problem is just as real for middle-class as for lower-class students, and it extends far beyond school prayers and pledges to every corner of the educational network. In our classrooms are individual children with individual minds. All too often their real interests, capabilities, and outlooks are ignored in favor of educational material that has what Maier would call a high *valence index:* material that groups of educators find attractive. To the extent that a youngster matches that material, he is educated. If he does not match the material, no alternative educational systems may be available to him.

The problem is easier to see in the case of deaf children (Chapter 17), who are simply not educated at all in many communities until they are old enough to learn lip-reading. Their need for a preschool language which is natural and easy—a manual language—is simply ignored; many special educators of the deaf find lip-reading more attractive, perhaps because it is nearer to a middle-class ideal of normalcy. It is even easier to ignore "inconvenient" characteristics of normal children.

Good principles of sound education must reach well beyond class influences to the nature of the human child who is being taught. We can illustrate this by considering class and ethnic influences as they relate to three characteristics: mental abilities, attitudes toward cognitive tasks, and prejudice.

Mentality and Ethnicity

In 1965, Lesser, Fifer, and Clark published an important study of the different patterns of mental abilities in children from various class and ethnic groups. Their tests, which were constructed especially for this study, used experiences and ideas that were common to all social-class and culture groups in New York City, where the experiment was carried out. Four mental abilities were emphasized: verbal, reasoning (analogies, classifications), numerical, and spatial. Thus, the tests were in the tradition of multi-aptitude batteries, rather than in the *g* tradition (see Chapter 9). Examples of each test follow. Since children were tested in whatever language they found most comfortable (any of four Chinese dialects, for example), words were carefully chosen to be translatable.

Verbal

EXAMINER: I have some words here, and I want you to tell me what they mean:
What is an *apple?*
What does *bench* mean?
What do we mean when we use the word *decorating?*

Reasoning

EXAMINER (laying out some sample pictures): These pictures tell a story about a little boy who painted a chair, but the pictures are mixed up. I'd like to have you put the pictures in a line so that they will tell a good story.

Numerical

EXAMINER (showing a picture): There are five children on this side of the street (points). When these two children get to this side of the street (points), how many children will be on this side (points)?

Space

EXAMINER: Now here are some pictures with airplanes. See this airplane (pointing)? Its trail (pointing) shows the path it is following. This trail shows it is going in a straight line. Here it goes into a cloud (points). If it follows the same straight line, where will it come out of the cloud—here, or here, or here, or here (pointing)?

All the subjects were from first grade and were between 6 and 7 years of age. There were 320 of them, 80 from each of the cultural groups; 40 of the children in each cultural group were middle class, and 40 were lower class. Locating these children was not a simple matter. Twenty-three community agencies were involved, from the New York City Planning Commission to Batten, Barton, Durstine and Osborn (the advertising agency). Determination of social class was based on occupation of family head, residence, and education of family head. Occupational categories, for example, ranged from lawyer or doctor to semiskilled and unskilled worker.

Testing was private and extensive. Children were generally seen for about 30 minutes at a time on three separate days. All the tests were given in the same order in whatever language the child preferred. Examiners called the tests "games," and were warm and friendly. The examiners found, as many researchers have, that their greatest rapport problem was resolving the disappointment of children who were not included in the study. Motivation, in other words, was keen.

The results of the study are shown in Figure 15.9. It can be seen immediately that the patterns of mental abilities are different for the four cultural groups, but that these patterns are the same for both middle-class and lower-class children *from the same ethnic background.* In most studies of culture and mental abilities, social class and ethnic group are treated as equivalent and thus confused. Ordinarily, for example, Puerto Rican and Negro children in New York used in psychological studies are from lower-class groups. When they are compared to white middle-class groups and when differences are found, we cannot tell if the differences arise from social class or from ethnic background. The Lesser study shows us that once an ethnic pattern of mental abilities has emerged, it will be the same—regardless of social class. Social class affects the *level* of the abilities, but it does not affect the *patterns.*

Social class may, however, have more of an effect in one group than in another. As Figure 15.9 shows, social class made a great difference in the black group, but less of a difference in the Chinese group. Further, the relationship of the ethnic groups to each other may shift when social class shifts. In the middle-class groups, for example, the Jewish children and the black children are higher than both the Chinese and Puerto Rican children in verbal ability. On all the other tests, the Jews, Chinese, and blacks are ahead of the Puerto Ricans. Among the lower-class groups, however, the black children have fallen below the Chinese in verbal ability and below the Puerto Rican children on all the other tests.

What is responsible for these differences? One might speculate indefinitely, but it will take many years of careful research before we know for sure. A study of family factors in Puerto Rican households that will be reported below suggests one way in which cultural influences could affect responses to cognitive situations.

Work Attitudes and Ethnicity

In the same year that the Lesser study was published, Hertzig, Birch, Thomas, and Mendez (1968) began a longitudinal study of Puerto Rican working-class families as compared with white, middle-class suburban

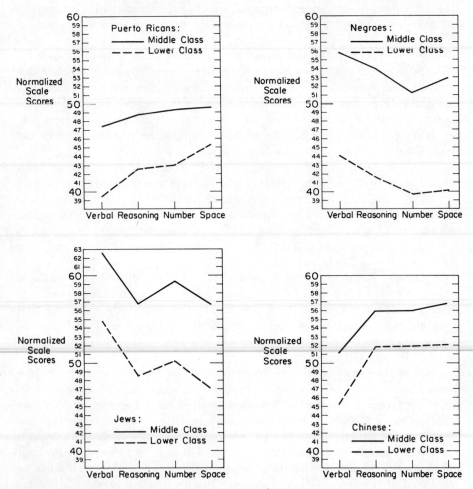

Figure 15.9 Patterns of mental ability scores for middle- and lower-class children. (Lesser, Fifer, and Clark, 1965, pp. 65–68)

families in the New York area. (This was a study in which ethnic background and social class were confounded, a point to which we shall return.) Hertzig and her colleagues followed Puerto Rican babies born into 53 families from the time of their birth. At the age of 3 years, it was decided to give both middle-class and Puerto Rican children intelligence tests—the Binet IQ test.

Although the groups as a whole differed in mean IQ (122 for the middle-class group, 96 for the Puerto Rican group), Hertzig selected children of the same IQ in order to compare their behavior toward the IQ task itself. She compared their behavior on the following bases: When confronted with a test item, called in this study a *cognitive demand,* a child has an initial choice: he can either work or not work. If he decides to work, he may talk about it or he may not talk; similarly, if he decides not to work, he may or may not talk about it. If he works and talks about it, he may make a limited remark or he may spontaneously extend his task verbally ("My sister has beads like this"). If he is not working but is talking, he may be making excuses, saying something negative ("No I won't"), saying something irrelevant ("I want to get a drink of water") that really functions as a substitute for work, or—and this is a most interesting category—talking about his own incompetence ("I haven't learned how to do this yet"). And, of course, he could be making requests for help. If he is not working and not talking, he may be shaking his head, walking over to the water fountain, seeking aid nonverbally, or just sitting there.

The categories of behaviors toward the IQ test were therefore those shown in Figure 15.10. The behaviors were recorded by observers who were not involved in the testing itself. They sat quietly in a corner of the

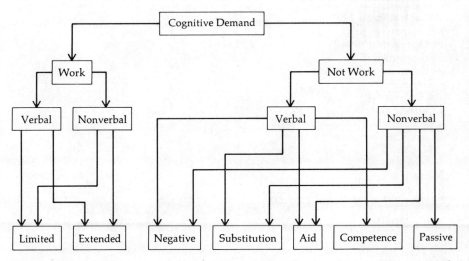

Figure 15.10 Possible responses to the cognitive demands of an IQ test. (Hertzig, Birch, Thomas, and Mendez, 1968)

room and wrote down exactly what the children did. Afterwards, the behaviors were coded into the categories by other individuals who had not observed the actual testing and who did not know who was Puerto Rican and who was not.

The responses had nothing to do with whether or not the child was correct; the experimenters were interested in the children's style of behavior toward the test in a broader sense. Some of the results are shown in Table 15.4. As you can see, there were many differences between the Puerto Rican and middle-class children (who had been selected from the larger group to match on IQ, remember, so these are not IQ differences) in their style of responding. The middle-class children made more work responses, especially to verbal test items; the Puerto Rican children made a few more work responses to nonverbal test items. The middle-class children made many more spontaneous verbal comments about what they were doing and attributed their lack of response (when that occurred) to their lack of competence significantly more often than the Puerto Rican children did. That would seem to be quite an important difference: If you can talk about your lack of competence, you are more likely to overcome it. The Puerto Rican children were more likely to substitute a verbal irrelevancy for a work response or simply to sit there passively.

Table 15.4
Some Differences Between Middle-class and
Puerto Rican Children, Style of Response to IQ Test

	PROPORTION OF RESPONSES (IN PERCENTAGES)	
	MIDDLE-CLASS CHILDREN	PUERTO RICAN CHILDREN
Work responses	73%	68%
Work responses to verbal test items	87	73
Work responses to nonverbal test items*	87	91
Verbal extensions	71	38
Verbal nonwork responses		
Negation*	22	18
Competence	31	11
Substitution	38	59
Aid*	9	12
Nonverbal nonwork responses		
Negation	20	10
Substitution*	48	44
Passive	32	45

SOURCE: Based on data in Hertzig et al., 1968.
    *These were the only differences between middle-class and Puerto Rican children that were not statistically significant.

The next problem was to try to understand where these differences came from. As already noted, they could not be attributed to differences in

IQ, since that was controlled. Nor could they be attributed to language difficulties; as in the Lesser experiment, children were tested in whatever language was most comfortable for them. Nor could the differences be attributed to shyness or insecurity with the examiner; the examiner was an old friend who had been visiting the home once a month since the children were born. In fact, it was to these home visits that Hertzig finally looked for a clue to the experimental results:

> One hypothesis is that the child-rearing practices and life styles of the Puerto Rican group differ from those of the middle class in ways that may foster the development of the behavioral differences found. . . .
>
> In the middle-class group, the mothers were much concerned with the age at which their children could assume responsibility for and exhibit skill in carrying out activities of daily living and self-care. They often expressed values that indicated that, in their view, the earlier a child was able to feed himself, dress himself, tie his shoes, and so forth, the better. Precocity in task-mastery had high prestige and status value for these families. . . .
>
> The atmosphere in the Puerto Rican homes was quite different. . . . Many Puerto Rican mothers actively discouraged the efforts of their children to feed or dress themselves. . . . "If I do it for him, I get done faster." . . . They also indicated that they "liked to keep their babies, babies."
>
> Although there was at least as much conversation and verbal exchange in the Puerto Rican as in the middle-class homes, the use of language appeared to differ in at least two respects: first, in contrast to the middle-class mothers who described tasks to be done, in the Puerto Rican homes verbalization tended to be social and affective rather than task-directed. Further, whereas the middle-class mothers tended to make sure that verbal task-directed instructions were understood and carried out, the Puerto Rican mothers tended not to insist that instructions or directions be acted upon.
>
> Patterns of play . . . appeared different in the two groups. Whereas middle-class parents considered toys a source of educational experience, Puerto Rican parents regarded them as amusements. . . . In contrast to the middle-class group . . . the Puerto Rican parents generally did not introduce the children to a new toy or game and intervened only if the child developed difficulties. Again in contrast to the middle-class parents, who encouraged mastery, intervention in the Puerto Rican group was directed toward solving the problem for the child; little effort was expended in directing the child toward solving it himself.
>
> These characteristics of family atmosphere and parent-child interaction all may contribute to the production of a life style in the Puerto Rican group that fosters the development of the behavioral patterns observed in response to demands for cognitive functioning. It may be that the Puerto Rican children come from a person-oriented rather than a problem-oriented culture and that they lack sufficient opportunity for the . . . development of successful problem-solving behavior under conventional educational conditions. The style of the culture may be one in which verbalizations are heavily weighted to communicate affective and social contents rather than task-directed ones, with the result that the ability to engage in verbal behavior in response to a cognitive demand fails to develop in the same way that it does in the middle-class children. (Hertzig, Birch, Thomas, and Mendez, 1968, pp. 45–46)

Education and Ethnicity

If these speculations are correct—and that is a big *if*—then the family-style differences may help account for the relatively poor performance of even the middle-class Puerto Rican children on the Lesser tests (Figure 15.9). At least the research suggests how cultural differences in approach to cognitive problems may produce differences in mental ability. This is not to suggest that these differences are not real or lasting; they are probably both. Lesser and Hertzig each conclude, in their respective reports, that *educational methods may need to be changed to suit the cognitive styles of different ethnic groups,* for we cannot count on the styles to change. The sad fact is that children with patterns of mental abilities—whether ethnically produced or not—which do not match traditional educational methods may never develop their full potential. These children simply fall further and further behind "matched" children as the years of traditional schooling go on.

We cannot assume with any confidence that ethnically special children are deficient, but we must be willing to face the fact that they are culturally different. School procedures and materials should take these differences into account. This same requirement holds true even for children who may superficially appear to fit more comfortably and effectively into a traditional educational setting. Good manners in this respect may be a far cry from genuine education. Once we begin to pay close attention to the *actual* responses of pupils to educational materials, differences arising from any source—sex, family background, social class, ethnic group—can be quite naturally taken into account. Alternative educational materials that suit such differences should become as common in schools as alternative sizes and styles are in clothing shops.

Educating minds in an academic sense is not the only problem faced by schools serving ethnically different groups. There is also the problem of educating the concepts, attitudes, and feelings that contribute to prejudice.

Prejudice

The roots and treatment of social prejudice have long interested psychologists. We face this problem in such extensive and explosive ways in the United States today that we often feel overwhelmed by our own ignorance and helplessness. Actually, we know quite a bit about what causes prejudice and about how to overcome it.

Educators who are actively involved in school racial problems are urged to study carefully a review by Proshansky (1966) called "The Development of Intergroup Attitudes." They will be surprised to discover how much research has already been done on this problem and how much is known about ways to combat it. Armed with this information, an educator with a special interest in human relations will find he is in a much better position to test a variety of solutions to particular school situations. Of course, the really hard work is not in the reading, but in the careful selection and courageous application of psychological principles.

First of all, by *prejudice* we are referring to negative attitudes that are directed toward groups perceived to be characterized by "typical" racial, religious, national, or cultural-linguistic behaviors. Whether or not they are really characterized by special behaviors is not the issue. If you do not like someone because he behaves in an unpleasant way, you are not considered to be prejudiced—*unless* you have developed the expectation that almost everyone in a particular ethnic group is likely to behave in that same unpleasant way.

Awareness of the fact that people of different ethnic backgrounds may behave in special ways (but not prejudice) emerges very early. It is visible in a child's language, choice of dolls, or playmates by about the age of 3 (Stevenson, 1967). Like other forms of cognitive development, these ideas become more detailed and better integrated as children grow older. By the age of 15 or 16, prejudiced concepts, like any other concepts, may be formally operational in Piaget's sense: An extensive system of prejudiced ideas and arguments may be tightly organized (Proshansky, 1966).

But although the *form* of the development—from isolated, fragmented, concrete actions to a logical system—may follow natural laws of cognitive growth, the prejudiced concepts themselves are learned. To put it more accurately, prejudiced concepts are *taught* to children by their own cultural groups. They are taught the way anything is taught—by example, discussion, threats of punishment, rewards, encouragement, and so forth. Members of cultural groups sustain prejudiced attitudes in each other for the same reasons that they sustain attitudes and cultural norms of any sort—because they are rewarding or reassuring in some way. All the group dynamics discussed in this chapter apply to the cohesion of an "in-group" against an "out-group." So do the social learning principles discussed in Chapter 10.

There are exceptions. Some children resist prejudicial teaching of any sort; some children respond to the teaching of other cultural groups, becoming prejudiced against their own, even though they have been exposed to the new teaching less frequently. It is not always easy to explain these exceptions, but they may have something to do with personality characteristics and with intelligence.

A Theory of Authoritarianism   One psychological theory of prejudice, as put forth in a book called *The Authoritarian Personality* (Adorno et al., 1950), places great emphasis on personality characteristics that may be shared by prejudiced people. An excellent nontechnical summary of this view is available in Brown, 1965, pp. 477–546. Without going into the special terminology, we can form an idea of this personality by summoning back some familiar concepts from earlier pages of this text:

The Freudian defense mechanism called *projection*—seeing character-istics in other people that you disapprove of or fear in yourself (projecting them to other people), especially as regards sex and aggression

External locus of control—believing that fate or outside forces are re-sponsible for things that happen to you

Low index of integration—having a few, very set principles of analysis and an inflexible viewpoint

Extremely rigid middle-class values

Self-esteem arising primarily from a comparison of oneself with others

According to Adorno and his colleagues, personality characteristics of this sort consolidate themselves into an extremely prejudiced outlook. The individual, sensing in himself "bad" impulses of a sexual and aggressive nature, avoids recognizing them by projecting them onto other people. Which other people? Scapegoats or underdogs, people who are tradition-ally and safely disliked (they do not usually fight back). Since the scape-goats are now seen as having "dangerous" sexual and aggressive impul-ses, repressive techniques ("keeping them in their place," "protecting our neighborhoods," "protecting our women") are socially sanctioned. Natu-rally, it is all right to repress people who have all those nasty inclinations.

Although this description is an oversimplification and is certainly not true of all prejudiced people, it explains a good deal. The extreme, irra-tional hatred displayed by the Arkansas mothers who fought school de-segregation seems powered by forces other than ordinary social learning. It is one thing to believe that blacks are inferior because you never learned any better; it is quite another thing to let yourself be seen nationwide on television screaming hideously at a tiny black child. When prejudice reaches such a peak, it must be in response to forces that—like nightmares—are located in the person rather than in the situation.

General Conditions and Cure of Prejudice It is also a well-known fact that prejudice declines as intelligence and education increase (see Brown, 1965, pp. 518–523). Many individuals who grew up in communities where prejudice was taught as a matter of course have been intelligent enough to throw off such teaching as they grew older. Others changed after they got to college. Sometimes there are conflicts in throwing off old attitudes of any kind; as we know, an individual with a relatively high integration index (see Figure 14.8) may suffer more internal conflicts because he can see more than one point of view. Conflicts about prejudiced attitudes are natural as one goes through the process of outgrowing them. The impor-tant point is that they are usually outgrown by intelligent people, unless social or personality pressures are very strong.

So we have, then, three basic conditions that can lead to prejudiced behavior: (1) The rules of a cultural group, rules governing behavior toward an out-group, which are taught, like table manners, to all children of the group; (2) personality disturbances producing an irrational fear and hatred of underdogs who are believed to be "dangerous"; and (3) simple ignorance. It is important to recognize the differences between these causes, because the cure for one will not necessarily be an effective cure for the others.

To begin with (3), simple ignorance (if that is all it is) can usually be overcome by straightforward educational techniques ("I never saw a colored man before. . . ." "I never understood how Jews worship before. . . ." "I didn't know that the man buying a house on my block was a lawyer; I thought all Negroes were dumb and dirty. . . ."). The problem with simple ignorance is that it is usually laced with some of (1) or some of (2). Cultural rules, which are learned at a very early age, can have emotional elements that are hard to shake. ("I know it's wrong, but I *feel* funny when I sit next to them on the bus. . . .") Straightforward education is not likely to be effective in this case unless it involves some emotional reeducation. Group therapy techniques—role playing, sensitivity training, face-to-face confrontations—can be extremely effective forms of emotional reeducation, if they are carried out under professional supervision (Levinson and Schermerhorn, 1951; Levinson, 1954; Culbertson, 1957; Katz et al., 1956). Films or TV presentations (Goldberg, 1956; Kraus, 1960) that help individuals see through the eyes of the minority group can also be helpful, because they change emotions.

But of course an exploration of personal emotion is just what a truly authoritarian personality could not stand: His entire personality is glued together by his conviction that "bad" things are in other people, never, never in himself. A therapeutic program that asks him to examine his own feelings will strike terror into the heart of a true authoritarian and make him more prejudiced than ever—especially against psychologists, psychiatrists, psychoanalysts, "eggheads," "free-thinking" ministers, and anybody else who represents a self-analytical point of view. The authoritarian is especially intractable when he is also unintelligent or uneducated, as is frequently the case.

It is important to understand that people who suffer from violent prejudice are in fact suffering from emotional illness, or neurosis, that may be severe. Even the most dedicated human relations expert may not be able to help, any more than he could help with a physical malignancy. Violent prejudice is indeed a cancer; it is feeding on the individual's own energies and psychological resources. In addition, it feeds on innocent and helpless people, which is why we cannot tolerate it.

Authoritarian personalities, like other personalities, are attracted to each other (refer back to the principles of group dynamics). Authoritarian groups like the Ku Klux Klan are dangerous and must be legally restrained. Less visible groups that may dominate a community must also be handled as one would handle immature children who lack inner self-controls—by imposing external controls. Rules must be made and enforced to protect innocent people from the personal nightmares of others.

The problem of educators who find themselves in an authoritarian community is not one of curing the prejudice, but one of standing firm while the controls are installed. In addition, they must provide human relations programs for the ignorant and the socially conditioned—programs that "wean" them, in effect, from roles established by an authoritarian culture. This may mean installing school reeducation programs that involve parents as well as children and bringing in professional psychological or psychiatric personnel for the retraining period. One thing is certain: Educators must take hold of these problems and not sweep them under a genteel, middle-class rug. The problems brought about by ethnic conflicts may continue to ferment as long as differing ethnic groups are in the school. The school of the future with its many educational programs tailored for ethnic, social, and cognitive styles must also come to terms with the basic problem of democracy itself—the problem of teaching diverse ethnic groups how to live in mutual harmony and respect.

SUMMARY

For several years now, J. McV. Hunt, a psychologist of great breadth and wisdom, has been referring to what he calls "the problem of the match" (Hunt, 1961, 1963, 1964, 1965, 1966). He is referring to the problem of selecting and presenting educational materials that engage students. Quakers have another way of phrasing it: they refer to materials or events that "speak to one's condition."

Speaking to the condition of students of different ages, inclinations, and backgrounds is indeed a complex issue. In Part III, we have been considering some of these complexities; reviewing and summarizing the principles is one way of surveying "the problem of the match."

One of Hunt's main points, and one that we have seen illustrated repeatedly in these chapters, is that motivation and cognition are inseparable. They are really two ways of looking at the same phenomenon—just as molecular motion and geometrical form might be two ways of describing the same table. Everything we do is infused with motivation of one sort or another. We could no more turn off our motivational systems than we could turn off our hearts—at least without serious damage to our brains.

In our formal education system we have somehow lost sight of this basic fact and have viewed motivational problems as problems of obedience, control, direction, and persistence within the setting of a fixed schedule and sequence of procedures. Perhaps to a large extent because of this, we seem to have produced many citizens who rather blindly follow the requests of those they perceive to be authorities of one sort or another. Milgram's experiments indicate just how serious the implications of national docility can be. The restive movement of our college students—and, increasingly, of our high school students—is perhaps a healthy sign that natural motivational systems are reasserting themselves.

Principles of behavioral control—conditioning, modeling, reinforcement procedures, and so forth—are not in themselves bad or dangerous. There are many things an enlightened, independent citizen should know and practice that can be controlled in these rather subtle ways. Conditioning principles are dangerous when they are applied unknowingly and haphazardly. The child who does not understand how to please an authority, but who learns only that no matter what he does, the authority will react negatively and unpredictably, is being conditioned into a type of anxious docility abhorrent in a democracy. The student who learns from his first day of school that rewards, in the form of good grades, may be withheld from him no matter how hard he works is learning how to be a school drop-out. If educators are to apply principles of behavioral control effectively and democratically, they must thoroughly examine the reinforcement systems and schedules operating in their own schools. They must also examine the school modeling opportunities, real and potential. For the most part, we can assume that schools are producing the negative motivational behavior they get by failing to recognize and to channel appropriately the natural motivations students bring with them into the classroom.

What are these natural systems? First of all, there are achievement and competence motives—drives for survival and for mastery of the environment—that have been built into our species through evolution. The intensity of such drives varies (perhaps genetically, to some extent) with the situation, with training, and with the child's general culture. In general, individuals respond to success by setting new goals to make themselves better in one way or another; they respond to failure in more unpredictable ways. They may change their goals realistically or unrealistically; they may suffer a dangerous depression. In any case, the teacher's main job is to help the student formulate realistic and attractive plans. When goals become "cognitively available," to use Prentice's term, natural achievement drives may be unleashed.

One danger in education is the failure, on the part of teachers and administrators, to recognize the true nature of achievement. Many educators have (and transmit to students) a faith in magic—the magic that a teacher's interest and concern will produce achievement. False encouragement in a belief that expectation will magically produce changes in IQ has been offered by Rosenthal and Jacobson (1968). The errors in their data and conclusions are explained by Snow (1969), who will soon publish a more detailed criticism. Magical expectations will not change IQs, and such a false promise may deflect educators from the hard job of improving the real educational situation. One aspect of this job is to encourage teachers to welcome truly competent thinking in their classrooms—to welcome students with the competence to argue with and to doubt the teacher himself.

The second major natural motivational system has to do with a need for sensory variation. Boredom is a need for a change in stimulation and a powerful motivator. Some individuals, for reasons that may be partly biological (biochemical) in nature, may have a greater need for stimulation than others and may respond to arousal of various kinds in a less intense way. But any student sitting in a dull classroom will be (according to the results of basic research on these questions) less able to think well or to plan, more likely to suffer from mild hallucinations or daydreams, and more susceptible to indoctrination of various kinds. The actively engaged mind must be in a state of sensory stimulation optimal for that mind. It will not work well otherwise.

Curiosity and exploratory behavior, sometimes of a very absorbed nature, will follow such engagement of the mind. Berlyne (1960) has shown that all curiosity motivators have in common a type of *collative* requirement—the mind is required to pull together moderately conflicting elements of one kind or another. Humor and art are also characterized by their collative aspects, when they are successful. Ideally, we would like education to follow self-motivating cycles: An individual is intrigued by a puzzle, works hard to solve it (increasing his knowledge at the same time), and then becomes intrigued by a higher-level puzzle based on his new knowledge. Both Piaget and Berlyne have developed intricate theoretical systems for explaining self-motivating learning cycles, and their application in classrooms is an important research problem. One thing is certain—the joy of discovery that can result from such a cycle is extremely powerful. It far outweighs the joys of a straight A report card.

In addition to these basic motivational considerations, "the problem of the match" involves a consideration of the person in society. The intellectually growing child is also growing in his personal outlook and emotional reaction system. Stages in this growth have been described by several theorists. Freud emphasized the "family romance" of the child's developing relationship with his mother and father; Erikson emphasized more general problems of trust, autonomy, and identity; and White has directed attention to changes in competence. These phases of personality change are associated with the phases of cognitive change described in Part I, and should similarly affect the educator's choice of appropriate materials and procedures.

Sometimes particular aspects of the personality characterize or dominate a child's classroom behavior. We considered the dimensions of impulsivity, anxiety, aggressiveness, dependence, self-evaluation, and cognitive styles, examining in each case the relevant theory and research. Knowledge of these dimensions and what affects them may help educators deal effectively with them in a classroom setting.

The final aspect of "the problem of the match" involves the child's social milieu. We considered, first of all, how the child's psychological ecology may be very different from the environment that is perceived by an outsider. Lewin's field theory provided a framework for that analysis.

We then examined more closely the effects of authoritarian vs. democratic social climates and the evidence that the democratic climate was more effective in many ways—although the authoritarian climate (in keeping with the fact that Mussolini "made the trains run on time") turned out more actual work. According to Piaget's analysis, children are going through important stages of natural moral development during the elementary school period, and a democratic atmosphere may encourage and channel these natural forces.

The forces themselves were analyzed in more detail in the section on group dynamics—forces of attraction and coalition, communication, and group problem solving. These forces are clearly complex, and they do not operate effectively in a laissez-faire setting. Good leadership, in the form of teacher understanding and guidance, will be necessary. Nevertheless, educational settings that can enlist these powerful social forces, rather than repress them, may also unleash great natural energies that will motivate and steer learning.

Other social forces, however, are at work outside the classroom. "The problem of the match" must come to terms with the fact that ethnic groups may differ in patterns of mental abilities. Some groups may be more talented in verbal than in spatial materials, and the opposite pattern may hold for other groups. Because they may remain constant in both high and low social-class settings, these patterns are not a simple matter of deprivation. One example of the way in which ethnic forces might work was provided by a study indicating that person-oriented, nonachievement-oriented family styles may produce mental differences in children. An appropriate educational setting should respond to these differences, not attempt to ignore or overcome them. Noneducation is all too often the result of our failure to recognize the extreme middle-class orientation of traditional schools.

Ethnically centered education means we must face the problem of prejudice. Some forms of prejudice are probably responsible for the middle-classness of the educational system itself, and more dramatic and dangerous forms are now plaguing the American school system. In cases in which the psychological roots of prejudice are neurotically intractable, external laws must be imposed to protect the rights and opportunities of minority groups. In cases in which prejudice has been learned (or nonprejudice has never been learned) and is therefore responsive to relearning, opportunities to experience the feelings and outlook of an out-group or an in-group may produce striking changes in attitude. External enforcement will not be necessary because internal transformations will take place. If possible, the school should assume a leadership role in teaching ethnically different groups to live together in a democratically fruitful way.

We can see that "the problem of the match" embraces every aspect of the human condition. Perhaps that is why education is the most exciting human activity in the world.

Part IV LANGUAGE

An organism that is intricate and highly
structured enough to perform the operations
that we have seen to be involved in linguistic
communication does not suddenly lose its
intricacy and structure when it turns to
nonlinguistic activities. In particular, such an
organism can form verbal plans to guide many
of its nonverbal acts. The verbal machinery
turns out sentences—and for civilized men,
sentences have a compelling power to control
both thought and action.

GEORGE A. MILLER
NOAM CHOMSKY

The remarkable fact of human language—like the remarkable fact of perception or skilled movement—is too often taken for granted. We are usually much more interested in what we are talking about than in the way we are talking, or even in the fact that we are talking at all. Looping back over a conversation and examining its formal structure may seem difficult, dull, and irrelevant. In reality, such an examination is not difficult, once a few basic concepts are understood, and it is certainly not irrelevant. The great inductive systems of human thought are nowhere so clearly displayed as in human language.

Dullness is, of course, a matter of viewpoint: There are those who see language as a mathematical puzzle; there are those who see it as a manifestation of profound evolutionary forces; and there are those who see intimate connections between language and metaphysics. Once we escape from language as a nineteenth-century pedagogue might have defined it, our viewpoints may change quite radically.

The overlapping areas of psychology and linguistics have combined in recent years to produce a new field called *psycholinguistics.* The leader from the area of linguistics is Noam Chomsky (1957, 1965). The leaders from psychology are George Miller (1962, 1965) and Roger Brown (1957, 1958, 1965). All have been followed by a veritable fleet of colleagues and students, many of whom have performed classic studies that we will discuss in the chapters that follow. Although most psycholinguistic forms and terminology come from linguistics, concern with language as a human system comes from psychology. In the area of development, we stopped assuming children spoke only a garbled form of adult language and started listening to what they actually said. What they actually said turned out to be both systematic and universal. It seems that all babies begin to speak in about the same way at about the same time, regardless of their nationality. The characteristics of this universal developmental system may provide us with important clues to a basic human learning process.

Chapters 16 and 17 deal with these developmental and evolutionary problems and explore the role of learning. Psycholinguists emphasize the difference between *performance* and *competence* in language, very much as cognitive psychologists might distinguish between *knowledge* and *behavior*. The general verbal knowledge stored in the head of a language user—as well as the process of acquiring it—may be distinct from the particular verbal skills revealed in any bit of language behavior. Skinner, of course, takes sharp issue with that assertion. We will look at his arguments as well.

Chapter 18 takes us into the important area of meaning: How can we tell if verbal statements are actually comprehended? What is the mental structure of comprehension? What happens to language when meaning rules are violated?

Language is a social process; much language behavior is also social behavior. Perhaps that is why styles of thinking seem to differ between some social groups—because both their language and their social use of language may differ. The current emphasis upon social deprivation and language remediation highlights this issue. Should standard English supplant the dialects of minority groups? In Chapter 19, we will develop several lines of argument and put forth a number of possibilities.

In conclusion, we will take up some specific questions about the role of language in the classroom. In general, of course, human education could not happen without language—language as a symbol system and as a process of thinking. The growth and education of language capacities is almost another way of describing the growth and education of the mind.

Chapter 16 THE DEVELOPMENT OF LANGUAGE

Several comprehensive studies of language development (McCarthy, 1954) provide detailed accounts of language characteristics in children. We will not attempt to recapitulate those studies here. By the time a child reaches preschool, so many things have happened to him linguistically that a complete account would fill many volumes. The emphasis in this chapter will be on the process of his language development as it relates to his continuing language development, for it is this continuation that is of special importance to his teacher. The chapter relies heavily on the work of Mc-Neill (1969).

Language development actually proceeds on several levels: *Phonologically* the child is learning to discriminate, create, and selectively combine speech sounds; *morphologically* he is learning to handle individual words and their special variations; *syntactically* he is discovering how to put words together in sentences; and *semantically* he is learning what those sentences mean. The first stage of language development seems to be primarily phonological.

THE BABBLING STAGE

At approximately 3 months of age, the normal child begins to make cooing and babbling noises. Why? Perhaps because it is fun. Like the circular reactions defined by Piaget (Chapter 13) or the competence motives described by White (Chapter 11), the young infant's discovery and practice of his own vocal sounds seems to be an end in itself. What may be discovered during this period? Perhaps something like the following:

One can have control over vocal sounds.
Some are different from others.
Some are long and some are short.
Some sounds are connected to others.
They make things happen (Mommy smiles, for example).
They make sounds happen from someone else.

Although the infant is not explicitly aware of these discoveries, he may nevertheless be preparing himself for the special sounds of his own language.

Rheingold's Experiment

Were these discoveries conditioned? Did Mommy decide, "Today I am going to teach baby that babble sound X is long and rattly, and that babble sound Y is short and high-pitched. Every time he makes sound X, I will smile. Every time he makes sound Y, I will pat his tummy. Then he will learn to distinguish between the sounds." It is doubtful if such plans are formulated, but some kinds of reinforcement that may have important effects do occur. This has been demonstrated experimentally by Harriet Rheingold and her associates (Rheingold, Gewirtz, and Ross, 1959).

Their experimental subjects were 3-month-old infants who lived in an institution, but who were well developed, healthy, and socially responsive. For the first few days of the experiment, baseline data were collected. The number of vocalizations each baby made were counted. During the count, one experimenter leaned over the crib with her face (which was expressionless) about 15 inches from the baby's. Then the experimental period began. The experimenter reinforced the baby's vocalizations by doing three things: (1) Smiling broadly, (2) saying "tsk, tsk, tsk," and (3) gently pinching the baby's abdomen. All this took about a second. At first, the baby was reinforced for every single vocalization, but as time went on, only some of the vocalizations were reinforced. (A mother might behave

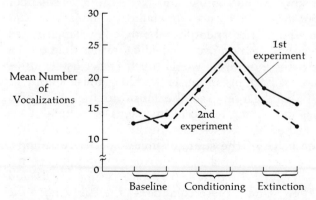

Figure 16.1 Mean number of vocalizations by infants in the Rheingold, Gewirtz, and Ross (1959) experiment.

similarly—reinforcing her baby's very first vocalizations every time they occurred, but reinforcing less frequently as the baby's vocalizations became more numerous.) The final part of the experiment was an extinction period. The experimenter again leaned over the crib with an expressionless face, and did not smile, "tsk," or pinch tummies.

The main result concerned the amount of vocalization—did it increase during the reinforcement period and decline during the extinction period? Figure 16.1 shows this was indeed what happened. The number of vocalizations increased sharply during the brief conditioning period and dropped just as sharply when reinforcement was discontinued. When Rheingold repeated the experiment on a second group of babies, the same effect occurred. There was also another interesting result. Rheingold recorded the number of emotional responses—frets, fusses, cries, and other signs of infant unhappiness. These emotional responses increased during the extinction period.

Surely this signifies that some pleasurable learning does occur during the babbling stage and that parents or caretakers can help increase it. Further, when a mother responds to her baby conversationally, she is not only encouraging him to vocalize, she may be providing him with important information about the nature of his language.

Friedlander's Experiment

Older babies can make quite delicate discriminations between types of vocal feedback and may even show preferences for one type over another. Would you expect a baby to prefer his mother's voice to a stranger's voice? Friedlander (1967) developed an ingenious method for finding out. He equipped a playpen with two transparent plastic cylinders attached to a tape recorder outside. When the baby handled a cylinder, he activated the sound of something on the tape recorder (Figure 16.2). Sometimes one cylinder turned on his mother's voice, and the other turned on a stranger's voice; sometimes one cylinder turned on his mother's voice, and the other turned on music. By making paired comparisons of this sort, Friedlander was able to find out about infant preferences for auditory stimulation.

In developing his method, Friedlander tested only a few babies (aged 11 to 15 months) and reported data on each individual, rather than on the group as a whole. One baby showed he would much rather listen to his mother than to a selection of Bach organ music (there are those among us who would agree), but that he preferred the music to the voice of a stranger. Friedlander was not willing to accept that complex cultural judgment at face value and pushed his investigation further. He contrasted the voice of mother and the voice of the stranger under special conditions. The mother was recorded speaking in a flat, dull voice, using impersonal words. The stranger spoke in a bright, happy voice, using words and phrases that the baby knew. Under these conditions, the baby chose the stranger's voice more frequently.

Was this because he failed to recognize his mother's voice? Friedlander thought that might be the case. One of his slightly older babies preferred the mother's voice no matter how flat and uninteresting, and Friedlander thought such a preference might display a *conservation* ability like that described by Piaget (see Part I). Perhaps the ability to recognize familiar voices in unfamiliar disguises is an important landmark of infant language development.

Might the unfamiliar sometimes be preferred over the familiar? Friedlander found that one of his babies strongly preferred listening to his

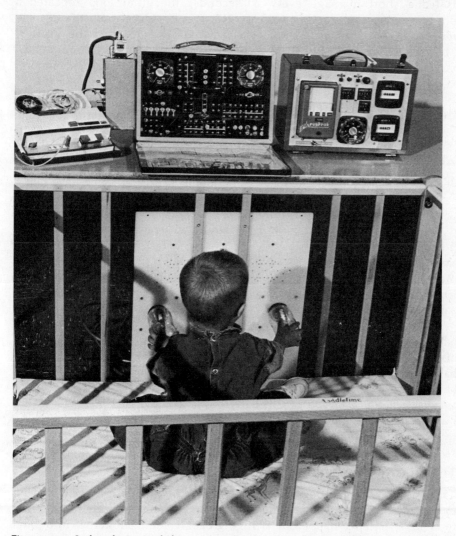

Figure 16.2 In his playpen, a baby uses Friedlander's PLAYTEST apparatus to listen to his favorite recording. (Photo courtesy *The Capital Times,* Madison, Wisconsin, May 12, 1969)

mother's voice in an unfamiliar guise (she was reading aloud the regulations of a local municipal skating rink). He hypothesized that what he called this "listening appetite" for unfamiliar or complex materials would serve to expand a baby's range of linguistic information. After all, if a baby only wanted to listen to something familiar, he might never hear anything new.

To test this further, Friedlander recorded a spirited conversation among the baby's father, mother, and a family friend. Two loops activated by the cylinders were then prepared from this recording. One loop repeated a short message every 20 seconds; the other loop repeated a longer, more complex message every 240 seconds. Over a month of experimentation, it became clear that the baby at first preferred the shorter, more redundant loop, but then switched his preference to the more complicated loop. (The loops were not always activated by the same cylinders, so the baby was not merely switching positions.)

> The evidence seemed to warrant the interpretation that the baby was . . . listening to the voice feedbacks with sufficient attention to their fine inner structure to detect the subtle differences between them. After sampling the two, he listened more at first to the one that had the fewer differences in its stimulus properties and hence was more easily assimilated. Then, having learned its content sufficiently to become familiar with its parts, he shifted his attention to the longer message, which gave him a more varied linguistic diet with which to satisfy . . . a more discriminating appetite. (Friedlander, 1967)

So we meet again the basic motivational system discussed in Part III, the practice-expand-practice cycle. First the baby listened to what was easier for him to follow because it repeated frequently. When that became thoroughly digested, he moved on to more complicated material. As Friedlander pointed out, the pattern leads to a disturbing question: What is the baby learning when he listens to "baby talk"?

Piaget might argue that baby talk, being easily assimilated to the baby's own babbling system, is an important form of encouragement. One of the films made by Uzgiris and Hunt (1966) shows several examples of babies "talking back" (cooing and vocalizing) to baby talk, but not talking back to ordinary adult vocal tones. Probably the rule here is to *encourage vocalization any way you can.* If baby talk encourages it, then talk away. But when baby begins to look at you as if you are an idiot, it may be time to start reading him the municipal skating rink regulations.

THE BEGINNING OF SPEECH

True speech seems to begin as a pattern of intonation like those occurring in questions, exclamations, and statements. The child appears to be trying to make a sentence happen by stringing babble sounds together into tonal patterns. Some children become quite accomplished speakers of these patterns and produce highly intoned strings of babbles that resemble sophis-

THE DEVELOPMENT OF LANGUAGE **347**

ticated adult conversation. Gradually, the child gains control over the components of the babble-strings and produces sets of true *phonemes,* or sound units.

The number of possible phonemes is limited because there are limits to our physiological capacity for making sounds. We make some with the lips, some with the tongue, some in the back of the mouth, and so on. Babies seem to begin with *p* and *b* sounds, probably because they involve lip movements (including one's own) that can be easily discriminated. Between the twelfth and eighteenth months, normal babies gain enough control of sets of phonemes to produce a few recognizable words.

Hidden Meaning Rules

Of course, a word is more than a set of phonemes; it also has meaning. Early words seem to be something like *labels.* At least they are responded to ("No, that's not Daddy, that's the milkman") as if they were labels. Adults, in fact, teach labels quite extensively.

There are some surprising aspects to this teaching process. In an article entitled "How Shall a Thing Be Called?" Roger Brown (1958b) points out that we seldom question the labels we teach children. A four-legged creature with a wagging tail and soft fur is labeled *dog* for a child, or possibly *Prince,* but seldom *quadruped.* This is partly because most adults believe children cannot handle long words, but it is not the only reason. The prickly thing with long green leaves is labeled *pineapple* for a child, not *fruit. Fruit* is a shorter word, but it is a more general term, and adults also believe children should hear specific terms. There are exceptions. Adults seldom label those shiny round things *dimes* or *pennies,* but use instead the general term *money.* Why? Because the distinction between dimes, nickels, pennies, and quarters is not important to a young child. He will not be buying or selling anything for quite a while. The uses important to a young child are more general: *money* is something not to put in your mouth or down the heating register. When specific functions develop—when money becomes something you put in a bubble gum machine at the supermarket—then *penny* may be taught as a specific label:

> The names provided by parents for children anticipate the functional structure of the child's world. This is not . . . something parents are aware of doing. When we name a thing there does not seem to be any process of choice. Each thing has its name, just one, and that is what we give to a child. The one name is, of course, simply the usual name for us. Naming each thing in accordance with local frequencies, parents unwittingly transmit their own cognitive structures. It is a world in which *Prince* is unique among dogs and *papa* among men, *spoons* are all alike but different from *forks.* It may be a world of *bugs* (to be stepped on), of *flowers* (not to be picked), and *birds* (not to be stoned). (Brown, 1958b, pp. 16–17)

The early labels that a young child learns are therefore not simply names for things; they are infused with functions. The function is part of the name.

Emergence of the Holophrase

Recall the earlier point that speech seems to begin as a pattern of babbles, which then differentiate into true words. In a similar way, a young child may start with a whole-word sentence, which then differentiates into parts. For example, "Milk!"—a one-word sentence—may really mean, "Please get me some milk in my special pink cup with the blue flower on it that I like." We can tell this is what the child really means from his behavior; if we handed him milk in the yellow cup with the white daisy, he might throw it on the floor. One-word sentences of this sort are called *holophrases*.

A young child gradually learns to separate the "thing idea" from the "function idea" in the words he is using. Thing ideas turn into nouns, and function ideas turn into verbs. Later, function ideas may differentiate still further into modifiers (like adjectives and articles) and into relation words (like prepositions). When the child becomes able to put specialized words together, he invents sentences.

EARLY SENTENCES

Just as adults may be unconscious of the hidden functions in labels they teach children, so grammarians may be unconscious of differences between their own rule systems and the rules people really use. To a grammarian, there may be one "right" way of constructing a "good" sentence, but there are actually many rules for constructing sentences. The fact that a young child may not construct sentences by adult rules does not mean that he has no rules at all. Modern psycholinguists no longer consider child grammars to be poor forms of adult grammars; they look upon children as speaking exotic languages of their own.

Consider the following sentences:

Here allgone.
More up.
Mommy sandwich.
Throw Daddy.

Can you understand them? Chances are you can, at least if you imagine some appropriate context (like a ball that the child is trying to throw to daddy). Yet these sentences certainly do not obey the rules of adult grammar; they are very poor sentences from that standpoint.

Suppose we were to try to describe the rules they *do* obey. Psycholinguists who have done just that made a remarkable discovery: *All children invent the same basic grammar at about the same time.*

Pivot Grammar

Between the ages of 18 months and 2 years, young children begin to use one set of words (not the same set for individual children) as if they were *pivots* onto which other words could be "hooked." These other words are said to be *open class* words, and they often seem to have a nounlike quality. There are many more open class words than pivot words. The very first sentence-making rule is therefore something like the following: Take a word from your pivot list (like *more,* for one child) and attach to it any word from your open list (like *milk, cookie,* or *dolly* for that same child), thereby making sentences like *More milk.* or *More cookie.* or *More dolly.* We can represent the rule this way:

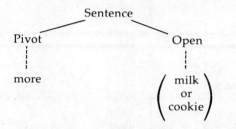

Of course the child cannot formulate the rule in so many words, but his sentences sound *as if* that rule were guiding him.

Table 16.1 shows lists of pivot and open class words collected from three children—those studied by Braine, Brown, and Ervin (Miller and Ervin, 1964) independently of each other. Each child had unique lists and could construct unique sentences from them, but all the sentences seemed to follow the same pivot-open rule. According to Slobin (McNeill, 1969), the pivot-open rule also appears in the first sentences of Russian, Bulgarian, Croatian, French, and German children. There seems to be a universal tendency for children to invent sentences of this type. Note how the pivot-open rule seems to be another manifestation of the early coordination of schemas, as described by Piaget (Part I). Perhaps the invention of pivot sentences is a natural outgrowth of a young child's general cognitive style.

Why do we say "invent"? Primarily because the children could not possibly be imitating these sentences. No adult ever uses pivot-open sentences; no child ever hears that kind of sentence unless he happens to be listening to another toddler. It seems unlikely that our great linguistic systems are transmitted through toddlers. Most psycholinguists find it easier to believe in something like a "language instinct" (Chomsky, 1965) than to believe that the complexities of grammar are learned through imitation. We will have more to say about this after we consider what happens next in the evolution of sentences.

Differentiation of Grammatical Classes and Rules

About two and a half months after Brown's child in Table 16.1 was first recorded, he was recorded again. He was using all the words in his original pivot list, but he was no longer using all of them as pivots. Some of the words (*a* and *the*) were being used as articles—that is, they occurred where articles are supposed to occur, with reference to nouns. Other pivot words were now functioning only as demonstratives. The child was pro-

Table 16.1
Pivot and Open Classes Developed by Three Children

BRAINE'S CHILD		BROWN'S CHILD		ERVIN'S CHILD	
PIVOT	OPEN	PIVOT	OPEN	PIVOT	OPEN
allgone	boy	my	Adam	this	arm
byebye	sock	that	Becky	that	baby
big	boat	two	boot		dolly's
more	fan	a	coat		pretty
pretty	milk	the	coffee		yellow
my	plane	big	knee		come
see	she	green	man		doed
night-	vitamins	poor	Mommy		
night	hot	wet	nut	the	other
hi	Mommy	dirty	sock	a	baby
	Daddy	fresh	stool		dolly's
		pretty	tinker-		pretty
			toy		yellow
				here	arm
				there	baby
					dolly's
					pretty
					yellow

SOURCE: McNeill, 1966, p. 22.

ducing sentences like "That a horsie." He never said, "A that horsie," as he might have before when he was using both *a* and *that* as all-purpose pivots.

About two and a half months after the second recording, when the child was recorded for the third time, he was no longer using adjectives or possessives as pivots. Now he had six grammatical classes of words at his disposal: articles, adjectives, demonstrative pronouns, possessive pronouns, and nouns and verbs, which had been around since the days of the one-word sentences or holophrases. The child had developed an extensive personal lexicon, or dictionary.

The child's sentence-production rules had also become more complex. Instead of just one pivot-open rule, he had rules like this:

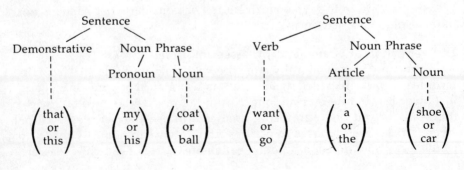

These are still very simple sentences, compared to the complex ones generated by adults. And yet, within the simple grammars of the young child, we find the same *basic grammatical relations* as are found in the adult speech forms of all languages. A child's language seems to grow because he is seeking the special forms these relations happen to take in his own language. Children apparently come equipped with a "language sonar system" for detecting the special forms of their own language. When they detect a form that expresses a basic grammatical relation, they incorporate it. What are the basic grammatical relations?

Nouns can have actions associated with them.
Actions can be directed toward objects.
Nouns and actions can be modified.
A sentence has a head, or main point.

All languages contain these relations, and children never invent sentences that violate them. Language develops as children discover the many ways in which these basic relations may be represented in their native language.

THE DEVELOPMENT OF TRANSFORMATIONS

In psycholinguistics, the basic grammatical relations are referred to as the *deep structure* of the language. The special forms that the relations may take are called the *surface structure*. Thus, the deep structure of the sentence "The ball was hit by the boy" may be "Boy hit ball." That is, the basic relation of subject, action, and object may be transformed into a statement called a *passive*. But the basic relation remains basic.

The *transformations* occur sequentially. First, an auxiliary verb (a form of *to be*) must be inserted in the basic sentence, and there is a special transformation rule for that. Then, the locations of *ball* and *boy* must be reversed (from *boy hit ball* to *ball was hit by boy*). There are also rules for changing *to be* into the appropriate tense and person (*was*) and a rule for inserting the necessary preposition (*by*). These rules are much more complicated than you may imagine.

A description of how a basic sentence is transformed into a surface form reads very much like a list of steps in a mathematical proof. There is a rule for step 1, a rule for step 2, and so forth. But it is important to understand that such rules refer to a speaker's linguistic *competence*, not to his *performance*. We do not go down a list of rules (muttering to ourselves) when we say "The ball was hit by the boy"—rules like, "Reverse ball and boy . . . insert new verb. . . ." Our language sounds as *if* we knew rules like that, in the same way that a baseball player looks *as if* he knew some complicated formulas for calculating curve balls. The formulas describe what the ball does and what the baseball player does, but they do not describe what goes on in the baseball player's mind.

We do, however, have some rules for generating transformed sentences. Although we do not understand exactly how the mind uses them, we know they exist. Consider the nonsense sentence, "The wugs zibboed the vetch." Now, transform that into a question: "Did the wugs zibbo the vetch?" What were your transforming rules? Insert a form of *do* (*did*); change the order of the words; change the tense ending of zibboed (drop the *ed*); and make a questioning intonation. How about the sentence, "The bips cavied the doop." Would you transform that into a question by the same rules? Obviously, you carry around within you rules for creating a large number of transformed sentences. It seems more sensible to assume that you store and apply those rules, rather than to assume that you store and retrieve each of the many sentences they could generate.

Further, we seem to have transformational abilities of other sorts. Imagine the back of your own head. That particular image (bald spot and all) required you to transform your own point of view. Are you right-handed? Take a pencil in your left hand, and write your name upside down. That action requires you to perform a series of perceptual and motor transformations of a basic system (your name written right side up). Walk backwards; recite the alphabet backwards; answer the question: "What if children suddenly became the ruling class of our society?" You contain within yourself a variety of transformational systems that you can apply in many ways. A system of linguistic transformations may be just another special case of a general transformational skill.

Development of Negative Transformations
The stages in the development of transformation abilities are incompletely understood, but the evidence thus far points to the same kind of pattern discussed earlier. The child seems to begin with an overall urge to speak in a transformed way and gradually learns how to do so. Consider the development of the ability to perform a negative transformation—to transform sentences like "The boy hit the ball" to "The boy didn't hit the ball."

The first indication of this ability appears about the same time as pivot sentences appear. As McNeill (1969) has summarized the process, the child may begin by saying:

> No . . . wipe finger.
> No a boy bed.
> Wear mitten no.
> Not a teddy bear.

The child seems to have a *negative operator* (*no* or *not*) which he then attaches to his standard sentences in a pivotlike way. This same early negation system has been observed in French, Russian, and Japanese children.

A few months later, there may appear to be a wider variety of negative sentences:

> I can't catch you.
> Don't bite me yet.
> I no want envelope.
> No pinch me.

The use of the words *can't* and *don't* may sound as if the child has learned some complicated rules about auxiliary verbs and contractions, but the child may actually be using these words as simple carriers of negative information, in much the same way as he uses *no* and *not*. We know this because the child never uses *do* in other (nonnegative) sentences as a separable helping verb. It will still be a few months before he seems to understand that *don't* is a combination of *do* and *not*. When he reaches that stage, *do* will appear in other sentences, separate from the *not*. At the same time, sentences like "No pinch me" will have disappeared. The child is apparently transforming these basic negative ideas into more sophisticated forms like "Don't pinch me," based on his new understanding of helping verbs and contractions.

Of Latts and Wugs

This is probably the pattern for all transformational growth: The young child begins with a global urge (like the urge to express negative ideas) and bit by bit, month by month, discovers its customary forms of expression. By the time he is 3 years old, the child is a veritable treasure house of transformational rules. Two famous experiments illustrate this process.

One of them, carried out by Brown (1957), presented children with the nonsense stems *niss, sib,* and *latt.* These stems could be used in ways that made them appear to be verbs, mass nouns, or count nouns. For example, the sentence form, "That person is latting," turns *latt* into a verb. "That is some latt," turns *latt* into a mass noun. "That is a latt," turns *latt* into a count noun.

THIS IS A WUG.

NOW THERE IS ANOTHER ONE.
THERE ARE TWO OF THEM.
THERE ARE TWO _____.

Figure 16.3 Drawing used by Berko (1958) to elicit children's knowledge of morphological rules.

Brown presented 3- and 4-year-old children with materials and statements of this sort to find out if they could recognize the grammatical differences in the way the nonsense stems were used. The children pointed to pictures that illustrated different uses of the stems. The preschoolers were quite accurate. If the stems were used as verbs, most of the children pointed to pictures of actions. If the stems were used as nouns, most children correctly pointed to pictures identifying them as mass nouns or count nouns. This showed that the children had rules for making identifications of this sort and that they could apply these rules to new situations.

A second well-known experiment was carried out by Berko (1958). She presented her subjects with nonsense figures accompanied by such statements as: "This is a wug. This is another wug. Now there are two of them. There are two____." (Figure 16.3 shows some of the material.) Children, even 2-year-olds, promptly say "wugs," thereby demonstrating that they carry within themselves a rule like: "To form a plural, add s."

Berko tested many other rules of tense and inflection (*morphological* rules). For example:

Past tense. (Man exercising.) "This is a man who knows how to gling. He is glinging. He did the same thing yesterday. What did he do yesterday? Yesterday he____."

Adults may hang suspended between *glinged, glang,* and *glought,* for we carry rules for past tense irregularities within us. But the preschooler, who has not yet learned these irregularities, promptly says "glinged."

Preschool Grammar

Although 3- and 4-year-olds have not yet finished their language development, they are well on the way. Menyuk (1963, 1964a) analyzed the natural speech of young children in various normal situations and found that many sophisticated transformational systems are in use by that time. Some of the transformations she heard children use are listed below:

Negation:	He isn't a good boy.
Auxiliary *Be* placement:	He is not going.
Do:	I did read the book.
Pronoun in conjunction:	David saw the bicycle and he was happy.
Question:	Are you nice?
Inversion:	Here is the toothpaste.
Separation:	He took it off.
Possessive:	I'm writing Daddy's name.
Conjunction:	Peter is here and you are there.
Conjunction deletion:	I see a red book and a blue book.

Menyuk (1964b) also recorded the speech of children who had been diagnosed as having defective speech. They made errors like the following:

Verb phrase omission:	This green.
Verb phrase substitution:	He tries to take the knife from falling.
Verb phrase redundancy:	He'll might get in jail.
Preposition omission:	He'll have to go the doctor's.
Noun phrase redundancy:	I want it the paint.
Noun form omission:	She has lots of necklace.
Particle redundancy:	The barber cut off his hair off.

These errors jar us into consciousness of our own transformational expectations. We expect young children to use certain language forms by certain ages. When they do not, we instantly recognize that their language development has gone wrong.

Is this an error of biology, or of environment? Have the children heard these improper forms? Probably not, any more than they heard pivot grammars. Has there been a failure of motivation to learn correct speech? Unfortunately, we know very little about the answers to these questions, but in Chapter 17 we will consider some of the issues.

Chapter 17 THEORIES OF LANGUAGE LEARNING

By the time they reach the age of formal schooling, normal children have within their language repertoire almost all the adult speech forms. And *they have accomplished this with no formal instruction.* Again, we come up against the remarkable capacity of the human child to learn complex information-processing systems without formal teaching. But has no teaching at all occurred? Let us look first at the two major theories of language learning and then consider in more detail exactly what language tutors may do. One states that language learning is an innate, biological process; the other, that it is a conditioned process.

EVOLUTION VS. CONDITIONING

Most of the material in the previous chapter has emerged from the studies of those who favor an evolutionary approach to language development. But psycholinguists did not choose to become evolutionists; for the most part, they found themselves forced into that position by the facts they discovered. Lenneberg has summarized their findings:

> Language has the following six characteristics. (i) It is a form of behavior present in all cultures of the world. (ii) In all cultures its onset is age-correlated. (iii) There is only one acquisition strategy—it is the same for all babies everywhere in the world. (iv) It is based intrinsically upon the same formal operating characteristics [basic grammatical relations and transformations from deep language structures to surface forms] whatever its outward form. (v) Throughout man's recorded history these operating characteristics have been constant. (vi) It is a form of behavior that

may be impaired specifically by . . . brain lesions which may leave other mental and motor skills relatively unaffected. (Lenneberg, 1969, p. 635)

These characteristics suggest that language learning is a biological process built into our species by the forces of evolution. Chomsky stated the position this way:

> On the basis of the best information now available, it seems reasonable to suppose that a child cannot help constructing a particular sort of transformational grammar . . . anymore than he can control his perception of solid objects or his attention to line and angle. (Chomsky, 1965, p. 59)

Chomsky's Language Model

To explain how the child does this, Chomsky has postulated a Language Acquisition System (LAS) rather like the system diagrammed in Figure 17.1. Each child is presumed to come equipped biologically with an LAS—a basic ability to formulate systems for generating sentences. The child samples the environment around him for examples of his native language. He formulates some ideas or hypotheses about the nature of this language. He then "outputs," or expresses, examples of his ideas. These examples are tested and are sometimes corrected by a tutor (a peer or an adult, often a parent). On the basis of his tests, the child may revise his hypotheses. He formulates new ones and tests them again. He gradually builds up a mature inner language-generating system, one that fits his linguistic environment—that is, he learns to speak his native language fluently.

Presumably LAS evolved as part of the total evolution of the human brain. Since we have no difficulty in attributing the total brain to evolutionary forces, we should have no difficulty in attributing language to

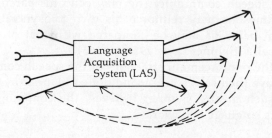

1. The child samples from his linguistic environment.

2. He formulates hypotheses about the nature of language.

3. He outputs some examples of his hypotheses. The fate of these examples may then feed back into his acquisition system, altering his hypotheses and "re-tuning" his sampling system.

Figure 17.1 The Language Acquisition System postulated by Chomsky (1965) and McNeill (1966), with modifications.

them as well. But many psychologists would disagree. They see language as a separate acquisition. Language, they say, is learned like any other cultural habit.

Skinner's Language Concepts

The foremost proponent of this point of view is B. F. Skinner. As we saw in Chapters 5 and 10, Skinner views human behavior as an intricate interlocking system of operants that are controlled or maintained by reinforcements. Whenever we see a particular pattern of behavior, we know there are reinforcements somewhere in the environment, or in the history of the individual, that are responsible for it.

Verbal behavior is no exception. In his major work on the subject, Skinner (1957) details his conception of the contingency systems that control two major types of verbal behavior—*mands* (for com*mand,* or de*mand,* or contra*mand*) and *tacts* (for con*tact*). *Mands* come about primarily in response to inner states of deprivation or aversive stimuli (such as fear or punishment). "Please pass the salt" is a mand; so is "Cheez it, the fuzz." "The salt is on the table" and "The fuzz wear blue suits" are tacts; they are controlled by objects or events.

According to Skinner, the probability that such verbal behavior will appear is a complex function of the reinforcement situation. The speech community has reinforcement traditions that function as cultural controls—obscene language is usually punished, for example. The audience or the listener provides reinforcement of various kinds: approval, taking action, emotional responses, money (for novels), and so forth. The speaker may also reinforce himself, especially by continuing his own behavior. He may self-reinforce correct verbal behavior and extinguish incorrect forms. Sometimes he may reinforce behavior that exactly mimics the behavior of the speech community (he may echo his parents, for example); at other times he may reinforce his own idiosyncratic responses. "'Artistic' verbal behavior may be compared with that of the musician playing for himself," Skinner says (1957, p. 165).

Of course, the reinforcement strategies of the speech community or of the individual have themselves been conditioned by prior systems of reinforcement. By such means, Skinner believes, the community maintains and passes on its language behavior.

Language Conditioning Studies

One great problem with this point of view is the difficulty in specifying exactly what is learned (what is the stimulus? what is the response?) and what the reinforcement is. If we say that the existence of verbal behavior means there must be reinforcement somewhere, then we can always find something to label "reinforcement." But this is not a scientific procedure; we may be inventing reinforcements to satisfy our claims and not really proving anything at all (Chomsky, 1957).

A more scientific procedure would be to select a type of verbal behavior, systematically reinforce it, and see if it becomes more frequent. A number of experiments have done exactly that (Krasner, 1958). For example, one experimenter instructed his subjects to tell imaginative stories about a man, a woman, and an animal. The experimenter had decided in advance to reinforce any mention of animals. Every time the subject said something about an animal, the experimenter nodded and said, "Mmm-hmm." The subjects, of course, were not told that any reinforcements were being dispensed. Nevertheless, they significantly increased their statements about animals.

In another experiment, self-satisfied ("I am happy," "We enjoyed it") statements were reinforced in an interview session. Again, although the subjects were not aware of the reinforcements, they increased their self-satisfied statements to a significant degree (Salzinger and Pisoni, 1957). In still another experiment, groups of psychology students fanned out all over a campus, selecting categories of verbal behavior and reinforcing their friends and roommates. They reinforced (by saying "Umm-hmm" or "Good" or by writing down a word) such things as plural nouns, adverbs, travel words, and words of living things and got significant results in almost all cases (Wilson and Verplanck, 1956).

Despite such results, psycholinguists are reluctant to attribute all language learning to operant conditioning. The fact that verbal behavior can be conditioned does not prove that conditioning is the way that language naturally develops. For one thing, the rate of increase in words or ideas in response to reinforcement is really quite slow compared with normal rates. When children first begin speaking in pivot sentences, they may put together over a thousand different word combinations in a given month (Braine, 1963a). Suppose you were to try to learn a thousand 2- and 3-word combinations, by rote, in Arabic? How much time, during that month, might it take you? How much repetitive drill would you need to remember each combination perfectly? Of course, if the combinations had something in common, you might be able to figure out a system or pattern that would speed your learning.

Braine's Theory of Language Patterns
One theory of this sort has been developed by Braine (1963b), who believes that children learn—from such cues as intonation and stress patterns—the characteristic *order* of words in certain standard sentences (simple declaratives, questions, passives, and the like). Having learned that order, they can then generate an indefinite number of novel sentences which conform to it. But as Braine's critics (Bever, Fodor, and Weksel, 1965) have pointed out, certain ideas other than order must enter into sentence comprehension. For example, "The kangaroo cost ten dollars" and "The child blew the kazoo" are both instances of simple declarative orders. "The kazoo was blown by the child" and "Ten dollars was cost by

the kangaroo" are both examples of passive orders—yet we recognize immediately that something is wrong with the last statement, something other than its order. Now we have to account for the fact that the child has also learned something special about kangaroos and costs. And so the list of *individual things learned* grows and grows, until it is too long for a lifetime.

Is Language "Imprinted"?

To avoid this pitfall, psycholinguists say that individuals come equipped biologically with the ability to generate and comprehend language; the only learning they do concerns the particular forms of their native speech. That kind of learning, the evolutionists say, is more like *imprinting* than conditioning, or than any other kind of learning favored by traditional learning psychologists.

Imprinting is a species-specific behavioral process that occurs during a critical period. One type of easily imprinted response in some animals is following behavior; others involve eating and nesting activities. The infant seems to come equipped with a set of behaviors that are "unlocked" by specific environmental cues. Such behavior is not practiced like other kinds of learning, but seems to come into existence swiftly and intractably—that is, once imprinted, the behavior is difficult to dislodge.

There is much about language learning that seems to follow a similar pattern, although it is of course more complicated, since we are altogether a more complicated species. Apparently, the brain critically "awakens" to special language stimuli between the ages of 1 and 3 years. If a child—for reasons of deprivation or deafness—is not exposed to language during that period, he may not develop language as easily or fully as he otherwise would have. During this critical period, the child's very rapid ability to learn to produce original sentences does not seem to come from practice, as traditional learning theory would require. And there are other problems with the traditional view.

Is Language Imitated?

For example, it is not easy to show that children learn language by imitating adults, although that is often what they seem to be doing. Actually, it can be very difficult to persuade a child to imitate something he does not already know how to say. One illustration of this is given by McNeill (1966).

> CHILD: Nobody don't like me.
> MOTHER: No, say "nobody likes me."
> CHILD: Nobody don't like me.
>   [Eight repetitions of this dialogue]
> MOTHER: No, now listen carefully: say *"Nobody likes me."*
> CHILD: Oh! "Nobody don't likes me."

Before a young child has developed a particular grammatical form, it may be very difficult to induce him to imitate it. Imitation is therefore probably not his natural method of learning that form. However, *imitation may be a useful remedial system for children whose language has not developed naturally,* as we will see. Imitation may also be useful in second language learning.

Evolution vs. conditioning could be argued at great length. In fact, this is one of the most fruitful arguments of modern psychology, for it is forcing psycholinguists and learning psychologists to reexamine their assumptions and data. We cannot settle the argument here, although it is clear that some learning and some teaching must be involved in full language development, evolution notwithstanding. In the next section, we will take up the role of tutors (such as parents or teachers) in reinforcing, expanding, enriching, and drilling language skills in children.

THE ROLE OF TUTORS

In our previous discussion of babbling, two principles emerged: (1) Reinforcement may encourage behavior (as in the Rheingold experiment) and (2) reinforcement may provide information (as in the Friedlander experiment). Both principles undoubtedly continue to operate during more advanced language development, but we can refine (2) a bit more: information about one's own language development may be (2.1) information about grammatical usage or (2.2) information about putting one's world into words. A third tutorial function is that of providing the opportunity for disciplined practice. First, let us examine the information principle.

Expansion and Enrichment

Consider what happens when a parent hears a child say, "Dere milk." The parent may respond (reinforce) by saying, "Yes, there's the milk," or, alternatively, "Yes, and I'll bet you're thirsty, aren't you!" In the first case, the parent has *expanded* the child's sentence to a correct grammatical form, but has added no new information. In the second case, the parent has *enriched* the child's conception of the situation, but without correcting his grammar.

The urge to expand or enrich a child's speech may be almost irresistible. We often feel impelled to say *for* a child what we think he is trying to say for himself. A good parent may intuitively recognize that a child is testing his own linguistic ideas, as the LAS diagram indicates. The feedback provided by the attentive adult may be critically important to the child's language development. If he gets no feedback, or gets only inappropriate or discouraging feedback, his language acquisition system may be impaired.

In a real-life situation, expansion and enrichment may occur simultaneously, but experimentally, we might ask the question: Which type of feedback produces the most grammatical improvement? Is it better to provide the child with a clear, grammatically correct version of what he is trying to say? Or is it better to enrich his ideas of what he is talking about, and never mind his grammar? The answer to such questions may be crucial to the economical design of Head Start programs, for example. Should we hire specialists to correct the children's grammar? Or will any wise conversationalist do as well?

One attempt to compare the effects of expansion and enrichment was made by Courtney Cazden (1965). She spent 40 minutes a day for about three months talking with children (between 2 and 3 years of age) in a Boston day care center. Since there were thirty children to every adult, Cazden felt sure that the children were not receiving sufficient linguistic stimulation and that her tutorial sessions, though brief, would have an effect. Some of the children were linguistically expanded, and some were enriched. Some examples from an expansion session follow:

Expansion

CHILD: She sitting down.
TUTOR: She's sitting down?
CHILD: He go in a water.
TUTOR: And he's going in the water?
CHILD: Yeah. Eeee . . .
TUTOR: What did the mother do?
CHILD: Fall out.
TUTOR: She fell out?
CHILD: Yeah.

As the examples show, the tutor simply reflected back to the child a correct grammatical version of what he was trying to say. One would certainly feel that this simple procedure would help the child become aware of important grammatical features, while not interfering with his own self-expression. In the enrichment sessions, the tutor's language was much more complicated.

Enrichment

CHILD: A kitty.
TUTOR: Yeah, he goes "meow-meow."
CHILD: Boy.
TUTOR: Yes, he's taking a bath.
CHILD: A flag.
TUTOR: Yeah. It's waving in the breeze.
CHILD: Dere car.
TUTOR: That's right. That's the kind that cleans streets.
CHILD: My cake fall down.
TUTOR: But it's a solid cake. It's all right.

One might expect that the enrichment sessions would be poor ways of inducing grammatical improvement, since a correct version of the child's own speech was never presented to him. That was what Cazden herself expected. But surprisingly, the children who had been enriched developed better grammar than the children who had been expanded; they were better able to imitate complex sentences, to use longer sentences, to use more complex noun and verb phrases, and so forth.

Upon reflection, Cazden decided this was not so surprising after all. Consider again the LAS diagram (Figure 17.1) and the examples of expansion and enrichment sessions. The child whose early attempts at speaking are only expanded hears less of his native language than does a child whose speech is being enriched. The expansion sessions provide the child with more limited sampling opportunities. Further, the sessions may be confusing. The young child's mind is on the thing he is talking about, not on how he is talking about it. When he says, "There dog," his mind is on something soft and fuzzy (even though he may be mistakenly referring to a squirrel). When the expanding tutor responds, "There is a dog," the child might misunderstand. (Is an *isadog* different from a regular dog? Maybe *isadogs* are the ones with the bushy tails.) The enrichment tutor, on the other hand, is sharing the child's interest and may be more understandable. The grammatical information (as well as the world information) may be easier for the child to assimilate. But is *ease* always important?

It was pointed out earlier that children imitate only what they already know how to say (that was why Cazden used sentence imitation ability as a measure of grammatical improvement). Imitation is not the child's natural method of learning a language, but in the case of subnormal development, more intensive remedial tutoring may be necessary. We have so far discussed the enriching tutor and the expanding tutor. A third kind of language teaching may be in the form of *tutorial drill.* A tutor in this role may not have an easy time of it.

Tutorial Drill

Typically, deprived children will have a great deal of trouble with . . . for example . . . the statement "This is a table" . . . perhaps reducing the statement to something like "Diii table." Call their attention to the omitted parts of the statement. Repeat the statement five to ten times, clapping to accent the missing parts. Repeat the same statement often. . . . It may take some severely deprived children three months before they are able to produce even a reasonable semblance of an identity statement. . . . Efforts to get them to repeat statements should continue, however, with the stimulus being presented very rhythmically and slowly. (Bereiter and Engelmann, 1966, pp. 140–141)

The Bereiter and Engelmann approach to language training has aroused considerable controversy. It is essentially a speech retraining method, although the attempt is made to teach a kind of speech that will improve logical thinking. Whereas the expanding tutor provides a correct version of the child's own language, the drill tutor may select special aspects of language to concentrate on. These aspects may not be familiar to the child at all, much less invented by him. That is why drill is necessary.

This approach seems so contrary to the way children naturally develop language that one wonders how it could be justified. Surely, our aim in remedial language teaching is not merely to teach children to talk as well as parrots. Teachers who urge language drills believe that something much more important than parrot talk is happening. They insist that the mind itself develops as a result of the forced development of language. To understand how this might be so, we will need to explore some views of the effects of language on thought. Chapter 18 is devoted to that topic, and we will return there to the question of tutorials and IQ.

Before moving on to the problem of comprehension and meaning, we ought to consider certain other conditions of language deficiency for which tutorials are obviously necessary. Although children suffering from these difficulties are usually placed in special classes, they sometimes appear in regular classes. Some discussion of *deafness, articulation defects, stuttering,* and *childhood aphasia,* as these handicaps relate to normal language development, may therefore be helpful.

DISTURBED LANGUAGE DEVELOPMENT

Consider again the LAS diagram in Figure 17.1. If this represents the language learning system of the normal child, then hearing and speech disorders will have an obvious effect. A child with a speech disorder (a disorder of articulation and word formation) will have an *output* handicap that may take various forms. A child with a hearing disorder will have both an *input* (language sampling) and an *output* handicap. The deaf child will not be able to sample his own language adequately, nor to monitor his own hypotheses about the form that language should take. This is obviously the more severe handicap.

Language in Deaf Children

The degree of language deficiency in our deaf population is appalling:

> The profoundly deaf person who has been so since before the age of language learning may know quite a number of isolated words, but with rare exceptions will he be able to form or comprehend sentences or paragraphs which approximate the complexity of Grade 4 reading level.
>
> The linguistic deficiency of the deaf consists more precisely in their inability to handle linguistic ordering or structure. Reading tests below the Grade 4 level are recognized as sampling only fragmentary aspects of the living language. Thus comprehension of Grade 4 reading as measured by present standardized tests may be proposed as a criterion of linguistic competence.
>
> According to this criterion, the percentage of deaf pupils who have linguistic competence, as can be seen in [the table below], reaches a max-

imum of only 12 per cent, a number which may be somewhat inflated by the presence of pupils in the . . . sample who had lost their hearing after the acquisition of language, or who were not profoundly deaf. . . .

Silent Reading Achievement of Deaf Pupils*

Age	Number of Pupils	Reading Grade Level (median)
10.5–11.5	654	2.6
11.5–12.5	849	2.7
12.5–13.5	797	3.1
13.5–14.5	814	3.2
14.5–15.5	1035	3.3
15.5–16.5	1075	3.4

*Note that between the ages of 10 and 16, the deaf children did not advance even one full grade in reading ability.

It should be noted that a 14-year-old deaf youngster with a reading level of Grade 3 is not comparable to a hearing peer who may have difficulty in reading. The hearing individual enjoys a comfortable mastery of the language, even though he may be retarded in reading. For the deaf, on the other hand, the reading level *is* the ceiling level of linguistic competence. It is quite inappropriate to designate this latter condition as retardation in reading. It is properly termed incompetence or deficiency in verbal language, a condition very rare among the hearing but almost universal among the deaf. (Furth, 1966, pp. 14–15)

The Need for a Manual Language Teachers interested in deaf children will, of course, take special courses in the methods and technology of their instruction. In doing so, they will discover (as all teachers do) some enlightened and some archaic instructional systems—systems that do not take adequate account of developmental principles. Among the latter is the current emphasis in the United States on lip reading and speech—that is, on "normal" language as compared to the sign language and manual alphabets that would be natural to a deaf person. No manual alphabet or sign language is formally taught in any American school for the deaf, although the children usually manage to transmit sign language to each other informally.

It cannot be proved that this instructional inadequacy is responsible for the language deficiency described above, but it surely must be an important contributing factor. Many young deaf children have no exposure to language at all, in any form, until they enter a school for the deaf at the age of 6 or 7. There they are given formal instruction in grammar—a type of learning very different from natural language learning, and even from second language learning, since the child has no natural language habits to capitalize on. At the same time, the child is given instruction in speech production. Not only has the critical period for language learning passed, but the type of instruction (when it finally occurs) utilizes the one perceptual system that does not work!

Ideally, the parents (and siblings) of a deaf child should themselves learn sign language and use it extensively. The very young child (age 2 to 3) can learn sign language as naturally as he could have learned a spoken language, were it perceptually available to him. Once this communication system is established, cognitive development can proceed normally; speech sounds and lip reading can be taught as a second language, and reading can follow a relatively normal course of instruction. By denying deaf children the manual language fluencies that are easily available to them, we start them down a path of cognitive retardation from which they may never recover. The fact that this denial occurs because manual languages are considered (by hearing teachers) to be "unnatural," "queer," or "stigmatizing" does not alleviate the tragedy.

> It is not surprising that the deaf themselves are somewhat resentful toward the society that constantly tells them they should not live and communicate as they do, but should learn the speech of society and mix freely with the hearing. They feel instinctively that without sign language most of them would indeed be unable to communicate anything but the most primitive and obvious needs. There would be no possibility of forming a meaningful community based purely on verbal exchanges. It is therefore in the deaf community that the deaf person finds opportunity for social, emotional, and intellectual development and fulfillment. (Furth, 1966, p. 16)

Neurologically, symbolic development should be possible to any organism in whom cross-modal connections are possible. As Geschwind (1964) has argued, connections between the manual or tactual systems and the visual systems should make a genuine language possible to the deaf. Failure to provide systematic training in this sort of language during the critical period for its development may permanently impair symbolic abilities.

Speech Disorders

The child whose hearing is normal but who suffers from an articulation (output) disorder is in a more favored position. The severe retardation experienced by most deaf persons may be spared him, although speech difficulties are more often found in retarded than in normal populations. Speech difficulties are also more often found in boys—as are reading difficulties (see Part V). They may run in families, and they often follow early childhood illnesses with high fevers.

As with all psychological disorders, controversy has raged over the role of parents in producing and healing them. There is a school which argues that speech difficulties are caused by overanxious mothers and too much pressure. There is another school which argues that the speech difficulties are a physiological accident and that anxiety in the mothers *results* from the child's problems.

Whatever the cause, the teacher of a child with articulation disorders must cope with that child in the classroom, not in the hospital or in the home. Although this text cannot provide detailed instruction in speech training, other books can. (A good one is *Speech Disorders,* by Berry and Eisenson, 1956.) Since most of us find it difficult to ignore articulation defects, the best way of responding to them may be correctly. There are some simple principles of "engineering" lip, tongue, and throat movements that will produce the correct sounds. The teacher who can quickly and efficiently demonstrate these to a child and help him practice them is surely a better teacher than one who maintains an embarrassed indifference.

The emotional aspects of articulation instruction would seem to be no greater than the emotional aspects of helping any child with any kind of learning problem. Naturally, we do not want to publicly shame or otherwise punish a child who has a disorder he cannot help. But the teacher who offers help, affection, and encouragement in overcoming a handicap is hardly likely to make matters worse.

The stuttering child is a different problem. Here, there are no simple engineering principles and probably little that a nonspecialist can do other than offer some degree of protection and support. The stuttering child (like any child) needs to feel he has friends and abilities that are respected. Both teacher and friends (if possible) should demonstrate a capacity for tolerating stuttering—they should be willing to wait out repetitions and blocks, and not fill in words and phrases. Normal class participation should be encouraged.

> Many young stutterers are excused from oral recitations in school either because the teacher is impatient and cannot wait for the stutterer's replies or is oversympathetic and does not wish to embarrass the stutterer. It does not take very long for some stutterers to decide that there are exemptions and immunities associated with stuttering which might be worth maintaining. (Berry and Eisenson, 1956, p. 293)

As we will see in later chapters, the use of language in discussions and dialogues may be critical to cognitive development in a school setting, but there may be ways other than oral recitation in which children with speech disorders can use and extend their language. It is especially necessary that they do so. According to the data summarized by Berry and Eisenson, children with articulation disorders do tend to have lower IQs and less satisfactory school records than children whose speech is normal. This is not likely to be true of stutterers, however; by college age, stutterers may actually be superior in IQ to the general college population.

Occasionally, teachers discover children whom they suspect of being *aphasic*—that is, sometimes unable to produce speech at all. This is a type of brain damage, and it has been discussed in Part I, along with some other related language disturbances (agraphia, dyslexia). In general, a rich language environment will be the best therapy a regular classroom teacher can provide for an aphasic (or slightly aphasic) child, along with some special drill materials in speaking and writing—but these should be administered privately. Practice is necessary, but a special tutor (an older child or a parent) may be as good at supervision as the teacher.

A Summary of Teaching Strategies

These four conditions—deafness, articulation disorders, stuttering, and aphasia—illustrate a single basic teaching principle: *Language must be heard and used if it is to grow.* The teacher's way of stimulating this use will vary with the nature of the developmental handicap:

Type of Handicap	Teaching Principle
Deafness	Provide a substitute language (manual speech), followed by the additional languages of speech, lip-reading, and reading.
Articulation disorder	Teach correct mechanical methods for producing the speech sounds.
Stuttering	Accept stuttering and encourage language usage anyway.
Aphasia	Keep child in a rich language environment, but provide special speech, spelling, and writing drills in private.

Only through the development of language can we share in the meaning and logic systems of the race. Failure to do so means not only exclusion from certain areas of society, but mental crippling. As Lashley (1963) said, "Certainly language presents in most striking form the integrative functions that are characteristic of the cerebral cortex and that reach their highest development in human thought. . . ." If language ability is defective, we must do everything in our power to fix it.

Chapter 18 VERBAL MEANING

Now that we have some basic information about the form and process of language development, we can look more closely at the problem of meaning, which is, after all, most of what language is all about. The technical name for this field of study is *semantics.*

In general, as discussed in Part I, meaning implies a connection between information stored in one part of the brain (or in one type of neural pattern) and other information. If we understand the meaning of the word *box,* then we have connected the squiggles *b, o,* and *x* with tactual and visual memories of something square and hollow. The study of semantics goes beyond this to the problem of words in sentences. As we will see, the perception of sentence meaning is governed by principles other than simple neurological ones.

In the first section of this chapter, we will take up the problem of verbal comprehension—how it develops and how it may be described theoretically. Note that *comprehension* itself is a very broad term, which has already been discussed in Parts I, II, and III from a variety of standpoints. Here we are focusing upon such things as the comprehension of verbal instructions or questions; reading comprehension is deferred until Part V. The last two sections of this chapter are devoted to the major factors affecting comprehension: association networks and rules of meaning. What we probably do when we comprehend verbal material is sort through a network of associations in accord with certain rules of meaning. This may be similar in many respects to the basic processes of searching and classifying discussed in Part II, but their special verbal applications require further explanation.

THE DEVELOPMENT OF COMPREHENSION

Earlier, it was stated that children generally imitate only what they already know how to say. We must now qualify this by distinguishing between imitation, production, and comprehension. The fact that a child can imitate a sentence—or produce it—does not mean he has comprehended it.

Fraser, Bellugi, and Brown (1963) performed the first modern experiment on comprehension. They showed young children (about 3½ years old) pictures that illustrated ten grammatical contrasts—like the contrasts between singular and plural, subject and object. The children responded in three ways: They pointed to the pictures, they imitated the experimenter, or they produced descriptive sentences of their own. The sentences to which they responded were simple ones, like "The sheep is eating" vs. "The sheep are eating," or "His wagon" vs. "Their wagon." These exemplified the grammatical contrasts. All the sentences could easily be said by 3-year-olds; that is, the grammatical forms were already within their repertoires.

The results of the experiment were clear: Children could imitate the sentences (by rote) before they really understood them—that is, before they could point to the pictures that correctly illustrated the contrasts. Thus, a child might say "The sheep are jumping" without errors, but point to the picture of the single sheep jumping, rather than to the one of two sheep jumping. He did not really understand what he was saying. This became especially clear when he was asked to produce descriptive sentences of his own.

One might argue that the child did not really understand the task—that is, he might not have understood the correspondence between plural language forms and plural picture forms—but an understanding of such a correspondence *defines* comprehension for this particular situation. Comprehension always requires a relation between something said and something done (or something else said, in the case of an older child or adult). This is what Luria and others have called the *pragmatic* function of language.

Directive Self-instruction

Luria (1959, 1961) has been a pioneer in studying the development of this pragmatic function. He began a series of experiments by giving very young children (between 1 and 1½ years) simple instructions they could easily follow like "Give me the cat," referring to a toy. But then if Luria placed a toy fish between the child and the cat, the request "Give me the cat" lost its directing power. The child would hand the experimenter the fish.

> The directive function of the word will be maintained only up to the moment when it comes into conflict with the conditions of the external situation. While the word easily directs behavior in a situation that lacks

conflict, it loses its directive role if the immediate orientational reaction is evoked by a more closely located, or brighter, or more interesting object. (Luria, 1959, p. 342)

We recognize this behavior as the hallmark of the very young pre-operational child who is still controlled by iconic stimuli. Essentially, the child's problem seems to be that of learning how to integrate *word* and *action* in the face of misleading visual cues. As the child approaches the age of 2, he becomes able to follow these simple instructions (that is, instructions to make simple discriminations). His next milestone will be that of learning to verbally organize his actions in advance. He may be given an instruction like, "When the light goes on, press the ball." The instruction activates what Luria calls a *pretriggering verbal system*. According to the Soviet experiments, this pretriggering system requires cognitive controls that a young child will not develop before the age of about 3.

> The younger children . . . appear unable to realize that synthesis of separate elements which is required by the instruction formulated in the sentence. Each individual word contained in the sentence evokes in the child an immediate orienting reaction, and as soon as he hears the beginning of the sentence *When the light flashes* . . . the child begins to look for the lights with his eyes; when he hears the end of the sentence . . . *you will press the ball,* he immediately presses the device in his hand. At this stage the separate words have already acquired an effective triggering function, but the creation, by means of words, of a preliminary pretriggering system of connections, which requires the inhibition of immediate reactions and their separation into individual fragments, turns out to be unattainable. (Luria, 1959, pp. 346–347)

Luria and others have attempted to train pretriggering systems in very young children by drilling them in simple self-instruction. That is, the child learns to say "Press" when the light comes on, and then to follow his own direction. Later (Chapter 19) we will hear more about the use of explicit and implicit speech in problem solving. Here, we need only note that *the development of a child's ability to comprehend verbal instruction* (that is, to coordinate his own actions with verbal instruction) *is probably related to the development of his own self-instructional capacity.*

Huttenlocher's Studies

As in all areas of cognitive development, there is no final stage of perfection. Comprehension failures of a more complex sort may continue to occur. A recent series of experiments by Huttenlocher (Huttenlocher and Strauss, 1968; Huttenlocher, Eisenberg, and Strauss, 1968) explored one aspect of this problem. The children in Huttenlocher's experiments followed instructions like "Make it so the red block is over the green block" while looking at some block shelves. One block (either green or red) had been placed on a shelf; the child was holding the other block. Sometimes the child held the block that was actually the object of the sentence (the green block in the above example; sometimes he held the block that was the subject. As we will see in a later experiment by Clark, the interpretation of sentence meaning generally proceeds from subject to object. Perhaps for this reason, the children in Huttenlocher's experiment took correct action (placed the block correctly) when they were holding the block that was the subject of the instruction. But they made frequent errors when they were holding the block that was the object of the instruction—they treated the object-block as if it were the subject.

Again, the child's problem seemed to be that of forming an alliance between word and action in the face of misleading perceptual cues. Even at the age of 8, Huttenlocher's subjects had difficulty with instructions that did not match their natural action tendencies. When they were holding the green block and the instruction "Make it so the red block is over the green block" actually required them to place the green block *under* the red one, errors were frequent.

Analysis and Coordination

These simple experimental situations may not seem to have much relevance to school work, at least beyond kindergarten. But the principles illustrated here—*analysis* and *coordination*—continue to govern the comprehension of more complex verbal material. When we comprehend verbal material, we must first analyze it into its grammatical and meaning components. We must then coordinate the results of our analysis with behavior. The behavior need not be concrete, as it is with young children; it may be other verbal behavior. But unless such coordination occurs, comprehension cannot be shown to exist.

The coordination of meaning and action has been discussed at length in Part I. Our main emphasis here is on the first principle of verbal analysis. What affects this analysis? What guides it? In the next two sections, we will review some of the answers to these questions.

ASSOCIATION NETWORKS

The words in a sentence have many meanings. How can you explain what they are? Probably by using other words. You might put those other words into sentences, or you might just call them out—you might say aloud all the other words a given word made you think of. If you did that, you would be generating a list or network of *verbal associations.*

Psychologists who study associations (Deese, 1966; Clark, 1970) have discovered that such networks are not random, but are lawful in various ways. For example, given the word *dark,* a large number of people will respond with the word *light* because it is an antonym (opposite in meaning to *dark*) and also because it is the same part of speech as *dark* (both *dark* and *light* are nouns).

Principles of Association

These examples illustrate two important principles of associative meaning: (1) The principle of contrast and (2) the principle of grouping. Apparently, they are fundamental cognitive principles of classification (see Chapter 8) that also appear in verbal associations.

The appearance of these principles is not independent of age, however. Young children (under the age of about 7—that magical period of shift from preoperational to concrete operational thinking) do not give the same kinds of word associations as adults do. Their associations are more like *relational classifications* (see Figure 14.6). The technical term for them is *syntagmatic* (from syntax, or word order), which means that the associations seem influenced by sentence position. Thus, the young child says *night* when asked to give an association to *dark.* Here the association is more like that of adjective to noun than that of noun to noun, as in the adult case.

When associations are in the same form class (the same part of speech), they are called *paradigmatic.* Children begin to switch from syntagmatic to paradigmatic associations as they move into their eighth year. This shift is difficult to explain, but it seems to be closely related to the child's increasing awareness of the meaning (semantic) features of words (McNeill, 1966). For a young child, the meaning of a word seems to have a great deal to do with his use of the word. "A hole is to dig," "A lap is to sit on" are the kinds of definitions young children give when you ask them what *hole* means or what *lap* means. When a child becomes able to describe the features of words—by saying, for example, that a hole has features of roundness, deepness, and dirtness—he is more likely to give paradigmatic associations to words. Paradigmatic responses would be *analytic classifications.*

Models of Meaning

The principles or rules that govern the types of associations we make are something like a *meaning structure.* Various ways of diagramming this structure have been tried. The one in Figure 18.1 is taken from Kiss and shows a possible relationship between words that are usually associated with each other. Deese (1966) diagrammed the associative structure for

Figure 18.1 Diagram of a meaning structure. (Kiss, 1968, p. 711)

butterfly as shown in Figure 18.2. His system is derived from factor analysis, a statistical technique for analyzing correlation patterns. In Deese's diagram, all the associations are paradigmatic (all the words are nouns, like the stimulus word *butterfly*). In Kiss's diagram, some of the associations are syntagmatic (the associations *warm* and *hold,* for example). Presumably, Kiss's associations are more likely to have been given by a young child.

Classroom Illustrations Although our ideas about such meaning structures are still tentative, we do know that they affect school learning. Two experiments will illustrate how.

We have all had the experience of thinking that we have seen or heard something before, when in fact we have not. (That was not Aunt Lulu getting off the bus, it was a stranger who made us think of Aunt Lulu. But a week later we may mistakenly tell Aunt Mabel, "I saw Aunt Lulu getting off the bus last week.")

Wallace (1967) gave both normal and retarded subjects a list of words that have fairly common associations. *Sugar,* for example, frequently brings forth the association *sweet.* Later in the list, the word *sweet* itself would appear, and the subjects would be asked if they had seen that word before. The normal subjects often erroneously said they had. The retarded subjects, who apparently did not generate the *sugar-sweet* association to begin with, did not make the same error.

The experiment makes an interesting point about the nature of retardation, but we will not pursue that topic further. The main concern here is that our normal tendency to generate associations to words can lead us to make errors of certain kinds. On a more advanced level, we may have the same problem with ideas. Some people—often creative people—associate many ideas to a stimulus idea (an exam question, for example). This stream or set of associations may interfere with their ability to recognize

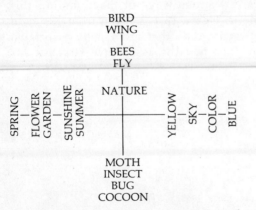

Figure 18.2   An associative structure for *butterfly.* (Deese, 1966)

the right answer from a multiple-choice list. (If you have such problems, it may be of some comfort to know that retarded people do not.)

In another experiment, Samuels (1968) gave fifth- and sixth-graders a reading test based on two paragraphs: One paragraph was made up of high association words—that is, words that are frequently found together. The second paragraph was made up of low association words.

High Associations. They were all happy to be together again. Outside the moon and stars shone brightly in the June sky, and the green grass sparkled in the night.

Low Associations. They were all relieved to be together again. Outside the moon and lake appeared clearly in the June evening, and the green house sparkled in the valley.

Samuels measured both the time it took the children to read the paragraphs and their ability to correctly answer questions about them. [A typical multiple-choice question would be: The green __?__ sparkled. (a) house, (b) plants, (c) grass, (d) emeralds.] Samuels found that it took the children significantly longer to read the low association paragraph and that they made more errors on questions about their reading.

Experiments of this sort show us one way of analyzing what we mean by *ease* or *difficulty* of verbal material. Easy verbal materials may have been *frequently* associated, whereas difficult ones may have been *infrequently* associated. Of course, the frequency of association may vary between individuals. The middle-class child, who has a rich network of associations to formal school material, may find questions about it quite easy. The lower-class child, whose associative network (to formal school material) may be sparse and weak, may experience difficulty.

Athough the Wallace experiment with retardates shows us that associations can sometimes cause interference and errors, the Samuels experiment shows us that having a rich set of associations usually makes school learning easier. Skillful (and compassionate) teachers will therefore try to build up children's verbal associative structures in many ways, perhaps most effectively through tutorial verbal enrichment, discussions, and class dialogues.

Emotional Connotations of Words
One further aspect of associative structures should be mentioned: The emotional aspect. When we hear the word *war*, for example, we not only associate other words to it, but we also associate feelings and values. War has a connotation of goodness or badness; it has connotations of strength and connotations of activity. Osgood (Osgood, Suci, and Tannenbaum, 1957) has devoted many years to the development of a scaling technique he calls the *semantic differential*. The technique shows how words differ (for different people) in *evaluation* (goodness or badness), *potency* (strength or weakness), and *activity* (active or passive). For example, the word *war* might have a profile on the semantic differential scales for a

group of average Americans like that shown in Figure 18.3. It might have quite a different profile for a group of revolutionists. How might the word *violet* be scaled? How about *Aunt Lulu?* You can see that this particular scaling technique makes systematic comparisons possible between different people, different words, and different cultures.

In one recent experiment, association speeds (reaction times) were measured for words that had been rated for pleasantness-unpleasantness by a semantic differential technique (Pollio and Gerow, 1968). Some of the pleasant words were *house, pretty,* and *soft.* Some of the unpleasant words were *rough, pain,* and *war.* All the words occurred with equal frequency in the language—that is, both the pleasant and the unpleasant words were highly familiar. Nevertheless, *associations to the unpleasant words took more time to produce.*

The effects of context were also studied in this experiment. Target words (the words to which an association was given) were actually embedded in lists of other words. The subject first read through a list of words and gave an association only to the word that made a light go on (the experimenter's signal). If the subject first read through a list of unpleasant words, his association to a target word occurred more slowly, even if the target word was pleasant. Similarly, if the subject first read through a list of pleasant words, his association to a target word occurred more quickly, even if the target word was unpleasant.

The experiment indicates that emotional aspects of words may affect our ability to associate other words to them—probably because the associations are being routed through different (emotional) areas of the brain. As we know from Part I, tiny differences in "brain processing time" may make enormous differences in our ability to integrate information. Presumably, then, words or ideas that have unpleasant associations may be more difficult for a student to tie in with other ideas. Further, if previous associations have been unpleasant, this "mood" may also interfere with efficiency. Problems of this sort and their relation to learning have been discussed in more detail in Part III.

A Summary Note

The preceding materials have illustrated the basic fact that verbal associations are not random; they are governed by laws we are only just begin-

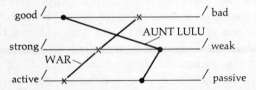

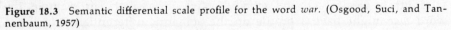

Figure 18.3 Semantic differential scale profile for the word *war.* (Osgood, Suci, and Tannenbaum, 1957)

ning to understand. When a word or a sentence is meaningful to us, we must have selected, from a large set of possible associations, certain particular ones. Consider the ambiguous sentence "They are stirring spoons." If we select one set of associations, we will perceive that sentence to mean "Those are spoons to stir with." If we select another set of associations, we will perceive the sentence to mean "Those people are stirring (the pile of) spoons." Why do we select one set of associations instead of another? What governs the selection process?

RULES OF MEANING

Consider the following five natural sentences (from Clark and Begun, 1968).

1. The rain ended the game.
2. The man fought the animal.
3. The secretary wrote the minutes.
4. The child caught the ball.
5. The girl attracted the boy.

Aside from the articles (*the*), each sentence contains a subject, a verb, and an object. In the natural sentences, each verb goes naturally with its subject and object. To construct unnatural sentences, we could switch around the subjects, objects, and verbs of the different sentences. For example:

1. The child wrote the animal.
2. The man fought the game.
3. The secretary ended the minutes.
4. The rain caught the ball.

Some of these sentences seem to be more sensible or meaningful than others—that is, some of them are obeying the rules of meaning better than others.

What are the rules of meaning? Research on the psychological (as opposed to the philosophical) aspects of this question is only just beginning. Generally, the research is taking an empirical form: Rather than specifying what the rules of meaning ought to be, experimenters are trying to find out what they are, just by asking.

The five natural sentences above were taken from a long list of natural "good" sentences made up by college students. The unnatural sentences were composed by switching the natural sentences around in systematic ways. Ratings of meaningfulness were then obtained from more college students. The experimental students (who did not know which were the original natural sentences and which were the switched sentences) correctly rated the natural sentences as the most meaningful. This result shows that rules of meaning are shared and can be transmitted. Even more interesting, however, were the switches that appeared to decrease meaning in the unnatural sentences.

Unnatural sentences that preserved the verb-object agreement were judged to be relatively meaningful, no matter what subject was attached to the verb-object pair. Even when subject and verb were the natural ones, introduction of an unnatural object reduced the meaning of the sentence to a significant degree. When subject and object were the natural ones but an unnatural verb connected them, the sentences became even less meaningful because both the verb-object and the subject-verb relation were violated.

Clark also constructed a different kind of unnatural sentence by substituting object-nouns for subject-nouns. "The ball caught the child," for example. As the college students judged them, these substitutions radically destroyed the meaning of the sentences. On the basis of his findings, Clark concluded that the following are some basic rules of sentence meaning:

1. The subject must belong to the right class of things—that is, it must commonly be the kind of thing that acts or does, not the kind of thing that is acted *on* or done *to*.

2. The predicate as a whole must make sense.

3. The subject and the predicate must form a meaningful combination.

Such theorizing tells us that deep structure is not merely a syntactic structure; it is also a meaning structure. The rules of meaning, then, will be closely related to the rules of grammar. In processing the meaning of a sentence, we seem to "go down" a phrase structure tree in three stages (Figure 18.4). Within the framework of association theory, we might say that we carry within our heads sets of associations to words we know. When we hear these words in a sentence, the deep structure of the sentence sets up a classification system. The system inhibits or discards associations that are not appropriate when the words are combined in this particular sentence. The system may also stimulate new associations producing comprehension of something new, as in poetry, for example.

Remembering Meaning

In one experiment, Sachs (1967) showed that memory for the "sense" of verbal material may be superior to memory of its form, even when the sense alterations are small. In her experiment, Sachs had college students listen to tapes of connected discourse (excerpts of nonfiction). After a paragraph or two, one sentence from the discourse was repeated. Sometimes that sentence was identical to the one heard originally; sometimes it was changed in meaning; sometimes it preserved the original meaning, but was changed in form. To illustrate:

Original sentence:

There he met an archeologist, Howard Carter, who urged him to join in the search for the tomb of King Tut.

Meaning change:

>There he met an archeologist, Howard Carter, and urged him to join in the search for the tomb of King Tut.

Form change (meaning preserved):

>There he met an archeologist, Howard Carter, who urged that he join in the search for the tomb of King Tut.

In all cases, only one or two words were changed. The students instantly detected the changes if they altered the sense of the paragraph, but failed to detect them otherwise. The result shows that we have extremely sensitive systems for storing the meaning of verbal material—systems that are not identical to our systems for storing syntactical information.

The Katz and Fodor Model One way of describing these processes is the following (from Katz and Fodor, 1963): Within each individual there may be a system for categorizing or *marking* words in systematic ways. (This is essentially a classification system.) All words, first of all, can be categorized grammatically—they are nouns, verbs, adjectives, and so

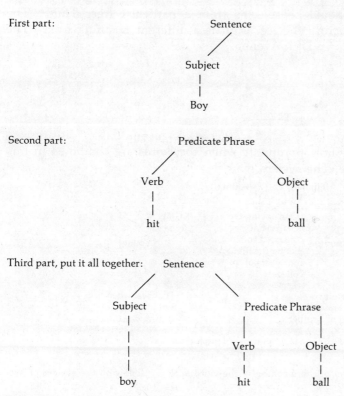

Figure 18.4   A phrase structure tree sequence.

forth. These *syntactic* markers can be called the first or top level of the categorizing hierarchy.

On the next level, *semantic* markers characterize the most general meaning features of the word. The word *jewel,* for example, may be semantically marked as *concrete* or *metaphor.* Under the marking of concrete, we would find meanings related to diamond operations; under metaphor, we would find meanings related to personal value, as in "She was a jewel of a mother." Semantic markers are the broad categories we find in dictionary entries following the part-of-speech designation.

Within each path opened up by a semantic marker, there are other markers. These have been called *distinguishers.* A distinguisher specifies exactly what is different about a meaning a word may have—that is, exactly how it differs from other meanings the same word may have. The full meaning of the word *bachelor* is displayed in Figure 18.5.

The diagram is from Katz and Fodor (1963), who have used it as an example of the kind of processing a semantic theory must be able to explain. This is one description of the way in which we seem to sort meanings. We have broad classifications (semantic markers) and narrower feature lists (distinguishers) that we use to designate what we mean by words. The way in which a word is used in a sentence signals us as to which meaning should be selected from a particular tree. Thus, "The bachelor hurried across the ice" signals a different meaning from "The bachelor hurried down Fifth Avenue."

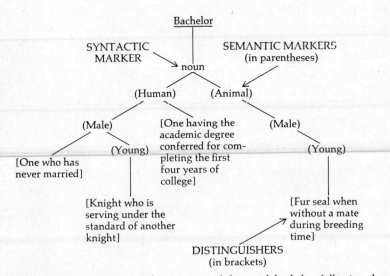

Figure 18.5 A diagram of the meaning of the word *bachelor,* following the system of Katz and Fodor (1963).

Extracting Meaning

To summarize the principles discussed thus far: The ability to comprehend verbal material—whether statements, questions, instructions, connected discourse, poetry, drama, or expository prose—seems to have three components (plus the requirement that the results of the following analysis then be coordinated with some other kind of behavior—pointing or saying something).

1. The ability to analyze or segment the material into manageable "chunks"—whether words, grammatical phrases, or action units

2. The ability to generate a set of associations to each chunk—probably in a treelike, nonrandom manner

3. The ability to choose from these associations those that are mutually compatible for the particular sentence

For example, in comprehending the sentence "The bachelor hurried across the ice," we must first segment the statement into its syntactical parts—subject and verb phrase. We then generate associations to the words in these segments, and finally we select associations at the base of each association tree that "go together" correctly. This entire process takes place swiftly and unconsciously, but we can partially objectify it by studying language in which it has gone wrong.

Pathological Meaning Structures

Consider the following samples of schizophrenic speech:

> It is hard to speak with a language which has an idiom of opposition. I mean insofar as there are so many bulwarks in historical content representative of a, the revolutionary victory won over an English prosidium.*
> It's made this country great in its self-containment. It might be of interest but it's hard to understand what I mean through a nonutilization of English grammar books. A small faction usually arises to call themselves leaders, forever after apologizes for it, who oppose learning. I don't know whether that's wholly correct or not, but Jimmy Cagney in one of his movies specified the fact that people who come up from the depths usually have a right to authority. The depths of the Anglo-Saxon language has no use for anything that is nonutilized, that is nonutility. What I mean is that progress is foolish when you consider the fact that through language and leadership you can augment the process of future generations being of foreign parentage. (Laffal, 1965, p. 132)

> I fancy very much some fruit, oranges, apples, bananas. I want fancy cakes . . . rock cakes, bread pudding jam tarts, doenuts chocolate-eclairs, I would like a pot of honey. I would like some sandwiches of real butter. Ginger bread I like ginger biscuits fancy biscuits ginger breads. I want. . . . I trust you will have me home, very soon. I hope all is well at home, how is Father getting on. Never mind, there is hope, heaven will come, time heals all wounds, Rise again Glorious Greece and come The Hindoo Heavens,

---

*The neologism *prosidium* may be a combination of the words *prose idiom* and *presidium,* which would combine the patient's preoccupations with language and with government.

The Indians Heavens The Dear old times will come back. (Critchley, 1964a, p. 361)

Washpots prizebloom capacities—turning out—replaced by the head patterns my own capacities—I was not very kind to them. Q. C. Washpots under-patterned against—bred to pattern. Animal sequestration capacities and animal sequestired capacities under leash—and animal secretions. Q. C. (Critchley, 1964a, p. 361)

The three examples, quoted from three different patients, show a progressive loss of meaning. The disorder in the first case is extremely subtle. All college and secondary school teachers have received student work that resembles it! Conscientious teachers may spend a long time trying to comprehend a meaning that seems to be in there somewhere. Asking the student about it later may bring forth the embarrassed admission, "Actually I don't remember what that meant either, but it seemed to make sense at the time!" With a few exceptions, nothing is wrong with the grammar, and the short-range associations seem quite compatible. "Speak with a language" makes sense; so does "idiom of opposition." But putting the two together into "It is hard to speak with a language which has an idiom of opposition" does not quite make sense. (That may have been what the patient found "hard" about it; perhaps he was trying to say that it is hard to say something and not reveal something about yourself at the same time. But that interpretation may result from *our* meaning skills, not the patient's.) This level of schizophrenic disorder illustrates a failure of component 3 above: an inability to select meanings that go together to make a longer-range sentence meaning.

The second example shows a more severe loss of longer-range sentential associations. The patient is simply stringing together short-term associations. Complex syntactical ability is absent. Both the first and the third component are weak; only the second one remains strong. The third example reveals the extent of the "word salad" that may result when all three components are almost destroyed: no grammar, a poverty of associations, and a complete inability to relate them properly. When all three processes are damaged, comprehension is nonexistent. Interestingly, thought also seems to be nonexistent. In the first two cases, some thinking appears to be occurring, although it does not flow normally. But in the third case, no thought at all could be said to exist.

The relation between language and thought is well illustrated by such disorders. In the next chapter, we will pursue this relation further, for as Vygotsky has said:

The relation of thought to word is not a thing but a process, a continual movement back and forth from thought to word and from word to thought. In that process the relation of thought to word undergoes changes which themselves may be regarded as development. . . . Thought is not merely expressed in words; it comes into existence through them. (Vygotsky, 1962, p. 125)

Chapter 19   LANGUAGE AND COGNITION

As discussed in Part I, language is a critically important way of handling information. We can represent our world by actions and images to only a limited extent. In order to represent it flexibly and powerfully, we must have symbols for it—and language provides these symbols.

Exactly how this symbolic representational system works is still largely a mystery. We know a bit here and a bit there, but most of this information (like most psychological information of any sort) can be put together in only a tentative way. In the first section below, we will take up the general topics of verbal mediation and inner speech, processes that are known to be correlated with problem-solving skills. In the two following sections, we will explore some special aspects of these general processes: the role of grammatical skills in mediating thought and the role of cultural influences on the use of language. We will also look closely at some experimental studies that have illuminated the effects of various kinds of verbal tutoring on IQ. Finally, we will take a look at the application of some of these principles in the classroom.

IMPLICIT AND EXPLICIT SPEECH

In Parts I and II, we considered several examples of the fact that speech may sometimes be used as a tool for accelerating problem-solving ability. In the Fisher experiment, teaching 2-year-olds labels for things they were feeling (with their hands) helped them recognize shapes. In the Gagné and Brown experiment, just talking aloud helped subjects discover a complex rule.

In a study by Tracy and Howard Kendler (1967), children learned to put a glass marble into a slot to get a steel marble, and separately learned to put a steel marble into a slot to get a candy. The question of main interest to the Kendlers was this: If we give a child only a glass marble and tell him to get himself a candy, what will he do? As adults, we would make the obvious inference. But 5-year-olds were at a loss.

The Kendlers hypothesized that the children failed to make the connection between the two situations because the stimulus materials and the outcomes were different. They decided to teach the children the common verbal labels "glass marble" and "steel marble" to see if that helped. It did. Children who practiced saying "glass marble" and "steel marble" as they practiced the original responses (getting a steel marble with the glass one, and getting a candy with the steel marble) were better able to use the two responses in combination.

Such experiments can be described generally as examples of the way in which a higher-order conceptual system, once taught to subjects, may make it possible for them to do a kind of thinking they could not otherwise do. One technical term for this helping process is *verbal mediation*.

Mediators and Signals

The notion of verbal mediation goes back historically to the days of John B. Watson and the early versions of behaviorism. Watson had the problem (as Skinner still does) of accounting for the fact that invisible thinking processes seem to be going on inside a person who is expressing no responsive behavior. One elegant way of solving (or sidestepping?) this problem is to argue as follows: Even though the individual is not responding in an overt way, he may be responding in a *covert* way. He may be making tiny vocal responses—perhaps so tiny they could not even be called silent speech. But those little vocal responses could constitute a "chain of command" that carries the individual from a stimulus to a response—that is, carries him from observation of a flame in the attic window to the cry "Fire!" or from the reading of an algebra problem to the exclamation "$\sqrt{-2}$!" several minutes later.

Neurologically, verbal mediation may be conceptualized as a cognitive process involving the speech area. Russian scientists consider such processes to make up the *second signal system* (Berlyne, 1963).

The *first signal system* refers to stimuli like bells, lights, or pinches. The second signal system permits "signals of signals"—the word *bell* may come to evoke the same response as the sound of the bell itself. The word *light* may come to function as a signal of a light signal. Russian psychologists have devised many experiments that show (they think) how this second system operates. For example, an experimenter might squirt cranberry juice into a subject's mouth when a signal occurs. Pretty soon, of course, the signal alone would cause the salivation the cranberry juice causes, even when the cranberry juice was no longer squirted. This technique (called classical conditioning, as you know from Chapter 10) can be used to study the second signal system. The cranberry juice might be squirted in conjunction with the word *correct*. After the word was thoroughly conditioned, the subject might hear a statement like, "The doctor cures sick people." Because that is a correct statement, the subject would salivate. If he heard the statement "At night the sun shines," he would not salivate. This might strike you as a peculiar way of studying higher mental processes, but how else could we show the existence of unconscious verbal reflexes?

Mediation vs. Production Deficiencies We need not limit our definition of verbal mediation to unconscious reflexes, but whether or not we do, physical development seems to play an important role. The Soviet investigations of the second signal system and American investigations of verbal mediation have both led to the discovery of an age factor in these processes. Children under the age of 6 may have difficulties with verbal mediation, when compared to older children. That is, they may not spontaneously use their own verbal abilities in problem solving or learning to the extent that older children do. Further, it may be especially difficult for younger children to learn verbal skills (like labeling).

You might well wonder whether this means younger children lack verbal mediation ability (neurologically speaking), or awareness of the fact that their verbal abilities are relevant to what they are doing. Certainly, neurological growth is a factor; but relevance is also a factor.

Flavell and his associates have been exploring this question. They have distinguished between *mediational* deficiency and *production* deficiency, which would imply a failure to produce appropriate verbal mediators when needed. In his first experiment, Flavell found that kindergarteners did not spontaneously use *naming* and *verbal rehearsal* to the extent that third-graders did in a simple picture recall task:

> The failure might have reflected an immaturity that was specifically linguistic in nature. . . . According to this line of explanation, there is more to language development than just a gradual mastery of its phonology, morphology, and syntax. The child who "has" a language, in the sense of having acquired such mastery, may still not know exactly when and where to use what he has, in rather the same way that an individual may "have" a concept or cognitive rule and yet not think to apply it on every appropriate occasion. . . . Thus, the genesis of language in its broadest sense may partly entail a progressive "linguification" of more and more situations. Initially, only a limited number of behavioral contexts call forth speech activity, but this number gradually increases as development proceeds. (Flavell, Beach, and Chinsky, 1966, pp. 296–297)

If this production deficiency hypothesis is true, we can see immediately why language tutorials might lead to improved problem-solving abilities. General practice on language might assist children to apply their language to new situations. Why not teach nonmediating children to use verbal mediators directly? Keeney, Cannizzo, and Flavell (1967) did exactly that.

In a simple picture recall task, the experimenters distinguished first-grade children who spontaneously verbally rehearsed the pictures from children who did not, and then taught the latter group to verbally rehearse. The children whispered the names of the pictures over and over again during a brief delay period (from 5 to 15 seconds). Originally, the nonproducers were not successful recallers. After rehearsal training, they were every bit as good as the children who spontaneously rehearsed the pictures. In a later test, all the children were given an opportunity to stop rehearsing if they wanted to. None of the spontaneous verbal rehearsers stopped, but all the experimentally trained rehearsers did—that is, the original nonmediators reverted to their old nonmediating habits. The brief training periods of most psychological experiments may not be sufficient to produce long-standing verbal mediation habits. A wider variety of experiences over a longer time period is undoubtedly necessary.

Vygotsky's Theory of Social, Egocentric, and Inner Speech

A major theory of the growth of verbal mediation skills has been developed by one of Luria's colleagues—Lev Semenovich Vygotsky—who died early in a promising career. Vygotsky's main contribution was a little book called *Thought and Language* (1962), which detailed his theory of the development of *inner* speech. According to Vygotsky, children learn how to talk about problems and solutions in a social context. As they begin to apply this speech spontaneously to their own problems, they talk to themselves aloud; this *egocentric* speech appears clearly around the age of 3. As children grow older, their egocentric speech disappears. Vygotsky believed that it turns into inner speech:

> Our experimental results indicate that the function of egocentric speech is similar to that of inner speech: it does not merely accompany the child's activity; it serves mental orientation, conscious understanding; it helps in overcoming difficulties; it is speech for oneself, intimately and usefully connected with the child's thinking.
>
> . . .
>
> . . . Between three and seven years . . . its vocalization becomes unnecessary. . . . In the end it separates itself entirely from speech for others . . . and thus appears to die out.
>
> But this is only an illusion. . . . [To say] that this kind of speech is dying out is like saying that the child stops counting when he ceases to use his fingers and starts adding in his head. . . . The decreasing vocalization of egocentric speech denotes a developing abstraction from sound, the child's new faculty to "think words" instead of pronouncing them. (Vygotsky, 1966, pp. 133–135)

In a major test of Vygotsky's hypothesis, Kohlberg and his colleagues (Kohlberg, Yaeger, and Hjertholm, 1968) monitored the speech of 112 middle-class children between the ages of 4 and 10. The experimental question was whether or not talking to oneself (egocentric speech) was systematically related to problem-solving ability and to age. As a measure of problem-solving ability, Kohlberg used both the Stanford-Binet IQ test and some Piagetian measures of operational development such as conservation tests.

Figure 19.1 shows Kohlberg's trend estimates for the development and decline of egocentric speech in bright and average children. The 4-year-old bright children were at their peak of egocentric speech, which declined from that age on. The average children did not peak until about the age of 7. From that time on, their egocentric speech also disappeared.

Kohlberg also found, as Vygotsky maintained, that there was a positive correlation between egocentric speech and *social* speech—that is, children who talked more to other people also talked more to themselves. This provides us with our most important clue to the training of verbal mediation abilities: Explicit verbal exchanges may be a way of developing verbal mediation skills, which can then "go inside" and become silent.

Inner Tutorials
We saw in Figure 17.1 that psycholinguists believe children engage in an active, inductive process of language learning—they sample the language around them and test their own hypotheses about what the rules of the language actually are. If their world is a loving and attentive one, they are likely to hear a great deal of language and to receive helpful feedback. The language and the feedback systems thereby grow rich and intricate.

If Vygotsky's theory is correct, both the language system and the social feedback system may "go inside." That is, the child may learn to internalize both his language and the tutorial relationship that he has with a parent, friend, or teacher. When the whole system has "gone inside," the child may have a substantial verbal mediating system that will carry him solidly through the problem-solving requirements of his school and his world. This process is schematized in Figure 19.2.

Although most of the interest in language development has naturally focused upon children, the same developmental processes may continue to

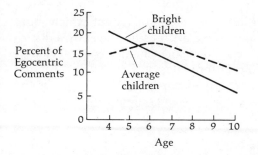

Figure 19.1 Age trends in the development and decline of egocentric speech among bright and average children. (Kohlberg, Yaeger, and Hiertholm, 1968, p. 718)

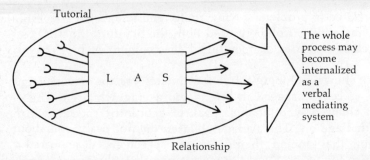

Figure 19.2 The Language Acquisition System (LAS) and the tutorial process as a verbal mediation system.

operate throughout life. When we move into an area about which we know little (say, nuclear physics), we must develop new verbal mediating systems for handling problems in that area—even mathematical problems. The most efficient way of developing such systems is probably a tutorial relationship, wherein we hear many examples of the kinds of problems facing us and talk them through to solution with our tutor. During such a process, we are actually formulating and testing many hypotheses about the nature of the field and about the nature of our systems for comprehending it. As the need for the tutor diminishes, we may still talk to ourselves for a while, very much as we used to talk to the tutor. We may even tell ourselves what the tutor used to tell us. Eventually, this phase of egocentric speech also passes, and the problem-solving process becomes quicker and more silent. We will have developed and internalized a new mediating system through the use of language.

This general picture of language and cognition is subject to many special variations, of which two in particular are of importance to teachers: (1) The effects that nonstandard language (such as dialects) may have on the development of verbal mediating systems and (2) the effects that particular social relationships (what we might call *tutorial biases*) might have on such development. We will consider each problem in turn.

THE LANGUAGE OF THOUGHT

The Bereiter-Engelmann language teaching program (about which more will be said shortly) is actually a special case of a position held by a distinguished scholar of anthropology and linguistics, Benjamin Lee Whorf. With some help from another famous anthropologist, Edward Sapir, under whom he studied in the late 1930s, Whorf developed what is known as the *linguistic relativity hypothesis.* It is a complex and subtle hypothesis, and we can best approach it by an example.

Whorf's Theory of Linguistic Relativity
As noted earlier in the experiment by Brown, children soon learn distinctions between mass nouns and count nouns. They can even apply their

knowledge of this distinction to nonsense terms and materials. But we were speaking of American children, Boston variety. Suppose we were to use American children, Hopi Indian variety? In this case, the experiment might turn out quite differently, for the Hopi language does not contain grammatical distinctions of exactly these sorts.

In the Hopi system, all nouns are individualized. They may be plural instead of singular (in which case a plural verb form is used with them). No nouns are really mass nouns, in the English sense. The Hopi word *water* does not mean a relatively formless substance that might take different forms, as in English statements like "a glass of water," "a drop of water," "a drink of water," and so forth. For a Hopi child, *kēyi* refers to water-in-the-shape-of-a-container (like a bottle or a glass), and *pāhe* refers to water-in-an-uncontained-form (like an ocean or a waterfall). The form or shape of the mass substance is implicit in its name. According to the linguistic relativity hypothesis, Hopi children would therefore have difficulty perceiving the distinction between mass nouns (which are independent of any form) and count nouns (which are not).

This has some important philosophical implications. The Hopi language does not provide for distinctions between *form* and *substance* the way the English language does. We have ways of combining form names (like *piece, drop, slice,* and *bit*) with substance names (like *bread, water, meat,* and *dirt*). Perhaps we perceive distinctions between form and substance only because our language contains such distinctions. That would be a special case of the linguistic relativity hypothesis, which generally asserts that *thought is shaped by the form of the language used for thinking.*

> The world is . . . a kaleidoscopic flux of impressions which has to be organized by our minds—and this means largely by the linguistic systems in our minds. We cut nature up, organize it into concepts, and ascribe significances as we do, largely because we are parties to an agreement to organize it in this way—an agreement that holds throughout our speech community and is codified in the patterns of our language. The agreement is, of course, an implicit and unstated one, BUT ITS TERMS ARE ABSOLUTELY OBLIGATORY. . . . No individual is free to describe nature with absolute impartiality but is constrained to certain modes of interpretation even while he thinks himself most free. (Whorf, 1956, pp. 212–214)

A Test of Whorf's Theory Brown and Lenneberg (1954) tried to test Whorf's hypothesis by the following experiment: They presented a group of college students with a large number of color chips and asked them to call out the name of the color as quickly as possible. Some colors were harder to name than others, and Brown described these as having *low codability*. The easily named colors were said to have *high codability*. A second group of subjects was then asked to remember the various colors by looking at a chip and finding it again on a large display board. As predicted, subjects had difficulty remembering (or recognizing) colors of low codability. Lenneberg and another colleague later used the same chips with a group of Zuni Indians, whose language does not contain different words for red and yellow. The Zunis frequently confused the red and yellow chips—something that was never done by the English-speaking subjects. A group of Zunis who spoke both Zuni and English also made red and yellow errors—not as many as the pure Zuni-speaking group did, but more than the English speakers did. Does this prove that our perception of nature is structured by our language?

Perhaps it would if there were other experiments of this type. But not many psychologists (or psycholinguists) have been interested in following up Whorf's hypothesis. Psychologists have been more interested in the effects of other psychological factors on behavior, and psycholinguists have been concentrating on the discovery of transformational rules.

Because basic grammatical relations are common to all languages, the differences that Whorf was talking about would occur in what we now call surface language forms. The distinction between the basic and surface features of language was made long after Whorf's death, but it might not have surprised him.

> The tremendous importance of language cannot, in my opinion, be taken to mean necessarily that nothing is back of it. . . . My own studies suggest to me that language . . . is in some sense a superficial embroidery upon deeper processes of consciousness, which are necessary before any communication, signaling, or symbolism whatsoever can occur. . . . (Whorf, 1956, p. 239)

Whorf and Piaget Whorf's findings suggest that some of the basic structures Piaget believes to be independent of language—such as the concept of time—may also be affected by linguistic systems.

In English, Whorf says, we make the abstract noun *time* in the same way that we make mass nouns—by dropping qualifiers such as "a period of" (time). We turn the particular "piece of bread" into the abstract *bread* by the same process. Time, then, is a countable sort of thing for us: we add units of time together and handle time generally in the same way we handle concrete and abstract nouns.

For the Hopi, however, *time* is more like an adverb than a noun. The Hopi does not say "in the morning," he says the Hopi equivalent of "morningly," or "when the morning phase is occurring." It suggests that the Hopi may remain in what Piaget calls a concrete operational stage of time conception. Time never becomes independent of the particular conditions of its experience—what Piaget calls "lived time." If Whorf's hypothesis is right, then only the English-speaking child could reasonably be expected to develop the formal operational concept of time, wherein time becomes independent of physical experience.

An Example Concerning Time Whorf (who was not familiar with Piaget's work, incidentally) believed that such differences in time language led to clear differences in behavior between Hopi- and English-speaking peoples. For the Hopi, the future existed only as it was contained in the present. A Hopi planner works within the present and lets the future take care of itself.

> One might say that Hopi society understands our proverb "Well begun is half done," but not our "Tomorrow is another day." This may explain much in Hopi character. . . . To us, for whom time is a motion on a space, unvarying repetition seems to scatter its force along a row of units of that space, and be wasted. To the Hopi, for whom time is not a motion but a "getting later" of everything that has ever been done, unvarying repetition is not wasted but accumulated. It is storing up an invisible change that holds over into later events. (Whorf, 1956, pp. 148–151)

One can easily imagine the differences in personality and motivation that such different time conceptions might produce.

> OUR [English] objectified time puts before imagination something like a ribbon or scroll marked off into equal blank spaces, suggesting that each be filled with an entry. Writing has no doubt helped. . . . We [have] for instance:
> 1. Records, diaries, bookkeeping, accounting, mathematics as stimulated by accounting.
> 2. Interest in exact sequence, dating, calendars, chronology, clocks, time wages, time graphs, time as used in physics.
> 3. Annals, histories, the historical attitude, . . . archeology, . . . classicism, romanticism.
> Just as we conceive our objectified time as extending in the future in the same way that it extends in the past, so we set down our estimates of the future . . . producing programs, schedules, budgets, . . . time wages, . . . rent, credit, interest, depreciation charges, and insurance premiums. No doubt this vast system, once built, would continue to run under any sort of linguistic treatment of time; but that it should have been built at all . . . is a fact decidedly in consonance with the patterns of the [Anglo-European] languages. (Whorf, 1956, pp. 153–154)

The patterns of what Whorf would call OUR language may (according to the linguistic relativity hypothesis) contain many subtle processes for shaping OUR thought. If this were true, then it would constitute a strong argument for altering the language forms of children who do not speak OUR language—that is, who do not speak standard English—and who therefore fail to achieve in OUR society.

Language and Cultural Deficiency

The problem of language deficiency is uppermost in programs of the Head Start variety. Baratz (1968) has reviewed (somewhat unwillingly) the literature supporting the view that children from disadvantaged areas are deficient in both language and the cognitive skills that a good language implies. Cazden (1966) has provided a more extensive review. Pedagogically, the leaders of this viewpoint are probably Bereiter and Engelmann (1966), since they have the most highly structured and well-publicized program for intensive correction of language deficiencies. Let us consider first the types of linguistic defects Bereiter-Engelmann believe to be true of the disadvantaged child. The following is a description written by one of their researchers:

> (a) He omits articles, prepositions, conjunctions, and short verbs from statements. For "This is a ball," he will say, "Dis ball." . . .
>
> (b) He does not understand the function of *not* in a sentence. An example: a child is presented with three objects and is asked to point to the cup, the spoon and the block. He does this and is then asked to point to "something that is not a cup." He points to the cup. . . .
>
> (c) He cannot produce plural statements correctly and cannot perform the actions implied by plural statements. . . . [In response to the instruction] "Find the balls that are big," all the children tested pointed to only one of the three big balls in the picture. . . .
>
> (d) He cannot use simple tenses to describe past, present, and future action. . . .
>
> (e) He is able to use *he* and *she* correctly for male and female figures but cannot use the pronoun *it* to refer to an inanimate object. . . . He misuses object pronouns, "Her done it" and "Him sit here" are common substitutions.
>
> (f) He does not understand many of the common prepositions and conjunctions. For example, over half of the children missed an item requiring them to point to an object *next to* a given object; fewer than half could handle a *between* task correctly. . . .
>
> (g) He can often perform a direction but is not able to describe what he has done. When asked to put a ball in the cup, he does so; when asked to tell what he has done, he might say, "Cup," "Ball the cup" or even "Cup in ball."
>
> (h) He does not realize that two or more words can describe one object. To him a boy is a boy, and it is not possible also to call him a person. Once he has learned to identify *pig,* it is difficult to teach him that the pig is also an animal. After he learned that a block is big, he has trouble accepting that the same block can also be described as red, and that one can say, "This block is big and red."
>
> Whether these language characteristics represent a language that is a valid but different language from standard English or whether they represent a substandard English dialect, incapable of being used for serious cognition, need not be argued here. What is evident is that such characteristics are not those of the language used in the public school. (Osborn, 1968, pp. 37–38)

Parenthetically, one might ask, "Then why not teach disadvantaged children in the language they *do* speak?" Although that seems a reasonable solution, there are at least two studies which show that comprehension may not be as great when disadvantaged children are taught in their familiar dialect as when they are taught in standard English—even when the teacher is the same person.

Dialects and Teaching Eisenberg and his colleagues (1968) recorded educated and uneducated speakers reading lists of familiar one-syllable words. The children who listened to these tapes were highly motivated—they had the goal of winning $50 in play money and a special toy for their class. They simply reported the words they heard the taped speakers say. Some of the children were white, some were black; some were lower-class, and some were middle-class. *All the children understood the educated speakers better—even the children of lower-class, uneducated parents.* The entire study was replicated with new subjects, and the same results emerged.

Stern and Keislar (1968) had a black actress record a series of lessons (on undersea animals) for Head Start children. These were daily lessons lasting about 11 minutes each for seven days. At the end of the period, the children were tested for comprehension of the materials. Half the children heard the lessons as recorded in standard English; the other half heard the lessons as recorded in their own dialect. *The dialect lessons were not as well comprehended:* The children who received them had an average test score of 18. The children who heard the lessons in standard English had an average test score of 22. (The tests were given in both standard English and dialect.)

It is not clear that all kinds of information would be better understood in standard English. These two experiments were limited to the sort of formal language one finds in school. As Osborn points out, this is the language young children must learn to understand if they are going to succeed in school:

> The following examples from teacher's manuals are for lessons that are to be taught the first days of school in first-grade classes: "Lead the group in a discussion about relative size by asking questions such as 'Are the two big cars the same size? Are the two little cars the same size? Is the first car in the row bigger than the second?'" . . .
>
> In order for the child to have even the faintest chance to follow these instructions, he must as a bare minimum understand such key words as *two, big, same, little, first, row, bigger, second, last, which.* . . .
>
> . . . To teach the child to function in the language used in the above examples is to require profound change in the child's linguistic and cognitive behavior. It is our position that if this is to be accomplished in the short period of time the child will spend in kindergarten or preschool class, there must be a rigorous program of highly organized and structured direct language instruction. (Osborn, 1968, pp. 38–39)

In the Bereiter-Engelmann language program, the children sit in groups of five with a teacher, practicing language for 20 minutes a day. They drill identity statements, negative statements, plurals, prepositions, conjunctions, and so forth, in a very systematic way—that is, the teacher follows a strict program. Sometimes the children speak in unison, and sometimes they speak individually. The teacher praises and corrects in a friendly but firm manner.

Does this kind of training work? Do these children become better able to *think?*

Language Training and IQ

If we measure thinking ability by using the Stanford-Binet IQ test (and that is a reasonable way to measure it under some conditions; see Chapter

9), then according to Osborn (1968), tutorial drill by the Bereiter-Engel-mann method improves thinking. In 1969, three groups of children had been in the Bereiter-Engelmann program for two years. Group I achieved a 10-point IQ gain (over the two-year period), from a mean of 95 to a mean of 105. Group II made a mean gain of 25 IQ points—from a mean of 95 to a mean of 120. Group III made a gain of 12 points, from a mean of 91 to a mean of 103. In addition, all groups were one or two years ahead in reading, arithmetic, and spelling on standard achievement tests. Of course, many other things had happened to the children during those training years. How do we know that the language training program was substantially responsible for the improved IQ? In particular, the children were also receiving training in reading, arithmetic, and spelling in special tutorial sessions devoted to those subjects. Perhaps the training in the par-ticular subject skills was really training in reasoning; and perhaps the rea-soning training produced the improvement in both IQ and language.

This brings up the more general question of the influence of cultural intention on language. Perhaps the linguistic relativity hypothesis—and the modified forms of it represented by Bereiter-Engelmann—are over-looking an alternative view: Perhaps a different mode of thinking pro-duces a different use of language, instead of the other way around.

THE INFLUENCE OF CULTURAL INTENTION

We noted earlier that a major influence on Whorf's thinking was Edward Sapir, an anthropologist who specialized in the study of language. One can read in Sapir's writings some of the seeds of Whorf's linguistic rela-tivity hypothesis (see, for example, Sapir's paper called "The Grammarian and his Language," reprinted in 1960, some of which is quoted below). But Sapir's broad study of languages did not lead him to conclude that cultural (or racial) distinctions of any sort could reliably be attributed to language. There are many examples of similar cultures (among Indian tribes, for example) that have quite dissimilar languages. And of course there are examples of dissimilar cultures that speak similar languages (among the English-speaking peoples, for example). Sapir believed any language was so constructed that it could respond to the intentions of any speaker. And he believed one language system could be translated into another—though not without changing a "feeling of orientation" toward the world.

Sapir also believed that *certain language forms might be available in a language long before the ideas they contained were consciously recognized by the speakers of the language.* The concept of causation (another of Piaget's basics), for example, may be expressed quite unconsciously in the language of primitive societies that have not yet developed formal, scientific concepts of causality. In another of Sapir's examples:

> It would be absurd to say that Kant's *Critique of Pure Reason* could be rendered forthwith into the unfamiliar accents of Eskimo or Hottentot,

and yet it would be absurd in but a secondary degree. What is really meant is that the culture of these primitive folk has not advanced to the point where it is of interest to them to form abstract conceptions of a philosophical order. But it is not absurd to say that there is nothing in the formal peculiarities of Hottentot or of Eskimo which would obscure the clarity or hide the depth of Kant's thought—indeed, it may be suspected that the highly synthetic and periodic structure of Eskimo would more easily bear the weight of Kant's terminology than his native German. . . . All languages are set to do all the symbolic and expressive work that language is good for, either actually or potentially. (Sapir, 1960, p. 444)

Dialects and Social Meaning

Modern sociolinguists like William Stewart (1967a, 1967b, 1968) take sharp issue with the implication that the dialects of disadvantaged children from black ghettos or Appalachia structurally prevent good, clear, logical thinking. On the contrary, Stewart says, the dialect may code delicate meanings that standard English cannot make.

> Many speakers of non-standard American Negro dialects make a grammatical and semantic distinction by means of be, illustrated by such constructions as *he busy* "He is busy (momentarily)" or *he workin'* "he is working (right now)" as opposed to *he be busy* "he is (habitually) busy" or *he be workin'* "he is working (steadily)," which the grammar of standard English is unable to make. (Stewart, 1967a, p. 4)

Mountain dialect speakers make a similar (but not identical) distinction by means of the prefix *a-*.

> This prefix shows that the action of the verb is indefinite in space or time, while its absence implies that the action is immediate in space or time. Thus, *he's a-workin'* in Mountain speech means either that the subject has a steady job, or that he is away (out of sight, for example) working somewhere. On the other hand, *he's workin'* in Mountain speech means that the subject is doing a specific task, close by. (Stewart, 1967b)

These examples suggest that one of the major learning problems faced by disadvantaged children may be their *teacher's* ignorance:

> Although English teachers, speech therapists and other language-oriented educators are now dedicating themselves more than ever to the task of helping disadvantaged children—and especially disadvantaged Negro children—acquire proficiency in standard English, very few of these dedicated professionals have demonstrated any real understanding of the language characteristics of the communities from which these children come. For their part, teachers of English to Spanish-speaking Mexican, Puerto Rican or Cuban children know that an understanding of the structure of Spanish will give insights into the problem which such children have with English, and these teachers would be shocked by any suggestion that a comparative approach to the language of the school and the language of the child is unnecessary. In contrast, teachers of English to disadvantaged Negro children have generally remained aloof from the serious study of non-standard Negro dialect.
> This lack of interest . . . is in large part the product of a normative view of language which has long been the mainstay of traditional teacher

training. Either overtly or by implication, the teacher-to-be is taught that the kind of usage which is indicated in grammar books, dictionaries and style manuals (and which is presumably followed by educated speakers and writers) represents a maximum of structural neatness, communicative efficiency, esthetic taste and logical clarity. Once this normative view has been inculcated in the prospective teacher . . . then the teacher will quite naturally regard departures from the norms of standard English as departures from structure, clarity, taste, and even logic itself. (Stewart, 1968, p. 4)

Note that Stewart does not recommend that standard English *not* be taught to disadvantaged children. On the contrary, he considers such teaching essential and has devoted much professional time to research in this area. Stewart's point is simply that the dialects spoken by disadvantaged children are fully adequate to logical thinking and to academic learning—*provided* the children can understand what is being said to them in the classroom and what is being expected of them academically. The cultural differences between lower-class and middle-class children may (in Stewart's view) cause at least as much learning difficulty as the language differences do.

Bernstein's Theory of Restricted Language
A British sociologist, Basil Bernstein (1958, 1961), has put forth a line of argument that is being taken seriously by a number of American educators (although not by Stewart). Although Bernstein did not preface his theory in this fashion, we might relate it to the problem of social induction discussed in Chapter 15. The child who is inductively learning his language is inductively learning the social rules of his society at the same time. He is learning, in fact, a great deal about the social use of language. Bernstein's sociological investigations have revealed, he thinks, that lower-class people use language primarily to confirm and extend social relationships, rather than for logical reasoning. The middle class, Bernstein says, uses language for more logical purposes.

Although Bernstein has said that this cultural use of language is related to the grammatical form of the lower-class dialects, he has presented no real evidence that this is true. In view of Stewart's insistence that lower-class dialects are adequate for all forms of logical reasoning, we will not pursue Bernstein's grammatical opinions, for they would just lead us back to the linguistic relativity hypothesis. Instead, we will examine Bernstein's argument that the social use of language may impair its efficiency for logical thinking.

According to Bernstein, lower-class language is much more intimate, emotional, and restricted than middle-class standard forms. The dialect depends on a fabric of shared meaning for both its emotional and communicative power. Think, for example, of your private language with an intimate—each gesture, each intonation, is so quickly understood that it does not have to be spelled out.

Tolstoy's Love Scene One charming example is found in Tolstoy's love scene between Kitty and Levin.

> "I have long wished to ask you something."
> "Please do."
> "This," he said, and wrote the initial letters: *W y a: i c n b, d y m t o n.* These letters meant, "When you answered: *it can not be,* did you mean then or never?" It seemed impossible that she would be able to understand the complicated sentence.
> "I understand," she said, blushing.
> "What word is that?" he asked, pointing to the *n* which stood for *never.*
> "The word is *never,*" she said, "but that is not true."
> He quickly erased what he had written, handed her the chalk, and rose. She wrote: *I c n a o t.*
> His face brightened suddenly: he had understood. It meant: "I could not answer otherwise then."
> She wrote the initial letters: *s t y m f a f w h.* This meant: "So that you might forget and forgive what happened."
> He seized the chalk with tense, trembling fingers, broke it, and wrote the initial letters of the following: "I have nothing to forget and forgive. I never ceased loving you."
> "I understand," she whispered. (Tolstoy, *Anna Karenina*)

An extremely restricted verbal exchange becomes possible because meaning is communicated in other ways. In fact, the communication *depends* on these other ways. A common background of experience and emotion must be shared by the speakers, or communication will not happen at all.

A Harlem Conversation As in the case of Kitty and Levin, the major function of a private language may be to signal the existence of emotional and social bonds. The present emphasis upon "soul talk" in black communities may have this function. In the following quotation, Malcolm X clearly signals his contempt for a would-be black leader who was incapable of speaking the language of the ghetto.

> There was an example of this that always flew to my mind every time I heard some of the "big name" Negro "leaders" declaring they "spoke for" the ghetto black people.
> After a Harlem street rally, one of these downtown "leaders" and I were talking when we were approached by a Harlem hustler. . . . He said to me, approximately, "Hey, baby! I dig you holding this all-originals scene at the track . . . I'm going to lay a vine under the Jew's balls for a dime — got to give you a play . . . Got the shorts out here trying to scuffle up on some bread . . . Well, my man, I'll get on, got to go peck a little, and cop me some z's." And the hustler went on up Seventh Avenue.
> I would never have given it another thought, except that this downtown "leader" was standing, staring after that hustler, looking as if he'd just heard Sanskrit. He asked me what had been said, and I told him. The hustler had said he was aware that the Muslims were holding an all-black bazaar at Rockland Palace, which is primarily a dancehall. The hustler in-

tended to pawn a suit for ten dollars to attend and patronize the bazaar. He had very little money but he was trying hard to make some. He was going to eat, then he would get some sleep. (*The Autobiography of Malcolm X*, p. 310)

A Summary of Bernstein's Principles If the purpose of a private language is to signal the existence of a shared emotional and sociocultural bond, will it restrict the thinking of the individuals who speak it? Bernstein believes that it may and offers the following reasons:

1. The private language orients the speaker toward group norms and principles, rather than toward the logic of the communication. The speaker's line of reasoning is of less importance than his social relationships and the social authorities. To challenge the language is to challenge the group, perhaps at one's peril.

2. Such an orientation may restrict the methods of verbally organizing information and concepts.

3. It may reduce intellectual curiosity and courage.

4. It may limit vocabulary development and produce a high degree of redundancy and repetition.

5. It may focus attention on concrete aspects of a situation ("the Jew's balls," for example), rather than on the abstract aspects.

6. It may encourage short attention spans, because meaning results not from a long line of reasoning, but from brief references.

7. It may discourage the individual from searching for ways of organizing and expressing his *unique* experiences.

8. It may reduce the length and complexity of completed thoughts.

9. It may retard the development of verbal planning skills and lead to poorly organized and dislocated thinking. Thoughts may be strung together like beads on a frame, rather than following a preplanned sequence.

Classroom Implications

All told, a private language may be said to severely restrict the range of thinking possibilities open to the speaker. Bernstein further describes the distressing plight of the private-language speaker in the formal-language (school) situation:

> It can be seen that attempts to change the system of spoken language of children from certain environments will meet with great resistance, passive and active. It is an attempt to change a pattern of learning, a system of orientation, which language originally elicited and progressively reinforced. To ask the pupil to use language differently, to qualify verbally his individual experience, to expand his vocabulary, to increase the length of his verbal planning function, to generalize, to be sensitive to . . . implications . . . these requests when made to a [private] language user are very different from when they are made to a formal language user. For the latter [the middle-class child] it is a situation of linguistic *development*, while for the former it is one of linguistic *change*. . . . The [private] lan-

guage speaker is called upon to make responses to which he is neither oriented nor sensitized. His natural responses are unacceptable. It is a bewildering, perplexing, isolated, and utterly defenseless position which ensures almost certain failure unless the teacher is very sensitive to the child's fundamental predicament. (Bernstein, 1961)

Marion Blank's Program

Sensitivity to the predicament would lead a good teacher to try to help a disadvantaged child develop more abstract language functions. One researcher who has been involved in such a teaching program is Marion Blank. She and her co-workers have been interested in teaching Head Start children to use language in a logical, abstract manner (as Bernstein would recommend). Whether or not the children used correct grammatical forms or articulated them clearly was not the major issue. Any form of speech would do, as long as it was being used to *think, reflect,* and *make inferences,* not just to describe immediate experience.

> The first goal of the teaching was to have the child recognize that information relevant to his world was not immediately evident but could be and *had* to be sought from his previous experience. Thus he was taught to question, to probe, to investigate. For example, the teacher put on her coat at the end of a session. The child said, "Why are you going home?" The teacher replied, "How do you know I am going home?" to which the child said, "You're not going home?" This response meant that the child had dropped any attempt at reasoning. . . . To encourage the child to pursue the matter, the teacher said, "I *am* going home, but what makes you think I am going home? When you get ready to go home, what do you do?" The child said, "I get my coat." A discussion then followed to solidify the significance of these observations. Thus Socratic dialogue was employed instead of didactic teaching.
>
> Various teaching methods were devised to achieve these goals. A common denominator of all the methods was that the child was confronted with situations in which the teacher used no gestures; to accomplish the task correctly, the child had to understand and/or use language. Another consistent factor was that the child was led to produce an independent response relevant to a situation created by the teacher and to extend the situation set forth by her. This extension focused on having the child discuss situations which did not exist in front of him at the moment. . . . Some of the major techniques used are described below:
>
> . . .
>
> **Imagery of future events.** . . . The child was required to think through the results of realistically possible but not present courses of action. The child might be first asked to locate a doll that was on the table. After the child completed this correctly, the doll would remain on the table, and the child might be asked, "Where would the doll be if it fell from the table?"
>
> . . .
>
> **Awareness of possessing language.** Frequently young children are only passive recipients of instruction. This deficiency means that they are unaware that they can independently invoke language to help order their world. This weakness can be overcome by techniques such as asking the child to give commands to the teacher. The teacher might say to the child,

"What shall I do with these pencils?" "Now *you* ask *me* to draw something." "Now tell me what the doll should do this afternoon."

   . . .

Common inexpensive objects readily available in the child's environment were the only ones used in the teaching. . . . The materials were used only as points of departure from which the child could discuss increasingly abstract (non-presently-existing) situations which were relevant to the materials. The same materials, when used alone by the child without supervision, might prove useless in terms of the aims of the study—namely, the avoidance of aimless, scattered, stimulus-bound activity. (Blank and Solomon, 1968, pp. 383–385)

Another Assessment of Language Training and IQ

In evaluating the effects of their method on IQ, Blank and Solomon were careful to include a control group. Whereas each member of the experimental group spent 15 to 20 minutes daily in individual tutoring sessions like those described above, each member of the control group spent the same amount of time in individual, untutored play sessions. The teacher was there and was warm and friendly, but did not "initiate or exchange any cognitive interchange" (Blank and Solomon, 1968, p. 385). These sessions continued for four months. Before and after the tutoring period, the children's IQ was tested on the Stanford-Binet.

In the experimental group, the average change in IQ was 14 points—the mean IQ moved from 98 to 112. In the control group, which had no training in the logical and abstract use of language, the mean IQ change was 2 points.

These IQ changes must also be evaluated in conjunction with the dramatic behavioral changes that accompanied these rises. For example, three of the children were so excessively withdrawn that they had not uttered any coherent verbalizations during their entire time in school. . . . Within 1 month after the program was started, all three were speaking clearly, coherently, and appropriately. . . . No comparable changes were noted in [similar] children from the control group. . . .

Even among the children who were relatively well functioning, striking improvements were found. For example, on the Stanford-Binet Test the pretest response of one girl in describing a picture was "a lady, a horse"; the posttest response was, "The mother is trying to catch the dog with the clothes, the dog takes the clothes, and the mother was trying to get it." This response illustrates the growth from simple labeling to a coordinated, sequential story construction. (Blank and Solomon, 1968, pp. 386–388)

It also illustrates the fact that *verbal abilities are a large portion of the intellectual skills measured by standard IQ tests.*

The Role of Teacher Preference

Any kind of language training (Bereiter and Engelmann style, or Blank style) seems to improve IQ as measured on the Binet test. The fact is that at the present time, both tutorial methods seem to work equally well—that is, drilling children in correct grammatical (and logical) statements or requiring them to use language as a vehicle for inductive reasoning. This means, apparently, that a teacher can feel free to choose the method most compatible with goals and personal style.

Many teachers do not find the Bereiter-Engelmann "pressure cooker" (Pines, 1967) method compatible. Some may not find the less structured Blank method compatible. At present, there would seem to be no scientific reason for choosing an incompatible method—that is, for forcing oneself to develop an uncomfortable teaching style. If research eventually proves one method to be superior to the other, then it is time enough to force oneself to change.

One general point does seem clear, however. We must never lose sight of the fact that nonstandard language and nonstandard language functions are not haphazard botches of standard forms. They are distinct, evolving systems of their own that have come into existence through natural inductive processes, just as standard forms have. The existence of this natural system is the teacher's greatest ally, as well as his greatest problem. Changing language, by any method, means changing—in both small and large ways—almost every aspect of thought. The remarkable fact is that this can be accomplished at all.

LANGUAGE IN THE CLASSROOM

Teaching language, or teaching about language (as in poetry), involves the same pedagogical problems as teaching anything else—problems of development, basic systems, motivation, and the use of language itself. This section on psycholinguistics should be relevant to general teaching goals and strategies, including (but not limited to) those of teaching language.

There are, however, certain special questions that do come up when language is discussed—the problem of teaching a foreign language, for example. Should it be taught "naturally," the way language itself develops? And what about the study of literature—does psycholinguistics have any suggestions?

In this short section we will attempt answers to a few of these questions, but any teacher who specializes in language instruction should have been discovering the relevance of psycholinguistic principles to classroom practice from the beginning of Part IV.

Tests of Verbal Skills

In the study of language development, a good teacher inevitably wonders if there are tests that will reveal the extent of a student's language maturity. A second question is whether or not such tests should be used as a standard classroom procedure.

Most aptitude or IQ tests contain sections assessing verbal ability. These will usually include measures of vocabulary, of verbal reasoning ability, and of special verbal classes such as *opposites* or *similes*. In addition, there are an increasing number of preschool tests that measure both language development and the ability to use language in particular ways, like labeling. A number of preschool tests also attempt to discriminate between a child's auditory or aural skills and his speech skills. A teacher who has studied the principles of cognitive psychology should be able to make a fair start at choosing such tests for himself. Guidance counselors or consulting psychologists of several varieties can offer additional advice. As long as the test itself is a good one and the teacher is willing to take on the additional responsibility of scoring and interpreting, there is no reason not to use it. On the contrary, any device for helping teachers become aware of individual differences among their students is all to the good.

Unless the student is a mute preschooler or otherwise unresponsive, however, he will probably reveal his own language abilities quite clearly within the first two weeks of school. His reading, writing, spelling, and composition skills can probably be judged as accurately from standard classroom assignments as from a standardized test. For a good teacher, a test is often a way of confirming what he already knows about a student. It may well be that a teacher—or a group of teachers—could devise special assignments to be administered early in the school year, for the purpose of providing a relatively comprehensive picture of students' language skills. These assignments would be especially valuable if they were related to the final objectives of the course and if they led to special individualized instructional programs. Pedagogical energy should, perhaps, be channeled more in this direction than in the direction of routine administration of commercial tests.

Teaching Grammar/Linguistics
The dissemination of modern psycholinguistic principles into school grammars has taken place with remarkable speed. For example, the *Grammar 1, Grammar 2* series, published by Ginn in 1967, provides excellent coverage at the secondary level of much that has been discussed in this text. Surely there can be no question but that these principles should supplant traditional grammar pedagogy.

Of course, such a change means that many language arts teachers must return to school to bone up on the new grammar. They will join a distinguished army of returnees, teachers studying new math, new science, and new social studies.

All these "new" pedagogies have a common characteristic that is illustrated by the new grammar: emphasis upon matching academic processes to students' natural learning processes. The teaching of biology now tries to capitalize upon a student's natural curiosity and his natural need to classify and organize information. Social studies utilizes students' natural inquiry systems and applies them to historical information. Mathematics begins with a child's natural theory of relationships and patterns (see Part V). The new trend in teaching grammar is similar: bring the student's natural language-learning systems into the classroom, and out in the open, where they can be explored and analyzed.

Teaching a Second Language

A few years ago, Carroll (1966) reviewed studies comparing the new audiolingual methods of teaching a foreign language to the old grammar-translation methods, which emphasize writing and reading. These studies show exactly what one would expect: students who have been trained in an audiolingual method are better on listening-speaking tests of their new language ability than students who have been trained in the old method; students who have been trained in reading and writing are better on grammar-translation tests than students trained in the new audiolingual methods. As Carroll points out, it is comforting to know that students learn what we teach them, but the question "Which method is *best?*" cannot be answered in any absolute sense. It must be rephrased, "Best for *what?* Listening and speaking? Or reading and writing translations?" Most significantly, Carroll adds:

> The one area of psychological research in grammar that I believe may be promising for foreign language teaching is the study of the development of grammar in the child's native language learning, because it carries the implication that a profitable method of foreign language teaching might be based on a developmental concept in which the several stages of second language learning would correspond to different degrees of completeness in grammatical development. That is, instead of requiring the student at a given stage to make sentences that are well-formed according to the complete adult grammar, he would be required only to make sentences conforming to the grammar prescribed for that stage. The grammar would then evolve through a number of stages until an adult form is reached. (Carroll, 1966, p. 36)

This very plausible and exciting suggestion has not, to my knowledge, been acted upon as yet. It is certainly true that a study of grammatical development does not lead to an audiolingual pedagogy (which emphasizes limitation of adult forms to a far greater degree than occurs normally), although such pedagogy is usually advertised as being more naturalistic than the grammar-translation methods. If we were really to apply natural language-learning principles to foreign-language teaching, we would come up with something like individualized pivot grammars using those foreign words which were most meaningful and necessary to individual students. The pivot grammars would gradually be differentiated into more complicated sentence forms, as the student's need for the more complicated forms increased. On the elementary level, this could be related to specific concrete projects, like block-building or cookie-making. On the secondary level, it might be related to a social studies project. For it is generally true that natural language learning never occurs in a real-life vacuum, the way it does in schools.

The Bilingual Child in School

The child who learns two languages more or less simultaneously has been able to capitalize on his own natural language-learning powers. Two questions of classroom relevance can be raised: (1) Do two languages improve thinking ability? (2) Should second languages be taught the way they are naturally learned by bilinguals—by simply plunging the child into a second language environment and letting him learn as best he can?

The answers to both questions are Yes, with qualifications. It used to be believed that knowing two languages might set up a kind of interference or linguistic "static" that would disturb reasoning ability. A recent study by Peal and Lambert (1962) disproves earlier evidence supporting the interference hypothesis. Additional, more technical studies like one by Kolers (1963) suggest reasons for this—for example, that separate verbal memories may exist for each language. In the Peal and Lambert study, bilingual children (approximately 10 years old) were significantly superior to monolingual children on many different measurements of reasoning ability:

> Intellectually, [the bilingual's] experience with two language systems seems to have left him with a mental flexibility, a superiority in concept formation, and a more diversified set of mental abilities, in the sense that the patterns of abilities developed by bilinguals were more heterogeneous. It is not possible to state from the present study whether the more intelligent child became bilingual, or whether bilingualism aided his intellectual development, but there is no question about the fact that he is superior intellectually. . . .
>
> Because of superior intelligence, these bilingual children are also further ahead in school than the monolinguals. . . . Their superior achievement in school seems to be dependent on a verbal facility. (Peal and Lambert, 1963, p. 20)

Partly because of these findings, Lambert has been involved in an experiment to teach a second language to first-graders by having the second language used as the sole medium of instruction (Lambert and MacNamara, 1969). Although the full results of this study will come over a longer period of time, the first-year results are now available, and they show that the progress of the children was remarkable. The subjects were English-speaking children who attended a French first grade. At the end of one year, they could read as well in French as French-speaking children attending a French first grade, and their mathematical skills compared favorably with those of both French and English controls. Their verbal association skills were just as swift in French as in English. Their French-speaking skills were not up to native ability, but good progress was shown. English-speaking skills (which were native) were in no way impaired, nor was English comprehension. Experiments of this sort may point the way toward a type of second-language instruction that will make formal teaching obsolete.

Teaching Standard English as a Second Language

For many children who speak a nonstandard English dialect, standard English may be learned very much as French was being learned by first-graders in the Lambert study. Why, then, do many of these children show academic and linguistic impairment compared to standard speakers of English? Should formal attention be paid to the problem of teaching nonstandard speakers, or should we just let them pick up standard English as best they can?

The answer is that formal attention should and must be paid to the problem. One great advantage of learning a truly foreign language is that discriminations between it and one's native language can easily be made. Learning a second dialect of a native language requires far more difficult discriminations that nonstandard speakers may be unable to discover without help. The conflicts between the way a word is spelled in a standard textbook and the way the child hears it may produce chaos in the head of a dialect speaker—chaos that remains undetected by his teacher, or at least ignored. (It is usually a simple matter to detect, from a child's written work, the influence of his dialect on his spelling, for example.)

Note here that we are not discussing the problem of the social use of language or the social implications of a dialect. Nor are we discussing the influence of the dialect on thinking ability. We are talking only about the purely mechanical problems of differences in sounds and grammar that may exist between standard and nonstandard language forms.

Most parents and teachers agree that children should learn standard English, even though they may not use it all the time. Their facility with standard forms will make textbooks (which are written in standard English), lectures, audiovisual materials, and classroom dialogues with standard speakers much easier to comprehend. Once this is understood, the teaching of standard English to anyone who is going to continue attending standard English schools becomes a necessity. And of course it should take place as early as possible.

To date, no formalized curriculum seems to have been developed, although resources exist. (See, for example, Shuy's *Social Dialects and Language Learning,* and other publications available from The National Council of Teachers of English and the Center for Applied Linguistics.) In general, all the techniques for teaching a foreign language—pattern drills, for example—can be used for the teaching of standard English. This means, of course, that the characteristics of the dialect should be understood by the standard English teacher, just as the characteristics of a foreign language should be understood by anyone teaching English to a foreign-language speaker. It is in this area of *dialect description* that adequate standard English curricula may need to be built.

Literary Analysis

The problem of adequate description of natural language also seems basic to the teaching of literary criticism. Even scientific journal articles, whose language seems to be stripped down to the bare bones, actually follow a rather elaborate style that can be understood only by studying articles from the journal of choice. This is a problem of recognizing the "natural language" of one scientist communicating with another. Formal plans for analyzing this natural language are really descriptive systems (Woodford, 1968).

Similarly, good style (as defined by Strunk and White, 1959, for example) means obedience to the principles that describe the writing of good stylists. Good poetry, drama, and literature all are defined, in poetry, drama, and literature analysis, by (1) sampling the natural language of poets, dramatists, or novelists; (2) extracting and classifying the principles that describe their respective languages; and (3) presenting these principles as hypotheses backed by supportive examples.

This generalization leads to an interesting test of the "good" literary specialist: Does his system (for analyzing poetry, literature, or drama) truly refer to the natural language of his target group? Or does it refer primarily to a private jargon (of words and ideas) used by other literary specialists? In many cases, students of literature seem to learn a private literary jargon, rather than the language of the authors who interest them. Presumably, such jargon-educated students will then be subject to the cognitive limitations that afflict any private-language user—they may have only the advantages of a comfortable in-group feeling!

Literary Composition

In Part VI, we will discuss the general question of creativity, of which literary composition is but one part. Here, we might make the single point that systems for good writing can be learned inductively, just as syntactical and meaning systems are learned. However, one major problem in providing for the inductive learning of literary systems is "tuning" the sampling device of the LAS. A bright student may be tuned by home experiences or personal inclination to samples of good literature. He may have an intuitive "feel" for what makes an author good, and he may be able to express this intuition quite effectively in his own work.

A duller student (and the dull students, of course, are the ones who force us to do the hard work of analyzing our pedagogical methods) may not be able to follow suit. He seems not to be properly "tuned," and providing him with a list of rules ("A paragraph must have a topic sentence. It is to be followed by three sentences that develop the topic sentence.") does little good.

The most successful method for coping with this problem appears to be a modeling one. The instructor provides a model paragraph. The student is then free to insert his own words into the model. By doing so, the student becomes sensitized to those mysterious rules of "good form" that skilled writers are actually using. The following material from a program developed by McCabe is an excellent example of this method:

In the first phase of work using a paragraph model, the teacher . . . works slowly and carefully with his pupils in an analysis of his model. As each part of the paragraph is analyzed, the student develops an original sentence in imitation of that part. Finally, he has a complete paragraph. In subsequent lessons, the guidance of the teacher is gradually withdrawn as he notes the ease with which his pupils handle their paragraphs.

As the single paragraph composition is mastered, it will be possible to move into compositions containing more than one paragraph. Appropriate models are provided. Models for specialized kinds of compositions such as book reports can be developed and used.

In his work with students, the author has noted that as students develop proficiency in use of a model, they tend to depart from a rigid adherence to its lines. An unexpected consequence . . . and an immensely pleasing one, has been a reduction . . . of characteristics ordinarily not thought to be associated with the composing aspects of composition writing. That is, the quality of the handwriting in terms of legibility improves, the number of mechanical errors decreases, and the number of misspellings decreases! Perhaps these phenomena reflect a decrease in general frustration at writing compositions.

During the school year 1962–1963, the author was one of a group of teachers who developed a model paragraph in such a program. The model is as follows:

> The Siamese is the most interesting cat as a pet. When a cat owner brags about his blue-eyed friend, he usually has a Siamese in mind. Because of its unusual coloring, its fondness for killing rodents, and its love of a good swim, it is always the subject of some interesting doings. Its love of swimming is probably its most interesting feature, since cats usually dislike water. Its many unusual characteristics make its owner the object of envy of other catkeepers and this is despite the fact that the bathroom is out of bounds when someone is taking a bath.

Using this model as a starting point, both teacher and pupils experienced success in improving the composition product. A first single paragraph composition (before special instruction) was submitted by an eighth-grade student.

ENGLISH

I did my composition on Joan Smith. Joan lives at 103 Norcorss St. Shes 13 and one of 4 children 2 brothers and two sisters' Her only Ambition now is to be a housewife. She likes all foods. Her favirate sport is softball.

The first composition (uncorrected) after experience with the model read as follows:

HORSES

Studying horses is the most fasinating subject as a hobby. When a horse owner talks about his chestnut brown hunter, he usully has a good horse in mind. Because of its ability to jump great heights, its prancing grace, and its love of a good run it is always indulged in some interesting doings. Its love of jumping is probably is greatest feature, Since most animals as big as the horse can't jump at all. Its wounderful characteristics make a horse-owner the envy of many animal owners and this is overlooking the fact that the horse can not be penned in by a small fence, because he will be up and over in no time.

After two more such essays, the student had obtained a mastery of the form. The next stage was the development of two parallel paragraphs:

My father was brought up the hard way. He was born in the Old Country. He was eleven when his father died, from then on it meant work for him and his older brother. They both had come to America and worked on farms. There was never too much time for enjoying the things most boys had.

* * *

My father's brother-in-law was brought up the easy way. He never had to work. He would just come home from school, do his homework and go out with the boys. He had, as you might call it, a very easy life as a boy.

Notice that the writer has departed from the precise lines of the model. Notice too the decrease in mechanical and spelling errors. The final composition in the series embodies two parallel modeled paragraphs in an original frame consisting of an introductory paragraph, a transitional paragraph and a conclusion.

COMPARISON OF THE GREYHOUND AND THE POODLE

In these two paragraphs I will compare the racing greyhound and the poodle, a house pet.

The greyhound is a racing dog. It is the fastest of all dogs. When the owner of a racing dog talks about his powerful, long-legged friend, he has a greyhound in mind. The dog is short-haired and may be tan, brindle, white, bluish, or spotted. There are different types throughout the world. The dogs weigh from sixty to seventy pounds, but are usually very fast, although they are difficult to care for and expensive to own.

I have told you the facts about keeping greyhounds; now I will tell you about the poodle.

The poodle is a different type of dog. It is usually a pet, and most poodles are smart animals. Poodles can be white, black, grey, blue or brown. Their hair is curley or frizzy and usually clipped or cropped in special ways. The poodle originated in Germany in the 1500's and is expensive to raise and own.

It is easy to see that although a greyhound and poodle are quite different in many ways, they have one characteristic in common; they are both expensive and demand a lot of care and time from the owner.

All these writing samples are reproduced in the form in which they came to the teacher's desk, before revision. (McCabe, 1965, pp. 43–46).

Model method of teaching composition skills have many additional applications; they would, for example, seem to serve as ideal guides to special language generation. Some further use of models in creative writing will be discussed in Part VI.

SUMMARY

We have approached language as a dynamic, ongoing process, rather than as a static structure of words. As a process, language illustrates many basic processes of thinking and mental development.

The infant "babbler" is learning to hear and to create fine distinctions between speech sounds; he is also learning about the social and rewarding aspects of language—that is, if he has a loving and attentive tutor. As true speech begins and grows, it seems to be characterized by a global urge to speak in a particular way, which gradually becomes differentiated—that is, the child gradually learns how to express that urge by using the rules and lexicon of his native language. In the course of this differentiation, the child invents and applies some interesting rules and words of his own: holophrases, pivot grammars, primitive sentences of various types, rules for word endings (morphological rules), and so forth. But all these developments conform to certain basic grammatical relations found in all languages throughout the ages.

Because of the age-related consistencies in language development, many psycholinguists believe it is an innate, biological process. The basic inductive process of sampling from one's environment, formulating hypotheses about the nature of the samples, and then generating examples and tests of the hypotheses seems dramatically illustrated by the language acquisition system (LAS, in Chomsky's terms). Other psychologists (such as Skinner) argue against this view and insist that language is a social habit, learned like any other social habit. Whether or not this is so, it is certainly true that language tutoring is helpful. Tutors may expand a child's grammatical skills, enrich his verbal descriptive systems, or drill him in specific language forms. Lack of tutoring will impair language development.

Biological damage will also impair it. Deafness, articulation disorders, stuttering, and aphasia will impair both language and mental development if remedial help is not provided. The deaf child in particular is doomed to mental retardation if ways cannot be found to provide him with a manual language during the critical period (around 2 to 3 years) of language development.

Meaning, or *semantics,* also results from systems that are learned and applied inductively. These systems interact with syntactic systems, but they are not identical to them. A syntactically "good" sentence may be semantically "bad" (as in "Ten dollars was cost by the kangaroo"), showing that meaning rules and syntactic rules are not the same.

Comprehension of meaning also implies two processes—the analysis of the sentence and the coordination of the analysis with some other kind of behavior. The analytical process involves segmenting or "chunking" a sentence into parts (like subject and verb phrase), generating associations to these parts, and then selecting mutual associations that are compatible—that is, that go together in a sensible way. Examples of schizophrenic speech illustrate this system by showing us what language sounds like when the system is absent.

Schizophrenic speech also shows us that language disorders appear to be thought disorders. The intimate connection between language and thinking has been studied in various ways. American psychologists frequently study what they call *verbal mediation systems;* Soviet psychologists refer to many of the same processes as *second signal systems.* The ability to generate or to use verbal representations (like labels, self-instructions, and so forth) is closely related to problem-solving abilities and to learning abilities of various sorts. Practicing the verbal representations aloud (talking to oneself, or to a tutor) gradually leads to their internalization. The verbal systems become silent, swift, and automatic. At this point, the systems stop looking like language and look like thought.

Some anthropologists and psychologists have therefore argued that the form of language (as in a dialect, for example) will affect the form of thought. If a child cannot say *not,* it is argued, then he will lack the concept of a negative. There is some experimental evidence that drilling such a child in more flexible and logical language forms will, in fact, improve his thinking, but the evidence is not conclusive.

Other sociologists and psychologists have argued that good thought can occur in any language form, provided that good (flexible, logical) thinking is encouraged by the child's culture. One problem with many lower-class cultures, for example, may be an emphasis on social rather than logical language functions. In the same sense that a "gentleman's C" may inhibit intellectual development, lower-class social pressures may inhibit or discourage the intellectual use of language. These pressures, not the language itself, may hinder learning.

General principles of language development and usage may affect many kinds of classroom instruction, not merely instruction in language. Similarly, principles found elsewhere in this text can be applied to language instruction. Overall, language must be considered both to reflect and to shape the total thinking process that we study from many different vantage points throughout this book.

Part V PICTURES, PATTERNS, AND CODES

Our eyes are general-purpose instruments for feeding the brain with comparatively undoctored information, while the eyes of animals possessing simple brains are more elaborate, for they filter out information which is not essential to their survival, or usable by the simple brain. It is this freedom to make new inferences from sensory data which allows us to discover and see so much more than other animals. . . . We do not perceive the world merely from the sensory information available at any given time, but rather we use this information to test hypotheses of what lies before us.

R. L. GREGORY

When you look at a picture, what do you see? How do you see it? When you look at a word, do you do the same thing? Are the processes of reading words different from those of "reading" pictures? What about mathematics? Do you read an equation in algebra the same way you read an algebra word problem? Do pictures and concrete materials assist mathematical thinking or interfere with it? Do they assist or interfere with reading?

Questions of this sort have shaped Part V. Why are they discussed together? In Part IV we saw that learning standard English may be in some ways more difficult for a dialect speaker of English than for a native speaker of French because the discriminations between standard and dialect English may be hard to make without special help. A similar problem exists among the various mental processes of word reading, picture "reading," and mathematical thinking. In many ways they appear to be similar, when in fact there are critical differences among them—so critical that to excel in one (say, reading) may mean to fail in another (say, mathematics). One way to illustrate this is through sex differences in aptitudes.

"Boys Can Figure, Girls Can Read"

As reported in *The Development of Sex Differences* (Maccoby, 1966), in 18 studies of reading ability that compared boys and girls, girls were more proficient in 10, boys were more proficient in 6, and no differences between the sexes were recorded in 2. In 21 studies of mathematical reasoning, boys were more proficient in 11, girls were more proficient in 1, and no differences were recorded for 9. In 18 studies of spatial abilities, boys were more proficient in 12, no differences were recorded for 6, and girls were ahead on none. In 74 studies of general verbal abilities (including articulation, spelling ability, vocabulary), girls were ahead on 48, boys on 16, and no differences were recorded for 10.

These results illustrate a well-known but little-understood fact in psychology: Girls are generally better than boys on tests of verbal aptitudes and skills, and boys are generally better than girls on tests of mathematical and spatial skills, which in themselves bear an interesting relationship to each other. Is mathematics more visual than verbal? The fact that girls are usually superior to boys on tests of verbal abilities and reading would suggest that reading is more like a verbal skill and mathematics, more like a spatial skill. Differences between the sexes in these skills suggest that certain predispositions or aptitudes for certain types of cognitive processing may have biological foundations.

But this possibility is only a guideline for future investigations; it is certainly not an explanation, nor is it an infallible rule. As college admissions officers know, girls usually score higher on the verbal portions of national examinations than on the mathematical portions. The opposite is true of boys. But there are always exceptions.

> When Samuel Johnson was asked which is more intelligent, man or woman, he replied, "Which man, which woman?" This is a vivid way of expressing the wide individual differences found within each sex, with the consequent overlapping. . . . In any psychological trait women differ widely from one another, and men likewise vary widely among themselves. . . . Even when one group excels another by a large and significant amount, individuals can be found in the "inferior" group who will surpass certain individuals in the "superior" group. (Anastasi, 1958, p. 453)

However, the group differences between boys and girls are quite real, and they focus our attention on the real differences between reading/verbal abilities, and quantitative/spatial abilities. Efforts to prove that these differences are primarily *environmental* in origin have not been especially successful.

Differences in interests between boys and girls seem to be present almost from birth. Because of these differences, little boys may play with materials (like tinker-toys) that help develop their spatial abilities; little girls may play with dolls (and do their talking for them) in a way that develops their verbal abilities. But it is difficult to prove that later (college-level) spatial and verbal skills result solely from these earlier forms of practice. The differences in practice may have resulted from an inborn difference in aptitude—little boys might choose tinker-toys because of their spatial aptitude; little girls might choose dolls because of their verbal aptitude. Both groups might enjoy practicing skills that are biologically natural to them.

In any event, we will not pursue further the intriguing implications of sex differences in verbal, quantitative, and spatial abilities. The sex differences merely illustrate the fact that the abilities themselves are different. In the chapters ahead, we will try to understand how and why.

In Chapter 20, we will examine the general process of visual perception, especially the perception of pictures. In Chapter 21, we will analyze the reading process. In Chapter 22, we will be concerned with the process of graphic symbolization—reading charts, diagrams, and the like. And in Chapter 23, we will examine various kinds of mathematical thinking. These are the pictures, patterns, and codes of the modern school child.

Chapter 20   PROCESSING PICTORIAL INFORMATION

As Chomsky has said, a child may not be able to help constructing a certain kind of verbal syntax any more than he can help his "attention to line and angle" (a kind of visual syntax). Much of visual perception seems controlled by certain automatic reactions. The color red is *red*, for example; it leaps out as an unavoidable sensation. A circle is a circle, lines stop, angles are sharp, curves are not, and so forth. Actually, we know quite a lot about these visual phenomena and the factors that govern them.

VISUAL SYNTAX

The wedding of psychology and linguistics (psycholinguistics) was only one of several similar weddings in the history of psychology. In the late nineteenth century, the attempt to combine the methods and technology of physics with those of philosophy led directly to the founding of psychology itself. This first branch of psychology was called *psychophysics,* and it was concerned with the measurement of sensation, including visual sensation. From careful and intensive work in the psychophysical tradition, we have derived a large body of knowledge about visual perception and the laws that govern it.

We will not attempt here to do more than hint at the power and complexity of these laws. The interested reader is referred to a good little book by Gregory (1966) called *Eye and Brain* for more details and for additional references. In the following paragraphs, we will present only a few basic principles of visual perception.

Gestalt Laws

In the early part of the twentieth century, a new school of psychology developed around principles of "wholistic," organic perception. We have already met one representative of this school in Heinz Werner (Part I). The Gestalt psychologists devised ingenious ways of demonstrating their theory that the brain has built-in systems for organizing visual information. Figure 20.1 shows three of the Gestalt laws of organization—the law of proximity, the law of similarity, and the law of closure.

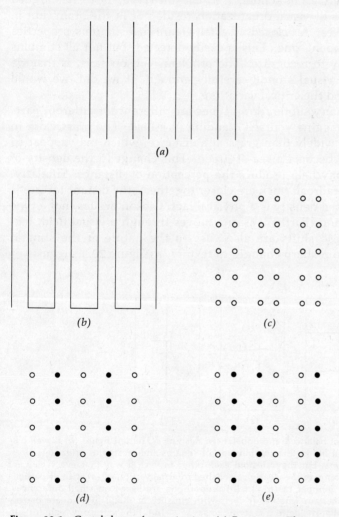

Figure 20.1 Gestalt laws of organization. (*a*) Proximity: There seem to be four pairs of two lines, rather than eight separate lines. (*b*) Closure: The four proximity columns have been destroyed by the addition of the horizontal lines. Now we see three rectangles and two irrelevant extra lines. (*c*) Proximity: We organize the circles into three columns. (*d*) Similarity: We see vertical rather than horizontal lines. (*e*) Proximity and similarity in opposition: This perceptual grouping is unstable.

As shown in the various parts of Figure 20.1, relationships between the visual stimuli (the lines or the circles) may "trigger" our brains into organizing them into columns, boxes, vertical rather than horizontal lines, and so on. Presumably, these laws operate in real-world perception as well. Two of their applications are shown in the excerpt from Arnheim (1966) in Figure 20.2, and in the illusion shown in Figure 20.3.

Cues of Texture

In opposition to the Gestalt school, J. J. Gibson (1950, 1966) has argued that many principles of visual organization reside not in the brain, but in the stimuli themselves. A "closed" Gestalt figure has stimulus properties different from an "open" one. This is easily detected, but not all stimulus variables are so easy to recognize. The problem, Gibson says, is that we do not analyze our visual stimuli carefully enough. If we did, we would always be able to find the critical variations.

For example, many subtle *textural* cues are different for different parts of a visual scene. Imagine yourself standing in a field. The grass close to you is spaced more widely than grass at a distance, which may appear so close together as to become a sea of green. This change in the density of the visual texture may help produce the perception of distance. Similarly, the distant ties of a railroad track are closer together—the distant texture is denser. This increased density is a physical fact, Gibson argues, not a type of mental organization. Further, as one moves through a visual field, textures shift; and these shifts are also cues to the nature of the stimuli. Edges may result from sharp changes in texture, as Figure 20.4 suggests.

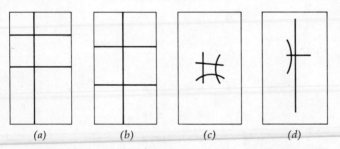

(a)   *(b)*   *(c)*   *(d)*

Figure 20.2 Examples of balanced and unbalanced designs. "The left figure (a) is well balanced. There is plenty of life in this combination of squares and rectangles of various sizes, proportions and directions, but they all hold each other in such a way that every element stays in its place. . . . Compare the clearly established internal vertical of (a) with its pathetically wavering opposite number in (b). In (b) proportions are based on small differences, which leave the eye uncertain whether it deals with equality or inequality, square or rectangle. We cannot tell what the pattern is trying to say. . . . In (c) the pattern, which drifts in space without anchor, approaches, on the one hand, the symmetry of a crosslike figure . . . and, on the other, the shape of a kind of kite. . . . Both interpretations, however, are equally inconclusive. They have none of the reassuring clarity of (d)." (Arnheim, 1966, p. 11, from "The Design Judgment Test" by Maitland Graves, © 1946 The Psychological Corp.)

Figure 20.3   An example of the principles of proximity and similarity in the production of an illusion. Do you see a fish design, or the word *summer* and its reflection?

Depth, Perspective, and Constancy

Changes in texture and changes in slope contribute greatly to our perception of depth and perspective. The slight difference in viewpoint between each of our eyes is primarily responsible for depth perception. This can be demonstrated by means of special prisms that reverse the viewpoints—the left eye now sees from the right eye's angle, and vice versa. With these prisms, depth *reverses* (up to a point—we do not see noses as holes, for example). Other important cues to depth and perspective are *interposition* (objects in front of other objects are closer to us) and *shadowing*. The direction of illumination produces shading that helps us characterize the objects of perception.

Because of the fact that texture, slant, and shadow change with light and distance, it is really quite remarkable that aspects of the scene stay the same to us. People who walk away from us do not seem to shrink in size, for example. A white object may seem as white to us in a dim light as in a bright one. A round object (such as a table top) may look round to us, when in reality we are seeing more of an ellipse—unless we are near the ceiling, looking straight down on the table. What accounts for these constancies?

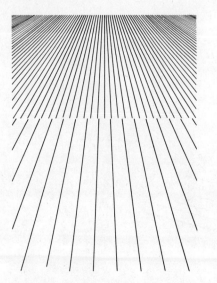

Figure 20.4   Abrupt changes in texture cue the perception of an edge. (Gibson, 1950, p. 93)

Scientists suppose that the brain is able to combine information of various kinds—including, for example, knowledge of what an object is—in a way that is sufficient to maintain its identity or sameness. This ability has important implications for sanity. Suppose the perceptual world constantly changed size, shape, brightness, color, and depth as it moved, or as you moved. Adjusting to such a world would be extremely difficult. One might well choose not to try to adjust at all, but to withdraw or to behave with hysterical abandon. How else might one survive inside a kaleidoscope?

It should not surprise us to learn that some doctors believe schizophrenia is accompanied by a loss of the visual constancies. Perhaps the bizarre behavior of many psychotics will someday be understood as the natural reaction to severe perceptual flux and disorganization arising from biochemical disorders. We can experience a bit of cranial confusion by staring at "impossible" figures like those in Figure 20.5, in which both perspective and depth fluctuate. Imagine living in a world composed of objects like these.

Seeing Movement

As mysterious as constancy is the perception of visual movement itself. What are the cues? Presumably they lie in changes in the relationship of an object to its background. These changes may be further complicated by movements of the observer's eyes or head, or by other physical movements (such as rotation) that affect the brain's organizing power. (Turn round and round to the right for a minute or two and then stop; the world will now revolve to the left.)

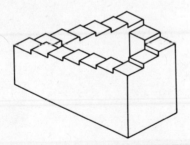

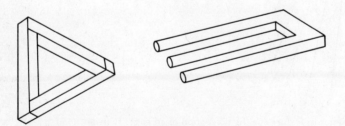

Figure 20.5   Impossible figures resulting from distorted use of depth and perspective cues.

Two physiologists, Hubel and Wiesel (1962), made the extremely important discovery that *individual visual brain cells* may be "tuned" to particular movements. That is, one cell may respond to horizontal movement; another, to vertical movement. Hubel and Wiesel discovered this by taking electrical readings from the individual brain cells of a cat by means of tiny recording devices. One important implication of their study is that (at least up to a point) velocity may be perceived directly without any guesses about time. (It has been believed that some kind of time estimate is involved in the perception of speed.)

When something "out there" moves, particular brain cells may be stimulated, and movement perception may result. But what about the movement of our own eyes? Reading the lines of this book, for example, ought to stimulate some of the same cells. But there is no perception of movement. Apparently other visual systems cancel this perception when it is not initiated by something "out there." Probably the same system that commands the eyes to move (across a line of type) also cancels self-perception of the movement. But lines may get wavy with fatigue. This suggests that the inner "command" systems may sometimes work in the opposite way and cause movement experiences when there are no outer stimuli.

> The world swings round when we are fatigued or suffering from the less pleasant effects of alcohol. This was described by the English wit, Sheridan. Two friends led him to the front door of his house, in Berkeley Square, and left him. Looking back, they saw him still standing in the same position. "Why don't you go in?" they shouted. "I'm waiting until my door goes by again . . . then I'll jump through!" replied Sheridan. (Gregory, 1966, p. 104)

Seeing Color

In view of the Hubel and Wiesel discovery, one might guess that a similar system would hold for color perception: perhaps there is one nerve cell for each color. This convenient theory cannot possibly be true. We can see almost as well in colored as in white light. If there were just one color cell firing, good vision would hardly result.

Actually, there are only a few color receptors, and the major problem in developing an adequate theory of color vision is to explain how those few receptors can handle so many different colors. How can the same set of cells register purple, lavender, and blue? How are we able to make such discriminations?

> The possibility that the full gamut may be given by only a few "principal" colors is shown by a single and basic observation: colors can be mixed. This may seem obvious, but in fact the eye behaves very differently in this respect from the ear. Two sounds cannot be mixed to give a different pure third sound, but two colors give a third color in which the constituents cannot be identified. Constituent sounds are heard as a chord, and can be separately identified, at any rate by musicians, but no training allows us to do the same for light. (Gregory, 1966, p. 119)

Color mixing has been the fundamental principle of color vision theory for well over a hundred years, but the precise details of the theoretical system have still not been worked out. The basic notion is that there are three types of color-sensitive receptors that respond selectively to red, green, and blue (yellow occurs from a mixture of red and green, believe it or not). All colors are then seen by a mixture of signals from the three systems.

Figure-Ground Perception

Another Gestalt principle is that something always seems to be the focus of attention; other aspects of the scene recede into the background. Of course this may change—the focus may shift. One famous illustration is the drawing shown in Figure 20.6. As we stare at it, the vase seems to be the figure against a black background. Then suddenly the "background" becomes the figure, and we see two profiles against a white background (the former vase). This shifting back and forth is a good way of experiencing the compelling, locked-in quality of the Gestalt relationship rules.

Other researchers believe these perceptual operations are linked to personality characteristics: They insist that people who have difficulty separating figure and ground may be more "field-dependent" (see Chapter 14) and have somewhat less mature personalities. Whether or not this is true, one thing is certain: The sex differences are around to plague us again. Girls generally have a more difficult time analyzing perceptual materials and discovering the figures that may be embedded in distracting backgrounds than boys do.

Good Form

A final, important Gestalt rule is the principle of good form—the tendency we seem to have to complete incomplete forms (to see Figure 20.7 as a

Figure 20.6 Figure-ground perception is illustrated by the alternation of the central focus. Sometimes it is a white vase, other times it is two profiles. This is Rubin's "Peter-Paul Goblet."

Figure 20.7   The Gestalt principle of good form.

typewriter, for example), to perceive asymmetrical (unbalanced) forms as symmetrical, and so forth. This "pull" toward balanced wholes may be why unbalanced ones seem particularly interesting (see Chapters 13 and 25 for discussions of infant preferences and creativity in such matters).

Conclusion

These principles have been only brief samples of the laws governing much of our visual perception. The laws operate as a kind of "syntax" that does not seem to be entirely under conscious control, any more than recognition of the subject and action of a sentence seems entirely under conscious control. But of course some learning is involved, at some point in the individual's development. The *experience of hearing* one's native language is essential to the proper construction of the grammar that one then uses automatically; the *experience of seeing* similarly affects the organization of our visual world. But, once constructed, the organization may be extremely powerful. As we will see later, these visual "syntactical" systems may sometimes interfere with verbal systems to the detriment of the educational process.

FEATURES VS. MODELS

How do we recognize a familiar face? One possibility is that we carry around inside our heads stored images of people we know. When we see someone, we may match their face against our stock of images, much as we might match a piece of fruit to a wax model. If a match is discovered, then recognition happens. ("Aunt Lulu! What are you doing out here in the middle of the desert?") It seems a reasonable theory, but there are some drawbacks. How then can we explain the mysterious fact that we sometimes recognize people who have changed physically—gained weight, grown older, and so on. Some parts of the old image may match the changed face, but not all of them will. If recognition still happens, it would suggest that we carry around inside our heads something like *lists of features,* rather than *models.* These lists would not read like FBI descriptions; they might be quite personal and idiosyncratic. (My set of features for recognizing Aunt Lulu might be very different from Uncle Arn's.)

Figure 20.8 Records of eye movements show which pictorial features were focused on by the viewer. (G. A. Miller, 1962a, pp. 52–53)

Eye Movements and Constructions

The kinds of features we pay attention to are illustrated by the eye-movement tracks shown in Figure 20.8. George Miller described the process in this way:

> Records of eye movements show clearly that the unified integrated experience we get when we look at a scene is something we must actively construct out of dozens of short, quick snapshots aimed at different parts of it. Our attention shifts rapidly from one point to another until gradually we become familiar with all the parts and the relations among them. (Miller, 1962a, p. 51)

Modern scientific views of how we look at pictures (Neisser, 1967) generally agree that seeing is basically a *constructive experience.* That is, if we could slow down the process of picture looking and study it in detail, we would discover that the mind puts together, in a unified way, selected information brought in by the eyes. In the example in Figure 20.8, the eyes focused on the lips, eyes, and hair of the girl; and on the bears and trees of the other picture. The mind put this selected information together and constructed a picture out of it. The first part of the pictorial comprehension process, then, will be an analytical one—we must locate and select the critical features.

Natural visual "syntactical" systems help us here: visual tendencies to closure, to figure-ground perception, to use textural cues, and so on operate automatically to help us locate critical features. And the eye movements involved in the scanning process also play an important role. Suppose the picture you were scanning moved with your eyes so that the image on your retina never varied. In that case, due to something like retinal fatigue, parts of the picture would fade out or disappear.

This fading-out process is almost like the picture-construction process in reverse. That is, in constructing a picture, our minds put together infor-

Test Picture   Examples of Fade-outs

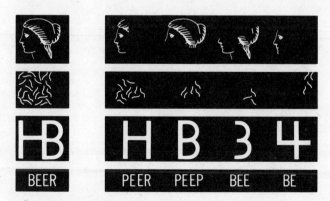

Figure 20.9 Examples of fade-out patterns resulting from a fatigued eye, showing that fade-outs occur in meaningful chunks. (Pritchard, 1961)

mation about critical features; in fading out, our minds appear to lose information about critical features systematically, not haphazardly. Figure 20.9 shows examples of systematic fade-outs from Pritchard (1961). Clearly, the mind chooses what parts of the pictures the eyes will stop seeing, just as it chooses (during the construction process) what parts the eyes will start seeing.

Subliminal Emotional Influences

It is possible to influence the eye-mind relationship experimentally by other techniques. For example, look carefully at the illustrations in Figure 20.10, from a paper by Guthrie and Wiener (1966). Figure A$_1$ is exactly like

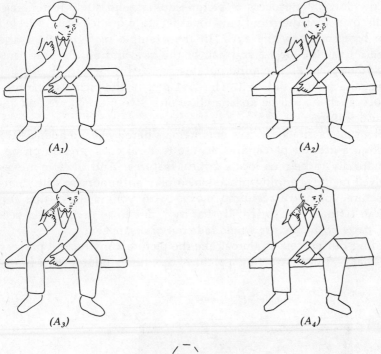

Figure 20.10   Influencing eye-mind relationships. (Guthrie and Wiener, 1966)

A_2, except that it is composed of rounded lines instead of sharp, angular ones. Figures A_3 and A_4 have guns in their hands; in addition, A_3 is rounded, while A_4 is angular. Now look at figure B. Gaps have been left in the figure—he could be "filled in" as rounded or angular, and as having or not having a gun.

The Guthrie and Wiener technique for using the figures was this: One of the completed figures (A_1, A_2, A_3, or A_4) was shown to a subject for a brief period in a special apparatus called a tachistoscope (which carefully controls the time of looking). The period of looking was so brief that the subject did not have time to register exactly what he saw. Immediately after this very brief look at one of the A figures, the B figure was exposed for a longer period of time, and the subjects were asked to make mood and character judgments about him. For example, they were to decide if B seemed to be helpful or harmful, pleasant or unpleasant.

The results showed that the brief exposure of the A figures influenced the mood and character judgments of B. If the subject had seen the angular A figures, he was more likely to perceive B negatively—as unpleasant and harmful. If he had seen the rounded A figures, he was more likely to perceive B positively—as helpful and pleasant. Interestingly, the presence of the gun did not influence perception; for these subjects, in this situation, it did not appear to be a critical feature. Because of the high speed of picture exposure, the meaning of the gun probably did not have time to register. What did register were the "syntactical" properties of the lines (sharp or rounded), and these cues operated as the critical features.

At slower speeds, of course, meaningful objects like guns will have a pronounced influence on perception, but they do so because of processes of association. This consideration moves us from the "syntactics" to the "semantics" of perceptual comprehension, a topic we will discuss in the next section. There are many other factors that influence our choice of critical perceptual features or cues—expectation, set, emotional reactions, needs, and hopes, as well as learning experiences of various kinds—which we will not review here. Once the critical features have registered perceptually, the flow of associations or concepts begins.

PICTORIAL COMPREHENSION

In Chapter 18, we suggested the following outline of the verbal comprehension process:

Analyzing the phrases into syntactic units (subject, verb phrase, and so forth)

Generating associations to the syntactic features

Selecting associations that make mutual sense in context

Coordinating the results of the process with some other behavior (doing or saying something)

(The last point has been more extensively considered in Part I.) Figure 20.11 shows how a similar scheme can be used for organizing a discussion of pictorial comprehension.

The feedback principle shown in Figure 20.11 refers to the continual self-testing process involved in concept attainment of any sort (see Figure 8.1). Looking at pictures, listening to conversation, reading a book, making a scientific discovery—all these are concept-attainment processes. Concepts, in turn, affect critical-feature analysis. Our ideas about why bears climb logs, for example, would affect our feature analysis of the picture in Figure 20.8; we might search for evidence of hidden honey. The matter of feedback becomes especially important in reading comprehension, which will be analyzed in a later chapter.

Effects of Ambiguity

As in verbal comprehension, associations of many types may be triggered by the "subject" or figure of a picture. One way to show this is to keep the

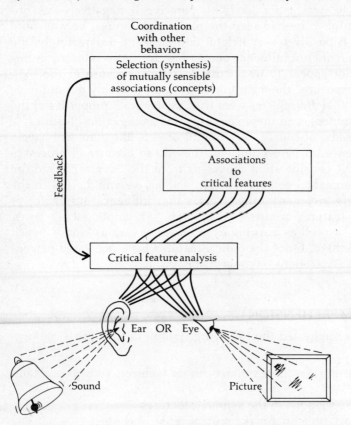

Figure 20.11   Schematization of the perceptual comprehension process in verbal and visual modes.

figure so ambiguous that it does not control or limit the associations. In an experiment by Bruner and Potter (1964), slides of ordinary objects (like a shoe or a fire hydrant) were shown *unfocused* to groups of subjects. Some subjects saw extremely unfocused slides; some saw slightly unfocused slides. The subjects were asked to identify the slides. After their initial statements, they viewed the slides again, this time in a more focused state. Again they were asked to identify what they had seen.

The study showed that viewers who had first seen the slides in a slightly blurred condition were able to identify them correctly fairly soon, even though they were still not in sharp focus. If viewers were first shown the slides in an extremely blurred condition, the slides had to be much more sharply focused for recognition finally to occur. It was as if the ideas or hypotheses or associations triggered by the extreme blur prevented comprehension of the true picture.

A similar type of interference may be produced by pictures that provide an excess of details; our minds may become so cluttered that they miss the main point. Dwyer (1967) carried out an experiment testing the effects of different types of pictorial representation (line drawings, shaded drawings, and photographs) on learning. One important aspect of this experiment was Dwyer's definition of learning. He used several different kinds of tests (knowing terminology, being able to draw a model of what was learned). Far too many educational experiments neglect to evaluate more than one kind of learning.

The pictures Dwyer used in a lesson about the physiology of the heart are shown in Figure 20.12. The slides accompanied a taped lecture, and both were carefully timed so that all groups heard words and saw pictures for the same amount of time. Group 1 saw only labels—the names of the parts of the heart that were shown in the illustrations. Group 2 saw line drawings; Group 3 saw shaded drawings (which added depth and perspective, as we know from our discussion of visual syntax); and Group 4 saw photographs. The presentation of the material lasted 40 minutes, and 39 slides accompanied the recorded lecture. The subjects were college students. Immediately following the presentation, all groups took four tests: (1) A heart-model test requiring identification of the parts of the heart

Table 20.1
Results of Four Tests on the Physiology of the Heart

	MEAN TEST SCORES			
TYPE OF SLIDE	3-D MODEL TEST	TERMINOLOGY	DRAWING TEST	COMPREHENSION
Labels	10.5	11.4	7.5	11.5
Line drawings	16.3	14.2	14.3	13.6
Shaded drawings	15.5	14.4	14.8	13.8
Photographs	8.4	8.9	10.2	10.9

SOURCE: Based on data in Dwyer, 1967.

shown in a three-dimensional model; (2) a terminology test composed of fill-in questions; (3) a drawing test requiring the subjects to draw a diagram of the heart and place the various parts in correct relationship to each other; and (4) a comprehension test requiring a thorough understanding of the heart, its parts, and its internal functioning. The results of the tests are shown in Table 20.1.

The excessive detail of the photographs decreased learning, compared to the learning produced by the drawings. On all except the drawing test, even the label slides (with no pictures at all) led to higher scores. (If one is going to be asked to draw something, any kind of picture may be more

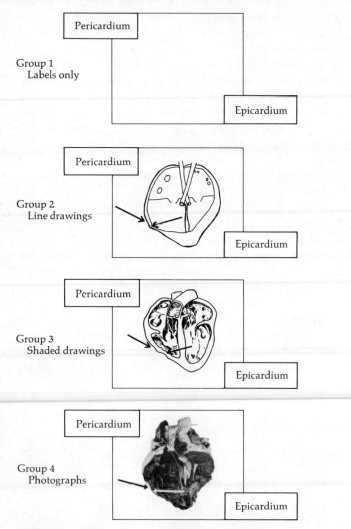

Figure 20.12 Different types of slides accompanying a taped lecture on the physiology of the heart. (Dwyer, 1967)

helpful than none at all.) But in general, the labels were not as effective as the line and shaded drawings.

Ambiguity in the Classroom

Both experiments (the Bruner and Potter blurred-slide experiment and Dwyer's heart-slide study) illustrate an important aspect of pictorial processing: Pictorial cues stimulate a rich flood of mental associations. Under

KLANSMAN'S ATTORNEY—Matt Murphy Jr., attorney for klansman Collie Leroy Wilkins, displays gun he claims to have taken from FBI informer Gary Rowe Jr. Murphy says he'll connect gun to case. Right, Klan's Robert Shelton.

Figure 20.13 Picture used in an assignment carried out by an eighth-grade student, with student and teacher commentary. (Photo courtesy United Press International)

some conditions, it may be difficult for students to consolidate selected associations into a single, clear concept, and it therefore behooves a teacher to choose visual aids with extreme care. A good summary of the educational pitfalls has been provided by M. D. Vernon in her small but comprehensive book, *The Psychology of Perception* (1962).

Pictorial comprehension differs from *graphic* comprehension (the comprehension of graphs, maps, diagrams, and the like, to be discussed in Chapter 22) in one particular way: There is no single correct verbal interpretation. Pictures should be introduced into a curriculum for the purpose of expanding and enriching associations, rather than constricting them. An anecdote associated with Figure 20.13 illustrates what can happen when a teacher is inflexible. It is a newspaper photograph of Matt Murphy, the Ku Klux Klan lawyer involved in the Liuzzo case—Violet Liuzzo was a Detroit mother of five children who was shot and killed in Selma, Alabama, during the 1964 civil rights demonstrations. In the car with the Klan assassin was an FBI informer who had witnessed the murder. The gun shown in the photograph was the one taken from the informer.

The picture was brought to class by an eighth-grader as part of an assignment on communication in mass media to select a newspaper photograph that implied something beyond its immediate caption. The student had written: "This picture is anti-Klan because it shows Robert Shelton, Klan leader, and a Klan attorney in the same picture, showing how he enforces his policy of anti-civil rights, as in the Liuzzo case. It shows how ruthless the Klan is." Unfortunately for the student, his teacher happened to be a member of a conservative political organization. The teacher wrote, in red pencil: "No—shows implication that FBI agent is guilty."

Two opposing views of a newspaper picture might have stimulated a good class discussion, if the teacher had been willing to permit it. Instead, she gave the student a C on the assignment and closed the discussion. Pictorial comprehension involves the arousal and consolidation of personal ideas—that is both its power and its danger.

Chapter 21 PROCESSING THE CODE OF WRITTEN LANGUAGE

Skillful readers (like those reading this book) may find it difficult to conceptualize the problem of learning to read. Remember how it was back in the old days when you stared at those newspaper squiggles and wondered what they meant? To recapture that feeling, consider Figure 21.1:

"V‡‡⅃,⊥+⅃. V‡‡⅃ +∧ ∧⊏⊗ ⊔⊸X⅃.
⊆‡⊸ ⊸⊸+∧X⊏ ⅁⊗ ⊥⊏‡‡∧ ⊏⊔⅃."

Figure 21.1 (McKee, 1948)

433

Look at those words. Get a feeling for them. Plan to recognize them again as wholes. Can you understand them? No? Does the picture help? If not, you may be experiencing some of the frustration and confusion with which millions of children in this country live day after day because of poor reading pedagogy.

Sight-reading Methods

The so-called look and say, sight reading, or meaning methods of teaching reading may be responsible for a high degree of illiteracy among American children (Chall, 1967). Look-and-say methods tend to force a child to rely on model-matching procedures—he must hunt for a word that matches another word or that "matches" the picture. Model-matching, as explained earlier, is probably not the natural human system for perceptual analysis and comprehension. Such a pedagogy may force a child to inhibit the development of his natural reading skills and may result in a type of mental crippling.

There are also other problems. Look-and-say methods use a great many pictures. As we have seen, however, pictures tend to stimulate associations of their own that may interfere with the *language* associations necessary to reading comprehension. This hypothesis was supported in a series of studies reported by Samuels (1967). Children who learned to read the words *boy, bed, man,* and *car* were distracted by pictorial representations of the words. Learning from simple file cards was more effective. Samuels tested this possibility in both laboratory and classroom settings. In the classroom setting, the presence of pictures was especially damaging to the learning efficiency of children who were below the median in reading ability.

Learning to read a word is not the same thing as learning to understand a picture. A written word is a special alphabetical code for a sound; a written sentence is a special alphabetical code for a pattern of sounds or intonations. Those sounds—which are the sounds of our spoken language—then open the way to the language association system. Pictures, which open the way to a visual association system, may produce disastrous interference. Finally, look-and-say methods, in discouraging children from attending to the code, may prevent them from developing self-help systems for attacking new words.

Model of Code-reading Processes

Figure 21.2 shows four aspects of the code: (A) letter-sound association systems, (B) spelling pattern sight-and-sound systems, (C) word-sound systems, and (D) phrase-sound systems. Each of these can be built from the preceding system. The more complex systems require more skill and become fluent at a later age. The advantage of the build and simplify aspects of the systems is that they make self-remedy possible. One can, for example, "sound out" an unfamiliar word or "word sound out" an unfamiliar phrase until the language associations flow correctly, and one suddenly comprehends what he has been saying. This, again, is partly a matter of brain connections; it is not a mystique.

Much of the controversy over reading methods (see the excellent summary by Fries, 1963, pp. 1–34) arises from a belief that there is only one proper code method of teaching. Actually, all codings are necessary at different stages of a child's development. System A, for example, will be quite boring to a six-year-old, but fascinating to a three-year-old. But the six-year-old who has skipped system A may not be as fluent a reader as one who has not. Some reading methods skip large chunks of the basic process. Only the very bright child will be able to fill in the missing material and teach himself the code.

Most of the evidence for these statements has been reviewed by Jeanne Chall in *Learning to Read: The Great Debate,* published in 1967. Her conclusions—that fifty years of research show that a code-emphasis

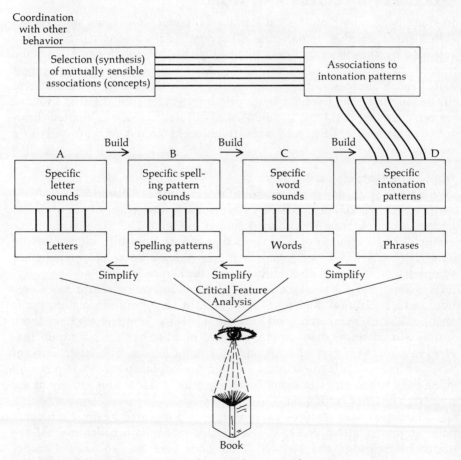

Figure 21.2 Schematization of the paths to reading comprehension.

method of teaching reading is superior to a meaning or look-and-say emphasis—were based on empirical studies of classroom behavior. In addition to such studies, there is a growing body of laboratory research that supports their results.

A science of reading independent of classroom life, just as immunization research is independent of the hospital clinic, is gradually coming into existence. It has three broad aspects: (1) The discrimination of the visual code units—letters, spelling patterns, and words; (2) the connection of the visual units with sound and speech units; and (3) the flow of information through the mind, cued and guided by the visual-auditory-speech connections. This flow may be directed by short phrases or by longer units such as sentences and paragraphs, but unless it is initiated by the code components, the process cannot be described as reading. We will look at some of the research in each of these three areas.

RECOGNIZING LETTERS AND WORDS

In their exploration of the cat's brain (Chapter 20) Hubel and Weisel (1962) made another remarkable discovery: Individual visual cells were activated by slits (bars or lines) tilted in particular directions. A slit tilted toward the left would cause one cell to fire; a slit tilted toward the right would cause another to fire; a horizontal slit would cause still another to fire. Assuming that a similar brain cell architecture is also found in man, we can conclude that letters composed of different groups of slanted, horizontal, and vertical lines may activate different groups of brain cells in a reading child.

Alphabetic Features vs. Models

Leading the way into these research areas, Eleanor Gibson and her students at Cornell University have developed a feature chart of our alphabet letters. A sample from this chart is shown in Figure 21.3. The letter *A,* for example, has a column of plus signs that differs from the column for the letter *E.* An *A* has a horizontal line, two oblique lines, an intersection, symmetry, and vertical discontinuity (it is broken or interrupted by vertical lines). The letter *E* has a column of "plusses" indicating that it has a vertical and a horizontal line (more than one, in fact), an intersection, cyclic change (like *B*), symmetry, and horizontal breaks. Some letters have more features in common than others, and the number of these common features reveals the *degree of confusability* among letters. The letter *E* is not very confusable with the letter *C; C* is more confusable with *U.* We will come back to the problem of confusability after looking more closely at the processes of letter recognition.

The problem of features vs. models was discovered again when computer engineers attempted to develop letter-recognition programs. As reported by Selfridge and Neisser (1963), one plan was to store a model letter (say an *A*) in the computer and instruct the computer to match in-

FEATURES	A	B	C	E	K	L	N	U	X
Straight segment									
Horizontal	+			+	+				
Vertical		+		+	+	+	+		
Oblique /	+			+					+
Oblique \	+			+			+		+
Curve									
Closed		+							
Open vertically								+	
Open horizontally			+						
Intersection	+	+		+	+				+
Redundancy									
Cyclic change		+		+					
Symmetry	+	+	+	+	+			+	+
Discontinuity									
Vertical	+				+				+
Horizontal			+			+	+		

Figure 21.3   A sample of Gibson's feature chart. Each letter is characterized by those features marked "plus" in its column. (Gibson, 1965)

coming letters to the model. If it matched, the computer was to "recognize" the new stimulus as an *A*. But as Figure 21.4 shows, such a program raises many problems. The incoming *A* might be a different size or tilted at an angle. It might be a lower-case *a*. It might be an *R* more like the model *A* than *a*, but not really an *A*.

In order for it to handle these details, the computer had to be given a list of features such as these: "If it's pointed at the top and has a bar

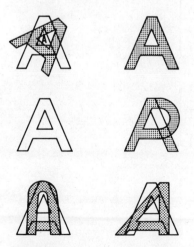

Figure 21.4   How does a model-matching system know when it sees a new *A*? (Selfridge and Neisser, 1960)

across it, call it *A*. If it's round at the top and has a bar across it, and its 'legs' are the same size, it's still an *A*." Figure 21.5 shows how such a feature list might be diagrammed. In the EPAM (see Chapter 7) tradition, we might store a series of tests inside the computer. Each letter must run the gamut of the tests: Does the letter have an open space at the top? Does it have a crossbar? Does it include a vertical line? For *A*, the answer to the first question is No; the answer to the second is Yes; and the answer to the third is No. When the same three tests are applied to *H*, *V*, and *Y*, different patterns of Yes and No answers appear.

That is all very well for computers, you may think, but surely people do not sort input letters (stimuli) through a series of feature tests. Or do they? One experiment that attempted to answer the question was carried out at Cornell by Anne Pick (1965), who was interested in measuring children's ability to learn to recognize previously unknown visual stimuli. Because she could not use the familiar alphabet, she used materials developed by Gibson called *letter-like forms*. Although these forms use many of the same features (Figure 21.3), they are not true alphabetic letters. Figure 21.6 shows the standard (*a*) and the variations (*b*) that the kindergarteners were first trained to recognize. Pick theorized that the children were learning these discriminations in one of two ways: (1)

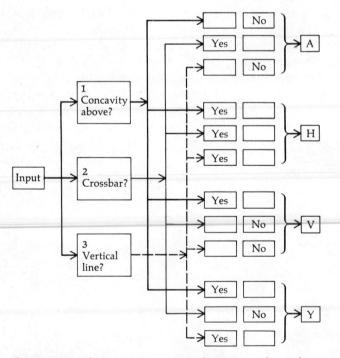

Figure 21.5   A feature-testing system. It recognizes letters by sorting them through a series of tests. (Selfridge and Neisser, 1963, p. 246)

STANDARD FORM

(a)

TEST FORMS

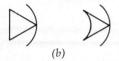

(b)

Figure 21.6   Letter-like forms. (Pick, 1965)

Model matching: The children may have been matching the test forms to a mental model of the standard as a whole. (2) Feature testing: The children may have been attending to changes in particular features of the test stimuli—curved lines in the illustration. She chose between these two hypotheses on the basis of transfer tests. Half the children received new test forms (rotations and reversals), and half learned new materials that had the same types of feature changes (straight to curved lines). Figure 21.7 shows the two.

If the children had been model matching, Group I should have had the highest transfer score, for they were simply seeing the same model in new positions. If the children had been feature testing, Group II should have had the highest transfer score, for although they were seeing a new model, its features were being changed in a familiar way.

Group II was ahead, proving, Pick believes, that feature testing is the basic process involved in recognizing these letter-like forms and in visually discriminating among them. Because the children had practiced feature testing, they were able to transfer their new skill to a form they had never seen before and quickly learned to recognize the same types of feature changes in that new form.

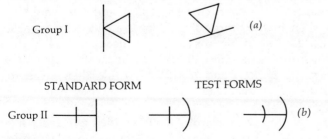

Figure 21.7   More letter-like forms. (a) New test forms, (b) new materials. (Pick, 1965)

Letter Confusability

This brings us back again to the question of *confusability,* because some feature changes are going to be more difficult to discriminate than others. Children may confuse *p* and *q, b* and *d,* which differ in the *direction* of critical features, as well as *E* and *F,* which differ in the *number.* They are not likely to confuse *E* and *q,* because the features involved in that comparison are very different. The difficulty of recognizing differences between letters will depend on which letters are compared.

In a recent experiment by Dunn-Rankin (1968), 315 second- and third-grade children made judgments about groups of letters like the following:

Target Letter	Comparison Letters	
	Which letter (in each pair) looks most like the target letter?	
e	a	b
	y	c
	w	d
	u	e
	t	f

All possible pairs of letters were compared to each target letter (with the exception of the letters *j, q, v, x,* and *z,* which appear infrequently in early reading materials). The results of Dunn-Rankin's study are shown in Figure 21.8. The target letters are shown at the bottom; as one reads up the vertical line the letters become less and less confusable. Thus, *m* is high up the line from *e,* showing that *m* is not easily confused with *e;* but lower on the line from *w,* indicating that *m* is much more easily confused with *w.*

This study can provide several kinds of useful information. First, it is often necessary for teachers to prepare reading materials that differ in degree of confusability. If a child is just learning his letters, *low confusables* (maximum contrast) may be easier for him to recognize. If he knows his letters well, he may still need to drill *high confusables* to become clearly aware of the fine distinctions between them. The Dunn-Rankin chart helps take the guesswork out of the teacher's preparation.

A second application of these results has to do with the construction of words. It can be seen from the chart that *stop, slop,* and *slap* would be highly confusable. In their investigation of children's ability to recognize differences between words, Calvin Nodine and his colleagues studied the effects of confusability. In order to eliminate the role of meaning, Nodine constructed pseudowords like *EROI* and *IEMO.* He could then measure the ability of children to deal perceptually with "words" they had never seen before.

In the first study, Nodine and Hardt (1969) verified the fact that young children (prereading 5-year-olds) had more difficulty recognizing differences between words made up of high confusables (*OEFU* vs. *OFEU*) than between words made up of low confusables (*OFWS* vs. *OWFS*), even though, as the illustrations show, the comparison pairs were composed of the same letters. The experimenters also discovered that the children took longer to make decisions about high-confusable words. To study this further, Nodine and Evans (1969) measured the eye movements of another

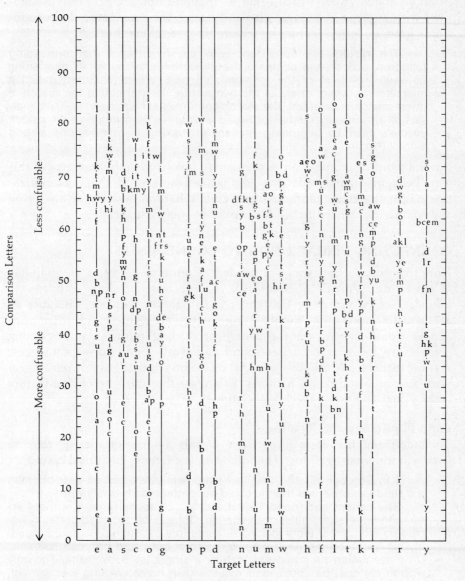

Figure 21.8   Confusability scales developed by Dunn-Rankin (1968, p. 992)

group of young children as they compared pseudowords. The experimenters recorded eye movements on videotape and studied the tape in slow motion. For high-confusable words, the children scanned more and fixated more frequently, and for longer periods of time, than for low-confusable words. Decision time was therefore increased.

Of special significance was the implication that children have a well-developed strategy for solving problems of this sort. They did not "wholistically" match entire words—that is, they did not compare one pseudoword with another in a single glance. Instead, they compared the pseudowords letter by letter, feature by feature, in a serial manner:

> The results are consistent with the hypothesis that prereading [children] search and compare pseudowords letter by letter, alternating between members of the [comparison] pair. When [children] detect a mismatch between letters of the two words, they terminate the search. If no mismatch is detected, the search continues exhaustively. . . . The analysis of eye movements has provided a tentative description of the search process used by beginning readers in making discriminations among words. (Nodine and Evans, 1969, pp. 40–41)

Natural word-discrimination systems may involve search strategies of this sort. Pedagogical methods that emphasize whole-word-shape memorization might therefore conflict with a child's natural system for analyzing and comparing the distinctive features of his new visual code.

CONNECTING VISUAL UNITS TO SOUND UNITS

Note that this section was not headed "Connecting Letters to Sounds," "Connecting Words to Sounds," "Connecting Spelling Patterns to Sounds," or "Connecting Sentences to Intonation Patterns," because all are equally necessary. Emphasizing particular sight-sound correspondences would depend on the degree of reading proficiency. Beginning readers are focusing on letter-sound and word-sound correspondences; mature readers are usually focusing on connections between phrases or sentences and intonation patterns. Whatever the unit, the critical feature is the visual-auditory-speech association.

Brain Physiology and Reading

To understand the basic importance of this association, let us refer to some clinical investigations. The following is a famous historical case:

> [On October 25, 1887] . . . an extremely intelligent 68-year-old man . . . suddenly observed that he could no longer read a single word. . . .
>
> The patient had [good] visual acuity, . . . spoke fluently without error, and understood all spoken speech. Objects were named perfectly, including pictures of technical instruments in a catalogue. He could indentify his own morning newspaper by its form but could not read its name. On presentation he could not identify a single letter by name. The only written material he could read was his own name. Writing was correct, both spontaneously and to dictation, but what was written could not be

read back. . . . His writing was rather like that of a blind man, larger than normal and with poor orientation of the lines.

Although the reading of isolated letters was impossible, the patient could identify them by name after tracing their contours with his finger; if the examiner formed letters by moving the patient's hand through the air, he could name the letters produced in this way. . . .

A rather surprising contrast was the fact that even at the beginning of the illness [the stroke], he could recognize individual Arabic numerals, but had trouble reading several numbers simultaneously and in doing arithmetic calculations. With the passage of time all his difficulties in reading Arabic numerals and in doing even the most complex written calculations disappeared while his difficulties in reading letters persisted unchanged.

. . .

The remarkable discrepancy between the loss of letters and preservation of numbers arouses one's interest in other visual symbols. The patient who had been a skilled musician now showed a total inability to comprehend musical notation, but could write a scale or particular notes to command. The ability to sing and play instruments was unimpaired.

The patient was observed carefully over the next four years. During this time he continued actively and very successfully in business, kept on writing, played cards skillfully, and learned and performed new music by ear. He had no difficulty in orientation even when going to strange parts of Paris.

On January 5, 1892, another [stroke] . . . left him with [damaged] speech and incapable of writing. He died at 10 A.M. on the sixteenth of January and an autopsy was performed . . . twenty-four hours after his death. (Geschwind, 1962, pp. 117–118)

Geschwind quotes this case as one of the earliest illustrations of a type of brain damage that can result in "pure word blindness"—that is, word blindness unaccompanied by speaking and writing difficulties. The physician who performed the autopsy (Dejerine) left a careful description of the condition of the patient's brain. The original stroke damage—the stroke that left the patient word blind for four years—is shown in Figure 21.9.

First of all, both the right and the left side of the brain can see, but only the left side can process language in most normal adults. The stroke made the patient's left side blind and also damaged the "bridge" that connected right-sided vision to the language area. Although the patient could see with the right side of his brain, he could not connect the letters he saw to the language areas on the left side. Unlike some of the patients discussed in Part I, the patient described by Geschwind could name other *things* he saw; his difficulties were solely in naming *words*. Geschwind believed that objects and pictures, being richer in tactual associations than letters, could find other ways of connecting with language.

It has been reported clinically that similar types of brain damage also affect *color* naming (Geschwind & Fusillo, 1966). The ability to connect a color perception to a spoken label appears to involve the same system used for letter-sound and word-sound connections. (Of course, we must not jump to the conclusion that a child who does not know color names is potentially word blind. It may be that nobody has taught him what the color names are.)

One may wonder if the sight of the letter, word, or color is connected to *auditory* or to *speech* brain areas and patterns. Evidence thus far suggests that both may be involved. Birch and his colleagues devised an auditory-visual tapping test that clearly shows the ability to connect visual signals to a heard pattern is important. Hintzman (1967) carried out an experiment which shows that reading and remembering nonsense words may involve silent speech. We will take up each experiment in turn.

Birch's Theory of Auditory-visual Integration and Reading

The latest version of Birch's auditory-visual integration test is shown in Figure 21.10. Subjects first heard the tap patterns shown in the left-hand column. As they listened, they saw three dot patterns, as shown in the right-hand column. Their task was to select the dot pattern that matched the tap pattern. (The correct selections are underlined in the illustration.)

Performance on this auditory-visual tapping test is highly correlated with reading ability. Table 21.1 shows the correlation coefficients of both

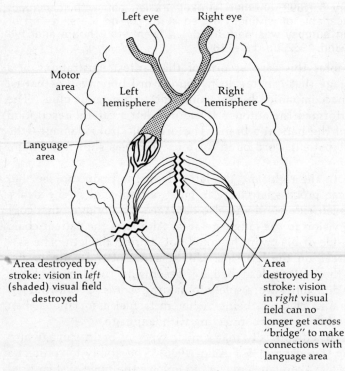

Figure 21.9 Diagram showing the type of brain damage resulting in loss of reading ability. The patient cannot connect words that he sees only with the right side of his brain to the word sounds stored in the language area on the left side of his brain. (Geschwind, 1962, p. 123, with modifications)

Table 21.1
Correlation of Auditory-visual Pattern Integration with Reading Achievement Scores

GRADE	WORD KNOWLEDGE		READING COMPREHENSION	
	CORRELATION (r)	PROBABILITY	CORRELATION (r)	PROBABILITY
2	.37	< .01	.44	< .001
3	.55	< .001	.42	< .001
4	.57	< .001	.46	< .001
5	.57	< .001	.49	< .001
6	.55	< .001	.43	< .001

SOURCE: Kahn and Birch, 1968, p. 463.

word knowledge and comprehension (as was measured by the Metropol-
itan Reading Achievement Tests) with the auditory-visual tapping scores
in grades 2 through 6 (ages 7 through about 12). These data are from an
article by Kahn and Birch (1968).

It can be argued that both reading and auditory-visual tapping abilities
depend on basic intelligence and that basic intelligence is what the two
kinds of tests really have in common, but it is possible to control statistically for the influence of basic intelligence and to show that it is not the

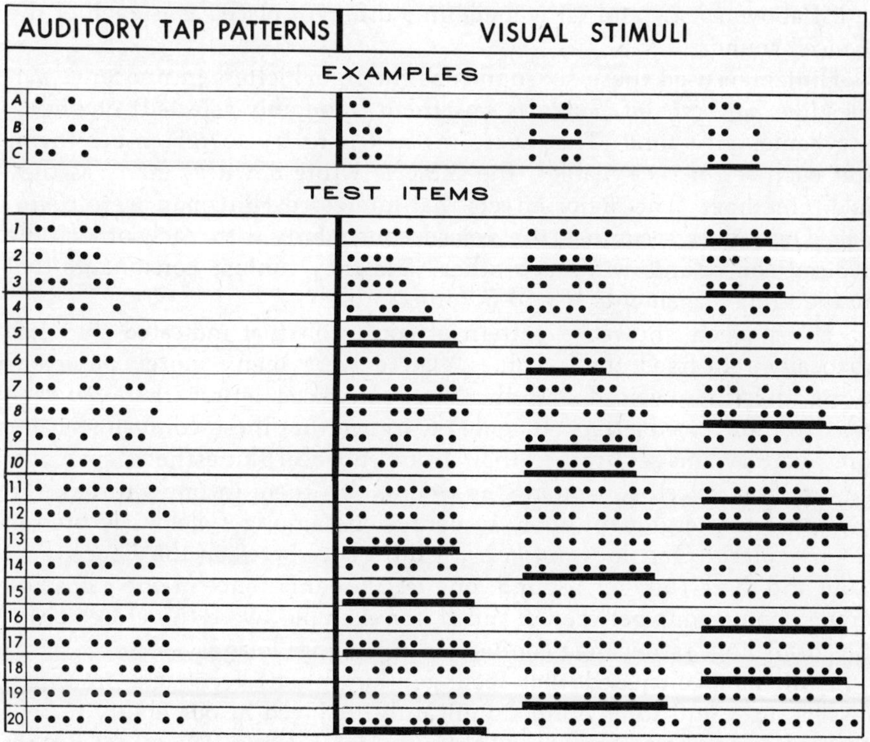

Figure 21.10 Auditory-visual tapping test developed by Herbert Birch and his colleagues
(Kahn and Birch, 1968, p. 461)

major cause of the relationship between auditory-visual integration ability and reading ability. Birch has done so (Kahn and Birch, 1968); he has also shown that the use of verbal labels (saying, "tap, tap" or "one, two" to oneself) does not account for the correlations shown in the table. The children who did count had lower auditory-visual scores than those who "just felt" the auditory-visual patterns, those who tried to visualize the auditory patterns, or those who could not explain what system they used.

Subvocal Reading

Despite these results, some degree of silent vocalization may be involved in reading skillfully. The Hintzman (1967) experiment suggests how. To understand what Hintzman did, we must review two aspects of articulation: *voicing* and *place of articulation*. Voicing refers simply to the involvement of the vocal cords:

Voiced Sounds	Unvoiced Sounds
B (as in bed)	P (as in put)
D (as in dog)	T (as in took)
G (as in good)	K (as in keg)

Placement refers to position in the mouth. Each of the voiced sounds in the list above (*B, D,* and *G*) is made in a different place, as is each of the unvoiced sounds.

Hintzman used these six sounds as the initial letters in nonsense syllables like *baf, kaf, taf.* Subjects saw them (randomly selected) on slides, six syllables at a time. They were instructed to try to remember them. After each set of six syllables, the subjects wrote down as many as they could remember. The major effects that interested Hintzman were *confusions.* Did subjects confuse the voiced consonants with each other? the unvoiced consonants with each other? Did they confuse consonants that had the same placements (*P* and *B,* for example)?

The subjects showed a pattern of confusion that indicated they had subvocally rehearsed the syllables. There were many more confusions among the three voiced and the three unvoiced letters than between voiced and unvoiced letters. It could be argued that these confusions came from auditory images, rather than from subvocal (kinesthetic) practice; one can *hear* voiced consonants as well as *feel* them in one's throat. But how could that argument apply to confusions among syllables located in the same place? One does not *hear* the difference between the *P* (puh . . .) sound and the *T* (tuh . . .) sound; one *feels* the difference in one's lips and tongue. Confusions between *P* and *B,* for example, were therefore confusions of feeling, rather than confusions of auditory images.

Hintzman concluded that feelings (kinesthetic feedback) in throat muscles, lips, and tongue are significantly involved in our ability to register and remember words or syllables we are reading. We might further conclude that good reading pedagogy will take the natural kinesthetic feedback systems into consideration and not try to eliminate them, as methods emphasizing silent reading often do. Just because advanced, skillful readers do not make obvious lip and tongue movements does not mean that no kinesthetic feedback is involved. Quite possibly, beginning readers who do make exaggerated movements and vocalize clearly will be better able to distinguish among sounds that involve similar movements and will become more skillful readers. That is what Chall (1967) means when she says that good reading methods for beginners should not imitate those of mature readers. Beginners need to learn the steps that lead to skills; if they merely try to imitate the skill, they may skip the very steps that guarantee it. An experiment by Jeffrey and Samuels (1967) illustrates this point.

Beginners and Phonic Blends

In order to study children's ability to learn a code that was absolutely new to them, Jeffrey taught his kindergarteners Arabic. One group of children learned four Arabic words; the other group learned four Arabic letters. Both groups then learned four new Arabic words (transfer words). The details are shown in Figure 21.11.

The group that had received letter training learned the new transfer words more quickly than the group that had received whole-word training. In fact, the letter-trained group got one or two of the transfer words right on their very first trial—the first time they had seen the new words. None of the children in the word-trained group were able to do that. Over all trials, children who were above average in IQ learned the new list in about 10 trials if they had had letter training; high-IQ children who had had word training required about 22 trials. The pattern was the same for low-IQ children: those with letter training learned the new words in about 17 trials; the others required about 32 trials. A method that capitalized on children's natural tendency to learn features produced more efficient readers.

Jeffrey emphasized the importance of another aspect of the children's training: drill in phonic blends. All the children, including the whole-word group, were drilled in the sound combinations of the transfer words (*ME, SE, MA,* and *SA*) prior to word or letter training. The whole-word trained children were apparently not able to use the phonic-blend training; the

Initial Training Words	Pronounced	Training Letters	Pronounced	Transfer Words	Pronounced
ﺏ ﺯ	MŌ	ﺏ	M	ﺏ ﻥ	MĒ
ﺍ ﺯ	SŌ	ﺍ	S	ﺍ ﻥ	SĒ
ﺍ ﻭ	BĀ	ﻭ	A	ﺍ ﻭ	SĀ
ﺍ ﻥ	BĒ	ﻥ	E	ﺏ ﻭ	MĀ

Figure 21.11 Arabic letters and sounds used by Jeffrey in his phonics experiment with kindergartners. (Jeffrey and Samuels, 1967)

letter-trained children were. Letter-sound correspondences as well as letter training were important to reading efficiency.

Summary
Visual-auditory-speech connections are critically involved in the reading process. We have seen this illustrated most dramatically in the case of the word-blind patient, who was later found to have suffered damage to systems connecting visual and auditory areas. When these areas were disconnected, the patient's ability to read was destroyed. In the Birch studies and in the Hintzman experiment, the relationship of reading ability to visual-auditory and visual-speech processes was further documented. The Jeffrey experiment applied this evidence specifically to reading training.

The relationship is important on all reading levels. So far, we have considered the most elementary units—sight-sound connections between *phonemes* (small sound units) and *graphemes* (small written units). When we move to large units—connections between the sight and the sound of spelling patterns and whole words (Figure 21.2)—the relationship becomes more complicated.

SPELLING PATTERNS AND WORDS

A casual inspection of our written language may suggest little correspondence between spoken and written forms—or grapheme-phoneme correspondences. This is misleading; the correspondences are much higher than one would think. Their discovery has been made possible by computerized analyses. Computers have been programmed to list all the times *a* has an "ah" sound when it occurs in the first syllable of a word, the second syllable, between two consonants, with an *e* at the end of the word, and so forth. It is possible to count all the possible sounds, in all the possible combinations, in the general vocabulary of educated Americans. (There are between 17,000 and 20,000 words in such a spoken vocabulary.)

The most recent computerized print-out of these lists is contained in a volume published by the Office of Education in 1966, called *Phoneme-Grapheme Correspondences as Cues to Spelling Improvement.* The director of the project was Dr. Paul Hanna of Stanford University. Dr. Hanna and his colleagues verified an earlier estimate that over 80 percent of the sounds in our spoken vocabulary (phonemes) are spelled consistently (represented by a consistent set of graphemes). But the principles involved (the consistencies) also take into consideration the position of a sound in a word, the stress given a word, and so forth. For example, the *i* sound (as in *pin*) can be represented in twenty-two different ways graphemically (there are twenty-two different ways of spelling that sound). However, the letters *i* and *y* actually represent that sound 91 percent of the time; the other representations are rare. Further, if the *i* sound (as in *it*) occurs in the initial position (as in *in* and *ill*), 89 percent of the time it will be represented by *i*.

If the sound occurs in the final position (as in *baby*), 60 percent of the time it will be represented by *y*.

If accent is also taken into consideration, the *i* sound in the initial position will be represented by the letter *i* over 98 percent of the time. *Y* does not represent this sound at all in accented syllables, except in such rarely used words (there are only five of them) as *larynx* and *polyp*.

The remarkable fact is that skillful readers and spellers have apparently learned these rules inductively, in some cases in spite of school training that deemphasizes the natural phoneme-grapheme consistencies. Psychologists have been studying this phenomena with reference to what are called *spelling patterns.* The hub of this research is Cornell University, and its originator is Eleanor Gibson.

Gibson's Spelling Pattern Studies

As Dr. Gibson defines it, a spelling pattern is a letter sequence (such as *ing, con,* or *ough*) that reliably predicts sound. The prediction rules come both from the patterns and from the location of the pattern in a word (for example, *gh* sounds different at the beginning than at the end of a word—as in *ghost* and *enough*). The patterns and the rules are apparently known by all skillful readers.

> The question . . . is how the correspondence rules are learned. Two quite different possibilities suggest themselves. The obvious one, which fits the usual educational procedure, is that the child begins by memorizing whole words. He learns by rote, with flash cards, and so on, to associate the printed CAT with the equivalent spoken word. Later, perhaps in second or third grade, his teacher introduces some phonics, and teaches him how to "sound out" and analyze a word. (This procedure is called "word attack.") Now he might begin to formulate some correspondence rules. On the other hand, the correspondence rules might develop in the way that grammar appears to develop. . . . A child speaks grammatically nearly as soon as he speaks at all, even though the sequence is short and the grammar very simple. . . . Perhaps as soon as a child gets the idea that writing and printing stand for the sounds of his spoken language, he begins to induce for himself the predictive regularities, even though the words are short and the rules, therefore, quite simple ones. One would not expect that he would formulate the rules verbally, any more than a child of four does the rules of grammar. (Gibson, Osser, and Pick, 1963, p. 143)

To decide between these two possibilities, Gibson followed the procedure of testing children's abilities to read nonsense words they had never seen before. If the sight-sound rules were operating for first-graders, Gibson reasoned, the children should be able to read pronounceable spelling patterns—even of nonsense words they had never seen before—better than they could read unpronounceable ones. If the sight-sound rules had not yet been learned, the children should not show any special facility with pronounceable patterns. Some examples of pronounceable and unpronounceable nonsense words are shown below:

Pronounceable	Unpronounceable
TUP	PTU
NUS	NSU
TAC	TCA

These syllables were presented quickly on a screen (a tachistoscope). The children said them, or spelled them, or both.

The fact that the first-graders made far fewer errors on the pronounceable syllables showed that the sight-sound rules were apparently operating for them, despite the lack of formal instruction.

> Tentatively, it is concluded that a child in the early stages of reading skill typically reads in short units but has already generalized certain consistent predictions of [sight-sound] correspondence, so that units [pronounceable spelling patterns] which fit these simple "rules" are more easily read. As skill develops, span increases. . . . The longer items involve more complex . . . rules and longer [spelling patterns], so that the generalizations must increase in complexity as the span increases. . . . This generalizing process undoubtedly promotes reading efficiency and could be facilitated by presenting material in such a way as to enhance the regularities and speed up their incorporation. (Gibson, Osser, and Pick, 1963, p. 146)

The new, so-called linguistic methods of teaching reading are based on research of this type. An example is shown in Figure 21.12.

Surprisingly, Anne Pick and her colleagues discovered that the same kind of sight-sound rules also governed the abilities of blind subjects reading Braille. These subjects took much more time spelling aloud unpronounceable words than pronounceable ones. Apparently they had also learned "sight"-sound grouping principles.

Learning to Spell

Dr. Gibson and her colleagues believe the spelling pattern is the basic unit of word-*reading:* spelling patterns may be the critical features (Figure 21.3) most frequently selected, even by advanced readers. However, the principle that sight and sound go together in an orderly way can be illustrated by letter-sound, word-sound, and phrase-intonation correspondences (Figure 21.2). It may be that learning the principle—on any level—is the critical factor. Dr. Hanna emphasizes this in his suggestions for spelling-pattern instruction:

SOME SUGGESTIONS FOR THE SPELLING COURSE OF STUDY

First grade is not too early to expect children to make initial examination of the code by which they carry on intercommunication. The average child enters first grade with an understanding and speaking vocabulary of from 5,000 to 10,000 words. But a literate person needs also to communicate by writing. Just as the child learns to speak by first making those sounds easiest to enunciate, so his first writing efforts should be based on those graphemes that most regularly represent the phonemes of his language.

A Lot!

"I am hot,"

    said the pot.

"I am wet,"

    said the pet.

"I am cut,"

    said the nut.

Get the pot.

    The pot is hot.

Get the pet.

    The pet is wet.

Get the nut.

    The nut is cut.

I got the nut.

    The nut was cut.

I got the pet.

    The pet was wet.

I got the pot.

    The pot was hot.

I got a lot!

7

Figure 21.12 A page from a new primer that emphasizes spelling patterns. (Rasmussen and Goldberg, 1964, p. 7)

The first grade spelling program ought, therefore, to start with a presentation of the beginning and ending consonant sounds, and the "short" vowel sounds, both regularly exemplified in appropriate monosyllabic words in his oral vocabulary. He should also be taught to form carefully the upper and lower case alphabetical letters that represent the phonemes he is learning to identify in words.

As the child develops, more challenging correspondences may be introduced: (1) single sounds spelling with two different letters, (2) consonant beginning and ending clusters, and (3) other correspondences of increasing complexity.

The second grade spelling program ought to lead the pupil to the discovery of rules and generalizations which help explain both consistencies and peculiarities of phoneme-grapheme behavior as illustrated in various spellings of "long" vowel sounds, formation of plurals and third person singular, irregular spellings of "short" vowel sounds, and the beginning concept of syllabication. Further, the second grade pupil should be introduced to the importance of alphabetical order and its relation to dictionary usage.

The spelling program in subsequent grades should continue to expand the pupil's knowledge of the orthography of his language and be concerned with increasing emphasis upon examination of factors that

The farmer planted *beepers* in his field
Rabbits love to eat beepers.
Mrs. Jones made curtains the orange color of beepers.

Beepers means ___ Carres ___

Watching T.V. sometimes makes me very *poud*.
If I am poud in school, I cannot do my work well.
"Oh, you make me poud!" said Mary in a cross voice.

Poud means ___ tierd ___

LIST ALL THE THINGS THAT WOULD HAPPEN IF

EVERYONE WANTED TO BE AWAY FROM PEOPLE, AND BE ALONE

1 It would be verry lony

2 Babies would Oid

3 Evry one would starve

4 there would be know teacher

5 there would be no friends

6 the priqpals

7 No egocashin

8 You would be sacecard and brod

Figure 21.13

influence the correct choice of graphemic representation in increasingly complicated words. . . .

The instructional area most likely to be neglected in the spelling programs is that of pupil discovery of the behavior of phoneme-grapheme correspondences in his language, and the rules and generalizations upon which the orthography is based. The inductive approach should be given the importance it deserves; and the teacher, rather than initiating the rule or principle to be learned, should encourage the pupil to extract it from close examination of words which illustrate the generalization being presented in a particular lesson. . . .

By using the resources of linguistic analysis, one can enlarge and deepen the scope of the spelling programs. Children can be expected to be able to spell, in the elementary grades, a vocabulary of from 6,000 to 12,000 or more words, depending upon the size of usable oral vocabularies. By building into the child the analytic power that comes from a knowledge of the structure of the American-English orthography, there will be almost no limit to the eventual size of his spelling vocabulary. (Hanna, Hanna, Hodges, and Rudorf, 1966, pp. 128–129)

Idiosyncratic Sight-sound Rules

To many readers, the technical discussion thus far may sound distressingly mechanized. Letters have sight-sound rules; spelling patterns have sight-sound rules; words have sight-sound rules. In addition, there are rules within rules: The rules for letters depend on where they occur in spelling patterns; the rules for spelling patterns depend on where they occur in words. Rules, rules, rules, all for children to learn. The remarkable thing is that they do learn them, just as they learn the complex grammatical rules of their spoken language: *but they may be the wrong rules.*

The child's language is the reading and spelling teacher's greatest ally or his greatest adversary. The reading and spelling child is listening to himself first. If he has not been taught the correct system for transcribing his own voice sounds into written forms, he will make up a system of his own. As Figure 21.13 illustrates, children will use rules, whether they are taught to or not. Unless the teacher begins with this principle, he will produce inadequate, half-taught language writers. (Refer back to Chapter 19 for material on learning standard English as a second language.) The problem is not whether to teach children rules; the problem is how to guide them into the natural selection of the correct rules. As you can see from the examples in Figure 21.13, there is nothing defective about the thinking of these fifth-grade children, but they are using a dialect that is not reflected in standard English orthography.*

READING COMPREHENSION

On the whole . . . *written materials contain less of the language signals than does talk.* In the graphic representations of language there are

---

*Further discussion of these problems may be found in *Teaching Black Children to Read*, edited by Joan Baratz and Roger Shuy, and published by the Center for Applied Linguistics (1717 Massachusetts Ave., N.W., Washington, D.C. 20036) in 1969. It is highly recommended.

left out such language signals as intonation and stress and pause. These are important features of the signals of meanings, especially of social-cultural meanings. If one is to read with comprehension . . . *he must learn to supply those portions of the signals which* are not in the graphic representations themselves. He must supply the significant stresses, pauses, and intonation sequences. A large part of learning to read is a process of learning to supply rapidly and automatically the portions of the oral signals that are not represented in the graphic signs. It is not simply a matter of speed and fluency. It shows itself in oral reading in what has been called reading "with expression." This oral reading "with expression" consists . . . of supplying the tone sequences, the stresses, and the pauses that in talk mark the word groupings that signal the total range of meanings. Real reading is not solely a passive process. . . . Real reading is *productive reading*—an active responding . . . that the written text requires to fill out its full range of signals. The simple question *When did he come?* can have the major stress upon any one of the four syllables, within a single intonation sequence.

When did he｜co＼me

When did｜he｜come

When｜did｜he come

When｜did he come

Each of these stresses would signal a particular different meaning. Nothing in the graphic shapes of the written representation of the question . . . provides the clue.

. . .

. . . The process of receiving a message through "talk" is a responding to the language signals of [one's] native language code—language signals that make their contact with his nervous system by *sound vibrations through the ear*. The process of getting the same message (the same meanings) through the "reading" of "writing" is responding to the *same set of language signals* of the same language code, but language signals that make their contact with his nervous system by *light vibrations through the eye*. (Fries, 1963, pp. 130–132)

As Figure 21.2 illustrates, we may think of this reading comprehension process as a matter of (1) making connections between written phrase patterns and intonation patterns, (2) generating associations to the language patterns (in ways that are probably similar to the semantic systems discussed in Chapter 18), and (3) selecting mutually sensible associations. This brings about the vivid imaginative realization described by Fries.

Developmental Problems

It is at this level (Figure 21.2) that special problems of cognitive development or neurological handicap may become apparent. Usually when we say "Johnny can't read," we mean he cannot "make sense of" the groups of words called phrases or sentences. He may be able to sound out the letter-sound and the spelling-pattern correspondences, but still fail to get the meaning when he puts words together in groups. He may be failing to connect the phrase patterns received visually to the intonation patterns stored in the auditory-speech areas of his brain. As we know from Geschwind's reports, such a comprehension failure may occur because of neurological damage. The same kinds of neurological "disconnections" may be involved in developmental *dyslexia*—the type of word blindness that seems to be present from birth in some people, especially boys, and that may be inherited (Critchley, 1964b).

Even more general, however, are problems of simple development. As we know from Chapters 1 and 4, associative systems are not present in full from birth, but must grow. Most of this growth has usually been completed prior to the time a child enters formal school at the age of 6. It is because of the exceptions that educators have developed the concept of "readiness." Children who can quickly learn letter-sound, spelling-pattern sound, and word-sound connections may still have difficulty integrating these units into meaningful phrases because they may not yet have sufficiently well-developed associative brain power. The problem may be especially frequent in children under the age of 6, but it may also occur in children 8, 10, and 12 years old.

Readiness and Practice

Whether we are dealing with normal development, slow development, or actual handicaps, *practice is still necessary. If we simply "wait until a child is ready," he may never be ready.* That message comes to us repeatedly from the sources discussed in Chapter 4, and it is illustrated again by experiments like the following:

Consider the *logographs* (whole-word symbols) shown in Figure 21.14. Unlike words composed of alphabet letters, these whole-word symbols do not have to be decoded (the child does not have to go through a preliminary step of alphabetic recognition). When the logographs are put into simple sentences, as in Figure 21.15, the child's ability to comprehend can be studied, even though he may be too young to have learned his alphabet. (He must first have learned his logographs, however.)

The logographs are surprisingly easy even for 3-year-olds to learn. Table 21.2 shows that the average score for a group of 3-year-olds was 5.7 correct out of a possible 8. By the time children are 5 years old, their score is almost perfect. (All children in this study learned the logographs in three trials lasting less than 4 minutes.)

Table 21.2 also shows, however, that the youngest children had great difficulty comprehending the meaning of sentences composed of logographs like those in Figure 21.15, even though they knew each logograph in the sentence. They demonstrated their comprehension in the following manner: After they had learned their logographs, eight sentences were presented to them, one by one. The child first read a sentence aloud—*jump over block,* for example. When he could read it correctly, the experimenter said, "All right, now let me see you *do* it." A block had previously been placed on the floor, and the child had previously practiced jumping over it.

On hearing that instruction, a 7- or 8-year-old child will walk over to the block and jump over it. A younger child is more likely to jump up in the air, make a sort of gesture for *over,* and then point to the block on the floor. He fails to integrate the logographs into a meaningful whole, and instead demonstrates each part separately. We know this because he does not coordinate his reading behavior with actions that would demonstrate such integration. Table 21.2 also shows that brain-damaged children of 12 years may not be able to perform these integrations at a normal 6-year-old level. This result again suggests that the problem is at the associative level, since the brain-damaged children could learn the sight-sound correspondences of the logographs as well as normal children could.

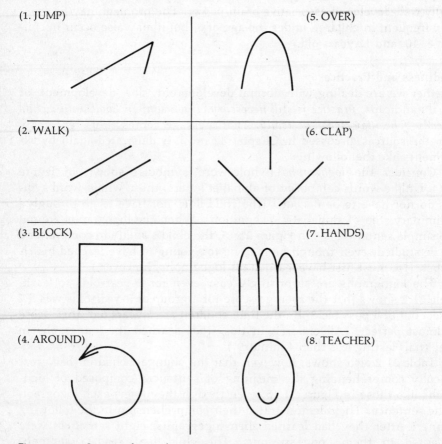

Figure 21.14   Logographs used in experiments on reading comprehension. (Farnham-Diggory, 1967)

Table 21.2
Logograph Learning and Sentence Integration

AGE	COMPREHENSION TRAINING	MEAN LOGOGRAPH SCORES (8 LOGOGRAPHS)	MEAN SENTENCE COMPREHENSION SCORES (8 SENTENCES)
3 to 4 years	No	5.7	1.9
4 to 5 years	No	7.1	2.8
5 to 6 years	No	7.7	4.1
6 to 7 years	No	7.7	4.4
8 to 9 years	No	7.8	5.9
5 to 6 years (children from black ghetto)	Yes	5.7	5.9
9 to 13 years (brain-damaged)	No	7.6	5.2

SOURCE: Based on data in Farnham-Diggory, 1967, 1970.

Denner (1970) recently administered these same tasks to average readers, problem readers, and Head Start children who were expected to become problem readers. He found that all his groups performed equally well on the enactive, pictograph, and logograph tasks, but not on the synthesis task.

> . . . The same problem readers and nonreaders who were able to grasp the meaning of the logographs found it very difficult to translate a string of logograph symbols into a unified act. . . . One might say that these children do not read sentences but a series of individual words; and the sentence meaning is some conglomerate of individual word meanings rather than a unified contextualized conception. . . . The average readers seemed to appreciate that words derive their meaning from the sentence context. (Denner, 1970, p. 886)

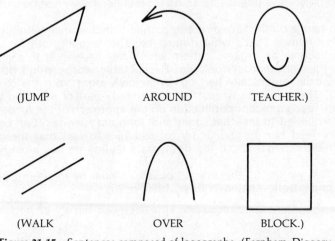

Figure 21.15   Sentences composed of logographs. (Farnham-Diggory, 1967)

Can these associations and integrations be taught? Two experiments have indicated they can be. A group of researchers at Syracuse University (Hall, et al., 1969) successfully taught young children to coordinate these sentences and other research also showed that 5-year-old black children from an urban ghetto could be taught to perform these sentence integrations at a level that surpassed that of third- and fourth-grade suburban children (Farnham-Diggory, 1970). In both cases, the children first practiced the behavior associated with the integrations (they practiced jumping over blocks, for example). This may have increased the associative potential of the logographs; even though the children already knew the actions (how to jump over blocks), the *overlearning* that resulted from their practice increased the associative power necessary for *sentence* comprehension.

Language Experience and Comprehension
The so-called language-experience approach emphasizes the role of enriched associations in the reading comprehension process. Good descriptions of the method are provided by Stauffer in *Directing Reading Maturity as a Cognitive Process* (1969a) and *Teaching Reading as a Thinking Process* (1969b). A similar approach is documented in Sylvia Ashton-Warner's *Teacher:*

> Organic reading is not new. The Egyptian hieroglyphics were one-word sentences. Helen Keller's first word "water," was a one-word book. . . . Out in the field of UNESCO today, it is used automatically as the only reasonable way of introducing reading to primitive people: in a famine area the teachers wouldn't think of beginning with any words other than "crop," "soil," "hunger," "manure" and the like. . . . Of course, as I'm always saying, it's not the only reading; it's no more than the *first*. The bridge.
> It's the bridge from the known to the unknown; from a native culture to a new; and, universally speaking, from the inner man out. . . .
> First words must have intense meaning for a child. They must be part of his being.
> How much hangs on the love of reading, the instinctive inclination to hold a book. *Instinctive!* That's what it must be. The reaching out for a book needs to become an organic action, which can happen at this yet formative age. Pleasant words won't do. Respectable words won't do. They must be words organically tied up, organically born from the dynamic life itself. They must be words that are already part of the child's being. "A child," reads a recent publication on the approach of the American books, "can be led to feel that Janet and John are friends." *Can be led to feel.* Why lead him to feel or try to lead him to feel that these strangers are friends? What about the passionate feeling he has already for his own friends?
> . . . These first words . . . these first books . . . must be made out of the stuff of the child itself. (Ashton-Warner, 1963, p. 25)

The creative zest of the language-experience approach can hardly be better described.

Early in the process, children also begin to dictate their own stories, and later to write them (on the typewriter, using primer-sized type, if possible). Stauffer (1969a) recommends two books about that kind of pedagogy: *Helping Children Write* (Applegate, 1961), and *They All Want to Write* (Burrows, Ferebee, Jackson, and Saunders, 1952). Integrative processes may be practiced in still other ways. Stories about a single topic may be packaged together, for example. Private word files may be kept and combined in new ways. Stauffer has recommended the use of a Pupil Word Card Holder that may be used for stories or messages:

Peggy . . . had set up the following story on her Word Card Holder:

I	like	pets

The	Turtle	is	a

pet in	our	room

Do	you	like	pets	?

Peggy

Placing the words on a Holder had many advantages. First, since the cards adhered to the surface, they stayed in place. Second, the holder could be moved about with ease without upsetting the word arrangement. Third, pupils could swap holders and thus exchange stories. Fourth, the words could be removed with ease and refiled for future use.

Pupils could write notes to each other. Edna wrote a note to Patsy:

May	I	read	your	turtle	story	?

Patsy put the answer on her Holder:

Yes

. . . Dick, with the help of Bill [who was a better reader] put this question on his Holder:

May	I	use	the	easel	to	paint	my	picture	?

At this stage Dick could read only three words in that question

May	I	picture

but he knew what the question asked. Even though the teacher was busy in a private pupil conference, Dick walked up to her and waited quietly

until she could turn to him. Then he handed his Holder to her. She read
the message, added the word

$$\boxed{\text{yes}}$$

and returned the Holder to him. . . . This was communicating with a purpose. (Stauffer, 1969a, pp. 201–202)

Language Experience and Code Methods Compared

Like most reading "controversialists," teachers who believe in the language-experience approach argue that they teach all aspects of the reading
process sooner or later. But clearly this approach emphasizes the reading
skills located in (D) of Figure 21.2. As Fries (1962) and Chall (1967) point
out, if associative enrichment (language experience) is emphasized to the
exclusion of the sight-sound rules of letters, spelling patterns, and
words—(A), (B), (C) of Figure 21.2—the average child, having been deprived of the basics, may never develop true reading fluencies.

> No one should quarrel with any of the assertions given by . . . reading
> experts concerning the need to make careful provision for "the cultivation
> of a whole array of techniques involved in understanding, thinking, re-
> flecting, imagining, judging, evaluating, analyzing . . . reasoning, and in
> making emotional and social judgments." Nor should he object to efforts
> to stimulate and strengthen any or all of these habits and abilities through
> the *use of reading*. But we certainly confuse the issue if we insist that this
> *use* of reading . . . *constitutes the reading process.* . . . Every one of the
> abilities listed may be developed and has been achieved *by persons who
> could not read.*
>
> . . .
>
> . . . To learn to walk the child must first achieve such muscular coor-
> dinations as will enable him to keep his upright balance by pushing with
> his feet upon something solid. To learn to swim he must first gain such
> muscular coordinations as will enable him to keep his balance while lying
> prone and pushing with his hands upon the water. In both situations, all
> consideration of the *uses* to be made of the skill of walking or that of
> swimming must be postponed until the first stages of the learning process
> have been mastered. (Fries, 1962, p. 118)

It is easy to see how the use of swimming (in a relay race, for example) might intensify the confusion of a beginner; it is sometimes less easy
to see how a similar emphasis on the use of words might confuse a beginning reader, who has not yet mastered the code. Just as the relay race
could be won by running around the side of the pool by a child who had
not yet learned to swim, so language experiences may be more quickly
achieved by avoiding reading—if the beginning reader is permitted to
achieve them in this way.

Comprehension—the enriched associative processes of reading—must
be approached through the *reading code system,* not through a bypass.
The child does this by gradually building up longer and longer sight-sound
systems (phrases) as his skills increase. As he builds, he must also prac-

tice comprehension—by practicing the behaviors associated with the phrases he is reading.

The Eye-voice Span and Comprehension

Once the child has become able to connect language patterns with written patterns, his language may help guide his perceptual processes. In the beginning, the pronounceability of spelling patterns may help guide his perception of them. In stages of advanced comprehension, the feedback processes may operate to guide efficient perception of whole phrases.

Harry Levin, also of Cornell University, has been investigating these feedback processes experimentally by means of the *eye-voice span*—that part of a phrase you could continue to recite right after the light was turned off your book. In young children, only one or two words can be recited. In adults who are good readers, whole phrases can be and usually are recited. That is, good readers have what Levin calls an *elastic* span that expands or shrinks with phrase boundaries. Judging by their recall after the lights were turned out, subjects would have read up to a comma, a conjunction, a period, or any other phrase marker. For example, the eye-voice span is longer for passive than for active sentences. In a sentence like "The ball was hit by the boy with the white hat," good readers would have seen all the words following the word *by,* which operated in this case as a phrase boundary.

> . . . Reading is a process of *hypothesis-making* and *confirmation.* In this respect, reading is similar to talking. When we talk, you make guesses about what I am going to say next so you don't listen to every word. But you do sample my speech and you trust your sampling strategy as long as the discourse fits your expectations. As the fit lessens, you begin to sample more densely. You listen more closely, in the same way that you begin to read every word. (Levin, 1967, pp. 128–129)

This description is reminiscent of the Language Acquisition System diagrammed in Figure 17.1. It too can be more systematically presented as a concept acquisition flow chart like that diagrammed in Figure 21.16. One begins with a phrase, transfers it to temporary storage (memory), takes in the next phrase, integrates it with the previous one, and asks the question (covertly), "Does this integration make sense?" If it does, the third phrase is added in; if it does not, one computes a new concept correcting the peculiarity, adds in the third phrase, and so forth.

Black English

But what of the dialect speaker of English? Again, we can see how the integration or concept-attainment process may be crippled in a reader whose personal phraseology (spoken language) differs from the phraseology of a standard English text. The logical way to help dialect speakers develop reading comprehension skills is to let them practice on materials that match their natural phrasing systems. Some examples follow from Wolfram and Fasold:

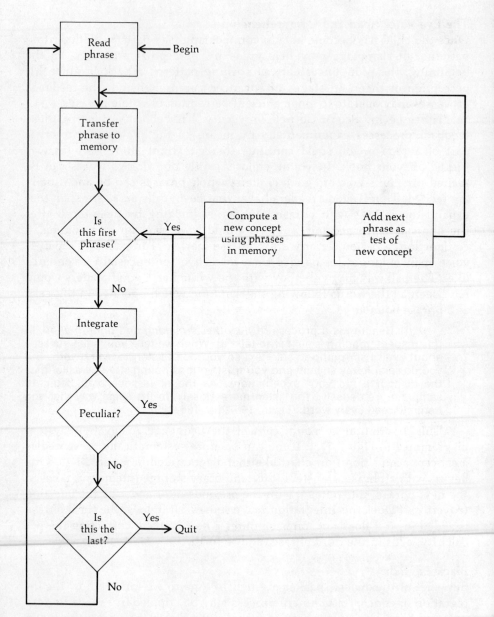

Figure 21.16 Flow diagram of the reading comprehension process, based on the concept-attainment diagram of Part II (Figure 8.1).

Standard English Version	**Black English Version**
(Child is looking at her reflection in a puddle.)	

"Look down here," said Suzy. "I can see a girl in here. That girl looks like me."	Susan say, "Hey, you-all, look down here, I can see a girl in here. The girl she look like me."
David said, "I do not see a girl."	David say, "I don't see no girl."
. . .	. . .
Nicodemus said to him, "How can this be?" Jesus answered him, "Are you a teacher of Israel, and yet you do not understand this? Truly, truly I say to you, we speak of what we know, and bear witness to what we have seen; but you do not receive our testimony."	So Nicodemus say, "How you know that?" Jesus say, "You call yourself a teacher that teach Israel and you don't know these kind of things? I'm gonna tell you, we talking about something we know about cause we already seen it. We telling it like it is and you-all think we jiving." (Wolfram and Fasold, 1969, pp. 138–155)

Note the black English examples do not violate standard English sight-sound rules; they merely permit the natural phrasing system of a nonstandard speaker to guide the concept-attainment process. Additional examples and details may be found in Baratz and Shuy, *Teaching Black Children to Read* (1969).

Chapter 22 PROCESSING MAPS, GRAPHS, AND DIAGRAMS

Pictures represent more or less exactly what we see. Language does not: the written word *chicken* looks nothing like a chicken (although the words *cockle-doodle-doo* sound vaguely like the rooster crow they represent). Graphic representations—maps, graphs, diagrams—seem to be midway between the two: they are less visually literal than a picture, but more visual than language. Perhaps just for this reason, they may cause special processing problems, for we must often talk to ourselves about graphic representations if we are to understand them.

In this chapter, we will take up first the relation of graphic representational ability to cognitive development, as described by Piaget, Draw-a-Person IQs, and the like. We will consider also the effects of motivation and of previous learning (or the absence of it) on these representational abilities. Although little has been done to explore children's maplike abilities, we will look at what there is and relate it to cognitive development and to social and racial factors. Finally, we will consider some specific recoding problems: recoding of numbers in graphs and of mathematical information in diagrams. This will help prepare us for the mathematical processing systems to be discussed in Chapter 23.

THE DEVELOPMENT OF GRAPHIC REPRESENTATIONAL ABILITIES

Piaget and his colleagues believe the ability to *operate images* follows general operational development; it does not precede it. We must therefore not expect young children to do better thinking about maps or diagrams than they can do about other kinds of problems. In fact, a young child may become "perceptually stuck" or distracted by visual materials and may not be able to relate them analytically to other information. One way to demonstrate this phenomenon has been shown by Inhelder (1965).

Show children two pieces of cardboard like this and make sure they are able to draw them:

Then say, "If I push the upper square a little bit to the right (indicate direction, but do not touch squares), can you do a drawing that shows me what the two squares will look like?"

Preoperational children (approximately 4 years old) tend to "conserve a frontier" by doing the following:

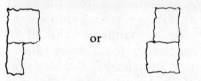

They may continue to do this even after seeing the correct representation:

But by the time a child is about 6, he will correct his own representation when shown a correct model.

Similarly, anticipations of rotated or somersaulting objects are difficult for young children. They cannot perform mental operations on images of things, until their general operational development has advanced. (We will pursue Piaget's theories further in Chapter 23.)

Representational Skills and IQ

Although Draw-A-Person IQ tests have nothing to do with Piaget's theories, they represent another version of the idea that general mental development precedes graphic representational ability. The most famous of these tests is Goodenough's (Harris, 1963). The child is asked simply to draw a picture of a man—the best picture he is able to make. The drawing is then scored for a long list of characteristics: Head present? arms present? fingers shown? correct number of fingers shown? There are about fifty items, including some that evaluate motor coordination (lines firm and correctly joined?) and eye detail, and norms showing how many points a child of a given age usually gets. One can estimate IQ from these scores, which show a fairly high correlation with the Stanford-Binet. About 50 percent of the variability (range of scores) on the Draw-a-Person test can be predicted from the Stanford-Binet (see Anastasi, 1968, pp. 249-250, for more details). Typical changes in draw-a-person ability with age are shown in Figure 22.1.

Other Influences on Drawing Skills

Some charming studies have shown that draw-a-person abilities are affected by motivation and expectancy. In one experiment, children between 4 and 8 years old drew pictures of Santa Claus before and after Christmas. Figure 22.2 shows some examples of the results.

The study most likely to make us cautious about draw-a-person IQs was that carried out by Cameron in 1938. He asked medically trained adults (physicians) to make drawings of a man riding a horse. One of the drawings is reproduced in Figure 22.3. Note the elements missing: facial features, fingers, and arms—not to mention parts missing from the horse (two more legs, for example). Even more revealing was Cameron's transcript of the "artist's" monologue, which hardly sounds like that of an adult: "This is General Sherman—(*of the horse*) looks more like a duck—(*of the man*) I'll make him a cowboy (*no change made*)—there! (*Quite obviously pleased with the work*)" (Cameron, 1938, p. 170). It is clear that although operational development is reflected in graphic representation ability, it must be disentangled from matters of motivation and basic drawing ability. Like any other complex coordination, that of image and hand may take considerable practice. Other measures of IQ (like a medical school diploma) may tell a different story.

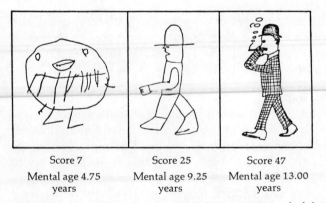

| Score 7 | Score 25 | Score 47 |
| Mental age 4.75 years | Mental age 9.25 years | Mental age 13.00 years |

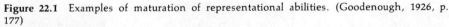

Figure 22.1 Examples of maturation of representational abilities. (Goodenough, 1926, p. 177)

GRAPHIC SYMBOLIZATION

When we say that a drawing is inadequate, we are actually recognizing that something observed or remembered has not been fully translated into a two-dimensional graphic form. In creative art, the artist himself is free

Figure 22.2 Changes in three children's drawings of Santa Claus before and after Christmas. (Solley and Murphy, 1960, p. 166)

Figure 22.3 Childish drawing from a scientifically trained adult who was an experienced horseman. (Cameron, 1938, p. 169)

to decide which aspects of his subject are to be translated and what the rules of the translation will be. Picasso, for example, may decide that only the angular features of a chair are to be recorded; distance between the angles, colors, solidity may be ignored. Further, he may decide how the angles will be recorded. If he chooses, he can represent the angles as curves or as opposite angles—anything in the chair that "goes out" may be represented as "going in."

Such freedom is not found in the type of material generally called "visuals" in classrooms—maps, diagrams, charts. Academic visuals are characterized by the requirement that a one-to-one correspondence must exist between critical features of the concept and its graphic representation. The types of representation used are also usually limited to conventional graphic symbols. Both principles are illustrated in the maps shown in Figure 22.4.

Map-making Skills and Culture

The part of the figure labeled (a) is a map of his house and school in Nepal (India) drawn by a 15-year-old Limbu boy. In fact, the house and the school are not on the same road, and the map is wholly inadequate. It contrasts sharply with the (b) map. Dart and Pradhan, from whose study the illustrations are taken, explain why:

> The "maps" we obtained from the Nepalese respondents are all very similar to each other and to the example shown in Figure 22.4(a). Always they include a recognizable *picture* of "my house," and of "the school," the two being connected by a line which seems to denote *the process of going* from one to the other, not the spatial relationship of one to the other. Thus, the two buildings . . . are not in fact on the same street or path, being separated by several street intersections and other landmarks,

none of which appear on the map. In contrast we show [Figure 22.4(b)] a map typical of those drawn by American children in response to the same instructions. Here both house and school are represented by abstract symbols, not pictures, and there is a clear effort to show spatial relationships and to provide needed spatial clues. The propensity of the Nepalese for making maps . . . which are *sequential* rather than spatial constructs is not limited to school children. In a land of foot trails, where literacy is too low to justify the use of signs, this propensity has been a source of consternation to more than a few travelers of Western upbringing! We, too, in reply to our inquiries as we traveled, were given instructions of "maps" which, like a string of beads, list in correct sequence the places we should

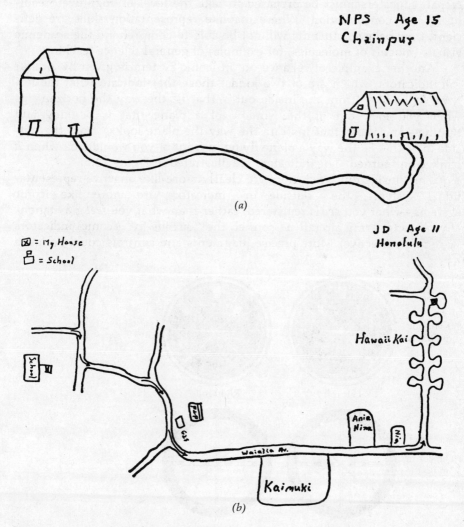

Figure 22.4   Maps drawn by (a) a 15-year-old Nepalese boy and (b) an 11-year-old American boy. (Dart and Pradhan, 1967, p. 653)

pass through without giving any clue as to distances, trail intersections, changes of directions, and so on. Our interest is not in the accuracy or potential usefulness of this . . . but in the light it may shed on a way of thinking. . . . (Dart and Pradhan, 1967, p. 653)

Enactive vs. Iconic Representation

As we know from Part I, in Bruner's theory the Nepalese representational system would be described as still predominantly *enactive,* as compared to the more *iconic-into-symbolic* level of development displayed in the map of the 11-year-old American youngster. Dart and Pradhan feel that to introduce the teaching of science, in particular, into underdeveloped areas like Nepal, educators must be prepared to take the level of cognitive "readiness" into consideration. Where maplike representation skills are deficient, they believe, students will not be able to comprehend the academic visuals (models of molecules, for example) of general science teaching.

Another example of reliance on an iconic system is given by aircraft roll indicators, which are of two kinds: those that indicate what the horizon looks like "from the inside out"—that is, the way the horizon tips when you look out of the window of a plane that is banking and turning—and those that indicate the way the plane looks "from the outside in"—that is, the way a plane flying in front of you would look when *it* banked and turned. The indicators are illustrated in Figure 22.5.

The "inside out" indicators are clearly more like enactive representational systems; the "outside in" indicators are more like iconic systems—what you *see* is registered, rather than what you *feel* gravitationally. Among Army aircraft personnel, the "outside in" (iconic) indicators were most effective. More precise judgments and controls could be made

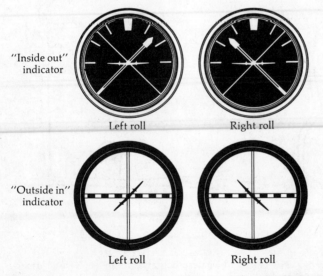

Figure 22.5   Examples of airplane indicators. (Chapanis, Garner, and Morgan, 1949, p. 158)

to displays of that sort than to the "inside out" (enactive) displays. Presumably, the iconic indicators matched the mental level of the pilots better than the enactive indicators did.

Symbolic Representation

The use of iconic materials will not ensure comprehension of academic visuals that have *symbolic* meanings. Vernon (1945) carried out an extensive study of the ability of 90 Army men, 89 RAF airmen, and 52 female teachers college students majoring in art to comprehend graphic information of the sort diagrammed in Figures 22.6 and 22.7. The subjects studied the figures for several minutes and then answered questions about what they had seen. They were not very sure of their interpretations:

> It is often not sufficiently recognized by those who advocate visual methods of presentation that the graph and the chart are no [less symbolic] . . . than are verbal and mathematical statements. But whereas nearly everyone in the course of their upbringing acquires some fluency in making verbal statements of ideas and meanings, only the specially educated are able to interpret general factual information from graphs and charts.
>
> Consequently, it is not surprising that this interpretation was often found to be difficult, and the subjects were slow to make it spontaneously without explicit instructions. In particular, there was a tendency to describe the appearance of the graphs or charts, rather than to report on the information they were intended to convey. Thus [about 35 percent of the reports] . . . contained irrelevant description of appearance—what the

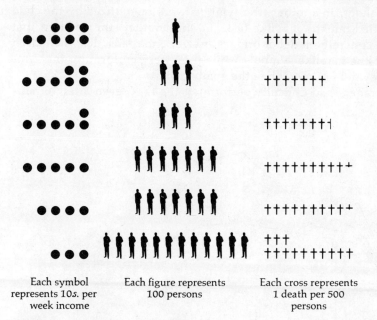

| Each symbol represents 10s. per week income | Each figure represents 100 persons | Each cross represents 1 death per 500 persons |

Figure 22.6 Graph of population, income, and mortality shown to British army personnel and student teachers. (Vernon, 1945, p. 148)

symbols of the charts or the curves of the graphs looked like. . . . The subject might be so preoccupied with appearance as to pay no attention to meaning. . . .

. . .

It follows in using such graphical material for instructional purposes, it is necessary to point out quite definitely how it is to be interpreted and what relation it bears to the data that are being presented. (Vernon, 1947, pp. 147–148)

Vernon felt that adequate instruction involved symbol explanations (what stands for what); verbal associations (enriched verbal knowledge of the events being graphed); and well-organized systems for selecting and relating this information. We can recognize a somewhat more general version of Figure 21.2, part (D): Symbols used in charts or graphs must be systematically connected to language association systems if comprehension is to occur. Learning to "read" graphs means learning to respond to them as *codes,* rather than as pictures.

Iconic vs. Symbolic Codes

A map is also a code from which pictures may distract the viewer. One set of studies (Farnham-Diggory, 1970) explored the development of maplike thinking skills under conditions of distraction by highly salient graphic symbols. The children were asked to make a bridge crossing a river with a road on each side, by using symbols they constructed from black strings (Figure 22.8).

In one study, the symbols were placed before the child so that he could refer to them; in another, the symbols were memorized by the child before he carried out the maplike task; in still another, the children first practiced on a concrete model of bridges, rivers, and roads. These children also looked at the maplike symbols while they were performing the symbolic task. They did not memorize the symbols first.

Second-graders had difficulty performing the task, even after 10 min-

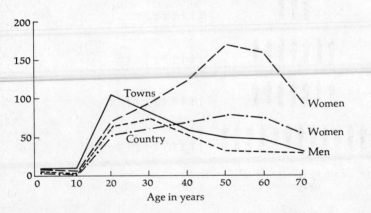

Figure 22.7 Graph showing deaths at various ages from tuberculosis of the lungs of people living in towns and in the country (Vernon, 1945, p. 149)

utes of play on the concrete materials, if the symbols were placed before them. They were better able to solve the problem if they memorized the symbols first and then worked on the problem. The language of the instruction could more effectively guide their maplike operations. If the symbols were constantly visible, they distracted the children from relating them properly.

Something like "picture-processing dominance" may interfere with our symbolic abilities on graphic materials. When we see a map or a chart, we generally expect to understand it in the same way that we understand pictures, and picture-comprehension habits may be quite strong because of all the practice we may have had. We expect to get the message of a chart instantaneously. When the message does not come through, we may become confused about what remedial steps to take. They are usually these:

1. Clarifying the nature of the code—of what symbol stands for what concept

2. Clarifying the nature of the relationships among the symbols—how this is more than that at one point in time, but not at another

3. Clarifying a proper sequence of interpretative steps—what should be looked at first, second

We must therefore develop a verbal program for threading our way through academic visuals. We must learn what to *say* about what we are seeing and in what order to say it. The verbal program is another version of the iconic-to-symbolic transition described by Bruner: "It may be true that a picture is worth a thousand words, but if the object is to locate its functional equivalent in another context then perhaps one word is worth a thousand pictures if it contains the conceptual key" (Bruner, Olver, and Greenfield, 1966, pp. 28–29).

Summary

In the first part of this chapter, we looked at the development of symbolic imagery and noted Piaget's belief that this is an outgrowth of general operational development. From Piaget's point of view, the use of graphic

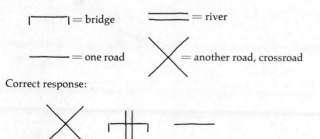

Figure 22.8   A set of graphic symbols. (Farnham-Diggory, 1970)

symbols is an advanced operational skill. Throughout this book, we have argued that schools can provide experiences which ensure the development of advanced operational skills and that the lack of these early experiences may inhibit development. This viewpoint would fit with that of Piaget, but not the further statement that graphic comprehension, like reading comprehension, involves the connection of graphic symbols to *language*. (Piaget does not think important operational developments are dependent on language.)

As we have seen, *pictorial* comprehension does not depend on language, although language may be necessary to focus and limit pictorial associations. *Reading* and *graphic* comprehension both depend on language: Words and graphic symbols are really codes for verbal statements, which they present in visual form.

Now, what about mathematics?

Chapter 23 PROCESSING MATHEMATICAL INFORMATION

Psychological history may eventually show that Piaget was really talking about mathematical abilities all along. Certainly, his nonverbal operations are best illustrated by mathematical processes. Graphic information processing is very different from the kind we employ in geometry, for example. Some graphic symbols may be involved in both cases, but the concepts they represent are quite different. In graphic presentation of data (Figures 22.6 and 22.7), the symbols are "hooked" into verbal systems; in geometric graphs, the symbols are "hooked" to mathematical rules. These rules can be described in words, but they are not basically verbal in nature. They develop intuitively through interaction with objects in a three-dimensional world; we know "in our bones" about things in space. Learning the geometrical system for describing things in space therefore means that we "hook" special mathematical symbols to the "bone" concepts, not to words. Similarly, the concepts necessary to arithmetical operations (like those of ordering, counting, and dividing) seem to be grounded in sensorimotor experiences, rather than in language. And in algebra we find operations upon operations—numerical symbols, relations, and the like—in ways that exactly illustrate what Piaget means by formal operational development.

Of course, sensorimotor and spatial experiences will not automatically lead to the development of complex symbol systems—especially to those possessing the formal rigor of mathematics. It may well be that the opportunity to study formal mathematics encourages and strengthens operational capacity in a way—and to an extent—that cannot be duplicated by other studies. Thinking about mathematics, then, may be a mode of thinking that, as Piaget has always argued, takes us well beyond language into a realm of pure logical awareness.

THINKING ABOUT GEOMETRY

Piaget is fond of saying that human mathematical abilities develop in a way that parallels the *logical* development of mathematics itself, but is opposite to its *historical* development. Historically, Euclidean geometrical systems developed before topological geometry, but inside the head of a child, topological concepts "bloom" before Euclidean ones do. That order (topological to Euclidean) is also now considered the natural order of mathematics itself. What does all this mean?

Topological vs. Euclidean Concepts

Topological concepts have to do with such things as openness, closedness, overlappingness, and intersection. Figure 23.1(*a*) shows some examples. These concepts are *logically* prior to those illustrated in the Euclidean diagram in Figure 23.1(*b*). You can see that notions of within, overlapping, and so forth are actually involved in the one Euclidean figure.

According to Piaget, the topological concepts are also *developmentally* prior to Euclidean ones. By the age of 3½, most children can copy the intersecting circles; for Piaget, this is evidence that they have the concept of intersection, even though they cannot yet work with it in Euclidean terms. Similarly, Piaget says, very young children have the concept of openness and closedness long before they have the Euclidean concepts of

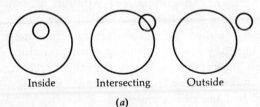

Inside   Intersecting   Outside

(*a*)

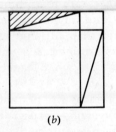

(*b*)

Figure 23.1 Topological and Euclidean concepts from *Piaget Rediscovered*. (Ripple and Rockcastle, 1964)

triangles, squares, and circles. This can be demonstrated by asking 3½-year-olds to copy the two rows of shapes shown in Figure 23.2.

According to Piaget, the child's conception of geometry will be built on his topological notions. In other words, we should not think merely of a child's *readiness* for topology before Euclid, but of his conceptual foundations: The topological experiences may actually prepare him for Euclidean formulations.

The Child's Construction of Euclidean Space

Piaget does not believe, however, that the basic Euclidean notions are formally taught. He believes we "construct Euclidean space" for ourselves and later match it up to academic geometry. This construction of Euclidean space begins when a child notices that a fixed system of reference is necessary for certain kinds of measurements. If he is asked to measure the height of a stack of boxes, for example, his natural reaction may be to compare the height to some point on his own body. When he is a little older (say, about 7) he may invent an independent measuring unit of some kind.

In one preschool, a 5-year-old child attached sixteen Unifix blocks together, making a "stick" that looked like this:

His choice of sixteen was quite arbitrary; it just happened to be a number which interested him that day. He then discovered that he could use his "rod" to measure other things: Something might be "one sixteen," "two sixteens," or "six sixteens" long. The child's behavior revealed the beginning of his natural Euclidean intuitions.

Many other basic concepts enter into the construction of Euclidean concepts: conservation of distance and conservation of length, for example. One conservation-of-distance experiment may be carried out in the following way: As shown in Figure 23.3, two tracks along which both experimenter and child can move their respective "streetcars" have been constructed. The experimenter's track is mostly vertical; the child's is hor-

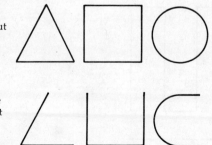

Young children copy these as similar *closed* figures, but cannot distinguish the differences in shape.

Young children copy these as similar *open* figures, but cannot distinguish the differences in shape.

Figure 23.2

izontal. The experimenter says, "I'm going to move my streetcar to here," and moves it to the position shown in the top half of the figure. He then says to the child, "Now move your streetcar so that it has traveled the same distance as mine," or words to that effect. A preoperational child will match the location of the experimenter's streetcar, as you see in the top part of Figure 23.3; he apparently has no conception of distance as something independent of location in space.

The lower part of Figure 23.3 shows another of the experimenter's maneuvers. He moves his streetcar straight up so that spatial matching by the child would mean that the child's streetcar would not move at all. And indeed, the preoperational child gets confused by a maneuver of this sort. He moves his streetcar out a little bit, and then back a little bit, but he will not be able to break away from his dependence on his spatial matching system. He will not be able to make the Euclidean inference that distance is independent of its spatial location.

Teaching Geometry Intuitively

Good geometry teaching will begin with intuitive experiences and lead students into an awareness of the power of formal rules. The importance of geometry as a reasoning system then becomes very clear.

Figure 23.4 illustrates a type of geometrical problem of interest to first-graders. How can the areas of the various forms be determined? The quadrilaterals are easy; all we do is count squares in the underlying grid.

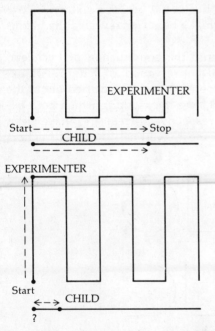

Figure 23.3   A diagram of the conservation-of-distance experiment. (After Piaget, 1964)

But what about those circles? And the free-forms? It can be a time of great excitement when the discovery is made that a string, placed around a curving outside edge, can later be stretched along the grid and measured as a straight line. But how can that information give us the area?

On a more advanced level, consider the Bridges of Königsberg problem:

> The city of Königsberg (now Kalinigrad) in East Prussia is located on the banks and on two islands of the river Pregel. The various parts of the city were connected by seven bridges. On Sundays the burghers would take their promenade around town, as is usual in German cities. The problem arose: It is possible to play this "*Spaziergang*" in such a manner that, starting from home, one can return there after having crossed each river bridge just once? (Ore, 1963, pp. 23–24)

"Walking out" the problem enactively would surely prove an impossible chore, even if we used only a reduced model of the town and the bridges. A map would help. The one presented by Ore is shown in Figure 23.5.

The existence of the map now translates the problem into a paper-and-pencil test: one can draw round and round, across one bridge after another, which is easier than walking. One can even conveniently describe the goal as "starting anyplace, drawing across all the bridges only once, and ending up back where one started." But an even more powerful and efficient system arises when one recodes the map into a symbolic graph, as shown in Figure 23.6. Note the line AD on the graph refers to

Figure 23.4 How shall we measure the areas of forms?

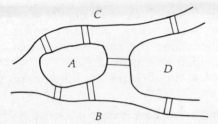

Figure 23.5   The Bridges of Königsberg problem. (Ore, 1963, p. 23)

the bridge crossing from *A* to *D* on the map; the segment *AC* refers to one of the bridges crossing from *A* to *C* on the map, and the curved segment *AC* refers to the second bridge (it might have been drawn as a straight line, except that it, like the first *AC* bridge, must terminate at *A* and *C*, and a curved line is the only way to make that happen).

Now we have not merely a paper-and-pencil test, we have something much more powerful—if a mathematical rule discovered and proved by the eighteenth-century mathematician Leonhard Euler is known: Graphs can be traversed completely in one single circular path *only* if each corner (vertex) has an even number of edges. Counting, one immediately sees that the vertex at *A* has three edges; so do the vertices at *D, B,* and *C*. Therefore, it is not possible to traverse the graph, the map, or the bridges themselves in one single walk without retracing one's steps somewhere. Such is the power of symbolic graphic systems, once the symbols are fully understood. Note, however, that the symbols do not seem to be connected to language, but represent, instead, sensorimotor and spatial experiences. Although the awareness of this relationship may be guided by language, the experiences themselves are not limited to language. We will come back to the complexity of the relationship between language and mathematics in the discussion of thinking about algebra. First, let us consider arithmetic.

THINKING ABOUT NUMBERS

Suppose we wanted to teach a robot to count. How might we do it? That is a good question not only for mathematics teachers, but also for children.

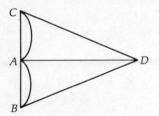

Figure 23.6   A symbolic graph of the same problem. (Ore, 1963, p. 24)

Paul Berry has presented a charming example of this pedagogical technique:

> The experimenter explains the procedure to the child as follows: "Now we will play at a special way of doing counting. I'm going to pretend that I don't know anything at all about how to count. I'll have some things in front of me, and I am supposed to count them. You have to tell me what to do. I am pretending to be very stupid, and my memory is very bad, so you have to tell me each little thing to do, one at a time, and then I will do whatever you say."
>
> . . . Experimenter had a tray of about 30 beans scattered more or less randomly. The child was a six-year-old first-grader.
>
> CHILD: Pick a bean. (Experimenter singles out a bean to look at but does not touch it.)
>
> CHILD: Say the first number. That is "one."
>
> E: One.
>
> CHILD: Remember that.
>
> E: You want me to remember it? I have a very bad memory. If you want me to remember it, I'd better write it down.
>
> CHILD: OK, write down 1. (E writes down 1.)
>
> CHILD: Pick another bean.
>
> E: I don't understand.
>
> CHILD: Pick out a bean. The way you did before.
>
> E: OK. I've got a bean.
>
> CHILD: Write down the next number.
>
> E: Where?
>
> CHILD: Write it where you wrote that other one. Cross out the first one and write this instead. (E crosses out the 1.)
>
> E: What am I supposed to write now?
>
> CHILD: Write the next number.
>
> E: I don't know the next number.
>
> CHILD: The next number is 2. Write 2. Now go back and do it again. (This continues until 7 beans have been counted.)
>
> CHILD: What bean are you counting? (E points to it.)
>
> CHILD: Is that the same one you counted before?
>
> E: I don't know.
>
> CHILD: You don't know! You're supposed to keep track of them.
>
> E: You didn't say that.
>
> CHILD: Well, it's no good if you don't keep track of them.
>
> E: What should I do now?
>
> CHILD: We'll just have to start over. Pick out a bean.
>
> E: OK.
>
> CHILD: No, really pick it up. (E picks it up.) Write down 1. Pick out a bean.
>
> E: What am I supposed to do with this bean in my hand?
>
> CHILD: Just keep holding it. Pick out a bean. (E holds out the bean already in his hand.)
>
> CHILD: No, not that one, pick out a bean *that's on the tray*. (E picks out a bean from the tray, adding it to the first one in his hand.)
>
> CHILD: Write down the next number, which is 2. (This continues . . .)
>
> CHILD: Write down the next number.
>
> E: I don't know what that is.
>
> CHILD: Well, what number have you got now?
>
> E: I've got 6 written here.

CHILD: Well, 7 comes after that. Write down 7.

E: You'll have to tell me what to write down every time.

CHILD: All right.

E: Why don't you tell me how you get the next number to write down, and I'll be able to do it myself.

CHILD: Well, 7 comes after 6.

E: Yes, but how do you know that?

CHILD: You just know it, that's all.

E: How can I get to know it too?

CHILD: You'll just have to learn it.

E: But I can't remember things.

CHILD: Well, I'll tell you all the numbers right now, and you write them down. Then you will know all of them.

E: OK.

CHILD: 1, 2, 3, 4, 5, 6, 7, 8, 9, 10, 11, 12, 13, 14, 15, 16, 17, 18, 19, 20, 21, 22, 23, 24, 25, 26, 27, 28, 29, 30, 31 . . . that's really enough, you won't need more than that. (At the next instance.) Write down the next number.

E: What is it?

CHILD: Look on your list.

E: What should I look for?

CHILD: Look for the next number.

E: How can I? I don't know what it is.

CHILD: What was the last number you had?

E: 7.

CHILD: Look for that, then.

E: I've found it.

CHILD: Write down what comes after it; that's right, 8. (Berry, 1964, pp. 398–400)

Components of the Counting Process

The child's inventions illustrate many aspects of the counting procedure that we take for granted:

1. There must be a one-to-one correspondence between a list of integers and a set of things.

2. We must go down the list in a particular order.

3. We must keep track of our place on the list and within the set of things.

4. There must be decisions about where to start, where to stop, and where to look for more things to count.

5. The list of integers is separate from the set of things and can be applied to other sets of things.

Young children cannot handle all these aspects of a counting procedure simultaneously. The list of integers is usually learned before the one-to-one correspondence is understood. When a very young (preoperational) child says, "This is as many as that," he may mean that "this" is taking up the same amount of *space* as "that."

Conservation of Number

The birth of the realization that the list of numbers in the child's head (a list he can display simply by counting aloud) must be systematically connected to the set of real-world items generally appears around the age of 6. It is one of the earliest conservations to appear. Like the others discussed in Part I, Piaget says that number conservation also depends on the birth of the concept of reversibility. The child who is free of the iconic pull of things in space has achieved that freedom by realizing that things moved to a new position can be moved back to the old position and that the movements cancel each other out. Because the movements sum to zero, they cannot affect number.

Serialization Abilities

Once a child has developed a true concept of number, he can begin to put numbers together with other numbers operationally. Addition, multiplication, subtraction, and other number manipulations become possible. But he must also understand the concept of *seriation,* or ordering.

> Ten wooden dolls of the same thickness, which can stand up or lie down, of clearly differing heights, the tallest being at least twice as big as the shortest, and ten sticks, also varying in size, but with less difference between them, represent the material. Ten balls of plasticine, also of clearly differing sizes, represent the rucksacks corresponding to the dolls. . . .
>
> The first problem . . . is to find the correspondence between the dolls on the one hand, and the sticks or balls on the other when the sets are not in order. The child is told that the dolls are going for a walk, and the correspondence is suggested, but without explicit reference to size. For instance, he is asked to arrange the dolls and sticks so that each doll can easily find the stick that belongs to it. (Piaget, 1965, p. 97)

Preoperational children have great difficulty with such problems. They may get part of the series arranged properly, but cannot handle it all. The child moving out of the preoperational stage may show the beginnings of a system; he may carefully compare two or three items at a time. The fully operational child will, however, keep track of gradations in the whole series. He may, for example, first choose the smallest of the dolls and sticks, then choose the smallest of those that are left, then choose the smallest of those that are still left, and so forth.

As we know, Piaget believes these developing systems depend not on language, but on sensorimotor and spatial experiences. One experiment (Farnham-Diggory, 1970) illustrating this follows: The experiment utilized the materials shown in Figure 23.7—6 wooden blocks, varying in size from small to medium to large, and 6 dot cards, with one, two, or three dots drawn on them. The blocks were arranged in the order shown in the figure, and the pile of dot cards was placed before the child with the instruction, "Put the dots with the blocks, the way they're supposed to go." No further explanation or instruction was given; the child was left to decide for himself what "supposed to go" meant. If he figured it out properly, he placed the cards with the dots in the order illustrated.

Because 4- and 5-year-old children have difficulty with this task, some procedures to help them were developed. These were pretraining experiences expected to prepare the child's mind to recognize the block-and-dot solution spontaneously; the solution was never taught directly. One kind of pretraining experience involved verbal drill: Children were drilled in comparing blocks and dots by saying "This is more than this" (about a large block and a little block, or about a three-dot card and a one-dot card) or by saying "This is big and this is little" (about the same materials). Each child practiced these statements thirty times; then he was presented with the block-and-dot task. Surprisingly, this verbal drill did not help nonserializing children to serialize spontaneously. They continued to put the dot cards randomly with the blocks, instead of putting the one-dot card with the littlest block, and so forth.

Another kind of pretraining was more successful. It was similar to the doll procedure described by Piaget above, except that more materials and fewer gradations were used. The dolls were of only three different sizes. Children practiced putting trucks of three different sizes with the dolls, putting elephants of three different sizes in the trucks, giving each doll an appropriate bubble pipe, giving each bubble pipe an appropriate number of pipe cleaners (the smallest pipe got only one pipe cleaner, the middle-sized pipe got more, the largest pipe got the most), and each doll an appropriate number of beads. After practicing on these materials, the children were given the standard block-and-dot task.

They were better able to perform it; the concrete materials apparently helped. They were also helped by practicing actions related to the blocks and cards. The experimenter would say things like, "When I show you this card (one dot), it means take a baby step." (The child then did so.) "When I show you this card (three dots), what does it mean?" (The child took a giant step.) Sensorimotor training was more successful than verbal training in helping young children develop serializing skills.

"New Math" Applications

The dependence of young children (and even of some adults) on concrete arithmetical experiences is an important component of "new math" pedagogy. There are many ways of helping children understand the logic of arithmetic through concrete exercises, and any of these methods are a

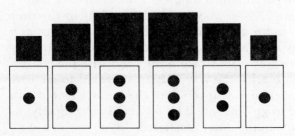

Figure 23.7 Blocks and dots used in the serial learning task. (Farnham-Diggory, 1970)

great improvement over the old system of giving children lists of arithmetic rules to be learned by rote, without any understanding at all. The "new" pedagogy is valuable not because it is more enjoyable (which it is), but because it matches the child's natural system for developing an intuitive sense of arithmetic. Further, as in the case of formal geometry, the formal rules of arithmetic may be valued for their power and efficiency only after a measure of intuitive struggle.

Thus, $4 + 4 = 8$ can be illustrated (in Stern, 1949) as:

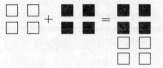

Such an illustration provides not only concrete block-manipulating experience, but also visual experience—an image the child can recall in the absence of the blocks. According to Bruner and Werner, as well as Piaget, images may be a necessary step in the transition from enactive to symbolic information-processing systems. Further, the efficiency of the symbols ($4 + 4 = 8$) may be especially appreciated after practice on their concrete equivalents.

A similar device is shown in Figure 23.8. The dial across the top part of the figure contains buttons that control the hand on the number dial. When button 1 is pressed, the dial hand moves one space clockwise; when the button 2 is pressed, the hand moves two spaces, and so forth. Practice on such a device helps children "see" how $1 \times 2 = 2 \times 1$, for example. The left side of the equality would be represented by pushing the 1 button two times; the right side would be represented by pushing the 2 button 1 time. In both cases, the dial hand will end up in the same place.

There are equally effective systems for teaching subtraction and division, and even the more complex aspects of arithmetic. Arithmetic teaching programs that guide children through complex principles by starting on an intuitive, concrete level and moving to the formal rules are now available under the Cuisinaire, Montessori, and Unifix labels. Lovell's (1966) small book, *The Growth of Basic Mathematical and Scientific Concepts in Children,* provides a good review.

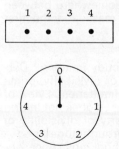

Figure 23.8   Practice on the concrete equivalents of symbols. (Fehr, 1953, p. 25)

Imagery In Advanced Mathematics

On a more advanced level, imagery still seems to persist as the fundamental "substance" of mathematical reasoning. Einstein wrote to Hadamard:

> The words or the language, as they are written or spoken, do not seem to play any role in my mechanism of thought. The psychical entities which seem to serve as elements in thought are certain signs and more or less clear images which can be "voluntarily" reproduced and combined. . . . The . . . elements are . . . of visual and some of muscular type. Conventional words or other signs have to be sought for laboriously only in a secondary stage. . . . The play with the mentioned elements is aimed to be analogous to certain logical connections one is searching for. (Einstein, in Hadamard, 1945, pp. 142–143)

Hadamard himself described several instances of the use of imagery in arithmetical reasoning. Take, for example, the classical Euclidean proof that there cannot be a final (last) prime number. A prime number, you will recall, cannot be divided by any number other than itself and 1. Seven, for example, is a prime number; so is two. Proving that there is no final prime number requires the following steps: First, one imagines that all the prime numbers have been multiplied together to make a giant number. To this number (called M), the number 1 is added. This giant number M will be a prime, because it is not divisible evenly by any of the numbers composing it; there will always be 1 left over. No matter what "ultimate prime" might be imagined, it can always be exceeded by including it in the construction of M and adding 1 to it. That is, it can always be exceeded by another prime. Therefore, there is no ultimate prime. Hadamard describes his personal imagery in this problem:

Steps in the Proof	My Mental Pictures
I consider all primes from 2 to 11, say 2, 3, 4, 5, 11.	I see a confused mass.
I form their product $2 \times 3 \times 5 \times 7 \times 11 = M$.	M being a rather large number, I imagine a point rather remote from the confused mass.
I increase that product by 1, say M + 1.	I see a second point a little beyond the first.
That number, if not a prime, must admit of a prime devisor, which is the required number [the largest prime in the series].	I see a place somewhere between the confused mass and the first point.

> What may be the use of such a strange and cloudy imagery? Certainly it is not meant to remind me of any property of divisibility, prime numbers and so on. . . . I need it in order to have a simultaneous view of all elements of the argument, to hold them together. . . . It does not inform me on any link of the argument (i.e., on any property of divisibility or primes); but it reminds me how these links are to be brought together. . . . The imagery is necessary in order that the useful hookings, once obtained, may not get lost. (Hadamard, 1945, pp. 76–77)

Thus, in arithmetic as in geometry, the relationship of symbols and images may be more critical than the relationship of symbols and language. True, language is involved, but it may not provide what Hadamard called "the useful hookings" to the extent that imagery does. But what of more advanced mathematics? In algebra, for example, the manipulation of symbols seems to be more closely related to language than to images. Is that, in fact, the case?

THINKING ABOUT ALGEBRA

Consider a typical algebra word problem:

If the number of customers Tom gets is twice the square of 20 per cent of the number of advertisements he runs, and the number of advertisements he runs is 45, what is the number of customers Tom gets? (Paige and Simon, 1966, p. 83)

Setting up the equations for this problem requires no knowledge of the meaning of *customers, advertisements,* or even of *Tom.* We could as easily have used nonsense words:

If the number of glubs X biks is twice the square of 20 percent of the number of quonks he dobs, and he dobs 45 quonks, how many glubs does he bik?

On the other hand, sometimes the substantive ideas are relevant. Consider the next two problems taken from the same source:

A man has 7 times as many quarters as he has dimes. The value of the dimes exceeds the value of the quarters by $2.50. How many has he of each coin?

A board was sawed into two pieces. One piece was two-thirds as long as the whole board, and was exceeded in length by the second piece by 4 feet. How long was the board before it was cut? (Paige and Simon, 1966, pp. 84, 87)

In the first problem, knowledge of the relative values of quarters and dimes is necessary to the solution, because otherwise the student cannot handle the part of the equation stating that "the value of the dimes exceeds the value of the quarters." But the substantive information may also be disturbing: the equation will turn out to be $(10x - 7) 25x = 250$. The solution is a negative number, and no such things as negative quarters exist. Similarly, in the second problem the solution will be a board of negative length.

In their study of the cognitive processes involved in algebra word problems, Paige and Simon (1966) made the following discoveries:

1. Some students seem to handle the problems in a predominantly verbal way, making direct translations of problem statements into equations.

2. Other students appear to use auxiliary representations—imagery, drawings, or related information—that assist them in setting up the equations.

3. To some extent, the two kinds of students can be detected through the use of contradictory, or physically impossible, algebra word problems. Though both groups of students may be able to solve the problems correctly and efficiently, students from the second group are more likely to detect the contradiction. They detect it because their auxiliary representational systems make the contradiction visible.

Algebra word problems are especially interesting—and, for some people, especially difficult—because they seem to straddle both verbal and mathematical symbolic processes. Consider some of the verbal associations generated by the word *root:*

> Suppose, for example, that John Curious, a junior high school pupil, encounters the word *root.* This word represents a sound which in turn represents a thing. In accordance with his experience to date, the thing *root* suggests to John is that part of a tree which grows underground and fixes, supports, and nourishes the tree. For him the phrase *root of an equation* may seem far-fetched. If, to date, his life in school has encouraged his natural curiosity and not, as is often the case, stifled it through memorizing and verbalizing, John may seek to get at the root of this word *root.* Did he not hear in Sunday school that "the love of money is the root of all evil"? Why did the teacher of Latin recently refer to the Latin root of the English word *percentage*? Clearly, a tree successfully transplanted roots itself firmly in the earth. Is this related at all to the mild upheaval of earth occurring when a hog is said to root? Don't cheer-leaders exhort all pupils to root for the team? What has all this to do with the root of an equation? "Come to think about it," muses John, "we found square roots of numbers last year. Is the root of an equation a square root?"
>
> The teacher who really helps pupils with language in mathematics will go beyond the minimal requirements of the situation in which the words "root of an equation" are to be taught. Merely to tell John that a root of an equation is a known quantity which satisfies the equation when substituted for the unknown quantity in the equation will not suffice. Such a statement is concise, correct, and clear—to an adult versed in mathematics. But to John, whose experiences with mathematical language are slowly spiraling and spelling meanings for him, an adult's pat phrases and neat formulations may be practically meaningless. However, if his instructor requires textbook talk and/or teacher talk, John can memorize it. Better still, he can receive credit for his memorizing unmeaningful language; he can, in fact, if he memorizes well, even win school honors and rewards from his parents.
>
> How, then, should the teacher help pupils to understand the word *root*? In the first place, pupils should have much experience with many equations and should have discovered for themselves that in some cases a single value satisfies the equation and in other cases two or more solutions can be found. In discussing and summarizing their work, pupils will probably need a word which they can use to distinguish the answer(s) to the equation from other kinds of answers they obtain in mathematics. Then, and no earlier, should the name be given. The *idea* that one or more values satisfies an equation is important. After it has been discovered, the name of such values is an easy matter. (Brune, 1953, pp. 162–163)

Operational Thinking in Algebra

The students who are having "much experience with many equations" are performing symbolic operations *on other operations* that are neither linguistic nor concrete in nature. While some imagery may still be useful, the literal meaning of language and the concrete meaning of linguistic referents (the things referred to) may be both irrelevant and distracting. One experimental demonstration of the operational thinking of algebra has been provided by R. R. Skemp of the University of Manchester:

> Algebra is concerned with the study of the properties of *number* in general, that is, with statements which are true of any and every number, and not only of particular numbers. It is further concerned with the properties of arithmetical operations in general, irrespective of the particular numbers on which the operations are performed. Thus, while arithmetic is concerned with the uses and results of its operations on numbers, algebra turns its attention to the operations themselves, and to the properties held in common by all operations of a particular kind. (Skemp, 1961, p. 46)

If this is true, then measures of operational thinking capacity should predict ability to solve algebra problems.

To test that hypothesis, Skemp devised a test showing three levels of operational thinking: (1) Performing operations, (2) combining concepts, and (3) combining operations. Sample test items are shown in Figure 23.9. The top two rows (A) show a simple concept discovery task. Three examples of the concept are followed by three nonexamples and three test figures. Which one of the test figures is a true instance of the concept? (B) illustrates a combination of the two concepts shown in (A); (C) shows a set of operations, which are then applied in (D); in (E), operations are combined. Skemp gave this test to junior high school students and correlated their performance with their scores on a standard mathematics examination. The correlations are shown in Table 23.1.

Table 23.1
Correlation of Test Scores with Mathematics Achievement

	CORRELATION WITH MATHEMATICS EXAMINATION
Performing operations	.42
Combining concepts	.58
Combining operations	.72

SOURCE: Based on data in Skemp, 1961.

As the complexity of the operations increased, so did the predictive value of the test, which suggests that *operations upon operations* are the cognitive abilities basic to mathematical thinking. This, of course, is Piaget's position. He might even argue that algebraic operations should not be taught until children have entered the stage of formal operations at about the age of 12 or 13.

Accelerating Operational Thought About Matrices

Although it is true that certain kinds of abstract thinking cannot be done easily before the age of 12 or 13, the foundations of algebraic thinking are now taught almost from the beginning of mathematics instruction. (See, for example, Z. P. Dienes' *Building Up Mathematics,* 1964, and other

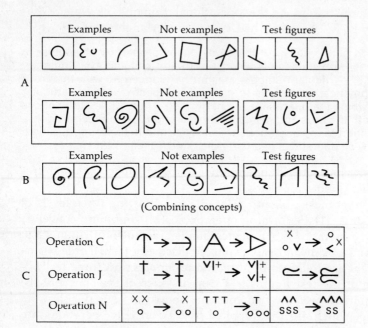

Figure 23.9 Sample test items from Skemp's test of operational thinking. (Skemp, 1961, pp. 51-52)

books by the same author for excellent examples of the ways to teach principles basic to all forms of mathematics in the very early grades.) For example, operations on numbers can be taught within the framework of a simple matrix an average first-grader could construct (from the work of David Page, 1962):

60	61	62	...						
50	51	52	53	54	55	56	57	58	59
40	41	42	43	44	45	46	47	48	49
30	31	32	33	34	35	36	37	38	39
20	21	22	23	24	25	26	27	28	29
10	11	12	13	14	15	16	17	18	19
	1	2	3	4	5	6	7	8	9

The teacher may begin by saying, "We are going to have a sort of secret code for writing numbers. It uses that table. Here is a number in code: 5 ↑. What number do you guess this stands for?" From there, it is possible to progress to 5 + 13 ↓ (answer: 8); 11 ↓ + 11 ↓ + 11 ↓ (answer: 3); 50 ↓↓ (answer: 30); 4 →↑ (answer 15), and so on. Practice of this sort helps develop the capacity to perform *operations on operations* that will flower when a child is older. Note, however, that these first-grade lessons capitalize on sensorimotor and spatial ideas (up and down) as aids in constructing abstract representational skills.

Conclusion

Mature algebraic thinking requires the ability to scan and manipulate symbols, to substitute one symbolic operation for another, and to recognize equivalences among operations that may appear to be different. Like language, algebra has a syntax—a system of entities and permissable relationships that will generate a large number of "good sentences." But it is not a linguistic syntax; it is produced and controlled by a set of *axioms,* or fundamental, governing mathematical rules.

Perhaps someday the problem of the relationship between the *axioms* of mathematics, the *deep structure* of language, and the *operations* of Piaget will be solved. At this point in time, the solution seems far out of reach. Once a problem has been defined, however, the highly creative minds that are capable of solving it usually emerge. The nature of such creativity is, in fact, the final topic of this book.

SUMMARY

Thinking about pictures, graphs, written words, and written mathematical symbols is not a single, unitary process. In fact, the different systems may conflict with one another. One severe problem with so-called reading readiness training, for example, may be the emphasis it places on pictures, graphic symbols, rather than on words. Because pictorial and graphic thinking conflict with reading, such "training" may do more harm than good.

Boys may find pictorial and mathematical thinking easier than reading; girls may show the opposite pattern. This is one reason why girls may get better grades in elementary school, where verbal skills are emphasized. By high school, where quantitative skills come into their own, boys begin to excel.

Pictorial thinking seems to have a "grammar" of its own: Visual cues trigger the brain into organizing information. Cues of texture, perspective, light, movement, color, and the like control many aspects of pictorial comprehension. The basic pictorial process is one of feature testing, rather than one of model matching. We recognize or understand a picture by "checking off" critical features, not by matching it as a whole to some remembered image. However, the cues may generate associations of their own that interfere with a particular concept. The use of pictures as teaching aids must be handled carefully; students may be more confused than enlightened by conceptually cluttered visuals.

Reading is very different from picture processing because it uses a code. Learning to read means learning to use a written code for the spoken language. Classroom research has indicated that code methods teach reading more successfully than look-and-say or noncode methods. Basic research would support the same proposition.

Learning the code is also a matter of feature testing, but the features are quite different from those involved in picture processing. Some alphabetic and word features are highly confusable, for example, and should be carefully practiced. At all levels, the connection between the written forms (graphemes, words, sentences) and the spoken forms (phonemes, word sounds, intonations) should be emphasized. This is essentially a matter of building neurological associative structures. When connections between the sight of a word and its auditory or spoken representations are weak, reading fails to occur.

Unlike pictorial comprehension, reading comprehension must be firmly tied to language comprehension, for the meaning of a printed phrase arises from verbal associations. (Images may occur, but they are probably generated by word sounds, not by word shapes.) However, practicing only the language comprehension process (as in the language-experience methods) may not teach reading either.

"Reading" graphs and maps is more like reading words than pictures. The strong pictorial elements of graphic or maplike materials may interfere with reading comprehension. Learning to read graphs means learning a code (though not an alphabetic one) and then learning to tie the coded material into language comprehension systems.

Mathematical thinking is also codelike in nature, but the code is neither graphic nor verbal. Mathematical symbols are "hooked" to intuitive mathematical ideas that may need to be practiced first. Learning mathematics means exercising sensorimotor schemas and then combining these schemas into operations, as Piaget would describe them. The process may be greatly aided by images—but not literal ones. As Hadamard says, "cloudy imagery" helps hold the mathematical argument together.

The conflict between mathematical and verbal thinking may be revealed by the difficulty some students have with algebra word problems, which require both verbal and iconic processing. Early training (in elementary school) in algebraic thinking may free students from a total dependence on verbal symbolism and prepare them for symbol processing of a mathematical nature.

Because of these basic differences among verbal, spatial, and pictorial processes, practice in one kind of thinking is not enough. An education that emphasizes only verbal skills will fail to develop the brain's symbolic potential. An education that is limited to pictures or mathematics will produce a similarly lopsided mental capacity. Mathematics provides a kind of training that cannot be obtained by any other means; so do reading and picture analysis. One will not substitute for the other. A comprehensive education requires comprehensive symbolic experiences.

Part VI THE CREATIVE PROCESS

The end to be reached, then, in any creative
process, is not whatever solid or silly issue the
ego or accident may decree, but some specific
order urged upon the mind by something
inherent in its own vital condition of being and
perception, yet nowhere in view.

BREWSTER GHISELIN

How do we know when someone has been creative? The simplest answer may be to point to what the individual has produced. If he regularly produces pictures, poems, or short stories, we say he is creative. But must they be good productions? Are we willing to say that someone who turns out bad paintings is as creative as someone who turns out good ones? How about people who paint by numbers? Are they creative? Probably we would argue that they are not, since they are only following someone else's recipe. But does that mean creativity can occur only where there is novelty? How much novelty is necessary for a product to be defined as creative? Is a sonnet (which has a fixed form) less creative than free verse? Are the Old Masters less creative than the Impressionists, who invented a new form? Are those who imitate the Impressionists uncreative?

If we discussed these problems for a while, we could probably come to some agreement about how we would define and rate creativity. We seem to have personal theories of creativity, just as we have personal theories of personality and motivation. But personal theories can be very wrong, and they can produce a dangerous perceptual set. For years, "everybody knew," and could see illustrated in any classroom, that intellectually gifted children were weak and puny, had bad eyes, were sissies, poor sports, and introverts. It was not until careful research was done (beginning with Terman in 1925) that "everybody knew," and could see illustrated in any classroom, that gifted children were above average in physical ability and health, as well as in social skills and general adjustment.

Where shall we go for careful research on the creative process? There are a number of research reports on parts of the creative process—the ability to generate a large number of ideas (fluency), for example—as we shall see. But so far no one has devised a way of carrying out a research project on the entire process from the germination of an idea to its final flowering. The closest we have come to such research is in the self-reports of creative people.

Psychologists owe a great debt to Brewster Ghiselin of the University of Utah; he has collected papers, letters, interviews, and diaries of thirty-eight men and women of recognized creative ability (Ghiselin, 1952). Careful study of these reports reveals a number of surprising similarities. First of all, each creator refers to some kind of *element universe*—ideas, images, things to paint, tunes, rhythms—to which he is especially sensitive. These elements are the building blocks of his creative productions. Although their elements may be very different in kind (from musical themes to stone shapes), many creators appear to share a "bubbling-up" sensation that may or may not be predictable. In addition, most creators refer to the problem of *ordering* or *organizing the universe of elements.* Mere bubbling is not enough; the real creative enterprise is to bring these elements into unified harmony. Although this may involve tedious periods of trial and error, most creators seem to be sustained by an intuition that a solution is possible. Yet when it comes, the solution may have a quality of *illumination* and *surprise.* In addition, most creative artists report what seems to them to be *unconscious incubation periods* in which some of their creative work proceeds without their full awareness.

In the chapters to follow, we will consider each of these aspects of the creative process, attending to self-reports of creative artists, to laboratory studies, and to classroom applications. We will also consider the relationship of creativity to intelligence and to social factors. As often as possible, samples of relevant curricula will be presented.

Chapter 24 THE UNIVERSE OF ELEMENTS

When I am, as it were, completely myself, entirely alone, and of good cheer—say, travelling in a carriage, or walking after a good meal, or during the night when I cannot sleep; It Is on such occasions that my ideas flow best and most abundantly. When and how they come, I know not; nor can I force them. Those ideas that please me I retain in memory, and am accustomed, as I have been told, to hum them to myself. (Mozart, in E. Holmes, *Life of Mozart*)

I learnt to paint from copying other pictures—usually reproductions, sometimes even photographs. When I was a boy, how I concentrated over it! Copying some perfectly worthless scene reproduction in some magazine. I worked with almost dry water-color, stroke by stroke, covering half a square-inch at a time, each square-inch perfect and completed, proceeding in a kind of mosaic advance. . . . Hours and hours of intense concentration, inch by inch progress, in a method entirely wrong—and yet those copies of mine managed, when they were finished, to have a certain something that delighted me. (D. H. Lawrence, *Assorted Essays*)

. . . I have always paid great attention to natural forms, such as bones, shells, pebbles, etc. Sometimes, for several years running, I have been to the same part of the sea-shore—but each year a new shape of pebble has caught my eye, which the year before, though it was there in hundreds, I never saw. Out of the millions of pebbles passed in walking along the shore, I choose out to see with excitement only those which fit in with my existing form interest at the time. A different thing happens if I sit down and examine a handful one by one. I may then extend my form experience more by giving my mind time to become conditioned to a new shape. (Henry Moore, in M. Evans, *The Painter's Object*)

The quality of my memory is characterized, I believe, in a more than ordinary degree by the intensity of its sense impressions, its power to evoke and bring back the odors, sounds, colors, shapes, and feel of things with concrete vividness. Now my memory was at work night and day, in a way that I could at first neither check nor control and that swarmed unbidden in a stream of blazing pageantry across my mind, with the millions of forms and substances of the life that I had left, which was my own, America. (Thomas Wolfe, *The Story of a Novel*)

Each of these quotations has provided us with a glimpse of its author's element universe, which appears to have two important aspects: (1) it is profuse—there is *a rich flowering* of ideas and concepts; (2) it reveals *a period of intense preparation* for later creative integrations. We will take up the latter topic first.

PREPARATION: THE INTENSIVE ACQUISITION EFFORT

According to Anne Roe (1943) and many others, creative people work extremely hard, and they work all the time—nights, weekends, and holidays mean very little to the individual engaged in a creative enterprise. Ghiselin has this to say about what he calls the *intensive acquisition effort;* it should be carefully noted:

A great deal of the work necessary to equip and activate the mind for the spontaneous part of invention must be done consciously and with an effort of will. Mastering accumulated knowledge, gathering new facts, observing, exploring, experimenting, developing technique and skill, sensibility, and discrimination, are all more or less conscious and voluntary activities. The sheer labor of preparing technically for creative work, consciously acquiring the requisite knowledge of a medium and skill in its use, is extensive and arduous enough to repel many from achievement.

Creative workers reporting their processes of production often inadvertently conceal the amount of conscious and voluntary work by their failure to stress it or to consider it in much detail. . . . We are led to underestimate the labor of invention by the appearance of the finished product. Freed of every irrelevance, especially the sweat and litter of the workroom, the work of thought or art or ritual stands as the simple formula of a subjective action. The impression it gives of unlabored force is not to be trusted. . . .

Even the most energetic and original mind, in order to reorganize or extend human insight in any valuable way, must have attained more than ordinary mastery of the field in which it is to act, a strong sense of what needs to be done, and skill in the appropriate means of expression. It seems certain that no significant expansion of insight can be produced otherwise, whether the activity is thought of as work or not. Often an untutored beauty appears in the drawings of children and we rightly prize the best of them because they have wholeness of motive, but they have scarcely the power to open the future for us. For that, the artist must labor to the limit of human development and then take a step beyond. (Ghiselin, 1952, pp. 17–18)

When we look at a piece of sculpture by Henry Moore, we do not think of the hours and hours he has spent studying natural forms in preparation for his own unique integration of them. When we read a novel by Wolfe, we ignore the intensive preparatory experiences that moved him to create the novel in the first place. And so it is with all creative productions—they are preceded by prodigious quantities of "stuff": A universe of elements is first constructed.

Wallas' Preparation Period

Another philosopher of creativity, Graham Wallas, wrote an important book called *The Art of Thought* in 1926. He described the intensive acquisition period as a period of *preparation*—the first of four stages (so Wallas thought) in the creative process.

> The stage of Preparation . . . includes the whole process of intellectual education. Men have known for thousands of years that conscious effort and its resulting habits can be used to improve the thought-processes of young persons, and have formulated for that purpose an elaborate art of education. The "educated" man can, in consequence, "put his mind on" to a chosen subject, and "turn his mind off" in a way which is impossible to an uneducated man. The educated man has also acquired, by the effort of observation and memorizing, a body of remembered facts and words which gives him a wider range in the final moment of association, as well as a number of those habitual tracks of association which constitute "thought-systems" like "French policy" or "scholastic philosophy" or "biological evolution," and which present themselves as units in the process of thought. (Wallas, 1926, p. 82)

From Wallas' standpoint, then, all formal education is a preparation for creativity since it provides a universe of facts, theories, and scientific systems that might be useful in subsequent creative enterprises. From another standpoint, we might wonder if the *motivation to learn and remember prodigious amounts of information* may not be the basic key to later creative production. In some cases, this may be highly specialized information; in others, it may be more general. But in all cases, the potential creator seems to go through an early stage of voracious absorption of some kind of information, and/or an almost obsessive practice of some basic skill.

Whatever its form, this *intensive acquisition effort* does not sound very much like the sentimentalized descriptions of "creativity" found in some education books. From these, one would think that a "creative classroom" is a place of playfulness and freedom, not one of intense concentration and purposefulness. Some educators, in fact, seem to use the word *creative* as a synonym for nonwork, when in reality it may describe the hardest work of all.

Because a rich element universe is characteristic of creative productions, some psychologists believe this richness to reveal the existence of creative talent. That is, they believe the ability to generate a universe of elements may be a personality trait that can be detected on standardized tests. If your ideas flow freely on one topic (the theory goes), they will flow freely on other topics, making you a generally creative person.

DIVERGENT THINKING

In Part II, we reviewed the arguments of theorists who believe intelligence is made up of different components and is not a single, unitary process. A component theory can easily be extended to include *divergent* thinking. Guilford (1959) has done so within the framework of his structure-of-intellect model. Although, as we will see, Guilford believes creativity cannot occur in low IQ people, he considers creative thinkers to have special mental qualities that are not found in uncreative people, even those with high IQ. He has labeled them *divergent* rather than *convergent*. Divergent thinking is expansive, fluid, flexible; convergent thinking is more focused and integrative. Although both skills are necessary to successful creativity, Guilford's so-called creativity tests have emphasized the divergent variety.

> The unique feature of divergent production is that a *variety* of responses is produced. . . . Winston Churchill must have possessed this ability to a high degree. Clement Attlee is reported to have said about him . . . that, no matter what problem came up, Churchill always seemed to have about ten ideas. The trouble was, Attlee continued, he did not know which was the good one. (Guilford, 1959, p. 479)

Divergent thinking has two aspects: *fluency* and *flexibility*. Suppose you were asked: "Name all the uses you can think of for a brick." You might say, "Build a wall, build a house, build a chimney, build a privy." You would get a score of 4 on fluency because of the four different things you suggested to build, but you would be scored only 1 on flexibility because you described only one function for bricks—that of building.

According to Guilford, there are many kinds of fluencies and flexibilities. *Associational* fluency, for example, might be tapped by asking subjects to list all the words they can think of that mean about the same thing as *good* or that mean about the opposite of *hard*. Or one might ask, "How many different ways can 2, 5, 1 and 11 be related to produce the number 8?" *Expressional* fluency is revealed by tests of this sort: Given the initial letters W___ c___ e___ n___, how many sentences can you produce?

Concepts of fluency and flexibility can also be applied to figures or pictures. What Guilford calls *adaptive* flexibility is tapped by the match problem. Given the arrangement in Figure 24.1, take away exactly four matches and leave exactly three squares. Since nothing is said about the size of the squares, the subject's adaptive flexibility is tested by his spontaneous recognition of the fact that the size of the squares need not all be the same.

Adaptive flexibility can also be demonstrated verbally. Subjects can be asked to produce shifts or changes in meanings and to develop novel ideas. One of Guilford's most famous tests of this skill is described in the following excerpt:

> The Plot Titles Test presents a short story, the examinee being told to list as many appropriate titles as he can to head the story. One story is about a missionary who has been captured by cannibals in Africa. He is in

the pot and about to be boiled when a princess of the tribe obtains a promise for his release if he will become her mate. He refuses and is boiled to death.

In scoring the test, we separate the responses into two categories, clever and nonclever. Examples of nonclever responses are: African Death, Defeat of a Princess, Eaten by Savages, The Princess, The African Missionary, In Darkest Africa, and Boiled by Savages. These titles are appropriate but commonplace.... Examples of clever responses are: Pot's Plot, Potluck Dinner, Stewed Parson, Goil or Boil, A Mate Worse Than Death, He Left a Dish for a Pot, Chaste in Haste, and A Hot Price for Freedom. (Guilford, 1959, pp. 474)

Fluency and flexibility certainly seem to have something important to do with creativity, but we must be careful not to consider such tests to be literal predictors. Some highly creative authors have not been clever about producing titles for their own materials—F. Scott Fitzgerald, for example. One of his early titles for *Tender Is the Night* was *Dr. Diver's Holiday;* another was *The World's Fair* (Mizener, 1949). He considered calling *This Side of Paradise* by the title *The Demon Lover.*

Of course, Fitzgerald might have produced many ingenious titles for Guilford's plots. Doing a test and producing titles for one's own compositions are two different things. The example merely points up the difficulties involved in relating Guilford-type tests to other kinds of creative behavior. We call these difficulties *validity problems.* Validity is a special technical term which asks the question: "Do tests of divergent thinking identify people who behave creatively in the real world?"

THE PROBLEM OF VALIDITY

In one experiment, Piers, Daniels, and Quackenbush (1960) administered some of Guilford's tests to 114 seventh- and eighth-grade students and correlated their scores with teacher ratings of creativity. Teachers rated the students on a 5-point scale ranging from *extremely creative* to *extremely uncreative.* The experimenters explained to the teachers that by *creativity* they meant:

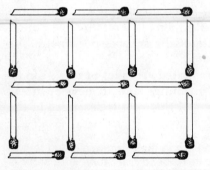

Figure 24.1

. . . the capacity of the individual to avoid the usual routine, conventional ways of thinking and of doing things and to produce a quantity of ideas and/or products which are original, novel or uncommon and which are workable. It must be purposeful or goal-directed. It may involve the forming of new patterns and combinations of information derived from past experience, and the transplanting of old relationships to new situations, or the generation of new relationships. (Piers, Daniels, and Quackenbush, 1960, p. 347)

That sounds like a description of the same kind of fluencies sampled by Guilford's tests, but oddly enough, the teacher ratings did not agree at all with the fluency test scores. In fact, the teacher ratings did not even agree with each other—for there were three teachers rating each student. The authors considered this result to be "disappointing and illustrative of the difficulties involved in this area . . . due to the vagueness and variability in the popular conception of what is meant by creativity."

From your own experience, would you guess that the lack of relationship between the Guilford tests and the teacher ratings was caused by the tests or by the teachers? That is, did the tests fail to detect creativity the teachers recognized? Or did the teachers have faulty concepts of creativity in their students? How would you explain the fact that teachers could not agree on the degree of creativity possessed by individual students?

In another attempt to validate Guilford-type creativity tests, Harris (1960) administered them to engineers in the General Motors Corporation. You can see in Figure 24.2 that Harris constructed a test of associational fluencies relevant to engineering. He then asked supervisors to eval-

TYPE I

LIST AS MANY POSSIBLE USES AS YOU CAN FOR THIS OBJECT

TYPE II

LIST AS MANY POSSIBLE USES AS YOU CAN FOR THESE TWO OBJECTS WHEN THEY ARE USED TOGETHER

TYPE III

WHAT IS THIS? LIST AS MANY POSSIBILITIES AS YOU CAN.

Figure 24.2 Examples of item types from Harris' test of creativity in engineering. (Harris, 1960, p. 255)

uate the creativity of the engineers and correlated the test scores with the ratings. In this study, there was better agreement between the two types of creativity scores, but the relationship was still not very strong. On the average, only about 12 percent of the variation in one measure of creativity (the test scores) could be predicted by the variation in the other measure (the supervisors' rankings); *88 percent of one measure could not be predicted by the other.* Such findings do not hold out much hope that a simple measure of fluency ("How many uses can you think of for this gidgie-gadget?") will enable us to discover people whom experts are going to call *creative* in the real world. Of course, you may argue, the experts can be wrong—and indeed they can be. But no matter what criterion of creativity you use, tests of divergent thinking do not seem to predict clearly who will achieve that criterion and who will not.

Nevertheless, the belief that Guilford-type fluencies are a clue to creative ability persists in educational and psychological circles and a number of training methods have been devised to increase them.

TRAINING GUILFORD-TYPE FLUENCIES

Myers and Torrance (1962) have published a series of workbooks they believe will develop creativity in children. Two of their fluency exercises are reproduced in Figure 24.3. Although it has not been demonstrated that classroom exercises of this sort actually develop true creativity in children, they may be a source of ideas for teachers.

Some laboratory experimentation has also been done on the factors affecting the production of Guilford-type fluencies. The major work has been carried out by Maltzman and his associates. In their basic experiment, Maltzman and his colleagues (1960) first administered a free association list of twenty-five words to their college-student subjects. These were common words that did not usually evoke uncommon associates—for example, *pencil, boy, sweet,* and *bake.* Using this list, it was possible to equalize experimental groups on the basis of their pretest originality. After the subjects participated in various training procedures, they were given a second free-association test list so that possible increases in their originality could be assessed. Guilford's Unusual Uses test was administered right after the second association list.

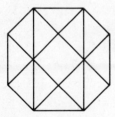

Jerry drove his car to the lake one day when he felt like swimming. He parked his car by the side of the lake, got out of the car, and jumped into the water. After about ten minutes he came out of the water. Just as he reached into his car for a towel, a policeman told him he was under arrest.

Think of as many facts as you can which might have been left out of this little story that would account for the policeman's action. . . .

How many triangles can you find in the figure?_____

Figure 24.3   Fluency exercises from Myers and Torrance (1962).

The following training and control procedures reveal the factors that Maltzman believed might affect originality training (the groups were composed of different people):

Group 1: Same Response Practice. The group received five additional presentations of the same (first) training list, with instructions to try to give the same response (associate) each time.

Group 2: Different Response Practice. The group also received five additional presentations of the same training list, but this time their instructions were to try to give a different response each time.

Group 3: New Unfamiliar Word Practice. This group continued to give free associations to 125 new words that did not occur frequently in their experience.

Group 4: New Familiar Word Practice. This group also continued to give free associations to new words (125 of them), but this time the words were familiar ones.

Group 5: No Practice. This was the control group; these subjects went from the first free-association list to the second with no practice of any kind.

What results might we expect from the training procedures compared to the control procedure? It seems plausible to assume that Group 1, which simply repeated the same responses (to the extent that they could remember them), would not show much increase in originality, even with a new list of words; and perhaps the group (Group 4) that practiced giving free associations to familiar words would not show as much originality improvement as the group (Group 3) that practiced giving associations to unfamiliar words. After all, the latter group might even be learning new words. But what about the second training group? And, most important of all, how might any of these groups perform on the Unusual Uses test? Remember, all five groups were being given that test as well as a second association list.

Table 24.1 gives us the results. Group 1, as anticipated, showed significantly less originality than all the other training groups on the second list.

The reason that a high association-test score was equivalent to low originality was because responses were scored in terms of the number of subjects giving them. For example, suppose the stimulus word was *boy*. If 80 out of 100 subjects responded "girl," then *girl* would receive a score of 80. If 1 out of 100 subjects responded "Oedipus," then Oedipus would be scored 1. Thus a more original response had a lower number, which stood for its low frequency of occurrence.

Groups 2, 3, and 4 did not differ from each other in originality of associations to the second word list, but they were all better than Group 1 and the control group (Group 5). Apparently, any kind of practice in free associating will improve originality on the same kind of task.

But what about the Unusual Uses test? Was the pattern of experimental results similar to the pattern on the second free-association task? No, as we see from the second column of Table 24.1; Group 2, *which had*

*had practice giving new associates to the same word list five times over, pro-
duced more unique ideas on the Guilford test—an average of 4.75 of them.*

Table 24.1
Mean Number of Original Associations and Unique Uses Following Training

GROUP	MEAN NUMBER OF ORIGINAL ASSOCIATIONS TO SECOND WORD LIST (LOW SCORE = HIGH ORIGINALITY)	MEAN NUMBER OF UNIQUE USES ON GUILFORD'S WORD LIST (HIGH SCORE = HIGH ORIGINALITY)
Group 1	70.90	1.03†
Group 2	54.49*	4.75‡
Group 3	56.44*	2.72
Group 4	53.40*	2.27
Group 5	76.38	2.58

SOURCE: Based on data in Maltzman, Simon, Raskin, and Licht, 1960.
*These three groups showed significantly more originality than Group 1 (same response practice) and Group 5 (controls).
†This group produced significantly fewer unique responses than any of the other groups.
‡This group produced significantly more unique responses than any of the other groups.

Creative Strategies

We used to be taught that transfer occurred because of "identical elements" shared by two tasks. What were the identical elements of the free-
association training and the Unusual Uses test? Certainly not the same
words, because the same words did not appear in both tasks. In another
experiment, Maltzman also found that even when a subject practiced the
Unusual Uses task itself, his originality on that very task was not as great
as his originality following practice of the Group 2 variety, practice
"dredging up" new responses to the same old list of words. Possibly the
Group 2 subjects developed a *strategy* for doing so, and that strategy was
transferred to the Unusual Uses test.

What might such a strategy involve? Probably some system for
searching (one's memory, the room, the view outside the window) for
new ideas. Ridley and Birney (1967), who provided subjects with strategic
guideposts to aid in searches, found these procedures even more successful than Maltzman's in increasing fluencies. For example, subjects
were told to transform the objects in the Guilford test. "Burn it, cut it,
paint it, etc. What uses of your object do these transformations suggest?
An example is: a brick (with a hole in it) as a pencil holder" (Ridley and
Birney, 1967, p. 159).

A demonstration that the development of a strategy might increase
Guilford-type fluencies suggests that intelligence may be an important
fluency-producing factor. That suggestion, however, has not met with
popular acclaim.

THE ROLE OF INTELLIGENCE

There is a dangerous myth circulating that should be scotched without further hesitation—the myth that creativity and intelligence are unrelated. It
seems to have begun with the publication of a book by Getzels and

Jackson (1961), which purported to show that "low IQ" children of "high creativity" were more spontaneous, amusing, and generally interesting (though less popular with teachers) than "high IQ" children of "low creativity." It should be instantly pointed out that by "low IQ," Getzels and Jackson meant an *average IQ of 127* and by "creativity," simply scores on Guilford-type fluency tests.

In a more recent book along the same lines, Wallach and Wing (1969) argue that "low IQ" subjects do not have as many "talented accomplishments outside the classroom" as "high productivity" (on Guilford-type fluency tests) subjects do. In this case, IQ was considered to be revealed by scores on the Verbal and Mathematical Scholastic Aptitude tests. These scores for the sample as a whole were 619 (verbal) and 645 (mathematical), on the average. The entire sample was taken from a group of students who had already been admitted to Duke University, which has relatively high admission requirements. Clearly, the "low IQ" group was not really low compared to the general population.

In an earlier book, Wallach and Kogan (1965) again argued that "low IQ" children who were high in "creativity" were different in various respects from "high IQ" children who were low in "creativity." Unfortunately, they do not provide us with actual IQs, but they do say that 94 percent of the children were from professional and managerial backgrounds, and they give us the children's scores on national achievement tests, scores that place the children in the top 4 percent of the national grade school population. These are clearly not low IQ children, regardless of the authors' decision to label them as such.

There are other rumors and references throughout the educational literature about the notion that creativity and intelligence have nothing to do with each other and that a highly creative child may not be especially bright. The two fallacies in this argument have already been indicated: (1) The fallacy that measures of fluency or productivity on Guilford-type tests are valid measures of creativity; (2) the fallacy that low IQ people are actually included in a test sample.

The fact is that Guilford-type fluencies *are* correlated with IQ—if the full IQ range is included. (We will defer the question of whether or not these fluencies fully measure creativity.) Guilford himself has summarized the issue this way:

> The relation of creative abilities to intelligence, as traditionally known and measured, has been investigated quite a number of times, usually by means of correlating scores from traditional intelligence scales with scores from tests of divergent-thinking abilities. Almost invariably the conclusion is that the correlation between creative potential and intelligence is positive but [moderate]. . . . But the relationship is nonlinear. . . . [viz.] Individuals with a high intelligence score may have scores on divergent-production tests ranging from low to high, but individuals with low intelligence scores very rarely have high divergent-production scores. From these facts we may state . . . that being high on what is measured by

intelligence tests is a necessary condition for high creativity, but it is not a sufficient condition. . . . No one can be very low in intelligence score and also be very creative. (Guilford, 1966, p. 74)

Again and again, where it is claimed that "low IQ" students are demonstrating "high creativity," it will turn out that "low IQ" means *low relative to students with extremely high IQs*. In other words, within an above-average population of intelligent people, fluency scores may vary considerably; within a below-average population, fluency scores will be low. Even when fluency is not the sole measure of creativity, the same basic relationships seem to hold. Barron (1969) has published the scores on a Concept Mastery test (not an IQ test, but closely related) for groups studied at the Berkeley Institute for Personality Assessment and Research, as well as for some other groups. They are shown in Table 24.2.

With the foregoing facts clearly in mind, let us backtrack a bit. You will recall from Part II that *IQ is what IQ tests measure*. A particular highly creative individual may have information of a very selective sort, information not adequately sampled by a standard IQ test. Further, individuals with a high degree of spatial ability may have difficulties with tests that emphasize verbal skills alone. Finally, there is the problem of cultural background: IQ tests standardized on middle-class populations may not fairly assess the intelligence of disadvantaged populations because the terminology and style of the test is unfamiliar. Of course, children from such backgrounds will have difficulties in middle-class schools, and their IQ test score may be an accurate predictor of school achievement for that reason; but creative children from disadvantaged backgrounds may appear

Table 24.2
Scores on Concept Mastery Test, Groups Differing in Degree of Creativity

GROUP	MEAN SCORE
Creative writers	156.4
Creative women mathematicians	144.0
Stanford Gifted Study	136.7
Representative women mathematicians	124.5
Graduate students, Univ. of Calif.	119.2
Research scientists	118.2
Medical students, Univ. of Calif.	118.2
Ford Fellowship applicants	117.9
Creative architects	113.2
College graduates, Univ. of Calif.	112.0
Public Health education applicants	97.1
Spouses of Stanford gifted	95.3
Electronic engineers	94.5
Undergraduates, lower division, Stanford	77.6
Military officers [captain and up]	60.3

SOURCE: Barron, 1969, p. 40.

to have lower IQs than they would actually have if the IQ test were culturally appropriate. Because of this, *their creativity may be a better index of their true intelligence than IQ tests are.*

For reasons of this sort, we would do well to think of creativity in students as a quality separate from intelligence, but we must not expect it to be a *substitute.* Intelligence can take many forms, a lesson Irvine teaches in this charming excerpt from *Apes, Angels and Victorians* (1955):

> Nobody would have been surprised if Huxley had explained evolution. Nearly everybody who has read the facts is a little surprised that Darwin did, and clever people from Samuel Butler to Mr. Jacques Barzun have demonstrated that he shouldn't have. Huxley had more talents than two lifetimes could have developed. He could think, draw, speak, write, inspire, lead, negotiate, and wage multifarious war against earth and heaven with the cool professional ease of an acrobat supporting nine people on his shoulders at once. He knew everything and did everything, and in his own time seemed a movement and an epoch in himself. In short, he enjoyed all the luxuries of genius. Darwin possessed only the bare necessities. He was a slow reader, particularly in foreign languages. He could not draw. He was clumsy and awkward with his hands, and despite his interest and belief in experiment, he was in some way oddly careless and inefficient. He had great faith in instruments, yet his instruments were mostly crude and makeshift. His children astounded him by proving that one of his micrometers differed from the other. He could not make a speech and dreaded appearing in public. . . . His conversation was an adventure of parentheses within parentheses which often produced a stammer and sometimes terminated in unintelligibility and syntactical disaster. He wrote fairly clear and interesting English only by slowly and painfully improving the impossible. . . .
>
> How could such a man escape ordinary failure much less achieve spectacular success? How could he possibly discover a great principle like natural selection and bring to completion a long work on organic evolution? Perhaps he succeeded — partly at least — in explaining evolution for the delightfully English reason that explaining evolution was a tradition in his family. In any case, his idea grew like a tradition — slowly, almost inevitably. . . . In 1837 he opened his first notebook on the mutability of species. From that moment he was a man living with an idea — a decent, safe man living with a shockingly indecent, horribly unsafe idea. (Irvine, 1955, pp. 71–72)

Darwin, of course, muddled through. And in chapters ahead, we will see that the mental requirements of genuine creativity are sufficiently great that no truly unintelligent person could master them. If an individual of great creative achievement does poorly on an IQ test, then we may well look to the test as an inadequate measure of his real intelligence.

Chapter 25 ORDERS AND CONNECTIONS

A CLASSROOM EXERCISE

The general difficulty with exercises in divergent thinking is that any old kind of fluency is not the hallmark of an element universe. Henry Moore's fluency in generating natural forms, Wolfe's fluency of sensations and images, and Mozart's parade of little tunes were each in the service of personal creative enterprises. One would guess, then, that *practice in generating ideas relevant to a creative enterprise of importance to the student* would be the best creativity training. This is because what one *does* with the ideas (as compared to simply *having* them) is the next important step.

The following excerpt from the Arts Curriculum for Able Students, developed by the Fine Arts Department of Carnegie-Mellon University, shows how a fluency exercise (the collection of sounds) can be tied to a particular creative goal:

> This unit is an attempt to make students more aware of, and more curious about, the sounds around them. The student should notice the tremendous variety of sounds to which he is exposed every day. He should become curious about the various ways these sounds are produced, of the ways in which they differ from one another, and the ways they are similar. He should become aware of the importance of sounds as clues to what is going on around him. He should better appreciate the intimate association of sounds with the places and things that produce them. Finally, he should make some attempt to describe sounds so that others may recall them. . . .
>
> Send children outside the classroom to such places as the school

cafeteria, the playground, and shops to collect sounds. Children should bring back tape-recorded sounds, written descriptions of sound, and/or sound-making objects. Once recordings have been made, many activities can be built around them. Students can try to guess the object which made each sound and how it was made. They can try to guess the location of the recorder when the recording was made. They can find similar sounds, thus opening up a discussion of why they seem similar. They can describe the sound in their own words to sharpen their awareness of words which describe sounds. Probably the teacher will want to spend some time on each of these activities. The description and classification problems will recur in another form later, so these activities can serve as an introduction to this process. . . .

Suggested final project: take the children on a field trip and have them make a sound reportage. The class can choose a subject such as SOUNDS AT THE ZOO, A TRIP TO THE AIRPORT. The class could gather the material by recording the sounds, taking pictures, or bringing back objects which would help the aural and visual re-creation of the event being reported. (Rice and Winsand, 1966, p. 98)

The excerpt serves to warn us that the construction of an element universe does not complete the creative process. As the children come marching back to the classroom, their tape recorders bulging with sounds, the question looms: *What is the teacher to do now?*

ANSWERS FROM THE MASTERS

If I continue in this way, it soon occurs to me how I may turn this or that morsel to account, so as to make a good dish of it, that is to say, agreeable to the rules of counterpoint, to the peculiarities of the various instruments, etc.

All this fires my soul, and provided I am not disturbed, my subject enlarges itself, becomes methodised and defined, and the whole, though it be long, stands almost complete and finished in my mind, so that I can survey it, like a fine picture or a beautiful statue, at a glance. Nor do I hear in my imagination the parts *successively,* but I hear them, as it were, all at once. What a delight this is I cannot tell! (Mozart, in E. Holmes, *Life of Mozart*)

What is mathematical creation? It does not consist in making a new combination with mathematical entities already known. Anyone could do that, but the combinations so made would be infinite in number and most of them absolutely without interest. To create consists precisely in not making useless combinations and in making those which are useful and which are only a small minority. Invention is discernment, choice. . . . The mathematical facts worthy of being studied are those which . . . reveal to us unsuspected kinship between other facts, long known, but wrongly believed to be strangers to one another. (Poincaré, *The Foundations of Science*)

To my distress and perhaps to my delight, I order things in accordance with my passions. What a sad thing for a painter who loves blondes but denies himself the pleasure of putting them in his picture because they do not go well with the basket of fruit! What misery for a painter who detests apples to have to use them all the time because they harmonize with the table cloth! I put in my pictures everything I like. So much the worse for the things—they have to get along with one another. (Picasso, in *Cahiers d'Art*, C. Zervos)

And when I understood this thing, I saw that I must find for myself the tongue to utter what I knew. . . . And from the moment of that discovery, the line and purpose of my life was shaped. The end toward which every energy of my life and talent would be henceforth directed. . . . It was as if I had discovered a whole new universe of chemical elements and had begun to see certain relations between some of them but had by no means begun to organize the whole series into a harmonious and co-herent union. From this time on, I think my efforts might be described as the effort to complete that organization. . . .

From this time on the general progress of the three books which I was to write in the next four and a half years could be fairly described in somewhat this way. It was a progress that began in a whirling vortex and a creative chaos and that proceeded slowly at the expense of infinite confu-sion, toil and error toward clarification and the articulation of an ordered and formal structure. (Thomas Wolfe, *The Story of a Novel*)

Components of New Patterns

Once the element universe has been constructed or discovered, the job of putting the elements together into new patterns can begin. Studying the self-reports of creative artists suggests that there may be three major as-pects to this process: (1) The *intuition of an order*—the belief (despite pre-liminary chaos) that an organization of the creative elements will be pos-sible; (2) a period of *combinatorial play and self-testing,* wherein trial organizations are attempted and discarded; (3) techniques or *styles of or-dering* (which we, with Bruner, will call *puzzle forms*). Besides the applica-tions, the invention of puzzle forms is also important in creativity.

THE INTUITION OF AN ORDER

One's first intuition, when faced with a new body of material, is often nothing more than a sense of "wrongness" or "rightness." I look at a list of projects planned for first-graders learning about the Eskimo, for in-stance, and it strikes me at once that there is something wrong with some of the projects and something right about others. Putting plants in the icebox is right, but building a styrofoam igloo is wrong. By letting each item "speak" to me in a general way, I can categorize each project as right or wrong. But if I stop here, I am nowhere. . . .

Intuition, to be fruitful, must carry this sense of incompleteness, the feeling that there is something more to be done. It is most successful when it can be backstopped and disciplined by more rigorous techniques of problem-solving and problem formulation. For unless it operates in phase with more rigorous and verifiable methods, its deficiency is some combination of looseness and incorrigibility. . . .

Unexploited intuition that goes nowhere and does not deepen itself by further digging into the materials—be they human, literary, scientific, mathematical, political—is somehow not sufficient to bring the person to the full use of his capacities. Intuition is an invitation to go further. (Bruner and Clinchy, 1966, pp. 74–76)

Perhaps the most striking quality of creative intuition is the sense of compulsion that accompanies it. As Wolfe put it. ". . . from the moment of that discovery, the line and purpose of my life was shaped." The intuition that something "right" can be achieved with the creative materials at hand seems to awaken an intense need to achieve that "rightness."

What is this intuition? Presumably, it is the unconscious recognition of possible connections within the material. There is nothing magical about such unconscious awareness; it is probably similar to conscious awareness, though momentarily below the threshold of conscious recognition. Perhaps the compulsive quality arises from the discomfort of this subthreshold experience; one feels compelled to discover consciously what one already knows unconsciously. Step by step, constantly testing and revising, this discovery is approached.

Remote Connections

Just as Guilford has emphasized "element generating" (divergent thinking) as being the most important aspect of creativity, another psychologist, Sarnoff Mednick, has emphasized *connectivity* between elements. Mednick has constructed a test that samples a person's ability to recognize unusual or remote connections between ideas. He calls his test the Remote Associates Test (RAT for short).

> We may . . . define the creative thinking process as the forming of associative elements into new combinations which either meet specified requirements or are in some way useful. The more mutually remote the elements of the new combination, the more creative the process or solution. (Mednick, 1962, pp. 220–221)

For example, given the set of words *rat, blue,* and *cottage,* what additional word might they all have in common? The answer would be *cheese.* Other items from such a test might be:

Example 2:	railroad	girl	class
Example 3:	surprise	line	birthday
Example 4:	wheel	electric	high
Example 5:	out	dog	cat

The answers would be *working, party, chair* or *wire,* and *house,* respectively (all from Mednick's 1962 paper). As you can see, the RAT also requires the subject to generate a flow of associations, but it has the additional requirement that overlapping or similar associates be recognized. Perhaps because the RAT thus combines two aspects of the creative process, its validity is a bit higher than the validity of fluency tests. In one experiment, for example, Mednick reports that 50 percent of the variability in creativity among a group of architects could be predicted by the variability in their RAT scores. Although 50 percent is higher than the 10 to 12 percent reported for Guilford-type tests, RAT scores would still not seem to be a sure way of predicting real-life creativity. A more interesting use of the RAT has been in experiments testing the ability of high and low RAT scorers to unconsciously utilize information presented to them experimentally. We will return to these studies in Chapter 26, "The Role of the Unconscious."

Like the tip-of-tongue (TOT) phenomenon discussed earlier, RAT exercises help give us a feeling—in a small way—for the intuitive sense of connectivity that seems to be the engine of the creative process. Crossword-puzzle fiends may share this addiction in some degree, but the creative artist, in recognizing that a coherence or harmony is possible among ideas or elements he finds to be of great importance, is driven by a compulsion far more consuming.

COMBINATORIAL PLAY AND SELF-TESTING

In the 1930s, a psychologist named Patrick collected a number of "think-aloud" protocols of poets composing poems to a picture. In one of the protocols (from a poet who was well known at that time) the process of *self-testing* in pursuit of the poet's intuitive sense of "rightness" is quite evident.

> This [picture] might be India except for the foliage. It is an awfully old-fashioned picture. . . . The way the water comes down. . . . It might be called mist and water. . . .
> This is what I think. The cloud mist has touched this mountain and the water has run down from it. I can't touch it. I can't reach the waters in the deep pool. I can't touch the white top of the mountain. I stand in a dark place looking out at it in the high place. I think this is it.

> The gray mist has touched your white forehead.
> And the waters flow from your feet
> Down to the dark chasm
> But I am far away on the dark hill
> I cannot touch

> What I want to say is I can't touch your lonely . . . Can't touch your loneliness

> The gray mist has touched your white forehead
> And the waters flow down from your feet
> Down into the black chasm

> Scratch out "down"

> Into the dark chasm
> But I am far away on the dark hill
> I cannot touch your loneliness.
> The gray mist has touched your white forehead

> Change to

> The gray mist has touched your white forehead
> And the waters flow down from your feet
> Into the dark chasm

Change to black chasm, for I don't want two "darks" as "dark chasm" and "dark hill." ... I like to use Anglo-Saxon words. "The gray mist has touched your forehead." "Forehead" is better than "brow." (Patrick, 1935, pp. 52–53)

The same kind of self-testing is displayed by a painter as he steps back from his easel again and again to survey each newly added bit and by the composer who repeats a single theme with slight chord variations until he discovers the one that is "right." But note that this process is highly personalized; "rightness" and "wrongness" cannot be determined by anyone other than the artist himself.

Self-testing Through Play

The teacher's problem in helping students to develop self-testing systems is a difficult one. Uncritical acceptance of anything the student produces will not help. Condemnation of an attempt that does not meet the *teacher's* test is equally unsatisfactory. Perhaps the best strategy is that of encouraging an attitude of experimentation in the student. Einstein (in Hadamard, 1945) called this *combinatory play* the "essential feature in productive thought." Picasso seems to be referring to the same kind of combinatory play when he says that in his pictures, "things . . . have to get along with one another." As anyone who has studied Picasso's paintings knows, his "things" manage to "get along" very well indeed, for he invented new systems for harmonizing them. The experimental attitude that new systems are possible—and the willingness to try them out—seems essential to the discovery of creative integrations.

The Berkeley Creativity Program The excerpt on pages 516–522 is from the *Productive Thinking Program* developed by Covington, Crutchfield, Davies, and Olton (1967–1971) at the University of California, Berkeley. It shows one way of helping children develop self-testing schemes.

Combinations and Transformations

Reitman (1965) points out that the combinatorial play of a creative process may involve a series of transformations of the original problem. In the Jim-and-Lila exercise, for example, the children began with a collection (loose and randomly connected) of information, transformed that collection into a list of ideas, and then transformed the list into a tree—that is, into a hierarchy that made some items on the list more important than others. The transformations of the original problem may seem like a chain of new problems, but actually they are restatements in a new form of the original problem. The restatements suggest fresh, new ways of looking at the old problem. This ability to adopt fresh points of view is considered to be an important part of the creative process and often seems to have a playful or childlike aspect, but there is nothing childlike about the basic

As Jim considers other possibilities that might explain the disappearance of the rare coins, you try to think of some, too.

What other general possibilities can you think of to explain what happened to the missing coins?

While Jim and Lila are thinking about this, you think, too.

What are some particular ways by which the
coins might have accidentally disappeared?

Our problem is, What happened to the missing rare coins? We need to get a lot of ideas about this. We should open our fishing net wide to catch as many ideas as possible.

What's a good way to do that—and not miss the BIG fish?

Why don't we use that idea-tree Uncle John showed us? First we can think of all the **general possibilities** for what happened to the coins. Then we can think of **particular ideas** to include under each general possibility.

Good. And, afterward, we can check each of these ideas with the facts and cross off any that don't seem likely.

Yes. Then we can follow up the ones that do fit the facts.

Notice that Jim and Lila have taken time to decide on a planful way of working on the problem. Perhaps you did that, too, when you started.

Let's see what happens as Jim and Lila use the plan of the idea- tree to organize their work. It should help them to think of many ideas.

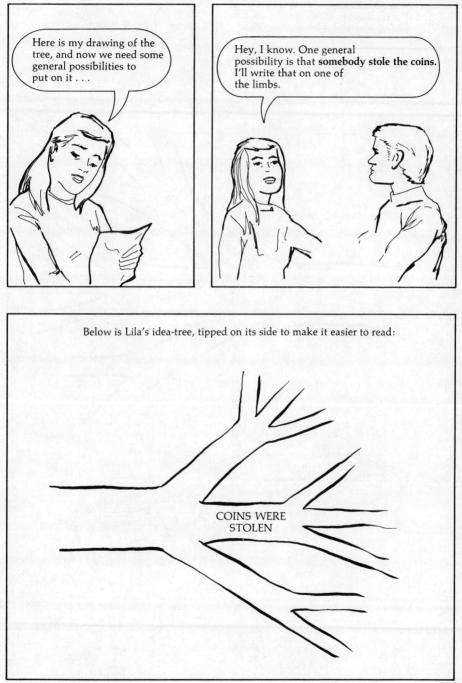

Here is my drawing of the tree, and now we need some general possibilities to put on it . . .

Hey, I know. One general possibility is that **somebody stole the coins.** I'll write that on one of the limbs.

Below is Lila's idea-tree, tipped on its side to make it easier to read:

COINS WERE STOLEN

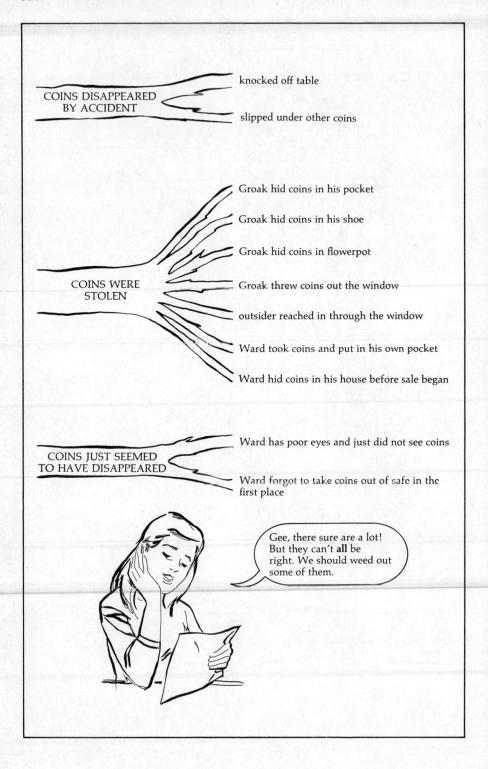

ability to handle a chain of transformed problems. As we know from Parts I and II, such a skill requires formal operational capacities of a high order. The concrete system provided for Jim and Lila by their teacher helps them practice the operational skill at a relatively young age.

The self-testing procedures in a creative exercise may frequently involve an intuitive sense of "rightness" that cannot be consciously explained. By being faithful to such intuitions, the artist may gradually evolve a unique personal style.

PUZZLE FORMS: CREATIVE STYLES

In the self-reports of creative artists, we have seen several examples of their sensitivity to the elements of their creative productions—pebbles, tunes, color sensations, and the like. It is less easy to find examples of an artist's awareness of his *style* of composition. Yet that style may be as clear, and as objectively describable, as the elements are. How is such a style practiced and evolved?

Bruner, referring to the formulations of an English philosopher named Weldon, believes that the style arises from the effort to solve problems:

> We solve a problem or make a discovery when we impose a puzzle form on a difficulty to convert it into a problem that can be solved in such a way that it gets us where we want to be. That is to say we recast the difficulty into a form that we know how to work with—then we work it. Much of what we speak of as discovery consists of knowing how to impose a workable kind of form on various kinds of difficulties. A small but crucial part of discovery of the highest order is to invent and develop effective models or "puzzle forms." It is in this area that the truly powerful mind shines. But it is surprising to what degree perfectly ordinary people can, given the benefit of instruction, construct quite interesting and what, a century ago, would have been considered greatly original models. . . .
> It is my hunch that it is only through the exercise of problem solving and the effort of discovery that one learns the working heuristics of discovery; the more one has practice, the more likely one is to generalize what one has learned into a style of problem solving or inquiry. . . . (Bruner, 1964a, pp. 93–94)

The holes in Henry Moore's sculptures resulted from his efforts to solve the problem of how to use space and air in working with stone. The style of painting called *Pointillism* was evolved by Seurat as a method of representing the physiological visual functions described by psychologists. Ernest Hemingway, under Gertrude Stein's tutelage, worked continuously on the problem of saying what he wanted to say as simply and sparsely as possible. The problems of modulation led Brahms to develop unique harmonic patterns. In each case, the artist developed puzzle forms or methods of coping with the special problems arising from his attempt to organize his own universe of elements.

Some literary examples of stylistic systems are given by Robert Graves, in a recent article on what he calls "the polite lie":

> For some years I earned my livelihood by writing historical novels. There are two different methods. One is to enliven a chunk of ancient history by making the characters speak and behave in modern style. The central event in an early-Tudor novel published a few years ago was the Field of the Cloth of Gold, at which the heroine, a maid of honor to King Henry, remarked brightly to her chivalrous hero: "I do hate parties, darling, don't you?" . . . The alternative method is suddenly to be possessed by a ghost . . . to relive his life and rethink his thoughts in the language that he himself used. . . .
>
> A period-style comes easily enough to whoever soaks himself in the contemporary literature and impersonates the characters. But what sort of English should be put into the mouth of an ancient Greek or Roman? . . . In my two Claudius novels, I relied on extant specimens of Claudius' literary style. . . . Suetonius records that Claudius wrote "ineptly" rather than "inelegantly." . . . I tried to reproduce the effect:
>
>> My tutor I have already mentioned, Marcus Porcius Cato; who was, in his own estimation at least, a living embodiment of that ancient Roman virtue which his ancestors had one after the other shown. He was always boasting of his ancestors, as stupid people do who are aware that they have done nothing themselves to boast about. He boasted particularly of Cato the Censor, who of all characters in Roman history is to me perhaps the most hateful, as having persistently championed the cause of "ancient virtue" and made it identical in the popular mind with churlishness, pedantry and harshness. I was made to read Cato the Censor's self-glorifying works as textbooks, and the account that he gave in one of them of his campaign in Spain, where he destroyed more towns than he had spent days in that country, rather disgusted me with his inhumanity than impressed me with his military skill or patriotism. (Graves, 1965, pp. 75–76)

The subtlety of appropriate stylistic systems is illustrated in other examples in the same article. In all cases the systems were evolved to solve problems of unification (of one sort or another) and operated as "puzzle forms" that could be applied to unlimited amounts of materials (scenes, dialogues). We could probably find in Graves' notes earlier versions that would show the evolution of his stylistic systems.

The fact that creative artists explain their styles as ways of solving creative problems suggests that it may not be possible to teach style directly. We may teach students to experiment with a variety of possible solutions, but the evolution of personal style will be an inevitable outcome of problem-solving procedures that are creatively valid for a given individual.

SOLUTIONS

The ultimate creative solution—the finished product—is really just one final synthesis, or test, of many. Sometimes it is not recognized as such until after it has occurred. But if it is to be called a creative solution, and not an ordinary bit of problem solving, it must have some special characteristics. Bruner (1964a) has suggested the characteristic of *effective surprise:*

> This I shall take as the hallmark of a creative enterprise. The content of the surprise can be as various as the enterprises in which men are engaged. It may express itself in one's dealing with children, in making love, in carrying on a business, in formulating physical theory, in painting a picture. . . . Surprise is not easily defined. It is the unexpected that strikes one with wonder or astonishment. What is curious about effective surprise is that it need not be rare or infrequent or bizarre and is often none of these things. Effective surprises . . . seem rather to have the quality of obviousness about them when they occur, producing a shock or recognition following which there is no longer astonishment. . . .
>
> I think it is possible to specify three kinds of effectiveness, three forms of self-evidence implicit in surprise of the kind we have been considering. The first is predictive effectiveness. It is the kind of surprise that yields high predictive value in its wake—as in the instance of the formula for falling bodies or in any good theoretical reformulation in science. You may well argue that predictive effectiveness does not always come through surprise, but through the slow accretion of knowledge and urge. . . . I will reply by agreeing with you and specifying simply that whether it is the result of intuitive insight or of slow accretion, I will accept it within my definition. The surprise may only come when we look back and see whence we have come.
>
> A second form of effectiveness is best called formal, and its most usual place is in mathematics and logic—possibly in music. . . . It consists of an ordering of elements in such a way that one sees relationships that were not evident before, groupings that were before not present, ways of putting things together not before within reach. Consistency of harmony or depth of relationship is the result. . . .
>
> Of the final form of effectiveness in surprise it is more difficult to write. I shall call it metaphoric effectiveness. It, too, is effective by connecting domains of experience that were before apart, but with the form of connectedness that has the discipline of art. . . .
>
> It is, for example, Thomas Mann's achievement in bringing into a single compass the experiences of sickness and beauty, sexuality and restraint in his *Death in Venice.* Or it is the achievement of the French playwright Jean Anouilh who in *Antigone* makes Creon not only a tyrant but a reasonable man. What we are observing is the connecting of diverse experiences by the mediation of symbol and metaphor and image. . . . Metaphoric combination leaps beyond systematic placement, explores connections that before were unsuspected. (Bruner, 1964a, pp. 19–20)

People often speak of *novelty* as the hallmark of creative solutions, but as Mednick (1962) pointed out, "7,363,474 is quite an original answer to the problem 'How much is 12 plus 12?'" It is not the fact of surprise alone that leads us to hail an achievement as creative; it is the effectiveness of the surprising solution. Many great scientific discoveries have what Bruner calls *predictive effectiveness*—they connect, by means of a scientific principle, many previously unconnected phenomena: The theory of evolution connects the turtles on Galapagos Island with the peas in a monk's

(Mendel's) garden, for example. (For a beautifully sensitive portrait of Darwin the creator, read *Darwin's Century,* by Loren Eiseley.)

Predictive Creativity in the Classroom

The following example is taken from *Teaching Aids for Elementary Mathematics,* by Turner. It suggests several lessons that could lead students into discoveries of predictive effectiveness having the "surprise" quality emphasized by Bruner.

> ... The history of mathematics tells how Fibonacci discovered this series in 1202 A.D. while he was trying to solve a problem in connection with rabbit breeding. Plant growth shows the series in the arrangement of leaves around the stem of some common grasses and also on the twigs of the beech, cherry, elm, pear, and willow trees . . . pine cones, tulips, and the rosette plants.
>
> The series could be approached by first studying leaf arrangements in the corn plant and grasses. As new leaves emerge, count the number of full turns before a leaf appears directly above any previous one. This is its cycle, and the number of leaves in the cycle compared to the number of turns in the cycle is a Fibonacci series ratio [see illustration below]. These curious ratios are always true for the plants given.
>
> Pupils can make interesting discoveries about the series. Members: 1, 2, 3, 5, 8, 13, 21, 34, 55, 89, 144, . . .

SOME PECULIAR CHARACTERISTICS OF THE SERIES

A. Additions after the 1's:

$$\frac{2}{3} = \frac{3}{5} \quad \frac{3}{5} = \frac{5}{8} \quad \frac{5}{8} = \frac{8}{13} \quad \frac{88}{13} = \frac{13}{21} \quad \frac{13}{21} = \frac{21}{34} \quad \text{etc.}$$

. . .

Plant	Fraction	Meaning
Ferns	1/2	In a full turn, 2 leaves
Grasses	1/3	In 1 full turn, 3 leaves
Beech Trees	1/3	In 1 full turn, 3 leaves
Cherry Trees	2/5	In 2 full turns, 5 leaves
Pear Trees	3/8	In 3 full turns, 8 leaves
Corn	3/8	In 3 full turns, 8 leaves
Willow Trees	5/13	In 5 full turns, 13 leaves

(Turner, 1966, pp. 36–37)

Creativity in Scientific Theory

Other kinds of creative solutions have the *formal* effectiveness of Bach's musical inventions, for example, or of topological geometry. See Chapter 23 for another example of creativity—Piaget's recognition of the fact that topological principles unfold in the mind of a child before Euclidean principles do, just as the logic of formal mathematics would predict. This is, of course, an example of creative thinking on Piaget's part; it is not an absolute fact. For this reason, we would say that much of Piaget's theorizing—his connections between child thinking and quasi-mathematical systems—has *formal* effectiveness, but not the *predictive* effectiveness that a theory like $E = mc^2$ has. Piaget's theories have a structure more like that of a formal musical system (say, a fugue) than that of an engineering rule.

Metaphoric effectiveness is nowhere more beautifully illustrated than in Bruner's own essay on Freud:

> For Freud, as for the Stoics, there is no possibility of man's disobeying the laws of nature. And yet for him it is in this lawfulness that the human drama inheres. His love for the Greek drama and his use of it in his formulations are patent. The sense of the human tragedy, the inevitable working out of the human plight—these are the hallmarks of Freud's case histories. When Freud, the tragic dramatist, becomes a therapist, it is not to intervene as a directive authority. The therapist enters the drama of the patient's life, makes possible a play within a play, the transference, and when the patient has "worked through" and understood the drama, he has achieved the wisdom necessary for freedom. . . .
>
> [But] success in transforming the common conception of man did not come simply from adopting the cause-and-effect discourse of science. Rather it is Freud's imagery, I think, that provides the clue to his ideological power. It is an imagery of necessity, an imagery that combines the dramatic, the tragic, and the scientific views of necessity. It is here that Freud's is a theory or a prototheory peopled with actors. The characters are from life: the blind, energetic, pleasure-seeking id; the priggish and punitive superego; the ego, battling for its being by diverting the energy of the others to its own use. The drama has economy and terseness. The ego develops canny mechanisms for dealing with the threat of id impulses: denial, projection, and the rest. Balances are struck among the actors, and in this balance are character and neurosis. . . . The imagery of the theory, moreover, has an immediate resonance with the dialectic of experience. True, it is not the stuff of superficial conscious experience. But it fits the human dilemma, its conflict, its private torment, its impulsiveness, its secret and frightening urges, its tragic quality. (Bruner, 1964a, pp. 153–158)

The Metaphors of McLuhan

There are many ways of giving students the experience of metaphoric effectiveness. Perhaps the foremost modern proponent of this sort of creative surprise is Marshall McLuhan:

> Electricity is not something that is conveyed by or contained in anything, but is something that occurs when two or more bodies are in spe-

cial positions. Our language derived from phonetic technology cannot cope with this new view of knowledge. We still talk of electric current "flowing," or we speak of the "discharge" of electric energy like the lineal firing of guns. But quite as much as with the esthetic magic of painterly power, "electricity is the condition we observe when there are certain spatial relations between things." The painter learns how to adjust relations among things to release new perception, and the chemist and physicist learn how other relations release other kinds of power. (McLuhan, 1964, p. 148)

Almost any quotation from McLuhan—and almost any illustration of his ideas (see Figure 25.1)—would serve to make the same point, that we may become freshly aware of the powers around us and within us by translating them into new representational forms. Neurologically, this can mean using parts of the brain that are not normally used in certain ways of thinking or perceiving. Artistically, the power of a written descriptive passage may lie in its ability to translate a visual or kinesthetic experience into a verbal one. The writer recodes his visual experience into words; the reader decodes the verbal experience into a visual one: He "sees" what the author is describing. In such a manner, as McLuhan frequently emphasizes, one representational system may enrich and extend the others.

Synectic Metaphors

Another student of the creative process, William J. J. Gordon has developed a technique he calls *synectics* for applying metaphorical systems in the production of creative solutions:

> For instance, a Synectics group was attempting to solve the problem of how to invent a new kind of roof. . . . Analysis of the problem indicated that there might be an economic advantage in having a roof white in summer and black in winter. The white roof would deflect the sun's rays in summer so that the cost of air conditioning could be reduced. The black roof would absorb heat in winter so that the cost of heating could be minimized. The following is an excerpt from a session on this problem:
>
> A: What in nature changes color?
> B: A weasel—white in winter, brown in summer . . .
> C: Yes, but a weasel has to lose his white hair in summer, so that the brown hair can grow in . . . Can't be ripping off roofs twice a year.
>   . . .
> B: Okay. How about a chameleon?
> C: That is a better example because he can change back and forth without losing any skin or hair. . . .
> E: How does the chameleon do it?
> A: . . . a flounder must do it the same way.
> E: Do what?
> A: . . . a flounder turns white if he lies on white sand, and then he turns dark if he lands on black sand . . . mud.
> D: . . . But how does he do it?
> B: Chromatophores. . . . In the deepest layer of the [flounder's skin] are black-pigmented chromatophores. When these are pushed toward the epidermal surface the flounder is covered with black spots so that he

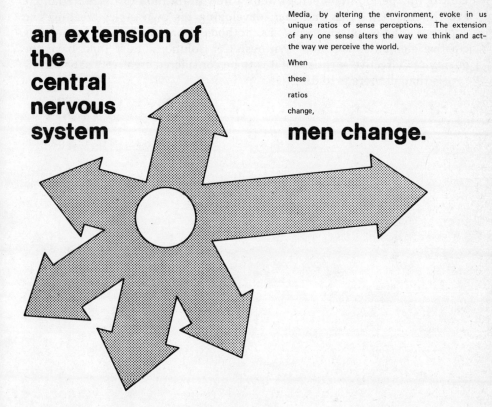

electric circuitry,

an extension of the central nervous system

Media, by altering the environment, evoke in us unique ratios of sense perceptions. The extension of any one sense alters the way we think and act—the way we perceive the world.

When

these

ratios

change,

men change.

Figure 25.1 Two pages of McLuhanese illustrating the power of analogies to stir our thinking. (McLuhan and Fiore, 1967, pp. 40-41)

looks black. . . . When the black pigment withdraws to the bottom of the chromatophores then the flounder appears light colored. . . .

c: You know, I've got a hell of an idea. Let's flip the flounder analogy over on to the roof problem. . . . Let's say we make up a roofing material that's black, except buried in the black stuff are little white plastic balls. When the sun comes out and the roof gets hot the little white balls expand. . . . They pop through the black roofing vehicle. Now the roof is white. . . . Just like the flounder, only with reverse English. (Gordon, 1961, pp. 54–56)

Summary
The creative process as described so far appears to go something like this: There is a period of intense preparation, or immersion, in whatever type of creative "stuff" the artist works with; this is followed by a flowering of

ideas about the "stuff"—a period of divergent thinking, or associating. During this period the creator intuits a new unification of his material. He experiments, tries this and that, developing his own style, creating and applying unique "puzzle forms" as methods of harmonizing or connecting creative elements. His final synthesis, or solution, must then have the quality of "effective surprise" if it is to be considered creatively satisfying.

Is that all there is to it?

Chapter 26 THE ROLE OF THE UNCONSCIOUS

We have been approaching the creative process as if it were a wholly conscious one. Of course it is not; but then, no kind of thinking is wholly conscious. Is creative thinking special in any way?

Certain aspects of unconscious functioning—sometimes called "inspiration," "incubation," and the like—are more often discussed in a creativity context. Further, the familiar notion that "genius is next to madness" implies that there may be some disturbing features to the creative unconscious—features akin to those of psychosis, drug states, and ecstatic religious experiences. If this is true, it might explain why some teachers have been unreceptive to the idea of creativity in the classroom—they may fear a release of uncontrollable psychic energies. Let us see if there are grounds for apprehension.

ENERGY AND FLUENCY

Think back for a moment to Freud's distinction between *primary* and *secondary* processes, which was covered in Part III. Primary processes, you will recall, are the stuff of which the id is composed; secondary processes—being abilities of the intellect—help consolidate the ego. Primary processes are blind and unsocialized; secondary processes are the systems whereby we cope with the world, including our own inner world.

It is believed (by Freud, among others) that artists are more closely in touch with primary process material than uncreative people. Some paintings, like some poems, for example, have the qualities of dreams, and dreams are pure primary process. The kind of "effective surprise" Bruner talks about characterizes certain slips of the tongue that Freud also believed to reveal primary processes. Professor Spooner's saying "Is the Bean dizzy?" might reveal an honest evaluation (at the primary process level) of a busy Dean.

Unleashing Unconscious Energies

We have also discussed Freud's concept of regression—a reactivation of early childhood conflicts that he saw as being of a special sort and that he believed could be recognized (though disguised and transformed) in works of art. In a brilliant example of metaphoric effectiveness, Freud (1947) saw in the works of da Vinci many elements of infant disturbances accounting, he believed, for both da Vinci's obsessional work habits and his choice of themes.

Although we may not agree with specific interpretations of this sort, we can recognize that some creative people can tolerate thoughts, feelings, and impulses which are greatly disturbing to others. An absence of repression may have two effects: (1) It may increase the flow of ideas and images (elements) available to the artist for creative operations; (2) it may also "unleash" (through activation of old brain emotion centers) powerful feelings and drives. These phenomena have been described by Ernst Kris, a famous psychoanalytic writer on the creative process:

> Schematically speaking we may view the process of artistic creation as composed of two phases which may be sharply demarcated from each other, may merge into each other, may follow each other in rapid or slow succession, or may be interwoven with each other in various ways. In designating them as *inspiration* and *elaboration*, we refer to extreme conditions: one type is characterized by the feeling of being driven, the experience of rapture, and the conviction that an outside agent acts through the creator; in the other type, the experience of purposeful organization, and the intent to solve a problem predominate. The first has many features in common with regressive processes: impulses and drives, otherwise hidden, emerge. The subjective experience is that of a flow of thought and images driving toward expression. The second has many features in common with what characterizes "work"—dedication and concentration. (Kris, 1952, p. 59)

The "opening up" of lower brain centers may be one important source of the intense energy to create often seen in practicing artists. But that is not the whole story.

Finding the Pattern in Unconscious Material

Psychotics are also "opened up," in the sense that their creative productions may reveal a clear flow of primary process material. Consider the differences between the following stories. One subject was a schizophrenic patient; the other was his normal control. Both were 16-year-old boys. The stories were about the same picture, that of a man standing under a street light at night, in rain or fog.

Schizophrenic

At midnight. Mr. Cox came home from work at 3:00 in the morning, He saw the street light on Midvale shining real bright as the moon shines. Once he came home and they were alley cats screaming in the alley on Midvale Avenue, and got everybody frightened as plain as day. Meanwhile, Denise and Robin were scared of the dark. The moment they walked to their windows and saw those alley cats pull in the screen, the screen off the doors, and knocking garbage cans over and pushing, pushing trash can over, knocking rake and shovel down, the moment they saw it, the moment they screamed. The first thing happened. They yelled until they woke up.

Normal

A hobo, standing on a corner. He's probably waiting for a bus or something.

In terms of our language analysis (Chapter 18), we would say that the schizophrenic subject had lost the ability to sustain meaningful long-term verbal associations, although his short-term associations were still intact. But what of his imagery and feelings? Surely we would describe his story as far more creative than that of his normal control. Or would we?

The normal subject lacks the fluencies necessary to a creative production, but he has the capacity to generate an explanation, or coherent form, for the few ideas in his head. The schizophrenic subject could not explain any connections—reasons, causes, relationships—among his richly flowing ideas.

As we know, an essential feature of the creative process is the harmonizing or ordering of the creative elements. Psychosis (whether natural or drug-induced) disrupts this ability. Kris, Freud, and others who have studied both psychotic and creative behavior agree that the *controlled* regression of a creative artist is very different from the *uncontrolled* regression of a psychotic. In the latter case, primary processes overwhelm the ego, and the disciplined ordering, self-testing, and stylistic processes essential to a genuine creative production become impossible. The difference is sometimes illustrated by the problem of communication.

The Hidden Audience

The psychotic may not be able to communicate. True art (according to Kris) cannot happen in that case. More important, a mentally healthy artist cannot happen either:

Inspiration—the "divine release from the ordinary ways of man," a state of "creative madness" (Plato), in which the ego controls the primary process and puts it into its service—need be contrasted with the opposite, the psychotic condition, in which the ego is overwhelmed by the primary process. The difference is clearest where the relation to the public is concerned.

Psychoanalytic investigation of artistic creation has abundantly demonstrated the importance of the public for the process of creation: wherever artistic creation take place, the idea of a public exists, though the artist may express indifference, may eliminate the consideration for an audience from his consciousness altogether, or he may minimize its importance. But wherever the unconscious aspect of artistic creation is studied, a public of some kind emerges. This does not mean that striving for success, admiration, and recognition need be the major goal of all artistic creation. On the contrary, artists are more likely than others to renounce public recognition for the sake of their work. Their quest need not be for approval of the many but for response by some. The acknowledgement by response . . . is essential to confirm their own belief in their work and to restore the very balance which the creative process may have disturbed. . . .

To the artist the public is . . . not only a distant and powerful judge. . . . He also puts himself into the place of the public and identifies in ego (and superego) with his audience. . . . While the artist creates, in the state of inspiration, he and his work are one; when he looks upon the product of his creative urge, he sees it from the outside, and as his own first audience he participates in "what the voice has done." Art, we said, always, consciously or unconsciously, serves the purpose of communication. (Kris, 1952, pp. 60–61)

In Kris's terms, then, the regression into a dreamlike state of associational fluidity must be in the service not only of the individual's own ego, but also of at least one other ego—a listener, observer, receiver—to qualify as genuine creativity. When the creative display (the story or the poem) is so private that no communication is possible, we may have something quite interesting from a psychiatric point of view, but we will have little that is creative.

This is the theory. Is it valid? If it is, a creative individual might show signs of both the regressive features that characterize a psychotic and the strong ego controls that characterize a healthy person. Just exactly that pattern was found when personality traits of highly creative architects and writers were compared with those of average architects and writers.

Creativity and Personality Tests

As part of extensive and continuing research into the nature of creativity, psychologists at the Institute of Personality Assessment and Research, Berkeley, have studied many individuals who were rated (by authorities in their respective fields) on degree of creativity. During one such evaluation, a group of architects took the Minnesota Multiphasic Personality Inventory—a test that can be scored for neurotic and psychotic personality traits. That is, neurotic and psychotic people are more likely than are normal people to answer MMPI questions in certain ways.

Table 26.1
Average Scores, Tests of Psychopathology and Ego Strength, Highly Creative and Average Writers

TRAIT MEASURED	HIGHLY CREATIVE WRITERS	AVERAGE WRITERS
Psychopathology		
Hypochondriasis	63	57
Depression	65	59
Hysteria	68	58
Psychopathic deviation	65	56
Paranoia	61	57
Abnormal fatigue	64	55
Schizophrenia	67	56
Hypomania	61	51
Ego strength		
Ego strength	58	52
Self-acceptance	63	54
Responsibility	52	50
Independence	63	60
Intellectual efficiency	54	52

SOURCE: Adapted from Barron, 1969, p. 72.

Table 26.1 shows the MMPI scores for highly creative and average writers. It can be seen that scores on the neurotic and psychotic test questions are higher for the more creative writers. Compared to normal populations, even the average writers had high scores on psychopathology:

> From these data one might be led to conclude that creative writers are, as the common man has long suspected them to be, a bit "dotty." And of course it has always been a matter of pride in self-consciously artistic and intellectual circles to be . . . eccentric. "Mad as a hatter" is a term of high praise when applied to a person of marked intellectual endowments. But the "divine madness" that the Greeks considered a gift of the gods and an essential ingredient in the poet was not, like psychosis, something subtracted from normality; rather, it was something added. Genuine psychosis is stifling and imprisoning; the divine madness is a liberation. (Barron, 1969, pp. 72–73)

An ego that remains strong and healthy in the midst of so many disruptive tendencies must be a very healthy ego indeed. As Table 26.1 shows, *ego strength in these writers was also extremely high.* Among psychotics with high psychopathology scores, ego strength is always much lower.

The study (which is reported in detail, along with several others, by Frank Barron in *Creative Person and Creative Process,* 1969) thus supports the hypothesis that readier access to primary process material may be associated with creative achievement *only* if the artist is strongly in control of this material. We are not afraid to dream if we are able to wake up at will.

THE CREATIVE PERSONALITY

The Berkeley researchers are building tentative profiles of creative individuals that agree only in part with common conceptions. Teachers on the lookout for creative youngsters in their classrooms may be helped to identify them by John Gardner's eloquent summary in *Self-renewal:*

> There are many kinds of creative individuals. Creative writers are distinguishable from creative mathematicians, and both are distinguishable from creative architects. Yet research suggests that there are traits which are shared by all of these and by most other highly original people.
>
> **Openness.** In studies of creative people one finds many references to a quality that might be described as "openness." At one level openness refers to the individual's receptivity to the sights, sounds, events and ideas that impinge on him. Most of us are skillful in shutting out the world, and what we do observe we see with a jaded eye. Men or women with the gift of originality manage to keep a freshness of perception, an unspoiled awareness.
>
> Of course this openness to experience is limited to those features of the external world that seem to the individual to be relevant in his inner life. No one could be indiscriminately open to all the clutter and clatter of life. The creative individual achieves his heightened awareness of some aspects of life by ignoring other aspects. . . .
>
> More significant than his receptivity to the external world is his openness with respect to his own inner life. . . . he has access to the full richness of one man's emotional, spiritual and intellectual experience. But the trait can be relevant even in the cases of men who appear to be dealing wholly with the external world. The creative engineer lets his hunches and wild ideas come to the surface, where the uncreative man would tend to censor them.
>
> **Independence.** The creative individual has the capacity to free himself from the web of social pressures. . . . He is capable of questioning assumptions that the rest of us accept . . . [But] it is easy to fall into romantic exaggeration in speaking of the capacity of men of originality to stand apart. Those who are responsible for the great innovative performances have always built on the work of others, and have enjoyed many kinds of social support, stimulation and communication. They are independent but they are not adrift.
>
> The independence or detachment of the creative individual is at the heart of his capacity to take risks and to expose himself to the probability of criticism from his fellows. Does this mean that he is a nonconformist? Yes, but not necessarily in the popular sense of the word. One of the interesting findings contained in recent research is that the creative individual as a rule chooses to conform in the routine, everyday matters of life, such as speech, dress and manners. One gets the impression that he is simply not prepared to waste his energy in nonconformity about trifles. He reserves his independence for what really concerns him—the area in which his creative activities occur. This distinguishes him sharply from the exhibitionists who reject convention in those matters that will gain them the most attention.
>
> **Flexibility.** Still another widely observed trait may be labeled flexibility. It is perhaps best seen in what has been called the playfulness of the man of originality. He will toy with an idea, "try it on for size," look at

it from a dozen different angles, argue to himself that it is true and then argue that it is untrue. Unlike the rest of us, he does not persist stubbornly and unproductively in one approach to a problem. He can change directions and shift strategies. He can give up his initial perception of a problem and redefine it. . . . He even manages to exercise a reasonable detachment from his own past attitudes and habits of mind, his own pet categories. (In the current fashion we talk much of the limitations on freedom that result from outside pressures and tend to forget the limitations imposed by one's own compulsions, neuroticisms, habits and fixed ideas.)

Related to this flexibility is a trait of the creative person that psychologists have called a "tolerance for ambiguity." The individual has a capacity to tolerate internal conflict, a willingness to suspend judgment. He is not uncomfortable in the presence of unanswered questions or unresolved differences. He does not find it difficult to give expression to opposite sides of his nature at the same time—conscious and unconscious mind, reason and passion, aesthetic and scientific impulses. . . . In his chosen field he does not have the brittle knowingness and sophistication of a man who thinks he knows all the answers. The advantage of this fluidity is obvious in that it permits all kinds of combinations and recombinations of experience with a minimum of rigidity.

Capacity to Find Order in Experience. The individual of high originality, having opened himself to such a rich and varied range of experience, exhibits an extraordinary capacity to find the order that underlies that varied experience, I would even say an extraordinary capacity to *impose* order on experience. . . .

This aspect of the creative process has not received the emphasis it deserves. We have made much of the fact that the innovator frees himself from the old patterns and have neglected to emphasize that he does so in order to forge new patterns. This, if you reflect on it, suggests a picture of the creative individual fundamentally different from the romanticized version. The image created by the beatniks and by most of their predecessors back to the nineteenth-century bohemians has led us to suppose that people of high originality are somehow lawless. But the truly creative man is not an outlaw but a lawmaker. Every great creative performance since the initial one has been in some measure a bringing of order out of chaos. It brings about a new relatedness, connects things that did not previously seem connected, sketches a more embracing framework, moves toward larger and more inclusive understandings. (Gardner, 1963, pp. 35–39)

Thus, in the genuinely creative personality, the energy and fluency of primary process material must be effectively integrated by strong secondary processes. The creative child in the classroom may not yet have developed the mature controls he will have as an adult, but the teacher who encourages him to develop them need not feel he is stifling the child's creativity. Similarly, the teacher who encourages well-controlled children to "let down their hair" and experience feelings and impulses more directly need not feel he is encouraging neuroticism, *provided that* the released energies are then channeled into a creative enterprise.

There is another important aspect of the creative unconscious—the phenomenon called *incubation*.

INCUBATION

Not all unconscious processes are of the free-flowing-energy variety. In some cases, according to the reports of creative people, problems are solved, confusions are straightened out, information is reorganized—all without the conscious awareness of the artist.

My father, an architect, landscape architect and civil engineer, was in the profession of creating designs that must take into account numerous topographical, esthetic, and engineering details. His procedure for developing a suitable design was as follows: First, over a period of many weeks, he would amass the information he needed from surveyor's maps, deeds, conferences with clients, and so on. When this preparation process was completed, he would work for a while with trial designs, an effort that made him discontented and tired. He would lie down on the sofa and read straight through copies of *Liberty Magazine, The Saturday Evening Post,* and *Collier's,* which at that time were all available at the newsstand for 5¢ each. By this time, he would be sleepy and would snooze for ten or twenty minutes. Coming awake suddenly and completely, he would have (he said) a complete picture of the finished design in his mind and would rush to his drawing board in order to get it down.

As a child, I was taught never to disturb this process, nor to wake my father from his naps on the couch with the magazines. My father knew little psychology, and nothing of Wallas' formulations or of the statements of other creative people. He had confidence in his system because he had discovered that it worked reliably for him.

Some other examples of incubation reports are taken from Patrick's 1937 paper. These are quotations from the artists, poets, and inventors she studied.

> (a) A poem is a spiritual irritation. It annoys me till it breaks out. . . .
> (b) I may get an idea for a poem from something that I see, which may be with me for a long time. For instance, I saw a nun leaning over a pool of flamingoes, and I got the idea of both being in captivity. I was a whole year trying to write that. I knew that it would be a sonnet or lyric, but that was all. . . .
> (c) At times ideas have bothered me for days and sometimes weeks until I set to work them out to completion, and then found that they amounted to invention. These are spontaneous ideas beyond the control of the individual. . . .
> (d) The study of a problem may take months or even years, taking it up and laying it down again a number of times—then when alone and at rest the substantial invention suddenly appears to my mind. . . .
> (e) I had worked on the problem until my mind and body were completely fatigued. I decided to abandon work and all thought relative thereto and then, on the following day, when occupied in work of an entirely different type, an idea came to my mind as suddenly as a flash of lightning and it was the solution. . . .
> (f) I almost always carry an idea round a while in my mind before I start to work. It keeps coming back several times while I am doing other things, and I can work it out later. Sometimes I lose it if I don't work on it.

In coming back it changes, and sometimes improves as it comes back. If I don't grab it I may get something different. . . .

(g) I incubate an idea for periods of two or three weeks. It may be for a month or more when I am not working on it. I think now of making a picture of Coconut Grove as it used to look, and I have been incubating that two years. Then I get to feel like I want to paint. I keep vaguely thinking of something like it to do. I am thinking now of a still life. This afternoon I may start on it. The idea recurs while I am doing other things, as I have thought of a still life for two or three weeks now. I think of the roundness of the fruit, and shapes against the glass bottle. It recurs in color, so when I am ready to paint I know what I want to do and do it very rapidly. A complicated thing becomes simple by thinking about it. I noticed a tree and did not think about it and before I knew it, I had all sorts of information for making it. . . . (Patrick, 1937, pp. 50–52)

Wallas' Stage of Incubation

Because of such reported experiences, Wallas (1926) decided there must be an incubation stage that invariably followed the preparation stage described earlier as the intensive acquisition effort. He considered incubation to have two major aspects: (1) A conscious decision on the part of the creator to stop thinking about a particular creative problem and (2) the subsequent takeover of the problem by the unconscious mind. After this incubation period, Wallas believed, came the stage of illumination—that is, the solution to the problem popped into consciousness, as it frequently did with my father.

Wallas felt it was important for conscious processes to "mix out" of the unconscious work and urged relaxation of various kinds:

Mental relaxation during the Incubation stage may of course include, and sometimes requires, a certain amount of physical exercise. . . . When I once discussed this fact with an athletic Cambridge friend, he expressed his gratitude for any evidence which would prove that it was the duty of all intellectual workers to spend their vacations in Alpine climbing. (Wallas, 1926, p. 90)

Despite the reports of creative people, the notion that unconscious mental work can go on and even improve if little attention is paid to it has been distasteful to experimental psychologists of both Wallas' time and our own. Efforts have been made to explain away the phenomenon of incubation in a variety of ways. It has been argued, for example, that nothing is really happening during those periods of inattention to the problem but rest. When the mind takes up the problem again, it can more quickly recognize the solution. Another argument has held that during the rest periods, wrong habits, now not being practiced, have weakened and dropped away. (How, one might ask, did the mind distinguish between the right habits and the wrong ones? Why did it not discard right habits as well?) Here is one version of the issue:

There is a very popular hypothesis which says that the unconscious mind is a fine source of original ideas: that one way to solve a problem is to forget it for a while, during which time the unconscious mind will work on the problem and present a solution, usually when the individual is not expecting it. In other words, the hypothesis is that while part of a man's mediation processes are busy with something else, other processes are solving the problem. . . .

What are the objective facts which this proposition about unconscious thinking is presumed to explain? Basically that a man works on a problem unsuccessfully, there is a period of rest from the work, and the problem is solved after this period of rest. Additionally, . . . the solution appears as the first trial after the rest period, in what has already been described [by this author] as the trial-and-error process of thinking. A further feature of the phenomenon, the appearance of the solution when the thinker was not working on the problem (frequently reported as coming "while I was shaving") may probably be disregarded as anecdotalism. The trouble with this "data" is, of course, that it does not include the millions of times men shave without solving problems. . . .

Not all psychologists accept the unconscious as an explanation. . . . Two more alternatives may be offered.

First, a solution on returning to a problem is, after all, one more trial in a trial-and-error process, and it must often be true that a man stops work just short of that one more trial.

Second, it has been suggested that any increase in stress interferes with problem solving. . . . If, for example, discouragement, frustration, or even intense concentration are stressful, and if these stresses disappear before the thinker returns to his problem, their absence might take away the inhibition which had previously prevented the finding of the solution.

These, then, are alternative hypotheses, more testable than those relating to the work of the unconscious mind, and experimentally minded psychologists will prefer them until there is some experimental evidence that the unconscious mind deals with problems. (Ray, 1967, pp. 45–46)

Which position on the incubation controversy do you find most plausible? Might it be possible to design experiments to distinguish between the two points of view?

THE EXPERIMENTAL STUDY OF INCUBATION

To demonstrate incubation as Wallas and the creative artists have described it, we would need to show that some kind of learning or concept formation happened during the period of inattention to the problem—learning that could not be accounted for simply in terms of recovery from fatigue or tension. Happily, some experiments of this sort have actually been done.

You will recall the Remote Associates Test (RAT) developed by Mednick and described earlier. Mednick and his colleagues have used that test as a method of studying incubation. They reasoned that the processes occurring during this stage were quite normal and could be shown to exist experimentally. For example, *unconscious use of information, attention to incidental information* (information not immediately relevant to a task at hand), *unconscious interest in novel relationships,* and *incidental concept formation* might all be said to occur during incubation. Mednick's experiments on these processes not only showed them to exist, but showed them to exist more in highly creative people (HCs) than in low creatives (LCs), as measured by his RAT tests.

Unconscious Use of Information

Mednick and his colleagues (1964) first carried out an experiment on what they called *associative priming*. The priming was accomplished by giving the subject a simple analogy question, such as:

   TV is to *channel* as *radio* is to s_____   (The answer, of course, is station.)

Since the answers were to serve as the priming stimuli, it was important for the subjects to get them right. They therefore used simple analogies cued by the first letter. The subjects were first given twenty-six remote-associate questions like the word sets illustrated above, only much harder. The subjects failed a good many of these, and the experimenter selected, for each subject, five of the failed items for priming, and five more failed items for controls (they would be repeated a second time to see if the repetition itself produced any improvement). The priming was accomplished by using the failed items as answers to the simple analogies. After this, the five primed and the five control RAT items were readministered. The important experimental question was this: How much change in RAT ability resulted from "stirring up" or "enriching" the associative process by the priming technique? The answer was *a significant amount,* despite the very small number of items involved.

Attention to Incidental Information

In a second experiment, Mendelsohn and Griswold (1964) investigated the ability of high creative (HC) and low creative (LC) subjects to absorb incidental information. Their subjects first learned a list of twenty-five words, while another list of twenty-five words played loudly on a tape recorder. Then the subjects worked on anagrams, some of which turned out to be the same as the words played on the tape recorder. Half the subjects were high creatives as measured by the RAT, and half were low. The experimental question was this: Would the HC subjects utilize the cue words on the tape-recorded list better than the LC subjects did? If so, then we could say that HC people were more open, or attentive, to general stimuli than LC people were. (There were no differences between the groups in actual memorizing ability; everyone remembered about the same number of words.)

The experimental results supported this view. The high creatives utilized the incidental anagram clues more fully than the low creatives did:

> We suggest that the results are attributable to differences in the reception and processing of stimuli by highly creative individuals relative to individuals of lower creativity. The data support the argument suggested earlier that HCs retain in usable form more of their prior stimulus experience. Two, by no means mutually exclusive, processes may underlie such a capacity. First, HCs may deploy their attention more widely and thus

receive a broader range of information with sufficient strength to influence their subsequent responses. Second, in dealing with present problems, HCs may screen out less of their "irrelevant" past experience.
(Mendelsohn and Griswold, 1964, pp. 435–436)

Unconscious Interest in Novel Relationships

In a third experiment, Houston and Mednick (1963) selected subjects from
a pool of college undergraduates who had already been administered the
RAT. Thirty HCs and thirty LCs were randomly chosen from this pool,
and were all given the following instructions:

> I am going to show you some cards, one at a time. On each card
> there are two words. I want you to look at both words and say aloud the
> one you like best. In response to each word you say aloud, I will say a
> word, or give you an association. For example, if I show you a card with
> the words "pencil" and "telephone" on it and you choose "pencil," I
> might say "paper." If you said "telephone," I might say "call." So, for
> each card you will choose one of the two words and say it out loud and I
> will give you a response word. (Houston and Mednick, 1963, p. 138)

Subjects were given to understand that this procedure had some vague relationship to something else that was going to happen next; otherwise,
they might have found the task too ridiculous to take seriously.

What was actually on the cards? On each card, one word was a noun,
and one was a nonnoun. If a subject chose a nonnoun, the experimenter
responded with some dull word—such as *black,* when the subject had
chosen the word *white.* But if the subject chose the word that was a noun
(like *father*), the experimenter responded with some interesting, incongruous associate (like *eggbeater*). Figure 26.1 shows how this treatment
differently affected the high and low creatives. The HCs quickly increased
the number of nouns they chose, and the LCs almost as quickly decreased
their choice of the same words. In later interviews, it was established that

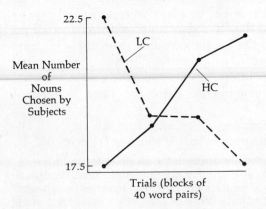

Mean Number
of
Nouns
Chosen by
Subjects

22.5

17.5

LC

HC

Trials (blocks of
40 word pairs)

Figure 26.1 Shifts in choice of words that produced novel reinforcement, by high and low
creatives, on the RAT test. (Houston and Mednick, 1963, p. 139)

none of the subjects was consciously aware of the relationship between his choice of words and the nature of the experimenter's response.

Incidental Concept Formation

In the last experiment we will discuss, subjects performed one concept formation task while their unconscious formation of another concept was actually being studied. This is how the experiment was explained to the subjects by experimenter Laughlin:

> Six words will be pronounced aloud. Four of these six words will go together in some way. These four words exemplify a concept. Listen carefully to the six words, and then figure out the concept or way in which four of the six words go together. Then write the concept word in the blank. For example, consider the six following words: "glue, paste, house, flypaper, rubber cement, gymnasium." The four words that go together in some way are "glue, paste, flypaper" and "rubber cement," because they are all "sticky." Thus, the concept is "sticky," and you should write "sticky" in the answer blank. (Laughlin, 1967, p. 116)

The alert reader will have noticed that the two discarded words, "house" and "gymnasium," also go together and exemplify a concept of their own. That was the second part of the experiment. After the subjects had gone through ten sets of the six words and selected the 10 four-word concepts, they were asked (without forewarning) to recall from memory as many of the secondary two-word concepts (and the words composing them) as they could. This was called *incidental* concept formation. Some time later, all the subjects were administered the RAT so that groups of high, medium, and low creatives could be formed.

The mean incidental concept formation score for the high creatives was 4.09; the mean for the medium creatives was 3.03; and that for the low creatives was 1.94—highly significant differences, statistically.

By this time, with so much evidence for superior learning on the part of so-called high creatives, you may be wondering whether RAT ability is not simply another name for general intelligence. Laughlin worried about this too, and he administered the Concept Mastery test to all his subjects. As one might expect, there was a relationship between IQ and RAT score, but only the latter predicted the incidental concept formation score. When subjects were divided into high and low IQ groups, their incidental concept means were 3.13 and 2.32, respectively; but when they were divided into high and low RAT groups, their incidental concept means were 4.09 and 1.94, respectively. The RAT variable apparently made a sharper difference than the IQ variable did. (IQ, however, matters, as we saw in a previous section.)

This careful series of experiments clearly shows that unconscious learning and problem-solving processes are not mystical "happenings," but straightforward cognitive abilities which can be studied experimentally. The kinds of thinking that may go on unconsciously probably do not differ (except, perhaps, in speed) from the kinds that go on consciously.

Trusting One's Unconscious Processing

One difference between a creatively productive individual and an ordinary thinker may be in the efficiency with which unconscious processing is used and trusted. It is almost as if the creative individual has "sublet" portions of his mind to different problems, all of which can be worked on unconsciously with check-ups, renovations, and collections carried out periodically by the "landlord." The analogy sounds highly unscientific—even a bit embarrassing. But as Bruner tells us, that may also be a characteristic of the relationship with his own mind evolved by a creative person:

> You begin to write a poem. Before long it, the poem, begins to develop metrical, stanzaic, symbolical requirements. You, as the writer of the poem, are serving it—it seems. Or you may be pursuing the task of building a formal model to represent the known properties of single nerve fibers and their synapses: soon the model takes over. Or we say of an experiment in midstream that *it* needs another control group really to clinch the effect. It is at this point when the object takes over. I have asked about a dozen of my most creative and productive friends whether they knew what I meant as far as their own work was concerned. All of them replied with one or another form of sheepishness, most of them commenting that one usually did not talk about this kind of personal thing. (Bruner, 1964a, p. 25)

Nevertheless, the teacher who understands something about the role of unconscious processing in creativity can help students come into a better understanding of their own abilities. Students struggling with a difficult problem can be encouraged to put their work aside for a while, to "let it stew by itself." Incubation can be explained and discussed, as can many other aspects of the creative process. Surely such instruction can be handled at least as straightforwardly as sex education—or can it be? Some people believe that efforts to quash creativity in children are fully as repressive as the Victorian attitude toward sex. In the next chapter, we will have a look at these arguments.

Chapter 27 ENVIRONMENT AND SOCIAL PRESSURES

No man, as they say, is an island; even the intensely personal process of creative production takes place within a culture and is influenced by it. An audience, as we have seen, plays an essential role in that process, for the existence of at least one other understanding person helps maintain the mental health of the artist and defines his production as a communication. Without a communicative intent, art may deteriorate into private fantasy.

But the response of the artist's culture may not be a positive one, despite his communicative intent. In this chapter, we will pay special attention to the response of a teacher to a creative child and of classmates to each other. We will critically examine some claims that creative students arouse hostility and retaliation.

In addition to responsiveness, a culture offers the creative person a special universe of elements. Gauguin, Faulkner, Joyce, Freud—all exemplify their unique social situations; indeed, every artist does. Let us begin with some implications of this fact.

CULTURAL ELEMENTS

In 1964, Iscoe and Pierce-Jones gave a Guilford-type fluency test to more than two hundred black and white children in Austin, Texas. The children were shown actual objects and asked to say all the things they could think of to do with them. Each child was tested individually. The authors described the environmental situation as follows:

> Due to the workings of geographical rather than administrative separation, the school-age children all came from segregated schools. The 5-

year-olds were obtained from nursery schools, also segregated. The public school settings for the Negro and white children were uniformly very good. The Negro 5-year-olds were obtained from a church-supervised, community-fund–supported nursery school set up to care for children of working mothers. The environment, although kind, was definitely much more crowded and less stimulating than the setting from which the white preschoolers were obtained.

All of the white children came from a lower class rather than middle class neighborhood. There was a significant difference in socio-economic level between the white and Negro children favoring the whites. In the southern part of the United States it is virtually impossible at present to equate on an income basis lower class whites with Negroes. One of the confounding factors is that a significant proportion of the Negro fathers are not steadily employed and it is the mother who usually represents the source of steady income. (Iscoe and Pierce-Jones, 1964, pp. 787–788)

(One might add that a similar difficulty exists in trying to equate lower-class whites with lower-class blacks in almost any section of the country.)

We have, then, a group of black children and a group of white children who are to be compared on a measure of divergent thinking. The two groups are similar to each other in age and sex; they differ in race, school environment, and home environment (lower income and fewer fathers who support the family in the black group). In addition, the groups differ in IQ. The experimenters administered the WISC to all children and found that the white group obtained a mean IQ of 103.37 and the black group, one of 91.6—a difference too great to be considered accidental. Will the groups also differ in creative thinking abilities as measured by Guilford-like tests? If so, what may be producing the differences? race, IQ, income, father-unemployment? Or will we be able to tell at all?

First, let us examine the fluency scores. Table 27.1 shows that the black children obtained higher fluency scores in all age groups except the oldest and the very youngest one (for which, if you recall, the nursery school setting was said to be "definitely more crowded and less stimulating" than that of the white nursery school). Table 27.1 also shows that when we put all the age groups together and look at the mean fluency scores for each item, *newspaper* and *cup* were responsible for most of the black superiority, with *table knife* next and *clock* last. In fact, the white children were slightly ahead on mean fluency of response to *clock*.

But now consider the flexibility scores. Table 27.1 shows that the superiority of the black children on fluency did not carry over to flexibility (although their scores did not fall significantly below the scores of the white children). Although black children were able to think up a great number of unusual uses for the experimental objects, these uses tended to be functionally similar—they might all refer to a "protecting" or to a "play" function, for example. The authors do not tell us exactly what these functions were, but they do say:

An examination of some of the categories used reveals rather striking differences. For the whites . . . the use of a newspaper for "personal inter-

Table 27.1
Mean Fluency and Flexibility Scores of Black and White Children, Six Age Groups

AGE GROUPS (YEARS)	FLUENCY		FLEXIBILITY	
	BLACK	WHITE	BLACK	WHITE
5	16.4	20.7	9.6	12.8
6	25.3	16.4	10.6	9.5
7	21.6	16.6	10.0	10.3
8	24.9	19.9	14.1	12.0
9	17.2	18.7	10.1	12.3
	Average black superiority in 3 age groups: 6.3		Average black superiority in 2 age groups: 1.5	
	Average white superiority in 2 age groups: 2.9		Average white superiority in 3 age groups: 1.9	
ITEMS*				
Newspaper	7.6	5.6	4.0	3.4
Cup	5.4	4.6	2.5	2.5
Table knife	5.1	4.9	3.0	3.3
Clock	3.3	3.6	1.3	2.1

SOURCE: Adapted from Iscoe and Pierce–Jones, 1964, pp. 790–791.
*Age groups combined.

est" was the most prominently chosen. For the Negroes . . . the "protective function" (such as covering floors) was the one most frequently used. Whereas the "soaking" function was employed only by 3 percent of the whites, it was employed by 24 percent of the Negroes. Similarly, using paper for polishing or cleaning was used by 7 percent of the whites and 25 percent of the Negroes. For the knife, it is interesting to note that the "aggressive weapon" category was used by 46 percent of the whites and only 35 percent of the Negroes. An alarm clock as a "waking up function" was employed by 65 percent of the whites, vs. only 32 percent of the Negroes. The clock as a "play-thing" was employed by 10 percent of the Negroes and only 2 percent of the whites. The cup as a "substitute for a pitcher" was employed by 40 percent of the Negroes and only 21 percent of the whites.

There are strong suggestions here that the originality of the uses proposed for familiar objects is related to the cultural background of the subjects. Newspaper has traditionally been the all-purpose material of the underprivileged. Thus, significantly more Negro children gave the use "put it on the bathroom floor when you take a bath" or "put fried stuff on it to take up the grease." Cultural relevancy cannot be escaped, and will have to be considered in future investigations of divergent thinking, originality and creativity. (Iscoe and Pierce-Jones, 1964, p. 795)

Of course, it does not necessarily follow that children from special subcultures will be more creative than mainstream children. The major problem is that they are not often given a chance to be creative at all—that is, they are not encouraged to utilize their special cultural information in creative ways. Kohl (1967) has shown us what can happen when they are.

Creativity in the Ghetto

Not long ago when I was teaching a class of remote, resistant children in a Harlem school, as an experiment I asked these children to write. I had no great expectations. I had been told that the children were from one to three years behind in reading, that they came from "deprived" and "disadvantaged" homes and were ignorant of the language of the schools. I had also been told that their vocabulary was limited, that they couldn't make abstractions, were not introspective, oriented to physical rather than mental activity. . . . I couldn't accept this mythology: I wanted my pupils to tell me about themselves. For reasons that were hardly literary, I set out to explore the possibilities of teaching language, literature, and writing in ways that would enable children to speak about what they felt they were not allowed to acknowledge publicly. Much to my surprise the children wrote a great deal; and they invented their own language to do so. Only a very small number of the children had what can be called "talent," and many of them had only a single story to write and rewrite; yet almost all of them responded, and seemed to become more alive through their writing.

. . .

I have subsequently discovered other teachers who have explored language and literature with their pupils in this way, with results no less dramatic. The children we have taught ranged from the pre-school years to high school, from lower-class ghetto children to upper-class suburban ones. There are few teaching techniques that we share in common and no philosophy of education that binds us. Some of these teachers have tight, carefully controlled classrooms; others care less for order and more for invention. There are Deweyites, traditionalists, classicists—a large range of educational philosophies and teaching styles. If there is anything common to our work it is the concern to listen to what the children have to say and the ability to respond to it as honestly as possible, no matter how painful it may be to our teacherly prides and preconceptions. We have allowed ourselves to learn from our pupils and to expect the unexpected. . . .

. . .

I discovered that everything I'd been told about the children's language was irrelevant. Yes, they were hip when they spoke, inarticulate and concrete. But their writing was something else, when they felt that no white man was judging their words, threatening their confidence and pride. They faced a blank page and wrote directly and honestly. . . .

. . .

Nothing the school offered was relevant, so I read the class novels, stories, poems, brought my library to class and let them know that many people have suffered throughout history and that some were articulate enough to create literature from their lives. They didn't believe me, but they were hungry to know what had been written about and what could be written about. . . .

. . .

They explored their thoughts and played with the many different forms of written expression. I freed the children of the burden of spelling and grammar while they were writing. If a child asked me to comment on the substance of his work I did not talk of sentence structure. There is no more deadly thing a teacher can do than ignore what a child is trying to express in his writing and comment merely upon the form, neatness, and heading. Yet there is nothing safer if the teacher is afraid to become involved. It is not that I never taught grammar or spelling; it is rather that the teaching of grammar and spelling is not the same as the teaching of writing. Once children care about writing and see it as important to themselves they want to write well. At that moment, I found, they easily accept the discipline of learning to write correctly. Vocabulary, spelling, and grammar become the means to achieving more precise and sophisticated forms of expression and not merely empty ends in themselves.

Here are two of Kohl's illustrations:

I am dreaming and crying in my sleep

I am dreaming because I have nothing better to do and crying because I am dreaming about a problem I had in school, you see I promise myself I'll be good and try to learn more, but everytime I come into the classroom (in my dream) my teacher right then and there starts to pick on me Louis this or Louis that. So I say to myself "Enough is too much, everyday the same old problem" why that's enough even to make a laughing hyena cry (wouldn't you if you were in my situation?)

Just as I was about to cry in my sleep for the second time unexpectedly a hand hit me right on my rear end (I knew it was a hand because I had felt this more than once) Of course I woke up. . . .

. . .

The first think I do in the Bathe room is to wash my face and comb my hair while my mother is ironing my shirt and pants. Oh by the way my mother's name is Mrs. Helen Frost (you can call her *ma* or Mrs. Helen cause that what I always call her and she doesn't get mad either). The next thing I do is eat my breakfast which consists of two or three jelly sandwiches and a glass of water or if I'm lucky I'll have a bowl of cereal with *can milk*. At this time it should be 8:30 time to go to school. P.S. 79 here I come I say as I start out of the door to my building. As I walk to the school . . . I begin to think of things that could but then again couldn't happen. For example: Maybe someday I'll be a scientist or a big business man or maybe even an engineer or then again the President of the United States or maybe even the mayor. . . . (Louis, age 11)

THE JUNKIES

When they are
in the street
they pass it
along to each
other but when
they see the
police they would
run some would
just stand still
and be beat
so pity ful
that they want
to cry. (Mary, age 11)
(Kohl, 1967, pp. 12–21)

If we compare Louis' story to that told by our schizophrenic 16-year-old, the difference in their integrative or ordering abilities is quite apparent. Louis' ordering principle was quite simple—a chronology from sleeping to waking to school. But the patient had no rule that we can recognize and could not have followed a chronological rule, even if we had asked him to. Similarly, although the images of both Louis' essay and

Mary's poem might not be available to a middle-class child, it is not merely the images that move us; it is their use, form, and organization that signify creativity in these tragic children.

It is not clear in Louis' case at least, and possibly not even in Mary's, that creativity would be correlated with a high score on a standard IQ test. Kohl reports that Louis was urged by guidance counselors to take vocational training rather than academic preparation in high school (he refused), so we might surmise that his school achievements were not outstanding by guidance standards.

The salvation of such children (if it is to happen) may be through creative endeavors rather than standard academic programs. The teacher who is willing (and able) to help students learn to find formal beauty in their special universe may be providing the only true intellectual guidance they will get.

Some teachers (and some administrators), however, would sharply disagree.

CULTURAL DISCORDS

Throughout most of his historic course *Homo sapiens* has wanted from his children acquiescence, not originality. It is natural that this should be so, for where every man is unique there is no society, and where there is no society there can be no man. Contemporary American educators think they want creative children, yet it is an open question as to what they expect these children to create. And certainly the classrooms — from kindergarten to graduate school — in which they expect it to happen are not crucibles of creative activity and thought. . . . From the endless, pathetic, "creative hours" of kindergarten to the most abstruse problems in sociology or anthropology, the function of education is to prevent the truly creative intellect from getting out of hand.

. . .

Creative intellect is mysterious, devious, and irritating. . . . Creativity is the last thing wanted in any culture because of its potentialities for disruptive thinking. (Henry, 1963, pp. 286–288)

Torrance takes a similar view:

From our data it can be inferred that all of the cultures . . . unduly punish the good guesser, the child who has intellectual courage, the emotionally sensitive individual, the intuitive thinker, the person who . . . is playful and childlike, the visionary individual, and the person who . . . is unwilling to accept things on mere say-so without examining the evidence. On the other hand, they seem to lavish unduly great reward for being courteous, doing one's work on time, being obedient and popular or well liked by one's peers, and being willing to accept the judgments of authorities. Teachers in the United States also appear to unduly discourage strong emotional feelings and unduly encourage receptiveness to the ideas of others. (Torrance, 1966, p. 163)

Unfortunately, it is not clear from the writings of many who are most passionately in favor of creativity in the schools just why it is not there. We all know unkind, rigid teachers who do in fact discourage creativity in classrooms. But such teachers also discourage learning, intellectual development, social maturity, independence, humanitarian impulses, respect for most human beings, and just about every other kind of worthwhile behavior. Why accuse them only of being anticreative?

Torrance feels strongly that creativity is being penalized in schools, and he has carried out a number of experiments which he believes prove his point. In doing so, he has actually raised another kind of validity problem—the problem of careless experimentation. We will illustrate this by considering one of his experiments in detail.

Troubling Experiments

Torrance's subjects were 125 elementary school pupils, 25 each from grades 2 through 6. The groups were formed in the following way: All the children had at some previous time been administered Guilford-like tests of creativity developed by Torrance. The children were ranked (compared to each other) on these tests, and each child was given an arm band in a color denoting his rank. (The children did not know what these arm bands signified.) White denoted the highest-scoring rank of 1; gold signified the rank of 2; red was 3; green was 4; and blue was 5. Experimental groups were then composed of one child from each of these levels (five-person groups).

Each group was given a box of science toys and toy parts, including such objects as sparklers, puzzles, and parts of a broken flying saucer. The group was given 25 minutes in which to explore and experiment, the objectives of which were to discover what could be done with the toys and why they function in special ways. In addition, each group was to plan and carry out a 25-minute demonstration (5 minutes was allowed for planning). After these steps were completed, each child in the group was asked to rate every other child in his group on the value of his contributions—that is, each child ranked four pieces of colored paper corresponding to the arm bands from most to least. (If he thought red contributed the most, for example, he put the red piece of paper at the top.)

The arm bands, of course, made it possible for the observers to keep track of who was doing what and when. Torrance describes the procedure only briefly and in very general terms:

> The experimenters tabulated the number of ideas initiated by each subject during the exploratory phase, and recorded all ideas demonstrated and explained during the demonstration period. Experimenters also described how the group organized itself and got underway with the task, what kind of roles developed for White (most creative), how the group went about planning the demonstration, what role or roles White played in planning, what role White was assigned in the demonstration, and other behaviors of the group—particularly actions directed toward White. (Torrance, 1963, p. 121)

The results of the experiment were also reported only in very general terms, and not all of them were statistically analyzed—in fact, it is not obvious exactly what was counted (movements? statements? when did one statement end and another begin?) or how a statistical analysis could have proceeded.

There are rules in statistical analysis that would make it improper mathematically to count many different responses from a single individual in the same way we count a single response from many different individuals. In the last case, the responses may be independent of each other statistically; in the former case, they may not be, and therefore they cannot be analyzed by an "independence-assumption" procedure. This point illustrates just one of the difficulties in understanding how reliable Torrance's results actually were. That is, if we were to repeat the experiment, would we get the same results?

Of the groups, seventeen of the Whites initiated what Torrance described as the "largest number of ideas in their respective groups during the exploratory phase." Since we do not know what "largest" actually meant, we cannot be sure if we would agree with Torrance's statement that "This provides a rough validation of the measure of creativity" obtained from the Guilford-type tests. If the tests did, in fact, predict more than 10 to 12 percent of the variability in the children's group creativity, then this would be important news—and surely we should be given the exact figures. How much difference (in group creativity) was there between White, Gold, Red, Green and Blue? Did the number of ideas (in the group) progress steadily downward by color rank? Torrance does not say. His main interest was in the behavior of the various groups, but because the descriptions are literary in form, it is difficult to abstract a consistent picture of either groups or individuals. For example:

> Each member of the third group [in second grade] grabbed a toy and as soon as it was dropped someone else picked it up. There was considerable bickering throughout the procedure and eventually each had a pile of toys in front of him. White and Green squabbled over the possession of toys. Very few ideas were initiated as most of the energy was expended in bickering. White engaged almost entirely in individual activity, making comments now and then. These comments made no impact whatsoever upon the group. The only organized action was the determination of sequence in the demonstration. No identification with the group, nor any cooperative behavior among members, was evident. There was almost no agreement about who made the most valuable contribution to the group's success. . . . Rankings were as follows: Red, Green, Gold, Blue and White. (Torrance, 1963, pp. 123–124)

On the basis of such descriptive material, Torrance concludes, "The uniformly unpleasant behavior of the most creative members suggests the need for teachers and parents to help highly creative children develop less obnoxious techniques for presenting their ideas and getting them accepted during the earliest school years. At this level, the most creative members are themselves responsible for much of their difficulty" (pp. 133–134). However, with reference to an older White (in a fifth-grade group) who apparently displayed considerable diplomacy, Torrance also says: "That creative people should be required to expend so much energy in 'being nice' in order to obtain a hearing for their ideas is regrettable." (The particular behavior was not included in the description of the group, so we cannot be sure what "being nice" actually meant in this case.)

Similarly, Torrance interpreted evidence of a group's acceptance of White as a leading contributor or chairman as a way of subverting White's creativeness by loading him down with paper or administrative work. "A group frequently exalts its most creative member by placing him in an administrative or power position. . . . Weighted down, they are unable to engage in the manipulation of materials and ideas that results in creative productivity" (Torrance, 1963, p. 134).

So in Torrance's view, creative people are "damned if they do and damned if they don't," but in point of fact the study produced no evidence that highly creative children were ignored, opposed, or ridiculed any more or less than other children in the experiment. The tabulation in Table 27.2 of each group's overall ranking of its White was compiled from the material in Torrance's article. It tells us that although there was a slight increase in "appreciation" (high ranking) for White as one goes from second to sixth grade, the overall difference (13 cases of relatively high and 12 of relatively low appreciation) was trivial. And even this trivial difference does not support Torrance's conviction that a creative child's peers will be hostile and rejecting of his contributions to the group project.

Although we may sympathize with the need to persuade some teachers and some school administrators to nurture creativity in their classrooms, we must not lose sight of the distinction between a sense of urgency and scientific facts. In the rush to discover and save creative children, we may be ignoring grave problems of validating their very existence. For example, it may be that some of these children are obnoxious at the age of 7, but so are a great many uncreative children. It may be that some creative children will be destructively inhibited by classroom disci-

Table 27.2
Number of Groups Ranking Most Creative Member as Relatively High
or Relatively Low in Value of Contribution to Group Project

GRADES	RELATIVELY HIGH (1ST OR 2ND)	RELATIVELY LOW (3RD, 4TH, OR 5TH)
Second	2	3
Third	2	3
Fourth	3	2
Fifth	3	2
Sixth	3	2
Total number of groups	13	12

SOURCE: Based on data in Torrance, 1963.

pline, but some may also benefit from it—and some children of both sorts may be disturbed by classroom permissiveness. It may be that some creative people have been persecuted, but so have a great many people who are not creative. And a large number of creative people have been greatly honored by their societies.

Psychological test specialists use the terms *false positives* and *false negatives* to describe prediction errors of the sort illustrated below:

| | | Creative? | |
		Yes	No
Persecuted by Society?	Yes	Predicted	False Negatives
	No	False Positives	Predicted

Whenever there are a large number of false positives or false negatives, we say that a strong correlation between the major variables (persecution and creativity, in the above examples) does not exist. The problem of validity in creativity research is of exactly this sort. Too many high creatives on one test turn out to be low on other measures of creativity (false positives); and too many low creatives (on the test) turn out to be highly creative on other measures (false negatives). Many of the relationships we believe to accompany creativity may not be supported by careful research. If we are to properly identify creative children, we must not let ourselves be blinded by favorable or unfavorable stereotypes about them.

Creativity in Adolescent Scientists

In a study of scientifically creative adolescents, a group of experimenters (Parloff, Datta, Kleman, and Handlon, 1968) were surprised to discover less evidence of social disruptiveness or nonconformity among the adolescents than among creative adults. The experimenters decided that adults who have achieved a measure of professional success can afford to become less conventional socially—but they warn us not to assume that unconventionality *produces* creativeness:

> Creative performance among the adolescents appears to be facilitated rather than inhibited by a measure of social skills and self-control. This finding is consistent with the view that the adolescent, unlike the adult, is faced with the practical necessity of coping with the world in which his success is, in fact, dependent upon his ability to maintain a reasonable degree of cooperation with those who control the resources he needs to achieve his goals. Society is understandably more tolerant of the demands, eccentricities, and flouting of convention of adults who have demonstrated their creativity than it is of similar behavior from the brash, unrecognized adolescent. The adolescent who is unwilling to make appropriate allowances for this reality may perforce have to devote much of his effort to struggle and rebellion, with a resultant loss of energy which

might otherwise have been available for creative productivity. An additional consideration is the possibility that the performance of the potentially creative adolescent may be facilitated rather than hindered by a self-discipline that permits him to learn principles, heuristics, and basic information, which he may then proceed to reintegrate and reorganize in a constructively creative fashion. It is important to recognize that although the more creative adolescent is sensitive to the feelings of others and aware of environmental constraints, he does not let such considerations limit his pursuit of an important goal; instead he may use such knowledge to work more effectively in achieving his ends. (Parloff, Datta, Kleman, and Handlon, 1968, p. 548)

A Concluding Note

Some specialists in the pedagogy of creativity do not believe that the major forces opposed to creativity in the classroom are evil teachers or heartless classmates; rather, they believe the problem to be one of ignorance of the nature of the phenomenon itself:

Perhaps the most commonly held belief concerning creative functioning is that the child will become creative of his own accord . . . if only he can be placed in a stimulating yet permissive and nurturing environment. The erroneousness of this view is due . . . to an oversimplification of . . . the conditions necessary for creative output. . . . In order to take full advantage of an unrestricting atmosphere, the child must first come to understand what constitutes creative ideas in the given situation and how he can achieve such ideas for himself. In short, he must learn *how* to think creatively. (Covington, 1967)

We have seen what a large order that is. But surely it is the most exciting educational challenge of our time.

SUMMARY

Our description of the creative process has focused on four central themes:

The Universe of Elements, or Building Blocks, Used by Individual Creators This universe is generated through mastery of a domain of information (described by Ghiselin as "the intensive acquisition effort"), through natural fluencies, and through intelligence. The psychologist most frequently associated with the notion of ideational fluency is Guilford, who has developed a number of fluency tests. He believes these tests sample a person's basic creative potential, but other research has indicated that scores on Guilford's tests do not clearly predict real-life creative behavior.

The Ordering, or Harmonizing, of the Elements Once the universe is generated, the problem of finding the connections begins. Most creators are driven by a strong intuition that such orderly harmonizing will be possible, but it may be years before they discover how to do it. Much self-testing is necessary, and this may be highly individualized: Achieving something that is "right" creatively is not the same thing as achieving something that is "right" academically. Sometimes the tests are really a series of restatements of the original problems; the creator sets up the problem this way and that until he finally develops a new way of looking at it. Creative styles may be considered personal solution templates for the kinds of problems a creator has defined. He may then use this template as a system for solving his problems. His final solution—if it is to be called creative—must have an element of what Bruner calls "effective surprise."

The effectiveness may arise from the great generality of the solution, from its metaphoric power, or from its formal power in describing a harmonious system.

The Role of the Unconscious Much of the "raw" energy of creativity comes from what Freud calls "primary process" material, but in the creator, unlike the psychotic, the material is shaped and integrated by "secondary processes" (ego controls and the like). This cortical control may have a great deal to do with the creator's need to communicate to a real or imagined audience; where communicative intent does not exist, psychosis may flourish. The creative person may be characterized by traits of openness, independence, flexibility, and so forth, but not to the exclusion of orderliness and self-control. He may also be characterized by his ability to develop a good "working relationship" with his own unconscious processes. The phenomenon of incubation, for example, may be deliberately cultivated by a creator; it may be his way of letting part of his mind work on one aspect of a problem, while another part is working on another aspect. Although some experimental psychologists have doubted that such "working arrangements" are possible, Mednick has experimentally verified the existence of such processes as unconscious attention to information and unconscious interest in novel relationships. His results suggest that incubation is indeed real, as highly skilled creators have insisted.

Environment and Social Pressures Once the creative process is clarified, the role of external cultural forces can be better understood. They may be both positive and negative. Cultural forces that increase a unique "universe of elements" may promote creativity; those that decrease intelligence may inhibit creativity. A disadvantaged environment may work in opposing ways on creatively inclined individuals. Although "folk psychology" has held that creative people are persecuted by their society, no good evidence in support of the argument appears to exist. We must be especially careful not to confuse uninhibited, careless, playful, childlike behavior with true creativity. Nor must we confuse orderly teachers with oppressive ones. An understanding of the creative process may lead to many important classroom innovations, but it can never lead to laissez-faire classrooms, for the creative process is not a laissez-faire operation. It is probably the most intensive classroom work of all.

In general, we must beware of confusing true creative behavior with sentimentalized notions of random self-expression. Even the most cursory glimpse of a truly creative production reveals the tremendous amount of mastery and planning that has gone into it. If we mislead children into believing that creativity "just happens," we will be dooming them to confusion and dissatisfaction over the failure of something magical to occur. Once we remove the magic from human creativity, its genuine glory can stand revealed.

Epilogue: THE DESIGN OF A FREE LEARNING ENVIRONMENT

This final section of the text will be more personal. There are two reasons for this: First of all, many people ask me, "How would *you* apply all those fancy psychological principles to the design of an educational system?" That is obviously a fair question, and it deserves a full answer. Second, one of my principles is that of individual creativity on the part of everyone involved in school programs. It would be contrary to that principle for me to present my educational design as if it were (a) the only correct one and/or (b) permanent. My only option is to present it to you informally as a process, not as a fixed product. I will, in other words, try to explain the thinking that has led me to make certain decisions and recommendations, as well as the recommendations themselves.

One more preliminary request: please read the rest of this book before you read this section. Many of my decisions are based on a wider framework of knowledge that will not be restated in this epilogue. For example, you will not understand certain decisions about the first-grade reading program unless you have read the material in preceding chapters. Nor will the dynamic program design model make sense to you unless you have read Part II. The purpose of this concluding section is to show you how the effort of such reading pays off in a practical sense.

What Is a Free Learning Environment?

As Silberman (1970) has documented, informal or "open" school programs are spreading in both England and America. The term *free learning environment* is simply a description of a new educational format that provides both freedom (from the child's point of view) and a learning environment (from the teacher's point of view).

The Pittsburgh Free Learning Environment Program

Our plan has been to set up a model program in a compass school, and then use that as the training and dissemination center for respective satellite schools. In each model school there is a nonteaching team leader, plus one teacher and one aide for every group of twenty-five children. (There are additional aides in the preschools, as required by federal guidelines.) A school board coordinator handles all problems of an administrative and public relations nature, and the university designer concentrates on the theoretical structure of the program. There is some overlap of functions, as there should be, but in general we have been able to cover a wide range of problems efficiently by separating areas of concentration in this manner.

The general development and dissemination plan has also been effective, primarily because it has been kept small enough for constant monitoring and experimentation. The basic theoretical model of sampling from a universe of educational possibilities, formulating some hypotheses and concepts, testing them, and then revising them on the basis of feedback applies to program development as well as to children's learning. We did not, in other words, generate an elaborate paper theory. We began with simple ideas and built the program organically on the basis of experience with those ideas.

The preschool (day care) and kindergarten levels of the program are now (1971–1972) ready for dissemination to satellite schools. The first- and second-grade levels, which have been developed in only one of the compass schools, are now ready for dissemination to the other four compass schools and will spread next year to the satellite schools. Third- and fourth- and fifth-grade level program development will be begun next year in a compass school and will be disseminated in the same pattern. Here in Pittsburgh we are working toward a 5-3-4 plan: 5 years of primary school, 3 years of middle school, and 4 years of high school. The extension of the free learning environment program to middle and high school is planned, but will not begin until the elementary phase is running smoothly. At present, the program is receiving Title I support.

In general, community and administrative support has been exceptionally harmonious. This is partly due to the school board coordinator's public relations skills, and partly to the fact that we are not trying to sell a program in advance of our own understanding of its virtues and defects. Further, we take seriously the concern that is frequently voiced by American educational administrators: "How can we be sure that an open school program will result in as much learning as a traditional program?" We are not educational romanticists. We do not delude ourselves that young children can reinvent and rediscover a culture as complex as ours. We are taking the responsibility for designing an environment and a teaching program that will result in more and better learning than a traditional program. Once such a program has been demonstrated and a realistic set of implementation procedures compiled, convincing administrators to adopt them is not a serious problem. Everybody wants good education to happen.

Before describing the details of our current free learning environment program, let me emphasize one point: Although I am accepting final responsibility for these ideas, I do not mean to imply that I invented them. On the contrary, I have learned as much from teachers and other public school personnel as they have learned from me.

The Preschool Level

At present, publicly supported preschool means day care or Head Start in most communities. Little public money is available for the preschooling of affluent children. However, public preschool for all is clearly on the way, and the following program is sufficiently general to be suitable for all classes of children.

From the developmental and motivational standpoint, preschool involves three major objectives for the children: (1) Learning what a non-family social learning situation is and how to cope with it, (2) beginning to differentiate one's own learning skills and interests, (3) beginning to coordinate those skills and interests in integrated learning activities.

The general physical design of the preschool can follow natural lines:

Block area
Housekeeping area
Water and sand area
Art area
Language stimulation area
Small motor area (for manipulative activities; this may be subdivided into a Montessori and non-Montessori area)
Large motor area (for tricycles, etc.)
Group lesson area (primarily for Peabody lessons)

The block and housekeeping areas are extremely important to symbolic development, since they provide opportunities for deferred imitation and symbolic actions of many kinds. Blocks, water, sand, and art are also important foundations for mathematical thinking.

The language stimulation area is a sort of library–talk corner, which may also include natural science materials and other conversation pieces. The paper by Blank and Solomon (1968) is required reading for our preschool teachers, and efforts are made to encourage children's language development in all possible ways.

The small motor area includes puzzles, beads, pegboards, and so forth. Many fine materials are now commercially available, and there is no point in listing a basic set. We bought everything we could, but avoided poor designs—materials that are too complicated for little fingers, too full of distracting, useless patterns, and/or too simple. Aside from those basic criteria, we found that the best way to choose materials was to watch what preschool children like to do. Fortunately, we had some funds for buying trial materials. If they were successful, duplicates were purchased for the other preschool classrooms.

The basic Montessori principles of care and organization in the handling of materials were extended to the use of all small motor equipment. Children learned from the beginning that all materials must be handled respectfully and replaced on a shelf or table after use. As Montessori well knew, and as much theory in Part I would support, the child who is disorganized in his activities is disorganized in his head. Organizing his actions also organizes his conceptual system. I worry whenever I walk into a messy preschool, even though I recognize that loving caretakers often believe a disorganized child is a happy child.

Teaching a child to be organized is not a mean thing to do, although it can of course be done meanly. When it is done lovingly and with praise, such activities as putting blocks away by size in a special location can be a matter of great pride and personal accomplishment to a young child. Permitting him to dump blocks noisily and messily is denying him that personal accomplishment. It is also misleading him into believing that noise and mess are socially acceptable in a school setting. That belief can get him into chronic trouble in elementary school.

Because it has a beneficial effect on general thinking about materials and children's learning, we recommend some Montessori training for preschool teams. We are not especially cultish in our Montessori outlook, however. We use the excellent manual *Montessori Matters,* published by the Sisters of Notre Dame de Namur, 701 East Columbia Avenue, Cincinnati, Ohio 45215. Some workshop demonstrations by Montessori-trained teachers were held. Materials can now be ordered from several American companies, and more cheaply from abroad. We like all our preschool children to go through the early self-care and home-care exercises (which require no commercial equipment), as well as the perceptual-motor exercises (Pink Tower, Broad Stair, and Cylinders). These exercises should be carried out exactly as described in the manual, so it can be useful to have a special Montessori area well separated from the housekeeping and small motor areas, which are freer.

Large muscle practice is of course important at the preschool level, and it should be available inside as well as outside. All kinds of jumping, hopping, skipping, and so on are scheduled and taught. As often as possible, eurhythmics are taught. Language training can often accompany large muscle training (inside the box . . . over the slide . . .). Music comes in here as well.

In general, all these activities, when separated into different areas of the room, will help young children begin to differentiate their own interests and skills. The concrete differentiation of separated room areas is very important from this standpoint. The young child learns that certain kinds of activities go on in certain places, and this helps him differentiate these activities from a general muddle of new social and academic experiences.

Some early integrative experiences are also necessary, however, and for this we have turned to the kit developed at the George Peabody College, in Nashville and available from American Guidance Service, Inc., Publishers' Building, Circle Pines, Minnesota 55014. Ask for *Level P Peabody Kit.* This substantial kit (two suitcases) includes everything guaranteed to delight preschoolers and to satisfy preschool teachers. All kinds of concepts are taught, and the charming lessons, of just the right length, are written out for teachers. In our preschools, one or two of these lessons are taught daily. There are some story and music experiences for the whole group, but otherwise children play and work individually, with teachers and aides functioning as assistants.

A word now about some of the more controversial preschool programs: We did not select them, but that does not mean we would give them a totally negative vote. If it is done properly, I see nothing wrong with the Bereiter-Engelmann type of pedagogy. I have not recommended it here, however, for two reasons: (1) It is a tiring program for teachers and for the children, and it is not clear (to me, at least) that the results are worth the effort. In general, I think that kind of effort can be put off until first grade (about age 6). By that time, of course, children *must* learn the basics of reading and arithmetic, forcefully if necessary. Given a limited set of resources, I would save them for first grade and make the big push then, if a push is necessary. (2) The Bereiter-Engelmann program arouses too much anxiety in many early childhood educators. It is not worth the public relations problems, in my judgment. There can be difficulties even persuading early childhood teachers to accept Montessori and Peabody, much less the more structured Bereiter-Engelmann or Gagné-type hierarchical drill programs. Let me say again that I would not agree with some early childhood teachers that these programs are intrinsically harmful. But I cannot see that they are enough better than the type of free learning preschool program we have outlined to be worth the struggle to install them. (And a final note: I think *Sesame Street* is wonderful!)

The Kindergarten Level

When a child has become sufficiently intrigued with concrete systems and symbols, he is ready to move into the kindergarten phase of our program. This normally happens around the age of 5, but some 4- and 6-year-olds are more suited for this program than for preschool or first grade.

Generally, kindergarten provides a sharper differentiation of cognitive skills and interests. The free learning kindergarten is divided into six areas: language arts, creative arts, social studies, mathematics, science, and perceptual-motor. There is no gross motor area because there is generally no room for one; but it would be a desirable area to have inside.

Most of our kindergarten children do their hopping, skipping, and jumping outside or in a gym.

Although much of the children's time is still spent in individual activities, group lessons are begun. The class is divided into three or four small groups. Once a week, each group has a lesson in three of the areas; the following week, they have lessons in the other three areas. The rest of the time, the children roam freely through the learning centers. That seems to be the most workable schedule for this particular program. The teacher must be sure to allow ample time for circulating through the areas and helping individual students. If too much of her time is tied up in small-group teaching, she will be exhausted and the children will be neglected.

Free learning activities, interspersed with small-group lessons, last for the first two hours of the kindergarten half-day. Then a half-hour large-group lesson period is scheduled. This includes discussion of materials and activities, singing, story, and a *Peabody Level 1* (also available from American Guidance Service) lesson. Following this period, the children go outside or to a gym for a half-hour large-muscle training period. That completes the kindergarten half-day.

More specifically, the language arts curriculum moves through a readiness program to preliminary instruction in reading. The readiness program includes stories, rhyming activities, language-experience charts, and sight-sound training. Reading instruction is of the simple, Montessori-type word-construction variety. Many games have been invented for this purpose. The following three books convey both the spirit and many of the techniques found in our readiness program: Brogan and Fox, *Helping Children Read,* published by Holt, Rinehart & Winston (1964); Henderson, *Reading Can Be Fun,* from the Exposition Press (1956); and of course Lee and Allen's *Learning to Read Through Experience,* from Appleton-Century-Crofts (1963).

The creative arts program is primarily media-oriented. The children are offered a wide variety of experiences (string-painting, crayon etchings, decorating gourds and trees, building from wood chips), but there is little emphasis on art concepts (that begins in first grade.) A similar curriculum could be generated by following the excellent suggestions found in the Whitman Creative Art Books, available from Western Publishing Company, Inc., Education Division, School and Library Department, 150 Parish Drive, Wayne, New Jersey 07470. (Both paperback and hardbound copies are available. The cheaper paperbacks will do quite well.)

The social studies curriculum is built around housekeeping materials and activities. We move in the traditional direction, from family to school and community. So far, there do not seem to be any adequate commercial curricula for this area in kindergarten (or even in first grade, for that matter). We have resorted to making pipe-cleaner families, magazine cut-out families, and are placing as much emphasis as possible on cooking, household activities, kinship and friendship patterns. These lead to good discussions of tools and roles. The overall aim is preparation for *Man: A Course of Study,* or some similar anthropological-sociological course developed for elementary school children, as well as for serious consideration of values and economics. I think we must be concerned with the problem of teaching inner-city children about nutrition, hygiene, and shopping strategies at the earliest possible time. Similarly, we must teach comparative American cultures, including black and Indian and Appalachian. The kindergarten curriculum provides groundwork (introductory concepts) for these objectives.

The mathematics curriculum emphasizes counting and set development. We like very much the Unifix materials and program, which are available through several commercial outlets. (For my own purposes, I order through Philip & Tacey, Ltd., 69–79 Fulham High Street, London, S.W. 6, because their catalog seems to me to have the most comprehensive, straightforward coverage of all kinds of educational materials.) We put blocks in the mathematics area, and teachers (or aides) often draw pictures of structures and post them. This is, of course, good basic training for geometry. Many other "manipulables" can be placed in this area for counting practice. We have classified other types of math readiness activities under perceptual-motor.

The science curriculum on the kindergarten level concentrates on construction materials (Lego, Tinker Toys, and Nut-Bolt materials), magnets, electricity, and whatever natural science is seasonable. The Harcourt, Brace & World *Concepts in Science Classroom Laboratory* and the Creative Playthings kits, such as the *Electrical Invention Kit,* are convenient, but an enterprising teacher can duplicate most of these materials at local lumber and hardware stores much more cheaply. If possible, we would have volunteer fathers help stock the science center and spend some time in it with the children. The problem with the Harcourt Brace materials is that children cannot get much out of them by themselves, although they love the laboratory demonstrations. With the help of a father, one can also provide dowels, planks, loose wheels, and so on for homemade wagons and other enterprises. This all provides excellent grounding for physical science concepts in the later grades.

The perceptual-motor area is a preoperational area containing materials that later "disappear" into mathematics, art, and science. This is where the children concentrate on the abstractions of color, shape, and various other kinds of perceptual-motor training. We have found The New York Times' company, *Teaching Resources,* 100 Boylston Street, Boston, Massachusetts 02116, a helpful commercial source. They have many kinds of materials in kit form, complete with detailed lesson plans. We like their Dubnoff materials for prewriting training and the Ruth Cheves kit for color and shape training. In this area, also, go the small-motor manipulative materials—puzzles, lottos, and the like. (Lotto, depending on the content, may also appear in language arts and social studies.) In addition, we have prepared a series of lessons on the balance beam and other kinds of physical coordination activities, which we classify as perceptual-motor.

As you can see, the free learning kindergarten is rich in materials and exploratory opportunities. We have no special theory about sequences in this respect. Some activities just naturally come before others (you have to learn to count before you can learn to add), but sequencing generally can be a matter of esthetics or teacher preference. The important point is for the children to be *busy* doing something *constructive.* If they are sitting around doing nothing, the kindergarten is not a learning environment, no matter how much work the teacher may be doing (lecturing or demonstrating). If the children are busy, but with haphazard free-play types of activities they could just as easily do at home, the kindergarten is also not a learning environment.

The free learning kindergarten program must be planned, however, preferably by the teachers themselves (or their supervisors), in some kind of advance workshop. Most teachers will not have time to run the program and invent it at the same time. The general procedure for planning is simple: (1) Divide the kindergarten room into six areas; (2) sort all available materials, and as many more as one can beg, borrow, steal, or buy, into the six areas (do not, of course, display them all at once); (3) bring children in; watch how they play with the materials and see what is necessary to guide them into more constructive play—what lessons need to be taught, what preparatory activities are needed, and so forth; (4) generate a sequence of activities for each center; (5) generate a set of lesson guides and independent study guides for the units in the sequence.

Figure E.1 contains examples of the format we have followed in writing our curriculum. Two forms (*a* and *b*) are for the small-group lessons, and one is for independent study activities (*c*). (The teacher, in that case, is referred to as a tutor; parents or college student volunteers can also be tutors.) The units in our sequence are referred to as Themes. There may be several lessons and a number of related independent study activities associated with a theme. We have thematic sets of lesson guides and independent study guides that the teacher can use in any sequence she wishes, as often as she wishes. Teachers' notes are written on the pages; space was left for that purpose.

You can see that the lessons may be more detailed than experienced teachers will need; but of course many teachers will not be experienced. Even if they are, they may need clear guidance in getting the program started. Students, student teachers, and volunteers can often follow lesson guides of this sort with no special supervision from the teacher.

In general, open school planning of any sort must be done carefully and in detail. We could not rely upon something magical to start the children learning. They just may not learn if the environment is not prepared with extreme care—or at least they may not learn anything they could not have learned at home with their grandmothers.

The Grade 1 Level

(Be warned: I will not be going beyond Grade 1 at this writing.) In many respects, grade 1 can be a continuation of the kindergarten program, particularly if many children have skipped kindergarten. That is, Grade 1 can be divided into six learning centers and stocked very much as one would

MATHEMATICS   Grade   K

COUNTING

Small Group Lesson 2

	Gp. 1	Gp. 2	Gp. 3	Gp. 4	Gp. 5	Makeups
Date						
Time						

Materials: Seals (flowers, birds, etc.) pasted on small pieces of oaktag
Small boxes of assorted toys and notions (as many as possible)
5 x 7 pieces of oaktag (or file cards) with dots going from 1 to 10 (use counter as template, and fill in with felt pen), e.g.,

Counters (several of each)
Unifix cubes
Pieces of yarn, different colors and lengths

What the Teacher Does	How the Children May Respond
Place materials on table before group. Explain, THESE TOYS ARE FOR YOU TO PRACTICE COUNTING. The following examples are suggestions of ways the teacher may proceed: CAN YOU COUNT THESE RED THINGS? (Place only a few—say, 3—red toys in front of child, unless you are sure he already knows how to count.) CAN YOU PUT ONE COUNTER ON THE ONE-DOT CARD? TWO COUNTERS ON THE TWO-DOT CARD? CAN YOU FIND ONE RED DOT (on the oaktag cards)? PUT ONE TOY ON THE ONE DOT. CAN YOU FIND THE CARD WITH TWO DOTS ON IT?	*One lesson takes a good deal of time — children like this and I don't want to rush through lesson.*
Present cards in scrambled order. CAN YOU SAY HOW MANY DOTS ARE HERE? REMEMBER TO TOUCH EACH THING THAT YOU COUNT.	

Figure E.1   Free learning environment curriculum formats.

stock kindergarten. Many of the same units can be used, at least for a while.

However, Grade 1 children soon clamor for more training in reading,

SOCIAL STUDIES   Grade   K
FAMILIES
Independent Study

Dates

Materials: Housekeeping materials
Assorted pipe cleaners, different colors
Pieces of file card
Paper clips
Felt pen
Box tops (for holding finished families in groups)
Teacher's prepared family

What the Children May Do	How the Tutor May Respond
Explore pipe cleaners.	SEE WHAT I MADE! I MADE MY FAMILY OUT OF PIPE CLEANERS. HERE'S THE FATHER, HERE'S THE MOTHER (THAT'S ME!). HERE ARE MY CHILDREN (name them). HERE IS MY SISTER, etc. Label with felt pen on a small piece of file card, The _____ Family. Hold label on pipe cleaner stand with paper clip.
Many children took part in this used charts and red tags gave stars beside name as project completed	WOULD YOU LIKE TO MAKE YOUR FAMILY? WHO WILL YOU HAVE TO MAKE? Show children how to make figures out of pipe cleaners, and stick them into clay bases. Make family label for the child. Or clip individual labels on each figure, if requested.
Make pipe cleaner family.	Talk to each child about his family. YOUR FAMILY IS SPECIAL. YOU HAVE A MOTHER, FATHER AND TWO BROTHERS. YOUR FAMILY IS SPECIAL. YOU HAVE A GRAND-MOTHER, A SISTER, AND A COUS-IN. YOUR FAMILY IS SPECIAL. YOU HAVE A MOTHER AND SEVEN SISTERS.
	Label individuals or families, as requested. Let children copy labels if they are interested in doing so.
	Put families in box tops, and display on divider shelf or on counter tops.

Figure E.1   (*Continued*)

writing, and arithmetic than the kindergarten program may have provided. In my view, reading is of primary importance. Whatever else happens in first grade, reading *must* happen. All one's resources, if necessary, should be poured into teaching the children how to read. Let me explain my thinking about the selection of a reading program.

One sometimes hears that good first-grade teachers should be able to invent their own reading programs and not have to rely on a basal program. This may be true, but the reality of teacher preparation in most of our colleges and universities must be faced: Many teachers are not trained

**LANGUAGE ARTS
EXPERIENCE CHARTS**
Small Group Lesson 3

Grade ___K___

	Gp. 1	Gp. 2	Gp. 3	Gp. 4	Gp. 5	Makeups
Date						
Time						

Materials: Experience charts
Felt pens

What the Teacher Does	How the Children May Respond
LOOK AROUND THE ROOM. SEE ALL THE THINGS WE HAVE LABELED? LET'S READ SOME OF THE LABELS . . . CHAIR, WINDOW, BOOK, etc. THE NAME OF SOMETHING IS AN IMPORTANT THING TO SAY ABOUT IT. BUT WHAT ELSE CAN WE SAY ABOUT IT? CAN YOU THINK OF ANYTHING WE COULD SAY ABOUT A (WINDOW) (CHAIR) (FISH) (FLOWER)? Let children make suggestions. Accept anything they say. Write their statements on the experience chart, one sentence to a line. YOU SAID SOME IMPORTANT THINGS ABOUT A ____. LET'S SEE IF WE CAN READ WHAT YOU SAID. Read the sentences on the chart. Let the children help you.	*It was easy to get the children to make suggestions for the experience chart, at first the answers were just 1 word but with a question about what the object does, etc. they became sentences.*

Figure E.1 *(Continued)*

to make up their own programs. They are, on the contrary, often told to "follow the manual" of a basal program. In addition, I think it is unrealistic to believe that making up a good reading program is that easy. It takes expert teachers years to develop a truly reliable program on their own.

My first effort has therefore been directed toward finding a good basal program, one that follows the principles outlined in Part V, but that outlines for the teacher in detail what to do first, second, and so forth and that also provides reading and writing practice for the children in some well-integrated fashion. Inner-city children in particular must be carefully taught good reading rules; they cannot be relied upon to discover these rules inductively by themselves. Even when discovery materials are provided (in sight-reading materials, for example), the rules that are displayed need to be clear and basic. That is, they should illustrate simple, basic spelling patterns, as opposed to "word shapes" or words of high frequency (such as *friend* or *people*) that are phonically confusing.

I think I have discovered two such programs. The first has been developed by Barbara Crane and is published by her own company, Motivational Learning Programs, Inc., 1909 Yardley Road, Yardley, Pennsylvania 19067. It is both a sight-reading and a phonics program, and it includes sight readers and workbooks for each child. The central characters are *Me* and *Efe,* a sort of dog. *Me* is a sort of person, sexless and raceless, and adored by young children. As is clear from the names of the two central characters, Mrs. Crane has begun her programs by teaching the *long* vowel sounds, which are much easier for children to discriminate (especially inner-city children who often have problems with auditory discrimination as a result of dialect differences, noisy households, or inattention habits). Miraculously, Mrs. Crane has generated a 500-word initial sight vocabulary based entirely on long vowel sounds (try it!). The children can begin reading immediately and can also begin to learn sight-sound rules. Writing practice is an essential part of the program. All the reading materials are in large print, of the sort the children themselves are learning. Writing practice can therefore be quite direct copying of words in the books. (Children love to copy in this way, as any first-grade teacher knows.)

There is an integrated readiness program that can be begun in kindergarten, but I would favor holding it for first grade. The program includes sight-sound training, puzzles, and so forth. One especially attractive feature is the consistency of pictures used in sight-sound training: The child does not have to solve the problem of deciding whether a picture of a vessel is a *boat* or a *ship,* for example. The picture will have been defined earlier, and that definition is held constant throughout the whole workbook.

The program goes through the second-grade level, which should be enough. By that time, the children should be able to read widely enough to do without a structured program. If they cannot, Mrs. Crane is developing a remedial program for all ages that should be available soon. This remedial program will be a flexible one that provides up to fifty drill pages for particular reading problems; it will not be a general, all-purpose program. (If the child needs an all-purpose program, he can start the basal program all over again.)

A second good basal reading program has been developed by Donald Rasmussen and Lynn Goldberg for Science Research Associates. It is called the Basic Reading Series. This was one of the first (now revised) so-called linguistic reading programs, which concentrate on the spelling-pattern concepts discussed in Part V. As in Mrs. Crane's program, children develop both sight-reading and word-attack skills immediately on highly redundant materials. (Redundancy, of course, provides the much-needed practice.) This program also has workbooks, tests, and enrichment materials. It uses short vowel sounds.

In addition to a basal program, children can begin immediately with other sight readers that embody simple, basic spelling patterns (plus a few irregular words). There are three sets of early reading materials that I like: (1) the Random House Dr. Seuss-type beginning reading books. (Some of these are harder than others; we selected only the super-easy ones for our first-graders. There are now about a dozen.) (2) The *Early Start Preschool Readers* published by Grosset and Dunlap. (3) The *Breakthrough* series, which must be ordered from Longman Group Limited, in London. These are small paper books that are especially charming.

In conjunction with these books, it is a simple matter to generate Dittos that give the children practice in reading and writing the words in the books. I like Dittos that provide both tracing and copying practice (Figure E.2). If the top half of the Ditto is a simple line drawing, tracing and coloring the drawing will provide additional fine motor practice with writing tools (felt pens are nice).

More generally, reading and writing should be happening as extensively as possible all over the first-grade room. Stories should be dictated to pictures and written on them. (See the references to books that detail informal language-experience procedures.) Drawers should be labeled. Charts should be printed and read repeatedly. As long as some basic rules are being carefully taught and as long as we can feel sure they will all be taught eventually, we can let children sample freely from a richer, more complex reading environment—especially the environment provided by their own language.

Figure E.2   A writing practice Ditto.

We can also let them practice writing anything they want to. One useful device for this purpose is an acetate board, a piece of heavy acetate held to a piece of cardboard with masking tape (Figure E.3). These can be of any size, and children may well want their own (rather like our grandmothers used to have their own slates). Cards with anything printed on them—names, labels, favorite words—can be slipped under the acetate, and the child can trace them with crayons. Rainbow tracing (one color after another) is popular. After tracing, the child can then copy the word on paper. In that way, he can learn to write what he wants to write, with minimal supervision from a busy teacher. Of course, it goes without saying that vast quantities of lined paper, pencils, crayons, and magic markers should be available.

In addition to all these materials, many other kinds of language-arts practice tasks should be available. We use wooden letters, rhyming games, phonics games, and so on. The Philip and Tacey catalog illustrates a paradise of word-practice games and materials that can help consolidate the developing reading skills of individual children. (The enterprising teacher can prepare many of these materials herself, but we favor the use of more elegant commercial materials whenever possible, for reasons of both esthetics and durability.)

In addition to the basic reading program, we also favor the adoption of a commercial mathematics program, which can then be extensively supplemented by concrete mathematical tasks and games. At present, I like the Houghton Mifflin *Modern School Mathematics* program. This can be started in kindergarten, or the kindergarten materials can be reserved for first grade. Unlike several other mathematics programs I have seen, these workbooks are clear (to children) and well-conceived, and I trust their sequence of concept development.

With this as a base, the teacher can generate Unifix exercises and

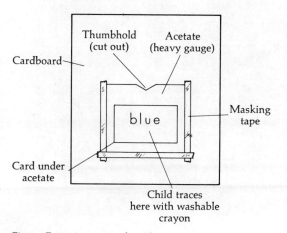

Figure E.3   An acetate board.

supplementary tasks of many kinds (Figure E.4). (See the Philip and Tacey catalog for interesting mathematics materials of all kinds.) Blocks and many of the materials classified as perceptual-motor on the kindergarten level can be placed in the first-grade mathematics area. Measurement projects are extremely popular (measure everything, and write it down). Practice in writing numerals can be encouraged through supplementary Dittos. Cuisenaire materials can be introduced late in first grade,

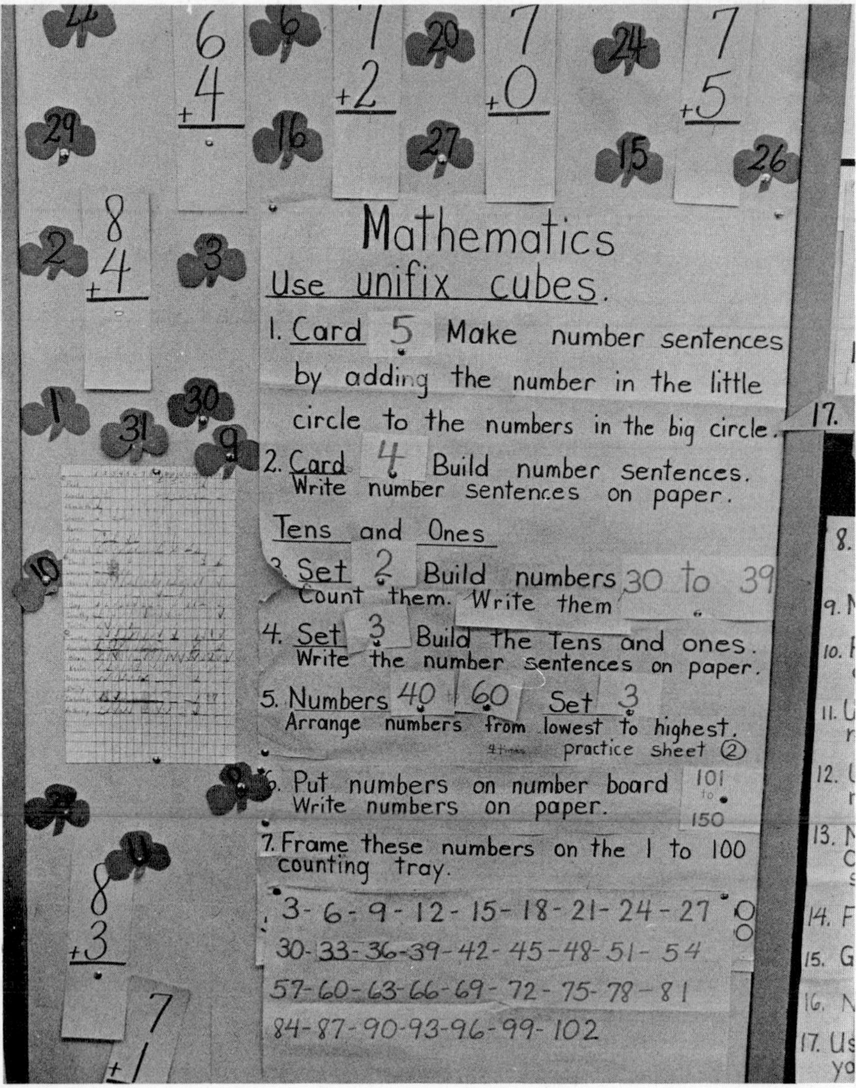

Figure E.4

but we have not found them as useful as the Unifix materials, nor as easily integrated with the basic mathematics program.

A good deal of mathematics will emerge naturally from the science program. We use the *Science Curriculum Improvement Study* (SCIS) kits, available from Rand McNally. The Grade 1 kits are *Material Objects* and *Organisms* (one kit is sufficient for a whole semester, and two first grades can trade off). These are highly recommended.

As far as social studies are concerned, the Shaftel program developed for Holt, Rinehart & Winston is a bare start. But at the first-grade level, so much time must be spent on language arts and mathematics that social studies is not easily scheduled anyway. We are trying to cover some important basic concepts through the development of integrated art–social studies–science projects, to be described next.

So far we have been discussing the differentiation and development of basic symbolic skills. What about their integration? One major value of the open school programs is their potential for the growth of child-designed, integrated projects. The children may build a store, for example, or a spaceship. Since room and time are allowed for such projects, much potential learning is possible through them. But often such learning does not happen, simply because the children are not able to guide themselves that effectively. To develop responsible integrated projects, we therefore turned to experts.

A local foundation has provided the modest funds necessary for bringing specialists together for the purpose of developing integrated primary school projects. Since most cities have such experts available and also have local foundations, this plan seems to be a good general one for stimulating responsible open school planning.

We chose three experts: one in the field of art, one in social studies, and one in mathematics-science. We suggested a theme, such as "City Adventures," and an outcome—a booklet that would provide a teacher with guidelines and suggestions. Consultants are requested to develop their concepts by teaching them, not by simply generating them theoretically. As each consultant teaches, the other two watch. Their project grows jointly in that way.

"City Adventures" moves toward the objective of building a city. In the beginning, however, the children learn to analyze important basic features of a city. In an art project, they learn to visualize details of their houses and other experiences—details they might have taken for granted—and experiment with ways of symbolizing them. In a science project, they experiment with construction problems and materials. In a social studies project, they analyze the significance of community arrangements and spatial relationships. They work gradually into the construction of a city of their own. The booklet will provide information about construction materials as well as about sequences of activities and teaching strategies.

We hope to sponsor and disseminate many integrated projects of this sort. We believe such projects, plus a good basic reading program and a good basic mathematics-science program, can provide a sound open school program—one that parents and principals alike will recognize as having solid educational value. (More about these values, and how to evaluate them, after a brief section on room arrangement and schedules.)

Organizing the Primary Free Learning Environment

Although many kindergarten rooms are large enough to incorporate comfortably six or more interest centers, many first-grade rooms are not. A small first-grade room can be roughly divided into four areas: the smallest one should be the group lesson area; the rest of the room can be divided into a language arts and social studies area, a mathematics-science area, and an art area. If the children are divided into four groups, they can be rotated through the four areas from time to time for a fair chance at every learning opportunity. Rotation may help organize the children initially, but after a while the procedure can be dropped.

We have found other useful organizational devices. A checklist may be kept: As a child performs a task, he checks off his name on that list. A teacher may list prescribed activities for a child, either posting it or keeping it in his file (or box, or locker, or "cubby"). A list of names may

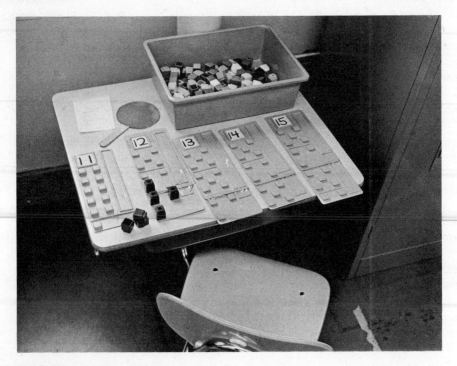

Figure E.5

be taped to a task or to the desk where a task is kept. One good system, especially for slow or immature children, is to place each task on a desk by itself (Figs. E.5 and E.6). The task stays there, and the children move from desk to desk, in their own time. Several of our classrooms have posted elaborate task charts of various kinds.

The need for such organizational procedures varies from class to class, from month to month, and from teacher to teacher. Some teachers can tolerate more uncontrolled child activity than others. As long as children are busy and interested, I see nothing wrong with whatever control procedures a teacher finds personally most comfortable. But as soon as teacher control begins to diminish and impoverish the children's learning experiences and expressive opportunities, program administrators should intervene.

Something should also be said here about noise control. The tomblike silence of traditional classrooms will not be found in a free learning environment. But the early noise of learning excitement will diminish as children develop skills of attention and concentration on individual tasks. We recommend as much carpeting and soundproofing as possible, however. We also recommend the installation of two or three carrels, where children can escape from too much social stimulation whenever they want to.

Figure E.6

The other standard noise-control procedures of turning off lights to produce silence or holding whispering periods are effectively used by our teachers to develop habits of quietness and courtesy while learning.

As far as lessons are concerned, we do not like more than one hour of formal teaching—distributed among four small groups, each of whom have a 15-minute lesson—in the morning, and a similar hour in the afternoon. There also may be a brief large-group period in the morning for announcements and general organization, and a longer large-group period in the afternoon (when the children are generally tired anyway) for a story, song, and show-and-tell. We like the joint show-and-tell system: "Will all of you who have something to share with the rest of us come and stand in front." The sharing may include art products and special lessons, as well as birthday announcements, and so on.

Except for these periods, the teacher spends her time circulating and guiding independent activities of various kinds. This is when the teacher will employ reinforcement strategies—praising here, withholding comment there. The teacher will be on the alert for opportunities to reinforce basic systems development (Part II). She will help the children develop and practice strategies of problem solving, remembering, scanning and holding information displays of various kinds, ordering and relating, and classifying. If the reading and mathematics supplementary tasks have been well selected, opportunities for this kind of practice will be numerous. In creative arts, there will be opportunities for helping children recognize the importance of generating ideas and of pulling them together in interesting ways, as discussed theoretically in Part VI.

The circulating teacher will also be on the alert for opportunities to encourage mature social interaction and personality development. She will encourage productive social coalitions and activities. She will suggest an activity here, a book there, thereby signaling the children concerned that she is interested in them as unique individuals with special interests of their own. She will become attuned to their developmental and personal characteristics, as outlined in Part III.

With a little practice, the free learning teacher soon realizes that she is doing an enormous amount of teaching. It may not feel like teaching, because she is not standing before a class of children, talking to them (and struggling to control them) all at once. But it is far more effective than traditional teaching. So when we say that small-group lessons (which are traditional in tone) should not take more than one hour morning and afternoon, we are not suggesting that teaching be limited, but that it become more creative and individualized than small-group teaching allows. (Some small-group teaching, however, is necessary for reasons of efficiency.)

In the higher grades, the same basic planning continues. We follow commercial reading and mathematics curriculums, but consider them only the bare skeleton of the basic reading and math programs. The additional reading and mathematical tasks and the projects integrating reading and math with social studies, art, and science provide extensive opportunities for children to learn in active, creative ways. As the children grow older and become better able to sustain long-term interest in projects of their own, they are encouraged to do so. As their own habits of self-organization and problem solving have deepened, the teacher will need to exert less and less direct supervision. Program designers will always try to keep abreast of the children's own inventions, so that adequate preparation and guidance can be provided for future classes. We are, in other words, letting the children help construct the program, but we are taking final responsibility for it.

Remedial Training

During kindergarten or early during Grade 1, we often find children who do not seem to have the perceptual organization necessary for symbolic activities. They may have great difficulty remembering color names, for example, or extreme difficulty with motor-spatial control, as in writing with a pencil or drawing.

In Pennsylvania, these children can be consigned to a "readiness room." In the free learning environment program, we prefer to think of this as a perceptual skills center, and we would like it to continue to be available, as a resource room, to children beyond first grade. In our program, eligible children from first through third grade spend a period a day in the center doing prescribed work.

Fortunately, many commercial materials, such as workbooks and equipment, are becoming available for programs of this sort (Fig. E.7). Our guiding philosophy in selecting such materials is that children with perceptual problems need intensive drill and close supervision. If a correct perceptual response (such as letter recognition) is not automatic, a rule must be learned ("count 3 for E; 2 for F"). Rules can be learned well only by supervised practice. Materials and program are selected to be consistent with this philosophy. In a sense, the perceptual skills center concentrates on and expands the perceptual-motor component of kindergarten and first grade.

Children who are slow or who have problems of emotional and social immaturity may not need the special help of a perceptual skills center. If the classes are not too large, they can be comfortably integrated into the regular free learning environment elementary program—and of course this is much better for them. The free learning environment provides enough room for individual differences to absorb some slow children and some hyperactives without too much disruption. Special preparatory or extra drill materials can be generated for slower children. The modeling provided by the normal children can be very beneficial to disturbed children. The fun of school (compared to a traditional elementary program) is a strong incentive for a slightly disturbed child to make a real effort to get

Figure E.7

himself under control. When a teacher can recognize this and praise him for it, his efforts will increase.

Further, the problems produced by boring, traditional elementary programs are not produced by the free learning environment. The child with high *nStim* can provide himself with adequate stimulation; the child who needs less stimulation can find a quiet corner (although this can sometimes be a problem a teacher should watch out for). The child with social problems has opportunities to test and revise his conceptions of proper social behavior, and his maturity will thereby increase. The child with a special talent and low interest in traditional school subjects will be able to develop in accordance with his own inner pattern. (Of course, he will have to master the basic skills of reading and arithmetic.)

Our remedial training program is therefore limited to children with clear evidence of perceptual disorganization. How do we assess this? There are several commercial tests available. We like a battery developed by Dr. Vivian Richman when she was a member of our school board's mental health department. This test has local norms obtained by Dr. Richman, and we like it for that reason, as well as for its basic design. Team leaders or perceptual skills center teachers can be trained to administer such tests to children designated by kindergarten and first-grade teachers.

But even with the help of such a test, the decision about remedial room placement can be difficult. There are often family factors or state regulations (age limits, for example) that must be taken into consideration. In general, we try to keep children in the regular classroom, if at all possible, on the assumption that this will provide them with maximal opportunities for sampling and constructing a normal outlook. In a free learning classroom, this is often what seems to happen. I have seen remarkable changes in severely disturbed or damaged children in only a few months.

Formal Evaluation

Like the curriculum, free learning environment evaluation procedures should grow organically out of the children's and teacher's activities, not out of a psychologist's disembodied theoretical system. There are three types of evaluation that concern us: (1) The self-evaluation of the children, (2) the evaluation of the children by teachers, and (3) program evaluation.

On the kindergarten and primary level, reflection and evaluation of one's own activities is a new experience, and we cannot expect formal operational capacities. Concrete checklists, files, collections, and workbooks of various kinds help children become aware of work they have completed and skills they have developed. Daily, during large-group meetings, teachers ask children to think over their activities. "How many of you visited the art center this morning?" In these ways, children are helped to become conscious of their own behaviors as a basis for self-esteem (Part III). As they grow older, they will be able to keep charts of their own accomplishments, graphs, records, and even books, and to make plans on the basis of them.

Teacher evaluation on the kindergarten level is presently in the form of checklists such as the one shown in Figure E.8. (This particular list was put together by Mrs. Laurie Dancy, of the school board's Office of Research.) We also use standardized tests. For the preschool, we like Bettye Caldwell's Cooperative Preschool Test, developed for the Educational Testing Service. For the kindergarten, we use the Stanford Early School Achievement Test (SESAT), Level 1. Both provide comprehensive checks on general mental growth, as compared to national norms.

On the primary level, reading and mathematical level tests are provided by the basic programs themselves. The children's level of proficiency can be assessed straightforwardly, and they can be routed through remedial or enrichment experiences when necessary. Equally straightforward testing of information and skills developed in science, art, and social studies can be carried out. I like the Cooperative Primary Tests developed by the Educational Testing Service for both basic skills and general information.

More difficult evaluations involve the special behaviors we expect free learning environment children to develop: problem-solving skills, independent study habits, self-governing behaviors, social and personal maturities, and creative abilities. Although teachers can rate such behaviors, some kind of objective testing would probably be more reliable. We are attempting to develop such tests now, but they are not yet ready for presentation.

Kindergarten   Language Arts Checklist

SCHOOL: TEACHER: DATE:

NAME OF CHILD	Recognizes name	Writes name	Dictates story	Handles book properly	Names common objects	Names pictures	Matches picture to label	Rhymes	Sequences	Makes letters on acetate	Matches initial sounds	Distinguishes initial sounds

Figure E.8   Teacher evaluation, kindergarten level.

One example of the kind of behavior we would like to assess was provided by an art teacher. He was able to compare a free learning environment class with a traditional class of children the same age. Of the free learning children, he said: "When I offer them new materials, they plunge in immediately and begin doing things. The children from the traditional class are more likely to stand around, waiting to be shown how to do something, or asking 'What are we supposed to do?' The free learning children also have another characteristic: they don't ask, 'Is this right?' They make up their own minds whether or not something is 'right.' If they like it, it's 'right.'" D. E. M. Gardner's (1968) book provides some good examples of maturity in art and other behaviors found in British open schools on relatively objective tests.

The final type of formal evaluation—that of the program—has concerned us most. This has involved assessment not of individual children, but of groups sampled randomly from free learning classrooms and from comparison (traditional) schools. Here we have been concerned with group means, rather than with individuals.

The first problem in evaluating an open school program is describing it in some sort of quantitative way. We developed two observational instruments for that purpose (Figures E.9 and E.10). The behavior of children as coded on the Pupil Behavior Record in a free learning environment is quite different from the behavior of similar children in a traditional classroom. Corresponding differences are found between free learning and traditional teachers.

The Pupil Behavior Record (Figure E.9) is a time-sampling device that sorts behavior into sixteen behavior categories and simultaneously into fourteen academic categories. The observer codes every 30 seconds. If four children and a teacher (who is coded on a different instrument, as explained below) are being watched, a coding occurs every 2.5 minutes, or twice in 5 minutes, for each individual. Over a two-hour period, that seemed an adequate sampling of behavior. Every 2.5 minutes is sufficiently frequent to provide a reasonably close watch, but not so frequent (as every 5 seconds would be, for example) as to be unnecessarily detailed. The Teacher Behavior Record (Figure E.10) is used simultaneously with the Pupil Behavior Record. It provides for eight managing categories (which are not coded academically) and three teaching categories (which are coded academically). All important teacher behaviors in a free learning environment were found to sort conveniently into one of these categories.

Of course, such instruments can be used to assess individuals rather than groups, but that is a time-consuming enterprise. For program evaluation, we sample (randomly) four to eight children from a classroom and combine their behavior records for an estimate of general class behavior. In addition, we use materials such as the Behavior Complexity Record and the Teacher Interaction Record (Figures E.11 and E.12) for evaluating other differences between classes and teachers.

Name of pupil_____ Date of birth_____

Date of observation_____ Age at time of observation_____ Sex_____ Race_____

School_____ Grade_____ Teacher_____ Observer_____

Time interval (tally rate)_____ Time: From_____to_____ Total time_____

WORK-ORIENTED	FREE LEARNING BEHAVIOR		
Independent activity			Total
Independent observing			
Social interchange	Teacher		
	Peer		
Spontaneous group activity	Teacher		
	Peer		
WORK-ORIENTED	**PLANNED GROUP**		
Planned group			SubTotal
NON-WORK-ORIENTED	**DURING PLANNED GROUP**	**DURING FREE LEARNING**	
Passive acceptance; waiting; bored			
Wandering around			
Independent irrelevant activity			
Social interchange			
Disruptive activity			
NEUTRAL	**WORK-ORIENTED**	**NON-WORK-ORIENTED**	
Cleaning up			
Caretaking			
Gross physical activity			

Total   A_____   F_____   _____ SS_____   Grand total [_____]
        B_____   H_____ Pg_____   S_____   Total planned group (W-O
        C_____ LA_____ PM_____   plus Non-W-O)
        E_____ M_____ Sc_____   _____
        Total free learning (W-O
        plus Non-W-O)

Figure E.9 Pupil Behavior Record.

Explanation of Categories

Time interval. The number of seconds (or minutes) between tallies. If four children and a teacher are being scored on a 30-second interval, there will be 2.5 minutes on a particular record as a tally rate.

Independent activity. School-type (generally cognitive) behaviors. They should be coded as detailed below under academic codes (LA = language arts, etc.).

Independent observing. Also school-type activities. Should be coded.

Social interchange. Only work-oriented (school-type) interactions. Questions, requests for help, "let me see your paper," etc., all should be categorized here. Should be coded.

Spontaneous group activity. Clusters of children, with or without a teacher, working together on school-type activities. They should be interacting as a group, although they may be working on different materials. If a child is sitting at a table with other children but is not interacting with them as a group, he should be placed in the above "Independent" category. Code.

Planned group activity. Group activities in which the children are required to participate. The teacher may also have preplanned the spontaneous group activities above, but if the children are not required to stop other things and enter the group, they should not be categorized as belonging to a planned group. Planned groups are usually "Circle time" in kindergarten, and traditional classwork in ordinary elementary and high schools. Code.

Cleaning up. Work-oriented but not academically meaningful; need not be coded, only tallied.

Passive acceptance. What good children do when they are not academically involved. They wait, without causing difficulty. They "conk out" by becoming glassy-eyed, yawning, putting their heads down, etc., but they don't cause trouble. Generally, this is not coded, only tallied — since it refers to nonwork behavior. Usually it is not important to know what work the child is *not* doing, only that he is not doing it. However, the behavior may be coded if the information will be helpful.

Wandering around. Moving about without any special purpose, not purposeful traveling. (The latter should be scored as independent activity and coded appropriately.) Wandering around is not coded, since it has no academic connotations.

Independent irrelevant activity. Nonwork (like doodling, jittering, etc.) that is not disruptive, but that is neither passive nor especially social. Not coded; if you could code it, it would be work-oriented independent activity.

Social interchange. Nonwork variety can be about anything but school-type activities, including social conversation, "Good morning," and the like. Not coded.

Disruptive activity. The usual disciplinary or nuisance behaviors. Not coded.

Caretaking. Activities associated with bathroom, water fountain, eating, resting, putting on rubbers, taking off rubbers, having coat buttoned, etc. Not coded.

Gross physical activity. Tricycles, sliding board, jumping around, relay races, etc. Not coded.

Academic codes:

    A = Arts and crafts

    B = Blocks, tinker toys, construction materials of all kinds

    C = Circle activities, including show-and-tell, flag salute, etc.

    E = Errand for teacher (taking roll down to office, for example), or putting up the milk list. If the behavior is not strictly of this nonacademic variety, it should be coded academically. For example, if a teacher asks a child to put his picture up on the bulletin board, that activity should be scored A not E. Or if the teacher asks the children to move their chairs back to the wall, that should be tallied under "Cleaning up," not E.

    F = Fantasy (as in pretend games, Batman activities, etc.) This is exclusive of housekeeping games, which are coded H.

Figure E.9 *(Continued)*

H = Housekeeping, including pretend games associated with housekeeping materials ("You be the baby and I'll be the mommy . . .")

LA = Language arts, including writing, alphabet learning, rhymes, language games like Scrabble, etc.

M = Mathematics, including chess or other games that have a clear basis in mathematical strategies of some sort.

♪ = Music, rhythms, songs.

Pg = Physical activities that are not gross and unplanned. For example, balance beams, or other circle games involving broad jumping, hopping, etc.

PM = Perceptual-motor activities such as puzzles, shape recognition, color naming, etc. Most manipulative activities (bead-stringing, pegboards, etc.) fit into this category.

S = Story, where children are listening to a piece of literature being read to them, either live or on tape.

Sc = Science (including gerbils, scales, planting bulbs, etc.).

SS = Social studies, such as discussion of community agencies (post office, fire house), parks, interpersonal concepts, etc.

Figure E.9   (*Continued*)

The Teacher Interaction Record may be summarized in various ways. Simple percentages may be computed of the amount of responsiveness to feelings and ideas, the most frequent types of questions, and so on, as well as combinations, such as the percentage of lecturing or commenting that specifically includes some reference to the feelings or ideas of children vs. the percentage that does not include any such reference. The Child Behavior Complexity Record and the Teacher Interaction Record are examples of the types of instruments we have developed for assessing changes in children and teachers. Our research has not yet proceeded far enough to report detailed results.

The use of group data for the purposes of program evaluation does not mean we have lost interest in individual children. On the contrary, we are attempting to develop sensitive measures of the capacities of young children to handle verbal, action, and pictorial information (see Part I) separately or in combination. If we can estimate their capacities in this regard, then we will be much better able to understand their response to free learning opportunities. Someday, our schools should be able to provide a variety of routes to educational achievement—routes defined not by general IQ, but by cognitive styles and talents. An essential part of our program is the basic research and test development leading to such objectives.

Teacher Characteristics

A free learning environment can be managed well by many different kinds of teachers. We began by expecting that only young, exceptionally intelligent, and creative teachers would be successful. This expectation (like most "magical" ones!) was not supported. Some older teachers of only average imagination and intelligence turned out to be outstanding free learning teachers; some younger, brighter ones were not successful. The

Name of teacher_____ School_____ Date_____

Time: From_____to_____ Total time_____ Observer_____

Time interval (tally rate)_____ Sex_____ Race_____ Age_____ Education_____

MANAGING BEHAVIORS		Total
Observing		
Social interchange		
Directing		
Controlling		
Interacting with adult		
Traveling		
Gone		
Handling materials		SubTotal

TEACHING			
Informal	Individual		
	Group		
Formal (lecturing, planned group, including small group)			

Activities code: A = arts/crafts, B = blocks/construction, H = housekeeping, LA = language arts, PM = perceptual-motor, M = math, Sc = science, ♩ = music/rhythms, Cl = cleaning up, E = errand, C = circle conversation, Pg = physical games, SS = social studies, S = story

Total A_____ H_____ _____ Sc_____ Grand Total

B_____ LA_____ Pg_____ SS_____

C_____ M_____ PM_____ S_____

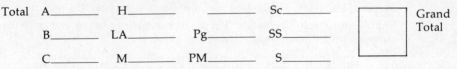

Explanation of Categories

Observing. Watching without interfering.

Social interchange. "How are you today?" and the like.

Directing. Instructions to children (not to adults) which may take the form of suggestions, questions, etc., but which have a manipulative function.

Controlling. Disciplinary actions; should be scored as "Directing" unless a clearly disciplinary function is manifested.

Interacting with adult. Giving aide instructions, speaking to principal, etc.

Traveling. In transit, without observing.

Gone. Not in the classroom.

Handling materials. Sorting music, putting away the paper clips, etc.

The next two categories refer to academically relevant behaviors, and should be coded (LA = language arts, etc., see Pupil Behavior code).

Informal teaching. Any kind of tutoring or guiding or outright instruction that does not take the form of a traditional planned lesson, where the children are pulled together in a planned group.

Formal teaching. Planned large or small group teaching.

Figure E.10 Teacher Behavior Record.

Name_____ School_____ Teacher_____ Observer_____

Age____ Race____ Sex____ Date____ Time: From____to____ Total_____

Int. No.			L?	Brief description of behavior	Material	Code
1	A Sc L P S M					
2	A Sc L P S M					
3	A Sc L P S M					
4	A Sc L P S M					
5	A Sc L P S M					
6	A Sc L P S M					
7	A Sc L P S M					

(For as many intervals as desired. A = Art, Sc = science, LA = language arts, P = perceptual-motor, S = social studies, and M = mathematics. Circle the letter describing the child's activity. L? = formal lesson; check if one is in progress.)

Directions for Coding

General code:

0   Passive behavior: Watching, staring into space.

1   Random behavior: Haphazard use of materials, purposeless wandering.

2   Simple purposeful behavior: Purposeful traveling, using materials in simple conventional ways, directed behavior.

3   More complex behavior: Interpersonal play, more complex use of materials (may be conventional), simple plans carried out.

4   Complex behavior: Carries out plan with several steps, but fumbles for appropriate way of doing so—false starts, much correction.

5   Complex behavior: Carries out plan with several steps with minimal back-tracking.

Examples for Each Kind of Material

Art materials:

1   Random formlessness; use of materials for sensory satisfaction (pounding, squishing); no discernible system for use.

2   Simple but poorly executed forms; decided system for use (applying colors in a definite order, etc.).

Figure E.11   Child Behavior Complexity Scale.

3   More complex forms with better control of the medium; two or three special details.

4   Definite forms, easily recognizable, or definite pattern requiring co-ordination of a set of details.

5   Coordination of complex ideas requiring several steps, including use of tools, templates, etc.

Cognitive materials:

1   Random or careless play with materials; indifference to the proper use of materials; throwing or breaking or otherwise mistreating materials; simple repeated action with no attempt at elaboration (pulling the rope back and forth through the pulley for five minutes at a stretch, for example).

2   Correct use of materials according to a simple plan, either pupil-initiated or teacher-initiated (putting Unifix cubes together to make long rods; following teacher directions to make sets of Unifix cubes, etc.).

3   More complex plan, either pupil-initiated or teacher-initiated, with poor control of materials (many false starts in bolting wheels to board; poor reproduction of patterns on peg- or geoboards, etc.).

4   More complex plan with good control of materials, or complex plan in several steps with many false starts.

5   Complex plan requiring several steps for execution, with good control of materials, giving a strong impression of forethought on the part of the child.

Construction blocks:

1   Helter-skelter messing with materials.

2   Simple constructions; simple plans for coordinating constructions (two or more children may be involved).

3   More complex constructions and coordination plans; anticipation of construction problems; but emphasis on fantasy rather than construc-tion.

4   Still more complex constructions and coordinations; clear spatial imagery and anticipation of problems.

5   Large-scale construction program that continues for long periods.

Social interaction:

1   Haphazard play, parallel or solitary play with little personal inter-action.

2   Parallel or solitary play with frequent short spates of social interaction; fantasized interaction (phone conversations).

3   Simple cooperative play using a common pool of materials; little co-ordination of roles; extensive conversation.

4   Cooperative play with assigned roles ("I'm the mother and you be my company"); role-appropriate conversation; cooperative problem solving.

5   Extensive working out of play roles, with cooperative use of materials, for long periods of time — perhaps over several days. Cooperative solv-ing of difficult problems.

Figure E.11   (*Continued*)

Teacher_____ School_____ Class_____ Date_____

Time: From_____to_____ Total Time_____ Interval_____ Observer_____

(Write description of activities/intervals on back of sheet after observation.)

Time Interval	Touch		Feelings			Ideas						Questions asking for Clarification of						
	M	Ch	Acc	Rej	Mis	Acc	Rej	Mis	Com	Lec	Dir	Info	Help	Thot	Feel	Pur	Word	Ans
1																		
2																		
3																		
4																		
5																		
6																		
7																		
8																		
9																		
10																		
11																		
12																		
13																		
14																		
15																		
16																		
17																		
18																		
19																		
20																		
Total																		

Figure E.12 Teacher Interaction Record.

Explanation of Categories

Time interval. Size of the observation intervals, usually 30 seconds. That is, during a 30-second interval, categorize (check category) all statements and physical contacts that occur. Thus, some teachers will have more differentiated records than others. (Categories may be checked more than once.)

Touch — Materials (M): Materials in use by the child who is the object of the interaction.

Touch — Child (Ch): Pats, hugs, guides hand, etc.

Feelings — Accepts (Acc): In Amidon-Flanders terms, "accepts and clarifies the feeling tone of the students in a nonthreatening manner. Feelings may be positive or negative. Predicting or recalling feelings is included."

Feelings — Rejects (Rej): Clearly recognizes but does not accept the feeling content of the child's behavior.

Feelings — Misunderstands (Mis): Responds to the feeling tone, but misunderstands or selects an irrelevant (tangential) feature as a cue. This category may be checked along with the accepting or rejecting category. That is, a teacher may accept a feeling, but misunderstand it; or she may reject a feeling, but on the basis of a misunderstanding of it.

Ideas — Accepts (Acc): "Clarifying, building, or developing ideas suggested by a student. As teacher brings more of his own ideas into play, shift to [Lecturing] . . ." (Amidon-Flanders).

Ideas — Rejects (Rej): This can include criticism or refusals of various types. However, if the *Accepts Feelings* category is also checked (or if *Rejects Feelings* is not checked), we will recognize a teacher who is guiding a student into more appropriate behaviors, but without damaging his morale.

Ideas — Misunderstands (Mis): Again, this category can be checked simultaneously with either *Accepts* or *Rejects Ideas* to describe the quality of the teacher's understanding of what the child is trying to do or say.

Comment (Com): Remarks that are not clearly a direction, a lecture (imparting information), or an answer to a question. ("It certainly is a beautiful morning.")

Lecturing, Teaching (Lec): Characterized by the intent to impart information. It may also be an answer to a question, in which case *Answer* is checked.

Directing (Dir): This category includes both direct and indirect forms of management. If a question such as "Would you like to get your chair?" is more of a direction than a question, it should be classified here. (Or it may be more a case of *Question Asking for Help,* in the judgment of the observer.) *Directing* will be checked along with *Accepts Feelings* or *Accepts Ideas* if the acceptance gets more elaborate. That is, when the teacher expands the child's ideas, she may give specific directions or suggestions that are too elaborate to be lumped under a simple category of *Acceptance.* Directing may also be scored in conjunction with *Rejection* or *Misunderstanding.* If none of the six previous categories are checked, then we assume a type of general or indifferent direction that is not being keyed (either positively or negatively) to the ideas or feelings of particular children.

Questions — Asking for Information (Info): "Did you have a nice time in the park yesterday?" "Is that a new coat?"

Questions — Asking for Help (Help): "Would you please bring me that tray?" "Can you hold that for me?"

Figure E.12   *(Continued)*

Questions — Asking for Clarification of Thought (Thot): Inductive questions designed to lead the child into a new awareness or concept. "What do you think would happen if you put that block over here?" "What do you suppose belongs here?" The teacher knows the answer, but wants the child to discover it for himself. Alternatively, the teacher may want the child to clarify his reasons for himself and for her.

Questions — Asking for Clarification of Feeling (Feel): "What's the matter, don't you feel well?" "Did something make you sad?" "Did you hurt yourself?"

Questions — Asking for Clarification of Purpose (Pur): "What did you do that for?" "Why are you going over there?" These are distinguished from inductive questions, because the teacher really does not know the answer. They are also distinguished from clarification of reason (above), when the teacher's intention is primarily to make the child aware of his own motives or intentions, rather than of his thinking processes.

Questions — Asking for Clarification of Words (Word): "What did you say?" "What did you mean by that?" The latter question would be classified as *Thot* if the teacher's main purpose were to make the child aware of his own meaning. If the teacher simply wants to understand the semantic content of a child's statement, her question would be classified here.

Answer (Ans): This category is used when a teacher answers a child's question.

Figure E.12   *(Continued)*

free learning environment permits teachers as well as children to bloom. Many of our teachers were surprised to discover their own resources and dedication to this newer method. (Originally, our teachers did not choose us; they were assigned to the project. By now, of course, some teachers are seeking us out.)

Our experience suggests, however, that there is one quality a good free learning teacher must have and all poor free learning teachers lack. It is not intelligence (beyond a certain minimum), creativity (again, beyond a minimum), college background (some of our aides, who have not even completed high school, are marvelous free learning teachers), or age. It is *energy.* Some older teachers, for example, simply do not have the physical strength for free learning operations. Some teachers have too many personal tensions and worries to have sufficient energy available for teaching. Their energy is tied up in personal concerns and defenses against their own anxieties. Some teachers are not able to organize themselves well enough to deploy their own resources effectively. They pour too much time into unnecessary operations.

For whatever reason, the common denominator of our good teachers is available, well-directed energy. Energy to notice and attend promptly to the individual needs of children; energy to generate a special, personal task for a child; energy to be pleasant and cooperative, despite numerous demands from the children; energy to direct aides and volunteers cheerfully and efficiently; energy to plan, plan, and replan ways of keeping the children busy and independent; energy to keep track of the effectiveness of lessons and other kinds of activities, to keep notes and written guides; energy to explain details of the program to parents and administrators; and above all, energy to respond warmly and sensitively to children.

Since the free learning environment is based on the natural capacities of children to learn and to grow mentally, it is especially necessary for a teacher to have the energy to nurture their intellectual needs. In a traditional classroom, the teacher is not required to spend so much time responding to individual intellectual needs. She can, instead, concentrate on presenting "canned" information to children as a group. This is much easier to do. In the free learning classroom, the teacher must constantly improvise; she must expand her own knowledge and become enough of an expert in all subjects to cope with the children's endless curiosity about them. This also takes a great deal of energy. Our teachers must "bone up" continually on science, mathematics, art, and so forth, and may soon feel the need for additional academic training.

The General Model for Program Development

As sketched here, our general model exemplifies the critically important *dynamic* aspects of free learning environment program development. Learning, for children, should be a dynamic process. Program development should also be such a process. Teachers should be continually building and revising aspects of their programs to fit the changing needs of their pupils. Program designers should be continually building and revising to fit the changing needs of teachers. The moment a program "freezes," education in its fullest sense will have begun to die.

A process program does not, of course, mean a disorganized program. Organization exists because of the dynamic hierarchy. A child samples from the environment of his classroom materials; a teacher samples from the environment of children sampling from classroom materials; program designers sample from the environment of teachers sampling from the environment of children sampling from classroom materials. In all cases, individuals are learning how to make judgments, formulate concepts, test hypotheses, and generally build minds on the basis of their sampling experiences. That kind of dynamic hierarchy is not disorganized; but it is very different from the hierarchy of a static curriculum through which everyone marches at more or less the same speed.

Difficulties in designing open school programs nearly always arise from attempts to fit a dynamic system into the traditional, static framework. Many administrators are afraid that a dynamic system cannot be an orderly educational system. The fact is it can be, because it is based on natural systems that orderly, educated people actually use, especially administrators.

The typical school principal is solving problems all day long; he is a problem-solving "machine." Teachers and pupils can also develop systems for handling changing information (problems) in efficient and creative ways, if they are encouraged to do so. *A dynamic educational system will inevitably evolve into an organized system if the minds involved in it are permitted to grow.*

The design of a free learning environment in a particular community, school, or classroom should grow out of the resources available to that particular community, school, or classroom. The model described here merely illustrates one way in which one school district has used its resources. Many other models that capitalize on the unique minds of available personnel are possible. The dedication of those minds to the development of free learning programs involves them in the same enterprise that engages the children: active learning, creative integration of ideas and materials, personal expression and individuation. That is the real meaning and importance of education: Either it is happening for child and teacher and program designer alike, or it may not be happening at all.

REFERENCES

Adorno, T. W., Frenkel-Brunswik, E., Levinson, D. J. and Sanford, R. N. *The authoritarian personality.* New York: Harper & Row, 1950.

Almy, M. and Cunningham, R. *Ways of studying children.* New York: Teachers College Press, 1959.

Amidon, E. The use of interaction analysis at Temple University. In Corrigan, D. (ed.), *The study of teaching,* pp. 42–54. Washington, D.C.: The Association for Student Teaching, 1967.

Anastasi, A. *Differential psychology.* New York: Macmillan, 1958.

_____. *Psychological testing.* New York: Macmillan, 1968.

Applegate, M. *Helping children write.* New York: Harper & Row, 1961.

Arnheim, R. *Art and visual perception.* Berkeley: University of California Press, 1966.

Aronson, E., Turner, J. A. and Carlsmith, J. M. Communication credibility and communication discrepancy as determinants of opinion change. *Journal of Abnormal and Social Psychology,* 1963, 67, 31–36.

Ashton-Warner, S. *Teacher.* New York: Bantam, 1963.

Atkinson, J. W. The mainsprings of achievement-oriented activity. In Krumboltz, J. D. (ed.), *Learning and the educational process,* pp. 25–66. Chicago: Rand McNally, 1965.

Atwood, G. A developmental study of cognitive balancing in hypothetical three-person systems. *Child Development,* 1969, 40, 73–86.

Babich, F. R., Jacobson, A. L., Bubash, S. and Jacobson, A. Transfer of a response to naive rats by injection of ribonucleic acid extracted from trained rats. *Science,* 1965, 149, 656–657.

Baldwin, A. *Theories of child development.* New York: Wiley, 1967.

Bales, R. *Interaction process analysis.* Reading, Mass.: Addison-Wesley, 1950.

Bandler, R. J., Madaras, G. R. and Bem, D. J. Self-observation as a source of pain perception. *Journal of Personality & Social Psychology,* 1968, 9, 205–209.

Bandura, A. Social learning through imitation. In Jones, M. R. (ed.), *Nebraska symposium on motivation,* pp. 211–269. Lincoln, Neb.: University of Nebraska Press, 1962.

————. Influence of models' reinforcement contingencies on the acquisition of imitative responses. *Journal of Personality & Social Psychology,* 1965, 1, 589–595.

———— and Menlove, F. L. Factors determining vicarious extinction of avoidance behavior through symbolic modeling. *Journal of Personality & Social Psychology,* 1968, 8, 99–108.

———— and Mischel, W. Modification of self-imposed delay of reward through exposure to live and symbolic models. *Journal of Personality & Social Psychology,* 1965, 2, 698–705.

————, Ross, D. and Ross, S. A. Imitation of film-mediated aggressive models. *Journal of Abnormal and Social Psychology,* 1963, 66, 3–11.

———— and Walters, R. H. *Adolescent aggression.* New York: Ronald, 1959.

———— and ————. *Social learning and personality development.* New York: Holt, Rinehart & Winston, 1963.

Baratz, J. Language in the economically disadvantaged child: a perspective. *ASHA: A Journal of the American Speech and Hearing Association,* 1968, 10, 143–145.

———— and Shuy, R. *Teaching black children to read.* Washington, D.C.: Center for Applied Linguistics, 1969.

Barron, F. *Creative person and creative process.* New York: Holt, Rinehart & Winston, 1969.

Bartlett, F. C. *Remembering: a study in experimental and social psychology.* New York: Cambridge University Press, 1932.

Bayley, N. Behavioral correlates of mental growth: birth to thirty-six years. *American Psychologist,* 1968, 23, 1–17.

Beilin, H. Cognitive capacities of young children: a replication. *Science,* 1968, 162, 920–921.

Bereiter, C. and Engelmann, S. *Teaching disadvantaged children in the preschool.* Englewood Cliffs, N.J.: Prentice Hall, 1966.

Berko, J. The child's learning of English morphology. *Word,* 1958, 14, 150–177.

Berlin, I. N. Learning as therapy. *Saturday Review,* October 15, 1966, pp. 78–93.

Berlyne, D. E. An experimental study of human curiosity. *British Journal of Psychology,* 1954, 45, 256–265.

_____. *Conflict, arousal, and curiosity.* New York: McGraw-Hill, 1960.

_____. Soviet research on intellectual processes in children. In Wright, J. C. and Kagan, J., Basic cognitive processes in children, *Monographs of the Society for Research in Child Development,* 1963, Serial No. 86, 165–184.

_____. *Structure and direction in thinking.* New York: Wiley, 1965.

_____. Curiosity and exploration. *Science,* 1966, 153, 25–33.

Berne, E. *Games people play.* New York: Grove, 1964.

Bernstein, B. Some sociological determinants of perception. *British Journal of Sociology,* 1958, 9, 159–174.

_____. Social structure, language and learning. *Educational Research, 3,* 1961.

Berry, M. F. and Eisenson, J. *Speech disorders.* New York: Appleton, 1956.

Berry, P. C. Pretending to have (or to be) a computer as a strategy in teaching. *Harvard Educational Review,* 1964, 34, 383–401.

Bever, T. Why two-year-olds are smarter than three-year-olds. Lecture given at Carnegie-Mellon University, February 23, 1968.

_____, Fodor, J. and Weksel, W. On the acquisition of syntax: a critique of "contextual generalization." *Psychological Review,* 1965, 72, 467–482.

_____, Mehler, J. and Epstein, J. What children do in spite of what they know. *Science,* 1968, 162, 921–924.

Bexton, W. H., Heron, W. and Scott, T. H. Effects of decreased variation in the sensory environment. *Canadian Journal of Psychology,* 1954, 8, 70–76.

Bieker, H. Using anecdotal records to know the child. In *1950 Yearbook of the Association for Supervision and Curriculum Development,* Washington, D.C., pp. 184–202.

Blank, M. and Solomon, F. A tutorial language program to develop abstract thinking in socially disadvantaged preschool children. *Child Development,* 1968, 39, 379–390.

Bloom, B. S. (ed.) *Taxonomy of educational objectives: cognitive domain.* New York: McKay, 1956.

_____ and Broder, L. J. Problem-solving processes of college students: an exploratory investigation. *Supplementary Educational Monographs, 73.* Chicago: University of Chicago Press, 1950.

Braine, M. D. S. The ontogeny of English phrase structure: the first phase. *Language,* 1963a, 39, 1–13.

_____. On learning the grammatical order of words. *Psychological Review,* 1963b, 70, 323–348.

Brooks, L. R. Spatial and verbal components of the act of recall. *Canadian Journal of Psychology,* 1958, 22, 349–368.

Brown, R. Linguistic determinism and the part of speech. *Journal of Abnormal & Social Psychology,* 1957, 55, 1–5.

———. *Words and things.* New York: Free Press, 1958a.

———. How shall a thing be called? *Psychological Review,* 1958b, 65, 14–21.

———. *Social psychology.* New York: Free Press, 1965.

——— and Lenneberg, E. H. A study in language and cognition. *Journal of Abnormal & Social Psychology,* 1954, 49, 454–462.

——— and McNeill, D. The "tip of the tongue" phenomenon. *Journal of Verbal Learning & Verbal Behavior,* 1966, 5, 325–337.

Brune, I. H. Language in mathematics. In Fehr, H. F., *The learning of mathematics,* pp. 156–191. Washington, D.C.: The National Council of Teachers of Mathematics, 1953.

Bruner, J. S. *The process of education.* Cambridge, Mass.: Harvard University Press, 1960.

———. *On knowing: essays for the left hand.* Cambridge, Mass.: Harvard University Press, 1964a.

———. The course of cognitive growth. *American Psychologist,* 1964b, 19, 1–16.

———. Some elements of discovery. In Shulman, L. S. and Keisler, E. R. (eds.), *Learning by discovery: a critical appraisal,* pp. 101–114. Chicago: Rand McNally, 1966.

——— and Clinchy, B. Towards a disciplined intuition. In Bruner, J. (ed.), *Learning about learning,* pp. 71–83. Washington, D.C.: Superintendent of Documents Catalog No. FS 5.212:12019. Published in 1966.

———, Goodnow, J. J. and Austin, G. A. *A study of thinking.* New York: Wiley, 1956.

——— and Olver, R. R. Development of equivalence transformations in children. In Wright, J. C. and Kagan, J. (eds.), Basic cognitive processes in children, *Monographs of the Society for Research in Child Development,* 1963, Serial No. 86, 125–141.

———, ——— and Greenfield, P. *Studies in cognitive growth.* New York: Wiley, 1966.

——— and Potter, M. C. Interference in visual recognition. *Science,* 1964, 144, 424–425.

Burrows, A. T., Ferebee, J. D., Jackson, D. C. and Saunders, D. O. *They all want to write.* Englewood Cliffs, N. J.: Prentice-Hall, 1952.

Cameron, D. E., Kral, V. A., Solyom, L., Sved, S., Wainrib, B., Beaulieu, C. and Enesco, H. RNA and memory. In Gaito, J. (ed.), *Macromolecules and behavior,* pp. 129–148. New York: Appleton, 1966.

Cameron, N. Functional immaturity in the symbolization of scientifically trained adults. *Journal of Psychology,* 1938, 6, 161–175.

Carroll, J. B. Research in foreign language teaching: the last five years. In Mead, R. G. (ed.), *Language teaching,* pp. 1–42. New York: MLA Materials Center, 1966.

Cartwright, D. The nature of group cohesiveness. In Cartwright, D. and

Zander, A. (eds.), *Group dynamics, research & theory,* pp. 91–109. New York: Harper & Row, 1968.

Cazden, C. Environmental assistance to the child's acquisition of grammar. Unpublished doctoral dissertation, Harvard University, 1965.

––––––. Subcultural differences in child language: an interdisciplinary review. *Merrill-Palmer Quarterly of Behavior & Development,* 1966, 12, 185–219.

Chall, J. S. *Learning to read: the great debate.* New York: McGraw-Hill, 1967.

Chapanis, A., Garner, W. R. and Morgan, C. T. *Applied experimental psychology: human factors in engineering design.* New York: Wiley, 1949.

Chomsky, N. *Syntactic structures.* The Hague: Mouton, 1957.

––––––. *Aspects of a theory of syntax.* Cambridge, Mass.: M.I.T. Press, 1965.

Clark, H. H. Word associations and linguistic theory. In Lyons, J. (ed.), *New horizons in linguistics.* Baltimore, Md.: Penguin, 1970.

–––––– and Begun, J. S. The use of syntax in understanding sentences. *British Journal of Psychology,* 1968, 59, 219–229.

Cohen, A. R. Cognitive tuning as a factor affecting impression formation. *Journal of Personality,* 1961, 29, 235–245.

Collins, B. E. and Raven, B. H. Group structure: attraction, coalitions, communication, and power. In Lindzey, G. and Aronson, E. (eds.), *Handbook of social psychology,* Vol. 4, pp. 452–525. Reading, Mass.: Addison-Wesley, 1968.

Corsini, D. A., Pick, A. D. and Flavell, J. H. Production deficiency of nonverbal mediators in young children. *Child Development,* 1968, 39, 53–58.

Covington, M. V. Promoting creative thinking in the classroom: the process of curriculum development. In Klausmeier, H. J. (ed.), *Contemporary research of significance to education.* Madison, Wis.: University of Wisconsin, 1967.

––––––, Crutchfield, R. S., Davies, L. and Olton, R. M. *The Productive Thinking Program.* Columbus, Ohio: Merrill, 1972.

Crandall, V. C., Katkovsky, W. and Crandall, V. J. Children's beliefs in their own control of reinforcements in intellectual-academic achievement situations. *Child Development,* 1965, 36, 91–109.

Critchley, M. The neurology of psychotic speech. *British Journal of Psychiatry,* 1964a, 110, 353–364.

––––––. *Developmental dyslexia.* London: Heinemann, 1964b.

Crockett, H. J. The achievement motive and differential occupational mobility in the United States. *American Sociological Review,* 1962, 27, 191–204.

Culbertson, F. M. Modification of an emotionally held attitude through role-playing. *Journal of Abnormal & Social Psychology,* 1957, 54, 230–233.

Dart, F. E. and Pradhan, P. L. Cross-cultural teaching of science. *Science,* 1967, 155, 649–656.

DeCecco, J. P. (ed.) *Educational technology.* New York: Holt, Rinehart & Winston, 1964.

Deese, J. *The structure of associations in language and thought.* Baltimore, Md.: Johns Hopkins Press, 1966.

DeGrazia, A. and Sohn, D. A. (eds.) *Programs, teachers, and machines.* New York: Bantam, 1964.

Denner, B. Representational and syntactic competence of problem readers. *Child Development,* 1970, 41, 881–887.

Deutsch, M. Socially relevant science: reflections on some studies of interpersonal conflict. *American Psychologist,* 1969, 24, 1076–1092.

Dewey, J. Theory of valuation. In *International Encyclopedia of Unified Science,* Vol. 2, No. 4. Chicago: University of Chicago Press, 1939.

Dienes, Z. P. *Building up mathematics.* London: Hutchinson, 1964a.

———. *An experimental study of mathematics-learning.* London: Hutchinson, 1964b.

Diggory, J. C. *Self-evaluation: concepts and studies.* New York: Wiley, 1966.

Dollard, J., Doob, L. W., Miller, N. E. and Sears, R. R. *Frustration and aggression.* New Haven, Conn.: Yale University Press, 1939.

Drever, James. Early learning and the perception of space. *American Journal of Psychology,* 1955, 68, 605–614.

Duncan, C. P. Transfer after training with single versus multiple tasks. *Journal of Experimental Psychology,* 1958, 55, 63–72.

Duncker, K. On problem solving. *Psychological Monographs,* 1945, Whole No. 270.

Dunn-Rankin, P. The similarity of lower-case letters of the English alphabet. *Journal of Verbal Learning & Verbal Behavior,* 1968, 7, 990–995.

Dwyer, F. M. Adapting visual illustrations for effective learning. *Harvard Educational Review,* 1967, 37, 250–263.

Eichenwald, H. F. and Fry, P. C. Nutrition and learning. *Science,* 1969, 163, 644–648.

Eiseley, L. *Darwin's century.* Garden City, N.Y.: Doubleday, 1958.

———. *The firmament of time.* New York: Atheneum, 1960.

Eisenberg, L., Berlin, C. I., Dill, A. and Frank, S. Class and race effects on the intelligibility of monosyllables. *Child Development,* 1968, 39, 1077–1090.

Engelmann, S. *Preventing failure in the primary grades.* Chicago: Science Research Associates, 1969.

Erikson, E. H. Identity and the life cycle. *Psychological Issues,* 1959, Monograph No. 1.

_____. *Identity: youth and crisis.* New York: Norton, 1968.

Farnham-Diggory, S. Self, future and time: a developmental study of the concepts of psychotic, brain-damaged and normal children. *Monographs of the Society for Research in Child Development,* 1966, Serial No. 103.

_____. Symbol and synthesis in experimental "reading." *Child Development,* 1967, 38, 221–231.

_____. Cognitive synthesis in Negro and white children. *Monographs of the Society for Research in Child Development,* Serial No. 135, 1970.

_____ and Bermon, M. Verbal compensation, cognitive synthesis, and conservation. *Merrill-Palmer Quarterly of Behavior & Development,* 1968, 14, 215–228.

_____ and Ramsey, B. Play persistence: some effects of interruption, social reinforcement, and defective toys. *Developmental Psychology,* 1971, 4, 297–298.

Fehr, H. F. Theories of learning related to the field of mathematics. In Fehr, H. F. (ed.), *The learning of mathematics,* pp. 1–41. Washington, D.C.: National Council of Teachers of Mathematics, 1953.

Feigenbaum, E. A. The simulation of verbal learning behavior. In Feigenbaum, E. A. and Feldman, J. (eds.), *Computers and thought,* pp. 297–309. New York: McGraw-Hill, 1963.

Feld, S. C. Longitudinal study of the origins of achievement strivings. *Journal of Personality & Social Psychology,* 1967, 7, 408–414.

Fenton, E. (ed.) *The Americans: a history of the United States.* New York: Holt, Rinehart & Winston, 1970.

Festinger, L. Informal social communication. *Psychological Review,* 1950, 57, 271–282.

_____. A theory of social comparison processes. *Human Relations,* 1954, 7, 117–140.

_____. *A theory of cognitive dissonance.* New York: Harper & Row, 1957.

_____, Riecken, H. W. and Schachter, S. *When prophecy fails.* Minneapolis: University of Minnesota Press, 1956.

Fisher, G. H. Developmental features of behavior and perception. I: visual and tactile-kinesthetic shape perception. *British Journal of Educational Psychology,* 1965, 35, 69–78.

Flavell, J. H. *The development of role-taking and communication skills in children.* New York: Wiley, 1968.

_____, Beach, D. H. and Chinsky, J. M. Spontaneous verbal rehearsal in a memory task as a function of age. *Child Development,* 1966, 37, 283–299.

Fraser, C., Bellugi, U. and Brown, R. Control of grammar in imitation, comprehension and production. *Journal of Verbal Learning & Verbal Behavior,* 1963, 2, 121–135.

Freud, S. *Leonardo Da Vinci.* New York: Vintage Books, 1947.

Friedlander, B. Z. The effect of speaker identity, voice inflection, vocabulary, and message redundancy on infants' selection of vocal reinforcement. Paper presented to the Society for Research in Child Development, New York, 1967.

Fries, C. C. *Linguistics and reading.* New York: Holt, Rinehart & Winston, 1963.

Fry, C. L. Training children to communicate to listeners. *Child Development,* 1966, 37, 675–685.

Furth, H. G. *Thinking without language: psychological implications of deafness.* New York: Free Press, 1966.

Gagné, R. M. *The conditions of learning.* New York: Holt, Rinehart & Winston, 1965.

―――― and Brown, L. T. Some factors in the programming of conceptual learning. *Journal of Experimental Psychology,* 1961, 62, 313–321.

―――― and Smith, E. C. A study of the effects of verbalization on problem solving. *Journal of Experimental Psychology,* 1962, 63, 12–18.

Gardner, D. E. M. *Experiment and tradition in primary schools.* London: Methuen, 1968.

Gardner, J. W. *Self-renewal.* New York: Harper & Row, 1963.

Gay, J. and Cole, M. *The new mathematics and an old culture.* New York: Holt, Rinehart & Winston, 1967.

Geschwind, N. The anatomy of acquired disorders of reading. In Money, J. (ed.), *Reading disability,* pp. 115–129. Baltimore, Md.: Johns Hopkins Press, 1962.

――――. The development of the brain and the evolution of language. *Monograph Series on Language and Linguistics,* 17, 1964, 155–169.

―――― and Fusillo, M. Color-naming defects in association with alexia. *Archives of Neurology,* 1966, 15, 137–146.

Getzels, J. W. and Jackson, P. W. *Creativity and intelligence.* New York: Wiley, 1961.

Ghiselin, B. *The creative process.* Berkeley, Calif.: University of California Press, 1952.

Gibb, C. A. Leadership. In Lindzey, G. and Aronson, E. (eds.), *Handbook of social psychology,* Vol. 4, pp. 205–282. Reading, Mass.: Addison-Wesley, 1968.

Gibson, E. Learning to read. *Science,* 1965, 148, 1066–1072.

――――, Osser, H. and Pick, A. D. A study of the development of grapheme-phoneme correspondences. *Journal of Verbal Learning & Verbal Behavior,* 1963, 2, 142–146.

Gibson, J. J. *The perception of the visual world.* Boston: Houghton Mifflin, 1950.

――――. *The senses considered as perceptual systems.* Boston: Houghton Mifflin, 1966.

Glidewell, J. C. et al. Socialization and social structure in the classroom. In

Hoffman, L. W. and Hoffman, M. L., *Review of child development research,* Vol. 2, pp. 221–256. New York: Russell Sage Foundation, 1966.

Goldberg, A. L. The effects of two types of sound motion pictures on the attitudes of adults toward minorities. *Journal of Educational Sociology,* 1956, 29, 386–391.

Goodenough, F. L. *Measurement of intelligence by drawings.* New York: Harcourt Brace Jovanovich, 1926.

Gordon, I. J. *Studying the child in school.* New York: Wiley, 1966.

Gordon, W. J. J. *Synectics: the development of creative capacity.* New York: Harper & Row, 1961.

Gottesman, I. I. Heritability of personality: a demonstration. *Psychological Monographs,* 1963, Whole No. 572.

Graves, M. E. *The art and color of design.* New York: McGraw-Hill, 1951.

Graves, R. The polite lie. *The Atlantic Monthly,* June 1965, 74–80.

Gregory, R. L. *Eye and brain: the psychology of seeing.* New York: McGraw-Hill, 1966.

Grimes, J. W. and Allinsmith, W. Compulsivity, anxiety, and school achievement. *Merrill-Palmer Quarterly of Behavior & Development,* 1961, 7, 247–269.

Guilford, J. P. Three faces of intellect. *American Psychologist,* 1959, 14, 469–479.

_____. Basic problems in teaching for creativity. In Taylor, C. W. and Williams, F. E. (eds.), *Instructional media and creativity,* pp. 71–103. New York: Wiley, 1966.

Guthrie, G. and Wiener, M. Subliminal perception or perception of partial cue with pictorial stimuli. *Journal of Personality & Social Psychology,* 1966, 3, 619–628.

Haber, R. N. Eidetic images. *Scientific American,* April 1969, pp. 36–44.

Hadamard, J. *The psychology of invention in the mathematical field.* Princeton, N.J.: Princeton University Press, 1945.

Hall, V. C., Salvi, R., Seggev, L. and Caldwell, E. Cognitive synthesis, conservation, and task analysis. *Developmental Psychology,* 1970, 2, 423–428.

Hanna, P. R., Hanna, J. S., Hodges, R. E. and Rudorf, E. H. *Phoneme-grapheme correspondences as cues to spelling improvement.* Washington, D.C.: U.S. Department of Health, Education and Welfare, Office of Education, 1966.

Harlow, H. F. The nature of learning sets. *Psychological Review,* 1949a, 56, 51–65.

_____ and Harlow, M. K. Learning to think. *Scientific American,* 1949b, Offprint No. 415.

Harris, D. B. The development and validation of a test of creativity in engineering. *Journal of Applied Psychology,* 1960, 44, 254–257.

_____. Children's drawings as measures of intellectual maturity: a revision and extension of the Goodenough Draw-a-Man Test. New York: Harcourt Brace Jovanovich, 1963.

Hayes, J. R. The maintenance of play in young children. *Journal of Comparative & Physiological Psychology,* 1958, 51, 788–794.

Haygood, R. C. and Bourne, L. E., Jr. Attributes and rule learning aspects of conceptual behavior. *Psychological Review,* 1965, 72, 175–195.

Heider, F. Attitudes and cognitive organization. *Journal of Psychology,* 1946, 21, 107–112.

Henry, J. *Culture against man.* New York: Random House, 1963.

Herbert, E. W., Galfand, D. M. and Hartmann, D. P. Imitation and self-esteem as determinants of self-critical behavior. *Child Development,* 1969, 40, 421–430.

Heron, W. The pathology of boredom. *Scientific American,* January 1957, 52–53.

––––––. Cognitive and physiological effects of perceptual isolation. In Solomon, P. et al. (eds.), *Sensory deprivation: a symposium,* pp. 8–33. Cambridge, Mass.: Harvard University Press, 1961.

Hertzig, M. E., Birch, H. G., Thomas, A. and Mendez, O. A. Class and ethnic differences in the responsiveness of pre-school children to cognitive demands. *Monographs of the Society for Research in Child Development,* 1968, Serial No. 117.

Heston, L. L. The genetics of schizophrenic and schizoid disease. *Science,* 1970, 167, 249–256.

Hicks, D. J. Imitation and retention of film-mediated aggressive peer and adult models. *Journal of Personality & Social Psychology,* 1965, 2, 97–100.

Hilgard, E. R. and Marquis, D. G. *Conditioning and learning.* New York: Appleton, 1950.

Hintzman, D. L. Articulatory coding in short-term memory. *Journal of Verbal Learning & Verbal Behavior,* 1967, 6, 312–316.

Holt, J. *How children fail.* New York: Pitman, 1964.

Homme, L. Contingency management. *Newsletter,* Section on Clinical Child Psychology, Division of Clinical Psychology. Washington, D.C.: American Psychological Association, 1966, 5, No. 4.

Hooper, F. H. Piagetian research and education. In Sigel, I. E. and Hooper, F. H. (eds.), *Logical thinking in children,* pp. 423–434. New York: Holt, Rinehart & Winston, 1968.

Houston, J. P. and Mednick, S. A. Creativity and the need for novelty. *Journal of Abnormal & Social Psychology,* 1963, 66, 137–141.

Hubel, D. H. and Wiesel, T. N. Receptive fields, binocular interaction and functional architecture in the cat's visual cortex. *Journal of Physiology,* 1962, 160, 106–154.

Hunt, E. Selection and reception conditions in grammar and concept learning. *Journal of Verbal Learning & Verbal Behavior,* 1965, 4, 161–169.

Hunt, J. McV. *Intelligence and experience.* New York: Ronald, 1961.

———. Piaget's observations as a source of hypotheses concerning motivation. *Merrill-Palmer Quarterly of Behavior & Development,* 1963, 9, 263–275.

———. The psychological basis for using preschool enrichment as an antidote for cultural deprivation. *Merrill-Palmer Quarterly of Behavior & Development,* 1964a, 10, 209–248.

———. Introduction: revisiting Montessori. In Montessori, M., *The Montessori method,* pp. xi–xxxix. New York: Schocken, 1964b.

———. Intrinsic motivation and its role in psychological development. *Nebraska Symposium on Motivation,* No. 13. Lincoln, Neb.: University of Nebraska Press, 1965.

———. Toward a theory of guided learning in development. In Ojemann, R. H. and Pritchett, K. (eds.), *Giving emphasis to guided learning.* Cleveland, Ohio: Educational Research Council, 1966.

Huttenlocher, J. Effects of manipulation of attributes on efficiency of concept formation. *Psychological Reports,* 1962, 10, 503–509.

———, Eisenberg, K. and Strauss, S. Comprehension: relation between perceived actor and logical subject. *Journal of Verbal Learning & Verbal Behavior,* 1968, 7, 527–530.

——— and Strauss, S. Comprehension and a statement's relation to the situation it described. *Journal of Verbal Learning & Verbal Behavior,* 1968, 7, 300–304.

Inhelder, B. Operational thought and symbolic imagery. In Mussen, P. H. (ed.), European research in cognitive development. *Monographs of the Society for Research in Child Development,* 1965, Serial No. 100.

——— and Piaget, J. *The growth of logical thinking from childhood to adolescence.* New York: Basic Books, 1958.

——— and Sinclair, H. Learning cognitive structures. In Mussen, P., Langer, J. and Covington, M. (eds.), *Trends and issues in developmental psychology,* pp. 2–21. New York: Holt, Rinehart & Winston, 1969.

Irvine, W. *Apes, angels and Victorians.* New York: McGraw-Hill, 1955.

Irwin, O. C. The amount and nature of activities of newborn infants under constant external stimulating conditions during the first ten days of life. *Genetic Psychological Monographs,* 1930, 8, 1–92.

Iscoe, I. and Pierce-Jones, J. Divergent thinking, age and intelligence in white and Negro children. *Child Development,* 1964, 35, 785–797.

Jaques-Dalcroze, E. *Rhythm, music and education.* New York: Putnam, 1921.

Jeffrey, W. E. Research on perceptual responses in children. University of California, Research Roundup on Children, July 14, 1960. (Mimeographed paper)

——— and Samuels, S. J. Effect of method of reading training on initial learning and transfer. *Journal of Verbal Learning & Verbal Behavior,* 1967, 6, 354–358.

Jensen, A. R. How much can we boost IQ and scholastic achievement? *Harvard Educational Review,* 1969, 39, 1–123.

John, E. R. *Mechanisms of memory.* New York: Academic Press, 1967.

Jones, R. M. *Fantasy and feeling in education.* New York: New York University Press, 1968.

Kagan, J. Reflection-impulsivity and reading ability in primary grade children. *Child Development,* 1965, 36, 609–628.

_____ and Moss, H. A. The stability of passive and dependent behavior from childhood through adulthood. *Child Development,* 1960, 31, 577–591.

_____ and _____. *Birth to maturity.* New York: Wiley, 1962.

_____, _____ and Sigel, I. E. Psychological significance of styles of conceptualization. In Wright, J. C. and Kagan, J. (eds.), Basic cognitive processes in children, *Monographs of the Society for Research in Child Development,* 1963, Serial No. 86, 73–111.

_____, Pearson, L. and Welch, L. Conceptual impulsivity and inductive reasoning. *Child Development,* 1966, 37, 583–594.

_____, Rosman, B. L., Day, D., Albert, J. and Phillips, W. Information processing in the child: significance of analytic and reflective attitudes. *Psychological Monographs,* 1964, Whole No. 578.

Kahn, D. and Birch, H. G. Development of auditory-visual integration and reading achievement. *Perceptual and Motor Skills,* 1968, 27, 459–468.

Karplus, R. and Thier, H. D. *A new look at elementary school science.* Chicago: Rand McNally, 1967.

Katz, D., Sarnoff, I. and McClintock, C. Ego-defense and attitude change. *Human Relations,* 1956, 9, 27–45.

Katz, J. J. and Fodor, J. A. The structure of a semantic theory. *Language,* 1963, 39, 170–210.

Keeney, T. J., Cannizzo, S. R. and Flavell, J. H. Spontaneous and induced verbal rehearsal in a recall task. *Child Development,* 1967, 38, 953–966.

Kendler, T. Development of mediating responses in children. In Wright, J. C. and Kagan, J. (eds.), Basic cognitive processes in children, *Monographs of the Society for Research in Child Development,* 1963, Serial No. 86, 33–47.

_____ and Kendler, H. H. Experimental analysis of inferential behavior in children. In Lipsitt, L. P. and Spiker, C. C. (eds.), *Advances in child development and behavior,* Vol. 3, pp. 157–191. New York: Academic Press, 1967.

Kessen, W. "Stage" and "structure" in the study of children. *Monographs of the Society for Research in Child Development,* 1962, Serial No. 83, 65–82.

Kiss, G. R. Words, associations, and networks. *Journal of Verbal Learning & Verbal Behavior,* 1968, 7, 707–713.

Koffka, K. *The growth of the mind.* New York: Harcourt Brace Jovanovich, 1946.

Kohl, H. R. *Teaching the "unteachable."* New York: New York Review of Books, 1967.

Kohlberg, L., Yaeger, J. and Hjertholm, E. Private speech: four studies and a review of theories. *Child Development,* 1968, 39, 691–736.

Köhler, W. *The mentality of apes.* New York: Harcourt Brace Jovanovich, 1927.

Kolers, P. A. Interlingual word associations. *Journal of Verbal Learning & Verbal Behavior,* 1963, 2, 291–300.

Kozol, J. *Death at an early age.* New York: Houghton Mifflin, 1967.

Krasner, L. Studies of the conditioning of verbal behavior. *Psychological Bulletin,* 1958, 55, 148–170.

_____ and Ullman, L. P. (eds.) *Research in behavior modification.* New York: Holt, Rinehart & Winston, 1967.

Kraus, S. Modifying prejudice: attitude change as a function of the race of the communicator. *Audiovisual Communication Review,* 1960, 10, 14–22.

Krech, D. The chemistry of learning. *Saturday Review,* January 20, 1968.

Kris, E. *Psychoanalytic explorations in art.* New York: International Universities Press, 1952.

Kushner, M. Desensitization of a post-traumatic phobia. In Ullmann, L. P. and Krasner, L. (eds.), *Case studies in behavior modification,* pp. 193–196. New York: Holt, Rinehart & Winston, 1966.

Laffal, J. *Pathological and normal language.* New York: Atherton, 1965.

Lambert, W. E. and MacNamara, J. Some cognitive consequences of following a first-grade curriculum in a second language. *Journal of Educational Psychology,* 1969, 60, 86–96.

Langer, J. and Rosenberg, B. H. Symbolic meaning and color naming. *Journal of Personality & Social Psychology,* 1966, 4, 364–373.

Lashley, K. S. *Brain mechanisms and intelligence.* New York: Dover, 1963.

Laughlin, P. R. Incidental concept formation as a function of creativity and intelligence. *Journal of Personality & Social Psychology,* 1967, 5, 115–118.

Lenneberg, E. H. *Biological foundations of language.* New York: Wiley, 1967.

_____. On explaining language. *Science,* 1969, 164, 635–643.

Lesser, G. S., Fifer, G. and Clark, D. H. Mental abilities of children from different social-class and cultural groups. *Monographs of the Society for Research in Child Development,* 1965, Serial No. 102.

Levin, H. Understanding the reading process. *Report of the 31st Educational Conference,* pp. 127–133. New York: Educational Records Bureau, 1967.

Levinson, D. J. The intergroup relations workshop: its psychological aims and effects. *Journal of Psychology,* 1954, 38, 103–126.

_____ and Schermerhorn, R. A. Emotional-attitudinal effects of an intergroup relations workshop on its members. *Journal of Psychology,* 1951, 31, 243–256.

Lewan, P. C. and Stotland, E. The effects of prior information on susceptibility to an emotional appeal. *Journal of Abnormal & Social Psychology,* 1961, 62, 450–453.

Lewin, K. *Field theory in social science.* New York: Harper & Row, 1951.

———, Dembo, T., Festinger, L. and Sears, P. S. Level of aspiration. In Hunt, J. McV. (ed.), *Personality and the behavior disorders,* Vol. 1, pp. 333–378. New York: Ronald, 1944.

Lindzey, G. and Byrne, D. Measurement of social choice and interpersonal attractiveness. In Lindzey, G. and Aronson, E. (eds.), *Handbook of social psychology,* Vol. 2, pp. 452–525. Reading, Mass.: Addison-Wesley, 1968.

Lippitt, R. and White, R. The "social climate" of children's groups. In Barker, R. G., Kounin, J. S. and Wright, H. F. (eds.), *Child behavior and development,* pp. 485–508. New York: McGraw-Hill, 1943.

Lovell, K. *The growth of basic mathematical and scientific concepts in children.* London: University of London Press, 1966.

Luria, A. R. The directive role of speech in development and dissociation. *Word,* 1959, 15.

———. *The role of speech in the regulation of normal and abnormal behavior.* London: Pergamon, 1961.

———. *Restoration of function after brain injury.* New York: Macmillan, 1963.

———. *Higher cortical functions in man.* New York: Basic Books, 1966a.

———. *Human brain and psychological processes.* New York: Harper & Row, 1966b.

Lynn, R. Temperamental characteristics related to disparity of attainment in reading and arithmetic. *British Journal of Educational Psychology,* 1957, 27, 62–67.

Maccoby, E. (ed.) *The development of sex differences.* Stanford, Calif.: Stanford University Press, 1966.

——— and Konrad, K. W. The effect of preparatory set on selective listening: developmental trends. *Monographs of the Society for Research in Child Development,* 1967, Serial No. 112.

Maccoby, M. and Modiano, N. On culture and equivalence: I. In Bruner, J. S., Olver, R. R. and Greenfield, P. M. (eds.), *Studies in cognitive growth,* pp. 257–269. New York: Wiley, 1966.

Mace, C. A. *The psychology of study.* Baltimore, Md.: Pelican, 1932.

Maffei, L. and Campbell, F. W. Neurophysiological localization of the vertical and horizontal visual coordinates in man. *Science,* 1970, 167, 386–387.

Mahone, C. H. Fear of failure and unrealistic vocational aspiration. *Journal of Abnormal & Social Psychology,* 1960, 60, 253–261.

Maier, N. R. F. Assets and liabilities in group problem solving: the need for an integrative function. *Psychological Review,* 1967, 74, 239–249.

Maltzman, I., Simon, S., Raskin, D. and Licht, L. Experimental studies in the training of originality. *Psychological Monographs,* 1960, No. 493.

Markle, S. M. *Good frames and bad: a grammar of frame writing.* New York: Wiley, 1969.

Massialas, B. G. and Zevin, J. *Creative encounters in the classroom: teaching and learning through discovery.* New York: Wiley, 1967.

Mattick, I. Adaptation of nursery school techniques to deprived children. *Journal of the American Academy of Child Psychiatry,* 1965, 4, 670–700.

McCabe, B. J. A program for teaching composition to pupils of limited academic ability. In Shugrue, M. F. and Hillocks, G. (eds.), *Classroom practices in teaching English,* pp. 39–46. Washington, D.C.: National Council of Teachers of English, 1965.

McCandless, B. *Children: behavior and development.* New York: Holt, Rinehart & Winston, 1967.

McCarthy, D. Language development in children. In Carmichel, L. (ed.), *Manual of child psychology,* pp. 492–630. New York: Wiley, 1954.

McClelland, D. *Studies in motivation.* New York: Appleton, 1955.

———. *The achieving society.* New York: Macmillan, 1961.

———, Atkinson, J. W., Clark, R. A. and Lowell, E. L. *The achievement motive.* New York: Appleton, 1953.

McGhee, P. E. and Crandall, V. C. Beliefs in internal-external control of reinforcements and academic performance. *Child Development,* 1968, 39, 91–102.

McKee, P. *The teaching of reading.* Boston: Houghton Mifflin, 1948.

McLuhan, M. *Understanding media: the extensions of man.* New York: McGraw-Hill, 1964.

McLuhan, M. and Fiore, Q. *The medium is the massage.* New York: Bantam, 1967.

McNeill, D. Developmental psycholinguistics. In Smith, F. and Miller, G. A. (eds.), *The genesis of language,* pp. 15–84. Cambridge, Mass.: M.I.T. Press, 1966.

———. The development of language. In Mussen, P. A. (ed.), *Carmichael's Manual of Child Psychology,* pp. 1061–1161. New York: Wiley, 1969.

Mead, G. H. *Mind, self, and society.* Chicago: University of Chicago Press, 1934.

Mednick, M. T., Mednick, S. A. and Mednick, E. V. Incubation of creative performance and specific associative priming. *Journal of Abnormal & Social Psychology,* 1964, 69, 84–88.

Mednick, S. The associative basis of the creative process. *Psychological Review,* 1962, 69, 220–232.

Mehler, J. and Bever, T. G. Cognitive capacity of very young children. *Science,* 1967, 158, 141–142.

_____ and _____. Reply to Piaget. *Science,* 1968, 162, 979–981.

Mendelsohn, G. A. and Griswold, B. B. Differential use of incidental stimuli in problem solving as a function of creativity. *Journal of Abnormal & Social Psychology,* 1964, 68, 431–436.

Menyuk, P. Syntactic structures in the language of children. *Child Development,* 1963, 34, 407–422.

_____. Syntactic rules used by children from preschool through first grade. *Child Development,* 1964a, 35, 533–546.

_____. Comparison of grammar of children with functionally deviant and normal speech. *Journal of Speech & Hearing Disorders,* 1964b, 7, 109–121.

Michaelson, G. Hippies head for the hills. *Parade Magazine,* December 14, 1969, 14–17.

Miles, R. C. Learning in kittens with manipulatory, exploratory, and food incentives. *Journal of Comparative & Physiological Psychology,* 1958, 51, 39–42.

Milgram, S. Behavioral study of obedience. *Journal of Abnormal & Social Psychology,* 1963, 67, 371–378.

_____. Some conditions of obedience and disobedience to authority. *Human Relations,* 1965, 18.

Miller, G. A. The magical number seven, plus or minus two: some limits on our capacity for processing information. *Psychological Review,* 1956, 63, 81–97.

_____. *Psychology: the science of mental life.* New York: Harper & Row, 1962a.

_____. Some psychological studies of grammar. *American Psychologist,* 1962b, 17, 748–762.

_____. Some preliminaries to psycholinguistics. *American Psychologist,* 1965, 20, 15–20.

_____. Psychology as a means of promoting human welfare. *American Psychologist,* 1969, 24, 1063–1074.

_____ and Chomsky, N. Finitary models of language users. In Luce, R. D., Bush, R. R. and Galanter, E. (eds.), *Handbook of mathematical psychology,* Vol. II, pp. 419–491. New York: Wiley, 1963.

_____, Galanter, E. and Pribram, K. *Plans and the structure of behavior.* New York: Holt, Rinehart & Winston, 1960.

Miller, H. L. and Woock, R. R. *Social foundations of urban education.* Hinsdale, Illinois: Dryden Press, 1970.

Miller, W. and Ervin, S. The development of grammar in child language. In Bellugi, U. and Brown, R. (eds.) The acquisition of language. *Monographs of the Society for Research in Child Development,* 1964, Serial No. 29, 9–34.

Milner, E. *Human neural and behavioral development.* Springfield, Ill.: C. C. Thomas, 1967.

Mischel, W. Preference for delayed reinforcement: an experimental study of a cultural observation. *Journal of Abnormal & Social Psychology,* 1958, 56, 57–61.

Mizener, A. *The far side of paradise.* Boston: Houghton Mifflin, 1949.

Montessori, M. *Dr. Montessori's own handbook.* Cambridge, Mass.: Bentley, 1964a.

―――. *The Montessori method.* New York: Schocken, 1964b.

Montgomery, K. C. The role of the exploratory drive in learning. *Journal of Comparative & Physiological Psychology,* 1954, 47, 60–64.

Moyer, K. E. Brain research must contribute to world peace. *Carnegie Review,* October 1968, 4–17.

Murray, H. A. *Explorations in personality.* New York: Oxford University Press, 1938.

Mussen, P. H., Conger, J. J. and Kagan, J. *Child development and personality.* New York: Harper & Row, 1969.

Myers, R. E. and Torrance, E. P. *Invitations to speaking and writing.* Boston: Ginn, 1962.

Nash, J. *Developmental psychology: a psychobiological approach.* Englewood Cliffs, N.J.: Prentice-Hall, 1970.

Neisser, U. *Cognitive psychology.* New York: Appleton, 1967.

―――― and Weene, P. Hierarchies in concept attainment. *Journal of Experimental Psychology,* 1962, 64, 644–645.

Newell, A. Thoughts on the concept of process. In Voss, J. F., *Approaches to thought.* A Symposium of the Learning Research & Development Center, University of Pittsburgh, 1967.

Nodine, C. F. and Evans, J. D. Eye movements of prereaders to pseudo words containing letters of high and low confusability. *Perception & Psychophysics,* 1969, 6, 39–41.

―――― and Hardt, J. V. Effects of letter confusability on the discrimination of pseudowords by prereaders. *Journal of Educational Psychology,* 1970, 61, 10–15.

Norman, D. A. *Memory and attention.* New York: Wiley, 1969.

Ore, O. *Graphs and their uses.* New York: Random House, 1963.

Osborn, A. F. *Applied imagination.* New York: Scribner, 1953.

Osborn, J. Teaching a teaching language to disadvantaged children. In Brottman, M. A. (ed.), Language remediation for the disadvantaged preschool child, *Monographs of the Society for Research in Child Development,* 1968, Serial No. 124, 36–48.

Osgood, C. E., Suci, G. J. and Tannenbaum, P. H. *The measurement of meaning.* Urbana, Ill.: University of Illinois Press, 1957.

―――― and Tannenbaum, P. H. The principle of congruity in the prediction of attitude change. *Psychological Review,* 1966, 62, 42–55.

Ott, J. F. The story of Esther. *Saturday Review,* October 15, 1966, 79, 92.

Overstreet, H. and Overstreet, B. *The strange tactics of extremism.* New York: Norton, 1964.

Page, D. A. *Maneuvers on lattices.* Conference on Mathematical Learning, Berkeley, California, 1962. Reprints available from Education Development Center, Cambridge, Mass.

Paige, J. M. and Simon, H. A. Cognitive processes in solving algebra word problems. In Kleinmuntz, B. (ed.), *Problem solving: research, method and theory,* pp. 51–119. New York: Wiley, 1966.

Paine, R. S. and Oppé, T. W. Neurological examination of children. *Clinics in Developmental Medicine,* Double Vol. 20/21. London: Heinemann, 1966.

Palkes, H., Stewart, M. and Kahana, B. Porteus maze performance of hyperactive boys after training in self-directed verbal commands. *Child Development,* 1968, 39, 817–826.

Parloff, M. G., Datta, L., Kleman, M. and Handlon, J. H. Personality characteristics which differentiate creative male adolescents and adults. *Journal of Personality,* 1968, 36, 528–552.

Parnes, S. J. and Meadow, A. Effects of "brainstorming" instructions on creative problem solving by trained and untrained subjects. *Journal of Educational Psychology,* 1959, 50, 171–176.

Patrick, C. Creative thought in poets. *Archives of Psychology,* 1935, No. 178.

———. Creative thought in artists. *Journal of Psychology,* 1937, 4, 35–73.

Patterson, G. R. A learning theory approach to the treatment of the school phobic child. In Ullmann, L. P. and Krasner, L. (eds.), *Case studies in behavior modification,* pp. 279–285. New York: Holt, Rinehart & Winston, 1966.

———, Littman, R. A. and Bricker, W. Assertive behavior in children: a step toward a theory of aggression. *Monographs of the Society for Research in Child Development,* 1967, Serial No. 113.

Paulson, A. A. (chm.) School phobia: workshop, 1955. *American Journal of Orthopsychiatry,* 1957, 27, 286–309.

Peal, E. and Lambert, W. E. The relation of bilingualism to intelligence. *Psychological Monographs,* 1962, Whole No. 546.

Peel, E. A. Curiosity and interest in motivating school learning. *Proceedings of the 14th International Congress of Applied Psychology, 1961,* Vol. 3, pp. 153–160.

Penfield, W. The uncommitted cortex. *Atlantic Monthly,* July 1964.

Pepper, S. C. *The sources of value.* Berkeley, Calif.: University of California Press, 1958.

Petrie, A., McCulloch, R. and Kazdin, L. The perceptual characteristics of the juvenile delinquent. *Journal of Nervous and Mental Disorders,* 1962, 134, 415–421.

Piaget, J. *The origins of intelligence in children.* New York: International Universities Press, 1952.

――――. *The construction of reality in the child.* New York: Basic Books, 1954.

――――. *Play, dreams and imitation in childhood.* New York: Norton, 1962.

――――. The development of mental imagery. In Ripple, R. E. and Rockcastle, V. N. (eds.), *Piaget rediscovered,* pp. 21–32. Ithaca, N.Y.: Cornell University Press, 1964.

――――. *The child's conception of number.* New York: Norton, 1965.

――――. *Six psychological studies.* New York: Random House, 1967.

――――. Quantification, conservation, and nativism. *Science,* 1968, 162, 976–979.

―――― and Inhelder, B. *The child's conception of space.* London: Routledge, 1956.

―――― and ――――. *The psychology of the child.* New York: Basic Books, 1969.

――――, ―――― and Szeminska, A. *The child's conception of geometry.* New York: Harper Torchbooks, 1964.

Pick, A. D. Improvement of visual and tactual form discrimination. *Journal of Experimental Psychology,* 1965, 69, 331–339.

Pierce, C. S. How to make our ideas clear. *Popular Science Monthly,* January 1878, 286–302.

Piers, E. V., Daniels, J. M. and Quackenbush, J. F. The identification of creativity in adolescents. *Journal of Educational Psychology,* 1960, 51, 346–351.

Pines, M. *Revolution in learning: the years from birth to six.* New York: Harper & Row, 1967.

Pollack, R. H. Some implications of ontogenetic changes in perception. In Elkind, D. and Flavell, J. H. (eds.), *Studies in cognitive development,* pp. 365–408. New York: Oxford University Press, 1969.

Pollio, H. R. and Gerow, J. R., III. The role of congruent and incongruent evaluative contexts in word association. *The Journal of Verbal Learning & Verbal Behavior,* 1968, 7, 122–127.

Polya, G. *How to solve it: a new aspect of mathematical method,* pp. 6–8, 12. Princeton, N.J.: Princeton University Press, 1945.

Prentice, W. C. H. Some cognitive aspects of motivation. *American Psychologist,* 1961, 16, 503–511.

Pritchard, R. M. Stabilized images on the retina. *Scientific American,* June 1961, 204, 72–78.

Proshansky, H. M. The development of intergroup attitudes. In Hoffman, L. W. and Hoffman, M. L. (eds.), *Review of child development research,* Vol. 2, pp. 311–372. New York: Russell Sage Foundation, 1966.

Rasmussen, D. and Goldberg, L. *A hen in a fox's den.* Chicago: Science Research Associates, 1965.

Raths, L. E., Wassermann, S., Jonas, A. and Rothstein, A. M. *Teaching for thinking: theory and application.* Columbus, Ohio: Merrill, 1967.

Ray, W. S. *The experimental psychology of original thinking.* New York: Macmillan, 1967.

Reese, H. W. (ed.) Imagery in children's learning. Symposium presented at the meeting of the Society for Research in Child Development, Santa Monica, March 1969.

Reitman, W. R. *Cognition and thought.* New York: Wiley, 1965.

Rheingold, H., Gewirtz, J. and Ross, H. W. Social conditioning of vocalization in infancy. *Journal of Comparative and Physiological Psychology,* 1959, 52, 68–73.

Rice, N. L. and Winsand, O. M. *A high school curriculum in the fine arts for able students.* Department of Fine Arts, Carnegie-Mellon University, 1966.

Ridley, D. R. and Birney, R. C. Effects of training procedures on creativity test scores. *Journal of Educational Psychology,* 1967, 58, 158–164.

Riesman, D. *Individualism reconsidered.* New York: Macmillan, 1954.

Roe, A. A psychological study of eminent psychologists and anthropologists, and a comparison with biological and physical scientists. *Psychological Monographs,* 1943, Whole No. 352.

Rohwer, W. D. Images and pictures in children's learning. In Reese, H. W. (ed.) *Psychological Bulletin,* 1970, 73, 393–403.

Rosen, B. The achievement syndrome. *American Sociological Review,* 1956, 21, 203–211.

———— and D'Andrade, R. The psychosocial origins of achievement motivation. *Sociometry,* 1959, 22, 185–218.

Rosenthal, R. and Jacobson, L. *Pygmalion in the classroom.* New York: Holt, Rinehart & Winston, 1968.

Rotter, J. R. Generalized expectancies for internal versus external control of reinforcement. *Psychological Monographs,* 1966, Whole No. 609.

Ryan, E. D. and Foster, R. Athletic participation and perceptual augmentation and reduction. *Journal of Personality & Social Psychology,* 1967, 6, 472–476.

Ryan, S. M., Hegion, A. G. and Flavell, J. H. Nonverbal mnemonic meditation in preschool children. University of Minnesota, 1969. (Mimeographed report)

Sachs, B. M. *The student, the interview, and the curriculum.* Boston: Houghton Mifflin, 1966.

Sachs, J. S. Recognition memory for syntactic and semantic aspects of connected discourse. *Perception & Psychophysics,* 1967, 2, 437–442.

Salapetek, P. and Kessen, W. Visual scanning of triangles by the human newborn. *Journal of Experimental Child Psychology,* 1966, 3, 155–167.

Sales, S. M. Need for stimulation as a factor in social behavior. *Journal of Personality and Social Psychology,* 1971, 19, 124–134.

Salzinger, K. and Pisoni, S. Reinforcement of affect responses of schizophrenics during the clinical interview. Paper read to the Eastern Psychological Association, New York, 1957.

Samuels, S. J. Attentional process in reading: the effect of pictures on the acquisition of reading responses. *Journal of Educational Psychology,* 1967, 58, 337–342.

———. Effect of word associations on reading speed, recall, and guessing behavior on tests. *Journal of Educational Psychology,* 1968, 59, 12–15.

Sapir, E. The grammarian and his language. In Mead, M. and Bunzel, R. L. (eds.), *The golden age of American anthropology,* pp. 440–449. New York: Braziller, 1960.

Sarason, S. B. et al.: *Anxiety in elementary school children.* New York: Wiley, 1960.

Scandura, J. M. and Durnin, J. H. Extra-scope transfer in learning mathematical strategies. *Journal of Educational Psychology,* 1968, 59, 350–354.

Schaefer, E. S. and Bayley, N. Maternal behavior, child behavior, and their intercorrelations from infancy through adolescence. *Monographs of the Society for Research in Child Development,* 1963, Serial No. 87.

Schain, R. L. *Discipline: how to establish and maintain it.* New York: Teachers Practical Press, 1961.

Schrag, P. Education's "romantic" critics. *Saturday Review,* February 18, 1967, 80.

Schroder, H. M., Driver, M. J. and Streufert, S. *Human information processing: individuals and groups in complex social situations.* New York: Holt, Rinehart & Winston, 1966.

Sears, P. W. and Sherman, V. S. *In pursuit of self-esteem: case studies of eight elementary school children.* Belmont, Calif.: Wadsworth, 1965.

Selfridge, O. G. and Neisser, U. Pattern recognition by machine. *Scientific American,* August 1960, pp. 64–5, 68.

Silberman, C. E. *Crisis in the classroom.* New York: Random House, 1970.

Simon, H. A. Motivation and emotional controls of cognition. *Psychological Review,* 1967, 74, 29–39.

——— and Kotovsky, K. Human acquisition of concepts for sequential patterns. *Psychological Review,* 1963, 70, 534–546.

——— and Newell, A. Computer simulation of human thinking and problem solving. In Kessen, W. and Kuhlman, C. (eds.), Thought in the young child, *Monographs of the Society for Research in Child Development,* 1962, Serial No. 83, 137–150.

Skeels, H. M. Adult status of children with contrasting early life experiences: a follow-up study. *Monographs of the Society for Research in Child Development,* 1966, Serial No. 105.

Skemp, R. R. Reflective intelligence and mathematics. *British Journal of Educational Psychology,* 1961, 31, 45–55.

Skinner, B. F. *Verbal behavior.* New York: Appleton, 1957.

———. Why we need teaching machines. In deGrazia, A. and Sohn, D. A. (eds.), *Programs, teachers and machines,* pp. 43–66. New York: Bantam, 1964.

———. Interview in *Psychology Today,* September 1967.

———. *The technology of teaching.* New York: Appleton, 1968.

Slobin, D. I. Imitation and grammatical development in children. In Endler, N. S., Boulter, L. R. and Osser, H. (eds.), *Contemporary issues in developmental psychology.* New York: Holt, Rinehart & Winston, in press.

Snow, R. E. Unfinished Pygmalion. *Contemporary Psychology,* 1969, 14, 197–199.

Solley, C. M. and Murphy, G. *Development of the perceptual world.* New York: Basic Books, 1960.

Staats, A. W. *Learning, language and cognition.* New York: Holt, Rinehart & Winston, 1968.

——— et al. Reinforcement variables in the control of unit reading responses. *Journal of the Experimental Analysis of Behavior,* 1964, 7, 139–149.

Stauffer, R. G. *Directing reading maturity as a cognitive process.* New York: Harper & Row, 1969a.

———. *Teaching reading as a thinking process.* New York: Harper & Row, 1969b.

Stern, C. *Children discover arithmetic.* New York: Harper & Row, 1949.

——— and Keislar, E. Effects of dialect and instructional procedures on children's oral language production and concept acquisition. Paper presented to the American Educational Research Association, Chicago, 1968.

Sterritt, G. M., Camp, B. and Lipman, B. Effects of early auditory deprivation upon auditory and visual information processing. *Perceptual and Motor Skills,* 1966, 23, 123–130.

Stevenson, H. W. Studies of racial awareness in young children. In Hartup, W. W. and Smothergill, N. L., *The young child: reviews of research,* pp. 206–213. Washington: National Association for the Education of Young Children, 1967.

——— and Odom, R. D. The relation of anxiety to children's performance on learning and problem-solving tasks. *Child Development,* 1965, 36, 1003–1012.

Stewart, W. A. Sociolinguistic factors in the history of American Negro dialects. *The Florida FL Reporter,* Spring 1967a.

———. *Language and communication problems in southern Appalachia.* Washington, D.C.: Center for Applied Linguistics, 1967b.

———. Continuity and change in American Negro dialects. *The Florida FL Reporter,* Spring 1968.

Strunk, W. and White, E. B. *The elements of style.* New York: Macmillan, 1959.

Suchman, J. R. Inquiry training: building skills for autonomous discovery. *Merrill-Palmer Quarterly of Behavior & Development,* 1961, 7, 147–169.

Sutter, E. G. and Reid, J. B. Learner variables and interpersonal conditions in computer-assisted instruction. *Journal of Educational Psychology,* 1969, 60, 153–157.

Tanner, J. M. Human growth and constitution. In Harrison, G. A. Weiner, J. S., Tanner, J. M. and Barnicot, N. A. *Human biology: an introduction to human evolution, variation and growth,* pp. 309–400. New York: Oxford University Press, 1964.

Taylor, D. W., Berry, P. C. and Block, C. H. Does group participation when using brainstorming facilitate or inhibit creative thinking? *Administrative Science Quarterly,* 1958–59, 3, 23–47.

Terman, L. M. (ed.) et al. *Mental and physical traits of a thousand gifted children,* Vol. I of *Genetic Status of Genius.* Stanford, Calif.: Stanford University Press, 1925.

Tolman, E. C. *Purposive behavior in animals and men.* New York: Appleton, 1932.

Torrance, E. P. *Education and the creative potential.* Minneapolis, Minn.: University of Minnesota Press, 1963.

_____. Implications of creativity-research findings for instructional media. In Taylor, C. W. and Williams, F. E. (eds.), *Instructional media and creativity,* pp. 147–178. New York: Wiley, 1966.

Turner, E. M. *Teaching aids for elementary mathematics.* New York: Holt, Rinehart & Winston, 1966.

Turnure, J. and Zigler, E. Outer-directedness in the problem solving of normal and retarded children. *Journal of Abnormal & Social Psychology,* 1958, 57, 379–388.

Ullmann, L. P. and Krasner, L. (eds.) *Case studies in behavior modification.* New York: Holt, Rinehart & Winston, 1966.

Uzgiris, I. C. and Hunt, J. McV. An instrument for assessing infant psychological development. Psychological Development Laboratory, University of Illinois, 1966. (Mimeographed report)

Vernon, M. D. Learning from graphical material. *British Journal of Psychology,* 1945, 36, 145–158.

_____. *The psychology of perception.* Baltimore, Md.: Penguin, 1962.

Veroff, J., Atkinson, J., Feld, S. and Gurin, G. The use of thematic apperception to assess motivation in a nationwide interview study. *Psychological Monographs,* 1960, 74, Whole No. 499.

Vygotsky, L. S. *Thought and language.* Cambridge, Mass.: M.I.T. Press, 1962.

Wagner, C. and Wheeler, L. Model, need, and cost effects in helping behavior. *Journal of Personality & Social Psychology,* 1969, 12, 111–117.

Waimon, M. D. The study of teaching behavior by prospective teachers. In Corrigan, D. (ed.), *The study of teaching,* pp. 55–63. Washington, D.C.: The Association for Student Teaching, 1967.

Waite, R. R., Sarason, S. B., Lighthall, F. F. and Davidson, K. S. A study of anxiety and learning in children. *Journal of Abnormal and Social Psychology,* 1958, 57, 267–270.

Wallace, W. P. Implicit associative response occurrence in learning with retarded subjects. *Journal of Educational Psychology,* 1967, 58, 110–114.

Wallach, M. A. and Kogan, N. *Modes of thinking in young children.* New York: Holt, Rinehart & Winston, 1965.

―――― and Wing, C. W. *The talented student.* New York: Holt, Rinehart & Winston, 1969.

Wallas, G. *The art of thought.* New York: Harcourt Brace Jovanovich, 1926.

Wapner, S. and Werner, H. *Perceptual development.* Worcester, Mass.: Clark University Press, 1957.

Watson, J. B. Psychology as the behaviorist views it. *Psychological Review,* 1913, 20, 158–177.

――――. *Behaviorism.* New York: Norton, 1930.

―――― and Rayner, R. Conditioned emotional reactions. *Journal of Experimental Psychology,* 3, 1–14, 1920.

Watson, J. D. *The double helix.* New York: Atheneum, 1968.

Weir, M. W. and Stevenson, H. W. The effect of verbalization in children's learning as a function of chronological age. *Child Development,* 1959, 30, 143–149.

Werner, H. *Comparative psychology of mental development.* New York: Science Editions, 1961.

―――― and Kaplan, B. *Symbol formation: an organismic developmental approach to language and the expression of thought.* New York: Wiley, 1963.

Wertheimer, M. *Productive thinking.* New York: Harper & Row, 1945.

Whimbey, A. E. and Ryan, S. F. Role of short-term memory and training in solving reasoning problems mentally. *Journal of Educational Psychology,* 1969, 60, 361–364.

White, B. L. The development of perception during the first six months of life. Paper presented to A.A.A.S., Cleveland, 1963.

―――― and Castle, P. W. Visual exploratory behavior following postnatal handling of human infants. *Perceptual and Motor Skills,* 1964, 18, 497–502.

――――, ―――― and Held, R. Observations on the development of visually-directed reaching. *Child Development,* 1964, 35, 349–364.

White, R. and Lippitt, R. Leader behavior and member reaction in three "social climates." In Cartwright, D. and Zander, A. (eds.), *Group dynamics, research & theory,* pp. 318–335. New York: Harper & Row, 1968.

White, R. W. Motivation reconsidered: the concept of competence. *Psychological Review,* 1959, 66, 297–333.

_____. Competence and the psychosexual stages of development. In Jones, M. R. (ed.), *Nebraska symposium on motivation, 1960,* pp. 97–140. Lincoln, Neb.: University of Nebraska Press.

_____. Ego and reality in psychoanalytic theory. *Psychological Issues,* 1963, Vol. 3, Monograph 11.

White, S. Evidence for a hierarchical arrangement of learning processes. In Lipsitt, L. P. and Spiker, C. C. *Advances in child development and behavior,* Vol. 2, pp. 187–220. New York: Academic, 1965.

Whorf, B. L. *Language, thought and reality,* Carroll, J. B. (ed.) Cambridge, Mass.: M.I.T. Press, 1956.

Wiener, N. *Cybernetics.* New York: Wiley, 1948.

Wilson, W. C. and Verplanck, W. S. Some observations on the reinforcement of verbal operants. *American Journal of Psychology,* 1956, 69, 448–451.

Winterbottom, M. The relation of need for achievement in learning experiences in independence and mastery. In Atkinson, J. W. (ed.), *Motives in fantasy, action, and society,* pp. 453–478. New York: Van Nostrand Reinhold, 1958.

Witkin, H. A., Dyk, R. B., Faterson, H. F., Goodenough, D. R. and Karp, S. A. *Psychological differentiation: studies of mental development.* New York: Wiley, 1962.

Wolfram, W. A. and Fasold, R. W. Toward reading materials for speakers of black English: three linguistically appropriate passages. In Baratz, J. C. and Shuy, R W. (eds.) *Teaching black children to read,* pp. 138–155. Washington D.C.: Center for Applied Linguistics, 1969.

Woodford, F. P. *Scientific writing for graduate students.* New York: Rockefeller University Press, 1968.

Yando, R. M. and Kagan, J. The effect of teacher tempo on the child. *Child Development,* 1968, 39, 27–34.

Zajonc, R. B. The concepts of balance, congruity, and dissonance. *Public Opinion Quarterly,* 1960, 24, 280–296.

_____. Social facilitation. *Science,* 1965, 149, 269–274.

Zeiler, M. D. Component and configurational learning in children. *Journal of Experimental Psychology,* 1964, 68, 292–296.

Index of Subjects

Acalculia, 56
Accommodation, 234
Achievement drive, 195–200
  and culture, 198–200
  and ego involvement, 195
  family influences on, 195–198
  imagery, 198–199
Aggression, 269–270
  and frustration, 273
  learning of, 270–272
  management of, 272–273
Algorithm, 82
Alpha capacity, 204
Anxiety
  coping in school, 264–266
  free floating, 262–263
Aphasic children, 364, 367–368
Assimilation, 234
Association
  classroom illustrations, 374–375
  meaning structure for, 373–374
  visual-auditory-speech, 442
Association areas, 6
Associational fluency, 501
Associative priming, 541
Associative structures, 373–375
  emotional aspect of, 375–377
Authoritarianism, 331

Behaviorism
  reinforcement principles of, 78
  theory of, 78–81
Brain
  auditory-visual integration in, 444–446
  damage to, 3
  evolution of, 5–6
  function of, 7
  physiology and reading, 442–444
Brain damage
  remedial strategies for, 57
Brain function
  Luria's theory of, 52–53
Brain map
  localization of mental faculties, 49

Centration
  perception of illusions, 18
Chaining, 85
Classical conditioning, 174–176
Classification process
  complex, 129–130
  frame of reference, 124, 126
  superordinate, 128
  thematic grouping, 130
Cognitive dissonance, 302

619

Index of Names